# ATLANTIC STUDIES ON SOCIETY IN CHANGE

## No. 39

Editor-in-Chief Béla K. Király
Associate Editor Peter Pastor
Assistant Editor Albert A. Nofi

WAR AND SOCIETY IN EAST CENTRAL EUROPE

Vol. XX

# REVOLUTIONS AND INTERVENTIONS IN HUNGARY AND ITS NEIGHBOR STATES, 1918–1919

Peter Pastor — Editor

Social Science Monographs, Boulder, Colorado
Atlantic Studies on Society in Change, Highland Lakes, New Jersey
Distributed by Columbia University Press, New York

1988

EAST EUROPEAN MONOGRAPHS No CCXL

Library of Congress Catalog Card Number 87-62415
ISBN 0-88033-137-2
Printed in the United States of America

# TABLE OF CONTENTS

## III THE HUNGARIAN REVOLUTIONS AND HUNGARY'S NEIGHBORS

## IV INTERVENTIONS AGAINST REVOLUTIONS

VII

# ACKNOWLEDGEMENTS

The Program on Society in Change conducts research, conferences, and publishes scholarly books. The National Endowment for the Humanities awarded it a research grant for 1978–81 and renewed it for another three year term (1981–84). Without this substantial and much appreciated support, the Program would not have existed. Additional contributions by Brooklyn College, the International Research and Exchanges Board, the American Council of Learned Societies, and the Open Society Fund helped us in completing the research and holding conferences.

Copy editing was done by Roberto Cambria and preparation of the manuscript for publication by Albert A. Nofi, Dorothy Meyerson, Frances Hetherington, and Maurice Leibenstern of the Program on Society in Change. The maps were drafted by Colonel E. Krasnoborski of the United States Military Academy at West Point, and Ms. Ida Etelka Romann.

Most of the essays contained in this book were read at the XVIII Conference on Society in Change held at the Janus Pannonius University at Pécs, Hungary, in June 1985. The University was a generous host, establishing the most pleasant atmosphere possible for this international, interdisciplinary conference. The Rector of the University, Professor Mária Ormos, offered efficient help in every way.

Péter Gosztony's essay was translated by William Batkay and Mario D. Fenyo translated the essays of László Fogarassy, Mária Ormos, and Martin Vietor, as well as Tibor Hajdu's "1918–1919: the Changing Image of Two Revolutions."

The work of the editor, Professor Peter Pastor, was greatly facilitated by the release time granted by his institution, Montclair State College of New Jersey, during the fall of 1984.

To all these institutions and persons, I wish to express my most sincere appreciation and thanks.

Highland Lakes, New Jersey  
August 20, 1987

Béla K. Király  
Professor Emeritus of History  
Editor-in-Chief

# PREFACE TO THE SERIES

The present volume is the twentieth in a series that, when completed, will constitute a comprehensive survey of the many aspects of war and society in East Central Europe. The chapters of this and forthcoming volumes have been selected from papers presented at a series of international, inter-disciplinary scholarly conferences conducted by the Brooklyn College Program on Society in Change in cooperation with other institutions of higher learning.

These volumes deal with the peoples whose homelands lie between the Germans to the west, the Russians to the east and north, and the Mediterranean and Adriatic Seas to the south. They constitute a particular civilization, one that is an integral part of Europe, yet substantially different from the West. The area is characterized by rich variety in language, religion, and government, and, not surprisingly, a similar variety can also be observed in concepts of national defense, in the nature of armed forces, and in ways of waging war. The study of this complex subject demands a multidisciplinary approach, and, accordingly, our contributors represent several academic disciplines. They have been drawn from universities and other scholarly institutions in the United States, Canada, and Western Europe as well as in the East Central European socialist countries.

Our comparative investigation of military behavior and organization attempts to ascertain what is peculiar to particular nations and ethnic groups, what has been socially and culturally determined, and what has resulted from the exigencies of the moment. We try to define different patterns of military behaviour, including decision-making process, attitudes and actions of diverse social classes, and the degree of restraint (or lack thereof) typically shown in war. We endeavor to present considerable material that can help us to understand how the process of social, economic, political, and techological change as well as changes in the sciences and in international relations influenced the development of doctrines of national defense and altered actual practice in such areas as military organization, command, strategy, and tactics. We also present data on the social origins and mobility of the officer corps and the rank and file, on the differences between the officer corps of the various services, and, above all, on civil-military relations and the origins of the East Central European brand of militarism. The studies will, we hope, deepen our understanding of the societies, governments, and politics of East Central Europe.

Our methodology takes into account the changes in the study of war and national defense systems which have occured in the last three decades. During

# PREFACE TO THE SERIES

that period, the study of war and national defense systems has moved away from a narrow focus on battles, campaigns, and leaders and now views a country's military history in the context of the evolution of the entire society. In fact, historians, political scientists, sociologists, philosophers, and other students of war and national defense have come to recognize the interdependence of changes in society and changes in warfare; they accept the proposition that military institutions closely reflect the character of the society of which they are a part. Recognition of this fact is a keystone of our approach to the subject.

Works in Western languages now provide adequate coverage of the diplomatic, political, intellectual, social, and economic histories of the peoples of East Central Europe. In contrast, few substantial studies of their national defense systems have yet appeared in Western languages. Similarly, though some comprehensive accounts of the nonmilitary aspects of the history of the entire region have been published in the West, there is as yet no comprehensive account of the area's national defense systems in any Western language. Nor is there any study of the mutual effects of the concepts and practices of national defense in East Central Europe. Thus, this comprehensive study of war and society in East Central Europe is a pioneering work. The present volume concentrates on the largely neglected, but unusually critical, period immediately following World War I, and is thus of particular significance.

As Editor-in-Chief, of course, I cheerfully take full responsibility for the comprehensiveness, cohesion, internal balance, and scholarly quality of the series I have launched. I intend this work to be neither a justification nor a condemnation of the policies, attitudes, and activities of any of the nations involved. At the same time, because the contributors represent so many different disciplines, languages, interpretations, schools of thought, our policy in this, as in past and future volumes, is to present their contributions without modification. In this sense, the volume is a sampling of the schools of thought and the standards of scholarship in the many countries to which our contributors belong.

Béla K. Király
Editor-in-Chief

X

# INTRODUCTION

## INTRODUCTION

A number of earlier publications in the series *War and Society in East Central Europe,* have already examined the revolutionary effect of World War I on East Central Europe. The military defeat of Russia and then of the Central Powers, brought about national revolutions in East Central Europe; as midwife to changes it gave birth to Czechoslovakia, rebirth to Poland, and new life to a Hungarian state without an Austrian coequal. Being on the side of the victors led to considerable territorial growth for Romania and Serbia, which soon after the war came to be known as Yugoslavia. Romania, Serbia, Czechoslovakia, and Poland gained new frontiers at the expense of the vanquished states.

The new political situation in East Central Europe made possible the intrusion there of some of the victorious great powers, namely Italy and France. In this, the more powerful France, with troops in the Balkans, took the lead. Its intention to dominate East Central Europe, however, cannot be separated from Paris' attempt to do the same in Russia and the Ukraine. Several contributions to this volume make it clear that these efforts were interrelated.

In the 1960s, following the lead of Arno Mayer, historians saw France's involvement in Russia as part of the Entente's goal of crushing the "forces of movement" embracing Bolshevism. But, more recent research stresses France's involvement in the area on the basis of traditional French imperialism. Thus, fighting Bolshevism became a rationalization for such a policy. The papers of Torrey and Munholland and of this writer also gravitate toward this view.

The crusading spirit of fighting Bolshevism in Russia and the Ukraine, and the shortage of French troops, forced France to enlist surrogate forces, such as Greek and Romanian troops. Fischer-Galati and Stavrou point out that both Romanian and Greek leaders supported intervention not because they feared world revolution and the spread of Bolshevism into East Central Europe, but for the sake of territorial aggrandizement. In return for toeing the French line, Romania and Greece counted on French support for their claims.

The threatening specter of Bolshevism was utilized as justification for Romania's expansion into most of Transylvania. As Torrey's essay indicates, the Romanians blamed the Károlyi government for spreading Bolshevism in that area, which Romania ostensibly intended to prevent through occupation. Hungarian archival sources amply demonstrate that the Romanian charges were baseless. In fact, it was Romanian expansionism that lead to the collapse of the Károlyi regime and to the rise of the Communist Hungarian Soviet Republic. This in turn, presented a perfect opportunity, as Fischer-Galati notes, for furthering Romania's political goals. After March 21, 1919, the crusade against Bolshevism called for the conquest of Hungary.

Before the rise of the Soviet Republic in Hungary, the two defeated states in East Central Europe, Hungary and Bulgaria, seemed to progress in a similar socio-political direction. Lampe shows that in Bulgaria statism as a solution, was favored; reforms from above was the order of the day under Stamboliski. And, Hungary took, it seemed, the same path under Károlyi. The February Land Reform Law that, owing to the fall of the Károlyi regime, was never put into practice except on the estates of Károlyi, was an executive, not a legislative act. The expected Socialist government following the aborted April 1919 elections also evinced the onset of statism in Hungary. Further similarities between Bulgaria and Hungary are indicated in Khristov's and Pastor's essay; since both Bulgarian and Hungarian territories were offered as compensation for supporting French policy, neither of these countries were asked to participate in the French intervention in Russia and the Ukraine.

The Hungarian Soviet Republic ushered in the only meaningful interwar European Communist system outside of the confines of the former Russian empire. This unique historical experience is the reason for this collection's stress of Hungary's revolutions.

The rise of the Hungarian Soviet Republic on March 21, 1919, was the result of the desperate reaction of Hungarians to what appeared to be a Carthagenian Peace. A Communist government in Budapest, it was assumed, could get the support of Moscow, which, as Torrey, Stavrou, Munholland, and Hajdu posit, was about to defeat the White and Entente forces in the Ukraine. It was expected that following victory, the Soviet Russian Red Army would then come to the aid of the Hungarian Red Army.

Although the statesmen around Hungary paid lip service to anticommunism in pursuance of nationalistic goals, Hungarian leaders, instead of working for the selfsame goals only by service in words to communism, took their Marxism seriously. Led by Béla Kun, they embarked on a doctrinaire Communist policy, domestic and foreign, which managed to alienate most social groups as indicated in the general overview presented by Ignác Romsics and the specific example of the engineers given by György Péteri. The desperate defense of national integrity was instrumental in establishing popular support behind the Soviet Republic in March 1919. The nationalistic component was perceived by most of the peace conferees in Paris. In fact, as Coppa shows, Benito Mussolini, the Italian Fascist leader, saw the pattern of National Socialism in the Hungarian example. Zsuppan finds that the British expected to ride out the storm and correctly assumed that the doctrinaire Hungarian communists would be their own grave diggers. Indeed, Romsics proves that this assessment was correct, for policies of the Hungarian Soviet Republic's government did alienate most social groups from the government.

Military intervention by Hungary's neighbors was supported by France, as were Hungarian counterrevolutionary organizations in French-occupied Szeged, as Tihany shows. Yugoslavia's reluctance in joining this Bolshevik crusade against Hungary is another indication that anti-Bolshevism was a mere cover for ulterior motives. Ormos suggests, and Kovačev demonstrates, that Serbia, satisfied with the occupation of Baranya, held no further claims against Hungary. Contesting with Romania the sovereignty of the Banat gave Yugoslavia additional reasons for abstaining from military intervention against Soviet Hungary.

Fogarassy sees in the Romanian military action in April 1919, the earliest intervention against Hungary. This action was made possible by the lack of movement on the part of the Soviet Russian Red Army in the Dniester area, which could have dissuaded Romania from fighting against Hungary. The evacuation of Odessa could have also contributed to the unleashing of the Romanian offensive. Stavrou argues that as a consequence of the Odessa fiasco, Greek troops were shifted to a defensive line on the Dniester. This redeployment, it appears, gave the Romanians the kind of security and confidence they needed in order to start operations against Hungary.

Whereas Hajdu attributes the failure of Trotskii's Red Army to link up with the Hungarians to bad military fortunes in spring and summer 1919, Ormos seems to accept this interpretation with a grain of salt. What seems to trouble her is that not only did Soviet Russia fail to provide military aid, but it also refrained from establishing diplomatic ties with Hungary. No prominent Soviet revolutionary leader was sent to bolster the morale of the Communists in Hungary.

We must also consider that the Red Army's bad military fortunes in the Ukraine, were neither due to outstanding abilities of the White military leaders, nor was it due to the high morale among their troops. Rather it sprang from defections from the Communist camp. The switching of sides of Hatman Grigoriev and others was caused by Communist actions that alienated a considerable segment of the Ukrainian population from the Reds. Therefore a combination of faulty Communist conduct of affairs in the Ukraine and in Hungary it can be argued, were the major cause of the collapse of the Hungarian Soviet Republic. Both Lenin and Kun would have had to change internal policies toward the peasants in order to help the Hungarian Revolution to survive.

On the battlefield, the Hungarian Red Army was successful against the Czechoslovaks in the Northern Campaign. Success in part was due to the fact that the Red Army was led by "specialists," professional officers, who according to Romsics and Szakály, were willing to serve the Red Army for patriotic reasons, even though people of their class had little sympathy for the Communist experiment. On June 16, 1919, in the wake of the Red Army's victory in the north, the Slovak Republic was declared in the eastern Slovakian town of Prešov (Eperjes), under the leadership of the Czech Communist, Antonin Janoušek. But, the withdrawal of Hungarian Red Army troops meant the collapse of this two-week experiment.

The departure of the Hungarian forces from Slovakia came as a consequence of the June 13 Clemenceau Memorandum. In his note to the Revolutionary Governing Council, Georges Clemenceau informed the Hungarian government of Hungary's new borders as decided by the Paris Peace Conference. The Hungarians were called upon to withdraw the Red Army from beyond the new frontiers in the north. In return he promised that following the Hungarian evacuation, the Romanians would withdraw from Hungarian territories. On June 19, upon Béla Kun's proposal the Congress of Soviets accepted the withdrawal of the Red Army from Slovakia, which began on the following day.

The judgment of historians on the wisdom of such a withdrawal is contradictory. Gosztony believes that the Northern Campaign boosted Red Army morale. The troops had patriotic pride, which, according to him was mistakenly deflated by Kun and the Communists. The battle flags, for example, were all red and did not include the Hungarian national colors. A halt to the campaign did not lead to a breathing spell, but in fact to the demoralization of the troops. Romsics also indicates that there was no further justification for the patriotic but anticommunist officers in the Red Army to remain loyal. Consequently, antigovernment conspiracies appeared even in the general staff. In the judgment of these historians, therefore, the decision to withdraw from Slovakia was a fatal mistake for the Soviet government.

Tibor Hetés, on the other hand, argues that by the time the Hungarian troops were withdrawn, the campaign had run out of steam and could not have been sustained any further. The ill-fated Tisza Campaign against the Romanians in July, as described by Nouzille and Torrey, could be marshaled as proof for either Gosztony's or Hetés's position. The easy defeat of the Red Army shows, as Hetés argues, that, for reasons of logistics, the Red Army was unable to mount a campaign. It is also evident that the government's failure to appeal to nationalism contributed to the low morale of the troops.

The Romanian victory led to the collapse of the Hungarian Soviet Republic and to the eventual rise of the counterrevolutionary Horthy regime, which intended to extirpate not only the achievements of the two preceeding revolutions, but, as Hajdu demonstrates, also embarked on a campaign to blacken the myth of the revolution. In this effort it succeeded well. Unlike the ill-fated revolution of 1848–49, the Liberal Democratic and the Communist revolutions of 1918–19 still do not project a positive image in the national consciousness of the Hungarians.

In addition to the efforts of the Horthy-era publicists, Hajdu also faults Marxist historiography for this state of affairs. During the 1940s and 1950s Béla Kun, the victim of Stalin's purges, was a non-person. The other extreme was reached in the late fifties and sixties, with the development of "Kunism," a cult which was fostered following the posthumous rehabilitation of Kun. The dubious veracity of these interpretations seem to create objections in the minds of most Hungarians. Pastor's examination of the recent historiography of Kun and the Soviet Republic points out that, following a brief respite when historians attempted to offer an objective interpretation, there has been a return to "Kunism." Hajdu also attributes the negative myth of the revolutions to a contemporary problem. In the perspective of almost 70 years, Socialist Internationalism, a goal of the Kun and the Communists, seems to have been a pipe dream. This is demonstrated by the state of affairs in 1986 in the Socialist Danube valley. For, at least two of Hungary's Socialist neighbors oppress their Hungarian minority to an extent unknown in the history of nationalities of the area.

It is hoped that this collection of essays will contribute to a better understanding of the Central European revolutionary events of 1918–19 on both sides of the Atlantic.

I
REVOLUTIONARY HUNGARY AND THE MILITARY

# THE MILITARY COLLAPSE OF THE AUSTRO—HUNGARIAN MONARCHY, OCTOBER 24 TO NOVEMBER 3, 1918

Márton Farkas

Our task is to summarize the last great defeat of Austro—Hungarian military forces on the Southwestern-Italian Front. This defeat, overlapping with the victorious liberal democratic revolutions happening in the hinterland at the same time, was a major cause of the collapse of the Habsburg empire. Military collapse was followed by a spectacular disintegration accompanied by revolutions. In the process of disintegration, the Habsburg state and military leadership were unable to suppress the revolutions and to foster a climate for a possible Habsburg restoration. Thus the Armistice clause, signed at Padua on November 3, 1918, in which the Entente Powers permitted 20 peacetime divisions "to restore the inner order and peace," was meaningless.

In the aftermath of the recent military catastrophe on the Piave in June and the so-called Black Day of the German army on August 8, 1918, the Austro—Hungarian Supreme Command reckoned on a great enemy offensive on the Southwestern Front. Reinforcing this view was the breakthrough of the Entente's Eastern Army in the Balkans on September 15, followed by the Bulgarian armistice on September 19.[1]

In the conference on the general military situation of the Central Powers (August 13—16, 1918, at Spa), German military leaders expressed, for the first time, the belief that they no longer expected to win the war, and that, therefore, a proposal ought to be made through a neutral country about starting negotiations to end the war.[2] The monarchy did even more: István Burián, the foreign minister, proposed immediate negotiations in his proclamation addressed 'To All Belligerents" on September 14.[3]

The German Supreme Command was indignant at the Burián Memoranddum, yet was forced to take an even more extreme step at the beginning of

October 1918. Namely, on October 4, it turned, with their allies, to President Woodrow Wilson, asking him to initiate and to urge immediate negotiations for an armistice and peace.[4]

The Austro–Hungarian High Command supported the offer of an armistice and peace with Italy. They considered that they had no prospects of offering successful resistance to the Entente troops marching forward on the Balkan peninsula, getting closer and closer to the southern borders of the Dual Monarchy. At the same time, they had to take into consideration the antimonarchial, revolutionary movements on the Home Front which became stronger and stronger, thereby becoming a threatening barometer of internal collapse. The Southwestern Army, still at their disposal and making up two-thirds of total available military forces, was completely exhausted both psychologically and physically, and a revolutionary spirit increasingly filled the souls of the soldiers. There was no chance to win, and any Entente offensive promised to have complete strategical and operational success. This would have meant total military collapse, surrender, and disintegration.[5]

The so-called memorandum-war between Wilson and Germany revealed the relentlessness of the winners on the threshold  of victory. This pushed the Central Powers toward further defeats and decreased their chances for further negotiations on favorable terms.

The Austro–Hungarian High Command was forced to try to avoid a last great Entente attack by initiating a "peace offensive."[6] Its activity in this respect was demonstrated by its willingness to satisfy all of Wilson's demands, although Wilson's memorandum to the new German government headed by Max von Baden, did not mention the Danubian Monarchy.

In response to one of Wilson's notes written to the Germans, Colonel General Arthur Arz, the Habsburg chief-of-the-general staff ordered the evacuation of the Venetian plain by October 17. Simultaneous with the preparations for evacuation, armistice committees were set up for the Southwestern and Southeastern Fronts.[7] Moreover, the High Command insisted on the immediate transformation of the monarchy  into a federal state. Consequently, the imperial manifesto (October 16) declared the Austrian part of the Dual Monarchy a Bundesstaat.

This initiative raised hopes of avoiding the planned Entente offensive and of bringing about the speedy conclusion of an armistice.[8]

However, such expectations were not realized. The Entente states, and most of all Italy, were neither satisfied with peace terms nor with the armistice proposals. Thus, conclusion of the war by a military victory called for the liquidation of the Austrian–Hungarian military forces on the Southwestern Front. The Italians believed that Habsburg military defeat was a very important prerequisite to the destruction of the military force of Germany. Moreover, Italy was interested in a military victory on the Southwestern Front because it might assure possession of those territories for which Italian irredentists clamored. Military successes, too, could strengthen Rome's position in Central Europe against the British and French who were busily pushing their own interests in the Balkans.

But, in this last great offensive against Vienna, Great Britain and France did not create difficulties for Italy. They did, however, have some differences with it as to the future of what came to be known as Yugoslavia, the Balkans in general, and Central Europe. These problems became sharper by the end of the war. The immediate Allied goal was the elimination of the Habsburg monarchy, yet these differences about the future undermined this mutual aim. Actually Italian victory on the Southwestern Front hastened the Enterites's final military victory, and so Franco—British plans concerning the Balkans and the Danube basin could be realized quicker. Their Italian ally, weakened by the war, could hardly be a danger to these projects and to the British and French anti-Soviet and anti-Russian intentions.[9]

The planned Italian offensive on the Southwestern Front was begun at 5 a.m. on October 24. When the detailed news about the attack arrived, complete confusion reigned in the Austro—Hungarian High Command who, completely caught off guard, had expected a cease-fire. After the initial shock wore off, the military leaders expected the collapse and disintegration of the army in the wake of the first blow. They feared the army's retreat into the hinterland, where the soldiers could join up with the troops stationed there, and so the "Russian catastrophe could be repeated... making total anarchy in the hinterland by a Bolshevik revolution."[10]

The shock can be easily understood, as the emperor and his retinue, acceding to the pressure of the High Command and of the commanders of the army, had made a last ditch attempt at avoiding battle. Emperor Charles turned to the Pope on the afternoon of October 23, asking his intercession with the Italian government to postpone the offensive, saying that "the war soon to be concluded will not be decided on the Venetian plain."[11] There was some hope rekindled after this appeal was made, for there was news coming through diplomatic channels about the kind reception given to an armistice delegation by the Entente, and the Vatican said, confidentially, Great Britain and France could accept the monarchy's request for a separate peace and for an immediate armistice. Although the terms would be very severe, this had to be done for strategic reasons and the monarchy should accept these. Vienna had to take this first step in order to have the Italian attack postponed. A similar telegram arrived from Sofia on October 23, sent by the English mission. In this, armistice was mentioned as the only condition for the postponement of the Italian attack.[12]

The emperor and his retinue hesitated; Gyula Andrássy, the new foreign minister, and the emperor himself did not dare to break with the Germans. Hesitation and fear led to the sending of a telegram to the Vatican, but this did not refer to the monarchy's appeal for an armistice, it only asked that the attack be postponed.

The Italian answer was the offensive. The demoralized High Command was paralyzed. The Bavarian communication officer delegated to the Austro–Hungarian High Command reported: "... they just let the things go on their own way and they were happy at not being disturbed in the headquarters."[13] Suddenly, on the afternoon of October 25, the High Command regained its confidence, as new reports told of unexpected resistance of the troops, especially on the front of the Belluno Group.

The good news started all kinds of speculations. Some saw the possibility for a favorable armistice and peace; others expected the survival of the unity of the army and the continued maintenance of discipline. Even the future of the monarchy was seen optimistically. A group of staff officers began to plan for the elimination of anarchy and the threat of Bolshevism in the hinterland.[14]

All hopes and considerations faded, however, by October 27. The army's resistance was broken, some of the troops revolted and some units, fleeing in disarray, started off to the hinterland. In a word, the High Command lost not only the battle, but the army.

The Italians' strategic aim was to break through the line of the Austro–Hungarian Sixth Army toward Conegliano-Sacile with a main stroke. This front line connected the Isonzo Army with the Tyrolese Army Group. The offensive was also aimed at tying down the main line of the army's reserves in the Vittorio-Conegliano-Sacile  region, so as to keep them out of further action.

For a successful breakthrough the plan required the rupture of the front at the junction of the two Austrian–Hungarian armies, the Isonzo Army and the Sixth Army, standing on Piave River. The second phase of the major stroke that was to follow the breakthrough, was an Italian thrust into the Feltre-Belluno basin from both sides of the Monte Grappa and from the area of Vittorio in order to roll up the Austrian–Hungarian–Tyrolese line through the Lugana valley.

It seemed reasonable to carry out minor attacks before initiating the major stroke aiming to knock out Austro–Hungarian reserves, which the

Italian high command believed to be at the lower end of the Piave. These were planned against the Austro–Hungarian Belluno Group and against the Austro–Hungarian Eleventh Army on the Tyrolese line, in the area of the Ariago plateau. The Italian strategic operational plan was formed after taking into consideration the logistical, support and troop strength of the armies facing each other. The catastrophically low supply of ammunition and troops of the Austro–Hungarians and the psychological influence of the defeat on the Piave were all taken into consideration by the Italian Supreme Command, along with the anti-Habsburg sentiments prevailing in the army and the war-weariness of the Slav troops. The revolutionary situation in the hinterland had a great impact on the soldiers' morale, and this fact was well known to Italian planners.

All these factors were weighed. Successful psychological warfare was also used at the start of the offensive. Selective propaganda equated the Entente's victory with the liberation of the Slavs. It intended to influence the Hungarian troops as well, harking back to the glory of the anti-Habsburg wars of liberation of the past and promised independence to Hungary. Italian propaganda also pledged to the Austrians liberation from German domination. Germany was identified as the only power responsible for the suffering of the war.[15]

The Italian command deployed 57 divisions – 51 Italian, three British, two French and one Czechoslovak, with 22 divisions in the first echelon, including the British and French divisions. Ten divisions were deployed in the second echelon, including the Czechoslovaks; and 16 infantry divisions were deployed as operational reserves, including four cavalry divisions in the third echelon.

The forces were put on full alert on October 14. The elite troops, including the British and French divisions, along with the Italian *Eight Army,* were to make the main thrust while the Italian *Twelfth* and *Tenth Armies* were positioned on the *Eighth's* right and left wing. These forces faced the Austro–Hungarian Sixth Army, the left wing of the Belluno Group and the right wing of the Isonzo Army. The Italian *Fourth Army* was charged with carrying out the diversionary strokes facing the middle and the right wing of the Isonzo Army. The Italian *Sixth Army* confronted the Austro–Hungarian Eleventh Army. The Italian *Third, First,* and Seventh Armies, having a role in the operations following the breakthrough, took their position against the middle and the left wing of the Austro–Hungarian Isonzo Army, respectively against the Austro–Hungarian Tenth Army in the Tyrolese Group.

The Austro–Hungarian High Command had no detailed, nor reasoned, plan against the expected Italian offensive. Badly affected by the severe domestic and foreign political crisis and counting on the success of diplomatic maneuvering, it did not ready the troops properly. Moreover, there was no intelligence about the date and the direction of the main stroke of the hostile offensive.[16]

The food and material supply of the Austro–Hungarian troops had only grown worse since the catastrophe on the Piave: soldiers were ill-fed and clothed. Staff officers' reports on the troops estimated the average weight of the soldiers as 55 kg; they judged their attitude and fighting spirit at minimum. According to these findings, the majority of the troops were "corrupted by Bolshevik and nationalist fallacies." Because of this general situation, the soldiers were unwilling, or unable, to offer real resistance. Actually, the High Command had to count on insubordination and the desertion from the lines and the disintegration of the army units.[17]

The Southwestern Army that should have numbered 1.5 millions, did not even reach 300,000 men. The forces were formally ranked into 57.5 divisions, but only a part of it, 37.5 divisions were on the Brenta–Treviso–Oderzo line, facing 42 Entente divisions.[18]

The Entente attack started on October 25 at 5 a.m., against the Austro–Hungarian Belluno Group and the Eleventh Army. The offensive's diversionary strike was initiated on a front 22-kms long between the Brenta and Piave, by the Italian *Fourth* and *Sixth Armies*. After a strong artillery barrage, the *Fourth Army* assaulted the Monte Assolone and Monte Pertica peaks from both sides of the Monte Grappa and occupied the key positions of the Belluno Group in very hard fighting, even resorting to hand-to-hand combat.

At the same time the Italian *Twelfth Army* descended from Monte Tomba to the valley of the Alano and broke through the Goniestream line. Italian troops experienced an unexpectedly tough resistance: initially, the Austro–Hungarian troops repelled the attacks, inflicting severe losses on the attackers. Both the Italian and the Austro–Hungarian Supreme Commands were surprised. But there was no secret in this development. It happened because the defenders were driven by their vital instincts and experience gained during four years of war and defended themselves while they had enough strength to do so. However, the enemy's dominance in materièl and manpower prevailed and resistance became weaker and weaker. The situation was similar along the line of the Eleventh Army on the Ariago plateau, where the Italian *Sixth Army* attacked between the Brenta and Astilo.

The two Italian armies, having the task of knocking out the Austro–Hungarian reserves in the direction of the main blow, stopped their attack after achieving this goal. Consequently, Austro–Hungarian troops could avoid the defeat. The Supreme Command, corresponding with the Italian intentions, concentrated the majority of its operational reserves, five divisions, behind the Belluno Group and the Eleventh Army. The correctness of this measure apparently was supported by a new attack of the Italian forces against the Belluno Group. However, wanting to possess the passes leading to the Feltre-Belluno basin from the south, the Italians proceeded to carry out the main blow on October 26.

While the Austro–Hungarian Supreme Command concentrated its attention on the lines in front of the Belluno Group, where nine Austro–Hungarian divisions were fighting against seven Italian divisions, General Armade Diaz, the Italian commander-in-chief, ordered the fording of the Piave in the evening of October 26. Thus began the enemy's main effort, which had a strategic impact within a few days.

Early in the morning of October 27, several units of the *Twelfth, Eigth,* and *Tenth* Italian *Armies* crossed the Piave and created three strong bridgeheads, throwing the Austro–Hungarian troops out of their positions. The Entente troops could break the front at three points from here at Valdobiaddenne, at Sernaglia, and in the region of the Monticano channel. The Austro–Hungarian counterattacks aiming to eliminate the Italian bridgeheads failed because the troops refused to obey and took flight.[19]

In spite of this, the Austro–Hungarian High Command ordered further counterattacks against the Sernaglia and Papadopoli bridgeheads. But, the counterattack could not be executed as the 34th Infantry Division, which was to carry out the attack at Sernaglia, refused orders on October 28, and the 11th Cavalry Division, which was assaulted from the flank by an Italian attack corps on the previous day, panicked and was completely dispersed; its members could not be regrouped in the rear. The attack against Papadopoli suffered the same fate: the mostly Hungarian troops of the 7th Infantry Division, the 43rd and 44th Rifle Division, the 36th Infantry Division, and the 10th Cavalry Divisions, consisting of mixed nationalities, rejected orders almost to a man, thereby taking themselves out of the operations. As a result of the successful Italian main strike, the front was pierced between the Belluno Group and the Sixth Army. Thus the road leading to the Belluno basin was open for the Entente troops.[20]

An equally impressive breakthrough was realized at the junction of the Isonzo Army and the Sixth Army. The Italian *Tenth Army* moving forward from the Papadopoli bridgehead broke the line of the Isonzo Army, first in the region of Vazoola and Oderzo, then it was wedged in along the Susegana–Corregliano railway and completely separated the above-mentioned two

Austro–Hungarian armies from each other. The High Command ordered a general retreat at 10 p.m. on October 28. The order stressed that ".. a defeat resulting in the dissolution of the military forces has to be avoided."[21] It was valid for the Tyrolese line, too. The High Command imagined that retreating troops could regroup at the so-called 1917 entrenchments, which was the front line before the breakthrough at Caporetto. Field commanders on the spot did not agree with this conception. As far as they were concerned, any further struggle was completely hopeless. Under the circumstances, immediate armistice and peace negotiations were favored, even at the cost of complete capitulation.[22]

Starting from this position, reinforced by the contents of the Andrássy note to Wilson sent on October 28, the Supreme Command sent an armistice delegation led by General of the Infantry Victor Weber. Captain Ruggera, a member of the armistice committee, established contacts with the Italian troops at 9'20 p.m. on October 29.[23]

Tactical commanders of the army, company officers felt relief: in order to keep a firm hand on the still obedient troops, they had to stop operations, and at the same time, had to reduce the rebel soldiers' influence. They expected to reestablish army morale and unity and wanted to turn it against the revolutionaries on the home front. In the order given to the armistice commission, Weber was asked to stress before the Entente representatives the urgent necessity of an armistice, lest the Austro–Hungarian army disband completely, overrun the hinterland, and Central Europe become prey to Bolshevism.[24]

When, on October 29, Weber dispatched Captain Ruggera to the Italian lines and Andrássy's request for a separate peace was transmitted to the Entente, General Arz, the chief-of-the-general-staff, sent a telegram to Paul von Hindenburg, his German counterpart explaining these steps, justifying them because of the disobedience and mutiny of the Austro–Hungarian 30th Division. But the Supreme Command's hopes for a quick armistice and separate peace failed to materialize. The same day the Yugoslav revolution blazed forth and that in Prague trimphed. On October 30, in Vienna, the heart of the monarchy, a workers' and soldiers' rising overthrew the Habsburgs. The next day, in Budapest, a liberal-democratic revolution led by Mihály Károlyi triumphed, attaining independence for Hungary. The soldiers stationed in Budapest played a very important role in this victory, and the Michaelmas daisy they put on their caps in place of the old imperial insignia, became a symbol of, and gave its name to, the revolution. In other Habsburg territories, Polish, Galician, among others popular movements, swept away the old administration. A common feature of all the uprisings was the divorce of the soldiers from state power and the securing of their armed support for the revolutions.

Thus, the supreme command, having lost control of the military forces stationed in the hinterland, tried everything to prevent the rout of the Southwestern Army still at the front. On October 30, it directed the troop commanders to stop immediately all fighting and to initiate negotiations on each sector of the front line.[25] The retreat had to be stopped by all means because the Italian attacks increased the spread of anarchy among the troops. Weber himself was ordered to bring about the suspension of the Italian operations even by accepting humiliating armistice conditions. Before issuing this order, the Supreme Command also asked the spontaneously forming national councils to send their men to the front lines in order to slow the disorderly retreat toward Austria.[26]

In accordance with their own interests, the national councils actually did not fulfil the Supreme Command's wish because they considered that a reorganized Southwestern Army would be the tool of Habsburg rule. The Hungarian response to the request was the Károlyi government's business. It did not approve of Weber's appearance on behalf of Hungary, but instead wanted to send a separate delegation under Károlyi's leadership, to Italian headquarters in Padua.[27] In order to have equal chances with other successor states at the peace negotiations, Béla Linder, minister of war, ordered an immediate cease-fire and the return home of the Hungarian units. Linder's command did not contradict the Supreme Command's because it was the latter that initiated a halt to the fighting.[28]

Nevertheless the Supreme Command refused to transmit Linder's command, as the armistice conditions seemed to be favorable beyond any expectation; for the Italian High Command recognized the monarchy as negotiator, although by November 3 it had ceased to exist as a unit, and allowed the Austro–Hungarian military command to maintain 20 divisions to uphold law and order.[29]

After some reflection, the Supreme Command decided to transmit Linder's command to the troops at 9:00 a.m. on November 2. Following it, at noon the surrender of the whole army was declared. The three-hour period between the two acts was insignificant with regard to the general situation, but later it was charged that Linder's command was the only reason for utter defeat. At the time, however, the tone and content of the telephone calls to Linder did not give the slightest evidence of the Supreme Command's disapproval or opposition.[30]

Neither Linder's nor the Supreme Command's orders could prevent the disintegrating armies from marching home. Nor had the Italian Supreme

Command not acted in accordance with the wishes of the Austro–Hungarian Supreme Command. Lieutenant General Pietro Badoglio told the delegates that the would cease hostilities only at 5:00 p.m. on November 4, following the signing of the armistice on November 3.[31] By so doing the Italians got an opportunity to occupy new, larger territories. At the same time 16.5 divisions still loyal to the Austro–Hungarian Supreme Command, were taken captive and declared prisoners of war.[32]

Arz and the military command immediately lodged a protest against this action, but protest grew weaker especially when the undisciplined troops in retreat reached Austrian territory, where starving soldiers looted and robbed. This brought the military command great relief: they were delivered from the trouble of coping with 16.5 undisciplined divisions.[33]

The Southwestern Army's return from the front was equally dangerous to the successor states. The soldiers were influenced by revolutionary ideas and they seemed to be inclined to repeat the events of the Russian October. Having seen its conservative plans evaporate, the Supreme Command tried to participate in the disarmament with all its strength. The strongest reason for this activity was to secure the victory for Wilson's ideas instead of Lenin's.

In Hungary, the Károlyi administration was very active in disarming the troops. Minister of War Linder gave orders for the disarmament on November 1. National Council members—cooperating with the Social Democratic party propagandists—promised agrarian reform to the soldiers arriving in the security zones, which were created at the borders between Austria and Hungary in the hope of accelerating the demobilization of the armed forces.

The soldiers of the Southwestern Army—41.5 divisions, approximately 1.5 million—arrived home in two enormous waves. Most came home before the second half of November; the return of the rest took place by the end of December. The POWs from Italy came home only in the postwar years. The return was not without difficulties: there were some atrocities inflicted by the Southern Slav, Bohemian, Polish, and Romanian formations on the civilian population in Austria. In areas inhabited by other nationalities the Hungarian formations suffered severe attacks by armed gangs which, under the influence of anti-Hungarian propaganda, had to believe that the Hungarians were responsible for the privations of the War. The slogan of these gangs was: "Hungarian pigs, you will pay for everything now!" Thus, the transit area became enemy territory for the homecomers.

Just after the war a great number of "scientific explanations" and historical falsifications were published about the collapse of the Southwestern Front and on the military defeat, which was seen as the cause for the disintegration of the Austro–Hungarian monarchy.

At the beginning of the twenties, Austrian and Hungarian variations of the German *Dolchstoss* [stab in the back] legend also appeared. On the one hand, this glorified the heroic soldiers at the front for their firmness and un-yielding endurance in the cause of the common fatherland, the monarchy; on the other hand, it slandered the troops and the people of the home front because they fell victim to certain traitors, Bolsheviks and nationalists, who had stabbed the heroically fighting army in the back, and so had undermined the centuries-old Habsburg monarchy, the common state of the peoples in the Danubian basin.

Together with the *Dolchstoss* legend there appeared the concept of faithful and unfaithful nations. Prominent in the latter group was the Hungarian nation. In their numerous memoirs, former Austrian military leaders have attributed the collapse of the front line to Hungarian units allegedly under the influence of the subversive elements of the hinterland. Special attention was paid to the disobedience of orders by the 27th Imperial-and-Royal Regiemtn and the 38th Hungarian Royal *honvéd* Division. In these memoirs, the final downfall was attributed to the cease-fire order of Béla Linder, minister of war of the Károlyi government. Historians of interwar Hungary confirmed this slanderous view of the Károlyi administration with their own arguments and selective decuments. Just before the outbreak of World War II, historians, however, tried to abandon the *Dolchstoss* legend and other falsifications.

After World War II the events of World War I attracted renewed interest, especially during the cold war period. The essays of this era have not been devoid of prejudice and political tendentiousness. The apotheosis of the Austro–Hungarian monarchy as the archetype of capitalist integration has often come into prominence in historians' works. Its utter defeat has been presented as an outstanding example for the disappearance of an important state in Central Europe. Austria–Hungary was seen as a lackey and victim of the aggressive ambitions of middle and great powers.

At the same time, objective historiography has affirmed the conclusion that the fall of the centuries-old Habsburg state served historic progress, although the new order: the birth of the successor states, has not solved all problems of the coexistence of the Danubian peoples.

## NOTES

1. László Zsigmond, "Díe Zerschlagung der Österreichisch–Ungarischen Monarchie und die internationalen Kraftverhaltnisse," in Aladár Mód, ed., *Etudes Historiques* (Budapest, 1960), pp. 332–33.

2. E. Gleise-Horstenau, ed., *Österreich–Ungarns letzter Krieg* (Vienna, 1937), Vol. VIII, 447–52.

3. Deutsches Zentralarchiv (Potsdam, Zentralarchiv der DDR), Stellvertreter des Reichskanzelers, Ausvertige Angelegenheiten 16.B.2.

4. For the text of the memorandum, see, Deutsches Zentralarchiv (Potsdam, Zentralarchiv der DDR), Stellvertreter des Reichskanzelers, Ausvertige Angelegenheiten 16. B. 2.–No. 2814; Hof, -und Staatsarchiv, Vienna, PA–I. 966-Krieg 25/33 KUM Nr. 4666, hereafter cited as *StA W*.

5. Hadtörténeti Levéltár, Budapest, AOK (Oberkommando) Chef des Generalstabes, Op Nr. 103.211–1918, hereafter *HL:* József főherceg, *A világháború, amilyennek én láttam* (Budapest, 1933), Vol. VII, 387.

6. Miklós Komjáthy, ed., *Protokolle des Gemeinsamen Ministerrates der Österreichisch–Ungarischen Monarchie (1914–1918)* (Budapest, 1966), pp. 687–80.

7. *HL*, AOK (Oberkommando) Chef des Generalstabes, Op. Feh. Nr. 1980, 1981–1918. "A fegyverszüneti bizottságok felállítása," AOK Chef des Generalstabes, Op. Geh. 1917–1918.

8. József főherceg, *A világháború,* p. 345; Dezső Rubint, *Összeomlás 1918* (Budapest, 1922), p. 307.

9. Bayerisches Staatsarchiv, Munich, MA–I–972–V.A.W. 25615717–Mu.

10. L. H. Kerchnawe, *Der Zusamenbruch der österreichische–Ungarische Wehrmacht in Herbst 1918* (Munich, 1921), pp. 72–73.

11. *Ibid.*, p. 59.

12. *StA W*, PA I. 966-Krieg 25/33. KUM Prot. 13154/57/1230 and the telegram of Count Czernin from Sofia, without entry number.

13. See, Bayerisches Staatsarchiv, Militararchiv, Munich, MA–I–972–V.A.W.–25615717/2-Mu.

14. Kerchnawe, *Der Zusammenbruch,* pp. 70–71.

15. *Ibid.*, pp. 182–203; Zoltán Czekus, *A világhábóú összefoglaló története* (Budapest, 1930), pp. 492–96; Ferench Julier. *A világháború magyar szemmel* (Budapest, 1933), pp. 270–75.

16. Kerchnawe, *Der Zusamenbruch,* p. 65.

17. *HL*, 11 AK Op. Nr. 2847/9; Kriegsarchiv, Vienna, 6. AK An. Abt. 6p. Nr. 60,000; no. Isonzo AK An. Abt. Op. Nr. 200; Op. Nr. 36,000; 6 AK an Abt. Op. Nr. 70,000; Op. Nr. 77,800.

18. Rubint, *Összeomlás,* p. 39; József főherceg, *A világháború,* p. 510.

19. Czekus, *A világháború,* p. 292.

20. J. Doromby, "Adatok a magyar csapatok szerepléséhez az 1918-i összeomlásban" *Hadtörténelmi Közlemények,* (1938), pp. 205–206.

21. Karchnawe, *Der Zusammenbruch,* p. 103.

22. *HL*, 6. AK Op. Nr. 1554/1.

23. *HL,* Verhandlungen Nr. 22. For the memorandum of Andrássy, see StAW, PA I 966-Krieg. 25/33. Friedensverkanstlungen, Telegr. Nr. 433.

24. Ferenc Nyékhegyi, *A Diaz-féle fegyverszüneti szerződés* (Budapest, 1922), p. 8—11; Márton Farkas, *Katonai összeomlás és forradalom* (Budapest, 1969), p. 271.

25. Kerchnawe, *Der Zusamenbruch,* p. 116.

26. *Ibid.,* pp. 118—19.

27. *HL,* Polgári demokratikus forradalom iratai. Hadügyminisztérium, 28,102/Elw. sz., and AOK Chef des Generalstabs Op. Geb. Nr. 2109.

28. *HL,* Polgári demokratikus forradalom iratai, HUM 28,102/Elw. sz., and AOK Chef des Generalstabs Op. Geb. Nr. 215o.

29. For the terms of the Padua armistice see *HL,* AOK Chef des Generalstabs Op. Geb. Nr. 2091 and 2162.

30. Kerchnawe, *Der Zusamenbruch,* pp. 134—38.

31. *Ibid.,* p. 137.

32. Nyékhegyi, *A Diaz,* p. 32.

33. Sándor Juhász Nagy, *A magyar októberi forradalom története* (Budapest, 1945), p. 213.

# WAR AND HOME DEFENSE,
# OCTOBER 31, 1918 TO MARCH 21, 1919

Ervin Liptai

The strength of the revolutionary workers' movement in the countries of the Central Powers increased gradually from the year 1917 and gained strength even after the Great War. At the same time the most bellicose and conscious elements of the workers in these countries not only swept away the war administrations and old monarchies but also, supported by a general hatred of the ruling circles responsible for the war, and by the despair of the people after defeat, attacked the whole capitalist social order. However, taking advantage of their victory and inflaming the forces of nationalism, the Entente allies were able to block these mass movements, thereby averting an armed assault against the ruling classes.

Despite its general eclipse, the ruling class in Germany was able to preserve its influence in the army; in Austria and Hungary, on the other hand, the ruling circles lost their most important mainstay, the army, by the end of October and the beginning of November of 1918. Consequently, fragments of the army were ready to crush the socialist revolution for the sake of the bourgeoisie in Germany, but were a nuisance to the Austrian and Hungarian ruling classes who wanted to do likewise.

After the victory of the liberal democratic revolution in Hungary the leaders of the political parties which had come to power, felt that most of their political aims had been achieved, or thought that any further problems could be resolved without the aid of armed forces. Indeed, they considered the army as a factor dangerous to the new system. They knew that their first and most important task was the disarmament and demobilization of the soldiers returning from the fronts in the deepest despair and intending to get even with those who were responsible for the war.[1]

The development of military policy of the new Hungarian liberal democratic administrations can be divided into three different periods. The first

—when Linder was minister of home defense—was the period of pacifism. This was quite obviously because the main motive force of the revolution in October 1918 was the antiwar feeling of the workers and soldiers; the revolution brought peace, independence, and democratic transformation to the country. On the other hand, this pacifism can be considered as the manifestation of the old antiwar feelings of the National Council. Moreover, the pacifism at the beginning of November was a conscious tactic of the administration, based on considerations of domestic and foreign affairs. The government wanted to break with the militarism of the Austro—Hungarian monarchy in the field of foreign policy. As far as home affairs were concerned, pacifist propaganda was a way to calm down the soldiers enthused by revolutionary ideas.

Pacifism, however, soon became untenable for the government owing to external reasons. Negotiations for a military convention with Entente representatives in Belgrade, and the territorial demands of the neighboring countries, made pacifist hopes illusory. The Entente powers, represented by France, and Hungary's neighbors demonstrated hostile intentions toward Hungary.

For this reason, the pacifist Minister of Home Defense Béla Linder was replaced by Albert Bartha, who embarked on the reorganization of the Hungarian army.[2] The army was ordered to stop the military advances of Czechoslovak and Romanian troops, who were bent on reducing Hungary's territorial limits. However, the Hungarian government was in no position to start a large-scale war against her neighbors, who were backed by the Entente. Instead it was forced to accept demarcation lines dictated by the Entente.

Nevertheless, Hungarian forces engaged in localized clashes with the Czechoslovak and Romanian armies. In these clashes, they were able to block the enemy for some time, namely up to the next memorandum from Paris, which approved *ex post facto*, the previously unauthorized advances of Hungary's neighbors.[3] These local encounters, however, had considerable importance. It may be assumed that, in the absence of such resistance, the armies of occupation would have grabbed greater chunks of Hungarian territory, which then would have been meted out to the aggressors. Consequently, the charges that the Károlyi administration disbanded the Hungarian armed forces and was unwilling to defend Hungary from advancing troops[4] are baseless and ahistorical.

Given the situation, with mass demonstrations of workers and peasants becoming more and more dangerous to political stability, the role of the army as the keeper of internal peace became very important. The effective force of the army, however, was made up of men from the five youngest age-groups and was not suitable for maintaining internal order. These young men were insubordinate and influenced by revolutionary feelings. This is the reason why Bartha attempted to attain his aims through a total demobilization of the armed forces, relying for support on police squads newly organized from the officers and NCOs of the old army.

Most of the 8000 professional and reserve officers still in service felt uncertainty in the new bourgeois democratic state and saw little or no future before them. Generally they did not agree with government policies, particularly with those concerning the army. So far as the workers' movement was concerned, they opposed the army, and judged it unpatriotic. Most officers were ready for counterrevolutionary escapades but they could do nothing because, unlike in Germany, there were no generals in Hungary who had gained a reputation in the Great War, or were at all popular with the people who could serve as the focus of counterrevolutionary activity. The reactionary officers' groups that did exist were organized mostly by unknown persons from lower ranks, and hence, could create nothing besides demagogic turbulence. Dissolving these groups was no problem for the administration.[5]

A smaller group of former professional officers collaborated with the liberal democratic administration, partly because they were more susceptible to democracy on the basis of their education and personal experience; partly, too, because, considering Hungary's foreign and internal situation, they became convinced that from political and organizational points of view the international and domestic workers' movement was the only force that could be matched against foreign expansion. Consequently, these officers of higher rank entered into the service of the bourgeois democratic administration and most served loyally even after March 21, 1919.[6]

For the members of the regulars who came mostly from the village poor, soldiering was more desirable than returning to civilian life, to unemployment and poverty. They tried to make military service both comfortable and advantageous. Their efforts in this regard necessarily turned them against the officers; opposition was deepened by the difference between the political thoughts and ambitions of the soldiers and officers. Common soldiers sympathized with the political movement of the working class and the village poor, but in some cases they were more radical: the soldiers were young, existentially independent, lived together and—what is the most important—unlike the organized workers, they were not influenced and guided by the hierarchy of the Social Democratic party and the trade unions.

The revolutionary movement among the soldiers was organized by the Soldiers' Councils. The administration and the management of the Social Democratic party both tried to control and direct these organs, but failed to do so. Under the circumstances, the Soldiers' Councils could not be the medium of strengthening the army; they worked toward disorganizing it. The Soldiers' Councils checked the use of the army against the growing forces of the socialist revolution, and their position taken on March 21 moved the leaders of the Social Democratic party to come to terms with the Communists and to decide on the proclamation of the Hungarian Soviet Republic. The government nominated József Pogány as leader of the Soldiers' Councils, a man who, having shifted to the left, was ready and able to go with the masses.

The road trod by József Pogány to this commitment to the proletarian dictatorship was much longer than that of the other leftist Social Democratic leaders. He learned much from the soldiers, and they gave him the impetus to shift to the left; he did not follow them but went with them and was a real defender of soldiers' interests in the elaboration of state policy. Pogány had disagreed with the Communist party before March 21, but, in spite of this, Béla Kun characterized him before Lenin as a man who fought on the side of the Communists even before the proclamation of the proletarian dictatorship.

In fact, Pogány with the help of the Soldiers' Councils, forced the resignation of Bartha, and later of Sándor Festetich.[7] This fact played an important role in Bőhm's succession as minister of defense. Bőhm, a Social Democrat, had new ideas about military policy and army organization.

It seemed probable that a Socialist minister of Home Defense would be able to collaborate with the Soldiers' Councils better than his predecessors and that the support of the organized workers would be strengthed as a result of his activity.

As far as his ambitions in terms of the army organization were concerned Bőhm followed Linder's footsteps. Yet, he declared important changes in the composition of the regulars, in the status of the army, and in the standards of army organization. His aim was to get rid of the soldiers of the old army who were unable to serve the purposes of the military administration; he planned to recruit from among the organized workers, and his intention was to create an army of the Social Democratic party.[8]

The first and main task was to overcome the aversion of the workers to the war and the army: the organization was to be supported ideologically. This support was embodied in the slogan "Revolutionary Home Defense." The Social Democrats endeavored to satisfy the workers who as a result of the revolution of October 1918, had become the masters of the country, and consequently the defense of Hungary's territorial integrity was very much in their interest.

Bőhm's attempt to organize an army failed for reasons similar to those of his predecessors . To some extent this failure can be attributed to the demoralization of the masses after the war. On the other hand, it is obvious that the organized workers were not really convinced that the country they had to defend was really theirs.

An utterly new situation arose when the Hungarian Communist party was formed on November 24, 1918. The Communist party did not consider the revolution to be finished after the events of the autumn of 1918 and tried to mobilize the working class for another revolution to lay the foundations of a socialist system. On the basis of Lenin's 1917 "April Theses" and in opposition to Bőhm's slogan about "Revolutionary Home Defense." the Communists declared that home defense could be revolutionary only if power was undoubtedly in the hands of the working class and the village poor, if the war did not serve for the maintenance of national suppression, and if the political management would totally break with the interests of the exploiters. They proclaimed that Hungary's enemies are not the workers and peasants of the neighboring countries but the exploiting classes. The objective ot the military policy of the Communist party was to gain the soldiers' support for the new administration, to win them over to the cause of the revolution, to organize the defense of the workers, and, ultimately, to foster the formation of the Red Guards.[9]

Undoubtedly, the results achieved by the Communist party in the field of the military affairs were more significant than those attained by the bourgeois parties. By the end of March numerous detachments of armed workers were ready to act for the socialist revolution and a majority of the army's formations was also on the side of the revolution. These were of very great importance in the bloodless takeover of March 21, 1919.

## NOTES

1. Hungary, National Archives, *Minisztertanácsi jegyzőkönyvek* K No. 27, Nov. 8, 1918, no. 42, hereafter cited as *MTJK;* Michael Károlyi, *Memoirs of Michael Károlyi. Faith Without Illusion* (New York, 1957), p. 126.

2. Pál Schönwald, *A magyarországi 1918—1919-es polgári demokratikus forradalom állam és jogtörténeti kérdései* (Budapest, 1969), pp. 172—74.

3. Mária Ormos, *Padovától Trianonig 1918—1920* (Budapest 1983), pp. 103—35.

4. Pál Schönwald, *A Károlyi Per* (Budapest, 1985), pp. 157, 187.

5. Vilmos Bőhm, *Két forradalom tűzében* (Budapest, 1947), pp. 94—95.

6. Ervin Liptai, *A Magyar Tanácsköztársaság* (Budapest, 1965) pp. 87—88.

7. Liptai, *A Magyar Tanácsköztársaság.* 68—70.

8. *MTJK,* K No. 20. Febr. 18, 1919.

9. Liptai, *A Magyar Tanácsköztársaság,* pp. 52, 78.

# THE EASTERN CAMPAIGN
# OF THE HUNGARIAN RED ARMY, APRIL 1919

László Fogarassy

The organizational meeting of the Governing Council of the Hungarian Revolution was held on March 22, 1919. Among its participants was Péter Ágoston, assistant commissar for foreign affairs, who kept a systematic diary in the period of the two revolutions and during the Romanian occupation. Ágoston had come to Budapest from Nagyvárad during the Károlyi regime and was an enthusiastic advocate of the principle of armed defense against the Entente and their allies. Quite understandably, therefore, in his notes on the first meeting of the Soviet Republic, he expressed disapproval of the fact that Vilmos Bőhm, who had proven himself a competent minister of national defense, was to become minister for the introduction of socialism, whereas József Pogány was to be appointed commissar for military affairs; for Pogány was the one who, according to Ágoston, "disorganized the army—and now he is the one expected to reorganize it, after all, we were getting ready to fight a war..." Nor was Agoston alone in this appraisal! Already in the course of the first cabinet meeting Ágoston had noted that although Sándor Garbai was the titular head of government, its true leader was Béla Kun. No one dared offer opinions, everyone wanted to hear what Kun had to say first. Kun gave Ágoston the impression of a leader who makes snap decisions, and was a true Machiavellian besides.[1]

The first cabinet meeting of the Soviet Republic discussed a number of matters. After the meeting was declared officially open, Garbai announced that Lt.-Col. Fernand Vix, head of the French Military Mission, inquired whether he might have to remain in Budapest, since, on the previous day, having been handed Károlyi's reply rejecting his demands, he had informed the Foreign Ministry official who delivered the note that he would be packing! Vix also complained about the restrictions imposed on his personal freedom, and announced his intention to move on board one of the two monitors the Entente had dispatched to Budapest. Szántó, assistant commissar for military affairs, objected to setting Vix free. On the preceding day Vix had requested by cable the dispatch of 15,000 Entente troops to Budapest from Belgrade. Now Szántó suggested that those guilty of transmitting the cable be arraigned in front of a statutory tribunal. The Council accepted this proposal. The Commissar for Food Supplies, Mór Erdélyi, then informed the Council that a supply of American lard meant for Hungary had already reached Zagreb, and that the personnel of the American mission in Budapest was prepared to travel there if provided a special train for the purpose. A decision to that effect was approved.

At a motion of Bőhm, Vix was to be promised freedom of movement and appropriate quarters, on the condition that he not send ciphered telegrams from Budapest. As regards military matters, the council took only one noteworthy decision: at the suggestion of Béla Kun, it entrusted Commissar of Military Affairs Pogány with the dispatch of civilian political commissars to the fronts, taking as model the practice of the French Revolution's Convention. After that, at the proposal of Szántó, the Council ordered the arrest of three high-ranking police officers who had played a prominent role in the persecution of Communists following February 20, 1919.

On Bőhm's motion, steps were taken for the arrest of the former wartime ministers Baron József Szterényi and Baron General Sándor Szirmay. Among other decisions taken it is worth mentioning the abolition of titles and ranks.[2]

Practically nothing transpired at this meeting that might have irritated the victorious powers. Only the day before, angry crowds had demonstrated in front of the building housing the Entente mission, against the Entente and against Lt.-Col. Vix, and it got to a point where Vix felt it necessary to telephone Bőhm to ask for an armed guard. The dispatched soldiers created the impression that Vix was a prisoner of the Hungarian government.[3] He was warned not to appear on the streets for the time being, for the sake of his personal safety.

Vix decided, nevertheless, to leave for Belgrade along with mission personnel. Before leaving he saw fit to issue a press release to the Budapest papers in which he denied that he had made any kind of statement regarding the future frontiers of Hungary in front of Count Mihály Károlyi. No one, however, took this denial seriously, but the mere fact that it could be published was an indication that the Soviet Republic, or rather its true leader, Béla Kun, was not eager to challenge immediately the Entente.

Lt.-Col. Ferenc Julier who was, from the beginning of January 1919 the commander of the 5th Section (Operations) of the Ministry of Defense, wrote in his memoirs:

Everyone hoped that the change in regime would bring about general mobilization and the immediate initiation of military operations. Our notions at the time may appear naive, to some today, but in March 1919 we could not have known how far the situation would degenerate. All we could see then was that the country was in agony and that we must grab whatever means were available to make her recover. I called together the officer corps of the section under my command after the above communication was received, and I confidentially revealed the situation to them that we might reach a unanimous decision regarding what attitude to adopt, as indeed we had always done. All my officers spoke to the effect that we must remain at our post, for the sake of the fatherland. There was but one officer who was unable to give a definite answer, because as he said, he still had to think about it. I am quite certain, however, that the overwhelming majority of the officers on active duty believed we must remain at our post.[4]

The first chief of staff of the Hungarian Red Army was Lt.-Col. Jenő Tombor. He was born on March 3, 1880, at Nyitra. The end of the war found him in Vienna, working in the head office of the logistical command. On November 20, 1918, his former classmate, Lieutenant-Colonel of the General Staff Boldizsár Láng, then military chief group leader, appealed to him to take over command of the Ministry of Defense's Operations Section. Later, on January 1, 1919, when Colonel of the General Staff Győző Lorx, head of Group II, resigned his post, Tombor was appointed to succed him on Lorx's own recommendation.[5]

Tombor probably gained the trust of the Socialists by persuading the officers in the group under his command, in January 1919, to to take a stand in solidarity with him against a purely bourgeois government, and that he communicated this stand to Károlyi, by passing the Minister of Defense Sándor Festetics. In February 1919, he joined the trade union of officers on active duty. Futhermore, Tombor referred to the fact—not without justification—that at that time the Socialists were the only entity capable of creating a strong army, or of instilling discipline in the old one.

Deputy Commissar (full Commissar from April 4) Béla Szántó became the leader of the Main Section of Operations. The relations between him and Tombor were not too bad. Whether Szántó actually took part in the overthrow of Commissar of Military Affairs Pogány (who was also the leader of the Main Section of Organization) cannot be known for sure, but it does not seem likely. The Revolutionary Council had decided to relieve Pogány of his command on April 3, since he had proven incompetent in organizational work; to be more exact, the council decided to transfer him to some other commissariat. Hence the protest march organized against Pogány on the following day was superfluous. The Pogány system of Soldiers' Councils was phased out only later, and gradually. A five-member board took over the reorganized commissariat of Military Affairs; but not a single one of them was a military expert, even though it would have been quite possible to find officers with Communist leanings to replace, say, the consistently ineffectual Rezső Fidler.[6]

On the very day of the spectacular fall of Pogány the special train bearing General Jan Christian Smuts arrived at the Keleti Railroad Station in Budapest. Béla Kun, Sándor Garami, Zsigmond Kunfi, and Elek Bolgár all met with the Entente representative. According to the report from General Smuts to Balfour, Béla Kun brought up two arguments in rejecting the Allied demands for a natural zone.

1. The area from which the Entente demanded that Hungarians should withdraw was defended mainly by Hungarian troops from Transylvania, *over whom the Government had but little influence* [italics mine] he could not issue an order he knows would not be obeyed.

2. Although the present government did not attach as much importance to the matter of frontiers as the general run of the population, if he were to carry out the demands presented by Vix he would fall just like the Károlyi government had fallen over the same issue.

If the Entente were to insist that Hungary pull back its forces, chaos would result and Entente troops would have to occupy not merely the neutral zone, but Budapest as well.

On his way back from Budapest Smuts stopped in Vienna and Prague, where he met with Karl Renner and Tomas Masaryk. When the Czech Ministry of Defense received information about what had transpired in Budapest, it issued an order to attack the Hungarian Soviet Republic on April 7, and, as a matter of course, informed the Supreme military council of the Entente about the order. On the very next day, however, *Supreme Commandant* Marshal Ferdinand Foch cabled that the lead elements of General Louis Franchet d'Esperey's Entente forces should occupy defensive positions until further orders, and therefore, the Czechoslovakian army should also remain on the defensive for the time being.[7]

The Operations Section of the Hungarian Commissariat for Military Affairs took the position, after all this, that general mobilization should be declared for as many classes as it could provide with equipment for the moment. The government, however, continued to insist on recruitment. Béla Kun did not even stress the need of establishing liaison between the Hungarian and Russian general staffs for the sake of military cooperation. No formal political or military alliance was signed between Budapest and Moscow.

Incidentally, Béla Kun was not an amateur statesman, as one might suspect from the aforesaid. Indeed, after the departure of General Smuts he counted on the possibility of war. Therefore, on April 7, he summoned Colonel Vilmos Nagybaczoni Nagy (the spokesman for the Transylvanian Division at the 1st Section of the Commissariat on Military Affairs) to present a realistic situation report on the mood and morale, the materiel situation, and the organization, of the Transylvanian forces. On the basis of personal meetings and discussions with the commanders and troops of the Transylvanian Division, Vilmos Nagy reported as follows: the proclamation of the dictatorship of the proletariat had been received generally with calm; the men were hoping that an attack against the Romanians would finally be launched, for the fighting spirit was there; the directive abolishing military ranks and decorations had loosened discipline, which had just been consolidated in the regiments that were not composed of purely Transylvanian elements—such as the 3rd and 39th Regiments from Debrecen, the 4th from Nagyvárad, and the 12th from Szatmár. The ban on wearing medals of bravery, in particular, provoked some irritation. The sermons delivered by the agitators sent out by the local directories were received with mixed feelings by the troops, especially since Red auxiliary troops had not been dispatched among them as yet. Moreover, as they were demanding uniforms, arms, ammunition, Vilmos Nagy got the impression that there were some Romanian *agents provocateurs* active among the Transylvanians, spreading the word that the Communists were out to confiscate all private property, including small holdings.[8]

It is worth mentioning here that the Revolutionary Governing Council appointed Frigyes Karikás as its political commissar at the the Transylvanian Division headquarters in Szatmár, whereas László Szamuely was sent to the headquarters at Nyíregyháza in the same capacity.[9]

On March 29, the Command of the Transylvanian Military District at Debrecen reported to the Commissariat for Military Affairs that the Romanians were concentrating troops along the northern sector of their Hungarian front, from which it concluded that their intention was to create a Romanian–Czechoslovakian corridor, thereby preventing the Hungarian Soviet Republic from establishing direct contact with the Russian Red forces.[10] In order to establish such contact, however, the Russian and Ukrainian Red troops would have had to penetrate into Eastern Galicia, where the West Ukrainian People's Republic had been proclaimed on November 13, 1918, with an area of about 40,000 square kilometers and four-million inhabitants —of whom about three-million were Ukrainians, the remainder Polish or Jewish, not counting the few of German descent. The relations between the Hungarian Soviet Republic and the White Ukrainian regime were not the worst. The two even reached an agreement according to which the West Ukrainians would commit themselves to ship large quantities of unrefined oil and gasoline to Hungary from the beginning of the second half of April.[11] On the other hand, their relationship with Poland and even Romania was bad. Thus, it was not especially in the interest of either Budapest or Stanislau, whether from the ideological point of view or from that of the creation of a Greater Ukraine (*Ruska Krajna*), to form some sort of an axis.

The Romanian *Consiliul Dirigent* meeting in Nagyszeben, in the area already occupied by the Romanian Royal Army, had ordered partial mobilization on February 4, 1919, calling up the classes of 1896, 1897, and 1898 for military service. The *16th* and *19th Division*s were formed with drafted Romanians and Saxons. Hungarians were not drafted, except those who reported voluntarily and presented evidence of Romanian origins. Even the mood of the German-speaking recruits was rather mixed; the prospect of having to fight against their former Hungarian comrades was not greeted with general alacrity. The Transylvanian troops in the Romanian Royal Army continued to don Austro–Hungarian uniforms for a long time for lack of materials, with Romanian rank insignia, whereas the officers received Romanian tassels to add to their old swords. German remained the language of command in several regiments. Officers from the Regat were assigned to the Transylvanian units, which had attained the planned peace effectives by March 27. The *16th and 19th Divisons* were raised to war footing after the proclamation of the Hungarian Soviet Republic, by calling up the classes of 1894 and 1895. April 1, 1919, was the first day of mobilization. When the classes of 1891 through 1893 were called up, the formation of the Transylvanian *20th* and *21st Divisions* got under way. The *16th* and *18th Divisions*, once raised to war footing, were placed under the Commander--in-Chief of the Transylvanian forces, General Mardarescu (*Comandamentul Trupelor din Transilvania*), from April 8th and 11th respectively. The commanding officers and chiefs of staff of these divisons were former officers in the Austro–Hungarian army.[12] The Saxon officers from Transylvania who enlisted into the Romanian Royal Army made good careers.[13] By mid-April the Romanian *Army of Transylvania* had at its disposal for operations against Hungary 64 infantry regiments, 28 cavalry companies, 192 batteries, one armored train, three aircraft squadrons, and two engineering companies.[14]

For the Hungarians, there were altogether 35 battalions, 20 batteries, two aircraft squadrons, some cavalry and three or four armored trains, of which four battalions and two batteries were facing the Serbians along the Maros River. In other words, the Romanian forces had a twofold advantage over the Hungarians in infantry, a threefold advantage in artillery, and an almost twentyfold advantage in cavalry. There were no Hungarian reserves east of the Tisza.

The fact that the Romanians had concentrated troops on the northern wing of their Hungarian front was first reported to the Commissariat of Military Affairs on March 29, by the command of the Transylvanian Military District in Debrecen. Immediately before the attack—that is between April 13 and 15—they noticed Romanian troop concentrations, and certain sections of the Hungarian front were under continuous fire. The statement of the Romanian General Staff, that the hostilities were initiated by the Hungarians, who were supposed to have attacked at several spots, notably in the valley of the Szamos at Sikárló, Cigányi, and Csucsa, as well as along the valleys of the Sebes and Kőrös, and at the narrows at Halmágycsucs, was pure invention. Yet, Romanian historians have become attached to this invention, either as a matter of comfort, as a matter of prestige, or out of ignorance—even two decades later, as seen in the writings of Kirițescu, among others.[15]

According to this account, on April 16 the Transylvanian Division met the first wave of the Romanian attack along the line Szilágycseh—Hadad—Bogdánd—Alsószopor. North of this line the Romanian *2nd Cavalry Division* and the *Olteanu Detachment* limited themselves, for the time being, to reconnaissance activities. The Transylvanian troops fought well. At Hada, they even captured the staff and commanding officer of a Romanian battalion. The Transylvanian Divison commander asked that the 21st Transylvanian Regiment be directed to Tasnád, and the Chief-of-General-Staff issued orders accordingly.[16] At 10 am, Colonel Károly Kratochwill gave the order for retreat.

Historical literature published since 1945 in Hungary has unanimously reproached Kratochwill for this order, which had a political background. From the military point of view, he justified this move on the grounds that the international battalions defending the narrows at Csucsa threw away their weapons at the sound of the first cannon and retreated, pillaging along the way, in the direction of Nagyvárad, thus leaving the right wing of the Transylvanian detachment exposed. The truth was, as the Romanian source also indicates, that the Romanian column penetrating from the north wedged itself into the narrows at Csucsa between the right wing of the Transylvanian Division and the Királyhágó group of the 39th Brigade. The group at Belényes put up a good fight against the overwhelmigly superior Romanian forces. During the last three decades Hungarian historians have not paid much attention to this episode; nor do the history books make special mention of the students at the military academy of Nagyvárad, (a company was composed of third- and fourth-year cadets), although even the Romanian historians have not denied them credit. On the other hand, attention has been focused on the defenders of the Csucsa line, exclusively on the basis of information contained in memoirs. It becomes clear from the latter that the 4th Armored Train played a distinguished role on this occasion.[17]

Panic broke out among the Kőösvölgy group of the 6th Division, and the three battalions stationed there retreated in dissarry. The 3rd Battalion of the 46th Regiment managed to hold out at Honcztő against an enemy attack from the direction of Zőldes. In his report, division commander Ákos Rab estimated that had the Romanians not attacked from the valley of the Maros River as well, their advance could have been halted.[18]

On April 17, the 6th Division, already in full disintegration, retreated some 50 km from the positions held the day before. The Romanians massacred the soldiers taken prisoner from this division.

> Our professional soldiers on monthly pay [that is, former officers and noncoms], stood their ground with determination and at the price of greatest sacrifices until the last moment, often left almost to themselves; many of the wounded, or among those that were exhausted shot themselves in the head in order to avoid Romanian captivity. According to the present experiences of the division command, the political commissars assigned to the units do not live up to the task which the Commissariat of Military Affairs hoped to achieve when it set up this institution, because of lack of individual merits. Irresponsibility, complete lack of military knowledge, and the fact that they are unable to endear themselves to the troops explain why this institution is definitely unseless. The squad leaders have clearly demonstrated at times that they are entirely lacking in competence and prestige in the course of activities preceding and during combat; the squads ordered to carry out scouting assigments often do not reach their destination, simply because their leader cannot read the map.[19]

Soldiers threatened to shoot down the officers and the political commissars who dared to stop them. Red Guard commander Molnár urgently requested from Szatmárnémeti the dispatch of the weapons and ammunition promised by the commissariat of Military Affairs, in order to arm the comrades there. He had sent as many armed men as he could from Szatmárnémeti to the front. At the same time, in order to maintain control, he was forced to summon police forces to Szatmárnémeti because the mood there was not conducive to resistance against the Romanians. Three hours later, Sándor Dénes, and János Kacsóf after him, reported that counterrevolution had broken out at Szatmárnémeti. According to the latter's report, several delegations came to demand to execution of a political commissar who had been arrested, and it was only thanks to Lt. Gusztáv Hautzinger, chief of staff of the 1st Transylvanian Brigade, that the executions did not actually take place.[20]

On the evening of April 17, the Transylvanian Division retreated to the line Huszt–Sárköz–Erdőd–Királydaróc–Tasnád–Magyarcsahol–Széplak. According to Ervin Liptai, reports regarding the heavy losses suffered by the Transylvanians were exaggerated, and the political commissars who filed these reports were spineless in his estimation.

It is true that the losses had been exaggerated. On the other hand, it is also a fact that the Romanians enjoyed numerical and material superiority all along the front. According to the situation report issued at 8 am the following day, the enemy had not penetrated the lines even at Csucsa; they probably refrained from attacking frontally because of the difficulties of terrain. The political comissar at Szatmárnémeti, Béla Papp, asked that urgent measures be taken because the situation was fast deteriorating; he urged that all organized workers of Szatmárnémeti, Nagykároly, Debrecen, and Nagyvárad take their weapons, otherwise the fate of Szatmárnémeti, Érmihályfalva, Nagyvárad, and Nagykároly was sealed.[21]

As of April 18, the Commissariat for Military Affairs ordered nine battalions and four batteries from various garrisons, including three international battalions, to proceed to the Romanian front. An operational group was supposed to have been formed from these units, independent of the Transylvanian Divison, in the vicinity of Érmihályfalva and, perhaps, of Nagykároly; after assembly was completed they were expected to launch a counterattack. The commander of this group was to be appointed by the headquarters of the Transylvanian Division, whereas Lt. Vilmos Nagy was appointed as chief of staff. Nagy however, declined the appointment, because he had no confidence in the troops dispatched to the front, and he had already received news about the flight of the internationals at Csucsa. He did not want to assume responsibility for the odium of a predictable failure.[22]

On April 18, the Transylvanians retreated to the line Királyháza–Szatmárnémeti–Érmihályfalva. Former Minister of Interior Vince Nagy who, as a resident of Szatmár was then political adviser to Kratochwill, testified that the commander of the Transylvanian Divison announced in the course of one of his visits that they would not be able to hold the line at Sikárló–Csucsa for long. He was forced to order a gradual, slow withdrawal, and intended to evacuate Szatmárnémeti.[23]

The headquarters of the Transylvanian Division moved that day from Szatmárnémeti to Mátészalka. There was heavy fighting around Kocsord and Szamosdob, in the area of the 1st Translyvanian Brigade. Here the Transylvanians, attacked in the rear by the armed Romanian population, had to retreat across a swamp, at times in water up to their chests, yet they succeeded in retrieving even their machine guns.[24] The left wing of the 39th Brigade was outflanked at Nagymajtény by a strong column of Romanian cavalry, and eventually broken through, as a consequence of which they had to surrender the town of Nagykároly without a fight. The Romanian *7th Division* was pursuing the 21st Brigade Group with strong artillery in the direction of Érmihályfalva. The 2nd Battalion of the 21st Brigade suffered heavy losses at Királydaroc. At Debrecen, 510 Red Guards, all former policemen, refused to obey orders to move to the front and mutinied. They had to be disarmed in the course of actual street-to-street combat with the 2nd International Regiment, which happened to be stationed in Debrecen at the time. The political commissar who signed the report on this incident asked that a general staff officer be sent to Debrecen to organize the defense, and reported at the same time that the mother, sister, and son-in-law of the *Consul Dirigent,* Iuliu Maniu, had been brought from Szilágysomlyó to Debrecen as hostages, in retaliation for the Romanian capture of the parents of Béla Kun. In May the relatives of Maniu and of Béla Kun were exchanged. All the officers of the Headquarters of the Transylvania Military District were placed under arrest when counterrevolution broke out at Debrecen. In the area patrolled by the northern group of the 39th Brigade, Magura Hill 915, east of Rév and near the Király pass, which was supposed to be defended by an international battalion, fell into Romanian hands almost without a fight. Discipline among the soldiers of the 101st Brigade was rapidly deteriorating; they commandeered trains and turned back in the direction of Békéscsaba. The report from the 6th Division mentioned guerrilla war waged by the Romanian population, and the headlong flight of its own troops. The enemy was advancing fast because they had cavalry, and even their infantry was motorized. The only reliable Hungarian contingent was composed of former railroad national guards.[25]

On April 19, the Governing Council of the Revolution ordered the general mobilization of the proletariat of Hungary with the appeal, "The Revolution is in Danger!" With the collaboration of the people's commissars the government organized rallies in the provincial towns and at the front. At these rallies, the participants were informed that the Russian Red troops had already crossed the frontier of Bukovina, and would soon join hands with the Hungarian Red Army. In fact, at that day's meeting of the Budapest Workers' Council, Béla Kun declared that the Russians were on their way to Czernowitz. The Commissar for Military Affairs telephoned Kratochvil to let him know that, because of the counterrevolutionary manifestations in the latter's jurisdiction, he was to brought before a revolutionary tribunal, and an emissary was to be sent to Szatmár to investigate the matter. This delegate turned out to be Captain of Hussars Tibor Szabó of Sáro, from the Commissariat of Military Affairs. It is typical of the chaotic situation that Szántó never issued any directive placing Kratochwill under arrest, or relieving him; he was satisfied with the fact that Sároi-Szabó was named deputy division commander the following day. Sároi-Szabó never reached Szatmár; he got only as far as Debrecen, where he took over command of the Military District of Transylvania.[26] That same day, remnants of the 1st Transylvanian Brigade rallied at Csenger, those of the 24th Brigade at Nagyecsed, and those of the 21st Brigade in the vicinity of Érmihályfalva. At Debrecen, two battalions of the Austrian International Regiment refused to proceed and threatened to shoot their commanding officer; finally they scattered in the city. The 1st International Regiment, on the left flank of the 39th Brigade, retreated after a short struggle and there were complaints of lack of discipline even in the southern group. On behalf of the city directory of Nagyvárad, Béla Katz informed the Commissariat of Military Affairs that the executive committee of the workers' council there did not feel up to the task of defending the city, because the troops fleeing in panic had damaged the morale of the workers.[27] On April 20, the Transylvanian Division headquarters at Mátészalka received instructions from the Commissariat of Military Affairs to transfer its seat to Debrecen. The 4th Battalion of the 1st Russian International Brigade, as well as the Naval Brigade, were among the reinforcements sent to Mátészalka that day. By that time the Romanians had reached the line Királyháza–Szatmárnémeti–Nagykároly–Nagyvárad–Tenke–Borosjenő Pankota–Világos–Szabadhely.

Commissars Vilmos Bőhm, Jenő Landler, József Pogány, and Béla Vágó showed up in Debrecen, as did Commissar Tibor Szamuely who traveled from Nyíregyháza to survey the situation. They held a general review of the troops from the balcony of the Bika Hotel; then Vágó, Pogány, Bőhm, and two local officials spoke to the crowd.[28] The military organizer of the defenses of Debrecen complained to the Commissariat of Military Affairs that the reinforcements meant for Debrecen were disentraining already in Püspökladány, so that in Debrecen the workers had to be assembled in military formations (supposedly Commissar Landler was the one who issued orders to that effect). He appealed to Chief-of-the-General-Staff Tombor to relate to comrade Béla Kun how incompetent and uninformed individuals taking similar measures would cause the complete collapse of the Hungarian Soviet

Republic, and recommended that those who perpetrated such acts be sentenced to death as traitors to the revolution and to the Soviet Republic.[29]

On April 21, the Romanians interrupted their military operations, because they felt the need to regroup their forces after five days on the offensive. This created the illusion that they would not cross the line of demarcation identified with Vix; that, however, proved to be a mistaken assumption. Since the Romanians had occupied Nagyszőllős and Tiszaújlak, the best troops had to be thrown in to protect the left flank of the 5th Division of Nyíregyháza. The 6th Division reported that the combat value of its troops was rather slight, there being not enough regular officers and noncoms. There was no sign of a will to fight, or any kind of enthusiasm or perseverence; the cause of all the losses suffered so far was the complete lack of discipline —the officers were not respected in the least.[30] Such was the situation in spite of the assignment to the division as commissar Ferenc Münich, one of the most dynamic political officers, and that there was no lack of subunits giving a good account of themselves!

On this day, eleven battalions and six batteries of reinforcements were sent to the Romanian front. At the cabinet meeting on the same day Vilmos Bőhm reported on his findings at Debrecen. At the proposal of Béla Kun, the Government of Councils established the Eastern Army Command, for the sake of the unified control of the troops beyond the Tisza; Bőhm was appointed to head the command and, at his suggestion, Aurél Stromfeld was appointed as its chief of staff. Tibor Szamuely was appointed the chairman of the statutory court-martial set up behind the lines; he was given plenipotentiary powers to discipline the undisciplined soldiers and head off counterrevolutionary activity.

On April 22 the Eastern Army Command assumed its functions at Szolnok. The Operations Section of the Commissariat of Military Affairs still had, at this time, control over the troops on the northern and southern fronts. Stromfeld urgently requested 100 former officers, including 40 former lieutenants and staff officers, from the Commissariat of Military Affairs for the general headquarters. On the basis of his findings at Debrecen, Bőhm immediately issued orders to every workers' and soldiers' council strictly forbidding them from intervening in or taking decisions on, any operational or military matter. He set up a school for political commissars at the general headquarters. As dilettantes, it was forbidden for them to interfere in military operations; those commissars who insisted on functioning in accordance with the former spirit of the soldiers' councils were simply sent back to Budapest.[31]

At the same time Bőhm issued orders to the effect that all units found between the Maros, Tisza, and Sebes-Kőrös were subject to the command of the 6th Division at Békéscsaba, all forces fighting in the area of the Sebes-Kőrös and Nyíradony were subject to the Military District Command of Debrecen, and all troops engaged between Nyíradony and Csap would be under the command of the 1st Divison (the headquarters of which was on their way to Nyíregyháza). The dispersed components of the Transylvanian command were to be reassembled. The 4th Divison at Püspökladány, three battalions, and one battery in the area of Balmazújváros would serve as reserves for the army, primarily for backing up the defenses of Debrecen.[32]

The Romanians reached the eastern boundary of the neutral zone indicated by Vix; they found justification for occupying this area in cabled instructions or French General Henri Berthelot. Then, for the sake of form, the Romanian leaders asked the Peace Conference for permission to continue their advance. They did not, however, wait for a reply, but proceeded on their own. By so doing they preempted the Hungarian counterattack planned by Stromfeld in the area between Nyíregyháza and Debrecen. The 6th Division retreated to the line at Kétegyháza. The Transylvanian Division surrendered Kocsord, Mátészalka, and Nyírmeggyes after heavy fighting.

Assembled for the defense of Debrecen were four battalions and one battery at Hosszúpályi and one battalion at Vámospércs, although, according to the directive issued on the previous day by the Eastern Army Command, a group of about one battalion-strength should have been dispatched in the direction of Berettyóújfalu to defend against a possible pincer movement from the direction of Nagyvárad, whereas the bulk of the defenses should have been concentrated towards the east. Sároi Szabó was probably expecting the main attack from the direction of Nagyvárad. In the afternoon, the Romanian *24th Regiment* broke through the front at Vámospércs, enjoying a threefold superiority in numbers; Hosszúpályi was under fire from other units of the Romanian *6th Division* at Nagyléta. The sirens of the factories at Debrecen were constantly sounding the alarm. Sároi Szabó sent a detachment to Nyírmártonfalva, two battalions toward Vámospércs, a battalion-and-a-half toward Ujléta, and three companies to Hosszúpályi. The bulk of the soldiers thrown into the fray, however, had been affected by the utter panic of the formations retreating from the firing line. Among those who held out in rearguard action were two Austrian companies of the 2nd International Regiment, and some workers' formations from the city.

At night, Sároi reported to the General Headquarters at Szolnok that he could not hold on to Debrecen, and undertook the evacuation of the city. The Romanians entered Debrecen on April 23. A delegation led by the

Bishop of the Reformed Church, Dezső Balthazár, received them. The former city council took over the administration from the directory and appointed Captain of Hussars Gábor Pálffy chief of police and commander of all law-enforcement agencies, and ordered all weapons turned in. The Romanian city commander issued similar orders, adding that the police and gendarmes should remain at their posts, without arms, whereas the Romanian city and local commands would provide armed guards to assist them in their task. All barracks had to be evacuated for the benefit of the Romanian troops, except for the barracks of the 2nd Hussar Regiment to which those officers, non-coms, and troops who had remained behind in Debrecen were now expected to move. Officers and noncommissioned officers were allowed to move about freely, without firearms or swords; they could wear their insignia in the street and could participate in social events.[33] It was mostly the inhabitants of Vámospércs and Tetétlen who suffered from the depredations of the Romanian troops after the fighting around Debrecen. The Czechs were on the move in the Ungvár area, occupying Ordarma with two battalions and one battery. The April 25 issue of the *Vörös Ujság* published news to the effect that these battalions had joined the Hungarian Red Army, but this was a gross mistake; the action, on the contrary, was the beginning of Czech intervention. A great military review was held in Budapest on the Vérmező, involving re-serve battalions composed of workers; some of them were to become workers' regiments on active duty and were dispatched to the front within a few weeks.

The directory of Debrecen fled at the very last moment to Füzesabony, whereas the Military District Command of Debrecen soon reported from Tiszafüred. The local authorities suggested that the floodgates at Tiszakeszi be opened to flood the plains of the Hortobágy, but this was vetoed by the Army Command.

Romanians occupied the villages to the East and South of Debrecen' Nagy-szőllős, Tiszaújlak, Mátészalka, Nyírmeggyes, Opályi, and Nyíracsád. The headquarters of the Romanian *7th Division* was at Nagykároly, those of their *6th Division* at Szatmárnémeti, and one of their cavalry brigades at Mátészalka.[34] Counterrevolution broke out at Munkács, with the proclama-tion of the Ruthenian Republic. Countermeasures were taken to put down the rebellion.

On April 24, the proletarian dictatorship once again held power in its hands at Munkács and Beregszász. In the area of Ungvár there was fighting with the Czechs, who were obviously trying to link up with the Romanians.[35] The headquarters of the 5th Division reached Miskolc. On this day, the headquarters of the Transylvanian Division was still at Nyírbakta. Stromfeld ordered that the troops hold out along the line Kétegyháza–Sarkad–Bakon-szeg–Hajdúszoboszló–Nyírbátor–Nagydobos–Szamos–Tisza, yet he himself did not believe that the Red troops would be able to halt the Romanians, otherwise he would not have at the same time ordered the military evacuation of the areas beyond the Tisza still in Hungarian hands.

The 4th Divison at Hajdúszoboszló (navy personnel and the Red Guard of Bihar County) was retreating of its own accord, without enemy penetration; the troops even commandeered transport by rail to Püspökladány. In the afternoon the International formation standing on the Földes–Sáp line likewise retreated without cause to Báránd, where it also attempted to commandeer railroad transport. Nevertheless, the general staff of the Brigade succeeded in turning the Internationals around back to Tetétlen. Headquarters dispatched two battalions and a battery from Püspökladány with the mission of recapturing Hajdúszoboszló from the Romanians.

The troops recaptured Hajdúszoboszló. The 2nd Armored Train was the first unit to re-enter the city bearing Tibor Szamuely. Szamuely had the mayor, the chief of police, and the manager of the savings bank hanged as leaders of the counterrevolution.[36] The reconnaissance units of the 1st Division were standing along the Hajdúhadház–Bokony–Nyíradony–Nyírm-hálydi line, whereas the Transylvanian Division was on the Nyírbogát–Nyí-vásár–Nyícsászár–Hodász–Orgróf Vay tanya–Nagydobos–Vásárosnamény line. At dawn, the Romanians captured Nagydobos and Hodász, not without fighting. Because of the strong enemy pressure the Transylvanians then retreated to the line: Kisléta–Pócspetri-puszta–Ofehértó–Nyírmada–Rohod–Ilk–Nagyvársány, whereas the bulk of the 21st Brigade Groups was in the Nyírjako–Ramocsaháza–Nyíribrony–Levelek area.[37] It should also be mentioned that all trace of the 1st Battalion of the 32 Brigade, from Budapest, a unit of the 1st Division which had been dispatched from Nyíregyháza to Haj-dúhadház, had been lost. It was found two days later in the area of Tiszapol-gár and Tiszapalkonya, a good distance from the front, busily engaged in pilfering.[38] According to a Romanian report, they had captured 2000 prisoners on that day and plenty of equipment. As they advanced along Ujkígyós –the bridge at Veszly–Doboz.

On April 25 the Naval Brigade was ordered back behind the lines to Karcag in order to sort out its units. One section of the Transylvanian Division was retreating while fighting at Nyírmada, behind the Lonyay Canal. Noting that the troops of the Transylvanian Division no longer had the capacity to resist, having been exhausted in the continuous fight, and with their equipment and clothing deficient, Stromfeld issued orders for them to draw back to the west bank of the Tisza at Rakamaz. Their section of the front would have to be taken over by the 1st Division. Around noontime Hajdúszoboszló was attacked anew by the Romanians. The Hungarians had to evacuate because of the passive, often antagonistic attitude of the population.[39]

The reconnaissance units of the 6th Division guarding Kétegyháza were pushed roward the Okígyós railroad station by the attacking Romanians. The Army Command ordered the establishment of bridgeheads at Szolnok, Tiszafüred, and Rakamáz, adding that the local directories were duty-bound to provide the necessary labor.

The 1st Division was forced into heavy defensive fights at Nagykálló; then, on April 26, along with the Foundry Workers' Battalion from Csepel, the 2nd Battalion of the 32nd Brigades, as well as about one battalion's worth of workers from Nyíregyháza, the division carried out an effective counterattack from Nyíregyháza in the direction of Nagykálló. Altogether three complete and two understrength battalions, plus three batteries, had taken part in the encounter. According to the wire report of the Hungarian Telegraph Service (MTI) they captured several machine guns and one cannon from the Romanians.[40] This action, however, did not alter the overall military situation in the least, and Nyíregyháza had to be evacuated too. That day the Transylvanian Division surrendered to the Romanian *2nd Cavalry Division* in the area Kotaj-Demecser.

Since the counterrevolutionary events at Szatmár, the command of the Transylvanian Division expected that it would become the victim of crossfire, because the Commissariat of Military Affairs refused to accept the pertinent reports of Kratochvil by way of justification. Therefore, in the morning of April 19, Kratochvil left Károly Kiss, a captain in the reserves, behind in evacuated Szatmár to act as a military intermediary. On the 20th, he sent military envoys to Nagykároly, to the headquarters of the Romanian *7th Division*. He requested a cease-fire and a halt to Romanian military operations, with the argument that his division was not "a Bolshevik formation," on the contrary, it was prepared to move against the Hungarian Red Army. General Dimitrescu answered that the was not empowered to conclude a cease-fire agreement, and if the Transylvanian Division wanted to put a stop to the fighting then let it lay down its arms unconditionally. The reply reached the division headquarters at Mátészalka on April 21, upon which Kratochvil sent the envoy back with a counterproposal. On this day the political commissars assigned to the division were obliged to flee their units. International troops at Debrecen wanted to disarm the division's vanguard at Debrecen—the Schupler Group or 21st Transylvanian Brigade—which had been dispatched from Ermihályfalva to Nyírbátor by rail through Debrecen.

This brigade was only able to extricate itself back to Érmihályfalva by threatening to put up resistance; from Érmihályfalva they reached the area of Nyírbátor after a lengthy march.

On April 24 an envoy handed over to the Transylvanian Division command the orders of the Chief-of-the-General-Staff of the Romanian Army. In these orders, the Romanians mentioned, as a condition of surrender, the prospect of interning the officers and troops until the termination of hostilities, after which, however, they would be released and allowed to go home. Their safety was guaranteed, and their possessions and complete freedom as well. The surrender agreement was signed on April 26, 1919, at Nyírbakta. About 6000 armed soldiers were present at the surrender at Demecser. The greater part of the artillery did not surrender, nor did the cavalry or fragments of various infantry units constituting about three to four battalions in total strength. All these troops either did not receive the appeal to surrender, or were not inclined to go into Romanian captivity. Many Transylvanian soldiers, once disarmed, escaped because of mistreatment by the Romanians who were occupied for a few days in transporting the Transylvanians, and the latter were disarmed only on April 28.

The general assertion found in the Romanian press and in Romanian military history, that the Romanian troops systematically surrounded and captured the Transylvanian Division is altogether invalid; for on that day, they had reached the Tisza only at one point, at Záhony, and smaller groups of Transylvanians that had been detached from their parent unit crossed the river unhampered at Versmart. When sections of the 1st Division launched a counterattack from the direction of Oros and Nyírpazsony against the Romanians advancing in the direction of Nyíregyháza, they also attacked the Transylvanians retreating in that area at Nyírtura. The Transylvanian side claims that they got into a crossfire during the retreat; the Reds were firing at them from the front, the Romanians from the rear. Even so, according to one of the dispatches, they strove to reach the Tisza, but they received news to the effect that the Czechs had occupied Tokaj, crossed the river, and reached Rakamaz. Since, on the basis of these rumors, it seemed they would be surrounded on yet a third side, they were prompted to give up the fight and "reach an agreement with the Romanians."[41]

On April 27, the Serbians also opened hostilities: crossing the Maros they occupied Nagylak and Makó, which were defended by only weak garrisons. Thereupon the Commissariat of Military Affairs also subordinated the 2nd Division to the Eastern Army Command, and the division was entrusted with the defense of the bridgehead at Csongrád. On this day, the Romanians did not interfere with the retreat, limiting themselves to reconnaissance activities. The still combat-worthy units of the 4th Divison (two battalions, four batteries) occupied the Hortobágy canal between Püspökladány and Karcag. Security units of the Military District Command of Debrecen (the Sároi detachment) were stationed at the Kishortobágy inn, while the bulk of the troops were stationed at the bridgehead at Tiszafüred. Fragments of the 1st Division (1st Battalion of the 22nd Brigade, of Csepel, the 2nd and 3rd Battalions of the 32nd Brigade, and some artillery) were on the Rakamáz–Balsa line. The bulk of the troops fighting at Nyíregyháza scattered, some of them commandeering railroad transport out of the town.[42]

On April 28, the 1st Division voluntarily gave up the bridgehead at Rakamáz. The Romanians renewed their pursuit of the Hungarian troops and their attack at Püspökladány created panic in the ranks of the 4th Division. The Army Command, however, dispatched three companies from the bridge at Ecsegfalva to Kisújszállás and, with the help of reserves, it was possible to carry out the retreat in a more or less orderly fashion.[43] General Constantin Presan, Romanian Chief-of-the-General-Staff, proposed to Marshal Foch that, since they were about to push the Hungarian forces across the Tisza and then send the bulk of their troops to the Dniester, a concentric attack should be directed against Budapest and the Hungarian forces should be disarmed completely. For this operation he offered altogether *two Romanian divisions,* adding that "if the allies do not commit anything to this operation the Romanian troops would stop along the Tisza, where they can withstand renewed attacks by the Hungarians most easily... ."[44]

Those remnants of the Transylvanian Division which had not participated in the surrender exercise began to rally in the area Kálkápolna–Füzesabony, exhausted, poorly equipped and armed, and with many untrained recruits among them.

On April 29, Serbian and French forces occupied Hódmezővásárhely, whereas on the left bank of the Drava Serbian units marched into Gola and took Hill 224 at Turbek (south of Mozsgo). The Romanians occupied Rakamáz, but the Verbőczy Battalion, the 2nd Battalion of the 39th Regiment, and the national guard units in the area were holding out at Tiszafüred. On the northern front, Czechs went on a general offensive along the line Lasztoc–Szendrő–Tornalja–Bánréve, so the Commissariat of Military Affairs placed the section of the front to the east of the Hernád River also under the Eastern Army Command, which entrusted the line of defense at Abaújszántó–Olaszliszka to the 1st Division.[45]

The Romanian positions were as follows at the time: within the *Grupul de Nord,* the *Olteanu Detachment* kept contact with the Czechoslovak forces at Ruska Krajna, the *2nd Cavalry Division* stood at Rakamáz, the

*16th Transylvanian Division* was west of Debrecen, the *7th Division* was occupying Püspökladány and standing along the Hortobágy canal. In the area of the *Grupul de Sud*, the *6th Division* had reached the Hortobágy canal also, the *2nd Division of Chasseurs* and the *7th Cavalry Regiment* were on the Gyoma–Szarvas line, whereas the *1st Brigade of Chasseurs* had reached Orosháza. The *18th Division Transylvanian* stood in the Debrecen–Nagyvárad zone as army reserve. The better part of its officer corps spoke Hungarian fluently.

The 4th Division deployed one detachment at the Szolnok bridgehead, whereas the bulk of its troops were in the area of Jászladány, Ujszász, Tápiószele, Jánoshida (units from the west of the Danube) or assembling in the area of Cegléd and Albertirsa (the 1st Regiment of Budapest, some Internationals, and naval units). The 6th Division was rallying in the area of Nagykőrös and Kecskemét.

On April 30, the stock of arms per battalion amounted to barely 100 rifles. Except for the bridgeheads at Tiszafüred and Szolnok, the Romanians had reached the Tisza everywhere. At Szentes the Romanian *1st Dvision of Chasseurs* pushed the security units of the 2nd Division beyond the Tisza and marched into Hódmezővásárhely. The Romanian *7th* and *16th Divisions* occupied the area around Csege. According to the report of the Sároi group, the enemy had been attacking all night–between April 30 and May 1–in the area of Tiszaszőllős and Egyek. The directory escaped from Törökszentmiklós, whereupon the company of Reds dispatched to that area marched back into Szolnok by nightfall. Its commanding officer was unable to control the unit because of the prevailing rumors.

On May 1, the Romanians stormed the bridgeheads at Szolnok and Tiszafüred, whereupon the General Headquarters of the Army Command had to transfer from Szolnok to Gödöllő; it reached there around 8 in the evening. A quarter of an hour later, it subordinated the Northern Front, up to Ipoly river, to the Eastern Army Command. Within four days, after the entire front was subordinated to it, the Eastern Army Command was transformed into an Army High Command, the Operations Section of the Commissariat for Military Affairs ceased to exist, and the officers assigned to it were reassigned to combat units. Lt.-Col. Tombor took over the direction of the Organization Main Group. Thus, the Romanian front became a sideshow,[46] and the focus of events shifted to the Northern Front. The losses suffered by the Romanians between April 17 and 30 were rather slight: 36 officers and 511 soldiers of whom eight officers and 92 soldiers had died; there were also 26 officers and 409 soldiers wounded, and one officer and eleven soldiers missing-in-action.[47]

On May 1, a very critical day for the Hungarian Soviet Republic, the troops defending Tiszafüred were still fighting heroically, yet the bridgehead had to be evacuated because the 3rd Battalion of the Red Regiment of Budapest had forsaken its positions. The remainder of the troops, along with the national guard of Tiszafüred which had joined them and were rallying at Poroszló,    took    over    the watch    on the    Tisza from Kisköre to Dorogma. On the other hand, most of the troops defending the bridgehead at Szolnok streamed back as a consequence of the Romanian attack, threatening to shoot down the commanders who attempted to stop them. The 68th Regiment of Szolnok and the 5th Battalion of Chasseurs from Budapest were praiseworthy exceptions. In the evening the retreating troops blew up a lesser railroad bridge crossing the Zagyva River.[48] The soldiers of the Red Regiment of Budapest also threatened to kill their own commanding officer because he insisted on holding the line.[49] On May 2, 1919, the news spread in Budapest that the Romanians had crossed the Tisza, and that the Hungarian Red Army was fleeing towards the city in complete disarray.

Prince Borghese suggested to the Hungarian Soviet government that they allow Czech legionnaire units to enter Budapest, in order to prevent the Romanians from doing the same. Václav Král deals extensively with Borghese's strange offer of "help," but we quote only the entry from the Ágoston diary for April 27, 1919:

The Entente ... meant to reserve Budapest for the Czechs, who were on good terms with the Italians. They suggested that we allow the Czechs in. They were under the command of Italian officers and thus it would not prove so humiliating if the Czechs were the ones to occupy us, as it would create the impression of an occupation by the Entente. Kun and I both rejected this proposal. Our view today is that the Russians will finally declare war on Romania, and then our situation would become easier. We already have their promise to that effect.

No such help ever arrived, but the Romanian front stagnated between May 2 and July 19, as the Romanians waited for reinforcements. The Hungarian leaders' attention turned to the Northern Campaign against Czechoslovakia.

## NOTES

1. From the fragments of Péter Ágoston's diary during the Károlyi Revolution and the Republic of Councils, from December 27, 1918. The manuscript collection of the Hungarian Academy of Science, MS 5060/c.

2. The legacy of Péter Ágoston, manuscript collection of the Hungarian Academy of Science, 5060/s. According to the minutes, the following were attending the meeting: Garbai, Kunfi, Ágoston, Szamuely, Rákosi, Erdélyi, Nyisztor, A. Illés, Vantus, Lukács, Kalmár, Bőhm, Bokányi, Pogány, Hevesi, Varga, Hamburger, Landler, Ládai, Rónai, Vágó, Dovcsák, Székely, Haubrich, and Fiedler—all commissars or assistant commissars. Ernő Seidler and Dezső Biró were present as recorders taking the minutes. The names of Kun and Szántó were omitted by mistake, whereas Csizmazia [sic] and the commissar from Ruthenia were absent.

3. József Kerekes, *Magyarország forradalmi harcai* [The revolutionary struggles of Hungary] (The military history of the operations of 1918–19). Manuscript Volume I, 128–29.

4. Ferenc Julier, "ellenforradalmi lélekkel a vörös hadsereg élén" [At the head of the Red Army with a counterrevolutionary spirit], *Magyarság*, July 6, 1927 (3rd installment). I have already reported on the essence of the parts between the two extracts (the conversation of Minister of Defense Bőhm with Colonel Stromfeld and Lt.-Colonel Tombor regarding the Vix note) in my essay, "The Unknown Transylvanian Division." I was relying on the justification of the sentence passed in the trial of Tombor. See, *Déri Múzeum Évkönyve* [Annals of the Déri Museum] (1971), p. 243.

5. Hadtörténeti Intézet Levéltára, hereafter cited as HIL, HoM bundle 711, item 374. Decision in the trial of Lt.-Colonel Jenő Tombor, August 18, 1920. After the biographical data comes a list of decorations earned in the war: the Knight's Cross of the Order of Lipót (Leopold); Order of the Iron Crown, Third Class, with Swords (twice); Military Cross of Honor, Third Class, with Military Adornment; Military Medal of Honor in Bronze, with Swords; Purple Heart with one stripe; Jubilee Memorial Medal, the Officers' Cross of the Bavarian Military Order of Honor; and the Turkish Red Crescent.

6. In the letter he wrote immediately before his death, Tibor Sárói Szabó (Zombor) asserted that during the Károlyi regime Béla Kun had promised him that after the proclamation of the dictatorship of the proletariat he would be entrusted with the command of the Hungarian army, whereas Otto Steinbrücke would be the leader of the Commissariat of Defense. In this regard, Dr. György [Georg] Lukács stated that the leadership of the Hungarian Communist party had never discussed this matter; this of course does not exclude the possibility that Béla Kun had indeed, unofficially, and without obligation, made such promises to Sárói and Steinbrück.

7. Elek Karsai. "Iratok a Smuts-misszió történetéhez," [Contribution to the history of the Smuts mission], *Levéltári Közlemények* (1967), 2; Václav Král, "The Interventionist War of the Czechoslovakian Bourgeoisie against the Hungarian Republic of Councils in 1919," (Bratislva, 1956), pp. 109, 149.

8. Vilmos Nagybaczoni Nagy, "Visszaemlékezés 1918–1919-re. Gondolatok 1963. március 21-én." [Memories of 1918–19. Thoughts on March 21, 1963] (manuscript), pp. 22–24. This manuscript reveals that Nagy was transferred from combat duty, in February 1918. In connection with the organization of the Hungarian uprising in Transylvania he writes (p. 8) that, according to the report received in the

Ministry of Defense on January 1919, there were from 8000–10,000 weapons available in the area of the valley of the Nyárad, Kolozsvár, the county of Kolozs, and the straits of Tömös, Békás and Gyimes.

9. Nagy, p. 26, as well as the *Nyírvidék* on April 2, 1919. He is quoting from "A polgári demokratikus forradalom és a Tanácsköztársaság Szabolcs megyében" [The bourgeois democratic revolution and the Soviet Republic in the county of Szabolcs], (Nyíregyháza, 1968), 61.

10. Lt.-General József Breit, "A vörös háború" [The red war], in Gusztáv Gratz, *A bolsevizmus Magyarországon* [Bolshevism in Hungary] (Budapest, 1920), pp. 233–34.

11. Archives of Military History, Budapest, Records of the Republic of Councils, container 88 (documents of the IV Army Corps), 307 hdm ikt, June 28, 1919. Its contents: On June 20, the Ministry of Socialist production reports in HÜNB to Haubrich, that there was only about a five-week supply of gasoline necessary for military operations. He requests that the vehicles department be cautioned to be most economical; furthermore, if possible to direct the operations in such a way that the railroad line leading to Stanislau be secured. The Republic of Council had reached a trade agreement in the second half of April with the Ukrainians for the shipment of large quantities of crude oil and gasoline to the Republic, but because of the occupation of the railroad line this agreement could not be carried out. The document was relegated to the archives on July 1 and, in any case, Stanislau fell into Polish hands two months earlier.

12. Otto Folberth, "Der rumänische Theissfeldzug gegen Räteungarn und die Siebenburger Sachsen,, *Südostdeutsche Vierteljahresblätter* (1969), pp. 220–23.

13. For greater detail, see, Viktor H. Muckesch, "Die Sächsische Garde in Siebenbürgen 1918. Eine Episode der siebenburgisch–deutschen Volksgeschichte," *Südostdeutsche Vierteljahresblätter*, Vol 20 (1971), Number 3, pp. 159–64.

14. Constantin Kiritescu, *Istoria razboiului pentru intregirea Romaniei 1916–1919*, Bucharest, no date, 2nd ed., III, 408. To complete the names I have consulted, HIL TK, container 55, the order of battle of the Romanian Army in 1919, VI, 27. At that time the army of General Cristescu was in Bessarabia; it comprised nine Romanian infantry division and two of cavalry, plus one French and one Greek division. In the operations across the Tisza in July the Romanians committed the following additional units: the other half of the *1st Cavalry Division*, the *1st Infantry Division*, and the *49th Brigade* of the *20th Division*.

15. Kiritescu, 409–13 (in survey)

16. *A magyar Vörös Hadsereg* [The Hungarian Red Army], selected documents, (Budapest: 1959), 133.

17. Tibor Hetés, *A 80. nemzetközi dandár* !The 80th international Brigade], (Budapest, 1963), 51–54.

18. HIL TK, container 5 (the documents of the Commissariat of military Affairs, 5th Section–situation reports). According to document 31 of the MVH, the 3rd Battalion of the 46th was engaged in the Honctő area, near Zöldes.

19. *Ibid.*, Situation report of April 17.

20. Lt. General József Breit, *A Magyarországi 1918/19 évi forradalmi mozgalmak és a vörös háború története* [The revolutionary movements in Hungary in 1918/19 and the red war]. (Budapest: 1919), III, 199–202.

21. HIL TK, container 5. Situation report received at 12:50 pm on April 17.

22. Recollections of Vilmos Nagy, pp. 26–28.

23. Dr. Vince Nagy, *Októbertől októberig. Emlékiratok, önéletrajz* [From October to October; memoirs and autobiography] with foreword by Lajos Zilahy (New York, 1962), 111. I should add that I was not able to use the documents of Károly Kratochwill, which are in the custody of the State Archives at Veszprém.

24. Endre Koréh, *"Erdélyért"; A Székely hadosztály és dandár története 1918– 1919* [For the sake of Transylvania; the history of the Transylvanian Division and Brigade, 1918–19] (Budapest, no date), 2/24.

25. HIL TK, container 5. Report dated April 18, 21:45 hours.

26. The letter from Tibor Sároi Szabó (Zombor) to the author contained no new data in addition to the information that he received his assignment from Béla Kun. There were proceedings against him instituted in front of the court-martial at Miskolc, but I have not yet succeeded in finding the pertinent records. He was, incidentally, acquitted.

27. See, footnote 25. It should be mentioned here that during the night from April 18 to 19, somebody gave instructions to the chief of police at the brigade headquarters for the assassination of the Romanians held as hostages, which they refused to carry out. For more detail, see Breit, III, 192–93.

28. *A Tanácsköztársaság Hajdú-Biharban 1919* (Debrecen, 1959), p. 414.

29. Kalman Incze, *Háborúk a Nagy Háború után. A béke háborúi*, (Budapest, 1938), I, 68; Károly Kratochwill, "A székelyt a forradalom sem győzte le," Endre Ajtay, ed., *A magyar katona. Századunk legszebb magyar csatái* (Budapest, 1943), p. 68.

30. *Ibid.*, p. 68

31. Vilmos Bőhm, *Két forradalom tűzében* [In the Crossfire of Two Revolutions] (Vienna, 1923), 306–10. The instructions issued to the political commissars are dated April 26. See MVH, 170–73.

32. MVH, 158–60.

33. *A Tanácsköztársaság Hajdú-Biharban, 1919,* 459–60.

34. HIL TK, container 65. Diary of military operations.

35. László Fogarassy, "Az 5. vörös hadosztály történetéhez. Védelmi harcok az északi offenzíva kezdetéig," *Borsodi Szemle* (1962), 48–54, (continued 1963), I, 73– 75.

36. HIL TK, container 65. situation report of April 24. Regarding the counterattack at Hajdúszoboszló, see Bőhm, 311–12.

37. In the above-mentioned situation report reference is made to Ibrány in lieu of Nyíribrony, which is probably a mistake. We can surmise the correct name from the fact that Nyíribrony is closer to Levelek, whereas Ibrány is east of the Tisza.

38. *Ibid.* It is reported from Kecskemét that the 38th Infantry Regiment and the Red guards there are not reliable. (Breit, III, 72). The military operations section of the Commissariat of Military Affairs states in its situation report for that day that the reinforcements sent beyond the Tisza amounted to 16 battalions and six batteries (actually, only 14 regiments); infantry battalions included the 1st of the 9th, 2nd/29th, 1st and 3rd/32nd, 1st/71st (replaced by the substitute units of the Trencsén Regiment escaped to Tata), 3rd/18th, 1st and 2nd/2nd international the 4th/1st International the 2nd/1st and 1st/2nd Naval, and 1st and 2nd/1st Budapest. Artillery batteries included the 3rd of the 1st Regiment, 2nd and 3rd/29th, 1st/18th, and 3rd and 5th/19th. Further battalions which later became involved in combat were still on their way, according to the summary, such as the 14th/44th, the 1st from Csepel, and a battalion of the 68th Regiment (VMH 182).

39. Bőhm, *op. cit.* Diary of military operations for April 25.

40. Diary of military operations for April 26. in Jolán Somogyi, ed., *A polgári demokratikus forradalom és a Tanácsköztársaság Szabolcs megyében* [The bourgeois democratic revolution and the Republic of Councils in the county of Szabolcs] compiled by Jolán Somogyi (Nyíregyháza, 1968), p. 69, 70.

41. Regarding the surrender, see, Kratochvil, 110–11; regarding the rumors of the Czech occupation of Rakamaz, Breit, III, 84.

42. Diary of military operations, April 27. Breit, III, 217.

43. Diary of military operations, April 28. According to a marginal comment dated April 30, during the battle at Rakamaz on April 28, most soldiers abandoned the bridgehead at dawn.

44. MVH, 192–93.

45. Breit, *A vörös háború,* 246.

46. László Fogarassy, "Adatok a magyarországi román hadszintér történetéhez (1919. május 2.–július 29)," *Herman Ottó Múzeum évkönyve,* VI. 335–53; In only wish to add that when Lt.-Colonel Henrik Werth brought the Romanian armistice conditions, Stromfeld, having perused them, declared:"This makes it quite clear that the Romanians are acting as the enemies not of Communism, but of Hungary, and therefore all Hungarians, no matter their political persuasion, must join hands to destroy this persistent enemy." (Breit, III, 133)

47. Breit, III, 128. It is possible that the source he had used whitewashes the events, because according to a Romanian historian during the Hungarian campaign the Romanian forces lost, between November 20, 1918 and August 20, 1919, 188 officers and 11,478 soldiers. Among these, 69 officers and 3601 soldiers died in combat. They suffered their most serious losses between July 20 and August 4, 1919 (Kiritescu, 488).

48. Breit, III, 136. Among the events of May 1, it is also worth noting: "The Sároi Group: yesterday two Romanian companies pushed it back from Kishortobágy to Csege. At the Szolnok bridgehead: at since 9 (May 1)... [illegible]."

49. Diary of military operations, May 1.

# THE NORTHERN CAMPAIGN
# OF THE HUNGARIAN RED ARMY, 1919

Tibor Hetés

Among the important issues of the history of the Hungarian Soviet Republic is the strategic military decisions which were made during its short life. Few in number, these decisions were affected by social and foreign policy considerations. Of all, the strategic Northern Campaign was most important. Its foreign policy considerations were portentous and had an impact on shaping military decisions.

The shift of foreign policy in the midst of a successful military campaign led to an eventual loss of the war, leading to the collapse of the Hungarian Soviet Republic on August 1, 1919.

* * *

On May 11, 1919, at a moment of favorable reports from Salgótarján, a council of the leading officials of the Hungarian government met in order to decide the strategic aims of the Hungarian Red Army. This council, owing to Hungary's unfavorable international position and military difficulties, had to make decisions under pressure.[1]

During the meeting, in the presence of Commissar of Foreign Affairs Béla Kun, Commissar of Military Affairs Béla Szántó, and Commander-in-Chief Vilmos Bőhm, Chief-of-the-General-Staff Aurél Stromfeld outlined the situation. He reported that, according to the intelligence gathered, the Romanians would continue their advance only after the arrival of reinforcements. This offensive would be coordinated with troops of the Entente approaching from the direction of Szeged and Gyékényes. News of the Entente forces' military activities were gathered from reports of the Commissariat of Foreign Affairs and the Headquarters of the Red Army. These reports established that large French forces were assembling in the south. The council, therefore, primarily discussed how to avert this possible combined attack.[2]

In the light of recently released archival material, it is evident that the suspicion of an Entente attack was not entirely misplaced. Hungarian intelligence reports, therefore, despite inaccuracies and exaggerations, reflected well the overall situation. Thus, the council's decision to consider the immediate danger and move against the Czechoslovak forces was correct. The advance of Hungarian troops, however did not begin until further reports reinforced conclusions drawn from the original ones. Actual deployment of Red Army troops did not begin until May 18.[3]

The military command, which stopped the successful operation in Salgótarján, did not abondon the idea of continuing the northern operations. On May 15, three days before redeployment, Stromfeld already gave orders to the III Army Corps to liberate the city of Miskolc, which was under Czechoslovak occupation. Plans for this offensive were readied between May 11 and 13.[4]

Both contemporaries and historians have described the decision to use force against the Czechoslovak army. But, some experts, disregard the very fact that the Czechoslovak army was proceeding with its own operation while the Romanian and the southern fronts were quiet. The Red Army, therefore, had little chocice but to engage the Czechoslovak forces. In addition to military considerations, political considerations also favored the Northern Campaign. Taking the initiative in the south would have been a mistake, for as Bőhm noted, an attack on French forces would have been a declaration of war on the victors of the Great War.[5]

Military arguments also spoke against an offensive against the Romanian Royal Army. At the end of April, it was not for matters of prestige that Stromfeld wanted to keep the bridgeheads on the Tisza River. He was already contemplating the next step: an attack on the Romanians. When these strategic positions were lost, however, the possiblity for a victorious offensive was discounted.

Since skirmishes with the Czechoslovaks were ongoing, the northern offensive actually needed only an increased punch to make it into an attack, or more precisely a counterattack, as it was the Czechoslovak army which had attacked first as it crossed the temporary demarcation line established by the Entente. Expectations of victory were heightened by military intelligence reports which clearly indicated that the Czechoslovak army represented the weak link in the chain of hostile armies encircling Hungary.[6]

On the other hand, some historians argue that the Red Army's offensive should have been restricted only to pushing the invaders back to the demarcation lines. Such a strategy, according to this position would have been useful in preserving the fighting spirit and power of the revolutionary army.

These arguments, however were incompatible with the dominant view of the times, which foresaw the onset of a world revolution.

The government had reached a consensus in connection with the plan of the Northern Campaign. There were differences only in the details of how to execute the plan. This involved the question of the direction of the main attack, on which opinion was divided.[7] One view favored starting the counterattack north-westward from Salgótarján to Nyitra. Another called for the Red Army to forge ahead via Miskolc to Kassa, and would have the advantage of preventing a possible link-up between Czechoslovak and Romanian armies. After much debate the second proposal carried the day.[8] But, Béla Kun favored the first alternative.[9] In fact, Stromfeld also had some serious reservation about the Miskolc–Kassa plan.

Stromfeld believed that the plan was dangerous as it could force the Romanians to come to the aid of the Czechoslovaks by linking up with them. At the same time, a victorious attack on the Czechoslovak flank would not destroy the Czechoslovak army.[10]

Bőhm, on the other hand, opposed an attack from the direction of Salgótarján, as he did not believe that the Red Army possessed adequate numbers of troops and fire power. Moreover, for him political considerations also militated against such a strategy; he further believed that the Salgótarján–Nyitra offensive would have necessitated the organization of a rear in Transdanubia, an area which was politically unreliable.[11]

The recapture of Miskolc was also important as it was a major industrial center. It would have created a very favorable situation for further military operations. Still, the possession of Miskolc and its surroundings would not have changed the strategic situation of the Hungarian Soviet Republic. With the exception of Stromfeld, who had strong reservations about the wisdom of an attack toward Miskolc and Kassa, the military leadership favored an attack in this direction for the same military and political reasons: to establish direct contact with the Soviet Russian Red Army.

Control of the mining district of Salgótarján and the stabilization of the situation there would have important consequences. It meant, foremost, security for the capital city of Budapest. Thus, the military consequences of victorious operations would have been strategically significant. Yet, political considerations were more important for the Hungarian Soviet government.[12]

Preparation for an attack toward Miskolc progressed favorably. On May 18, however, the enemy advanced toward Salgótarján. The first really complicated operational situation came to pass. Stromfeld's strategy, of combining boldness and daring, led to the Red Army's advance on Kecskemét, while it secured the situation in Salgótarján and initiated operations in Miskolc.[13]

On May 19, the 5th Division started its advance during the night and the following night it recaptured Pétérvásár. On the morning of the 20th the 1st Division also started its attack to recapture Miskolc. By the evening they arrived at the southern outskirts of the town. Some advance units pierced its defense perimeters. On the next morning the troops marched into Miskolc.[14]

This military victory of major import raised hopes for the beleaguered Hungarians. The reorganized Red Army won recognition and the soldiers' morale was boosted. It was assumed that foreign reaction to victory would have an impact on the international position of the Hungarian Soviet Republic.

The military follow up to this victory created some considerable soul searching. The Republic's military forces were dispersed along different fronts, and to expect further military victories seemed an illusion. On May 25, headquarters began to make preparations for the continuation of the Northern Campaign. Considering the overall situation, the Military Command decided to make all preparations in the area between the town of Losonc and the Tisza River, which held promise of developing into a broader offensive.[15]

Justification for the offensive, its aims and direction were recorded in Stromfeld's order of the day for May 26:

> For political and economic reasons, Headquarters decided to cut through the inner flank of the Czech-Romanian forces, first to defeat the Czechs and, after the Tisza crossing, to attack the Romanians.[16]

The military leadership hoped that the attack on the Czechoslovak Army would bring about victory within a week. Consequently, the area retaken could then serve as the rear for the operations east of the Tisza.

In connection with the direction of the offensive, the possiblity of joining up with the Soviet Russian Red Army arose again and this was seen as facilitaing the recapture of Romanian-held territories east of the Tisza from the direction of Csap. The offensive in the direction of Miskolc and Kassa and the break-through at the junction of the Romanian and the Czechoslovak forces was a realistic and militarily correct plan. At the outset of the offensive it was not known to the Hungarians that a Hungarian–Russian link-up was out of the question as a result of the changing fortunes of the war in the Ukraine.

On May 29, preparations on the Northern Front were completed and on the next morning fighting broke out all along the lines. On June 5, the troops were already fighting for Kassa. Having archieved the main purpose of the offensive, Stromfeld wanted to make preparations for crossing the Tisza by redeploying the divisions on the right flank. At the same time he continued to pay attention to the Northern Front.[18] True to his original fears, the Czechoslovak forces did not suffer a decisive defeat which would have forced them to abandon their original goals.

In response to the offensive against the Czechoslovaks, the Peace Conference sent off its first memorandum, bearing the name of its president, French Premier and Minister of War, Georges Clemenceau. This reached the Army Command on June 8, 1919. Although Entente pressure on the Hungarians should not be neglected, it is questionable whether it played a cardinal role in the postponement of the offensive against the Romanians. The offensive on the Northern Front continued, even though the Clemenceau Memorandum reproached the Hungarians for attacking the Czechs violently and subduing Slovakia without cause. In the same memorandum, Clemenceau, in the name of the Peace Conference, stated that the conferees are ready "to force Hungary to cease hostilities."

This indicates that it was not Allied pressure that prevented the Red Army from turning against Romania. Rather, the forces necessary to bring about such an operation were tied down by the Czechoslovak army. The "reckoning" with the Czechoslovak army was a prerequisite for the recapture of the territory east of the Tisza.[19]

The Hungarian Red Army had enough power to complete one operation, but neither the army, nor the country was able to sustain a war for a long time. For economic difficulties caused in part by the Entente blockade, lack of logistic supplies, unsuccessful recruitment and unpopular forced enlistment, made questionable the success of an extended war.

After June 9, military operations came into conflict with foreign policy needs. Military operations, the exchange of important diplomatic notes, and armistice negotiations were at a cross purpose with one other. Revolutionary romanticism clashed with historic reality. In this situation the military leadership wanted to develop a northwestern operation again; it had to give up its plans because of the hesitation of the political leadership. The Northern Campaign ran out of steam. Consequently, there followed rapid deterioration of the situation and final military defeat.

## NOTES

1. Tibor Hetés, *Stromfeld Aurél* (Budapest, 1967), p. 179.

2. Hadtörténelmi Levéltár, "Hadseregparancsnokság naplója," May 11, 1917, in *Magyar Tanácsköztárasság iratai* (hereafter cited as *HL*).

3. *HL*, May 17, 1919; Tibor Hetés, "Stromfeld Aurél katonai pályafutása" *Hadtörténeti Közlemények*, Vol. XXV, No. 4, (1978), 469.

4. Vilmos Bőhm, *Két forradalom tüzében* (Budapest, 1947), pp. 256–57; Jenő Landler, *A Vörös Hadsereg diadalmas útja és bomlása. Szemelvények a magyar hadtörténelem tanulmányához* (Budapest, 1955) II, 482–83.

5. Bőhm, *Két forradalom*, p. 255.

6. Tibor Hetés, ed. , *Stromfeld Aurél válogatott írásai* (Budapest, 1959), p. 222.

7. Bőhm, *Két forradalom*, p. 256.

8. Béla Szántó, "Részletek Szántó Béla volt Hadügyi Népbiztos visszaemlékezéseiből" *Hadtörténeti Közlemények*, Vol. VI, No. 1, (1959), p. 52.

9. Bőhm, *Két forradalom*, 256.

10. Landrer, *A Vörös Hadsereg*, II, 483.

11. Bőhm, *Két forradalom*, p. 256.

12. Hetés, *Stromfeld*, pp. 189–90.

13. *HL*, May 17, 1919.

14. Tibor Hetés, ed., *A Magyar Vörös Hadsereg: 1919. (Válogatott dokumentumok)* (Budapest, 1959), pp. 288–90.

15. Gábor Rohonyi, László Nagy, Gyula Tóth, eds., *Szemelvények a magyar hadtörténet tanulmányozásához* (Budapest, 1955), II. 422.

16. Hetés, ed., *Stromfeld Aurél válogatott írásai*, pp. 222-24.

17. Hetés, *Stromfeld*, p. 201.

18. HL, June 7, 1919.

19. Tibor Hetés, "Stromfeld Aurél élete, 1878–1927," in Hetés, ed., *Stromfeld Aurél válogatott írásai*, pp. 88–92.

20. Hetés, *Stromfeld*, pp. 219–20.

# BÉLA KUN AND HIS VIEWS
# ON STRATEGY AND DEFENSE

György Borsányi

Béla Kun started studying the issue of defense in the most regular way as a private in the 21st Kolozsvár Infantry Regiment. He took his first steps on the hierarchy ladder, up to the rank of master sergeant, during hard battlefield service in Galicia. Before he was captured on the Russian front, he spent 18 months in the Austro–Hungarian army. During this period he not only had the opportunity to reflect on the nature of militarism, but also obtained direct knowledge of the psychology of front-line soldiers as well as their needs and opportunities. He had also learned the enlisted men's special idiom and came to know what war was like from the bottom up. Thus he acquired the ability to feel empathy with the common soldier. All his experiences proved to be extremely useful later when the Hungarian Red Army was organized.

Following the Bolshevik Revolution, he threw in his lot with the Bolsheviks and he worked as an agitator among his fellow prisoners of war. In January 1918, he was at the Bureau of Prisoners of War, an institution formed under the Commissariat of Foreign Affairs. The following month he was commanding some troops in the defense of Petrograd. Soon after he became an important organizer of a propaganda effort that was to be done among the former prisoners of war still in Soviet Russia. During the summer of 1918, he commanded operations in the field. On July 7, he was commanding a platoon of 70 men during the defeat of the Left Social Revolutionaries uprising in Moscow. In August, he was in the Urals leading a Hungarian company against Kolchak. In September, he returned to the Urals at the head of a battalion.[1]

His activities in spreading propaganda among the prisoners of war, however, were much more important than his participation in actual military operations. He did multifaceted propaganda work, organizing training courses for propagandists, reading lectures, editing, writing articles and brochures.

One of his brochures *What do the Communists Want!* was even published in Germany that same year by the Spartacists.[2] A popular summary of the basic principles of communism, it propounded the well-known communist argument: "only weapons can fight weapons." The proletariat, he said, must take up arms and wrest power from the bourgeoisie. "After the victory of the revolution," he wrote, "[the] regular army will be replaced by a body of armed workers and peasants who will elect their own commanders from among the rank and file who are suitable for the posts."

These ideas, as well as those expressed in *Militarism*, appeared in print in the summer of 1918, along with *Who Pays for the War?* They reflect the contemporary ideological standards of the Communist movement. The pacificism of Social Democrats was heavily criticized in the conviction that the imminent world revolution would eventually bring peace for the entire world.[3] That those expectations later proved to be false was, of course, not Béla Kun's fault.

After having returned home as an acknowledged leader of the Communist Party of Hungary, he studied several aspects of the problems in connection with the military forces. His reasons for doing so were:

1. To demoralize and disorganize the military power of the bourgeois republic.
2. To win over to the Communist Party as many soldiers—whether either discharged or still in service—as possible.
3. To get ready for an armed uprising.

As for the first point, it was not very difficult to demoralize the bourgeois republic's army as it was the weakest of all its institutions. Similar influences from the right and the left made it impossible for the government to make the army efficient. Communists had been present in the Soldiers' Councils from the outset and did their best to prevent the army from regaining stability. They publicized Minister of Defense Albert Bartha's plans for introducing martial law and actively took part in the demonstration organized against Bartha and later against his successor, Sándor Festetics. The most effective weapon in their hands was the demand that the government should pay 5400 crowns remuneration to the soldiers who served during the war.[4] This sum was so large that the demand could not have been satisfied even if the bourgeois revolution had come into power in a particularly prosperous year. On the other hand, it gave them a good slogan. The soldiers, who echoed it obediently, sent deputations to the Ministry of Defense and bombarded the minister with it. This slogan, along with many others, contributed to the increase of Communist influence among the discharged soldiers, thanks to particularly successful propaganda. The Communist Party of Hungary's (CPH) ideology soon became dominant in the discharged soldiers' and non-commissioned officers' organizations as well as in the sailors' and railwaymen's militia. There was also a strong Communist grouping in the Budapest Workers' Guard.[5]

Béla Kun personally did a lot in order to win over the regular army's staff. It is well known how courageously he behaved on December 31, 1918, when while delivering a speech in the barracks of the 1st Infantry Regiment, his words were interrupted by gunshots.[6] He took no notice of the firing and finished his speech. Then, careless of the possible risks, he went to other barracks. The firmness he showed in this situation, and in many others, greatly enhanced his popularity as well as that of the CPH. This was all the more important as the Communist Party planned to seize power by force of arms. In order to achieve this aim, it had already bought weapons from the troops of the German Mackensen Army who were passing through the country en route to home. An armory was set up in Kispest, a suburb of Budapest.[7] Nor was the party in need of able and resolute men who would be the core of a Red Guard to be set up in the future.

Events, however, took a different turn. Kun was given another task to carry out. Instead of oganizing the uprising, he had to outline the ideological platform of the movement which was coming to power. He fulfilled that job while under arrest in the Budapest Central Prison, in a letter he sent out addressed to Ignác Bogár. In reality, the message was addressed to the leaders of the Social Democratic Party of Hungary. In his letter, he stressed that breaking with the "revolutionary defense policy" was a condition for bringing about the fusion of the two Marxist parties. He emphasized that war with Czechs, Romanians, or Serbians, should be avoided in any circumstance.

This position stemmed logically from the Communists' attitude toward the republic. Consequently, it considered a bourgeois war unnecessary bloodshed in order to maintain bourgeois class rule. Such an effort was by no means to be backed by the proletariat. Posterity, of course, evaluates post-World War I circumstances in a more complex way. Béla Kun's words about just and unjust war reflect a somewhat simplified interpretation of contemporary Marxist teaching. He stated:

A proletarian party's consent to waging a revolutionary war can be given only if:

a) all power is taken over by the industrial and agricultural proletariat;
b) there are no more capitalistic interests of any kind;
c) it is fully guaranteed that the war would not bring about a new form of oppression for any nations.[8]

During the post-World War I period, however, historical conditions have fundamentally changed, making it possible for a proletarian party to support a bourgeois government in case of war, as in the case of the fight against Fascism. Nevertheless, in the given situation. Kun gave a strictly ideological point of view.

In a letter written on the eve of the Communist takeover, Kun calls for the "abolition of the regular army" and for a "proletarian class army." These demands clearly show the influence of orthodox Marxism; the only surprising element in them is that Kun seems not to remember his experiences in the Soviet Union in 1918. There he was in the main current of events and knew very well the debates in connection with army organization. He also knew that in Soviet Russia they had eventually resorted to general conscription. He should have been aware of the fact that "armed proletariat" was an abstraction that included anarchists, the lumpenproletariat, and other social elements that might endanger the rule of the proletariat, as can be seen in the role that Mahno's, Petliura's, and Grigoriev's troops played in the Russian Civil War.

Some points in Kun's program remained matters of interest even after the proclamation of the Hungarian Soviet Republic. Besides performing the duties of the Commissar of Foreign Affairs, from the very first day, he took part in the decision-making process in connection with military affairs. Thus, he had a hand in having Pogány's decree on the Red Army accepted. It declared: "The Red Army should be formed by the already enlisted men and by those recruited from among organized workers." Recruitment as it is well known, had failed to fulfil hopes. The notion of electing commanders had to be changed soon, along with the assumption that all professional army officers were evil and had to be treated as potential traitors.

At the beginning of April, Kun became a member of the Council of the Defense Commissariat, and thus, was formally given a voice in the army leadership.[9] He was not, of course, to deal with the details of military operations. He concentrated on the most essential questions, and first of all, the issue of whether the Soviet Republic could count on any help from the outside.

Our proletarian dictatorship was not established on the belief that we would be able to defeat the Entente's military forces. We have never expected that the six divisions the armistice allowed Hungary will be sufficient to stop the offensive threatening us from every side. We have emphasized and emphasized again that we have tied the fate of our enterprise to the fate of the international proletarian revolution.[10]

Kun uttered these words a few weeks after the proletarian takeover. In the given situation the help of the international proletarian revolution was expected to come about in two ways. Either in the form of a Soviet–Ukranian Red Army offensive in Bessarabia or in a turn of events in Austria. Kun reckoned with both and also, instead of just waiting for their realization, he tried to precipitate their occurrence. Without going into further details about his connections with Soviet Russia, it is known that he sent a close associate, Ernő Bettelheim, to Austria, where his mission was to help the proletarian revolution win by a *coup d'état* which was, of course, unsuccesful. Nor did hopes for the immediate outbreak of a revolution in Germany materialize either.

Another issue of extraordinary importance was whether the government should surrender or not. The question arose when on May 1, Romanian troops reached the line of the Tisza and rumors reached Budapest that they had crossed the river at Szolnok. In the leading Council of the Republic opinions were divided as to whether or not it was reasonable to continue fighting. The speaker at the May 2 meeting of the Budapest Workers' Council was Béla Kun. He did not try to make the situation appear more favorable than it was. On the countrary, he depicted it in rather somber colors. "The majority of our troops." he said, "is unfit for defending the capital which is therefore thrown at the mercy of the Romanians." Then he posed the question: "Are we going to give Budapest up or fight for it! "[11] Impressed by his speech, the Budapest Workers' Council voted for the continuation of the war and for sending the workers' regiments to the battlefield. Kun's conduct was a very important factor although not the only one—in the campaign of resistance that unfolded in May and completed itself in the military expedition to northern Hungary.

Kun often went to Gödöllő, to the headquarters of Aurél Stromfeld. No decision of importance was made without his consent. He often visited units under training and met the soldiers. He proposed and the Governing Council accepted, the decision to refuse payment of allowances to unemployed veterans who would not enlist in the army. He had a decisive vote in personnel matters, too, as in the appointment of József Haubrich, Jenő Landler, Béla Vágó, and József Pogány, as battalion commanders.[12]

A significant point was his attitude toward the Clemenceau Memorandum. His position is, of course, very easy to criticize even today. It is possible to pick out one aspect of the situation and confront it with another one. When taking everything into consideration, however, there was no other answer to be given than Kun's. It is only natural that the delegates to the Congress of Councils—although with bitter afterthoughts—adopted it, as they were unable to come up with a better alternative.

The acceptance of the Clemenceau Memorandum, which called on the Red Army to withdraw from lands recaptured from the Czechoslovaks, gained some time for the Soviet Republic which could have been most valuable if the revolution in Germany had broken out or the Soviet Russian Red Army had started its offensive on the Dniester. But neither happened, and time would work against the cause of the Hungarian Soviet Republic. Thus, for Kun, the only thing that was left was preparation for defeat which, he was convinced, would not take long.

During the last days of July Kun stayed on the battlefield with the fighting troops and tried to maintain discipline in the midst of panic and disorder.

There he stood, facing the soldiers, trying out again everything that others had already tried to hold them back. He begged and posed threats, his voice faltered and cracked jokes, tried from here and from there, started over and over again. And again and again, he found himself facing a wall, a stiff, unmovable, massive human barricade. He tried to dissolve that wall by separating smaller groups to talk to—all in vain. Had but a single word been uttered against him or the proletarian dictatorship... No, it was worse than that, it was something more inaccessible than any suspicion or hostility; they were simply indifferent. They shrugged, not desperately only with disappointment. "It is for nothing we have driven the Czechs out," they said. "Where are the workers from Budapest?" they asked, and the question did not sound like reproach, it sounded like an argument. Hours passed, and Kun dropped his arms with the gesture of someone whose hands are bleeding because he wanted to strike fire from wood.[13]

On August 1, 1919, Kun announced to the Budapest Workers' Council the resignation of the Revolutionary Governing Council. That was the last action of Béla Kun as a leading personality of Hungarian political life.

## NOTES

1. György Borsányi, *Kun Béla, Politikai életrajz* (Budapest, 1979), p. 72.
2. Kun Béla, *Szocialista forradalom Magyarországon* (Budapest, 1979), pp. 56–77.
3. Kun, *Szocialista forradalom* pp. 78–84, 114–16.
4. Tibor Hajdu, *Az 1918-as polgári demokratikus forradalom* (Budapest, 1968), pp. 138–39; Vilmos Bőhm, *Két forradalom tüzében* (Budapest, 1946), pp. 91–96.
5. Hajdu, *Az 1918-as polgári demokratikus forradalom*, pp. 221–22.
6. Borsányi, *Kun Béla*, pp. 99–100.
7. Hajdu, *Az 1918-as polgári demokratikus forradalom*, p. 221.
8. Kun, *Szocialista forradalom*, pp. 164–70.
9. Borsányi, *Kun Béla*, p. 152.
10. Kun, *Szocialista forradalom*, p. 204.
11. Kun, *Szocialista forradalom*, p. 220.
12. Borsányi, *Kun Béla*, p. 166.
13. Ervin Sinkó, *Optimisták* I (Novi Sad, 1953), 93.

# THE COLLAPSE OF THE HUNGARIAN RED ARMY

Peter Gosztony

On July 6, 1969, Péter Ágoston, one of three people's commissars for foreign affairs of the Hungarian Soviet government and emissary extraordinary of the Revolutionary Governing Council, noted the following in his still-unpublished Diary:

> I signed the armistice agreement in Pozsony, and reached agreement with the French regarding the release of the prisoners-of-war. It did not enter General Mittelhauser's head that we would conclude an armistice with them. If however we are still going ahead and doing it, then surely it is because we went to support the Austrians, in order to establish to soviet system there. It seems that he has no inkling that the Red Army is now very weak and for this rason we surrendered those extensive territories in Upper Hungary... .[1]

Péter Ágoston was mistaken. The young Hungarian Red Army was forged during the Northern Campaign—in Upper Hungary—and the soldiers of the III Corps, the greater part of whom came from the Budapest factories, performed great deeds against the Czech forces. Within a few weeks the corps—50 battalions and 24 batteries led by Jenő Landler—had won back 2836 km$^2$ of territory of Hungary. On June 28, however, at Béla Kun's suggestion the governing council in Budapest took a decision whereby the upper Hungarian territories liberated by the Red Army had to be evacuated, or rather, the troops had to be withdrawn to the lines held in May. Kun trusted in the promise of Clemenceau, or rather, in the promise of the Paris Peace Conference of the victorious powers of World War I, according to which, in return for the evacuated upper-Hungarian territories, the Entente powers would approach the Romanians to give up the Tiszántúl territories they had occupied.[2]

The governing council's decision fundamentally broke the morale of the troops ordered back from upper Hungary. The mass of the soldiers greeted Béla Kun's decision with incomprehension and were even less willing to accept the reasons for it. How was it possible *voluntarily* to give up a territory reacquired in battle, when in exchange the ministers of distant countries were only holding out the promise of supposed compensation? No, it was not the time for public disturbances: under the leadership of their commanders, the troops carried out the withdrawal, but doubt was growing about the Soviet Republic, both among the simple Red soldier and his officers or rather, about the united Social Democratic-Communist party leadership standing behind it. Indeed, Commander of the Army Vilmos Bőhm resigned his post on July 10. He explained his reasons at length in his memoirs.[3] Even earlier, on July 1, Aurél Stromfeld, the outstanding Chief-of-the-General-Staff of the Red Army, had abandoned the general head-quarters at Gödöllő, and we also know of several divisional commanders who likewise voluntarily left their posts as a sign of protest over the with-drawal, which they characterized as unacceptable.[4]

Although an explanation of Béla Kun's behavior vis-à-vis Clemenceau does not belong here, let us note—in Béla Kun's defense, if you like—that he saw in the French prime minister's promise primarily the possibility of gaining time for the Soviet Republic: somehow in the way that Lenin did, when he made peace with the Central Powers in fall 1918 at Brest—Litovsk, on the basis of territorial concessions. But it is also possible that he was in-fluenced negatively, was "terrified," by those reports that informed him about the internal political picture of the Red Army, of Landler's III Corps, marching from triumph to triumph in upper Hungary. Kassa and Eperjes, that is to say, awaited the incoming Hungarian troops not only with under-standable enthusiasm, but even with houses bedecked with the national colors. A large part of the troops became drunk on patriotic feelings. In numerous units they demanded the setting up of the national colors along-side the red flag, symbol of Internationalism. Even Jenő Landler himself made a favorable recommendation in this connection, but this met with Béla Kun's incomprehension, indeed his determined refusal.[5] Kun and the people gathered around him (Tibor Szamuely, for example) stood ex-clusively on the ground of internationalism. They trusted and believed in the outbreak and quick victory of world revolution, as well as in the might of the Russian Red Army, which in those summer weeks stood on the left bank of the Dniester and reached to the foothills of the Carpathians. They thought that the Russians might soon provide direct military assistance to the Hungarian Soviet Republic.

In mid-July the governing council found itself in a grave situation. Although it had surrendered the liberated upper-Hungarian territories to the Czechs, it had not succeeded in taking possession of the Tiszántúl (east bank of the Tisza River). Therefore, they decided to enforce their wishes on the battlefield and to prepare the Red Army for the earliest possible offensive, the so-called Tiszántúl Offensive, against Romania. On July 12, the council ordered universal conscription. At the same time, troops pulled back from upper Hungary began deploying along the Tisza line.[6] I must and do agree with Dr. László Fogarassy of Bratislava, the outstanding researcher on the military history of the 1919 area, when I cite his statement that the Red divisions lining up against the Romanian Royal Army at that time stood in fact on the threshold of an "internal disintegration," the disintegration of military virtue.[7] In the divisions and brigades symptoms manifested themselves, which were similar to those that were observable scarcely a year earlier, in October 1918, in the Austro—Hungarian Imperial-and-Royal Army. Jenő Landler, from July 18 the new commander-in-chief of the Red Army, had to disband several workers' regiments (e.g., the 8th and 14th Regiments), because their military value was practically zero. Although other units were still "on their feet," their discipline (e.g., in the 11th Regiment) was terrible. There were also brigades (e.g., the 80th International Brigade) whose soldiers went on pillaging raids and could not have cared less about their officers or political commissars. Since the institutions dealing with augmenting and filling out the total personnel strength from the hinterland were not functioning adequately, the 7th Workers' Regiment, as such, had to be dropped from the order-of-battle of the Army of the Tisza. Landler had almost no reserves behind the troops massed for the attack. Although a large contingent of the 8th Division was in the camp at Hajmáskér, their leaders simply refused the order: they did not wish to participate in the offensive against the Romanians, while the soldiers of the 52nd Regiment, composed of the Pécs Mining Battalion, declared that they wanted to serve the Soviet Republic only in the liberation of Baranya county, in the reacquisition of their narrower fatherland.[8]

From such examples as these, it indeed appears that the Red troops massed against the Romanian Royal Army comprised a military force only "on paper." The Army of the Tisza however, also had divisions of outstanding capability, e.g., the Red artillerymen and the soldiers of those infantry battalions whose personnel strength in the main originated from the lost Hungarian territories. These units were motivated chiefly by their desire to regain their narrower fatherland in battle. We also know from contemporary military historical literature that they fought well! The successes of the first phase of the Tisza Offensive are to be put down chiefly to their account. Their reliability was not sufficient however to raise the battle morale of the *entire* Army of the Tisza.

General Staff Lieutenant-Colonel Ferenc Julier worked out the battle plan of the Tisza Offensive, the same man who carried through the Upper Hungarian Campaign with the III Corps, when he was the general staff officer of Jenő Landler, the present commander-in-chief of the Red Army. They knew each other: as the saying goes, they had sniffed gunpowder together in upper Hungary. Cooperation was good between the two men, notwithstanding that Landler was primarily a politician, a Communist, while Julier, as a professional officer, did not feel sympathy for Communism. For him the Soviet Republic, with its political arrangements and ideology, was and remained an alien world. Julier committed himself to the Red Army primarily out of patriotic feeling.[9]

The preparation for and course of the Tisza Offensive does not appertain to the subject of my presentation. The enemies of the Soviet Republic, the representatives of the Entente Powers in the Danubian basin, knew of the offensive, or rather, of its preparation, in time. The headquarters of the Romanian army on the Tisza also possessed adequate information. It was not Julier, therefore, who was the "traitor," as the Hungarian military and historical literature asserted later, after 1945 and indeed to the present day (although not so determinedly in recent times).[10] On July 21, in a letter addressed to Marshal Ferdinand Foch in Paris after the attack of the Red Army, General Louis Franchet d'Esperey wrote reassuringly: "The Hungarian offensive will collapse right at the outset!" Romanian reinforcements were on the way to the Tisza Front. He then added: "I can assure you that I give the Hungarian Soviets at most 2–3 weeks to live. If our offensive were not perhaps to bring the end of the Kun government, the untenable domestic state of affairs will bring it in any case... ."[11]

The Tisza Offensive of the Red Army began on July 20. The Romanian troops were stronger than the Hungarians; their equipment and discipline were also much better. According to the 1960 assessment of military historian Ervin Liptai, the Romanians had a two-and-a-half-to-one superiority as regards infantry. The superiority of their artillery and cavalry, however, was really overwhelming.[12] Despite this the Red Army—crossing the Tisza in several places, even establishing a deeper bridgehead in more than one place— fought successfully against the Romanians. III Army Corps troops led by Béla Vágó, for example, repeated at Szabolcs and Tiszaeszlár the bravura of the Upper Hungarian Campaign.[13] On July 24, however, decisive changes came about. The arrival of reserves, as well as certain redeployments, made it possible for General Gheorghe Mărdărescu, the commander of the Romanian troops, to stop the Hungarians, then drive them back in a counterattack.[14] This succeeded to such an extent that within six days the Romanians could even cross the right bank of the river at Tiszaeszlár and Tiszadada. The troops of the Red Army had urgently to be ordered back. Julier blamed himself, or rather, the bad battle plan, for the fiasco. He submitted his resignation, which, however, Landler did not accept. At Cegléd, on July 31, the supreme command of the Red Army convened in Béla Vágó's special train. Taking part in this, besides Landler, were József Pogány, Dezső Bokányi, Jenő Hamburger, Béla Kun, and, of course, Julier, who, looking at the situation that had developed through the eyes of the general staff, recommended stopping any kind of offensive and using the troops of the defensive.[15]

Other things were discussed as well—political affairs, the future fate of the Soviet Republic. The idea was broached as to whether, if the governing council were to resign and cede power to a more moderate political grouping, the Entente would be willing to have a substantive discussion and to halt the interventionist Romanian troops. Kun continued to favor unconditional struggle. The Red Army had again to be pressed on the offensive, he asserted in reply to Bokányi and Julier; he argued that so far the Romanians had come across the Tisza with only a small force; hence if the Red Army were to drive these back, it would be possible to hold the line of the river for a longer period. The Cegléd War Council indeed ordered a renewed attack by the Red Army—but meanwhile, by July 31, the internal disintegration of the troops had assumed frightening dimensions.

In his memoirs, Julier wrote that, while the withdrawal after July 25 of the Red troops who had crossed the Tisza proceeded under relatively organized conditions and thus a good part of the war material also managed to be saved, this situation changed radically on the last day of July. Something had "cracked" in the soul of the troops! Discipline had shattered; the taste for battle had sunk to zero. On July 31, Julier came back from the Tisza with this summary: "The troops did not want to fight any more at any price!"[16] Béla Kun had also arrived at a similar conclusion. After the Cegléd war council he rushed in his car through part of the Tisza front. At Szajol, where he attempted to instill spirit into the soldiers in a short speech, he found only deaf ears. We know from the memoirs of Ferenc Münnich, the political commissar of the Red Army, that the Red soldiers kept saying to Kun: "We have already fought enough! Fight yourselves, comrades!"[17] Even in the best case an immeasurable apathy dominated the spirit of the Red soldiers. They had been disappointed in their leaders, they had been disappointed in international solidarity, for—to give just a single example! —the "great internationalist proletarian demonstration," or rather, strike, announced with great fanfare for July 21 failed to come off anywhere in Europe, or rather, insignificant local movements here and there shriveled.

Several workers' regiments publicly declared that they were going home, they were not fighting any more! In other places the troops voluntarily abandoned their posts. Now they wanted only peace. In vain did Béla Vágó, on the basis of the decision of the Cegléd war council, assume command over the still-existing troops of the I and II Army Corps and take steps to prepare for an offensive. The military machinery had conked out. In the morning hours of August 1, from Szolnok south, virtually not a single unit was standing behind the Tisza on the Hungarian side. It was not even possible to speak of surveillance of the river! On this very day the Romanian army was making preparations to cross the Tisza line from Szolnok southward.

At this time the Red Army still had, on paper, 23 battalions and four artillery batteries. From these Vágó scraped together those troops with which he launched a counterattack against the Romanians at Szolnok on August 1.[18] They even succeeded in reseizing part of the city, but the success remained only a local success. On the other sectors of the front the Romanians, even if cautiously at first, continued their advance in a westerly direction—toward Budapest.

In Budapest, meanwhile, Béla Kun was arranging the liquidation of the Soviet Republic. On the afternoon of August 1, he was present at the session of the Budapest Central Workers' Council. The sights observed in the last two days at the front probably weighed heavily on his mind. Let it be said to his credit that he had the courage to look the facts in the face and to draw from them the conclusions given by the situation.

Already at this time Béla Kun had behind him the session of the party leadership and the governing council, at which it was decided to relinquish power. Only Tibor Szamuely stuck with Kun. Even the Trade Union Council had voted overwhelmingly in favor of giving up the dictatorship. There remained to Kun, therefore, the task of informing the Budapest Central Workers' Council. Zoltán Rónai informed those present of the resignation of the governing council as well as of the reformation of the trade union government. Then Béla Kun stepped to the dais. According to the extant minutes he began his speech as follows:

I no longer have a voice, I have only the belief that the proletariat that left not me, its leader, in the lurch, but left itself in the lurch, is still a proletariat that is not at fault, because it was not possible to make out of capitalism, out of this squalid, this loathsome capitalism, anything else than that squalid and loathsome system that there was in this country. I, comrades, I say that I have carefully weighed, have carefully thought over, what I should do, and now I still declare coldly and calmly: the dictatorship of the proletariat has collapsed here in Hungary. The dictatorship of the proletariat has collapsed economically, it has collapsed politically and militarily... .

Kun then passionately argued that his wish was to fight on the barricades for the dictatorship of the proletariat together with the masses. Rather death than giving up! "Of this I thought, comrades!" he said to the assembly. "But what are we to do? To step forward onto the barricades, without the masses?"[19] Kun's approximately 30-minute speech, which was not free of contradictions, merits attention for its honorable frankness. For it is possible to count on one hand the number of those politicians in our century who dared to face the total failure of their political experiments and drew the conclusions from this openly and frankly!

On August 2, ironworker József Haubrich became the commander-in-chief of the Red Army, after Vilmos Bőhm and Jenő Landler. To him there remained but the fragments of the army. Among his first measures was the putting in order of the "flag-business" that had dragged on since the Upper Hungary Campaign. Haubrich ordered that the battle flag of the Armed Forces (n.b.: no longer the Red Army!) henceforth should be red on only one side. The other side had to be the national colors. The other military measures did not produce much result. Haubrich, who temporarily also handled the war portfolio in the trade union—the so-called Peidl—government, soon lost authority over the army. But Julier stuck with him, and even Aurél Stromfeld, that noble soldier, for a time returned from his self-chosen Dunántúl isolation in order, if necessary, to extend assistance in blocking the continuing advance of the Romanians on Budapest. But a detachment that the headquarters at Gödöllő could have had at its disposal was no longer to be found! Mardarescu's soldiers entered Budapest without firing a shot on August 4. On August 6, a small counterrevolutionary group in the capital ousted the Peidl government from power, in a putsch. It is characteristic that the trade union government could not muster even one platoon of soldiers for its defense!

What became the fate of the still-remaining Red troops?

In the first week of August on territories controlled by royal Romanian forces Mardarescu's troops forced six combat divisions to lay down arms. Thus 40,000 soldiers and 1235 officers were captured. Only a few units —such as the 2nd Brigade, which crossed to the Dunántúl at Vác—succeeded in escaping capture. From the middle of August the National Army led by Miklós Horthy was already master in part of Transdanubia, the Dunántúl. In his memoirs, *The Collapse,* published in 1933, Miklós Kozma writes *inter alia* that during their advance on the Dunántúl a skirmish took place at Fajszna between a Red patrol and soldiers of the Moravek—Ostenburg Detachment.[20] In a recent study, however, Béla Kirschner reports on the circumstances of the liquidation of the Sátoraljaújhely directory, very far away from Budapest. Here the administative organization of the Soviet Republic learned on August 3 of the fall of Kun as well as of the formation of the Peidl government. At that time the local commissar for war proclaimed: "... Communism has disappeared. The Red Army is disarming. Everyone should return to his home!"[21]

Already by mid-August, it was no longer only the local directories, but the workers' councils as well, that had dissolved, melted away, by themselves. Even if here and there was found an agile local military leader who endeavored to keep the units entrusted to him under arms, at the news of the entry of the Romanians into Budapest and at the widespread reports according to which the Soviet Republic had been liquidated and Béla Kun had left for Vienna with the people's commissars, it ultimately proved impossible. Leaving behind their weapons, the soldiers melted away from their barracks. The history of the modern era knows few more total collapses than the August 1919 collapse of the Hungarian Red Army!

Let us still speak here about some of the causes of the military collapse of the Red Army, as the researcher sees them from a distance of seven decades.

The Red Army was, in effect, forged into a military force during the Upper Hungary Campaign. There, a defensive war was being waged. Besides the internationalist mentality, national sentiments also played a role. The leaders of the Soviet Republic, primarily Kun, were contemptuous of this spiritual motive, which had a powerful impact on the taste for battle for the troops. For, by far, the greatest number of soldiers of the Red Army were peasants. They did not understand internationalism. Nor did the Soviet Republic satisfy their hunger for land. What could have motivated their fighting, therefore, if neither defense of the homeland nor defense of the land played a role in this struggle? The workers' regiments fought well at first. Their discipline was also adequate. But after a short time they had enough of the front. They thought this way: in May they had voluntarily come to fight, they now also had the right voluntarily to leave the front. They were unruly. In some units anarchy raised its head. "Trade union discipline" was not able—at least in the long run—to substitute for military discipline.

As for the bulk of the officer corps, they entered into service in the Red Army guided by national sentiment. A secret, unvoiced, unspoken slogan sounded in them: "Even if we start into battle under red flags: by the time we reach the Carpathians our colors will be red-white-green!"[22] György Lukács the great Marxist philosopher—for a time a political commissar in the Red Army—correctly stated in a posthumously published piece in the weekly *Elet és Irodalom* in May 1975 that "... in 1919 the national element played a huge role—this Red Army was in essence a Hungarian army: it was defending against foreign attacks!"

The Red Army was at the same time also a people's army. Every sorrow and woe of the hinterland reached the soldiers and affected them grievously in spirit—thus, the starvation of the family, the various counterrevolutionary movements, Szamuely's terror measures, all of which—we know—weighed especially on the peasant districts. To this was added the transportation chaos in the hinterland, the propaganda of the Whites, the many deliberately alarming rumors also reaching the front, the frequent promises of the Entente, and not least the political division, the shilly-shallying, of the leaders in the governing council. All these factors severally and collectively had a negative impact on the troops.[23]

A clear military goal, the toleration of the national mentality even for tactical reasons, and—not least—the steadfastness of the hinterland were in my opinion the most important factors of military policy, the absence of which —as events demonstrated—decisively affected the operation of the Red Army and brought nearer the inescapable end, the fall of the Soviet Republic.[24]

In connection with the collapse, the disintegration, of the Red Army, posterity has not blamed the simple soldier. While circumstances permitted, he did his duty. For precisiely this reason I regard it as especially unfortunate that to this nameless, unknown Red soldier, who in 1919 defended Soviet Hungary against foreign invaders under difficult circumstances, against armies unleashed on the country by the imperialist Great Powers, to this soldier —aside from the figure of the Red sailor on the monument to the Soviet Republic in Budapest—a special statue has not yet been erected in present-day Hungary. Is the time not here to correct this?

## NOTES

1. Diary of Péter Ágoston, Manuscript Archieve of the Hungarian Academy of Science, MS 5060/D.
2. György Borsányi, *Kun Béla: Politikai életrajz* (Budapest, 1979), p. 185.
3. Vilmos Bőhm, *Két forradalom tüzében* (Budapest, 1946), pp. 310–22.
4. Tibor Hetés, *Stromfeld Aurél* (Budapest, 1978).
5. Ferenc Julier, *Ellenforradalmi lélekkel a Vörös Hadsereg élén.* Series of articles in the issues of the Budapest daily *Magyarság* that appeared between July 3 and July 17, 1927. The June 15 article gives an account of the "flag-affair."
6. On the details, see, Ervin Liptai, *A magyar Vörös Hadsereg harcai 1919* (Budapest, 1960).
7. László Fogarassy, "A Magyarországi Tanácsköztársaság katonai összeomlása," *Történelmi Szemle* (Budapest), 1981/1:20.
8. Fogarassy, p. 21.
9. He himself gives a fuller account of this in his memoirs: see, the June 12 and June 13 entries.
10. If he had been, the counterrevolutionary system would not have persecuted him after 1919. In the second half of 1919 Julier was in prison under remand. A court of honor finally ruled in his case, and cleared him. The National Army (and later the Hungarian Royal Army) did not accept him. His case was finally settled after 1932, when he received a regimental pension. Julier passed away from cancer in Budapest on April 25, 1944, at 66 years of age.
11. Cited in Borsáanyi, p. 190.
12. The strength of the Red troops fighting on the Tisza Front was 74 battalions (31,000 rifles) and 88 batteries (311 cannon). With the exception of divisional squadrons, they had no cavalry. The Romanian army in the Tiszántúl, on the other hand, was composed of 119 battalions (84,000 rifles), 60 cavalry squadrons (12,000 swords), and 98 batteries (392 cannon), the source for the Hungarian data is Liptai, p. 498; see further, *A magyar Vörös Hadsereg 1919. Válogatott dokumentumok* (Budapest, 1959); the source for the Romanian data is Mardarescu, *Campania pentru desrobirea Ardealului si occuparea Budapestei, 1919–1920* (Bucuresti, 1920).
13. For details see *Vágó Béla 1881–1981. Vágó Béla születésének 100. évfordulóján–Baján 1981. augusztus 10-én–tartott emlékülés előadásai* (Kecskemét, 1983), pp. 46–7.
14. Mardarescu, pp. 141–42.
15. Fogarassy, p. 32.
16. Julier, *Magyarság*, June 16, 1920.
17. In his memoirs written for the "general public," Ferenc Münnich gives a laconic and "delicate" account of this when he writes: "The withdrawal from the north undermined the discipline of the army. With Béla Kun we made an attempt to reestablish discipline, but this did not succeed, and further events led to the fall of the Soviet Republic. .." Ferenc Münnich, *Viharos út* [Budapest: Szépirodalmi Könyvkiadó, 1966], p. 75. My citation is from Münnich's memoirs shelved in the Hungarian Socialist Workers' Party's Institute of Party History, which Borsányi cites in his *Kun Béla*, p. 191.
18. On the details, see, László Fogarassy, "A magyar Vörös Hadsereg utolsó csatája–Szolnok, 1919. augusztus 1". Published in *Jászkunság*, 1961/Nos. 3–4.

19. Cited in Borsányi, p. 195.

20. Miklós Kozma. *Az összeomlás 1918–1919* (Budapest: n. d.), p. 393.

21. Béla Kirschner, "A Tanácsköztársaság kormányzótanácsa lemondása hatása a frontvonal mentén," *Századok,* 1968/Nos. 3–4:437.

22. Communication to the author by two veteran Hungarian army officers, who took part "with counterrevolutionary souls" in the 1919 Upper Hungary Campaign of the Red Army (Münnich, fall 1984).

23. Later, Soviet military policy also accepted the importance of these factors. Let us quote here Stalin's Order No. 55 from February 23, 1942, in which he expresses very clearly that "... the outcome of war will now no longer be decided by such secondary factors as the factor of unexpectedness, but by permanently operating factors: the consolidation of the hinterland, the spirit of the army, the quantity and quality of the divisions, the armament of the army, the organizing ability of the command staff.." Let us observe the sequence! Source: *Sztálin a Szovjetunió Nagy Honvédő Háborújáról* (Moscow, 1946), p. 39.

24. It was precisely László Fogarassy, in his study *A magyar Vörös Hadsereg utolsó csatája,* who pointed out that by the end of July 1919 the Entente's plan for a concentric attack was ready in case the Soviet Republic were not to draw back. French, Czech, and Serbian troops stood at the ready for such a purpose. The outcome of the intervention would not have been in doubt!

# THE JULY CAMPAIGN OF THE HUNGARIAN RED ARMY AGAINST ROMANIA AS SEEN BY FRANCE

Jean Nouzille

The successful Northern Campaign of the Hungarian Red Army against the Czechoslovak forces was halted as a consequence of pressure coming from the peace conferees in Paris. On July 7, 1919, the Allied Supreme Council in Versailles called on the Hungarian government to suspend hostilities against the Czechs. A week later, on June 14, the Entente ultimatum, signed by the President of the Peace Conference, Georges Clemenceau, ordered the Hungarians to withdraw to the previous demarcation lines. Béla Kun accepted it; a move which French officials saw as a way to gain time.

On June 24, Kun ordered the Red Army to cease fire and on June 30, it withdrew to a line which was fixed by the Peace Conference as Hungary's new frontier. This retreat provoked the resignation of several leading officers of the Red Army, including Colonel Aurél Stromfeld, who objected to the withdrawal from areas which were ethnically Hungarian. Stromfeld was replaced by Lieutenant-Colonel Ferenc Julier. As the Hungarian troops withdrew, French reports noted that the Slovakian Campaign had cost the Red Army 450 dead, 3691 wounded, and 471 troops captured by the Czechoslovaks.

Since the Clemenceau Memorandum ordered all belligerents to the previous lines, Kun assumed that the retreat of the Red Army would be followed up by withdrawal of the Romanians to the demarcation line. Since the Romanians did not seem to budge, on July 11, 1919 Béla Kun asked Clemenceau, the French prime minister, to use his influence with the Romanians to remove their forces from southern Hungary. Clemenceau's answer was negative. Consequently, Kun decided to use force to dislodge the enemy.

The decision to launch an offensive was made following a reexamination of the internal situation. It was believed that there was an improvement on the homefront as the two major insurrectionary attempts were brought under control. On June 5, 4000 peasants marched on the western town of Sopron. They had been stopped in Nagycenk by the Sopron garrison and then sustained heavy casulties at Kopháza.[1] On June 24, an insurrection broke out in Budapest. It was led by Captain Jenő Lemberkovics and Major László Bartha, the commander of the Ludovika Military Academy. The uprising soon collapsed due to its lack of popular support. The leaders of the insurrection escaped the firing squad only as a result of the intervention of Lieutenant-Colonel Guido Romanelli, the head of the Italian Military Mission in Budapest. Béla Kun used the occasion as a pretext for the exlusion from the Governing Council of some leading Social Democrats—Sándor Garbai, Vilmos Bőhm, Zoltán Rónay, and Sándor Szabados. He also reduced the number of People's Commissars from 36 to 11.[2]

Counterrevolutionary organizations also existed outside of the imperium of Soviet Hungary. The "Vienna Committee," an organization of anticommunist refugees, headed by Pál Teleki set up shop in the Austrian capital.[3] As early as May, French authorities reported the offing of a counter-revolution:

We cite the ex-Captain Gömbös as one of the active promoters of this future government. We hear the following names mentioned; Lukachich and Sóos from the military, and from among the civilians the conservative Andrássy and the Socialist Garami will take part in the civilian government.[4]

On May 5, 1919, another counterrevolutionary government was formed in Arad, under the leadership of Count Gyula Károlyi. Two days later, Captain Gyula Gömbös took control of the barracks in Szeged, and soon after of the whole town. The government of Gyula Károlyi then transferred itself to Szeged, and asked Miklós Horthy to take command of the "National Army." The latter did not create any anxiety for Béla Kun, as the size of this new army was very small.

Kun went on to fix the starting date for the offensive against the Romanian army for July 20. This was to coincide with the announced general strike of the western European labor unions protesting intervention in Hungary. This was scheduled for July 21.

The Hungarian command regrouped its forces to face the Romanians, whose withdrawal would be demanded by the Hungarian government.[5] The plan of the Hungarian offensive had two phases, the first phase involved the crossing of the Tisza River, the second was the building of bridgeheads and their expansion. The Tisza was to be crossed at Tokaj, Szolnok, Köteles, and Tiszafüred. The division crossing at Tokaj and Szolnok were to link up, forming an axis of Szolnok–Nagyvárad and Csongrád–Békéscsaba and To-kaj–Nagykároly. The Governing Council also intended to strengthen the Hungarian Red Army by creating two new divisions[7] and consolidating seventeen workers' battalions.[8]

On July 15, the Hungarian battle plans were passed to Lieutenant-Colonel Romanelli of the Italian Military Mission, who informed the Allies immediately. Thus, the Red Army was unable to profit from a surprise attack, nor from its initial numerical superiority.[8] Consequently, the combat went through three phases. From July 20 to 24, the Hungarians were on the offensive, from the 27 to 30, the Romanians started their counteroffensive, and from July 30 to August 1, the Red Army was routed.

As the Hungarian offensive began on July 20, the Romanian army, prepared for the attack from July 15, was ready to defend itself. All the Tisza River bridges were blown up and the Romanian army was deployed in depth.[9] Following an intense artillery barrage, the Hungarians crossed the Tisza according to plans, and took the Romanian outposts. During the first two days of the offensive they did advance toward their objectives, but on the third day, the offensive was slowed down owing to the strong Romanian counterattacks. Still, by July 24, the Red Army took Mezőtúr and Kisújszállás. A line was established along Mezőtúr–Túrkeve–Kisújszállás and Kenderes. Further south, troops recaptured Szentes.[10]

Until that day, the Romanian strategy was satisfied with just slowing down the Hungarian offensive. As the Red Army offensive stalled on the Szolnok–Nagyvárad axis, the Romanian command decided to bring most of its forces to this sector, including some troops transferred from Bessarabia. The Romanian maneuver included a simultaneous counterattack on the flanks on the troops that had crossed at Szolnok and on the bridgeheads at Tokaj and Mindszent. The successful offensive started on July 25. The following day the Allies suspended relations with the Hungarian Soviet Republic as the Romanian offensive rolled on, despite the Hungarian capture of Dévaványa. The Red Army began its retreat to the right bank of the Tisza River during the night of July 26–27.

By July 27, the Red Army retreat was complete and even rear guard elements were forced to retire to the right bank. Troops from the Northern Front and Budapest were hastily transferred to the Romanian Front to assure the orderly retreat of the troops and to prevent a Romanian crossing. On July 28, all Red Army forces were on the West Bank of the Tisza and the Romanians reached their former positions. In the conflict 3000 Hungarians were captured. According to reports to Paris, the most recently captured prisoners admitted that the morale among the Hungarian troops was very low as a result of the defeat. It was also reported that Hungarian troops withdrew in good order, except for the rear guards who ran, abandoning their weapons and supplies.[11] Romanian losses in the counteroffensive amounted to 3000 dead and wounded. On the same day the Romanians decided to profit from succes by making preparations to cross the Tisza and pursue the enemy to Budapest.

On August 1, the Romanian troops crossed the river and advanced 30 kilometers within a day, meeting little resistance from the retreating Hungarian troops. Only between Szolnok and Abony did remnants of the Red Army undertake forceful counterattacks. By the end of the day the Romanians reached the line of Abony–Tápiószentmárton–Jászberény and Komló–Heves–Tiszafüred.[12]

The rout of the Red Army coincided with the flight of Béla Kun and most of the leaders of the Soviet Republic. On August 1, the Socialist Gyula Peidl established a new government with Socialist ministers from the cabinet of Mihály Károlyi and Béla Kun. [13] This government was created with the encouragement of the Italian Military Mission.[14]

On August 2, Cegléd was taken by the Romanians and during the night of August 2, the Romanian troops reached the line of Pécel–Maglód–Üllő, 20 kilometers from Budapest. Kecskemét, however was still holding.[15] On August 3 and 4, the mopping up of Hungarian troops continued.[16] Mutinies among the Hungarian troops took place in Cegléd, Kistelek, and Kisújszállás.[17]

On the evening of August 3, Romanian cavalry troops entered the capital and on the next day an orderly occupation of Budapest was concluded. At 6:00 pm the Romanian commander, General Georghe Mărdărescu made his entrance to the city. The remnants of the Red Army, workers and police battalions, were immediately disarmed, public buildings were occupied, and the press was put under Romanian censorship.[18] When Colonel Romanelli, who, since the collapse of the Kun Regime, claimed to represent the Entente governments in Budapest, asked the Romanian commander to come to talk to him about Romanian intentions, Mărdărescu declined.[19]

On August 6, the Allied Supreme Council learned that the Romanian military authorities presented armistice terms to the Hungarians in the form of an ultimatum. The Council assumed that the armistice terms contradicted the terms of the Belgrade Armistice of November 13, 1918, which Hungary signed with the Allies and the Associated Powers.[20] In fact, the Romanian–Hungarian Armistice called on the Hungarians for the immediate disarmament of all Hungarian forces, handing over to Romania half the rolling stock of the Hungarian Railways and half of Hungary's river boats. There was also a demand for 20,000 wagon loads of wheat, the same amount of oats and barley, and 10,000 wagon loads of maize. The Romanians also wanted 200 cars, 400 trucks, and 30 percent of all Hungarian agricultural machinery.[21] Moreover, the Romanians laid claim on military equipment for 30,000 men.[22]

In response to the news, the Supreme Council informed the Hungarian, Serb, and Romanian governments of the establishment of a joint committee of four Allied generals, Jean Cesar Graziani (France), Harry Hill Bandholtz (United States), Mombelli (Italy), and George Gorton (Great Britain). Its role was to control the Romanian withdrawal and Hungarian disarmament.[23] On August 6, István Friedrich drove the Peidl government from power and established a counterrevolutionary government, proclaiming Archduke József as Regent of Hungary. Reaction to this change was swift. On August 12, Edvard Beneš, the Czechoslovak Foreign Minister wrote the following to the President of the Peace Conference, Premier Georges Clemenceau:

> I repeat it to you, Mr. President, what is going on in Hungary now under the care of Josef von Habsburg is extremely dangerous for the peace of Central Europe... this will lead exactly to the same result as under the Béla Kun government; that is to an extremely deep hostility of Hungary to all of the neighboring states.[24]

The defeat of the Red Army initiated a white terror in Hungary. Paris was appraised that:

> After the fall of Bolshevism, the troops in Pápa have arrested a large number of people. These persons were then transported to Sifok... . The same situation took place in Magyaróvár, where former red troops and workers have been arrested under the order of prince Lenyag [Lonyay?] Every evening they are horsewhipped and beaten black and blue by drunk officers... . Violent deeds have taken place even in Budapest... .[25]

This reaction was also accompanied by anti-Semitic violence which did not abate until September.[26]

On November 14, the Romanian troops began the evacuation of Budapest, and two days later, Admiral Miklós Horthy made his formal entrance to Budapest at the head of his army. By November 23, the Romanian army was beyond the Tisza[27] and at the intervention of Sir George Russel Clerk, the Entente representative, István Friedrich was forced to give up his seat in the cabinet presided over by Károly Huszár.

Born in great part out of the division of the former Austro–Hungarian army, strengthened by servicemen, volunteers, and Red Guards, the Hungarian Red Army was formed when Hungary was attacked by the Romanian and Czech armies. Following its first defeat by the Romanians, the Executive

Council reestablished discipline and appealed to the patriotic feelings of former officers. These, under the command of Colonel Aurél Stromfeld, led the Red Army to victory over the Czech forces. The Executive Council, however, made a mistake. Feeling assured of working class support, believing in internal stability, and influenced by the flush of victory over the Czechs, the Council and Béla Kun underestimated Romania's capacity to recover and to hurl back the Red Army in its hopeless attempt to recover the occupied territories.

The wars of the Red Army, as reflected in French reports, indicate good military qualities on the part of Hungarian officers and troops alike. In August 1920, the French Ambassador to Prague recalled:

... on the one hand, the not very heroic memory that the Czech soldier left in the annals of the Austrian–Hungarian Army during the last war, on the other hand, the strange ease with which the Red Army in full decomposition during Béla Kun's regime, has made the Czech battalions fall back...[28]

He added:

In the meantime, when we compare the Austrians with the Hungarians, now that they are divided, it is undeniable that superiority belongs to the latter. It is therefore, the Hungarians, who provided the real military might to the Dual Monarchy.[29]

The agressiveness of the Red Army and of Hungarian irredentism troubled the neighboring states to such extent that they created a *cordon sanitaire* around Hungary. As the French Ambassador to Prague reported to Paris:

The alliance recently signed between Romania and the two Slav States would bring again to the latter two considerable reinforcements; the Little Entente would struggle against Hungary not as three against one, but as six against one, (that is about fifty-two divisions against eight) ....They think that within a few days Budapest would be occupied, and the junction with Yugoslavia and Hungary through the famous corridor would no longer be needed.[30]

## NOTES

1. Archives de la Guerre, Vincennes (hereafter cited as *A G*), 7 N 2885, Telegram. no. 407/3, July 15, 1919.

2. *AG,* 7 N 2885, Telegram no. 449/3, June 27, 1919.

3. *AG,* 7 N 2885, April 18, 1919.

4. *AG,* 7 N 2885, May 8, 1919.

5. *AG,* 7 N 2885, Telegram, July 7, 1919.

6. *AG,* 7 N 2885, Ciphered Telegram, July 7, 1919.

7. *AG,* 7 N 2885, Telegram no. 584/3, July 11, 1919.

8. *AG,* 7 N 2885, Telegram no. 601/3, July 15, 1919.

9. Archives du ministere des affaires etrangeres, Paris, (hereafter cited as *AE*); Correspondance politique (hereafter cited as *CP*), Europe, 1919–1929, *Roumanie,* Vol. 48, folio 7, August 3, 1919.

10. *AE, CP, Roumanie,* Vol 48, folio 8.

11. *AE, CP, Roumanie,* Vol 48, folio 11.

12. *AE, CP, Roumanie,* Vol. 48, folio 19. August 5, 1919.

13. *AE, CP, Roumanie,* Vol 48, folio 21.

14. *AE, CP, Roumanie,* Vol 48, folio 21 and 66.

15. *AE, CP, Roumanie,* Vol 48, folio 26, August 6, 1919.

16. *AE, CP, Roumanie,* Vol. 48, folio 24.

17. *AE, CP, Roumanie,* Vol. 48, folio 25.

18. *AE, CP, Roumanie,* Vol. 48, folio 62, August 10, 1919.

19. *AE, CP, Roumanie,* Vol 48, folio 66.

20. *AE, CP, Roumanie,* Vol. 48, folio 33.

21. *AE, CP, Roumanie,* Vol. 48, folio 46.

22. *AE, CP, Roumanie,* Vol. 48, folio 57.

23. *AE, CP, Roumanie,* Vol. 48, folio 34.

24. *AE, CP, Tchécoslovaquie,* Vol. 45, folios 22–23.

25. *AG,* 17 N 518, Appendix, p. IV.

26. *AG,* 17 N 518, Compte rendu des évenements survenus du 15 septembre au 1er octobre 1919, p. 7, Szeged, October 1, 1919.

27. *AG,* 17 N 518, Bulletin de renseignement no. 9 du 22 november, 1919.

28. *AE, CP, Tchécoslovaquie,* Vol. 45, folio 12, August 12, 1920.

29. *AE, CP, Tchécoslovaquie,* Vol. 45, folio 14.

30. *AE, CP, Tchécoslovaquei,* Vol. 34, folio 207, December 28, 1920.

# THE HUNGARIAN RED ARMY AS SEEN THROUGH BRITISH EYES

Ferenc Tibor Zsuppan

In recent years, both native Hungarian and non-Hungarian historiography of the 1919 Hungarian Soviet Republic has made significant advances in unraveling the tangled web of frontier-making and military measures woven by the Paris peacemakers in 1919. Research has been particularly rewarding in the case of those historians, like Mária Ormos[1] and Peter Pastor,[2] who have investigated the role of the French in Hungary's affairs in 1918—19.

A comparable exercise regarding British involvement, however, has so far not been undertaken by historians. This paper will attempt a partial remedy, by filling in something of the military involvement of the British in the Entente's countermeasures against the Hungarian Red Army, even though this involvement may not have amounted to much more than mere reporting on the state of military matters in Hungary. In recent years, new material has become available in addition to the holdings of the London Public Record Office: the Scottish Record Office in Edinburgh, as well as Lloyd George's private archives in London, make it possible to trace the background of the highest British decision making. In addition, the historian is now better informed as to the "lessons" that the British establishment drew from its observations of the Hungarian Soviet Republic.

Normally, all governments gather information on other coutries in large part for no other reason than that it may prove useful at some hypothetical future juncture in the relationship with that other country. Surprisingly, this standard policy was not followed fully by the victorious Entente at the end of World War I vis-à-vis the defeated enemy, so strictly was the principle of imposed or dictated peace followed.[3] The Entente's relationship with defeated Hungary in 1918—19 is a good example of how neglect of information gathering can produce far-reaching and unexpected—and often irremediable—explosions of events. The British, like the other Allies, had woefully little information on the slowly gathering Bolshevik "menace" in either Austria or Hungary, before the Dictatorship of the Proletariat was declared in Budapest on March 21, 1919.[4]

The first step in assessing the relationship between the British element in the Entente and a defeated Hungary, is to turn to the armistice, or armistices, that applied to Hungary in November 1918, and in the succeeding months. It is immediately striking that neither the British Peace Delegation in Paris, nor the British Foreign Office in London, was aware of the fact that it was not the Villa Giusti Armistice of November 3, 1918 (concluded by the Italian General Diaz), but that of Belgrade of November 13, 1918 (concluded by General Franchet d'Esperey of the *Armée d'Orient*) that applied to Hungary. The reasons for this British unawareness were twofold: first, there was no British officer present in Belgrade on November 13, 1918. For, although Lieutenant General T. Bridges headed the "British Military Mission with the Allied Armies of the Orient" in Salonica, the earliest a British officer even approached Hungary's (former) southern boundaries was with the journeys of Major Temperley who travelled the Belgrade—Zagreb—Fiume—Laibach—Belgrade circuit on November 20–28, 1918, without, however, approaching Hungary or mentioning the Hungarians in his dispatches.[5] Reporting on Hungary or, more precisely, on the Hungarians' compliance with the Armistice of Belgrade was—not unnaturally—left to the French, as by November 22, 1918 the British were to forgo the French suggestion that they take part in Budapest's military occupation.[6] The French themselves did send a Military Mission, headed by a Colonel Vix, to Budapest at the end of November.[7]

The second, weighty, reason for the British War Office as well as the Foreign Office having so few first-hand reports from Hungary was—as we shall see later—the Italian insistence that the Belgrade Armistice be expunged from all recommendations of the meetings of the Military Representatives of the Supreme War Council, lest it affect adversely the validity of the Diaz Armistice and thus weaken Italy's case regarding the frontiers of postwar Yugoslavia.[8] Indeed, it is illustrative of Great Britain's unconcern at developments in Hungary that the central figure of the British administrative detail, Sir Maurice Hankey, was not to unearth the actual document of the Belgrade Armistice until April 1, 1919.[8] This almost total lack of firsthand knowledge must in large part explain the severe shock displayed by the British Peace Delegation's higher echelons when news of the declaration of the Dictatorship of the Proletariat reached Paris. Before that date, it seems that, of the few reports on Hungary available, only a typed version, itself dated January

17, 1919, of the interview of the Foreign Office Staff with the Inter-Allied Commission of Relief of German—Austria, had reached Prime Minister David Lloyd George's office, warning that "if Buda-Pesth is left to itself it will sooner or later explode." Lord Harding's annotation on the document, commenting that "It would be useful however to know rather more than we do as to what is going on at Pesth," indicates a belated recognition of inadequate information.[10]

Indeed, this general weakness in information gathering, based on the misconceived idea of nonrecognition of the regimes, could seriously have affected Britain's weight in the peace negotiating process in the long run, since, unlike, for example, France, Britain, was less involved in the actual business of imposing the new frontiers. The position was somewhat retrieved by Britain's former prewar military attaché to Vienna, Sir Thomas Mongomery-Cuninghame, being sent to Vienna at the end of January, 1919, to oversee and report on post-Armistice matters and on matters likely to affect political and economic issues and the later peaceful political reconstruction of the former Dual Monarchy.[11] Told also by his military superiors of the British Section of the Supreme War Council in Paris "to keep an eye on affairs in Hungary," and himself always alert to the danger of the spread of Bolshevism, Montgomery-Cuninghame traveled to Hungary on February 5, 1919, and during the three days of this stay, made the aquaintance of József Pogány (then President of the Budapest Soldiers' Council), and the Social Democratic Vilmos Bőhm. The former, Montgomery-Cuninghame, not uninfluenced by racial prejudice, deemed a "disagreeable" individual, who was using the Soldiers' Councils he had created to pursue his own "career and ambition."[12] Of Bőhm, Montgomery-Cuninghame wrote that he was "without trace of selfish aim," referring to "the originality of his mind," his "driving force" and "responsiveness."[13] It is noteworthy that the impression created by Bőhm on Montgomery-Cuninghame was to be a permanent factor in the relationship of the two men for the duration of the Dictatorship of the Proletariat. Montgomery-Cuninghame's first visit to Hungary already revealed, too, his main concern in relation to the likelihood of social and political instability in the former territory of Austria—Hungary: that is, the lack of a disciplined army in Hungary (as well as in Austria), proud of its own traditions, and to be regarded as essential for the maintenance of order if Bolshevism was to be avoided.

Montgomery-Cuninghame's second visit to Budapest at the end of February (although near contemporaneous with misleadingly reassuring reports from other parts of Hungary)[14] confirmed his fear of Bolshevism and of inevitable catastrophe: in looking forward to the likely outcome of planned elections (not in fact held) he noted the growing importance of a leftward shift in the political orientation, as well as the patriotic nature of socialists and communists alike, including, and especially, Pogány.

Thus it may happen that a Communist victory at the polls over the government may provoke an outbreak of hostilities between the Magyars and Roumanians, and on the other hand an outbreak of hostilities may mean a coup d'etat by the Communists.

Back in Vienna, it was clear to Montgomery-Cuninghame that the fact that the "Entente do not recognize the validity of civil stipulations in a military convention," and that, therefore, there could be no recognition of the integrity of Hungary either, must, inevitably bring about the fall of Károlyi, once the true situation was realized in Hungary.[15]

It Was Montgomery-Cuninghame's repeated warnings from Vienna, taken up by the British Director of Military Intelligence, that prompted the Director, at the beginning of March, to urge the recognition of the Austrian and Hungarian governments and at the same time the necessity of fostering co-operation between neighboring governments for the Danube Confederation.[16] Time was, of course, running out, and the Director's pleas were overtaken by events. His urgings went unheeded, and the delivery of the so-called Vix Note to Budapest on March 20 was, of course followed on the next day by the fall of the Károlyi regime, and the rise of the Dictatorship of the Proletariat.

The weakness of information analysis and dispatch within the British Peace Delegation, was highlighted by the failure to foresee the likely explosive impact of the Vix Note. At the same time that Montgomery-Cuninghame was making tentative steps to assess the situation in Hungary, and in advance of the note's delivery, British officers were participants in Belgrade in advance preparation for execution of the note's demands for a Hungarian withdrawal from the Armistice line facing the Romanians, and for the French General Paul de Lobit's taking command of the area between the Diaz Line and the Hungarian frontier. General de Lobit, the British officers reported, had already asked the British Military Attache in Belgrade, on March 14, to send an officer to join a control mission for the area, and although Captain Harold W. Temperley could not "permanently join mission," he helped it "as far as events allowed."[17] The next day (March 15), the gist of the Vix Note was known to the British officers, disclosed by the French Chief of Staff at Belgrade on the very morning of its arrival form Paris. Again, the French Chief of Staff reguested the attachment of a British officer at French Headquarters, to show allied unity, and again Temperley was considered for this post. More important, Admiral Ernest Charles Troubridge immediately agreed to show Anglo–French unity by sailing his monitors on the Danube under dual French–British colors.[18] The dependence here on French sources of information and directives is noteworthy.[19]

Similarly, for upward of ten days after the Vix Note's delivery, information on Hungarian internal matters arrived in Paris almost exclusively via the French, who controlled the lines of communication, and was usually out of date when it reached the British. For this reason, Colonels Twiss and Cornwall of the British Directorate of Military Intelligence in Paris, saw it as imperative that they interview Captain Nicholas Roosevelt of the United States Army, who had recently returned from Hungary.[20] The interview's significance lies in the fact that it was passed on by Maurice Hankey to both Lloyd George and Arthur J. Balfour on March 29[21] and must have had a direct influence on them in reaching the decision on April 1, 1919 to send General Jan Christian Smuts to Hungary. From Roosevelt's interview, the British gained the impression that there was in Hungary "intensely bitter feeling against the Tchecko-Slovaks and Roumanians," and that the nationalist frustration, perceiving "no other way of protesting, hoped to put pressure on the Entente to withdraw its decision by releasing the pent-up disorder in Buda-Pest." Another important conclusion drawn by Captain Roosevelt was that he was "inclined to discredit altogether the stories of a Russian Bolshevik invasion of Hungary over the Carpathians, or of any active cooperation between the two."

As the Hungarians were thus judged to be on their own for the moment, the attention of the British turned toward the state of the Hungarian Red Army[22] as the only potent instrument with which the Hungarians could translate their nationalism into an effective anti-Entente policy. At the time of the Proclamation of the Dictatorship of the Proletariat, the Hungarian Red Army was under reorganization under Bőhm, who employed Stromfeld and his specialists of the Ministry of Defense. At the end of March, the Magyars had a mere 18,000 troops facing 40,000 Czechs; the same number again faced 35,000 Romanians, and lastly 72,000 French and Serbians were opposed by 13,000 Hungarians.[23] Plainly, these forces were inadequate against the combined strength of their enemies. However, as there was little cooperation between the opposing forces, and as the Anglo–Saxon Powers were intent on preventing Budapest being overrun, a deadlock ensued, in the breaking of which the British (as we shall see) were to prove to be particularly effective.

British observations on the Hungarian Red Army's development may conveniently be divided into two periods: the preparatory one, from March 21, 1919 up to June 1, when the army attacked the Czechoslovaks, and the active period which followed.

During both periods, the British observers in Hungary were almost exclusively military personnel, for the Entente was prepared to communicate with the Council of People's Commissars only about the execution of the Armistice, that is, military concerns. Consequently, whilst their remit and reports covered, of course, other matters outside the scope of this paper, their military obervation was often acute.

By a twist of geography, British naval personnel too were involved with reporting on internal conditions inside Budapest, as Admiral Troubridge's monitors (confiscated from the Austro—Hungarians) were under the command of British officers. Thus, it was that Lieutenant Commander Williams-Freeman, whose reports will be drawn on hereafter, came to be in Budapest, staying on after March 21 partly through chance and partly to represent all Entente interests in Budapest, including residents and their property.[24]

When General Smuts arrived in Budapest on April 4, Williams-Freeman was, therefore, able to brief him on, amongst other matters, the state of the Red Army, the factions inside the ruling groups, and the degree of popular support the regime enjoyed. The army itself was judged central to the regime's survival which could not be of long duration, in Smuts' opinion (doubtless based on Williams-Freeman's reports), because "they are without an army and have little prospect of being able to create one." Similarly, the weakness of the Red Guard was noted: the large number of the unemployed who joined it, "having once received their enrollment fees and clothes, immediately disband and constitute a permanent and increasing element of disturbance." Confirmation of the reports was found in Béla Kun's admission to Smuts that the number of "troops who were defending the territory [of the area about the evacuated] was very slight."[25]

These reports, together with other information also indicating the probable early demise of the Communist regime in Hungary (General Smuts' own more specific recommendations—which somewhat resembled Oszkár Jászi's concept of a Danubian confederation—were dismissed out of hand by Lloyd George and Balfour on April 6),[26] contributed to the highest policy makers of the Paris Peace Conference shelving for a time Hungary and her problems. Another month would, in fact, elapse before the Council of Foreign Ministers, on May 9th, again discussed Hungary.[27] The assessment at this meeting, that the regime in Budapest was about to be toppled, was based partly on an American source (Professor Philip Marshall Brown),[28] and partly of British origin.[29] However, it was entirely on the basis of British information that British members of the Supreme Economic Council, on May 19,[30] advocated, and saw adopted, the continuation of the blockade of Hungary until a "government is installed there which gives some assurance of settled conditions." Where the British agents' reports were concerned, it is probably fair to say that, whilst in broad terms, most significance was doubtless attached to the reports of widescale social resistance to the Bolsheviks' policy, their hostage taking, and general reprisals, nonetheless, the fact of the existence of a Red Army in Hungary and that it constituted a potential, if as yet not an actual threat to the peacemakers' efforts, did also contribute to the Supreme Economic Council's resolution.[31] Whilst reports on Hungarian internal conditions began to accelerate in the number of telegrams sent by Montgomery-Cuninghame and Williams-Freeman from the second week of April onward, important military reports were also coming through in the same period. The British Peace Delegation was informed as early as April 10 that units of the Austrian *Volkswehr* had entered Hungary to aid the Hungarian Red Army,[32] and later, on April 21, a report was also received, based on Austrian War Office leaks, that the Székely Division was by then "marching with Roumanians against Hungarian government."[33] However, of utmost importance both to the Big Four and, even more, to their allies, the "Successor" states, was the detailed intelligence that Williams-Freeman was in the meantime in a position to hand over to Admiral Troubridge, notably, precise data of the actual armament of the Hungarian Red Army after April 11. He was able to specify that 167,000 rifles, 1600 machine guns, 30 mountain guns, 100 field howitzers of 15 cm calibre, and 167 heavy howitzers of 18 cm calibre were in the Red Army's possession. He noted, however, that the usefulness of the army was diminished by the "great shortage of ammunition." He, further, listed the arms of the Budapest Red Guards he noted, was "negligible as a fighting force": 2300 rifles, 418 machine guns, four mountain guns, 45 field howitzers and 14 heavy howitzers; he also noted 69 accurately known mines in the Danube.[34] This information, transmitted no doubt to French and Serbian staff officers in Belgrade, must have been of considerable importance for the Romanian Army, as it resumed its advance towards the Tisza River on April 16.[35]

The British observers continued to add to the above information with a number of telegrams sent throughout May and June to the British Director of Military Intelligence, who wrote, on June 19, 1919, on the accumulated file dealing with clandestine arms smuggling: "The supply of the Italian Mission in Vienna to the Hungarian Bolshevists of Arms and ammunition is confirmed from numerous sources, both from British and French."[36]

Whilst it may be asked whether knowledge of the armaments and military preparedness of the Hungarian Red Army contributed in any way to the wording and spirit of the resolution of the Supreme Economic Council, the verdict must probably in precise terms be a negative one. A more important contribution to that resolution was the communication from Montgomery-Cuninghame's messenger, Major Barrow, written on May 7 in Budapest, and certainly in the hands of members of the British delegates by the evening of May 18 (Hankey and Lloyd George were to see it on May 20, but the covering letter to them is dated May 19 by Sir William Mitchell-Thomson).[37] The letter's gist was that Bolshevik terror was increasing in Hungary, and that Entente foodstuffs would be likely to prolong the life of the regime, especially as its organizational efficiency was improving all the time. The British officers, however, in relaying rumors of intended coups by Magyar counterrevolutionaries and urging the intervention of Romanian and Serbian troops "as resistance by the Hungarians is impossible," were evidently drawing on their special knowledge of Red Army unpreparedness.

A new phase of reporting by the British observers in both Hungary and in the neighboring countries was now to be opened up suddenly by the new offensive of the Hungarian Red Army on May 30 in Eastern Slovakia.

The likelihood of increased Hungarian Bolshevik activity in neighboring countries had been indicated in Williams-Freeman's dispatches following his visit to Vienna on May 14. It must have been evident to him that after the Romanian army had halted on the Tisza by May 1, the Hungarian communists would be tempted by "foreign adventures" and by the possibility of concomitant propaganda campaigns abroad.[38] However, it would be wrong to assume that any British observer had predicted the north-easterly thrust of the Hungarian Red Army on May 30. Indeed, Robert W. Seton-Watson, who was at that time in Prague, telegraphed Balfour in Paris, on 9 June (after the Hungarian advance), to the effect that "Magyars selected psychological moment when French had scarcely taken command [of the Czechoslovak Army] and when morale of Czech Army had been undermined by prolonged and deliberate sabotage on the part of Italian officers."[39]

During the actual campaign, British observers proved more alert to the Hungarian Red Army's activities and the steps necessary to contain it.[40] From Prague, on June 8, a report from the British Military Attaché in the Czech capital conveyed the poor morale of the Czech Army, and the fear that the Hungarian army could not even be held. There is a note of real urgency:

...The fall of Kosice [Kassa], the crossing of the Danube at Parkany and steady advance towards Pressburg will illustrate the gravity of the situation... . Something should be done quickly, there is the Roumanian Army, and two French divisions

who could create a diversion to the East, which would immediately relieve the situation here as at present about three-quarters of the Magyar force is employed on the
Western Front."[41]

At this time, of course, consideration of the Hungarian situation was no
longer subject to delay. By the time the above telegram arrived, the Military
Representatives of the Supreme War Council were already discussing the Hungarian military threat (deliberations of June 7 and 8).[42] It is obvious that assessment of the strength of the Hungarian Red Army was based on combined
intelligence from all sources, but mainly from that supplied by General Maurice Pellé from Czechoslovakia and by General Franchet d'Esperey in Constantinople. British intelligence had an important part to play, however, since the
consensus taken at this meeting as to Hungarian armed strength of 120,000 to
140,000 men was arrived at after the British General Sackville-West insisted
on it, as against a lower French estimate of 100,000 to 120,000. It was
against these troops that the Entente was deemed to be able to throw in no
more than 84,000 men. It was as a result of this higher estimate of the Hungarian Red Army's strength that it was decided, in the words of General Sackville-West, that "it was most important to use all the forces at our disposal,
and consequently to bring in the Czechoslovaks."[43]

Similarly, that Lloyd George alone emphasized that the root cause of the
current conflict lay in the earlier Czecho-Slovak drive toward the only coal
district in Hungary, was due mainly to American and Italian observation,
although confirmed by British observers.[44] The significance of Lloyd George's
realization is, of course, that it played its part in his insistence that the
boundaries must remain fixed. When the Council of Four made it clear both
to Magyars and to their neighbors that there could not be further tinkering
with the boundary to the advantage of the latter, and the Hungarians obeyed
the instruction to withdraw from Slovakia, the Hungarian Red Army, although it had not enlarged Hungarian territory by one iota, had at least achieved recognition that the boundary was regarded as fixed once and for all.
Lloyd George's intervention, and the part British reports on the spot had
played in it, was vital.

Thereafter, the British representatives fully supported the French military
initiatives to force the Hungarians to reduce the Red Army's strength to the
level required by the Armistice.[45] The British, like the French, took the view
that they would only support the Hungarian demand for a withdrawal of the
Romanian forces from the Tisza once the above preconditions were fulfilled.
The British view, finalized between July 2–4, 1919, was based on the facts
that, one, the Hungarian Red Army's strength had now risen from 150,000
to 200,000 men; two, Béla Kun had declared general mobilization on June

21; three, Béla Kun broke the Armistice conditions; and lastly Béla Kun had acted in bad faith. In these reasons, Lord Hardinge, Allen Leeper of the Foreign Office, and the Director of Military Intelligence, concurred, all eventually carrying with them Balfour and Lloyd George.[46]

In reaching the above conclusions, the top echelon of the British delegation had drawn extensively on British officers' reports. On June 17, Montgomery-Cuninghame had reported from Vienna that the Communists planned a coup in Vienna;[47] subsequently, he noted that a few days later an agent had brought him the news that on June 17 an important conference took place inside the Hungarian Legation in Vienna, attended by Ernő Czóbel, and Béla Linder.[48] They discussed the possible redeployment of the Hungarian Red Army to western Hungary, in six to eight days, from its position in Slovakia, The aim was said to be to apply pressure on Pozsony [Pressburg] and Vienna. Similarly, a report from Williams-Freeman in Vienna, reaching Paris on July 4,[49] had a direct influence on British policymakers: advocating Kun's overthrow because he had refused to respect the Armistice conditions, the letter predicted that if Entente troops marched into Budapest, the Red Army would not resist them.

The British, therefore, had had no difficulty in concurring that the Hungarian Red Army must be substantially reduced. To the end of achieving the Armistice's conditions, the British enlisted the help of agents inside Hungary, among them Hungarian army officers.[50] Their willing participation reflected the general malaise and loss of purpose, and no doubt the officers' lack of trust in a regime which, apart from nationalist fervour, had nothing to offer them.

The opportunity for substantial information to be passed via the British to the Entente came with the creation of a unified Budapest command, established on June 7, when the Iron and Metalworkers Union took command of all troops in Budapest, including the police, fire brigade, and ambulance services: thus the IV Army Corps was created under the command of the leader of the Iron and Metalworkers, József Haubrich.[51] So far from the military command of Budapest being ever under close communist control, British documents in fact reveal that through Haubrich and his Chief of Staff, artillery Major Géza Lajtos, constant information was given, through the British, to the Entente, regarding both internal and military matters.[52] Similarly, when the Commander-in-Chief of the Hungarian Red Army, Aurél Stromfeld, retired from the scene in disgust at the withdrawal of his troops from Slovakia, his place was taken by Ferenc Julier,[53] a decidedly more cynical soldier, who —like so many—considered that the Soviet Republic could no longer work for Hungary's national interests. In a no doubt exaggerated view of the situation, it was claimed that at a given point almost the entire staff of the army was awaiting the moment when they could have the whole army annihilated by the Romanians, in order to get rid of Béla Kun and the Communists.[54] By July 15, Böhm himself, the Minister of War, would go to be Ambassador in Vienna and with Kun's cognizance and agreement, to make contact with the Entente and specifically with Montgomery-Cuninghame.[55] At the same time, Kun would use the tactic of indicating to Montgomery-Cuninghame, through Böhm, that he was ready to relinquish power, a step which would have rapidly brought about the dissolution of the army.[66]

In fact, with his sources of information among the Hungarians, Montgomery-Cuninghame already knew by July 5 that the Hungarian Red Army would soon be waging a war on the Romanians.[57] On July 8, Montgomery-Cuninghame's informant told him that "so long as Red Army remains armed, peace is impossible as army cannot be kept idle and cannot be disarmed by existing government."[58] The next day, Major Lajtos sent a message personally that Kun was supported by the following groups: "the terror troops, officially called detective detachment of the Home Office," 10,000 proletarians in the state's offices; "portions of the Red Army and the Red Guard." It is worth noting, too, that Major Lajtos judged correctly that "a coup attempted by the Army or an advance of the White Guard from Szeged is likely to lead to civil war"—presumably an oblique warning to the Entente not to deploy Horthy's troops in any capacity, a futile attempt, as it transpired.[59]

As the days passed, the quality of military intelligence from the Red Army's staff officers became increasingly valuable; for example, Colonel Montgomery-Cuninghame was informed on July 9 and 10, that although the Red Army consisted of nine divisions, the 4th Division had already been disbanded.[60] Then came the best intelligence of the entire sequence: on July 10, Montgomery-Cuninghame obtained the entire deployment order of the Red Army, the strength and location of the Magyar troops crossing the Tisza, and the fact that the attack against the Romanians was to take place between July 15 and 20.[61] As July 15 passed, Montgomery-Cuninghame's informant made clear the reason for delaying the attack: heavy artillery was still being moved between the Danube and the Tisza, but it was now calculated that the attack would start on July 20.[62] Significantly, the Romanians were, on July 15, already in possession, via Vienna, of a crucial piece of information: it was known that the 80th International Brigade, consisting of Austrian, Russian, and Serbian Communists, would cross the Tisza at TiszafÜred.[63] Clearly, the staff officers wished to have this focus of communist strength expunged from the Red Army. The Romanian General Staff, in possession of the strength and intended direction of the main blow on July 17,[64] was thus enabled to counterattack and withdraw when the Hungarian Red Army crossed the Tisza on July 20. By July 24, the attack had bogged down,[65] and on July 27 it was reported to Vienna that the Hungarian Red Army had withdrawn behind the Tisza, with the exception of the Szolnok bridgehead.[66]

A telegram sent from Vienna by Montgomery-Cuninghame to Paris on August 1 succinctly indicates the fate of the Red Army at the time when Bela Kun was contemplating his resignation:

23rd Regiment dissolved. Majority of cavalry including elements of 1st, 7th and 9th Hussars surrendered to Romanians. Bridgehead division Budapest Corps dissolved. Anti-aircraft guns sent forward to Theiss. From 4th Division 7th or 9th regiment transferred to Western Hungary for mutiny.[67]

On the afternoon of August 3, the Viennese Entente Missions knew by telephone that the Romanians were marching into Budapest.[68]

In looking back at the wealth of documentation in British archives on the Hungarian Soviet Republic and its Red Army, the strengths and weaknesses of British reporting become clear: the British officers did not, and could not, sympathize with the aims of a regime they were separated from nationally, historically, and by their own class viewpoint. There was, therefore, no attempt to gain an insight into the thinking of the Kun regime; yet, this very detachment gives their reports a vividness and a clarity not easily found elsewhere, since information on every aspect of the regime's life was censored in Hungary and is still difficult of access. In terms of simple factgathering, however, it is evident that the British achieved contact with sources of information vital to the further military decisions of the Entente.

The British officers, further, came to the conclusion—logically, from their viewpoint—that "unless Bolshevism is eliminated from Hungary before peace is signed and the French armies withdrawn, it will most certainly spread all over Eastern Europe."[69] In order to prevent this, British observers in and around Hungary endeavored tirelessly to have the regime replaced with something more commensurate with the Hungarian population's wishes: to this end, they had to expedite the Hungarian Red Army's defeat. How this was effected was shown in a series of articles (now, unfortunately, inaccessible) by Stromfeld's successor as Commander-in-Chief, Ferenc Julier, in 1927.[70] British documentation now evidently confirms such factors as the role of Hungarian army informants.

The British role in Hungary, whilst traditionally considered less prominent than that of, for example, the French, can now be seen as having decisively contributed to the downfall of the Kun regime.

# NOTES

1. Mária Ormos, *Padovától Trianonig. 1918–1920.* (Budapest, 1983).

2 Peter Pastor, *Hungary between Wilson and Lenin: the Hungarian Revolution of 1918–1919 and the Big Three* (New York, 1976).

3. Mihály Károlyi, *Az új Magyarországért* (Budapest, 1968), p. 252.

4. The victorious Entente's only policy was, in effect, a total refusal to recognize or to communicate with the Magyar governments after the Magyar October Revolution of 1918. Public Record Office (hereafter *PRO*) Foreign Office (hereafter *FO*) 371. 3139. 205128. M. de Fleurian's Note, form the French Embassy in London, to the British Foreign Office, December 12, 1918.

5. *PRO. FO* 106/1394.

6. *PRO. FO* 371. 3139. 191866. See also, *PRO. FO* 371. 3139. 195380. Lord Derby (Paris) to the Foreign Office. November 26, 1918.

7. Mária Ormos, pp. 76–77.

8. *PRO. CAB.* 25/125. Supreme War Council. Military Representatives. July 7 and 8, 1919.

9. *PRO. FO* 608/16. 6113. M.P.A. Hankey's letter to General Smuts, Paris, April 2, 1919. Hankey writes: "I had never seen the Convention of November 13th. Moreover, I have looked up the Cabinet Minutes (I had influenza at this time) and I can find no trace of it. In fact, I do not think it ever was officially communicated to the Allied and Associated Powers. ... I have carefully looked up the records of Quai d'Orsay Meetings to see if I could find any reference to it. I find only one. It was referred to in the original draft of the Report of the Military Representatives at Versailles, when they recommended the zone between the Roumanian and Hungarian Armies. In the final report, however, as approved by the Council of Ten, all reference to this Armistice was excised on the motion of Marquis Salvango Raggi, the Italian Representative."

10. This is to be found amongst Lloyd George's Papers (House of Lords Library) F/49/3/1.

11. Sir Thomas Cuninhame, "Between the War and the Peace Treaties," in *The Hungarian Quarterly*, Vol. V., No. 3. (Autumn, 1939), pp. 410–24.

12. *Ibid.*, pp. 419–20.

13. *Ibid.*, p. 419. For an entertaining account of Montgomery-Cuninghame's activities before and after the First World War, see, *Dusty Measure* (London, 1939).

14. *PRO. FO* 371. 3514. (1193). 44286. "A Note on the Political Situation of Hungary." Vienna, February 27, 1919.

15. *PRO. FO* 371. 3514. 44286. Montgomery-Cuninhame to Foreign Office. Vienna, February 27, 1919.

16. *PRO. FO* 608 (34/2/1/). 3877.

17. *PRO. FO* 371. 3508. 44804. General Plunkett (British Military Attache in Belgrade) to the Director of Military Intelligence. Despatched on March 19, 1919.

18. *PRO. FO* 371. 3508. 44850. General Plunkett to War Office. Belgrade, March 15, 1919. (Received in London on March 22, 1919).

19. The British gained information on the after effects of the Vix note in Hungary only on March 24. It was on this day that General Franchet d'Esperey's telegram from Constantinople, dated March 22, was passed on to them in Paris. *PRO. FO* 608/11. 5089.

20. *PRO. FO* 608/12. 5544.

21. Lloyd George Papers. F/23/4/45. On March 29, 1919, Hankey annotated this paper, before sending it to both Balfour and Lloyd George, as "of great interest and importance."

22. The first information the British peacemakers received of the nature of the Hungarian Red army seems to have been from Swiss sources. A certain Doctor Krno Czeck, who left Budapest on March 27 and who had spoken to Colonel Vix on March 22, reported upon arriving in Bern that the "Magyars had then about 70,000 soldiers in all. But new government is organizing a new army composed of Magyar red guards and international red guards. Hungarian government will if necessary recruit by force for this second army Russian prisoners of war and also Russians, Slovacs and Serbs [undecypherable]. New army is chiefly composed of unemployed who will receive 20 kronen a day and who enrol in large numbers... ." The Hungarian Red army was established by a decree of the Revolutionary Governing Council on March 24, 1919. E. Liptai, *A Magyar Vörös Hadsereg. 1919* (Budapest, 1959), pp. 81–84.

23. *Ibid.*, pp. 109–10. Report of the War Commissariat on the manpower of the Red Army. April 16, 1919. For the strength of forces opposing the Hungarians, see: Assessment of the Chief of the French General Staff (Communicated to the British on April 18, 1919) in *PRO. FO* 608/12. 8112.

24. Lieutenant-Commander Frederick A. P. Williams-Freeman, DSO, had already performed duties intermittently in Budapest since December 1918. *PRO. FO* 608/13. 7858. 7298.

25. *PRO. FO* 608/16. 6113.

26. E. A. Crowe wrote To Balfour on April 6, 1919: "I trust that General Smuts' proposal to start meeting with German and Austrian Representatives in Paris at once, without waiting for the definite decision of the Allied and Associated governments as to the terms of peace to be demanded, will be categorically rejected..." *PRO. FO* 608/16. 6113.

27. *Foreign Relations of the United States. 1919. Paris Peace Conference.* Vol. IV. pp. 693–95. (hereafter, *FRUS. PPc.*)

28. *FRUS. PPC.* Vol. XII. pp. 45–62.

29. *PRO. FO* 608/13. 8618. 8614. 8708. See, for example, *FO 608/13. 9328.* Montgomery-Cuninghame wired to Balfour: "Communists much elated at stopping Allies, [i.e., the Romanian offensive had been halted on May 1, 1919] unwilling to agree to change of government and state will maintain as centre for working propaganda for Bolshevism what is left of Hungary. Inhabitants of Budapest surprised at turn of events... ."

30. *FRUS. PPC.* Vol. V. pp. 706–707.

31. *PRO. FO* 608 (46/1/5) 9268. Montgomery-Cuninghame telegraphed Balfour from Vienna on May 5, 1919: "Arrests of hostages continue, and their condition, treatment and state of mind is such, as to demand the interest of the Entente in their fate and some warning to Béla Kun as to their security."

32. *PRO. FO* 608 (41/1/7) 7016.

33. *PRO. FO* 608 (41/1/5) 8066. Montgomery-Cuninghame (Vienna) to Balfour (Paris). April 21, 1919.

34. *PRO. FO* 608 (21/36/3) 8005.

35. *PRO. FO* 608/13. 7946. Montgomery-Cuninghame to Balfour. Vienna, April 20, 1919, reported the fall of Nagyvárad and Békéscsaba, and added that the "Hungarian troops have dispersed leaving only small forces holding their positions and that the

general situation from the point of view of war equipment is impossible." Marginal comments on this document indicate that the British were aware that Béla Kun had already asked the Russian Bolsheviks for attacks on the Romanians in Bessarabia on April 18, 1919.

36. *PRO. FO* 608 (41/1/3) 12657.

37. Lloyd George Papers. F/23/4/65.

38. Williams-Freeman wrote that "The military position of the Hungarians is improving principally owing to the cessation of all offensives against them, all ex-officers and men are forced to join the army, and discipline is gradually improving [...] The government are at present concentrating as many of their forces as possible gainst the Czechs near Salgótarján (coal mines) and also wish to retake Miskolc." *PRO. FO* 608/13. 13094.

39. *PRO. FO* 608 (46/1/12). 12385.

40. In Lloyd George's papers there are at least nine separate items dealing with the Czech campaign of the Hungarian Red army.

41. Lloyd George Papers. F/8/3/62.

42. See footnote 8.

43. See footnote 8.

44. *FRUS. PPC.* Vol. VI. pp. 281–87, 351, 399.

45. Ever since May 30, when the C.I.G.S. "recommended that immediate military action should be taken to overthrow the existing Bolshevik regime in Buda Pest," the subsequent British assessment of the military situation in Hungary was to remain on the same basis. For example, on June 26, the British Military Intelligence recommended the crushing of the Hungarian Red army, because "In organization, discipline and morale, it has improved beyond all recognition. Nationalism has reconciled many Hungarians to Bolshevism, and the whole spirit of the people is changing". PRO. FO 608/13. 13493.

46. *PRO. FO* 608/14. 14178.

47. *PRO. FO* 608 (41/1/7) 13786.

48. *PRO. FO* 608 (46/1/12) 13051. Montgomery-Cuninghame to Balfour, Vienna, June 19, 1919. Czóbel, Fenyő, and Linder had, at one time or another, been prominent personalities at the Hungarian Legation in Vienna ever since March, 1919.

49. *PRO. FO* 608 (46/1/5) 14380. Memorandum by Williams-Freeman, Vienna, June 30, 1919.

50. *PRO. FO* 608 (46/1/12). 14294. Montgomery-Cuninghame to Balfour, Vienna, July 2, 1919.

51. József Haubrich took overall command in Budapest as early as May 2, 1919. See, József Breit, "A vörös háború" in Gusztáv Gratz, *A Bolsevizmus Magyarországon* (Budapest, 1921), pp. 250, 289.

52. Montgomery-Cuninghame (Vienna) to Hoover (Paris), July 8, 1919. *PRO. FO* 608 (46/1/12) 14964.

53. The changing of the Commanders of the Hungarian Red Army was reported in a telegram by Montgomery-Cuninghame on about July 8, 1919. *PRO. FO* 608/9. 15448.

54. Géza Lakatos and Rudolf Fleischhacker: "A főhadiszállás", in Gusztáv Gratz, *A Bolsevizmus Magyarországon* (Budapest, 1921), pp. 291-3)3.

55. Vilmos Bőhm, *Két forradalom tüzében* (Budapest, 1946), pp. 340–41. Bőhm was in Vienna as early as July 14. However, officially it was only as late as July 21 that he finally took over as Hungarian Ambassador in Vienna.

56. On July 15, the American Commissioner in Vienna handed over a report to Montgomery-Cuninghame, written by an American officer, B. N. Barber. In it Barber wrote: "The discipline is declining from day to day, and the Hungarian Red Army is falling to pieces" as the Tricolor was being exchanged for the red banner. *PRO. FO* 608/12. 16088.

57. *PRO. FO* 608 (46/1/12). 14930. Montgomery-Cuninghame (Vienna) to Paris. July 5, 1919.

58. See, footnote 51.

59. Montgomery-Cuninghame (Vienna) to Paris. Vienna, July 10, 1919. (Major Lajtos' memorandum was compiled in Vienna on July 9, 1919). *PRO. FO* 608 (46/1/7) 16075.

60. *Ibid.*

61. Montgomery-Cuninghame (Vienna) to Paris. July 10, 1919. *PRO. FO* 608 (46/1/12) 15425.

62. Montgomery-Cuninghame (Vienna) to Paris. July 15, 1919. *PRO. FO* 608 (46/1/12). 15438.

63. Montgomery-Cuninghame (Vienna) to Paris. July 15, 1919. *PRO. FO* 608 (46/1/12) 15439.

64. British Mission in Bucharest to Balfour in Paris. July 18, 1919. *PRO. FO* 608 (46/1/12) 15898.

65. Montgomery-Cuninghame (Vienna) to Paris. July 24, 1919. *PRO. FO* 608 (46/1/12) 16259.

66. Montgomery-Cuninghame (Vienna) to Paris. July 28, 1919. *PRO. FO* 608 (46/1/12) 16474.

67. Montgomery-Cuninghame (VIenna) to Paris. August 1, 1919. *PRO. FO* 608 (46/1/12) 16995.

68. Montgomery-Cuninghame (Vienna) to Paris. August 3, 1919. *PRO. FO* 608 (46/1/12) 17140.

69. Scottish Record Office (Edinburgh). The Philip Kerr Papers. GD40/17/68. "Memorandum on the position in Hungary" by E. Ashmead-Bartlett. June 7. 1919.

70. Ferenc Julier, "Ellenforradalmi lélekkel a Vörös Hadsereg élén." *Magyarság.*

## II
## HUNGARIAN SOCIETY DURING THE REVOLUTIONS

# HUNGARIAN POLITICS AND SOCIETY ON THE EVE
# OF REVOLUTION

Gabor Vermes

In tracing the causes of a revolution, historians are likely to analyze conditions—poverty, social conflict, political tensions—that served as logical antecedents to a radical turn of events. Yet, in a period preceding a revolution, passionate attempts to exploit such conditions may not be at all frequent or consistent. Those who strive for change are often inhibited by excess ideological baggage, which leads them to cling to unrealistic objectives and keeps them from making flexible adjustments to changing circumstances. Others are hampered by their own concealed or half-denied but nevertheless strong attachments linking them to the very establishment that they are attacking. Some, seeing themselves as motivated by noble idealism, fail to realize that changes could not be achieved solely through their own display of exemplary moral and political behavior.

When various individuals and groups with these tendencies confront a government and an establishment which, out of conviction and stubborn defiance, refuses to budge or compromise, then the result is not a revolution but an impasse. Possibly, of course, fast-moving internal events may sufficiently radicalize pople and leaders to break such a stalemate, as in the French Revolution. Barring that, the stalemate can be broken only through the impact of an external event, such as a lost war. In that case, the truly interesting questions arise from the study of the impasse itself, because the character and outcome of any historical event, including a revolution, has to be at least partially explained in terms of the period that preceded it. It is, after all, not a negligible point whether a revolution is led by revolutionaries who have purposefully plotted for such a sharply defined objective or by reformers turned reluctant revolutionaries who have stumbled into it.

In the Hungarian case, the virtually paralytic impasse in 1918 had less to do with the numbing effects of a devastating world war. Rather, it derived from the peculiarities of Hungary in the era of Austro–Hungarian dualism, and this is where the retracing of steps has to begin.

The governing ethos of dualist Hungary was a belief in Magyar supremacy and Hungary's territorial integrity. Most politically conscious Hungarians accepted these as axioms, as the absolute and non-negotiable guarantees of national existence in the face of a perceived Slav and Romanian threat. Magyar domination, in this view, was justified both by history–the Magyars having been the only nation in the Danube basin capable of forming a state that had lasted over a thousand years–and by their superior economic, social, and political power, as well as by their culture. A liberal constitution was to provide full legal equality to Magyars and non-Magyars alike, prompting the latter to discharge their obligation of loyal citizenship to a unitary Hungarian national state.

Oppressive Magyar domination was inexcusable, both on pragmatic and moral grounds, for a small minority of Hungarians. They considered it both foolish and unjust to keep the non-Magyar half of Hungary's population reduced to a *de facto* second-class citizenship. They believed that a full extension of democratic political rights and social justice, initiated by Hungarian Radical and Socialists leaders, would enable them to act as the benevolent dispensersₗ of progress to all citizens of a rejuvenated country. However, not even this group envisaged the breakup of Great Hungary or the renunciation of Magyar leadership.

This shared belief in Magyar leadership has to be projected against the background of an economically and socially polarized society. There were, in dualist Hungary, vast differences between rich and poor, between the abject poverty of landless agricultural laborers and owners of dwarf holdings, on one hand, and the fabulous wealth of some landowners on the other, along with the stark contrast between squalid working class slums and pleasant middle-class comfort in Budapest. Nevertheless, Hungarian politics did not reflect this polarization. The safety valve of emigration eased the population pressure, and the presence of a constitution, political parties, and free press exercised a mitigating impact, despite a very restricted franchise and blatant electoral abuses. The nearly total obsession with matters of national honor and prestige vis-à-vis Austria was a genuine, if often vastly exaggerated, concern shared by most Hungarians, gentry, middle class, and peasant alike. Differences between the champions of the 1867 Compromise, the 67-ers, and the more independence-oriented 48-ers were more apparent than real. Noisy demonstrations in Parliament notwithstanding, both sides agreed on the essential defense of the established social order and political arrangements. Finally, the jointly shared belief in Magyar supremacy and Hungary's territorial integrity blunted the sharp edges of political polarization, in spite of deep disagreements over how, and within what future framework, this supremacy should be maintained.

Initially, World War I did not introduce new elements into this situation. On the contrary, a brief "union sacrée" toned down the pitch of acrimonious parliamentary cacophony that had characterized the prewar years. Count István Tisza, the powerful prime minister of Hungary, was in control. All efforts were concentrated on winning the war, with a concomitant postponement of all major legislation and parliamentary elections. This immobility suited Tisza well, because he could devote more time and energy to matters of foreign policy and military affairs. Furthermore, he was convinced that statesmen as war leaders had the obligation, provided that they had the will, to control events within their respective countries. Because he considered any radical rupture in the status quo a serious error, if not a crime, in peacetime, national unity and domestic stability appeared even more essential to him during the war.

Nevertheless, by 1915–16, the dynamic forces unleashed by World War I had made it increasingly evident that such forces could be stifled or slowed down but not stopped. For instance, Tisza could turn aside the granting the right to vote to all front-line soldiers only by commanding the docile parliamentary members of his majority party to reject it. This most popular demand was part of the general process of democratization, as the fully mobilized masses of a total war[1] became less and less content to function as mere passive spectators, not when so many of them were laying their lives on the line. As the war continued and war-weariness set in, groups and individuals alike expected to be rewarded for their sacrifices, and escalating demands accompanied rising expectations.

The young king, Charles IV, dismissed István Tisza as Hungary's prime minister in May 1917, precisely because he could see that certain political changes had to be made in the aftermath of the first Russian Revolution, generally perceived as the potential source of further revolutionary conflagration elsewhere. However, a heavy price had to be paid for long decades of sterile parliamentary debate in Hungary: no political party was prepared or able to step forward, combining a sufficient mass base, a progressive platform, and the necessary courage. "Suffrage reform failed," the writer Hugó Ingotus commented:

not now in July 1918, but last year in June, when the greatest concern of the first
suffrage cabinet was whether, among the young gentlemen dining at the Danube
promenade, A. should be a lord lieutenant and B a government commissioner, or B.
a lord lieutenant and A a government comissioner.... . Universal suffrage failed because more people supported than liked it.[2]

While Tisza retained his parliamentary majority, and thereby a strangle-
hold over any government, the prime ministership of several minority cabinets was in the hands first of Count Móric Esterházy, a well-meaning but
inept aristocrat, and then of Sándor Wekerle, a clever cynic who soon earned
the mistrust of nearly everyone on the Hungarian political scene. Other politicians who had played prominent roles for decades were torn between their
attachment to the status quo and their grudging realization of such a policy's
inevitable failure. Count Gyula Andrássy, Jr., attempted to solve this dilemma
by simultaneously uttering progressive slogans and refusing to act on them.
Count Albert Apponyi hoped that the French phrase, *"plus ça change, plus
c'est la même chose,"* would hold true in Hungary as well. "I wish to accomplish this suffrage reform," he said, "because then it will be ours. Whoever
creates the reform will enjoy its fruits. The Hungarian nobility emancipated
the serfs in 1848 and thus retained its influence thereafter."[3] Not even the
middle-class champion of universal suffrage, the leader of the small Democratic party, Vilmos Vázsonyi, lived up to the expectations of the progressive public. The more he became preoccupied with the prerogatives of his
office and then with the "Bolshevik threat," as minister of justice, then minister in charge of implementing the suffrage reform, and then minister of
justice again, the less attention he paid to the execution of his original mission. According to one opinion, that change of heart was a reflection not only
on Vázsonyi's ballooning ego, but also on the growing conservatism of his
constituency, the Jewish middle class of Budapest, fearful of a revolution and
prepared to defend the established order.[4]

As opposed to parliamentary-governmental paralysis, the war-induced
process of democratization appeared to favor those parties which became involved in it. However, all of these parties were weighed down by the various
legacies of the prewar era, and they were usually unwilling to reexamine and
throw their rigid ideological positions and organizational inertia overboard.
Catching up with the popular mood, rather than channeling it into desired
directions, was usually their mode of operation.

The so-called Károlyi party was a group that broke away from the Party
of Independence in July 1916. The split stemmed from the personality and
political views of Count Mihály Károlyi, whose forceful stand in favor of
universal suffrage, total national independence without the Habsburgs' right

to rule as kings, and peace, underlined by his desire for emancipation from German tutelage, set him and his friends against the moderate majority of the Party of Independence and its leader, Count Albert Apponyi. Károlyi's strikingly sharp personal imprint on this new party, however, proved to be detrimental on at least two counts. First, the party was never perceived as other than a maverick aristocrat's personal coterie of friends. As such, it could not duplicate the mother party's organizational strength, nor could it create a mass base. Second the leader himself became a solo performer, far ahead of his following. Károlyi himself attributed this fact to his own rapid progress as a people's tribune and social reformer, as well as the defective personal character and opportunism of many of his followers.[5] The entire party, Károlyi included, was imbued with Magyar chauvinism, regarding with suspicion any movement for autonomy by the ethnic minorities, hoping that democratization and social progress would eliminate ethnic hostility toward a new type of Hungarian state.

The Radical party, founded in June 1914, bore the marks of its founder, the sociologist Oszkár Jászi. In its unconditional promotion of economic, political, and social reforms, the party embodied the dreams and plans of progressive intellectuals. At the same time, this intellectual character proved to be its greatest liability, because the far-reaching reforms it was advocating, transcended the much more modest claims of the only class to which the party could appeal, the middle class, weak in self-confidence and uncertain of its political orientation. The Radical party traveled the furthest in accommodating the demands of the ethnic minorities for cultural autonomy, stopping short of contemplating their separation from Hungary.

The Hungarian Social Democratic party, with its tight organization, discipline, and strong influence among the industrial working class of Budapest in particular, was the most powerful of the three leftist parties in terms of its mass support, its lack of representation in parliament notwithstanding. Although there had been some attempts in the party's past to forge alliances with progessive intellectuals and left-leaning gentry politicians, governmental and middle-class hostility, coupled with Marxist convictions, engendered a fortress mentality in the leadership. Such an attitude logically led to obsessive preoccupation with trade union and internal party affairs, accompanied by the seemingly conflicting but understandable desire to break out of "quarantine." No one fought harder for universal suffrage than Hungarian Socialists, but the party leadership, lacking the means of reaching that objective, bickered and vacillated between the policy of continuing alone and searching for allies.

For instance, an alliance with Károlyi would have made eminent sense, and for some time, between the creation of the Suffrage Bloc in June 1917, and February 1918, such an alliance existed. However, these tenuous ties were broken by the Socialist leadership, which, at that point, made no distinction between a Károlyi, a Vázsonyi, and a Jászi, and by early 1918, it was ignoring them all.[6]

During the first several years of the war, with Socialist activities at a low ebb, party leaders were in the doldrums. "What prevailed among the comrades," Manó Buchinger recalled, "was sulkiness, a state of irritation, and an awareness of being downtrodden, which was caused by their sense of helplessness."[7] While the 1917 Russian revolutions electrified the party, their message left the Socialist-reformist leadership with a painful and insoluble dilemma: how to exploit the Russian example without following it. On January 18, 1918, for example, a general strike took place in Budapest, but when the notoriously unreliable Wekerle promised to accede to the workers' demands, the party leadership called off the strike.

On the issue of ethnic minorities, Hungarian Socialists pursued a policy similar to that of the Radicals, with the difference that Socialism was expected to usher in full realization of non-Magyar autonomy within the unitary state of Hungary. Social Democratic party leaders made this stand clear to their comrades at every international conference they attended.[8]

By the summer of 1918, power was again in Tisza's hands without his appointment to any official position. Ever since his removal from office in May 1917, he had held successive governments hostage as the leader of the Party of National Work, which had obtained an absolute majority at the last elections in 1910. Sándor Wekerle, his putative opponent, prime minister of three minority cabinets since August 1917, resolved the deadlock not by calling for new elections, but by virtually accepting Tisza's point of view on all important matters. The Suffrage Bill, fully enacted on July 19, 1918, raised the percentage of voters to approximately 13 percent of the total population from 7.7 percent under the 1913 law. For all practical purposes, this new law merely revised the previous one.[9] Tisza was triumphant that he had defeated all efforts to obtain universal manhood suffrage, and he was equally pleased over his "recent understanding" with Wekerle.[10]

Tisza's moderate opposition was in shambles. "It was not difficult for Tisza to win," Ignotus pointed out at the time, "when his opponents themselves were afraid of their own victory." Nor were they able to resolve the contradiction between their "abhorrence of modern trends and their simultaneous claim that the country required new policies in today's world." As Andrássy himself dejectedly concluded, "We outlived our time."[11]

The parties on the Left were better off only to the degree that belief in the righteousness of their cause could somewhat alleviate their sense of impotence. Another flare-up of strikes took place in the industrial belt of Budapest and elsewhere in the country in June 1918. The Social Democratic Party organized a Workers' Council, which in turn both stopped the strike and then proceeded to dissolve itself. Jászi continued to write and also to deliver speeches, while Károlyi withdrew to his estates during a good part of the summer and fatalistically waited for events to unfold.[12]

If all this sounded like sweet music in Tisza's ears, such sounds were deceptively siren-like. The foundations of state and society were gradually eroding, although, to be sure, the outward signs were not yet alarming. "We felt as if we were on a sinking ocean liner where no rescue service had been organized in advance," the writer Marcel Benedek wrote in his memoirs. However, he recognized that this analogy "was limping on both feet," because, although there had been much confusion in Hungary in 1918, nobody had yet realized the magnitude of danger, nor had anyone panicked.[13]

One likely reason for this superficial calm was the chronic nature of economic dislocation, as well as its uneven impact on various strata of the population. Certainly, by the summer of 1918, the lower middle and working classes were accustomed to continuous belt tightening, rationing, and shortages of all kinds. "The population of the capital is hungry," reported the journalist Lajos Róna in July 1918, "they stand in line for hours for bread... . Budapest, the heart of the country, is covered by dust and dirt." At the same time, the middle and upper classes got by. There was, after all, a thriving black market, and there were some people who, in Róna's words, "luxuriated in unbridled affluence." A similar discrepancy was present in the countryside, where landowners and rich peasants were able to take advantage of wartime market conditions, while the bulk of the peasantry suffered from forced requisitions, reduced rations, artificially set price ceilings, and diminished real wages in the case of the agricultural laborers.[14] Even if only a gradual deterioration, rather than a drastic change, took place by summer 1918, the level of material and psychological reserves was steadily sliding downward. "The state authority sunk further both in Austria and Hungary. The complicated mechanism of the Monarchy functioned less and less and broke down more and more."[15]

Another reason for the superficial calm was the apparent normality of the Hungarian political secene. The forms of constitutional life went on, as wartime restrictions were neither severely nor consistently applied. The forces of opposition were impotent in Tisza's shadow, but the parliamentary show continued. Speeches of the handful of non-Magyar representatives in parliament had become bolder, but they were delivered to bored and indifferent fellow representatives. This situation sharply contrasted with conditions in Austria, where, upon the restoration of constitutional government in May 1917, the *Reichsrat* had become the scene of a nearly continuous pandemonium. Various non-German representatives, including Czechs, Slovenians, Poles, and Ruthenians, were presenting their respective claims ever more assertively. Emperor Charles faced the choice of either suspending the constitution or eventually allowing for a confederation in place of Austrian German dominance. Well-meaning and intelligent as he was, he realized the futility of the first approach, but hesitated to embark on the second.

News from Austria rarely caused a stir in Hungary. This reflected conventional Hungarian thinking, which regarded the monarchy not as the organic union of two closely related political entities, but rather as two states jointly executing certain functions but otherwise operating totally independently. Not even to the 67-ers, Tisza included, was the 1867 Compromise an emotional investment. It was viewed as simply a functional device guaranteeing, through the Monarchy's great power status and the Common Army, Hungary's territorial integrity and Magyar supremacy.

Inasmuch as news from Austria awakened interest in Hungary, it was this aspect of increasingly dubious Austrian support that worried people. During the war, until the restoration of constitutional rule in Austria, dualism functioned relatively smoothly, because it rested on the cooperation of the Hungarian parliamentary government and the Austrian imperial bureaucracy. Although they engaged in frequent confrontations, both in fact had a vested interest in keeping the system going. Should Austria become a federal state, dualism would clearly lose its meaning.

Hungarian anxiety over Austria reached a peak in the summer of 1917. It seemed as if the convening of the *Reichsrat* signalled the sudden opening of a dike after a devastating drought. The level of protest somewhat abated by summer 1918, not because the non-Germans in Austria were receiving what they wanted, but because new developments in the military and related spheres of the war were shifting the center of meaningful political decisions away from Vienna.

The feverish political activities of Croatian, Czech, Italian, Polish, Romanian, Serbian, Slovenian, and Slovak emigré politicians in Entente countries bore results when the governments of those countries abandoned their last hope of ending the war quickly by concluding a separate peace with the monarchy. The Congress of Oppressed Nationalities was held in Rome in April 1918, with the official blessing of the Italian government. This congress reaffirmed the principal aim of liberating the peoples of the monarchy, and even differences between the South Slavs and Italians were temporarily shelved. Although Entente recognition was not immediate, the Allies did begin to appreciate both the propaganda and the military value of this movement, which received further impetus from the organization of Czechoslovak,

Polish, and Yugoslav legions fighting alongside the Entente armies. By early June, the Allied governments were endorsing the Rome resolution and thereby the creation of an independent Czechoslovakia, Poland, and Yugoslavia as their war aim.

These developments had a strong echo in the monarchy. On May 16–18, 1918, using the fiftieth anniversary of the Czech National Theatre in Prague as a welcome occasion, representatives of various nationalities held a meeting there and expressed their desire for national emancipation and the right of their nations to self-determination. This Prague resolution stopped short of demanding the monarchy's dissolution, but it did demonstrate that the gap between the program of exiles abroad and the aspirations of national movements within the Monarchy was rapidly becoming narrower.[16]

The military situation at the monarchy's major front in Italy deteriorated fast. "The army in the spring of 1918," reminisced Aurél Stromfeld, colonel of the general staff during the war, "had already collapsed and, after that, it was in its death throes." Such a strong statement was somewhat exaggerated, because the Common Army was still able to mount a major offensive in June 1918, on Piave River. However, the commander of this offensive. Field Marshal Svetozar Boroević, acknowledged that the army was essentially unprepared, men and horses were hungry, guns could barely be moved, and even if they could, the number of shells was limited to 4.9. per gun. The offensive failed utterly and resulted in the death, wounding, or capture of 150,000 men. This fiasco made it impossible for the Common Army to launch another major offensive. Nor was its defensive capability secured. Apart from meager food rations, the ammunition dispatched to the front dwindled to insignificance. Whereas in March 1917 alone the number of shells produced was 50,000, the figure for the entire first six months of 1918 dropped to 24,000.[17]

How did Tisza react to these and other ominous signs that could not but conjure up the spectre of devastating defeat! According to conventional wisdom, marks of statesmanship are foresight and adaptability to new conditions without relinquishing basic principles. But what if new conditions nullify everything for which a statesman has stood throughout his entire political career! In such cases, myopia becomes an understandable defense mechanism, and the statesman in question carries on business as usual, while using self-deception to avoid confronting the implications of threatening developments.

Tisza's big parliamentary speech on June 19, 1918, was standard fare, except for a measure of repetitive harshness. As always, he called for reconciliation between Magyars and non-Magyars. He criticized the insensitivity of

Hungarian teachers and government commissioners who were sent to Romanian schools and ecclesiastical meetings respectively and who made no effort to learn the Romanian language. According tot Tisza, such unnecessary provocations were bound to backfire. At the same time, he very strongly urged more stringent criminal proceedings against non-Magyar nationalist propagandists, along with the introduction of economic reprisals and cultural restrictions, measures he had not earlier advocated. Entente plans aimed at Hungary's dismemberment had evidently prompted Tisza to tilt his thinking somewhat in the direction of conservative authoritarianism. He spoke about the Entente's warmongering, the continued usefulness and necessity of the German alliance, and described the Hungarian nation's fight as a life-or-death struggle.[18]

This point of view possessed a certain intrinsic logic, best exemplified by the speeches and writings of Ferenc Herczeg, who reduced Tisza's somewhat lofty political rhetoric to common-sense propositions. Although Herczeg is now remembered as an author of historical plays and some lighthearted prose, he was also István Tisza's most effective political collaborator. "The dam-keeper is in control of the situation only as long as  the  dam is intact," Herczeg told the Parliament's Suffrage Committee on March 12, 1918:

Once the dam breaks, the flood is in control and not man.... . Universal suffrage would endanger Hungary's territorial integrity... . The optimists say that, if we treat the ethnic minorities well, they will love the country. But in fact they do, including the most fanatical propagandists among them, except that what they imagine their country to be is incompatible with the Hungarian conception of the state.[19]

Both Tisza and Herczeg claimed that the character of Magyar supremacy within the framework of the Hungarian state could not be drastically changed without annihilating the framework itself, along with Magyar preeminence. The underlying assumption of this judgement—the irreconcilability of multiple national aspirations and a strong unitary Hungarian state—was logically sound. However, the preservation of the status quo in Hungary was becoming increasingly untenable, as the instruments to accomplish this goal were progressively weakening. Furthermore, the soon-to-be-victorious Entente stood on the side of those who were determined to destroy that status qou.

To some degree reinforcing but also countering the Tisza—Herczeg line, resurgent right-Radical views gleefully registered the demise of Hungarian liberalism. The journalist István Milotay believed that his country faced a stark choice between the "Tisza regime and Hungarian bolshevism." Milotay lashed out against Hungarian Jews who, he claimed, were building a state within the state through their use of social and economic resources. A parliamentary speech by Count István Bethlen reflected a similar opinion. He castigated unassimilated Jews for their promotion of radical social reforms, as well as their defense of price hikes and shady trading practices. Even paragons of academic respectability, such as Professors Jenő Cholnoky and Győző Concha, added to this chorus through their characterization of Jews as rootless, destructive, and tradition-denying.[20] Anti-Semitism, which had been smouldering for some time, flared up with vehemence precisely because the very existence of Hungarian traditional life and values was felt to be at stake. Much as most Hungarian Jews absorbed and internalized traditions, a conspicuous minority appeared to defy them. As a growing number of conservative Hungarian nationalists preceived their country to be in danger, their level of tolerance dropped precipitously, and Jews were increasingly becoming the most obvious targets of their anger and frustration.

István Tisza, for all the wrenching anguish he felt for his country and for all the punitive measures he was prepared to employ against putative subversives, was unwilling to betray Hungary's liberal heritage, which was also his own. In a parliamentary speech on August 7, 1918, he categorically condemned anti-Semitism as dangerous, divisive, and unfair. "Everyone should be judged on his own merit," Tisza said, "and not on the basis of his religion or race... . in the beautiful regiment in which I had the honor to serve this past summer, there were two recklessly courageous Jewish officers." Minister of Defense General Baron Sándor Szurmay interrupted Tisza's speech at that point with a brief observation: "Many of them [Jews] have received the gold medal for bravery."[21]

In the meantime, the leftist parties continued to cling to their version of Social Democracy or Liberalism with guarded but tenacious optimism. The Socialists took comfort in their solid mass support and the anticipation that they would eventually obtain their primary objective, universal suffrage, while the Radicals and the Károlyi Party had faith in the universal blessings of a forthcoming Wilsonian peace that was to usher in an era of justice, fairness, and democracy. Responding to the speech of President Wilson in the United States Senate on January 22, 1917, in which he had endorsed the principle of national self-determination and "peace without vicotry," Márton Lovászy, a Károlyi Party leader, spoke in the Hungarian Parliament with approval. "The Hungarian nation," said Lovászy, "has no reason to complain about Wilson's emphasis, as its interests are in accordance with the interests of mankind." Fourteen months later, Ignotus, the most articulate spokesman for progressive intellectuals, rejected the idea that patriotism was an alien concept to him and his friends. "We want to have a country," Ignotus wrote, "which belongs to all and where every citizen can fully recognize his human and civil rights... . It is just as wrong for a Romanian or Serb to demand a separate territory, torn from the Hungarian state, as for anyone to do so on the basis of being a Catholic, a Greek Orthodox, or a Jew." Oszkár Jászi admitted that the establishment of a federal Hungary, where the Magyars would keep "their given and natural leading role," would not be easy. Nevertheless, he thought that such a state would be both possible and desirable because "federalism does not signify the growth of centrifugal tendencies; on the contrary, it would bring about a genuine and spontaneous cooperation between the Magyars and the ethnic minorities."[22]

While these attitudes appear to represent astonishing naïveté, it is necessary to place them within their proper historical context. World War I, horrible as it was, did not automatically and in all cases destroy the optimistic faith in reason and progress bequeathed by the eighteenth-century Enlightenment, especially to nineteenth- and early twentieth-century Liberalism. And even if that flame had been nearly extinguished by the horrors of war, was it not rekindled by the president of the country that would play an important role in any peace settlements?

A brief lull in mid-summer 1918 was followed by a rapid series of momentous events. On August 8, Entente armies broke through the German lines in France; on September 14, mostly French and Serbian troops launched an offensive in the Balkan Peninsula. Two weeks later Bulgaria capitulated, and French, British, and American divisions simultaneously kept up their relentless pressure upon slowly retreating German troops. On October 4, Germany and Austria-Hungary appealed to President Wilson for an armistice on the basis of his Fourteen Points, and twelve days later, Emperor Charles announced the federal transformation of Austria, transformation that had no bearing on Hungary's territorial integrity, but a concession that Wekerle had extracted from Charles. Subsequently, the Hungarian government broke all ties with Austria except for the person of the monarch. Tisza endorsed this arrangement in Parliament with a heavy heart. In the same speech on October 17, he admitted that the war was lost.[23]

Such fast changes provoked powerful emotions, ranging from bitterness and rage over defeat on the Right and Center, through intense anticipation of justice for a democratic Hungary on the Left. In no discernible way had these changes modified the myopia of the former or the romantic idealism of the latter. On October 17, Tisza still described those who were undermining the Hungarian state as a "tiny minority." In his judgement, Hungary's task was to convince the Western Powers and, above all, President Wilson that they had been misled about the true state of affairs in Hungary and that it was in their best interest, as well as the interest of progress and liberty, that the Magyars should fulfil their historic mission in the Danube Basin.

At the October 22 session of the Council of Ministers for Joint Affairs, We-kerle agreed to the unification of all South Slav territories, provided that those territories would be attached to Hungary. This claim was presented only a week before the Yugoslav National Council proclaimed the unity of all South Slavs in an independent state. The German general attached to Austro–Hungarian headquarters, August von Cramon, delivered a devastating comment on this kind of thinking when he ridiculed those Hugarians who still held to the magical belief that enemy armies would somehow stop at the "red-white-green frontier posts."[24]

In the meantime, progressive writers such as Miksa Fenyő wrote about the importance of not allowing the erosion of Magyar rights through the acceptance of "false accusations by Slav and Romanian propaganda," as such an erosion would preclude the realization of much needed reforms. Lajos Biró predicted Hungary's transformation into an "Eastern Switzerland," whose citizens would be devoted to it, even if some of their fellow co-nationals would live in flourishing states beyond the borders. In another article, he warned the civilized nations of the world not to support efforts that would impose "the peace of the sword" on Eastern Europe, reversing injustice and oppression.[25]

The facts of October 1918 are well known. By the end of the month, the older order had collapsed; the parties of the Left moved into the vacuum and assumed power in the revolution of October 30–31; it was a revolution without revolutionaries; certainly it seemed so at the top. When Károlyi wished to organize a peace demonstration in late September, the Socialist leader Ernő Garami told him that such a demonstration would be premature because it would provoke the king. When another Socialist leader, Manó Buchinger, returned from Vienna in October and recommended establishing workers' councils, his suggestion met with strong resistance from the other leaders. The negative reaction was even stronger when a trade union leader proposed arming the workers in late October. Károlyi, also in late October, was trying to convince Archduke Joseph to be the king of an independent Hungary. "When we found out that the explosion had come and a few hot-headed and impatient officers had commenced action on their own responsibility," Jászi late reaclled, "we were dismayed at the news."[26]

Hungarian reformers swept into power in the 1918 revolution were unprepared to dispel bewilderment and confusion, to overcome chronic vacillation, and to eliminate the discrepancy between effusive rhetoric and lack of dyanmic actions. "I built in 1918," Károlyi reminisced, "a golden bridge for old Hungary."[27] This bridge may not have glittered to landlords, business tycoons, or members of the Upper House, but it was indeed designed for all the citizens of Hungary. The builders of that bridge, however, were incapable of protecting, maintaining, and ultimately saving it.

## NOTES

1. On the question of total war, see Béla K. Király, "Elements of Limited and Total Warfare" in Robert A. Kann, Béla K. Király, and Paula S. Fichtner, eds., *The Habsburg Empire in World War I* Boulder, 1977).

2. *Nyugat* [The West], July 16, 1918.

3. Hungary. *Országgyűlés Nyomtatványai, Képviselőház, Napló* [Proceedings of the Hungarian Chamber of Deputies], XXXVI, 133–34, June 25, 1917.

4. Tibor Hajdu, *Károlyi Mihály. Poltikai Életrajz* [Mihaly Karolyi. A political Biography] (Budapest, 1978), p. 243.

5. Mihály Károlyi, *Egy egész világ ellen* [Against the Whole World] (Budapest, 1965), p. 141.

6. Hajdu, p. 246.

7. Manó Buchinger, *Küzdelem a Szocializmusért* [Struggle for Socialism] (Budapest, n.d.), I, 248.

8. *Ibid.*, II, 15, 17–18; Tibor Erényi, *Szocializmus a századelőn* [Socialism at the Beginning of the Century] (Budapest, 1979), pp. 362–63.

9. Kálmán Molnár, *Magyarország közjoga* [The Constitutional Law of Hungary] (Pécs, 1929), pp. 436–37.

10. Manuscript Archive, The Hungarian Academy of Sciences, 1019/285–305. July 20, 1918.

11. *Nyugat*. June 1, 1918; *Ibid.*, September 1, 1918; *Képviselőház, Napló,* XL, 336, July 9, 1918.

12. József Galántai, *Magyarország az Első Világháborúban* [Hungary in World War I] (Budapest, 1974), pp. 392–93; Hajdu, p. 264. One could make an argument that militancy at the grassroots level invalidates the idea of an impasse in Hungary in 1917–18. However, such a militancy was neither consistent nor was it effective in generating more than a transitory impact upon the political life of the country.

13. Marcell Benedek, *Naplómat olvasom* [*Reading My Diary*] (Budapest, 1965), p. 294.

14. Lajos Róna, *30 év az újságíró pályán* [30 Years in the Journalism Profession] (Budapest, 1930), III, 709; Julianna Puskás, "A nemzetgazdaság militarizálásának hatása a parasztság helyzetére Magyarországon az első világháború idején" [The Effect of the National Economy's Militarization upon the Peasantry during World War I] in Pál Zsigmond Pach and Pál Sándor, eds., *Tanulmányok a kapitalizmus történetéhez Magyarországon* [Studies on the History of Capitalism in Hungary] (Budapest, 1956), pp. 325, 331, 335, 357.

15. Gustav Gratz and Richard Schüller, *Der Wirtschaftliche Zusammenbruch Österreich–Ungarns* (Vienna, 1930), p. 88.

16. Galántai, pp. 407–408; Leo Valiani, *The End of Austria–Hungary* (New York, 1973), pp. 199–256; Z.A.B. Zeman, *The Break-up of the Habsburg Empire 1914–1918* (London, 1961), pp. 147-216.

17. *A Magyar Munkásmozgalom Történetének Válogatott Dokumentumai* [The Selected Volumes of the History of the Hungarian Working Class Movement] (Budapest, 1956), V, 259; László Szabó, *Mi okozta az összeomlást és a forradalmakat?* [What Caused the Collapse and the Revolutions?] (Budapest, 1922), pp. 94–95; Márton Farkas, *Katonai összeomlás és forradalom 1918-ban* [Military Collapse and Revolution in 1918] (Budapest, 1969), p. 180; Gratz and Schüller, p. 123.

18. *Képviselőház, Napló,* XXXIX, 391–398, June 19, 1918.

19. *Magyar Figyelő* [Hungarian Observer], VIII (1918), pp. 338, 342–43.

20. István Milotay, *Tíz esztendő* [Ten Years] (Budapest, 1924), pp. 116–17;

*Bethlen István Gróf beszédei és írásai* [The speeches and writings of Count István Bethlen] (Budapest, 1933), I, 137–38; *A Zsidókérdés Magyarországon. A Huszadik Század Körkérdése* [The Jewish Question in Hungary. The All-round Inquiry of the Huszadik Század] (Budapest, 1917), pp. 74, 78–82.

21. *Képviselőház, Napló*, XLI, 172, August 7, 1918.

22. *Ibid.* XXXIII, 357, January 24, 1917; *Nyugat*, April 1, 1918; Oszkár Jászi, *Magyarország jövője és a Dunai Egyesült Államok* [The Future of Hungary and the Danubian United States] (Budapest, 1918), pp. 80, 68.

23. *Képviselőház, Napló*, XLI, 290–291, October 17, 1918; *ibid.*, p. 292.

24. *Ibid.*, pp. 294–298; Miklós Komjáthy (ed.), *Protokolle des Gemeinsamen Ministerrates der Östereichisch–Ungarischen Monarchie (1914–1918)* (Budapest, 1966), pp. 696–703; August von Cramon, *Unser österreichisch–ungarischer Bundesgenosse im Weltkriege. Erinnerungen aus meiner vierjährigen Tätigkeit als bevollmächtiger deutscher General beim K. u. K. Armee-oberkommand* (Berlin, 1920), p. 187.

25. *Nyugat*, October 1, 1918; Lajos Biró, *A kezdet és a vég. Vezércikkek, 1914–1918* [The Beginning and the End. Editorials, 1914–1918] (Budapest, 1918), pp. 172–86.

26. Hajdu, p. 269; Buchinger, p. 23; Hajdu, p. 270; Oscar Jaszi, *Revolution and Counterrevolution in Hungary* (London, 1924), p. 32.

27. Quoted in Hajdu, p. 273.

# THE HOME FRONT DURING THE KÁROLYI REGIME

György Litván

In the dramatic October days of 1918 the Hungarian National Council and the coalition government formed by the Independent [Károlyi] party, the Radical party and the Social Democratic party—and led by Mihály Károlyi as prime minister—was the incarnation of the unity and the common hopes of the progressive and patriotic forces in the country. The newly independent, democratic Hungary was born amidst enthusiastic tears and fraternization, almost without bloodshed, in the October Revolution.

After a few weeks, in spite of the still great authority of Károlyi and all his efforts for cohesion and reconciliation, this unity was in ruins. Inside the cabinet, the Socialist and Radical ministers on one side and the Independents on the other, amidst mutual recriminations, paralyzed the work of each other. By the end of December the original coalition disintegrated. The Károlyi party split into a more middle-class, conservative, and nationalist wing and a smaller one which leaned leftward. The Radical party practically ceased to exist and invited its adherents to back Social Democrats. The latter, however, had to face frightfully growing new leftist opposition in the form of the young Communist Party of Hungary, founded by Béla Kun in November 1918.

The essence of the conflicts and antagonisms can be, with some simplification, summarized thusly: parties held different views on the succession to power and on solutions of the social, economic and political crisis. This was the great task of the nation for this century: to create a democratic Hungary and insert it into the new order of the Danubian area and that of Europe; to form, out of a multinational empire and part of the Habsburg monarchy, a Hungarian [Magyar] Hungary, living in peaceful coexistence with its emancipated neighbors; and a people's republic out of the historical kingdom characterized by extensive latifundia and other feudal vestiges.

The immensity and difficulty of the task would be extraordinary even under normal circumstances rather than in a feverish state of crisis that existed at the end of the Great War. It is wholly understandable that almost each of the necessary reforms—that of the agrarian structure, nationalization, the new fiscal system, the new constitution and the form of government, the demobilization and reorganization of the army, and so on—provoked passionate responses in the press, in public opinion, the parties and even inside the cabinet. The greatest tensions both within the government and between the cabinet and national public opinion which finally led to the collapse of the regime, however, was caused by the international situation.

Within a few weeks after the victory of the democratic revolution of October 1918, a national illusion collapsed. It was a wide-ranging, almost general belief that Károlyi, who was known as anti-German and pro-Entente since 1912, would be treated favorably by the Allies and that the non-Magyar nationalities of the country would readily accept the program of an "Eastern Switzerland" outlined by Oszkár Jászi, who had fought for their rights for a decade. By December, it turned out that a sentence was executed on historical Hungary which was not yet officially announced.

Czech, Romanian, and Serb troops, violating the Military Convention signed in Belgrade on November 13 with be consent of the Great Powers, strove to create a *fait accompli*. They occupied, without waiting for the peace treaties or the plebiscite promised by President Wilson, first the territories where their compatriots formed a majority, then areas of mixed population. Purely Hungarian inhabited lands were staked out on strategic or economic grounds.

All this was, naturally, a grave shock to the public, a dark cloud obscuring the political horizon, impeding the resolution of urgent tasks of inner social transformation. After all, it would be necessary to know the extent of the territory to be transformed and inserted into the new East Central Europe, on which the government had to organize land distribution, military conscription, and elections. The date of the general elections, for instance, the first time they would be held in Hungary, on the basis of universal suffrage and secret ballot, was postponed several times and fixed at last for April 1919 which the regime would not live see. The main cause of this hesitation was that the government did not want to confine the elections to the territory limited by ever-tighter demarcation lines, because this would be interpreted both inside and outside the country as a *de facto* renunciation of the occupied territories. Radical agrarian reform, a step of vital importance because it would also be the best means to consolidate the regime, was issued late partly out of similar constitutional considerations.

In examining the relationship of war and the home front, the most important points, however, were: what kind of diplomacy seemed to serve best the goal of foreign policy; how could the nation be preserved and integrated into Europe; and how could the regime and the democratic evolution of Hungarian society be consolidated? Károlyi and his left-wing ministers, projecting their own desires, started from the assumption that the faster and the further the country proceeded on the road of democratic change, the more confidence it could gain with, and the better treatment it could get from, the victorious Great Powers. So they pressed for the urgent initiation of the reforms.

On the other hand, conservative forces in the government and the aristocrats boasting of their Western relations, endeavored to curb and stop the process of revolution. They argued that this swing to the left would bring Hungary under the suspicion of "Bolshevism," and thus result in harsher treatment from the Allies.

It must be admitted that this group was right and Károlyi was wrong. For, French Foreign Minister Stephen Pichon warned, in a secret telegram at the end of November 1918, the ambassadors of his country and, through them, the allies of France: *"Il y a quelque impudence de la part du Comte Károlyi à essayer de masquer ainsi par une façade ultra-démocratique le but réel poursuivit par le Gouvernment hongrois lequel vise uniquement de maintenir dans l'asservissement des nationalités non magyares."*[1]

Nevertheless, the mistaken assumption of Károlyi and his friends would have had important domestic consequences had their plans been followed by swift and determined actions. But the right wing, which was encouraged by the international isolation of the government, demanded priority for the defense of the national territory and urged the suspension of planned social and democratic reforms. "The Károlyi Party looks on with growing anxiety," wrote the party's daily, "that the influence of the radical ministers strives to divert even Mihály Károlyi from the platform of the party which could create, in the near future, a situation of an almost inevitable open split in the party ranks."[2]

On the other side, Oszkár Jászi, minister of the nationalities, announced his intention to resign, because, in his view,

the present composition of the government is short of the kind of democratic resoluteness, daring initiative and revolutionary energy which could save our unhappy country in the present tragic situation... . At the same time, the counter-revolution is on the move. Inside the Independent party the old reactionary trend is active again and it organizes palace revolutions against my policy towards the nationalities and my plan of confederation. ...In such circumstances, the extreme leftist tendency, too, is getting stronger day by day. ...Facing this double danger of counterrevolution and anarchy, the government must, in my opinion, stubbornly persist on radical policy and realize as much of the aspirations of the broad masses as it is realizable under the present economic and intellectual stage of development in Hungary. That means, beyond the full political democracy, the dismemberment of the latifundia, possibly connected with [the] land-value tax and cooperative system; the nationalization of the biggest plants, and fair participation of the state, the workers and the owners with the other greater enterprises; the utmost protection of the interests of the working people. Under the present conditions anything exceeding this program is not realizable, anything less is not acceptable.[3]

Inside the cabinet, which met almost daily, the debates started and became heated mostly on the possibilities of national defense, the problems of the army, the interpretation of territorial integrity, and on the negotiations with the leaders of the national minorities and with the Allied commissaries. Trying to curb these controversies, Jászi proposed, at the outset, to make clear the government's position concerning the intrusions of the Czech, Romanian, and Serbian troops. "It is a nonsense to take up arms, if we are unable to offer successful resistance, as the demonstration of our weakness must have a very unfavorable effect," he emphasized.[4]

On November 28, Jászi reported to the cabinet his talks with Milan Hodža, envoy of the Prague government and member of the Slovak National Council, about the possibility of an autonomous Slovakian state which would retain some ties with the Peoples' Republic of Hungary. Here, the almost irreconcilable differences came out most clearly between, on the one hand, the Socialist and Radical ministers [Zsigmond Kunfi, Ernő Garami, Pál Szende, Oszkár Jszai], who regarded a federal solution both as an optimum and as desirable, and, on the other, the Independents [Márton Lovászy, Tivadar Batthyány, Dénes Berinkey, Ferenc Nagy, Barna Buza and the defense minister, Col. Albert Bartha] who opposed it as an excessive concession. They tried to insist on the complete territorial integrity of old Hungary. They were reproached mercilessly by the Socialist Kunfi: "Some people are still unable to face the consequences of the military defeat. Hungarian hegemony is lost, and we must draw all the conclusions." Next day, he pointedly asked the defense minister whether there are means for a solution other than an agreement; whether it would be imaginable to wage a successful war under French occupation, against the Czechs, who are backed by the Allies? Bartha acknowledged that there is no such possibility and no such Hungarian army to impose anything upon the neighbors of Hungary.[5]

Their debate continued during the following days, even after Hodža was disavowed by the Prague government, which declared that he had gone beyond his authority. In the December 1 cabinet meeting Jászi linked the problems of the external and domestic crises. Much more was at gamble than the loss of the Slovaks, as he warned his colleagues. "If anarchy will continue, everything will turn into chaos and there will be a general Bolshevism. The life of our children is at stake!" When his main nationalist opponent, Márton Lovászy argued in favor of tougher resistance by stressing that Hungary had nothing more to lose, as the cruel amputation of the northern, eastern, and southern parts of the country was already in progress. Jászi retorted that even dismemberment could take place either in an atmosphere of mutual hatred and final collapse, without the hope of any future communication and understanding, or under more peaceful conditions, with the future possibility of cooperation to serve the common interests of this great economic and geographic unit.

However, in spite of these rather utopian hopes, Jászi admitted that he recognized the weight of the counterarguments and offered his resignation, which the cabinet refused once more.

The minutes of the Council of Ministries, the press reports, and other sources reflect the sharpening of the inner conflicts, which followed closely the worsening of the international and military situation. "The policy of the French government is a hotbed of Bolshevism," Károlyi exclaimed on December 17.[6] It could have been also said: a hotbed of nationalism and of counterrevolution.

That is to say, the process of polarization continued. With the demonstrative resignation of the two respected Independent ministers, the original coalition was broken up, and the conflicts were transferred from the cabinet to the extra-governmental forces on the right and left. But, Károlyi still held the balance of powers for a time. In his unpublished notes, he wrote about the turn of 1918–19:

I strengthened the socialist positions in the army and in the government. I had to choose whether I should make a bourgeois anti-socialist policy or inversely. I chose the socialist policy, not merely out of conviction. Would I yield, this bourgeois cabinet would have been within two months the tool of the MOVE [a rightist officer's organization]. Several delegations of the MOVE came to offer their services to me. It would be very easy to gain them over, just as Horthy could gain them over later. I did foresee the policy of detachments and I did not shoulder it.[7]

At the same time, he did not foresee the other extreme possibility, that of Communist alternative, although he already noticed the appearance and the successful agitation of the Communist party in December 1918. In a speech declaring himself a partisan of limited private ownership, he rejected definitely, but not aggressively, the Communist solution. "We cannot introduce it in a time," he said, "when the whole of Europe did not yet turn to communism."[8]

Even as late as February 1919 he did not regard the Communist challenge as a close and practical menace. In a letter to Switzerland, destined for the information of the Allied diplomats, he wrote:

> It is due to the catastrophic economic situation promoted by the Allies that Bolshevism could unfold itself, though not in a dangerous degree. Similar conditions may produce an anarchy in any country. The danger lies not with the Bolshevism imported from Russia. This one grew out almost from its own ground, it was born from the misery...[9]

Károlyi, who later became very close to the Communists, considered them at this time with some sympathy, but as late as March 21, as sort of eccentric though well-meaning utopians. He did not yet recognize their practical ability for organizing revolutions and taking power. He thought that Social Democracy, backed by the organized working class, would easily drive them back or force them to cooperate. He hoped to avoid easily both counterrevolution and the new revolution by strengthening the governmental role of the Social Democratic party.

The swiftly growing force and importance of the young Communist party was recognized at the earliest by the two poles of the political scene.

One, curiously enough but understandingly, the extreme right. Right-wing radical editor, István Milotay, gave his Christmas article in his journal *Uj Nemzedék,* the caption, "Proletarian dictatorship or bourgeois rule?"; he tried to persuade the bourgeois parties to withdraw for a while from the government for the sake of the liquidation of the whole revolutionary process.

At the other end of the spectrum were those in, or near, the Galileo Circle. Impatient young intellectuals and students, who were, under the impact of the war and the news coming from Russia, were already on their way to breaking with the Democratic-Socialist and bourgeois Radicalprogressist camp. It was their review, *Szabadgondolat* [Free Thought], edited by Karl Polányi, which initiated and published the first serious and important debates—in December 1918 and in the first three days of 1919—on the Bolshevik ideology and movement which "arrived to Pest" during November 1918.

The first three articles of a special issue, published in December 1918, were written by the leading figures of the older generation of the Hungarian left: Oszkár Jászi, the then still Social Democrat Jenő [Eugen] Varga, and the still "bourgeois" philosopher Georg Lukács.[10] To the challenge of Communism and proletarian dictatorship, their answers were quite different. Varga embraced it on the basis of the Russian experiences. Jászi, as a principled democrat, rejected it definitely. Lukács' "Bolshevism as a moral problem" ended also in a refusal, though with many signs of deep attraction.

In any case, the essence of the choice was best seen and grasped by Lukács. The democratic way, he wrote in this article, is forcing Social Democracy to cooperate also with such classes and parties which are hostile toward its ultimate goals. This is an *outer* concession which must not become an *inner* one.

The fascinating force of Bolshevism lies in the liberation from this compromise. But those who become enchanted with it may not always know what they shouldered for the sake of avoiding this compromise. Their dilemma is whether it is possible to attain the good by evil means, to achieve liberty on the road of oppression. The choice between these two standpoints is, like every moral problem, a question of faith."

The author confessed that he "cannot share that faith." The mere fact that a few weeks later he joined the Communist party with a faith strong enough for a lifetime, shows the attractiveness of this idea and of this movement at this time. And this was enhanced the more, in February, by the detention of the Communist leaders, with the cabinet's approval, mainly with the view of reassuring the Allies. Their consequent mistreatment by the police forces gave further strength to the Communist cause. These events, according to an article of Karl Polányi, "showed the communist cause unexpectedly from a new side. There was something, possible justifying the communists. It was merely a possibility, but the masses started to tremble by its force."

This magnetic force, last but not least, was greatly strengthened by the hope that the victory of the Communist revolutions in Central Europe may cut the Gordian knot of insoluble national problems, frustrate the imperialist peace settlement for a new order, putting an end to national humiliation.

By March 21, 1919, these steps led to a total polarization, the explosion of an already unbearable tension, the surrender of a democracy between wind and water. Nevertheless, mindful of our original approach, here again we should not forget that the failure of the Hungarian democratic experiment was caused directly by the Allied note resembling an ultimatum—that is, the shocking effect of the Great Power's policy. And we must repeat that it was the same policy which increased the divergence in forces outside the government, undermining the Károlyi regime.

It took more than a half a century until this democratic experiment was duly recognized and reevaluated by historiography. One of its brave fighters, however, had already predicted this in the sinister years of persecution, on the fifth anniversary of the October Revolution in 1923:

Honest historiography and unbiased historical science will place the Károlyi rule, although it collapsed under the burden of heavy responsibilities, into one of the most noble chapters of Hungarian history, because of its spirit and its endeavors. This period directed Hungarian politics and social life into the road of the civilized development of mankind. The only way of evolution for Hungary, just as for other civilized nations, is democratization. This is a necessity which cannot be altered by setbacks and detours. October was an experiment to realize progressive Hungarian democracy. We must not doubt that the nation will return to its goals and to its spirit.[11]

## NOTES

1. Pichon's telegram of November 29, 1918, to the French ambassadors in London, Rome, and Washington. Archives du Ministere des Affaires Etrangeres, Paris. Europe 1918–1929, *Hongrie*, Vol 44, fol. 165–167.

2. *Magyarország*, Dec. 10, 1918.

3. Jászi's: official letter to M. Károlyi, Dec. 10, 1918. *Károlyi Mihály levelezése* I. *1905–1920* (Budapest, 1978), pp. 320–21.

4. Minisztertanácsi jegyzőkönyvek (Minutes of the Council of Ministers), Nov. 20, 1918. Magyar Országos Levéltár K 27. Box 119.

5. *Ibid.*, Nov. 29, 1918.

6. *Ibid.*, Dec. 17, 1918.

7. Párttörténeti Intézet Archívuma. Fond 704. Cited by János Jemnitz–György Litván: *Szerette az igazságot* (Budapest, 1977), p. 171.

8. "Beszéd a kommunista törekvésekről," *Magyarország*, Dec. 17, 1918.

9. Károlyi's letter to Pál Pálffy, Feb. 2, 1919. *Károlyi levelezése*, p. 405–407.

10. O. Jászi: "Proletárdiktatúra," *Szabadgondolat*, 1918. pp. 225–226.; J. Varga: "A bolseviki uralom jövő kilátásai," *Ibid.*, pp. 226–28.; G. Lukács: A bolsevizmus mint erkölcsi probléma. *Ibid.*, pp. 228–32.

11. Zoltán Szász: "Az októberizmus történelem-bölcsészeti kritikája" in, Barna Buza, et al., *Öt év múltán. A Károlyi-korszak előzményei és céljai.* (Budapest, 1923), pp. 207–22.

# THE HUNGARIAN STOCK MARKET DURING
# THE LIBERAL DEMOCRATIC REVOLUTION, 1918–1919

Suzan Glanz

On July 28, 1914 at the outbreak of World War 1, the Budapest Stock Exchange was officially closed. But by the middle of the first year of the war, a significant private trade had developed among the exchange members. This private trade was at first carried out in the reception room of the exchange building, then, with the permission of its directors, on the floor of the exchange itself. Eventually this informal trading received official recognition and continued throughout the war until the Hungarian Soviet Republic was established. The exchange was closed while the Soviet Republic was in existence and did not reopen until October 20, 1919.

During the three month prearmistice period stock prices, as measured by the market average, declined by 21.77 percent. However, in the three month postwar period the market declined by only 3.46 percent.

During the prearmistice period bank stocks fell by 22.6 percent, flour mill stocks by 30.33 percent, steel mill stocks by 10.92 percent, coal mine and brick works stocks by 16.83 percent, transportation stocks by 23.01 percent, and miscellaneous stocks by 26.5 percent. In the postarmistice period bank stocks declined by 3.69 percent, flour mill stocks by 19.14 percent, steel mill by 19.42 percent, coal mine and brick works stocks increased by 0.29 percent, transportation stocks rose by 13.45 percent, and miscellaneous stocks sank by 4.03 percent.[1]

In the period immediately following the armistice Hungary's future looked quite bleak. The country not only lost the war but it also faced the prospect of losing large amounts of territory. Furthermore, its economy was at a complete standstill and it was facing numerous labor strikes. Nevertheless, overall stock prices held quite firm during this period.

An explanation for the large decline before the armistice, is easy to come by, but not for the market's only slight decline after the armistice.

Postarmistice stock market behavior, however is more difficult to explain and could perhaps be best understood as simply as a sigh of relief from the burdens of war and a sense of optimism for the future. The country expected economic aid to come from the Allied countries as a result of the Paris Peace Conference. Another possible explanation for the market's behavior during this period would be that purchasing stocks was used as a haven from the rampant inflation during this postwar period.[2] The greatest loss in value was in the steel mill and flour mill shares. The fact that the value of steel mill stocks fell by 19.42 percent, is hardly surprising since most of the iron ore mines came under Czechoslovakia's control. Flour mill stocks declined sharply due to impending land reform (which never really came about) and loss of farm lands to annexations by Hungary's neighbors. As a result it was expected that the country would be left with excess capacity. Transportation stocks outperformed the market by a wide margin; a consequence of speculative buying in the aftermath of Italian buying of Austrian transportation stocks.[3]

In late July 1918, *Pesti Napló*, a Hungarian daily, reported that "due to uncertainty there is no observable trend in the market. The price ranges are generally narrow, and speculation seems to be in the Hungarian issues as the market in Vienna is nearly dead."[4] While reports from the war front were discouraging, the news on the domestic front was more encouraging. On August 4, it was reported that the Austro–Hungarian Bank would open a Spanish office on September 15 in order to promote trade between Spain and the monarchy. On August 7, Schlick–Nicholson, a Hungarian company, announced that it would build a new machine tool factory in Budapest. As a result the market gained in the first two weeks of August. In the third week of August, however, leaders of the Central Powers met to reach a common understanding regarding steps to be taken to reach an armistice with the Allies. The market reacted by trading at a slightly lower level because of the uncertainty of the peace terms. Only flour mill stocks closed higher for the week as it was announced that mill workers were now exempt from military call-ups.

The last week of August and the first fortnight of September saw a firmness in the market and an increase in trading activity, despite the bad news from the fronts. This was due mostly to the increasing activity of the new-issues market, especially among bank stocks. *Pesti Naplós's* market analyst wrote that "a number of firms are trying to take advantage of the strength of the stock market and the expectations are of stock splits and new issues." On August 25, the National Forestry Company (*Országos Fatermelő Rt.*) announced that it would call a special shareholders meeting for September 3, to raise its capital stock from six million to twelve million crowns. The National Bank (*Országos Bank*) also announced plans to raise its capital stock. However, on September 3, the Government notified the Hungarian Bank (*Magyar Bank*) that it would only allow a 20-million crown increase in its capital stock despite a request for a 40-million crown increase. On the very same day a government decree was signed limiting the issue of new stock. This dampened the interest in the market and prices fell.

On September 14, István Burian, joint foreign minister of the Austro–Hungarian monarchy, asked the Entente nations to begin discussions on the conditions for peace. He made it clear that a peace on the basis of Wilson's Fourteen Points would be unacceptable. Until mutually acceptable terms were proposed, he favored the continuation of the war. As a result, when the market reopened after a three-day break for the Jewish holidays, prices fell. In the following week the market recovered slightly.

War bulletins and rumors about impending changes in foreign policy made the market very nervous. From the battle fronts came news of the capitulation of the Bulgarian army, of the resignation of German Chancellor Georg Hertling, and of the Allied troops in the Balkans' imminent crossing of the Hungarian border. On the exchange a major dealer declared bankruptcy. As a result panic broke out and the market dropped 17.2 percent for the week. Many members asked the exchange's board of directors to close the market temporarily to prevent a further drop in prices. However on September 24, after a meeting, the Association of Securities Dealers decided to set maximum limits on inter-day fluctuations of 5 to 10 percent. This measure stopped the further plummeting of prices.[5]

On October 4, Burian sent President Wilson two notes suggesting an immediate cease-fire and accepting the peace terms based on the Fourteen Points. On the 6th, Berlin took the initiative by sending a note to President Wilson proposing a immediate armistice, with the Fourteen Points as a basis. On the 8th Wilson sent his response to the German government in which he asked for further elaboration. Next day, at 4 pm, the Hungarians learned of this message and interpreted this as a positive sign and expected a similar answer to their note (which, in fact, was only answered on the 19th).[6] The following day, the 10th the papers reported, that by 5 pm on Wednesday, the price of gold and diamonds on the "coffee house exchange" dropped sharply. A kilogram of gold fell to 18,000 crowns from the September price of 26,000, and the price of diamonds fell by 30 percent. On this unofficial exchange, the price of sugar also fell, to 20 crowns a kg from the previous 30 crowns. Interviewed real estate agents reported that in anticipation of peace many landlords withdrew sell orders.[7]

In the ensuing weeks the stock market continued to fall, reacting mostly to political events. At various times there were rumors that the market would be closed; all of which proved false. On October 17, István Tisza announced in parliament that "we have lost the war." thus acknowledging what many already knew. On October 24, a number of Stock Exchange members demanded that the market be closed due to the unsettled political conditions. But by a vote of 17 to 11, the Board of Directors decided to keep it open. In the last week of October, with the expectation that Mihály Károlyi, a parliamentary leader with a pro–Entente reputation, would be appointed prime minister, the market stabilized expecting that his appointment would hasten the peace process. On the 26th, Charles IV notified Kaiser Wilhelm II that he was going to sue for a separate cease-fire and peace agreement. Indeed, on the 28th, Foreign Minister Gyula Andrássy petitioned President Wilson for a separate peace. While movement was taking place on the international scene, during the night of 30–31, a bloodless revolution shook the streets of Budapest. Demonstrators demanded the appointment of Károlyi, who was the leader of the recently organized National Council. On October 31, former Prime Minister, István Tisza was assassinated by a band of disgruntled soldiers. That same day, Károlyi was appointed prime minister of Hungary, and the following day the market was closed for 24 hours.[8]

On Saturday, November 2, the Board of Directors, in light of the impending armistice and Károlyi's appointment, issued an optimistic statement saying, "that we hope that the stock exchange will play an important role in the rebuilding of the new nation and it accepts this role enthusiastically... and hopes that its leadership will lead with its existing autonomy intact, which in the current economic conditions is vital for fulfilling the nation's goals."[9] But despite the reasuring speeches, trading activity on the exchange declined sharply. On the 6th, only four stocks traded. On the 7th and 8th trading picked up slightly (ten stocks and 31 stocks, respectively). On the 9th, when news arrived that the Berlin Stock Exchange had closed, trading almost came to a complete standstill. Twenty stocks were traded on the 11th, seven stocks on the 12th; thirteen on the 13th, and only three on the 14th. At this time, it was considered whether to close the exchange completely owing to the extremely light trading. Instead, starting November 14, trading hours were reduced to 30 minutes a day (11'30 am to 12 pm); daily price limits were set to the previous day's low. On November 14, Hungary proclaimed itself a republic. However, the market did not react to the news, instead it took a wait-and-see attitude with trading activity held to a minimum.

Despite the further decline in trading volume the directors of the exchange, in a meeting on December 3, decided against closing the exchange.

They noted that market activity in Vienna picked up, and therefore, expected a similar increase on the Budapest Stock Exchange. This proved to be a pipe-dream, as the Hungarian economy came to a complete halt. Production ceased in nearly all industries, not only because of lack of raw materials, but also because of the political uncertainties. For example, Romania announced that it would allow shipments of lumber to Hungary only in exchange for food. And, Czechoslovakia prohibited the shipment of forestry products completely. In many factories workers demanded the resignation of managers. There were talks between the companies and the workers to meet these demands. News of impending strikes also spread. Only when the Government indicated that it would intervene, did market activity pick up again. On January 9, the committee of the Supreme Economic Council of the Paris Peace Conference, headed by Alonzo E. Taylor, with headquarters in Vienna, arrived in Buda-pest. It was expected that, as a result of this meeting, economic aid to Hungary would be approved. This, however, never came about.[10]

Economic problems, coupled with the apparent Allied hostility to the liberal-democratic government, led to a cabinet crisis at the end of December and early January 1919. A number of ministers resigned. In spite of the crisis atmosphere in Budapest, the upcoming opening of the Paris Peace Conference and the second Coolidge Mission's visit rekindled hopes that the Hungarians were not being neglected. To solve the political crisis, the National Council appointed Károlyi president of the republic. Because the Paris Peace conference was to start with preliminary talks already taking place on the 13th, it was still assumed that the Hungarians would partici-pate; consequently, the market reacted positively, and the number of stocks traded increased. On the 20th, price limits were abolished and the trading day was expanded from 11 am to noon.

Beginning in January, labor problems put a damper on prices in the stock market. Demands by workers to participate in management were spreading and at the same time production was still at a standstill. Workers also called for participation in wage policy decisions. In one extreme case, workers demanded to have their representatives present even at the opening of company mail.[11]

On January 21, it was announced that the workers of Schlick–Nicholson had successfully removed two managers and had replaced them with their own representatives. The Hungarian Trade Bank of Pest (*Pesti–Magyar Keres-kedelmi Bank*), Schlick–Nicholson's major stock holder, immediately announced that, in light of events, it would no longer approve any new loans. It was also anticipated that because of abolition of price limits and news that Yugoslavia had instituted agrarian reform, the market would react in a negative way. Nevertheless, it was only slightly down for the week. In the last week of January, trading volume increased, but prices were mostly unchanged. On January 31, Saturday trading was allowed again, making the trading week six days long.

On the news that the Italians were buying up shares of Austrian shipping lines, the prices of Hungarian lines also went up. This created a positive atmosphere in the market and the prices closed higher for the week. However, on February 13, it was announced that the Hungarian Agrarian Reform Law was to be published on the 15th; as a result the market fell slightly. The market reacted negatively to this reform because it called for the breakup of large farming estates. The market was also waiting for some statement from the National Workers Council, which was formed on February 8, to direct public work programs and this, too, put a damper on the market. On February 19 at 11:30 am, market activity was stopped by the bell of the secretary of the exchange. He announced that in sympathy with the Socialist demonstration and general strike the trading activity would stop for five minutes. When trading resumed prices fell.[12]

In the first week of March, the market remained stable, but when, on the 7th, the government announced plans to nationalize property, prices fell. On March 17, the government decided to begin nationalization and this resulted in large demonstrations supporting the government. The market's confidence was further shaken. Furthermore, a crisis was caused by the Vix ultimatum. This memorandum called for the creation of a neutral zone between Hungary and Romania, which meant that Hungarian troops would have to withdraw and as a result depriving Hungary of still more territory. This left the government no other alternative than to resign. As a result the market closed lower and on March 21, when the Hungarian Soviet Republic came to power, the exchange closed its doors for several months, even though it was not explicitly ordered to do so. This was done because, as the papers reported,

in the stock exchange building one of the executive committees of the Council of Commissars was assigned rooms. There are guards in the doorway, who allow only people with permits into the stock exchange building. The participants of the market are forced out into the street and into the coffee house in the building. But there is no talk of business.[13]

In taking account of the market's activity before and after the Armistice, and during the time of the Liberal Democratic Republic, it is evident that trading closely mirrored the political events that shook Hungary. Market activity before armistice reflected the pessimism and the uncertainty that Hungary faced. The market's only slight decline after armistice or just before the collapse of the Liberal Democratic Republic, reflected partly both the uncertainty of the political situation and a relief that the war was over. There was also some room for optimism, for at this time it was still believed despite evidence to the contrary that Wilson's Tenth Point, which dealt with "Autonomy in Austria–Hungary," would preserve all or most of Hungary's territory. This contributed to the market's relative good performance at a time when there was also increased buying of shares as a hedge against inflation. The coming of a Socialist-Communist fusion government on March 21, which intended to defend the integrity of Hungary, could also have strengthened stock prices. The closing of the stock exchange, however, was symbolic of the Hungarian Soviet Republic's ill-considered intent of destroying capitalism the quickest way possible.

## NOTES

1. These industry groups are the same as those used by the Hungarian papers carrying the daily quotes. All averages are simple unweighted arithmetic averages.

2. The traditional methods of measuring inflation were useless during this period (both before and after the Armistice) due to price controls on consumer goods. Even though the black market flourished during this period there are no statistics to measure it. However, the comparison of the value of a paper crown vs. a gold crown could perhaps give us some indication of inflation.

3. The stock market prices were taken from the daily papers, the Hungarian language, *Pesti Napló*, and the German language, *Pester Lloyd*, both published in Hungary. Although there were over 180 stocks listed on the Budapest Stock Exchange during the period under examination, the list was narrowed to just 52 companies because trading activity was very light and sporadic on the rest of the list. In order to be included on our list a stock had to trade at least twice a week. Once selected, these 52 stocks were classified into six industry groups; and since not all stocks traded on the same day and in order to permit comparison, weekly averages of the daily prices were calculated. Furthermore, weekly averages were calculated for each industry group, and an overall weekly market average was also calculated.

The stocks were classified by industry groups as follows:

| Industry group | Companies in group |
|---|---|
| Banks and savings and loans | 15 |
| Flour mills | 2 |
| Steelmills and machine tools | 5 |
| Coal mines and brick works | 8 |
| Transportation | 8 |
| Miscellaneous | 14 |
| Total | 52 |

4. *Pesti Napló*, July 31, 1918.

5. *Pesti Napló*, September 25, 1918

6. Victor S. Mamatey, *The United States and East Central Europe, 1914–18*. (Princeton, 1957) p. 324

7. *Pesti Napló*, October 11, 1918.

8. *Pesti Napló*, November 2, 1918.

9. *Pesti Napló*, November 2, 1918.

10. Gunst Péter, ed., *Magyar Történelmi Kronológia*. (Budapest, 1984), p. 441

11. *Pesti Napló*, January 10, 1919.

12. *Pesti Napló*, February 19, 1919.

13. *Pesti Napló*, March 23, 1919.

# ENGINEER UTOPIA: ON THE POSITION
## OF THE TECHNOSTRUCTURE IN HUNGARY'S WAR
## COMMUNISM, 1919

György Péteri

The new Socialist system in Hungary, hardly two months old, had to face, it seemed, what one of its leaders, Gyula Hevesi, called a "problem of intellectuals."[1] At issue were concerns expressed by the technical intelligentsia as to their role in the new system of industrial management. The minutes and resolutions of the May 29 and June 1, 1919, meetings of the National Association of Employed Engineers (AMOSZ) as well as repeated policy declarations of several of the People's Commissars (Béla Kun, Jenő Varga, and Hevesi) to the effect that the new institutions of proletarian power in factories and industrial plants must not interfere with the sovereignty of engineers in technical matters, confirm this impression.

The debate seems to have concluded with policy measures which strengthened central power and control over the councils of workers. Moreover, this interpretation rings true if we place it in the context of the emerging new system of industrial management.[2]

The new legal, institutional frameworks of economic activity, established at amazing speed, provided for a radical "upward" redistribution of management functions. The concept of industrial enterprise as such was declared a thing of the past, and management of economic resources became concentrated in the hands of central authorities. And, centralized state administration left but very little to be done at the microeconomic level. Even operative control over the purely technological process—the only function remaining at the level of plants and facatories—fell under the care of sectoral centers.

The vacuum of functions, in principle, notwithstanding, no fewer than four institutions competed for, and/or shared, power at the bottom level of the economic administration.

The production commissar, the embodiment of the principle of one-man management, represented "the whole proletariat in the plant where he has been placed as leader." In other words, he was the executive organ of centralized economic administration, providing "the link between the Commissariat [of Social Production] and the individual plants."

The councils of workers' control, product of the near past, were preserved in the new system rather unwillingly. A collegial organ, the members of which were elected by the workers themselves in the factory and were not approved, and/or appointed—as the production commissar—by the relevant sectoral center of the Commissariat. These councils were the legacy of a spontaneous movement of workers, radically reshaping the mode of management of capitalist industrial enterprise around the turn of the revolutionary years of 1918–19. A legacy the leaders of Soviet Hungary thought it best to relinguish claim to. This was strongly indicated already. The "Socialization" Decree no. IX of the Governing Council (March 26, 1919) already strongly pointed in this direction; for it defined as the major function of the workers' control, the establishment of "proletarian labor discipline" at the plants. That task took on greater emphasis later on during debates in May and June 1919; discussion ruled out all possible conclusions but the one—workers' control was an ill-fitting cog in the wheel of industrial management, and therefore, produced undesirable frictions.

No systemic reason, it seemed, existed, on the other hand, that could give rise to friction between the technological management and the production commissar. On the contrary, the very nature of large-scale industrial organization provided for the two. Workers' control, however, proved "a necessary evil" (Béla Kun), a source of disturbance in the otherwise smoothly working industrial system, a burden which, for political reasons (it was, after all, a workers' state) had to be carried until the eventual transition to "workers' management" (when the new political rule is consolidated enough to completely integrate economic activity into the state administration).

Joining the above triangular arrangement of factory management is a fourth element—the trade unions. We may, thus, arrive at a fairly consistent and verifiable understanding of the developments leading to the National Economic Council's resolution of June 11, that placed the organs of workers' control under trade-union guardianship. The unions themselves had been at loggerheads with the movement of workers' control for the obvious reason that the latter tended to trespass into fields on which the trade union apparatus based its power, and in which it made a living.

In fact, top political leaders went out of their way repeatedly to defend the sovereignty of specialists in technological matters against undue interference on the part of workers' control. This becomes more intelligible in the context outlined above, as part of the policies pursued with a view to strengthen bureaucratic centralization at the expense of direct, democratic control by the workers. And, within the same context, so does the unrest among organized engineers culminating late May and early June, as but one part of a polyphonic composition combining the arguments of engineers, trade union bureaucrats, and the political leadership, against workers' participation in economic management.

However plausible the above account might be for the descending phase of the career of workers' control in the revolutions of 1918–19, it is, unfortunately, quite misleading as a contextualization of the "problem of intelligentsia." Seen from a rather narrow and ahistoric perspective on industrial management, it is almost impossible to recognize that the trio of political leadership, engineers and trade-union bureaucracy, made for a unity of a very temporary and *ad hoc* character. The three components shared a common view that a "steward system" was as ill-adapted to the needs of effective management in industry as it was in the Red Army. But even on that point they were acting as three separate socio-political groups with conflicting interests and aspirations.

A proper understanding of the 'problem of intelligentsia' of Soviet Hungary, therefore, calls for a broader, historical perspective, one able to do justice to a relatively new and specific phenomenon on the horizon of modern Hungarian society, the emergence of engineer consciousness. This consciousness led to a movement that could mobilize about the half or two-thirds of the country's technical intelligentsia around an anticapitalist utopia with several features distinguishing it from the labor movement's visions of socialism.

Let us start with some basic statistical data concerning the absolute and relative size of the stratum we are dealing with. According to the 1910 census, of the 456,470 persons employed in mining, metallurgy, and industry 5.2 percent (23,859) were white-collar workers. A little more than a fifth (4198) were engineers and technicians. According to the 1920 census, which might better reflect conditions prevailing in 1918–19, of a total industrial workforce of 205,183, 8.5 percent (17,140) belonged to the white-collar category, in which the share of engineers and technicians was practically unchanged in absolute number, 3237.

It is important to note that Jews in pre-1914 Hungary (comprising, in 1919, a mere 4.5 percent of the total population)[3] were strongly represented among the ranks of white-collar private employees. Their share in mining was 17.9 percent; in the rest of industry, 43.9 percent, running as high as to 52.6 percent in the Budapest industrial agglomeration[4] (the largest single industrial region, where 37.2 percent of Hungary's manufacturing was concentrated.)[5] The engineering profession was becoming to an increasing degree a Jewish, lower-middle class career during the first decades of this century: in 1900, 1910, and 1920, the relative weight of people of Jewish origin in the total number of engineers was 23.9 percent, 37.6 percent, and 39.2 percent respectively.[6]

As engineers, if they pursued professional values and prestige, they found themselves entirely subjected to business considerations prevailing in the private firm that employed them: institutionalized research and development activity not yet existing outside the walls of industrial enterprise.

As Jews, they found the capitalist entrepreneurial career as the only open (but rather narrow) path of upward social mobility. Such a career might give one the satisfaction of becoming one's own master but could hardly be conducive to professional aspirations.

As part of the "socially unattached intelligentsia," engineers, too, had, ideologically, made, in search for a way out of their "middle-of-the-road position," a Mannheimian option: they could choose "first, what amounts to a largely voluntary affiliation with one or the other of the various antagonistic classes; second, scrutiny of their own social moorings and the quest for the fulfilment of their mission as the predestined advocate of the intellectual interests of the whole."[7]

Few engineers with professional self-esteem could opt for political affiliation with the bourgeoisie, the more especially since in Hungary it had been short on a political, ideological platform of any coherence. On the flip side of the coin, i.e., political affiliation with the workers' movement, led to a cul-de-sac as well, "since the Hungarian Social Democratic Party did not admit white-collar workers into any of the existing trade-unions," and since also, "the anti-intellectual trade-unionists rejected them as 'representatives of capital' in the factory."[8]

Thus, the conditions in late nineteenth- and early twentieth-century Hungarian society and politics provided a fertile ground for the emergence of a specific engineer consciousness, for such conditions were pushing the technical intelligentsia, interested in social, political problems, toward "becoming aware of their own social position and the mission implict in it."[9]

Some time around 1912–13, Gyula Hevesi, who was to become the mastermind behind the ideological and political mobilization of engineers during the war years, had come to the conclusion "that on my social level, where I find myself, amidst my:

> poor economic circumstances, all my aspirations for prominence, for an existence providing the possibility of research work along the lines of my own desires or, at least, the possibility of creative technical work, were hopeless. Moreover, even if I managed to create a great thing, it would, after all, only serve the power of usurpers. Discard, then, the physics, astronomy and inventions! There is a much greater problem here to be solved, a problem of which my individual grievance is but a tiny, though inseparable, part. *The task is to destroy the barricades that have been raised by today's society in the way of all who posses nothing but their talent and knowledge.*"[10] [Italics mine]

Throwing himself into contemporary sociology and economics, Hevesi gained reassurance in his disgust with private ownership by reading Henry George's *Progress and Poverty* (published in Hungarian in 1912), and derived much and decisive inspiration from Schumpeter's *Theorie der wirtschaftlichen Entwicklung* (first published in Leipzig, in 1912).

He was quick to develop further Schumpeter's theory of profit and the dynamics of capitalist economy into his own "theory" of production and exploitation. In Hevesi's understanding, three indispensable factors of production were Nature, Labor, and Know-how (the latter consisting of work method and, in general, techniques, including the technological knowledge necessary to produce the means of production). Capital did not figure among the necessary factors of production; the exploitation of labor was but a secondary phenomenon of the capitalist system deriving from "that the capital, in some way or another, has "expropriated the 'know-how', the third indispensable factor of production..."[11] Without *new* technique, *new* know-how, young Hevesi contended, entrepreneurial capitalism would be unable to profit from workers' expropriation:

> For the capitalist, therefore, it is not the technology in general what is of importance, but the technological change, the process of technological development or, in other words, the changes of 'know-how' brought about unceasingly and ever faster by discoveries and inventions in the workshops through generalisations based upon thousands and tenthousands of empirical and experimental observations. As the great bulk of these discoveries and inventions are made by engineers and technicians ... employed by the capitalist enterprise, the expropriation of technological progress that opens up newer and newer sources of extra-profit is based on the exploitation of this technical intelligentsia.[12]

Hevesi's understanding of the world, his endeavor to define the place of engineers in it, might very well fail to meet many of the criteria of a "good theory"—it was, indeed, eclectic, incoherent, and it could hardly claim to have covered but a fragment of the whole construction of Hungarian society. Nevertheless, its appeal to the group it was designed for, does not seem to have suffered by those deficiencies, for it did possess all the properties that make an effective ideology. It promised to elevate the group from its "unanchored" state of social desolation by providing them with a self-consciousness that turned their middle-of-the-road position from a source of despair into the starting point of a hopeful quest for a mission of universal significance. It gave the engineers an identity of being the Atlas of the Earth of Capitalism, upon whose shoulders the system was resting with its whole weight, and, at the same time, of an enchained Prometheus whose creative faculties were being exploited for wrong purposes and in the wrong way. In other words, Hevesi's anticapitalist Schumpeterianism was capable of meeting the basic requirements of a mobilizing ideology: it did equip the engineers with a consciousness, a conception of their own position in the social network and, at the same time, depicting for them an Enemy, the Capitalist, against whom they were not only allowed, but in their absolute right, to give full vent to their agression accumulated through many decades of their Odyssey in the No-Man's Land of Society.

Economic, social, and political developments in Hungary in the years of World War I, made possible, and also greatly accelerated, the evolution of the germ of engineer consciousness into a full-fledged radical movement with a strongly utopian attitude subjecting everything to the desire to change the prevailing order.

The elementary wisdom which holds that "the foremost precondition of a revolution is as great a famine as possible" as "it is very difficult to make revolution with full Comrades,"[13] pinpoints one of the most effective motives that were making various social groups highly receptive to radical ideas. The real-income position of the major wage- and salary-earning strata of Hungary's urban society, underwent a considerable deterioration in the wake of forced military mobilization of economic resources.

Real Incomes 1913–1918[14]

| Year* | Unskilled worker | Skilled factory worker | Civil servant | Private white-collar employee |
|-------|------------------|------------------------|---------------|-------------------------------|
| 1913–14** | 100.00 | 100.0 | 100.0 | 100.0 |
| 1914 | 86.8 | 82.6 | 82.6 | 82.6 |
| 1915 | 63.2 | 64.2 | 85.8 | 58.4 |
| 1916 | 49.5 | 55.8 | 58.6 | 45.2 |
| 1917 | 50.5 | 57.7 | 33.5 | 36.0 |
| 1918 | 46.2 | 53.4 | 33.0 | 32.9 |

*End-of-the-year data;          **Average for 1913–1914

The corollary of this deterioration had been not only an almost sevenfold increase of trade-union membership between 1913 and 1918,[15] but also the profound transformation in the character of trade unions from relatively tame organizations of economic defense to lively forums for the articulation of comprehensive political demands.

In 1917, the organization of engineers started gathering momentum, too. In May, the industrial section of the only existing white-collar union (*Magántisztvieslők és Kereskedelmi Alkalmazottak Országos Szövetsége*) broke away and formed the National Association of White-Collar Workers of Industry and Transportation (IKTOSZ). This union's leadership was to a great extent recruited from among radical engineers, several of whom were later to become founding members of the Communist party in Hungary. In December 1917, the engineers' section, with a membership of more than 1000, was established within IKTOSZ. And, finally, on November 18, 1918, that section became independent and formed, with more than 1500 members, a purely engineer union, the National Association of Employed Engineers (AMOSZ).

The process of establishing independent organizational frameworks for the emerging engineer movement, took place parallel with the development of a close alliance between engineers and the Socialist labor movement. Political cooperation with workers' unions and workers' groups acting independently of their unions, the activities of the Interfactory Committee, the left-wing Social-Democratic or, rather, Communist rhetoric of speeches, articles, and policy declarations by engineer activists as well as membership of leading engineers in the Social Democratic party and, then, in the Communist party, indicated the emergence of the alliance and, at the same time, the unquestionable possibility for the engineers' movement of merging into left-wing labor politics and, thereby, losing its own, specific ideological profile well before having had a real chance to develop it.

No doubt, radical and swift ideological, political adjustments were made by key personalities (Gyula Hevesi, József Kelen, Armin Helfgott, etc.) of the engineer movement in the direction of Leninist Marxism of the 1917—18 vintage. It is also a fact, that the AMOSZ, due to its most known activists' Communist party membership, was regarded as a basically Communist organization in the political bookkeeping of the period. Still, it would be a gross exaggeration to understand the relationship between AMOSZ and the rest of the revolutionary movement of late 1918, early 1919, in terms of a total merger of the former into the latter.

However wide both the Social Democrats and Communists opened their arms toward the intelligentsia in the late war years, the gesture could not develop into a deadly hug. Jenő Varga published articles in March and December, 1918, showing —by Hungarian Social Democratic standards— an unusually vivid interest and concern as to the relation between the workers' movement and the "class of officials," and urging, with reference to the disquieting experience of Soviet Russia, "the socialist education of Hungarian students, Hungarian intellectuals, and Hungarian officials." The newcomer Communists' attitude around the turn of 1918—19 was to extensively capitalize on all sorts of movements that might help them get a footing in the organizations of industrial wage and salaried employees and to cause as much trouble to the Social Democratic party and to the new, liberal-democratic regime as possible. Left-wing Social Democrats could hardly deal seriously with the integration of engineers, their foremost concern being how to stop the political landslide that threatened to undermine the party's control over the labor movement. The Communists, on the other hand, appear to have left the re-education of their political associates for a time when they would have already been helped into power by them.

No less important, to the engineers, the involvement in leftist labor politics hardly seemed to imply giving up, in any way, their ideology, their engineer identity, or their mission they believed to have in the postcapitalist world order. On the contrary, the *mesalliance* between engineers' technocratic anticapitalism and the ideas of bureaucratic State Socialism seemed to be a most promising, and an only too natural, marriage. As Armin Helfgott declared: "The source of evil is capitalism, which by now has become an anachronism. ... The principles of modern natural sciences are in full harmony with the ideas of socialism."[16] Indeed, the months leading from the establishment of the Károlyi regime to the declaration of the Soviet Republic, had been a period of further consolidation and development, rather than of fading away, of engineer consciousness. And this holds true of the whole movement, its Communist members included. The amazingly elaborate program for "Socialized Production" taking shape during January–February 1919, truly reflected the belief that "The socialist "production, the long dreamed-of ideal of the engineer, makes the pioneer role of the engineers in the Communist society obvious.„[17]

József Kelen's article of January 1919 contended that the prevailing economic crisis was rooted in the antagonism between the public interest (demanding maximal economy and productivity) and the private interest (seeking profit-maximization and risk-minimization). Under the circumstances of social, political instability, he wrote, the contraction of business enterprise was inevitable as risk-minimizing, dominated overriding profit considerations and thereby made the capitalist system incapable of ensuring social reproduction. "Therefore," Kelen drew the conclusion, "especially today, we need such a form of production as would be exclusively geared to the criteria determined by the public interest ..." And that "form of production" Kelen found "easy to outline":

> We have to rationalize, standarize and manage the whole production according to the actual needs. This part of the job is a technological and administrative-cum-statistical matter: the central management of agriculture, mining and manufacturing in accordance with the criteria of economy, productivity and consumption. ... all this has ceased to be just a theory, a utopia. This is a realistic program.[18]

Despite the fact that he abandoned Schumpeter—according to his own memoirs, around 1914–15, when he fell victim to a new passion he felt for Marx' *Wage, Labor, and Capital*[19] –Hevesi, too, continued with great enthusiasm to conceive a future where the technical intelligentsia would be able to come into a social position to which they had always been, by virtue of their profession, entitled but, due to the political power of the "capitalist usurpers," not yet admitted.

> Nothing more is to be done than to eliminate the profit considerations from production and to adjust the capacity of machinery to the social needs. To be able to do so, the owner of the factory or the director dependent upon him is to be replaced by such a technical manager—preferably someone from among the factory's engineers, to be elected by the workers—who both socially and professionally is reliable. The latter [professional] consideration is to weigh more as this factory manager will have a higher, controlling forum over him, a board to be elected by the workers and white-collar employees. To this board a member will be delegated by the central organ (which may be called, for example, Central Production Council (CPC)) taking care of the management of the whole production. It will not cause great trouble if the factory manager does not happen to be an eminent technical expert, for the rest of the technical management—being freed from the economic dependence on the enter-

prise management that prevails now—will be in a position to freely say their opinion of his activities before the factory board as well as before the elected collegium of workers or before the latters' plenary meeting.... For the management and control of the industrial branches and the whole production, a central organ, as I already said, will have to be established: the Central Production Council. Its members will be elected technological and scientific experts and, furthermore, representatives of workers and, in general, of consumers. This council will determine the general principles of production, it will dispose of all the raw materials and energy supplies and will distribute them among the different production branches in accordance with the interests of needs.[20]

Hungary was, of course, not the only country where the Engineer Utopia manifested itself. It must have been influencing the fantasy of radical intellectuals in Paris as well. Ilia Ehrenburg tells in his memoirs of a discussion that took place in the Café Rotonde in 1916, where Fernand Léger dropped the following remark:

The war will soon come to an end. The soldiers do not want to fight any longer.... The regions and countries destroyed will have to be rebuilt. I think, the politicians will be kicked out: they have gone bankrupt. In their place will be seated engineers, technicians and, maybe, workers too...[21]

Parallel in time with the revolutionary developments in Hungary, Thorstein Veblen was publishing, in the United States, a series of essays in *Dial*, reprinted later as *The Engineers and the Price System*.[22] His main theme was that "Twentieth-century technology has outgrown the eighteenth-century system of vested rights." Therefore, suggested Veblen, matters of industrial policy "should plainly be left to the discretion of the general staff of production engineers driven by no commercial bias". He concluded with "A Memorandum on a Practicable Soviet of Technicians," wherein he elaborated upon the new order "designed to correct the shortcomings of the old," where "politics and vested interests" distorted the workings of the industrial system.[23] Veblen himself was rather pessimistic about whether his ideas would soon come true in America. On the other hand, he was quite convinced, in general, that

the material welfare of all the advanced industrial people rests in the hands of these technicians, if they will only see it that way, take counsel together, constitute themselves the self-directing General Staff of the country's industry, and dispense with the interference of the lieutenants of the absentee owners. Already they are strategically in a position to take the lead and impose their own terms of leadership, so soon as they, or a decisive number of them, shall reach a common understanding to that effect and agree on a plan of action.[24]

What made the Hungarian experience during the time of war and revolutions specific, was the emergence of a movement of engineers who wanted to see it "that way," who took counsel together, and who, in March 1919, were much inclined to take their own succession to General Staff positions over the country's economy for granted. After all, as they informed telegraphically all the "technical-science workers" of the world on May Day 1919, "The Communist order means nothing else than the elimination "of the chance for any business speculation, and that the technical sciences in their purity will play the leading role in production."[25]

Returning to our point of departure, "the problem of intellectuals" in Hungary's Soviet Republic, we can now try and set free that issue from the limited context of plant management and to make an assessment of the position of engineer movement in the developments of "high politics" after March 21, 1919.

The first conspicous fact is that it was only the People's Commissars (mostly Hevesi, Kun, and Varga) who presented the issue to the public as if it had emerged from a conflict between the technical intelligentsia and manual labor. There is little evidence showing the engineers or the workers to have viewed the problem that way. On the contrary, during the debate of the AMOSZ-meetings of May 29 and June 1, remarks were made emphasizing that "The engineer's work, according to our experience, has always been respected (with a few exceptions) by the manual workers."[26] Ignác Pfeifer, spokesman for the unrest and discontent prevailing among the engineers, protested against "irresponsible elements" trying to set "manual workers against intellectual workers."[27] He came then closer to naming the source of evil by saying this:

For the technician to be able to fulfil his vocation, it is first of all necessary to acquire respect for him among the workers and in the bosom of the whole Soviet Republic. We feel the lack of this respect not among the self-conscious workers who have been working together with us for years, but in those measures and decrees that have been issued by the dictatorship of the proletariat. (Great applause.)

The distinction made by Pfeifer between workers and the "dictatorship of the proletariat" is indeed most important to understand the actual implications of the debate. Further help to guess the riddle may be brought from Chairman László Sajó's contribution to the meeting on 29 May:

First, we have to see to it that the engineers are granted such a position in the Communist order of production as they are, by virtue of their profession, rightly entitled to. Secondly, we have to find the ways and means of rendering the knowledge of engineers useful at all those places where not only special technological expertise is needed but also comprehensive economic and industrial considerations, and where decision-making, leadership and control are exercised.

He later added:

Those who will implement the Marxist idea are acting, in their policies, clearly in opposition to the Marxist understanding. If that happened so, as it did, then it was that situation which made the leaders of AMOSZ summon the meeting as a situation had been created in which the intelligentsia [*fejmunkások*] rightly feel their position, their living, but even the fulfilment of their task which is their duty in the proletarian society, endangered.[28]

The critique's immediate target was obviously the top political leadership. But its curious feature, a consistent abstinence from taking up *concrete* measures, decrees, or policies that were regarded to be deleterious to the engineers, shows that the aim was to convey the discontent of the engineer movement over their being, in general, excluded from (or, not being admitted to) the emerging new political class rather, than to press for particular concessions by the other side.

It was the gradual concentration of overall power and control into the hands of the bureaucracy of an administration merging all aspects of social reproduction into its field of competence that lay at the bottom of the engineers' grievance. In the process of rearrangements at the top level of society, a background in the organizations of a "blue-collar" labor movement bestowed on pretenders to power an unquestionable legitimacy, whereas the engineers, expecting to be automatically promoted to a hegemonic position by their expertise, found themselves standing on the platform and desperately waving to the "Train of History" they had missed again. The days of feverish planning for socialization of plants, for standardization, for "concentration of production into the most economic units," for large-scale rationalizations, etc., had been over, and instead of the technical sciences "in their purity" playing the leading role, they saw their influence rapidly losing ground, at the level of central management as well as in the factories, to the bureaucratic apparatus of blue-collar sectoral unions and career party officials succeeding to control positions in the name of "the dictatorship of the proletariat." Even the very existence of the engineers movement came to be threatened by repeated proposals to the effect that all white-collar organizations should dissolve and their membership should join relevant blue-collar organizations of the different industrial sectors.[29] By late May, this trend of the dynamics of political change had manifested itself in organizational-institutional terms, too. The former center of "Engineer Power," the People's Commissariat of Social Production, was merged into the National Economic Council, to become the latter's Division III responsible for the technical control of industrial plants, Divisions I and VII taking over the more strategic functions of central economic management. Gyula Hevesi and József Kelen, themselves being already political functionaries rather than engineer activists, had been "degraded" by this reorganization to the rank of group leaders within Division III from their previous position of People's Commissars of Social Production (then ranking as high as Antal Dovcsák, a trade union leader, who after the reorganization came to head the whole of Division III). No engineers figured among the Heads of Divisions or the Presidents of the National Economic Council.[30]

Engineers applied, in this context of belied hopes, I suggest, their understanding to the problem of plant-management, too. Trespassing in technical matters by production commissars (if they were workers), trade unionists, and councils of workers' control, made them realize how weak were the foundations of their position. And those who had not been aware enough of that weakness were enlightened in a rather persuasive way by Béla Kun during the month of May.

Kun was, from Soviet Hungary earliest days, firmly opposing engineers' pretension to political power. When he saw that, after the issuance of Decree IX of the Governing Council (on the socialization of industry and transportation), in many factories engineers had been appointed to the post of production commissar, he protested: "I emphasize again," he said on the April 8 meeting of the Revolutionary Governing Council:

that those who appoint engineers misunderstand the function that the engineer in the production is good for. ... If we don't appoint workers we are going to have a production bureaucracy, an engineer bureaucracy. The production commissar must truly be a representative of the proletariat. In this respect he considers a radical change to be necessary.[31]

Within the context outlined above, even Kun's otherwise rather confusing dabblings with the concepts of "workers' control" and "workers' management" conveys an intelligible message:

The workers' control is but the transition to workers' management. Today the production commissar represents the whole of the proletariat. There are separate technological organizations in the plants and there is the organization of workers' control. This has to be so, it cannot be otherwise, because this is a necessary transitory phase to the workers' management. *As soon as ... the elevation of such a generation of workers becomes possible as will be fully capable of performing the technological control of the plants and participate in the technological management itself, we go over to workers' management. Until then it would be a ridiculous semiradicalism to take a stand against the specialists and demand to place even the technological management into non-professional hands.*[32] [Italics mine]

None too bright perspectives for engineers! Kun's worker-demagogy—having much in common with the treatment the young Soviet Russia was meting out to the "specialists"—found its way straight into the program of the Socialist-Communist Workers Party in Hungary. There it stood: "The economy is taken care of by the proletarian state relying upon the trade unions and with the direction of the Supreme Council of National Economy. The factories' management is the task not of the technical bureaucracy but of the workers themselves."[33]

And, finally, Kun's speech delivered before the meeting of AMOSZ on May 29, 1919, made the place of engineer in the emerging mix of the new political class entirely clear for anyone who was able to decipher the code of radical end-of-the-war brochure-Marxism. Calling for a distinction between the questions of intellectual leadership and of the evaluation of intellectual labor, he proceeded to say this:

> Every Marxist is convinced that the proletariat can be made free only by itself. Thus, the question whether there is, there has to be, or there can be an intellectual leading class that leads the proletariat into its struggle, is decided. In the class struggle of the proletariat there cannot be and must not be a separate class which, as intellectual leaders, would lead the class struggle, because the ideology of the proletariat's class struggle, as Engels says, is nothing else than a reflexion of the class struggle going on in the society ... between the workers' and the employers' classes. Consequently, the bearer of this ideology cannot be anyone else but the working class itself. The representative of this ideology, of this collective class consciousness can be only the working class and not some separate leading class.

At this point Kun might have felt that he was soon cutting the ground from under his own feet, so he took a little detour explaining that:

> The intellectual leader, consequently, is the class-consciousness of the proletariat itself which *may be represented in the most pregnant and classic way even by such persons who are not from among the proletariat, whose situation is not a proletarian class situation. In our opinion, those whose Marxist belief is so firm that they are prepared to make every sacrifice in the revolution of the proletariat, those may represent the class consciousness of the proletariat notwithstanding the fact that they are themselves not proletarians.* But the intellectual leader is none else but the self-consciousness of the proletariat. [Italics mine]

Having earned in this rather tortuous way a "legitimacy" for the power of those "most pregnant and classic representatives of proletarian self-consciousness," Kun proceeded quickly to mete out a couple of blows to the engineers who sought positions of significance for themselves under the sun of revolution:

What I have never been able to agree upon with the engineer comrades, ever since I came home from Russia, was that they conceived the socialist society to be like the state led by the philosophers of Plato. Their preoccupation, as Plato's had been with the philosophers, was with what the role of the engineer would be and whether it would be he who would lead the society from capitalism to socialism. ... the question of intellectual leadership and that of the evaluation of intellectual work have constantly been confused by the engineers. For, the class struggle of the proletariat has not come to an end. It goes on, only now it continues not from under but from above against the capitalism, the bourgeoisie. Consequently, also in the future there remains to be only one intellectual leader: the class consciousness of the proletariat.[34]

So comes to its end, the intriguing episode of engineer radicalism in modern Hungary. Pursuing their own utopia, they allied themselves with the labor movement, and on many questions they promoted, with their own ideological weaponry, the cause of bureaucratic State Socialism. They were among those who sharply criticized the democratic movement of workers' control in the Budapest industry, saying that anything less than the complete nationalization of the means of production was only "miserable half-reforms." After March 21, the new system of industrial management—following large-scale nationalization—was established in accordance with their ideas, and the defense of "sovereignty of engineers in technical matters" helped to eliminate the remnants of industrial democracy. But, then, their turn came, too. The ambition to be "the more equal" of equal partners within the alliance with labor was frustrated. And, again, it was not the working class who frustrated it, but the very same, emerging political-administrative class that was at cross purposes with workers' control as well.

George Lukács pinpointed the most important feature of the developing new society writing that

the socialist organization of the economy means the cessation of the independence of economic life. The economic activity which, till now, was an autonomous process with its own laws that could be recognized but not directed by the human mind, becomes a part of the state administration. It becomes a part of a unified, planned process instead of being regulated by its own laws. For, the ultimate motive powers of this unified social process have ceased to be of an economic nature.[35]

The Engineer Utopia suffered of a gross misconception as to the character of those "ultimate motive forces," and thus, very few personalities of the movement could qualify as "pregnant and classic representatives of the proletarian class-consciousness."

## NOTES

The preparation of this study has been assisted by grants from the Jan Wallander Foundation for Social Research of the Svenska Handelsbank.

1. Gyula Hevesi, *Szociális termelés: A Magyar Tanácsköztársásg iparpolitikája* [Social Production: The Industrial Policy of the Hungarian Soviet Republic] (Budapest, 1959), pp. 72–73; *Idem, Egy mérnök a forradalomban* [An Engineer in the Revolution] (2nd ed.; Budapest, 1965), pp. 242–45.

2. This was my own way of viewing the problem, almost ten years ago: György Péteri, *A Magyar Tanácsköztársaság iparirányítási rendszere* [The System of Industrial Management of the Hungarian Soviet Republic] (Budapest, 1979), pp. 227–33; or, in the recent edition of the book in English: *Effects of World War I: War Communism in Hungary* ("War and Society in East Central Europe", Vol XVI [New York, 1984]), pp. 180–85. Having recently studied the sources pertaining to the debate again, now from the engineers' point of view, I feel I missed important points when writing the relevant parts of my book. This paper's aim is to try and repair that failure. The empirical foundations of this essay are by and large the same as those presented and documented in details in my book. This will make possible a certain degree of economy of documentation here. The best account of the political developments in 1918–19 is to be found in Tibor Hajdu, *Az 1918-as magyarországi polgári demokratikus forradalom* [The Bourgeois Democratic Revolution of 1918 in Hungary] (Budapest, 1968): *Idem, A Magyarországi Tanácsköztársaság* [The Hungarian Soviet Republic] (Budapest, 1969); Rudolf L. Tökés, *Béla Kun and the Hungarian Soviet Republic: The Origins and Role of the Communist Party of Hungary in the Revolutions of 1918–1919* (New York, 1967).

3. András Kovács, "A zsidókérdés a mai magyar társadalomban" [The Jewish Question in Today's Hungarian Society], in Viktor Karády *et al., Zsidóság az 1945 utáni Magyarországon* [Jewry in Post-1945 Hungary] ("Adalékok az újabbkori magyar történelemhez" (Contributions on Modern Hungarian History), Vol 4 (Paris, 1984)), p. 35.

4. *Ibid.,* p. 34.

5. György Spira and Károly Vörös, *Budapest története a márciusi forradalomtól az Őszirózsás forradalomig* [The History of Budapest from the March Revolution to the Autumn Rose Revolution, 1848–1918], *Budapest története* [The History of Budapest], ed. László Gerevich, Vol IV (Budapest, 1978)), p. 559

6. A. Kovács, "A zsidókérdés ...", p. 34

7. Karl Mannheim, *Ideology and Utopia: An Introduction to the Sociology of Knowledge* (London, 1976), p. 37

8. R. L. Tökés, *Béla Kun ..., pp.* 30–31. In point of fact, white-collar workers had by the turn of the century established several "trade-union-type" organizations, expecially after their first congress in 1896, when the *Magántisztviselők Országos Szövetsége* [National Association of Private Employees] was founded, which had rather close contacts with the SDP (Cf. László Faragó, "Magántisztviselők" [White-Collar Workers], article in *Közgazdsági Enciklopédia* [Economic Encyclopedia] Vol. III, (Budapest, (1929)), p. 890. It appears from Hevesi's memoirs, *Egy mérnök ...,* that engineers (and private industrial employees in general) *employed in factories* had been mostly unorganized until the first years of World War I.

# REVOLUTIONS AND INTERVENTIONS

155

9. K. Mannheim, *Ideology and Utopia* ..., p. 142

10. G. Hevesi, *Egy mérnök* ... , p. 62, emphasis added.

11. *Ibid.*, p. 64.

12. *Ibid.*, p. 65. For another account of Hevesi's 'Schumpeterian' critique of capitalism and of his engineer "class"-consciousness, see the memoirs of József Lengyel, *Visegrádi utca* [Visegrádi Street] (Budapest, 1962), pp. 53–54, quoted by R. L. Tökés *Béla Kun* ..., *p. 31.*

13. Remark made by one of the pupils of the Agitators' Training School, to József Révai's lecture on revolutions, April 19, 1919, *Országos Széchenyi Könyvtár* [MSS in the National Szechenyi Library, Budapest], Fol. Hung. 2194, Vol. II, p. 14

14. G. Péteri, *Effects of World War I* ..., p. 6

15. R. L. Tökés, *Béla Kun* ..., p. 227

16. Speech before the first meeting in December 1917 of the engineers' section in IKTOSZ. Quoted from G. Hevesi, *Egy mérnök...*, by R. L. Tökés, *Béla Kun* ..., p. 31

17. Imre Hoffmann, "A szociális termelés gazdasági szükségessége" [The Economic Necessity of Social Production] *Szociális Termelés* [Social Production], June 4, 1919, p. 5

18. József Kelen, "kommunizált termelés" [Collectivized Production], *Szabadgondolat* [Free Thought], January 15, 1919, pp. 41–43.

19. G. Hevesi, *Egy mèrnök* ..., p. 80.

20. G. Hevesi, "A termelés azonnali kommunizálásának műszaki lehetősége, gazdasági és jogi kiviteli feltételei" [The Technical Possibility of an Immediate Collectivization of Production and its Economic and Legal Preconditions], *Internationale*, Vol 1, no. 3–4 (February 1, 1919), pp. 48–49.

21. I. Ehrenburg, *Emberek, évek, életem* [People, Years and My Life] Vol. I, (Budapest, 1963), p. 188.

22. The edition used here: Thorstein Veblen, *The Engineers and the Price System*, (New York, 1925).

23. *Ibid.*, p. 100, 138–69

24. *Ibid.*, pp. 136–37

25. *AMOSZ*, Vol. I, No. 1 (May 1, 1919)

26. Editorial note to Jenő Varga's speech before the AMOSZ-meeting on May 29, 1919, *AMOSZ*, June 25, 1919, p. 16

27. *AMOSZ*, June 25, 1919, p. 9

28. *Ibid.*, pp. 20–21

29. "The AMOSZ cannot agree to the tendency of recent times which wants the intellectual workers in general but especially the engineers to merge into the blue-collar organizations." *'Pro domo'*, *AMOSZ*, June 25, 1919, p. 22. The need of engineers' *autonomy* was emphasized in the discussion between AMOSZ and MEMOSZ (the trade union of workers employed in the construction industry): Cf. "A mérnökök helyzete a szakszervezeti mozgalomban" [The Position of Engineers in the Trade Union Movement], *AMOSZ*, June 1, 1919, p. 14

30. Documents relating to the reorganization: *Az MSZMP Párttörténeti Intézetének Archívuma* [The Archives of the Institute of Party History of the Hungarian Socialist Workers Party Central Committee, hereafter *PIA*], 602. f. 9. öe., 15. öe. and 39 öe., furthermore, 600. f. 2/2. öe.

31. Minutes of the meeting of the Revolutionary Governing Council, April 8, 1919, *PIA*, 601. f., 1. cs. 10. öe., no. XI, p. 32

32. B. Kun's fourth lecture on modifying the party's program, in *A magyar munkásmozgalom történetének válogatott dokumentumai* (Selected Documents on the History of the Hungarian Labor Movement), Vol. 6/a (Budapest, 1959), p. 517.

33. *Népszava* [People's Voice], June 19, 1919

34. *AMOSZ*, June 25, 1919, pp. 11–14.

35. György Lukács, "Régi és új kultúra" [Old and New Culture], *Internationale*, *Vol. I, No. 6–7, (1919), p. 10*

# THE SOCIAL BASIS OF THE COMMUNIST REVOLUTION AND OF THE COUNTERREVOLUTIONS IN HUNGARY

Ignác Romsics

Hungary at the beginning of the twentieth century was an underdeveloped agrarian-industrial country. Sixty percent of its population lived off the land, therefore, the majority of its population were peasants. Nonagricultural owners of medium- and small-sized plots accounted for approximately 15 percent of the overall population. The proportion of urban workers is estimated to have been around 20 percent. About half were miners and industrial workers, while the other half worked in the service sector; this included domestic servants, maids, and day laborers.

A natural consequence of the Socialist character of the revolution was that the traditional ruling elite, owners of large- and medium-sized estates as well as the big- and medium-sized capitalists of industry and trade were opposed to the Soviet Republic from the moment of its establishment. Their more prominent representatives fled abroad in its very first days, and in the middle of April, founded the Hungarian National Committee in Vienna, also called the *Anti-Bolshevik Committee* (ABC); a coalition, with representatives from the defunct Party of Work, Constitution party, Independence party, People's party, and Christian Socialist party. Moreover, moderate, right-wing democrats of the Károlyi party of 1918 could also be found in its ranks. In harmony with historical traditions, 80–90 percent of the anticommunist leadership including the ABC's, were aristorcrats; the upper and middle strata of the middle class were pushed into the background. Count Gyula Károlyi, aristocrat, big landowner, politician, became the leader of the countergovernment in Arad [then in Szeged] formed on May 5, 1919. The counterrevolutionary centers which cooperated with one other were primarily striving for winning the armed support of the Entente powers. In comparison with their earlier conservative rigidity, they also showed a high degree of flexibility in their search for internal political allies. In order to regain full or partial power, they would have been ready to cooperate with the leaders of democratic movements among the lower middle class and peasants. They were also ready to deal with Socialist leaders who chose exile instead of cooperation with the Communists.

Naturally, the immediate opposition of the traditional elite to the Communist revolution was countered by the support given to it by the working class. As a consequence, the workers' comparatively high degree of organization and concentration in urban areas, primarily in Budapest, represented a much greater force than one would suppose from statistics. In addition, by the spring of 1919, other segments of the urban workers, such as the day laborers, domestic servants, maids, who earlier had not or hardly been supporters of the cause, became attracted to Socialism.

There was a rapid increase in the number of trade-union members from the end of 1918 onward. As opposed to the Social Democratic party, relying primarily on skilled workers and those having been organized for a longer period of time, the Communist party core, established in November 1918, was recruited mostly from those workers who were unskilled or were pushed to the periphery of society. These included wartime invalids and discharged and unemployed soldiers. At the beginning of 1919, the Social Democratic and Communist workers were opposed to each other on several issues. By the fusion of the two workers' parties, however—at least temporarily—some kind of unity of workers was formed which was very advantageous from the point of view of the revolution.

Among the old elites and the urban workers, therefore, was a high degree of political consensus. This type of solid consensus about the revolution did not exist among other classes.

Socialization and management of production methods made bankrupt, or threatened with bankruptcy, a significant part of the medium and small property owners just like the big landowners and big capitalists. True, in theory, socialization of industry affected only the factories employing more than 20 people. That, however, was not adhered to in several places, for different reasons. In practice, barber and shoemaker shops employing one or two people were also nationalized, and at places, attempts were made to organize artisans working without assistants into work shops. Besides, the factories, banks, pharmacies, hotels, and even movie theaters, were turned over to public ownership. Stores were not formally socialized, only "taken under supervision," that is, their inventories were registered, their prices were defined, and their incomes were controlled. From the merchants' point of view, of course, there was hardly any practical difference between socialization and supervision. Essentially, they had been turned into supervised employees of the state and ceased to be independent owners. As a consequence of all that, as well as some other measures taken, such as the confiscation of jewels or moving families of workers into flats inhabited by the middle class, the majority of urban medium and small property owners viewed the progess of the new order with animosity.

The leader of the Jewish lower middle class in Budapest, Vilmos Vázsonyi, true to the class he represented, did not enter into active counterrevolutionary activities. He stayed abroad until the very end of the Communist experiment. At the same time—at least in the first weeks—many rural small tradesmen, independent artisans working alone or employing one or two assistants, and at some places even small merchants too, were found among the advocates of revolution; they undertook active roles in workers' councils and directories as well. Naturally, the small property owners played a role in the revolution primarily in the places where the decrees of socialization were adhered to and no encroachments occurred.

Among the intelligentsia, it was the progressive artists and scientists, rural teachers as well as trade union and health insurance functionaries who had earlier Marxist ties, who supported the revolution most unequivocally. Several members of the central government and local governmental leaders came from these groups of intellectuals.

In contrast, veteran state administrators, police and gendarmerie officers, as well as the clergy of various religions, supported the counterrevolution from the very beginning. In accordance with their training and profession, they participated primarily in propaganda activites, while chief constables, court clerks, and gendarmery officers organized and directed concrete counterrevolutionary actions. As the Soviet Republic organized a new state apparatus and strove for the complete annihilation of the economic and ideological power of the churches, the strongly counterrevolutionary behavior of those groups needs no special proofs or explanation.

Among the opponents of the Soviet Republic, were the active officers and those in reserve, the number of whom increased during the war. This group was opposed to everything represented by the Soviet Republic just like the ruling classes, the churches, and the old state administration. The fact, however, that the Soviet Republic undertook to oppose the armies of the neighboring nations forced them to choose between anti-Bolshevism and the defense of their country.

Both Communists and nationalists had a common goal not to allow "...our ancient land to be taken away from us." These considerations moved many of them to take up arms in defense of the Soviet Republic.[1] This feeling of duty to defend the country, naturally, held true for other layers of the intelligentsia, as well as the middle and lower middle classes, but in no instance was the choice as critical as in the case of officers having chosen the defense of their country as their profession. A similar role was expected from the so-called refugees coming from the occupied territories.

The situation gave rise to a unique social phenomenon in that the Red Army was directed by people belonging to the same caste of officers as those making up the high command of the anti-Communist National Army in Szeged and the Austrian detachment of Colonel Antal Lehár. In this vein it is noteworthy that 15 out of the 35 colonel generals of the Hungarian army between 1938 and 1945, had served in the Red Army.[2] A third choice, simultaneous service in the homeland's defense and anti-Bolshevism, as the example of Colonel Károly Kratochwill and his Sekler Division demonstrates, did not exist in the given situation. For the powers involved refused to grant border adjustments or a Sekler republic, as was the price Kratochwill and his group demanded in return for overthrowing Soviet power by their march on Budapest.

The relationship between the peasantry and the Soviet Republic was basically determined by the settlement of the land question. The decree of April 3, 1919 of the Revolutionary Governing Council included the socialization of medium and large properties. According to a later decree and national practice, lands exceeding 75 acres were generally qualified as medium and large holdings. At the same time, partly for doctrinal reasons and partly for practical reasons, the decree prohibited the redistribution of land and also prescribed the organization of state farms and agricultural cooperatives on the socialized land.[3] Peasant reaction to the decree was far from unanimous.

The first group, the so-called rich peasantry possessing land over 75 acres, faced with the expropriation, shared the same antirevolutionary attitude as the other social layers deprived of their properties. True, that group accounted for hardly 2–3 percent of the whole peasantry. But, as a consequence of their prestige in the villages, their opinion was more important than percentages indicated. Under normal circumstances, the lower layers of the peasantry looked upon these big farmers as their natural leaders. The only exception to that rule was the layer of the poor peasantry connected to Social Democracy or Agrarian Socialism.

The lower segments of land-owner peasantry, the small and medium owners making up about one-third of the whole peasantry, were not concerned by socialization. They were potential allies for the Communists; at the same time, they were also greatly worried about the plans, proclamations, and alarming news concerning lowering the limit of property fated for socialization, and the unification of small holdings within the framework of cooperatives; also like the bourgeoisie and other segments of the peasantry, they had an aversion to the internationalist and anticlerical propaganda and phrasemongering of the Soviet Republic.

Besides settlement of the land question, the greatest unease and dissatisfaction in the country were evoked by the measures taken in relation to church policy, such as secularization of church schools, the elimination of clerical teachers, dissolution of religious orders, and attempts to stop religious education in schools. It was very characteristic of the different mentalities and the communication gap between the revolutionary leaders and the peasantry that, when the Governing Council did away with land tax, the small holders considered it not as a sign of support but the first step toward complete collectivization. But, since, in the first weeks of the revolution, they did not feel that they were in direct, but only potential danger, the overwhelming majority of them did not turn against the new system but rather joined the local revolutionary organizations and attempted to dull its "edge," as it were. Moveover—in case they had food stocks—they intended to exploit the food shortage in the towns by bag-trading and profiteering.

The poor peasantry or agricultural proletariat accounting far about two-thirds of the peasantry and somewhat more than one-third of the whole population itself, was divided into several layers. About two-fifths were owners of very small holdings of one or two acres; another two-fifths were landless day laborers; and one-fifth were so-called estate servants. Among the poor peasantry, only a few, counted in the tens of thousands, had been organized before the war, or sympathized with socialistic ideas and movements. Among these were those who became attracted to Social Democracy and Communist ideology during the Liberal-Democratic Revolution. They received and welcomed the Soviet Republic as their own, like to industrial workers.

They constituted a significant proportion of council members and leaders of the directorates in the villages and in the rural towns, and like workers, they fought in or alongside, the Red Army. That holds equally true for agricultural workers from the territory east of the Tisza who came from villages occupied by the Romanians. For them the conflict meant not only the defense of Soviet power but also a war of liberation. Certainly connecting the socialization of large- and medium-sized land holdings with land redistribution would have mobilized, for the revolution, the more passive part of the majority of the poor peasantry who took for granted the traditional order and hierarchy of the village. But, they were disappointed when no such policy was realized; their petitions and letters of complaint are moving reading even today.

Dissatisfaction among farm hands and day laborers was further increased by the fact that—although in the summer season they worked not 8 but 12 hours a day—unjustifiably low wages were set for them. Official wages for adult men was hardly more than 2 crowns per hour; industrial skilled workers received 4.0–8.50; unskilled workers 2.50–6.50.[4] Disappointment among poor peasants expecting land redistribution, had an impact on the mood of the more conscious agricultural workers who assumed a leading role in the revolution. Many, therefore, reassessed their relationship to the Soviet Republic.

In sum, we may state that the segments of workers, artisans, peasants and intellectuals supporting the newborn Soviet Republic unequivocally accounted for a statistically smaller proportion of the population than that which remained neutral or hostile to it. Among the population quite significant differences could be observed in the different regions and types of settlements. Comparatively solid revolutionary strongholds were Budapest, the big towns, and mining towns with a high concentration of workers. In contrast, a significant part of the agricultural districts, primarily in the counties between the Danube and the Tisza and in Transdanubia, played the role of hinterland of the counterrevolution. Among the agricultural regions, the power of the proletariat could primarily rely on certain territories east of the Tisza, e.g., the Viharsarok possessing a more significant Agrarian Socialist past. However, those parts fell under Romanian occupation by the end of April. Thus, it did not take long for the conflict to emerge between Budapest and the countryside, between the industrial areas and agricultural regions.[5]

Naturally—at least in the first weeks—external and internal counterrevolutionary trends had no significant social basis either. The poor peasantry was disappointed; the small and medium peasantry worried and antipathetic to the new system. But, for the time being, they did not support actively the counterrevolution either. In March and April the idea of overthrowing the Soviet Republic and of an armed counterrevolution occurred only to the landowners, rich peasants, chief constables, clerks of the Court, and a part of the officers; they had already initiated a great many counterrevolutionary actions. But, the radius of those actions almost never exceeded the administrative boundaries of a given settlement and lacked a significant social basis. Thus local revolutionaries put them down with little or no difficulty, generally within an hour or two. The only exception was, the attempted coup by officers and large farmers in Kecskemét toward the end of April, when counterrevolution won over to its side several thousands of peasants in and around Kecskemét. We can find an explanation for this in the uniquely

radical policy of the directorate in Kecskemét, a policy of total collectivization and the immediate realization of complete social equality.

That situation, comparatively favorable from the point of view of the revolution, had been significantly modified by the end of May, by the beginning of June. For, the Soviet Republic's mass basis had narrowed down; that
of the counterrevolution had been established and extended. Reasons for
changes in mood and behavior of the various segments of the population,
were diverse and different from one other. In one way or another, they
were all connected, however, to Hungary's very grave economic, diplomatic,
and military situation. The domestic policy of the Governing Council was a
cause for further alienation.

The evacuation of upper Hungary in June, had an especially depressing
effect on the officers, refugees, and intellectuals. The Red Army's potential to defend the territory was seriously questioned by the order to withdraw; no longer did one have to make the earlier obligation a choice between
defense of the homeland and anti-Bolshevism. From then on, the overwhelming majority of the officers and many others made a definite turn in the direction of the government in Szeged. The number of applicants to the count-
terrevolutionary army increased, and by the end of June, conspiratorial
groups of officers in Budapest decided upon an armed coup. Consequently,
the general staff of the Red Army became a real hotbed of plots against the
Soviet Republic.

The turn of literate Hungary in the direction of conservatism and extreme
right radicalism is very well reflected in three books published during these
months; later these works enjoyed mass success. Here, have in mind the political work of the Jesuit Béla Bangha, the twice-published *The Rebuilding
of Hungary and Christianity* (1920),[6] Dezső Szabó's bestseller, *The Village
Swept Away* (1919),[7] and Gyula Szekfű's historical-political survey, *Three
Generations.*[8] These three books, to a very great extent, laid down the basis
of the "Christian-national" ideology of the counterrevolution which soon
after came to power. The adjective "Christian" meant opposition to the tradition of free thinking based on the natural sciences and the anticlerical feeling and atheism of the revolutions; "national" was used in contrast to the explanation of social development on the principles of interests and classes with
the internationalism of the workers' parties.

Signs of disappointment and turning away from the revolution also manifested themselves in the circles of progressive artists and creative intellectuals.
Pacifist Mihály Babits who received a professorship after the victory of the
Soviet Republic, was unable to understand the phenomenon of revolutionary
terror; in his letters to his mother, in May, he wrote: "These circumstances
will be over sooner or later..." and "These are bad months but they may not

last long." "My world view", he said later, "was pushed completely in the direction of conservatism during the dictatorship of the proletariat."[9] Zsigmond Mòricz, who at the beginning supported the "new world" with enthusiastic reports, was discouraged primarily by the lack of land redistribution and the mood of the peasantry. We could go on citing examples which may be interpreted as signs of returning to liberal democracy.[10]

Change in the behavior of the small and medium peasantry was basically connected to the change in their financial situation and opportunities. The partly legal and partly underground free trade from which some peasants with significant foodstuffs profited handsomely in the beginning, deteriorated by May, and almost completely ceased to exist by June. A reason for this was the rapidly increasing shortage of industrial articles; another, the disappearance from circulation of the old money [so-called blue money], believed to be reliable. At the same time, the population in big towns, primarily Budapest, lived in privation. Thus, and in order to provide for the fighting army, the Soviet Republic was forced to resort to requisitioning. The reaction of the peasants was physical resistance, hiding the stocks, and feeding them to livestock and even destruction. Landowning peasantry was also pushed toward playing an active role in the counterrevolutionary movement by the fact that most of their representatives accepted by the councils and direcorates at the beginning of April, were dismissed one after the other from the local authorities in the course of May.

The changed situation was well reflected by the mushrooming of counterrevolutionary actions of differing character. Between May 15 and June 15, the national and rural press reported twice as many counterrevolutionary plots as in the two preceding months together. And these actions had not a few dozen but several hundred or even thousand participants or dissatisfied people. The radius and length of the counterrevolutionary actions also enlarged. The most significant counterrevolutionary uprising, the one next to the Danube in the vicinity of Kalocsa, lasted from June 18 to June 25; it extended to several villages of two counties; 10—45 percent of the population [altogether a mass in the order of magnitude of 10,000] participated in it. Therefore, the counterrevolution at the Danube could only be suppressed by a coordinated attack of several regiments of the Red Army.

That the originally counterrevolutionary strata and a significant part of the rural population "found each other," could be observed in several events in Transdanubia, for example, in the uprising in the vicinity of the Mura at the end of May and the beginning of June, financed by the Anti-Bolshevik Committee in Vienna. Naturally, the interests of the old ruling elite and the layers traditionally connected to them, and those of the landowning peasantry, did not coincide fully at all. The sole basis of their alliance was actually anti-Bolshevism; they had completely different ideas about the policy to be followed after the Soviet Republic's overthrow.

In opposition to the big landowners and capitalists, basically conservative and striving for restoration of pre-revolutionary conditions, as well as the officers, representing dictatorial ideas in addition to reinstating the *status quo* ante, the land-owning peasantry entertained definite desires for democracy, and thus made efforts to that end. So, in perspective, the different groups of the counterrevolution were also opposed to one another and the crushing of the revolution immediately brought these differences to the fore.[11]

By the beginning of June, the political attitude of the urban workers had also changed. The workers—as the anti-Soviet leader of the Social Democratic Party, Ernő Garami noted—believed in the spring of 1919 that "...they were able to attain whatever they wished."[12] As the international isolation of the Soviet Republic became more and more obvious, and as the internal difficulties increased, the initial optimism of the workers disappeared, and gave way to disappointment and pessimism. The Transdanubian railway workers' strike at the beginning of June was instigated by the Anti-Bolshevik Committee, and initiated by Hungarian State Railway's clerks. However, traffic was paralyzed by the simple railway workers who received their wages in "white money," and therefore suffered from deprivation.

Clashes between the population unprovided for, and the directorates, as well as military commands, became almost constant from the end of May in the agricultural towns in the territory between the Danube and the Tisza most devastated by the soldiers. Interest decreased in mass rallies; the trade union and the party halls became empty. In contrast, the number of churchgoers and the participants in church processions increased greatly.

Disappointment and turning away from the Soviet Republic characterized primarily workers who had recently joined the movement. However, a significant number of old organized workers did not see any other way out but by ending the dictatorship and returning to the earlier coalition and reformist social policy. Representatives of the National Party Congress at the beginning of June, deleted the names of most Communists and leftist Social Democrats from the official list of candidates and in their place wrote the names of right and moderate Social Democratic leaders opposing the policy of the Revolutionary Governing Council.

It must be emphasized that differences between the objectives of the workers turning away from the revolution and of the rightist middle class was greater than the differences in the goals of the land-owning peasantry and of the counterrevolutionary centers of Szeged and Vienna. The organized part of the urban workers and the conscious core of the poor peasantry were not won over to the counterrevolution either in June—July or after the fall of the counterrevolution. The officers' coup in Pest of June 24 was joined by the workers of one factory only.

Counterrevolution at the Danube did not spread further toward the west because the Social Democrats in Szekszárd—after the Communist directorate strongly opposing them at the time had already fled—defended the town from the attacking peasants. In the middle of July, when Bőhm was negotiating with Entente representatives in Vienna about elimination of the dictatorship and the conditions for the return to democracy, he stoutly refused the offer of the big landowner counterrevolutionaires to form a coalition with them.

In the days following the evacuation of northern Hungary, the top leadership of the Soviet Republic made a few weak attempts to strengthen and regain its position. Prohibition of alcohol was lifted; land tax reinstated; and poor peasants designed to receive small plots of a few acres. Measures were taken to solve the money problem and improve upon public food supplies. However, none of these measures could be carried out. For that reason, and because of the unfavorable external conditions, internal power relations could not be improved upon. In all, without arguing that the Soviet Republic was finally overthrown by the external enemy, I agree with those evaluations which state that by June—July, the Soviet Republic was on the way to defeat and had lost its internal social support.

## NOTES

1. *Czegléd,* March 23–24, 1919.

2. Sándor Szakály, "A második világháborús magyar katonai felső vezetés összetétele," *Valóság,* (1983), no. 8, p. 86; for a detailed analysis of the officer corps of the Hungarian Red Army, see, Sándor Szakály's essay, which follows in this collection.

3. Sándor Balogh, et. a., *Magyarország a XX. században* (Budapest, 1985), pp. 98.

4. Jenő Pongrácz, ed., *Tanácsköztársasági Törvénytár* (Budapest, 1919), Vol. II, 32–33/ Vol. III, 48–50.

5. Ignác Romsics, *A Duna–Tisza köze hatalmi-politikai viszonyai 1918–19-ben* (Budapest, 1982), pp. 88–109.

6. Béla Bangha, *Magyarország, újjáépítése és a kereszténység* (Budapest, 1920).

7. Dezső Szabó, *Az elsodort falu* (Budapest, 1919).

8. Gyula Szekfű, *Három nemzedék* (Budapest, 1920).

9. Lajos Sipos, *Babits Mihály és a forradalmak kora* (Budapest, 1976), pp. 75, 88.

10. For  discussion of the revolution's impact on the intellectuals, see in this collection the essay of Ivan Sanders, and Tibor Hajdu's "1919: The Changing Image of Two Revolutions."

11. Romsics, *A Duna–Tisza köze,* pp. 185–88.

12. Ernő Garami, *Forrongó Magyarország* (Vienna, 1922), pp. 63–64.

# THE OFFICER CORPS
## OF THE HUNGARIAN RED ARMY

Sándor Szakály

The historian exploring the Hungarian revolutions and counterrevolutions following World War I is bound to face, sooner or later the question of: who were the soldiers, and the military leaders, who participated in revolution and counterrevolution? Who were the commanders, the officers who organized, commanded the armies of the liberal democratic People's Republic and then the Soviet Republic as well as the counterrevolutionary governments?

Answers are not, as forthcoming, as easy, as one would think. The following may serve as an explanation. In the course of the almost seventy years which have elapsed since the liberal democratic revolution and the proclamation of the Soviet Republic, no work has analyzed completely the composition of the officers' corps of the armies of the People's Republic and the Soviet Republic. Nor do we have at our disposal studies exploring the question of how the leadership of the Red Army was organized. That issue is not discussed by the studies, monographs, and popular works dealing with the history of the 1918—19 revolutions and the battles of the Red Army. Most are content with listing the names of the leaders with the highest military ranks, their source of military training, and only in very few cases is there an evaluation of their careers.[1]

No comprehensive study or detailed analysis of the social background of the commanders or the officer corps of the Red Army has been made so far. The aim of this paper is to draw some preliminary conclusions based on some sources which may be used in a detailed study of the subject.[2]

The governments coming into office following the victory of the liberal democratic revolution in Hungary and their ministers of war, questioned the necessity and significance of the existence of the army, in order to implement the Wilsonian peace principles and put into practice their pacifist views,[3] Disarming the troops was also intended to curb possible radical actions by the armed masses returning from the front. They emphasized that democratic Hungary had no need for an extensive army based on universal conscription. They considered the army's main task as the maintenance of internal peace and order. A small volunteer army would suffice, it seemed, for to blunt revolutionary actions by the armed masses, disarmament of the army exceeding a million in number was already started by the Károlyi government. Disarmament was also included, by the way, in the terms of the armistice agreement.[4]

The disarmament of almost the whole army concerned the professional officer corps, and partly the reserve, officers too, most adversely. It was clear to everyone that Hungary would no longer be in need of the huge army it used to possess. And an army lower in number, weaker in arms, consisting of volunteers needed much fewer officers than were available.

As early as November 1918, the government began to reduce the number of officers—primarily professionals—at a time when the picture of the mercenary army to be set up was only being outlined and the necessary number of officers was not yet known. Measures taken in November—December 1918 were the pensioning off of all members of the corps of generals, elimination of the general staff, the corps of technical and artillary officers, and the dismissal of professional officers and reserve officers.[5]

Consequently, when the needed number of officers of the army to be set up was determined at approximately 8500, it turned out that the government had at its disposal only about 7500 officers. And only about forty percent of the 7500 were professional officers!

Naturally, to fill the gap between the available and the desired numbers was not an insurmountable task, for there were thousands of professionals and tens of thousands of reserve officers without jobs and employment. Some had started to study at universities or commercial academies, others had tried to find civil jobs, and many more had traveled home to their families living in the occupied territories. However, the undermanned officer corps was not replenished, as this could not yet be justified by the low strength of the armed forces. Public opinion was also against the organization of a large standing army. At the same time the constant erosion of the demarcation lines put an increasing number of officers into territories not under government control. One of the reasons for this was that different headquarters with significant forces of officers remained on the territories passing under occupation—under the command of Entente authorities—and only the troops were withdrawn. This fact had no real significance in the winter of 1918—19 but it created grave problems at the time of the development of the Red Army in the spring of 1919.[6]

That was the situation of the army and the corps of officers in March 1919, when, under the influence of external and internal circumstances, power was taken over by the Hungarian Party of Communists and the Social Democratic party and the Hungarian Soviet Republic was proclaimed.

One of the first measures taken by the Soviet Republic, the Revolutionary Governing Council, was to order the setting up of the Red Army.[7] It hoped to organize the Red Army as a class army, an army of the proletariat, but for the time being, the army could not do without the professional staff of the army of the previous era, who would have to go through several "tests."

In harmony with the practice of the liberal democratic period, the government wished, as much as possible under the circumstances, to create the Red Army from volunteers and to entrust it to the command of proletarian commanders. This way of organizing the army seemed to be feasible to the middle of April 1919, marking the end of comparative peace. However, offensives of the Romanian and then the Czechoslovak armies, approved and supported by the Entente powers, made the fast "proletarization" of the corps of commanders and officers illusory.

The war situation had become catastrophic by the first days of May 1919. The small numbers of badly armed troops who represented the Red Army, in name only, began to withdraw from the Eastern Front in rapid succassion. The best armed and strongest, the Sekler Division [the former 38th Divison] first withdrew after smaller defensive skirmishes, then it surrendered to the Romanian troops under the command of Károly Kratochwill. The Romanians interned the officers and soldiers, the majority of whom were not allowed to return to Hungary until 1920.

At this time the leaders of the Soviet Republic, which was in deadly danger, turned to the people of the country, primarily the workers, for help. They called upon the people to join the Red Army and thousands of them did, including hundreds of former professional and reserve officers. These former officers made up the high command and the officers corps of the Red Army, along side those who had previously joined the Red Army. Later, in view of the pressing shortage of officers, it was made compulsory for the former professional officers to join the army!

The question now arises as to why the officers undertook service in the army in spite of the fact that they just recently had been proclaimed "undesirable."

The answer to this question may be summarized in three points:

1. The Soviet Republic's political and military leaders undertook the task of defending the country: for the majority of the officers imbued with nationalistic ideas this meant the protection of Hungary's territorial integrity. The majority of officers serving in the army, or engaged in service, came from the territories occupied by the Romanian, Czechoslovak, and Serbian armies, or lying outside the demarcation lines. These officers saw the defense of their homeland and the liberation of the Hungarian territories under occupation as a just fight of self-defense of the Soviet Republic.

2. New opportunities for fantastic military careers arose for young captains, majors, and lieutenant-colonels, since the liberal democratic governments had pensioned off not only the generals but, from January 1, 1919, the majority of the colonels as well. Thus, the opportunities to reach high-military rank opened up before the officers ready to enlist in the Red Army, for which the majority of them would otherwise have had to wait for long years under "normal" circumstances.

3. Individual problems of subsistence. Those entering service could expect to make a living from exercising their profession. The lack of jobs, and partly of foodstuffs as well, forced the officers, mostly without property and trained in only military skills, to continue their military careers.

Almost all the officers who served in the Red Army brought up in their defense these three reasons before officer screening committees set up after the collapse of the Soviet Republic. In general, the committees accepted these arguments.

When investigating the composition of the Red Army's officer corps I consider it important to set up categories of origin for the officers and analyze their level of professional training. As I had a sufficient amount of data for approaching the question from this angle—taking as a basis the corps of professional officers—I think it worthwhile to emphasize a few essential considerations.

Investigating the places and dates of birth, we find that more than *fifty percent* of the officers came from the territories occupied by Entente troops. This, as we indicated above, defined the relationship of the officers of the defensive fight of the Soviet Republic. As to the distribution by age, it becomes clear that a great part of the Red Army commanders and officers were born in the years 1881—88. That means that the average age of the officers of higher ranks was between *32 and 38 years-of-age!* This needs emphasis, because these years are the most useful and fertile years of the soldiers' intellectual and physical abilities.

Investigation of family background, the question of social origins of the officers seems to be of importance, too because we read in several works that these officers came from the ruling classes of the monarchy which defined their counterrevolutionary attitude and their relationship to the dictatorship of the proletariat. That view oversimplifies matters. It is a fact that the overwhelming majority of the professional officers emphasized, in general, that they fulfilled their obligations as soldiers only—and not as committed advocates of Socialist ideals—but they could not, at the same time, be considered counterrevolutionaries. It may be stated that the overwhelming majority of professional soldiers came from the intelligentsia or from lower middle-class families of the Austro—Hungarian monarchy, practically from the same strata as did the majority of the leaders of the Soviet Republic, with the only difference that Jewish origin is almost impossible to find among the officers. For people of such background, the choice of the officer's profession, made at an early age, meant a step up in the social hierarchy. To give it up in the spring of 1919 would have meant a halt in their climb up the social ladder and perhaps a descent. In March—April 1919, it could not yet be forseen that the Soviet Republic was to last for 133 days only!

If we examine the proportion of officers having served in the Austro—Hungarian Army and in the war-time *honvéd*, we see that the proportions were about 50—50 percent among the officers of the Red Army. That was definitely favorable for the *honvéd* officers if we *compare* the proportions of officers between the Common Army and the *honvéd*. At the same it is to be pointed out that the former Common Army officers were of Hungarian origin almost without exception, and it is also a well-known fact that under the Károlyi regime, there was a merger between the former *honvéd* units and the Hungarian units of the former Austro—Hungarian army.

When examining the distribution of Red Army officers according to rank we must consider their former ranks for following the example of the Russian Red Army, officer ranks were abolished in the Hungarian Red Army. The majority of the officers held the ranks of captains and majors. The number of lieutenant-colonels was lower; the number of colonels almost negligible. This was the consequence of the pensioning off "program." We must also point out that these officers, young in age as well as rank, having served at the front for more than four months in the course of the four years of world war, offered in many cases training for, and service in, the general staff as well as an important professional preparation for the commanders of the highest ranks of the Red Army who were selected in general from the point of view of political considerations!

I do not consider it purposeful to examine the nationality distribution of the officers of the Red Army as, excluding the officers of the international units and subunits, more than 90 percent of the officers proclaimed themselves, Hungarian.

So far, I have attempted to draw a sketch of why the former professional officers undertook to serve a government considered alien by them, and to their original surroundings. In the following I shall try to show why the officers, the majority of whom had sincerely sworn to defend their homeland, turned away from the Soviet Republic and, in some cases, even against it.

It is well known that in the weeks of the defensive and then the offensive military operations of the Red Army, the former professional officers participated in the fight with full enthusiasm, but from the middle of July 1919 increasingly more officers reported ill and left service under various guises; moreover, some left the Red Army and offered their services to the counterrevolutionary government in Szeged.[8]

Seeking reasons, I believe that mention must be made, first of all, of the fact which "forced" Aurél Stromfeld to resign, too. The withdrawal was decided upon for political considerations following the successful liberation campaign in upper Hungary. Stromfeld's example evoked similar responses in the high command he headed and molded by his personality. Officers mostly coming from the occupied territories lost their faith in the liberation of the occupied territories.

Considerable weight—if not the greatest importance!—must have been given to the fact that there was already another government existing in Szeged with which the Entente might have been willing to enter into negotiations. Its army was in formation, and that army stood closer in form if not character to former professional officers than did the Red Army. The "attraction" to the Szeged army reached such dimensions in July 1919, that some officers —for example, Henrik Werth—offered their services to it.

Examining the question of turning away from, and against, the Red Army, we must not leave out of consideration the constant conflicts between the former professional officers and the political commissars who mostly lacked military training and experience. They interfered in military-professional matters and looked upon the former professional officers as saboteurs and counterrevolutionaries. They had commanders arrested and relieved at the least sign of suspicion. Such conflict and mutual lack of confidence became strong especially following the ill-fated counterrevolutionary attempt of June 24, 1919. The danger of that conflict seemed to be impossible to eliminate, as was emphasized, among others, by former Lieutenant-Colonel Ödön Schranz, head of the personnel department of officers of the War Comissariat, in his memorandum of July 10, 1919, addressed to War Commissar Béla Szántó.[9]

Following the Soviet Republic's defeat the Red Army officer corps become increasingly more passive and merged almost completely into the National Army, and then into the *honvéd* army being organized. Their assimilation though not without difficulty, took place in a short period of time. The former "red" and "white" officer soon formed the unified "Hungarian Royal *Honvéd* Corps of Officers." This may be stated in spite of the fact that we have data even from the second half of the 1920s to prove that the military careers of the former "red officers" were "followed with greater attention" than the careers of those who had not served in the Red Army.[10]

The commissions established to justify behavior during the revolutions did not, in general, condemn officers for having spent weeks or months in the Red Army, because the officers referred to duress almost without exception, and there were always people to verify it. Another recurrent argument offered in defense was the intention to protect the homeland, the sincerity of which we have no reason to doubt.

The question may arise as to why the new army being organized by the post-Soviet regime needed the officers who had served in the Red Army. Taking the data and facts into account, the answer seems to be simple. The overwhelming majority of the lieutenants and lieutenant-colonels of the professional corps of officers who had served in World War I, had served in the Red Army of the Soviet Republic; only a small number had avoided such service or were prisoners of war abroad, or served in the National Army. At the same time it is also a fact—clearly demonstrated by later military careers—that the professional qualifications of the officers who had served in the Red Army far exceeded those of the officers from Szeged. Another fact to be emphasized is that the majority of the officers of the National Army established in Szeged were not professionals but reservists. The majority were not needed by the new army. The army under reorganization needed young professional officers with war experience, for a higher number than necessary of older colonels and generals had offered their services to it.

It was this necessity that may be considered to have been one of the reasons why the military courts of the counterrevolutionary system sentenced very few professional officers to demotion, retirement or, as a more serious punishment, to prison. That they greatly tolerated the services of officers formerly in the Red Army and in the army of Károlyi's People's Republic, is well illustrated by the cases of Jenő Tombor, Ferenc Julier, and Albert Bartha. Regent Miklós Horthy ordered —"exceptionally and as a token of mercy"—that they be promoted in the active force, at the request of all three of them, and then put them in reserve as colonels from 1924, receiving full pension.[11]

Naturally, there were military leaders whose activities in the Red Army were not forgiven, for example, Aurél Stromfeld and József Kerekes.

This picture would not be complete if we made no mention of the professional officers who, following their service in the Red Army, became members of the high military leadership in the counterrevolutionary system. A significant majority of these officers had served in the Red Army to the satisfaction of the political and military leaders, until the collapse of the Soviet Republic, on August 1, 1919.

Hugó Solarz fought as a brigader general in 1919, and then later, as Hugó Sónyi, as a general of infantry was commander-in-chief of the *honvéd* army between 1936–40.

Döme Stojakovics, head of the intelligence and counterintelligence service of the Red Army in 1919, later as Döme Sztójay, lieutenant general, was the Hungarian ambassador to Berlin, then prime minister in 1944.

Gusztáv Erb, serving next to Stromfeld in the High Command of the Red Army in 1919, was later, as Commander of Army Corps, Gusztáv Hennyey, superintendent of the infantry and then foreign minister in the Lakatos government.

Rudolf Fleischacker served in the High Command of the Red Army, became head of the department of intelligence and counterintelligence in the period of the counterrevolution under the name of Rudolf Andorka, then Hungarian ambassador to Spain between 1939–41.

Ferenc Knausz, head of the southern-Slavic records of the Red Army in 1919, between 1941 and 1944 was Colonel-General Ferenc Szombathelyi, head of the high command of the *honvéd* army.

Sándor Bengyel, a captain, was chief of staff of a division and then of an army corps in the Red Army; later, as Sándor Bengyel-Győrffy, he was colonel general and minister without portfolio of public supplies in 1941–42.

Besides the well known are the following who were all lieutenant-generals or colonel-generals in the period of the counterrevolution: Alajos Béldy, Károly Beregfy, Albin Lenz, Béla Miklós, Zoltán Módly, István Náday, József Németh, Kálmán Révy, Géza Siegler, Lajos Veres...[12]

In summary, we may accept the statement that the corps of officers of the Red Army of the Soviet Republic was made up of lower-ranking professional and reserve officers of the Austro–Hungarian army and former royal *honvéd*. Service in the Red Army was primarily inspired by the defense of the homeland. For them, service to the dictatorship of the proletariat meant continuance of their military careers as well as—which they imagined to be free from politics—a means for making a living. Consequently, they suffered but did not accept the curbing of commander's and officer's prerogatives during the republic. When the opportunity opened up, seeing the hopeless situation of the system they had so far served as a necessity, they stood up for the counterrevolution representing the old social system which they were used to and accepted. The weeks, the months, they had spent in the Red Army remained only small episodes in their lives.

## NOTES

1. A selected list of works on the revolutions of 1918–1919 includes: Tibo Hajdu, *Tanácsok Magyarországon* (Budapest, 1958); Tibor Hajdu, *Az őszirózsás forr dalom* (Budapest, 1963); Tibor Hajdu, *A Magyarországi Tanácsköztársaság* (Budapes 1969); Tibor Hetés, *Munkásezredek előre!* (Budapest, 1960); Ervin Liptai, *A Magya Tanácsköztársaság* (Budapest, 1979); Ervin Liptai, *Vörös katonák előre! A Magyar Vö rös Hadsereg harcai 1919* (Budapest, 1979); Béla Köpeczi, ed., *A Magyar Tanácskö társaság 60. évfordulójára* (Budapest, 1979).

2. László Fogarassy, "Kik vezették az 1919-es Vörös Hadsereget?," *Borsoc Szemle*, 1 (1971) pp. 70–78. This is the only work that has some relevance to the topi In this essay, Fogarassy traces in minute detail the personel changes that occured in th military leadership.

3. Ervin Liptai, *Vörös katonák előre!* p. 19.

4. Maria Ormos, *Padovától Trianonig* (Budapest, 1983), pp. 26–75.

5. *Rendeleti Közlöny a magyar hadsereg számára* [*Szabályrendeletek*], no. 10 (1918), p. 711, no. 110, (1918), pp. 719–720, no. 9, (1919), p. 34, no 16 (1919), pp 74–75, no. 18 (1919), pp. 80–81.

6. The report of Ödön Schranz to Béla Szántó, July 10, 1919. Document in th possession of the author.

7. See the Revolutionary Governing Council's order of March 24, 1919, in Hetés Tibor, ed., *A Magyar Vörös Hadsereg 1919. (Válogatott dokumentumok)* (Buda pest, 1959), pp. 81–82.

8. On June 6, 1919, Miklós Horthy, the Minister of War of the conterrevolu tionary government at Szeged issued the order concerning the establishment of th Hungarian National Army. For the text, see, Tibor Hetés and Tamásné Morva, eds. *Csak Szolgálati Használatra! Iratok a Horthy-hadsereg történetéhez* (Budapest, 1968) p. 57.

9. Schranz to Szántó.

10. This type of report can be read about Captain Károly Berger (later Beregfy who was assigned to the high command; see, Hadtörténelmi Levéltár, Budapest (here after cited as *HL*), Honvédelmi Minisztérium Elnöki C. osztály 1920. i. tétel, 105785 sz

11. The decision was made in 1930, but was retroactive to 1924. see, *HL*, Kor mányzói Elhatározások, February 12, 1930, 85 titk. K. I. –1930.

12. For a detailed account of the careers of these officers, see Szakály Sándor "Az ellenforradalmi Magyarország [1919–1944] hadseregének felső vezetése. Adattá I. rész A–K," *Hadtörténelmi Közlemények* no. 2, (1984), and "Adattár L–Z," *Had történelmi Közlemények* no 3, (1984).

# 1919 IN LITERATURE

Ivan Sanders

"1919 in Literature" is a susupiciously broad and vague topic. This presentation is not quite as ambitious, or as all-encompassing, as its title suggests. I will not, of course, attempt to give an account of the treatment of the Hungarian Soviet Republic *in literature* (by which one may mean world literature), but will try to focus on the representation of this event in selected Hungarian works.[1] It would be no doubt interesting to investigate the reaction of writers in other countries to the revolutionary upheaval in Hungary, although I wonder if one would be able to uncover a significant amount of material. While a Hungarian Communist returning from the U.S. in the spring of 1919, did write in Budapest's *Red Gazette (Vörös Újság)* that "all of America rejoiced over the Hungarian proletarian dictatorship,"[2] it is safe to assume that such an assertion is the exaggeration of an overenthusiastic partisan.

The truth is that knowledge about the Hungarian Soviet Republic in the West has always been limited, and misconceptions, half-truths, and plain ignorance invariably played a role in the reaction to the event. Let me cite just one recent example. An English translation of György Lukács's *Gelebtes Denken,* or rather the long interview based on Lukács's autobiographical sketch, was published not long ago in England. The book itself, entitled *Record of a Life* in English, is not very carefully edited; in fact, it is full of errors and repetitions, but a recent review, in the American journal, *Dissent* (an antiestablishment, leftist publication), compounds these errors with misreadings and misinterpretations of its own. The reviewer presents a chillingly hostile view of Lukács as critic, ideologue, and politican, which is his prerogative, of course; what is indefensible, however, is that, while commenting on Lukács's ruthlessness as Commissar for Education in Béla Kun's government, the reviewer reveals his very spotty knowledge of what really happened in Hungary in 1919. For example, he is under the impression that Lukács was

the first and only person to call Kun's regime a dictatorship; he implie
that only Lukács, brazen radical that he was, had the nerve to call it tha
He talks about a full scale war between Hungary and Romania in 1919, an
believes that not only did the philosopher Lukács become Commissar fo
Culture, but that Bartók, Kodály, and Dohnányi were Commissars of Musi
which, according to him, made the Communist revolution "the most cultura
ly distinguished dictatorship in modern times."[3] Bartók, Kodály, and Dohn
nyi were, of course, members of the Musicians' Advisory Board (or *Direk
tórium)*, and not commissars.

As I said, my aim is to discuss the Hungarian literary response to th
Soviet Republic, and by this, I don't just mean what writers said and wrot
during the Republic. Much has already been written about this, as well a
about the cultural policies of Béla Kun's regime, the antagonisms betwee
Communist and Social Democratic writers, the polemics between independ
ent radicals like Lajos Kassák and the Communist leadership, and so on an
so forth.[4] I am interested in literary representations that transcend topica
political importance or literary-historical interest—representations, in othe
words, that became and remained important literary works in their ow
right. Needless to say, a great many works dealing with the proletarian dic
tatorship have appeared in Hungary between 1919 and the present, som
glorifying, other vilifying the event. Inevitably, many, too many, are trans
parently tendentious, didactic, propagandistic. I have chosen three works
three very different responses to a historical turning point, which reveal a
much, if not more, about the crisis of conscience the event engendered i
the authors than about the event itself. All three amount to much more tha
a political statement; they constitute a moral reckoning, an artistic credo
They may be termed representative works only insofar as they were writte
by three outstanding and influential twentieth-century Hungarian writers
The three works I will consider are a poem and a related essay by Mihály
Babits, a novel by Dezső Kosztolányi, and a short story by Lajos Nagy.

Mihály Babits, the *poeta doctus* of his generation and a towering figur
in the Hungarian literary life of the first decades of the century, at first wel
comed the revolutionary changes of 1918–19. He was appointed Professo
of Hungarian Literature by the Károlyi government but assumed his new po
sition only during the Soviet Republic. Babits's initial enthusiasm, howeve
gave way to painful second thoughts and doubts. A famous poem he wrote i
the summer of 1919 signals a retreat and a rejection of revolutionary up
heavals in general and the 1919 Communist revolution in particular. Th
poem, "Szíttál-e lassú mérgeket?" (Have You Breathed In Slow-Actin
Poisons?), which is still considered too controversial to be included in new

editions of Babits's collected works, is a passionate denunciation of enticing but fatal ideologies, a repudiation of words, which can be a deadly narcotic and an encitement to evil action. Babits warns against the enchantment of words, especially slogans, patriotic and political catchwords, which promise redemption but, when turned into deeds, deliver only chaos and tragedy. "Man, if you mean well," he says near the end of the poem, "take my advice and spit out the bloody words."

> And if you feel that the word, this deceptive seed
> is innocent still; if it sprouts in your soul's fertile field,
> better set fire to the field, and let doubt be
> parched and red-hot, like a flame over an arid plain.[5]

"Szíttál-e lassú mérgeket" may be seen as a general indictment of all potentially destructive ideologies, but as it was written weeks before the defeat of Kun's regime, its target was clearly a revolution that intended to bring about sweeping changes in the name of a political philosophy that—to Babits, at least—seemed seductively intellectual.

Babits's essay, "Hungarian Poet in 1919," written during August and September of that year, may be considered a companion piece to "Szíttál-e lassú mérgeket." The essay, too, is a tortured self-examination, the stock-taking of a repentant poet. In it, Babits argues that a writer cannot be a revolutionary; he is by nature a conservative, a preserver, a repository, of accumulated cultural values. "Who should be more fearful of Destruction, which is elevated to a governing principle in a Revolution, than he who stands on the pinnacle of Culture?" Babits asks. "Is not he the one who takes the most terrible fall if the structure collapses? Should he still become a revolutionist, a tool of the Dismantlers—the enemy of all that he cares for, all that constitutes his reason for being?"[6]

In the same essay, Babits, who before and after this critical juncture, was a sworn enemy of all forms of racial discrimination and intolerance, pins the blame for the disasters that befell his nation on restless and irresponsible strangers. Alluding unmistakably to the fact that most of the leaders of the Hungarian Soviet Republic were of Jewish origin, he writes: "Here they were again: the outcasts of nations, the unflappable consumers of culture, the ardent and argumentative Jews. They wanted to wipe the slate clean, and we feared a new dark age that would last a thousand years. They screamed for a new civilization, and set about destroying everything left intact by the War. And we, like a sick man, wake up with a start from one nightmare, roll over, and wait for another, even more terrifying nightmare to begin."[7]

Many critics consider the period in which Babits wrote this essay th
nadir of his literary career: the essay is seen as a shameful whitewash, a de:
perate recantation meant to appease the counterrevolutionary regime, which
it should be pointed out, was not impressed—it stripped Babits of his universi
ty post, and snubbed and even harassed the poet for quite a long time. Bu
Babits wasn't an opportunist; the essay and the poem reflect a larger dilem
ma—a dilemma that was a perennial one for the poet. How politically com
mitted should a writer be? Should he—can he—retreat into an ivory tower
These were the questions Babits grappled with all his life. Toward the end o
that life, in the late thirties, when confronted by a new menace: Fascism, h
did resolve the dilemma. In his last poetic work, the magnificent *Book o*
*Jonah (Jónás könyve)*, he reaches the conclusion that in certain circumstance
the poet must speak out, for, as he put it, "he who remains silent is in leagu
with the guilty" ("vétkesek közt cinkos aki néma").

Like Babits, the poet, novelist, essayist, Dezső Kosztolányi also sympathiz
ed at first with the Soviet Republic, but later repudiated it even more dra
matically than did Babits. For a time in the early twenties, Kosztolányi joine
the staff of a rightist, ultra-nationalist, strongly anti-Semitic newspaper, an
in a column entitled "Pardon me," he regularly lashed out against Commu
nists, fellow travelers, and anyone suspected of leftist leanings. These crude
personal attacks and Kosztolányi's journalistic activities in this period i
general damaged his reputation to a considerable extent. His change of hear
was seen as sheer opportunism. He was further compromised when it wa
learned that while fulminating against "godless," "rootless" revolutionaries an
their mostly Jewish supporters, he sent his wife to Vienna in order to ge
Lajos Hatvany, a wealthy Jewish writer and patron, to underwrite the foreig
publication of one of his works.[8]

*Édes Anna* (Anna Édes), written in the mid-twenties, was also a kind o
moral reckoning, an act of penance, and an attempt at self-purification. Th
novel, considered one of the masterpieces of twentieth-century Hungaria
fiction, is not about 1919, it is not a political novel *per se*, although the tim
and place—Budapest during the months following the defeat of the Com
munist republic—are quite important. Based on a spur-of-the-moment idea
suggested to the author by his wife, *Édes Anna* is about a model maid, Anna
Édes, who winds up murdering her employers. The novel is a kind of psycho
logical thriller with Freudian overtones, although, as we said, the social and
political background is sharply etched, and it is not so much the depth of the
psychology but the author's artistic economy, his resourceful realism, and his
profound moral awareness that raises the novel to the level of a masterpiece.

The opening and closing chapters of the book are not directly related to the action of the novel but nevertheless reveal a great deal about the temper of the times. The prologue-like first chapter is a grotesque parody of the rumors circulating, in the respectable upper-class neighborhood where the action is laid, about Béla Kun's hurried departure from Budapest after the collapse of his regime. According to these stories, Kun fled on an airplane piloted by himself, taking with him much of the gold and silver and other treasures he amassed during his brief reign. One heavy gold necklace was said to have fallen out of the airplane and been picked up by a vigilant citizen.

In the final chapter of the novel we find a wry bit of self-mockery. It has been months since the sensational murder; the shock of it has already worn off. A conversation is overheard between one of the neighbors of the victims and his politican friends. The subject of the conversation is the author himself, a resident of the same neighborhood. "He used to be quite a Communist," the neighbor, a lawyer by the name of Druma, comments.

> Really? said one of the politicians, surprised. Because now he's a devout Christian.
> That's right, added the other politician. I read it in a Viennese paper—he is a white terrorist.
> He was a Red all right, Druma repeated. He had dealings with one of those heathen commissars. He even had his picture taken with him at the Parade Grounds.

* * *

> I don't get it, the first politician said, shaking his head. What does the man want? Whose side is he on, anyway?
> Simple, Druma concluded. On everybody's and nobody's. However the wind blows. Before he was paid by the Jews, so he sided with them. Now the Christians back him. Smart man, that one... Knows what he's doing.[9]

The novel itself can be read as an indictment of the restored conservative order. The maid, Anna Édes, in employed by a high government official, Kornél Vizy, a conformist bureaucrat who reasserts his legitimate, historical rights with vengeful joy after the defeat of the Communist revolution. His wife is an unfulfilled, neurotic woman who out of boredom, and with a kind of morbid, vicarious pleasure, spends much of her time bickering with, or fretting about, maids who to her mind are either lazy or dirty or impudent

or immoral. But Anna, a peasant girl from the lovely Balaton region,
different. She is the model maid—quiet, industrious, alert, docile. Mrs. Viz
cannot believe her eyes. Yet her fundamentally suspicious nature, her ingraine
prejudices against servants do not allow her to treat Anna decently. Sh
does not exactly abuse her, but with her constant nagging and unreasonab
strictness she manages to torment and humiliate the girl.

It is against this treatment that Anna rebels instinctively and violently
stabbing her masters to death one night with a kitchen knife. It's an uncoi
scious act—a clear motive is never established. To a large extent Anna remain
an unexplained, unexplored character, a psychological puzzle, though this b
no means diminishes her tragedy. By failing to delve into her inner life, b
eliciting sympathy for her indirectly, showing the inhumanity of others tc
ward her, Kosztolányi confirms our feeling that despite the apparently sense
less murder committed by Anna, she is really the victim in this tragedy. Th
author seems to be saying that the fundamental evil of a master-servant rela
tionship is exacerbated by modern society's tendency to classify people ac
cording to profession, social position, etc., thereby depriving them of thei
individuality. Anna kills because with this act she violently reasserts he
"human selfhood." We can go even further and see the Vizys, despite thei
particularized and largely negative portrayal, as victims of the same dehuma
nization and alienation. Given the society they are a part of, they canno
possibly give into their impulse—momentarily present—to treat Anna wit
genuine humanity.

Yet, Kosztolányi rejects this world, this social order not in the name o
any political creed but as a Christian humanist. The character in the nove
who becomes the author's mouthpiece is an old, frail physician, Dr. Movisz
ter, the Vizys' neighbor, who is described by Kosztolányi as being "neithe
a bourgeois nor a Communist; a member of no political party, but a membe
of that human community which encompasses the whole world, the livin
and the dead." At Anna's trial, Moviszter is the only one who rises to he
defense. "My feeling is that they did not treat her in a human way," he say
in the courtroom. "They did not treat her as a human being but as a machine
They made a machine out of her.... They treated her inhumanly, atro
ciously."[10]

Unlike Babits and Kosztolányi, Lajos Nagy (1883–1954) was, from the
beginning of his career, an angry radical; but he came into conflict with the
illegal Hungarian Communist party in the 1930s, as well as with the post-
World War Two Communist establishment, for not having the proper party
spirit. Revolutionary romanticism and fervor were always alien to Nagy

his artistic temperament found its finest expression in a rigorously plain, even abrupt style of writing. His uncompromisingly critical outlook prompted his critics to call Nagy a "born dissenter."

One of Nagy's best stories, "May, 1919" ("1919 Majus"), written in 1932, is also a most penetrating look at a representative social situation and conflict at a critical point in the nation's history. The story is set in a small Hungarian town and focuses on a supposedly friendly gathering of some of the town's "better" people. The main character, István Petur, "a complete Hungarian gentleman," cannot wait for the Reds to be beaten; he has scores to settle, is seething with rage. Narrated with a remarkable economy of literary means, mostly in the form of dialogue, the story nevertheless offers a shattering portrait of Petur, a hollow, debased man, a macho bully, a psychopath, actually, who frightens and intimidates even his friends, who out of class loyalty, and because they are much too weak and passive, don't dare to resist him. Indirectly, the author passes judgment on these somewhat more human but ineffectual, corruptible friends, too. At one point, one of the friends, a painter from Budapest, muses to himself: "He'd have to be only a shade different, add on just a little bit, one iota, one tiny measure, to the way he was. And then he would whip out his gun (for then he too would probably have one), and shoot the man strutting before him."[11] As one of Lajos Nagy's critics pointed out, Petur, a member of the gentry class, represents a type that was depicted by writers before Nagy with considerable sympathy, or at least with resigned understanding. But in Lajos Nagy's portrayal the only things that remain of their bravado and gallantry are the empty swagger and the brutish, sadistic instincts.[12] During the course of the little nighttime revelry, Petur orders his servant about, wakes up the Jewish storekeeper next door, demands that he sell him some wine, and repeatedly taunts and humiliates the merchant. Infuriated by his refusal to drink with him, Petur aims his gun at the stoic Jew and shoots through the window behind him. His rowdy behavior attracts the attention of a Red guard patrolling nearby; later the local commander appears and promptly arrests Petur. Lajos Nagy's scrupulous realism is in evidence throughout. He makes no attempt to enhance the character of the Communist officer. The commander is a simple though firm man: but he is not particularly memorable or even sympathetic.

As I said at the outset, these three literary works—Babit's poem and related eassay, Kosztolányi's novel, Lajos Nagy's short story—can't be said to be wholly representative of the Hungarian literary response to the Soviet Republic of 1919. They are three outstanding literary works that happen also to deal with the experience of 1919. Eminent writers like Babits and Koszto-

Iányi, though hostile to the violence, the chauvinism, the generally oppressive character of the reestablished old order, had found the radicalism of 1919 frightening, too. And even Lajos Nagy, a politically far more committed writer, exercises great self-restraint in evoking, in 1932, the fateful summer of 1919.

The three works are no doubt valuable from a historical point of view, if only because they contain masterful portraits of the type of people who were to become active supporters of the Horthy regime. (Clearly, there is a connection between Lajos Nagy's István Petur and Kosztolányi's Kornél Vizy. Petur may be a more revolting character than Vizy, but they are essentially the same type.) What is also important to note is that all three works reflect—in Babits's case, of course, in a painfully self-incriminating way—the anti-Jewish feelings that became so characteristic of the counterrevolutionary period. In some sense, then, the three works I discussed may be called representative literary reactions to the events of 1919 after all. Since all three are complex and subtle works, they reveal more about the immediate impact as well as the wider ramifications of 1919 than the more explicit, literal treatments of the event.

## NOTES

1. I stress the word selected; I will not deal at all with some rather important literary representations of the 1919 Soviet Republic (e.g., Ervin Sinkó's *Optimisták,* József Lengyel's *Prenn Ferenc hányatott élete,* Lajos Kassák's *Egy ember élete,* etc.), which deal more explicitly with the historical events, and which may be considered literary documentations rather than artistic evocations of the period.

2. See Andor Garvay, "Szökés Amerikából," in Farkas József, ed., *"Mindenki újakra készül..."* vol. 3 (Budapest, 1960), pp. 539–66.

3. Paul Berman, "A Bloody Critic," *Dissent* vol.32 (Spring, 1985), pp. 242–44.

4. See Farkas József, *'Rohanunk a forradalomba'* (Budapest, 1957, pp. 220–35.

5. Mihály Babits, *Összes versei* (Budapest, 1942), p. 201.

6. .............., *Ezüstkor* (Budapest, [1938]), p. 162.

7. *Ibid.,* p. 151.

8. See Ferenc Kiss, "Kosztolányi és a *Pardon*-rovat," *Valóság,* Vol. 20 (June, 1977), pp. 18–35.

9. Dezső Kosztolányi, *Édes Anna* (Budapest, 1963), p. 286.

10. *Ibid.,* p. 287.

11. Lajos Nagy, *Kiskunhalom* (Budapest, 1968), p. 178.

12. See Miklós Szabolcsi, ed., *A magyar irodalom története* vol. 6 (Budapest, 1966), p. 397.

# THE CHURCH IN THE STORM OF THE REVOLUTIONS OF 1918–1919 IN HUNGARY

Leslie Laszlo

The collapse of the Austro–Hungarian empire in Fall 1918 created a radically new situation for the thousand-year-old Hungarian Catholic Church.[1] An important part in the ancient constitution,[2] a pillar of the traditional society, the church had now to find its place in a secular republic, bereft of prerogatives and privileges.

For the church hierarchy, just as for all other beneficiaries of the Dual Monarchy, the end of the millenium came swiftly and quite unexpectedly. Neither they, nor the lower clergy, nor the faithful, were prepared to face up to the social upheaval that was to sweep away the *ancien régime* overnight. To be sure, there were social reformers within the church, such as Ottokár Prohászka, bishop of Székesfehérvár, and Sándor Giesswein, canon of the Győr Chapter, who had inspired and led the Christian Social Movement and founded Christian Workers Organizations, but they were rather the exceptions among the much larger number of conservative prelates and clergy. These "Christian Socialists" had little impact on official church policy; their influence on the government was almost nil. Nevertheless, thanks to them, the anticlerical leaders of the liberal-democratic revolution did not mount a frontal attack against the Catholic Church, and even allowed it to play a certain role, albeit limited, in the "new order."[3]

When at the end of October, 1918, the National Council, headed by Mihály Károlyi, seized power, and on November 16, proclaimed Hungary a republic,[4] the new government, which was based on a coalition of the Károlyi party, the Bourgeois Radicals, and the Social Democrats, and in which elements hostile to religion played a major role, it was feared, would lay claim to the royal prerogatives of "supreme patronage" over the church.[5] These would have secured for the government a far-reaching influence over church affairs.[6] For this reason, Prince Primate, János Cardinal Csernoch convened a conference of the Bench of Bishops for November 20. The conference decided to bring about as soon as possible the establishment of an organization, to be called *Catholic Autonomy,* for the administration of church institutions and property, independent of the state. As in the case of the Protestant churches, the governing body of Catholic Autonomy would have also included members of the laity, to be selected at a congress convoked to this end.[7] At the same conference Ottokár Prohászka, who had never liked the great earthly riches of the church,[8] succeeded in persuading his fellow bishops to make the now inevitable sacrifices voluntarily, setting a fitting example to others. The Bench of Bishops, rising to the occasion, solemnly declared in its letter of greeting the new government that "the Church, for its part, in the service of democratic development and for the realization of land reform, willingly offers the lands in its possession which are suitable for this purpose."[9] The bishops designated Prohászka and Ágost Fischer-Colbrie, the like-minded bishop of Kassa, to carry on the discussions about church property with the government. These promptly established contact with Barna Buza, minister of agriculture, and offered officially Church lands amounting to over a million *hold.*[10] for distribution, asking merely that 100 *hold* be left to each bishop for meeting the needs of his household.[11] As it later turned out, this was less than the minimum finally established in the land reform law, which was in general 500 *hold,* whereas in the case of church lands it was 200 *hold.*[12]

Bishop Prohászka, although he also realized the perils of the situation,[13] greeted the republic with confidence and expressed the hope that in the new democratic order the Catholic Church could develop more freely than it had been able to under the *ancien régime.*[14] There was indeed no reason for excessive anxiety in the beginning. The new government was not expressly inimical to the chuches; the membership of the National Council included a Catholic priest and a Protestant minister[15] and also a representative of the Christian Social People's party.[16] However, moderate elements soon were increasingly relegated to the backgorund by radical innovators. Oszkár Jászi, minister of nationality affairs, who exerted a strong influence over Károlyi, was an early advocate of a total separation of church and state.[17] He was supported by the Social Democrats, who demanded secularization of church schools and abolition of religious instruction. To this end, they proposed the separation of educational from religious affairs, and creating two distinct ministries—the Ministry of Religion and the Ministry of Public Education.[18] As one result of the governmental crisis of January, 1919, which was brought on by the Social Democrats, this separation was indeed effected, and the Social Democratic party received the education portfolio, which it had so strongly desired.[19]

At the same time, the new Minister of Religion, the loyal Catholic János Vass, opened negotiations at the behest of the government with the Papal Nuncio in Vienna for the establishment of diplomatic relations between the Vatican and the newly independent Hungarian Republic.[20] Instead of the separation of church and state, they placed great importance on getting the Holy See to recognize the transfer of the right of "supreme patronage" to the new head of state, namely President of the Republic Mihály Károlyi. The government wished, in this manner, to assure the continued influence of the state over the church.[21] This could well have been the reason why the Council of Ministers was reluctant to agree to the proposals of Zsigmond Kunfi, the Social Democratic Minister of Education, directed at the abolition of religious instruction and the secularization of denominational schools.[22] These proposals could be put into effect only after the Social Democrats on March 21, 1919, took power with the Communists, led by Béla Kun, who had been trained as a Bolsehvik agitator while a prisoner of war in Russia.[23] Kunfi could now execute the governmentalization and secularization of education as People's Commissar of Education.

The Hungarian Soviet Republic[24] officially professed the principles of freedom of conscience and separation of church and state. Paragraph II of the Construction declared:[25]

The Soviet Republic protects the true freedom of conscience of the workers by separating completely the Church from the State and the schools from the Church. Each person may practice his religion freely.

However, the Communists made no secret of the fact that, in accordance with their Marxist view of the world, they regarded religion as a harmful superstition and an opiate serving to mislead the people, and that they meant to eradicate it completely. They forbade churches any participation in public life; they disbanded the Christian Social People's party; they abolished all religious associations and movements; and they established the ominously named Office for the Liquidation of Religious Matters for the purpose of closing religious schools, press, and publishing houses, and all movable and real property of the churches.[26] At the same time they robbed the churches of their press and restricted the practice of religion to within the four walls of the churches; they conducted an unbridled campaign of propaganda against God and religion. Desecration of churches and of objects serving religious purposes, as well as physical attacks on priests and nuns, were daily occurrences.[27] Communist authorities themselves came to see these activities as too much of a good thing and began to worry that they would alienate the people in this way.[28]

The situation became especially grave following unsuccessful counterrevolutionary outbreaks that flared up in June, since the Communists placed the blame for these primarily on the Christian Socialists, who were starting to reorganize themselves illegally and in secret, and on the anti-Communist agitation conducted by the clergy.[29] The increasing terror[30] prompted Prince Primate Csernoch to request the Holy See, in a letter addressed to the Cardinal Secretary of State, to exert its influence with the Allied Powers so that the Entente countries would take the Hungarian Catholic Church under their protection, in much the same manner as in the past the Christian subjects of the Porte had been under the protection of the European powers.[31] Before, however, a reply could have arrived to this unusual request, Béla Kun's rule of four months was brought to an end by the Romanian troops marching into Budapest at the Entente's behest.

The revolutions of 1918–19 proved to be but ephemeral interruptions in the *status quo,* which was fully restored after the triumph of the counter-revolution under Admiral Miklós Horthy. Though by the midthirties, currents for reform and renewal were stirring also within the church, and powerful social movements, including the half-a-million strong Catholic Agrarian Youth League, KALOT, were demanding far-reaching socio-economic changes, the hierarchy was as unprepared for the Armageddon of 1945, as it was in 1918. The Hungarian Catholic Church, like the Bourbons, neither forgot, nor learned from past history.

## NOTES

1. This study deals solely with the predominant Roman Catholic Church, to which over half of the population in Greater Hungary, and two-thirds in Trianon Hungary, owed allegiance. The other officially "received" churches, namely the Uniate, Calvinist, Lutheran, Unitarian, were not only numerically smaller, but also their nexus with the state was incomparably weaker—and conversely, their autonomy much greater—than that of the Roman Catholic Church. The latter preserved her quasi-established church status even after legal equality had been granted in 1848 to all "received" churches. For more details, see my "Church and State in Hungary, 1919–1945" (Ph. D. diss., Columbia University, 1973).

2. The Archbishop of Esztergom, Prince Primate of Hungary, was the First Lord of the Banner, next in dignity to the king. The bishops were *ex officio* members of the House of Magnates. The clergy had the status of public officials. The immense *latifundia* and other property of the Church were state supervised and protected. Collection of church taxes was enforced by state authorities. Catholic feast days were observed as public holidays.

3. During the war, Giesswein and other prominent members of the Christian Socialist and People's parties took active part in the League for a Lasting Peace. They did this in spite of the fact that among the Hungarian adherents of this international peace movement the anticlerical bourgeois radicals—Mihály Károlyi, Oszkár Jászi and his circle of friends—played the leading role. See, *Giesswein Emlékkönyv* [Giesswein Memorial Volume] (Budapest, 1925), pp. 170–71; József Galántai, *Egyház és politika, 1890–1918* (Budapest, 1960), pp. 152–54; Count Michael Károlyi, *Fighting The World: The Struggle for Peace* (New York, 1925), p. 219.

4. Gusztáv Gratz, in *A forradalmak kora: Magyarország története 1918–1920* [The Age of Revolutions: The History of Hungary 1918–1920] (Budapest, 1935), discusses the history of the Revolution of 1918, as well as of the Proletarian Dictatorship of 1919, from a conservative point of view, but with a striving for objectivity. A more comprehensive and more positive evaluation of the Károlyi era is provided by the account of an active participant, Sándor Juhász Nagy, Minister of Justice in 1919, in *A magyar októberi forradalom története (1918. okt. 31–1919. márc. 21)* [The History of the Hungarian October Revolution, October 31, 1918–March 21, 1919] (Budapest, 1945). In addition, much useful though often strongly partisan, material of a factual and of an evaluative nature can be found in the rich memoir literature, written mostly in emigration and published abroad, of the leading participants in the democratic Revolution. Thus, for instance, Count Michael Károlyi, *Fighting the World* and *Memoirs of Michael Károlyi, Faith Without Illusion*, trans. Catherine Károlyi (London' 1956); Oscar Jászi, *Revolution and Counter-Revolution in Hungary* (London, 1924); Count Tivadar Batthyány, *Beszámolóm* [An Account of My Life] (2 vols., Budapest, n. d.) Vince Nagy, *Októbertől–októberig (Emlékiratok–Önéletrajz* [From October to October: Memoirs–Autobiography] (New York, 1962); (New York: 1962); Wilhelm Bőhm, *Im Kreuzfeuer Zweier Revolutionen:* (Munich, 1924); Ernő Garami, *Forrongó Magyarország* [Hungary in Turmoil] (Leipzig, 1922). A more recent Marxist contribution is Tibor Hajdú's *Az őszirózsás forradalom* ("The Chrysanthemum Revolution") (Budapest, 1963); see also Gábor Vermes, "The October Revolution in Hungary: From Károlyi to Kun" in Iván Völgyes, ed., *Hungary in Revolution, 1918–19*, (Lincoln, Nebraska, 1971).

5. The Royal Supreme Patronage included as its most significant prerogative the right of the Apostolic King of Hungary to fill the vacant bishoprics and other prelacies with large benefices with his appointees. The Pope would be only asked then to expedite the bull of "preconization."

6. Indeed, one of the very first acts of the new regime was to convene a conference of jurists, including experts in canon law, which was to provide the appropriate legal underpinning for the claim. The conference dutifully reported that "the present government is entitled, in virtue of legal succession, to the exercise of the royal prerogative, notwithstanding the changeover to a republic. The governing authority inherited the fullness of the royal prerogatives and the conference unanimously held that the viewpoint according to which the government is in possession of the right of supreme patronage, is acceptable also to canon law." [Quoted in Andor Csizmadia, A magyar állam és az egyházak jogi kapcsolatainak kialakulása és gyakorlata a Horthy korszakban [The Development and the Practices of the Legal Relationship between the Hungarian State and the Churches during the Horthy Era] (Budapest, 1966), pp. 97–99.) However, this was not the bishops' view. As Primate Csernoch informed Valfré di Bonzo, the Papal Nuncio in Vienna, in the opinion or the Bench of Bishops, "the right of Royal Supreme Patronage could in no way be transferred to the revolutionary government, but, in order to settle the issues arising out of this question, negotiations with the Holy See should be started." (Quoted ibid., p. 98 n.)

7. See Béla Balázs, ed., A klerikális reakció a Horthy-fasizmus támasza [Clerical Reaction as a Buttress of Horthy Fascism] (Budapest, 1953), pp. 17–20; Giesswein Emlékkönyv, p. 29.

8. See, for example, his editorial entitled "Szekularizáció"[Secularization] in the April 24, 1898 issue of Esztergom, a political and general weekly under the editorship of Prohászka; published in Az igazság napszámában, [Laboring for Truth] Vol XXI of Összegyüjtött munkái [Collected Works], pp. 52–54; also, "Mi segít rajtunk?" [What Would Help Us?] article in the July 7, 1905 issue of the periodical Egyházi Közlöny; published in Az Ur házáért [For the House of the Lord], Vol XX of Összegyüjtött munkái, pp. 75–78.

9. Quoted in Batthyány, Beszámolóm, II, 99.

10. One hold equals 0.57 hectares, or 1.42 English acres. On the eve of the World War I, the Hungarian Roman Catholic Church owned 1,525,191 hold of land. Of this 836,823 hold belonged to the estates of archbishoprics and bishoprics, 416,792 to cathedral chapters, 33,790 to the abbeys and provostship, 40,874 to cathedrals and seminaries, 196,912 to religious orders. In addition, the three great Catholic educational foundations owned 243,624 hold. See, Béla Bangha, ed., Katolikus Lexikon [The Catholic Encyclopaedia] (4 vols., Budapest, 1931–33) I, 492, 507. After Hungary's territorial losses in Trianon, the Catholic Church with 851,321 hold was still the greatest landowner. The lands of the Catholic foundations after 1920 amounted to 121,537 hold. Ibid.

11. Mihály Kerék, A magyar földkérdés [The Agrarian Question in Hungary] (Budapest, 1939), p. 151; Jászi, Revolution, p. 81

12. The provisions of "People's Law XVIII of 1919 on the Allocation of Land to the Agricultural Population," promulgated on February 16, 1919, are presented in detail by Kerék in A magyar földkérdés, pp. 152–57.

13. His biographer, Antal Schütz, writes that Prohászka, reluctantly yielding to the persistent urging of those solicitous for his welfare, left Budapest in disguise on the

evening of the revolution and returned to Székesfehérvár. *Sion hegyén* [On Mount Sion] Vol. XXV of *Összegyűjtött munkái*, p. 99.

14. See his editorial entitled "az új idők áramában" [In the Currents of the New Times] in the November 19, 1918 issue of the Catholic daily *Alkotmány;* published in *Iránytű,* [Compass] Vol. XXII of *Összegyűjtött munkái,* pp. 202–205. Prohászka spoke and wrote with admiration and enthusiasm about the blessings of American democracy with which he had become personally acquainted during his missionary tour of America in summer 1904. He ascribed the great vitality of American Catholicism primarily to the generosity of the faithful and the zeal of the priesthood, but in great measure also to the freedom the Church enjoyed. *Utak és állomások* [Journeys and Stations] Vol. XVI. of *Összegyűjtött munkái,* p. 272; *Korunk lelke* [The Soul of Our Age] Vol. X of *Összegyűjtött munkái,* p. 103.

15. Namely, the Catholic priest János Hock, president of the National Council, and Zoltán Jánosy, a Calvinist minister from Debrecen; both were members of the Károlyi party. (Gratz, *A forradalmak kora,* pp. 9–11).

16. Károlyi wanted to include the Christian Social People's Party into his government, but yielded to the violent opposition of the Social Democrats and abandoned this plan. (Batthyány, *Beszámolóm,* II, 80–81.) See also, Jenő Gergely, "keresztényszocialisták az 1918-as magyarországi polgári demokratikus forradalomban" [Christian Socialists in the 1918 Bourgeois Democratic Revolution in Hungary] *Történelmi Szemle,* XII (1969) 26–65.

17. Batthyány, *Beszámolóm,* II, 54. Batthány asserts that Jászi even proposed that the churches be allowed to retain all their property, if only the separation of church and state were achieved.

18. Juhász Nagy, *A magyar októberi forradalom története,* pp. 396–98.

19. For the governmental crisis of January, see, Gratz, *A forradalmak kora* pp. 75–80; Juhász Nagy, *A magyar októberi forradalom története,* pp. 399–421; Garami, *Forrongó Magyarország,* pp. 94–88.

20. Batthyány, *Beszámolóm,* II, 195–96; Sándor Raffay, "Eltolódások az állam és az egyház viszonyában" [Dislocations in the Relationship of State and Church] *Protestáns Szemle,* XXXIII (1924), 15–16; Balázs, *A klerikális reakció,* p. 201.

21. Csizmadia, *A magyar állam és az egyházak.* p. 97. On the basis of his claim to the rights of supreme patronage, Károlyi relieved of their office the 21 members of the committee for the supervision of Catholic funds and foundations and appointed new members in their stead. (Batthyány, *Beszámolóm,* II, 226–28.) The ministerial council held on March 21, 919, during the final hours of the regime, dealt among other things, with ecclesiastical appointments; two priests were named canons, and two others were appointed professors on the Faculty of Theology of the University of Budapest. (Bőhm, *Im Kreuzfeuer,* pp. 280–82; Batthány, *Beszámolóm,* II 189, 196.)

22. Batthyány, *Beszámolóm,* II, 157–58.

23. For a detailed description of the *coup d'état,* see, Tibor Hajdú *Március huszonegyedike; adatok a magyar tanácsköztársaság kikiáltásának történetéhez* [The Twenty First of March: Data concerning the History of the Proclamation of the Hungarian Soviet Republic] (Budapest, 1959).

24. For the history of the Hungarian Soviet Republic, see, in addition to the works of Gratz, Jászi, Bőhm, and Garami, previously cited—Rudolp L. Tőkés, *Béla Kun and the Hungarian Soviet Republic* (New York: Praeger, 1967); Zsuzsa L. Nagy, *Forradalom és ellenforradalom a Dunántúlon, 1919* [Revolution and Counter-Revolu-

tion in the Dunántúl 1919/ (Budapest, 1961); and István Deák, "Budapest and the Hungarian Revolutions of 1918–1919", *The Slavonic and East European Review*, XLVI (1968) 129–40.

25. "The Constitution of the Socialist Republic of Federated Councils of Hungary" (Adopted by the National Convention of Federated Councils on June 23, 1919) can be found in *A Magyar Tanácsköztársaság jogalkotása* [The Legislation of the Hungarian Soviet Republic] edited by Pál Halász, István Kovács, and Vilmos Peschka (Budapest, 1959), pp. 55–72. Although the constitution came into force formally only three months after the Communists took power, the principles contained in it were practiced even prior to its formal adoption. Thus, for example, the separation of church and state was declared as early as March 22, 1919, at the very first meeting of the Governing Council, and measures were taken for its implementation. (See, the study by Lajos Számel entitled "Kulturális igazgatás a Magyar Tanácsköztársaságban" [Cultural Administration in the Hungarian Soviet Republic] in Márton Sarlós, ed., *A Magyar Tanácsköztársaság állam és joga* [The Government and Laws of the Hungarian Soviet Republic] (Budapest, 1959), p. 146.

26. The decrees of the Hungarian Soviet Republic concerning education and matters related to religion and church affairs have been collected by Katalin Petrák and György Milei in *A Magyar Tanácsköztársaság művelődéspolitikája* [The Educational Policy of the Hungarian Soviet Republic] (Budapest, 1959).

27. For details, see János Lieber, "A kommunista egyházüldözés Magyarországon" [The Communist Persecution of the Church in Hungary] in Károly Huszár (ed.) *A proletárdiktatúra Magyarországon* [The Dictatorship of the Proletariat in Hungary] (Budapest, 1920), pp. 151–62; Gratz, *A forradalmak kora*, p. 116; Baron Albert Kaas and Fedor de Lazarovics, *Bolshevism in Hungary* (London, 1931), pp. 140–44; and Sándor Jankovich, "Az Egyház a Tanácsköztársaság idején" [The Church during the Soviet Republic] *Katolikus Szemle* (Rome) XXI (1969) 15–24; 121–31; 234–43; 346–56.

28. Thus, to allay the storm of general indignation, Commissar of Education Zsigmond Kunfi, had to issue a decree on April 17. 1818, "on the free exercise of religion and on the proclamation of religious freedom" which he ordered to be read form all pulpits. In the opening lines of the decree he reminded everybody that "the Republic of Soviets regards religion as the private affair of each individual and assures to each the free exercise of his religion." Therefore, "the Republic of Soviets regards all those who prevent anyone from freely exercising his religion or interfere with his free exercise as enemies of the revolutionary order." *(A Magyar Tanácsköztársaság művelődéspolitikája*, pp. 22–24.) It is also reported that when the Prince Primate complained in writing to the government about the excesses, Béla Kun himself replied and promised to redress the situation. See the essay by Sándor Orbán entitled "Az esztergomi érsekség a proletárdiktatúra ellen és az ellenforradalom felülkerekedéséért, 1919" [The Archbishopric of Esztergom Against the Dictatorship of the Proletariat and for the Victory of the Counter-Revolution] in László Zolnai, ed., *A Tanácsköztársaság napjai Esztergomban* [The Days of the Soviet Republic in Esztergom] (Budapest, 1960) pp. 109, 11. Still, on June 21, 1919, People's Commissar György Nyisztor found it imperative to speak up at the National Congress of Councils against the outrages committed against the religious sentiments of the people and to make the perpetrators of such acts responsible for the alarming rise of anti-Semitism and counter-revolutionary movements. See, A Magyar Szocialista Munkáspárt Központi Bizottságának Párttörténeti Intézete, *A magyar munkásmozgalom történetének válogatott dokumentumai* [Selected Documents from the History of the Hungarian Workers' Movement] (Budapest, (1960), VI 2, 208.

29. Balázs, *A klerikális reakció*, pp. 22–27.

30. For an account of the Red Terror, see Gratz, *A forradalmak kora*, pp. 125–54; also Bőhm, a member of Béla Kun's government, *Im Kreuzfeuer*, pp. 418–48.

31. Excerpts of the letter are quoted by Balázs, *A klerikális reakció*, pp. 29–30. According to a footnote, the Hungarian text of the quotations is translated from the Italian original, classified as no. 2910/1919 in the archives of the Prince Primate.

# III
# THE HUNGARIAN REVOLUTIONS
# AND HUNGARY'S NEIGHBORS

# THE HUNGARIAN REVOLUTIONS AND AUSTRIA

Helén Gábor

At the end of the First World War, in autumn 1918, the Austro–Hungarian Monarchy, containing many nationalities, disintegrated. The newly formed national successor states enjoyed the support of the Allies for their wartime roles. Strengthening them was also in the peacetime interest of the Allied Powers, particularly France, which angled for a leading role in Central Eastern Europe, replacing a weakened Germany. With allies in the East, Paris intended to secure a solid advantage in victory, and hoped to isolate, if not liquidate the Russian Socialist revolution. In accomplishing these aims, France could rely on the young bourgeois states.

In the two countries of the erstwhile Dual Monarchy, Austria and Hungary, there ensued, within a short time, great political, economic and social changes. In both countries, a liberal democratic revolution had been victorious. Each became independent republics with coalition-governments in which Social Democrats obtained ministry portfolios. On March 21, 1919, Hungary went further when it stood on the path of the Socialist revolution, with the creation of the Soviet Republic of Hungary.

These historic changes had taken place in hard circumstances, for the Habsburg empire bequeathed a legacy of hatred of the neighboring nations and the consequences of the ravages of war. Austria's territory was reduced from $676,000$ km$^2$ to $79,538$ km$^2$, its population declined from 51 to six-and-a-half million.[1] Hungary's area before the World War I, was $282,870$ km$^2$ –together with Croatia-Slavonia, $325,311$ km$^2$ –from this $92,833$ km$^2$ had remained and a population of 18,264,533 (20,886,487 with Croatia) was reduced to 7,615,117. Previously Austria received foodstuffs from Hungary, Galicia, and Bohemia, and was provided with coal by Poland, Bohemia, and Germany. On account of the independence movements, the animosity caused by the war, the peoples of these regions sabotaged the transport of provisions; by November 1918 they stopped it. The monarchy stood in need of grain imports even before 1914. During the war production decreased, the Allies had put a blockade into force, which they lifted with regard to Austria at the end of March 1919, but not in respect to Hungary. In Austria the provisioning was particularly grave, because its own harvest met only 25 percent of, the need in flour, 20 percent, in potatoes, 33 percent, in meat, 5 percent in lard, and 7 percent in sugar.[2]

Within the monarchy, Hungary's industry developed unevenly. During the war, production served, in the first place, the needs of the front line, yet it was unable to satisfy them. From among the manufactured goods consumer goods disappeared. The population became ragged. With the formation of the national states, Hungary lost lands that supplied raw materials for industry. A considerable part of heavy industry was also lost. The country was in dire need of coal, iron, petroleum, salt, textiles, shoes, and many other articles. The governments of Austria and Hungary had recognized that in spite of political independence, the economic interdependence of Austria and Hungary remained, and that the goal of foreign policy was increased cooperation.

On November 5, 1918, the two countries worked out an agreement, which was finalized within twenty days. This was the first interstate agreement between independent Hungary and Austria.[3] According to this barter contract, Hungary was to deliver 5000 tons of grain, 3000 tons of potatoes, 40,000 head of sheep, 4000 cattle on the hoof, 1500 slaughtered cattle, and 500 horses for slaughter.[4] In return, Austria was to deliver paper, medicine, chemicals, iron, salt, and textile goods.[5] As delivery stalled on both sides, smuggling between borderland towns became all the more intensive, especially from Moson, Sopron, Vas, and Zala counties.[6] Hungary's foodstuff transports were hampered by the lack of adequate supply. In January 1919, an American official, Philip L. Goodwin, sent a report from Budapest to Archibald Coolidge in Vienna, in which he rendered account of Hungary's dire financial situation, of the lack of coal and raw material; he also mentioned the provisioning difficulties, concerning fats in particular.[7] It was characteristic of the situation in Hungary that the Minister of Provisioning prohibited even the Hungarian Legation in Vienna from purchasing at home, and suggested that: "The legation-staff should adapt itself to the conditions of Vienna."[8]

Trade between the two countries had been impeded not only by the shortage of commodities, but also by the controversy about contested western Hungary. Austrian Christian Socialists demanded annexation; they also sent propagandists to the area to convince its population that they should join Austria; and they even prepared for armed attacks to achieve their goals. The Social Democratic leaders, Chancellor Karl Renner, and

Undersecretary of State for Foreign Affairs Otto Bauer, rejected such a solution, on the basis that the Social Democratic party stood for the right to free self-determination of peoples. They did, however, reserve the right, "on the basis of the Wilsonian principles [to] ask at the Peace Conference that the population should be allowed to exercise freely its right to self-determination."[9] Finally the Peace Conference adjudicated Burgenland with a German majority to Austria, but its transfer took place only in November 1921.[10] At any rate, the controversy about the proper place of western Hungary induced the Hungarian liberal democratic government, and then the Soviet government, to pay more attention to the needs of the German-speaking population living in Hungary.

Relations between the two former leading Habsburg states were characterized not only by antagonism, but also, since their Social Democratic parties, now having entered into power, shared a common political fight for the past several decades. The feeling of solidarity did not collapse along with the empire; in 1918–19 they conferred jointly on many questions. The reputation and the authority of the Austrian Social Democratic party's leaders influenced the policies of Hungarian Social Democrats. Similarly, a close connection also existed between the Communist parties of both countries, established in November 1918, but here the situation was the inverse of that of the Social Democrats. The Hungarian Communists were more experienced, more conscious of their aims and goals. It was they who assisted the Austrian Communist party, which struggled for a long time with opportunist, putschist, and sectarian views. Austrian Communists thought that a "resolute" small group would suffice to gain power; they did not pay sufficient attention to the organization of the masses. Yet, the effect of its propaganda surpassed by far the circle of its numerically insignificant membership. That was due principally to the susceptibility of the workers to revolutionary ideas. The party's influence on the *Volkswehr,* the armed forces, organized by the Social Democrats was extremely strong, too.

On the surface, both governments' policies bore striking similarities, if we consider only the main tendencies. Both endeavored to win the favor of the Allied Powers for the improvement of the situation of their countries; their middle class impeded the revolutionary movements with the help of the Social Democrats; they strove to build up a system based on private ownership, similar to the democracy of the western imperialist countries. But, the development of the revolutionary movements of the two countries diverged in direction, and by March 21, 1919, the two countries had different social systems.

The excited reaction of the Austrian conservatives and of the partisans of liberal democracy to Communism in Hungary could be gauged by the title of the *Neue Freie Presse's* morning editorial of March 23: "Bolshevism is at the gates of the city of Vienna." It warned the Allied Powers: "Getting through to Moscow is rather difficult, but Budapest lies nearby, since the starting of service of express trains, it lies close even to Paris...". The Social Democratic Party's *Arbeiter Zeitung* on the same day explained in an editorial, that in spite of similarities circumstances were different in Hungary and Austria. Hungary had foodstuffs, Austria did not; if the two countries took the revolutionary path, the distress of the masses would increase. When the Austrian envoy in Budapest informed him of the great event, Otto Bauer instructed the envoy by telephone to tell Béla Kun that "German–Austria cherished always the best and friendliest intentions towards the Hungarian state. These feelings will undergo no change at all–regardless of the internal politics of the new government." He stressed that Austria would not interfere in the internal affairs of Hungary, but neither should Kun pursue a propaganda which would aim at influencing Austria's internal politics.[11]

As a consequence of the news of the events in Hungary, the workers of Vienna demonstrated in the streets by the tens of thousands in support of the Soviet Republic; they held meetings at which the Communist leaders spoke. In the provincial industrial regions, enthusiasm ran equally high. As the Communist movement boomed, the number of people joining the party increased. On March 28, the Austrian Communists wrote the following to their Hungarian comrades: "Over here the situation is also such that in 3–4 weeks important events, similar to those in Hungary, will happen...".[12] When the Austrian workers learned that recruitment into the Hungarian Red Army had begun, many people volunteered from the factories in Wiener–Neustadt and its surroundings.[13] On April 3, 1200 people led by Leo Rothziegel arrived in Budapest–workers, members of the youth federation, and most of them Red guardsmen of the 41st Battalion of the *Volkswehr*–to fight "for the cause of the international proletariat."[14]

Before the arrival of the volunteers, Austrian workers and soldiers offered the Hungarian proletarian dictatorship weapons, ammunition, airplanes.[15] Undersecretary of State for Military Affairs Julius Deutsch, warned Commissar of the Artillery Arsenal Leo Fischer, not to give weapons to the Hungarians, they must remain neutral; nevertheless, he organized the smuggling of weapons to Hungary by trucks and airplanes.[16] Julius Deutsch winked to a certain extent at the deeds of those who broke his prohibition; he was only occasionally compelled to take steps against them. Naturally, too, the Soviet regime sent its men to Austria to buy weapons and foodstuff. Some were caught, but many were not.[17] Otto Bauer noted in 1923: "Officially we could not deliver armaments to Hungary, but the Social Democratic workers of the Wiener–Neustadt region had smuggled a considerable quantity of armaments through the Hungarian frontier unimpededly."[18] The Christian Socialist deputies in the National Assembly justly accused Julius Deutsch and Otto Bauer of not putting an end to smuggling.[19]

Austrian Social Democratic leaders believed that, in Austria, the establishment of a Soviet regime would be unrealistic and "unseasonable." But Bauer, and in particular Deutsch, as sincere Socialists, sympathized with the Hungarian Soviet Republic. They also knew that the international position of their country would be more advantageous as long as a proletarian dictatorship existed in Hungary. The Allies would rather send provisions to hold Austria back from imitating the Hungarian example. It was also hoped that Austria might receive a more favorable treatment at the Peace Conference, and might have a better prospect for annexing western Hungary and the Burgenland.

Social Democratic leaders had been put in a tight corner by the Austrian workers especially on two occasions. For, workers launched a militant grassroots movement to bring about Socialist change, on April 18, then on June 15.

On April 17, demobilized soldiers, invalids, and the unemployed published several demands, followed by a demonstration which ended at the houses of Parliament. Here the atmosphere was already so explosive that the demonstrators clashed with police, smashed windows, and set fires. They even disarmed a few policemen who were shooting and lashing out at the crowds with the flat of their swords. The demonstrators attacked so fiercely that the policemen had to draw back into the parliament building and refused to continue the fight against the workers. Then Friedrich Adler arrived in front of the parliament and spoke at length to the workers. Adler exercised his prestige on the Communists, who then decided to ask the trade-union stewards of the factories if they were willing to support the demonstrators by a general strike. After the police withdrew, *Volkswehr* formations had been ordered to set things right. The masses had confidence in them because many of the troop had participated in the demonstration. The members of the *Volkswehr* mingled with the demonstrators and said: "Not today, comrades! "[20] —as if only the postponement of the action would be the matter in question. A part of the demonstrators left the scene of the struggle with disappointment. They had participated in a revolutionary action with the expectation that they might bring about the rule of the proletariat. The clashes of April 17 resulted in six dead and more than fifty wounded.[21]

The Allies' decision to force the reduction in the size fo the *Volkswehr* by 25 percent precipitated the events of June 15. The allies originally wanted this *demarche* carried out by May 31. Under the influence of the mass movements, its execution was postponed to June 15. The postponement did not calm the masses, and the Communists organized more successful mass demonstrations. On June 5, 25,000 workers and *Volkswehr* members participated before the *Votivkirche* where it had been decided that, if necessary, they would refuse the Allied demands by force of arms. Communist leadership decided to prepare an armed uprising by June 15, aimed at routing the government from power and proclaiming the dictatorship in the name of the proletariat. According to the plans, workers were to be mobilized in the industrial area situated not far from Vienna. They were to seize local power on June 14. Planners expected that under the influence of the events, workers in the capital would then revolt and would suit.

The Social Democratic leaders knew about the preparations and tried to stem the course of events by dividing the revolutionary forces. The police had also been informed and on the evening of the 14th, when the Communists came together to discuss in detail the following day's action, the police surprised them and arrested 130 persons as well as the Communist guard.

Next day, when the workers learned of the arrest of their leaders, they proceeded to the prison where they were being held. Here they found themselves face to face with the city guard and with a police line. The repressive organs of the government made use of firearms. Twenty dead and eighty wounded remained on the spot of the clash.[22]

To calm tempers—and because the failure of the uprising was already certain—Eldersch, the Social Democratic minister for home affairs, released the Communists. The Social Democrats did not want a trial, for they wanted to avoid an open break with the Communists. They, therefore, entrusted the matter to the so-called parity commission, which consisted, besides the chairman, of two lawyers and two Social Democratic and two Communist members.[23] Because of this, the Christian Socialists violently attacked the Social Democrats.

Undoubtedly, the Hungarian Ernő Bettelheim played a part in the events of June in Vienna. Bettelheim, as the deputy of the Communist International was in Vienna from May on. He soon became a member of the board of the Austrian Communist party, of its directorate of four. His role in the uprising gave a chance to the Austrian reactionaries to attack the activities of the Hungarian Legation in Vienna, and its envoy, Ernő Czóbel. Undersecretary of State for Foreign Affairs Bauer, was forced to yield to the strong conservative and Allied pressure, and asked for Czóbel's departure. Czóbel left Vienna on July 11.

Bauer forwarded to Béla Kun a long, friendly letter, in which he gave a detailed analysis of the foreign and internal situation which ruled out chances for a Soviet republic in Austria. Simultaneously he stated that, in spite of the differences of opinions and tactics, the destiny and the interests of the two countries were closely interwoven, as a Hungarian counterrevolution would be dangerous for a Socialist Austria and an Austrian conterrevolution would transfer Austria into a launching pad of an attack against Hungary.[24]

The fact that Austria not only received Hungarian counterrevolutionaries, but did not even hinder their arming, contradicts to a certain extent Bauer's statement. It was from Austria that the counterrevolutionary emigration initiated armed attacks against Hungary. They robbed the Hungarian Legation in Vienna; they provided assistance to the domestic counterrevolutionary movements; they set up ties with the counterrevolutionaries of Szeged. Neither imprisonment nor expulsion came as a result of their activities. The deeds and punishment of the Hungarian Communists in Austria, however, had been publicized. The kind of treatment they received had presumably been influenced by the Vienna representatives of the Allies.

But even the presence in Austria of the Allies and their repeated objections could not impede the continuous existence of diplomatic, economic, and commercial ties during the life of the Soviet Republic of Hungary. Although with Allied approval and with certain restrictions, it was the Austrian Social Democrats, who, after the collapse of the Hungarian Soviet Republic, rendered the right of asylum to the Hungarian Social Democrats and Communists and their families.

On July 25, Otto Bauer was forced to resign his post of undersecretary of state for foreign affairs. On the following day, he addressed a long letter to Renner, who sojourned at that time in St. Germain, at the Peace Conference. This letter constitutes another proof of Bauer's honest, humane Socialist state of mind.

He was worried about the possibility that the administration of the affairs concerning the Soviet Republic of Hungary could fall into hostile hands. Therefore, he proposed that his secretary, Kautsky, should remain in his place, and that every file related to Hungary should *ante expeditionem* get into the Kautsky's hands. He also proposed that Austria should abstain from a clash with Soviet-Hungary and that it should not have any connection with the counterrevolutionary government of Szeged. Bauer suggested that Austria should take upon itself to mediate between the Allies and Hungary and should prevent, if possible, the delivery of weapons to the so-called successor states. In case of the Soviet regime's collapse, all political refugees should obtain the right of asylum.[25] This last proposal was put in force within one week, as on August 1, 1919, the Kun regime collapsed in Budapest.

## NOTES

1. Erich Zöllner *Geschichte Österreichs. Von den Anfängen bis zur Gegenwart* (Munich, 1961), p. 541–42.

2. Otto Bauer, *Die österreichische Revolution.* (Vienna, 123), p. 118–19. In other sources, the rate of import-needs differs from that indicated by Bauer, but all of them state grave shortages.

3. *Országos Levéltár* (hereafter *OL*), [Hungarian National Archives]/ *Külügyminisztérium (Küm)* (Ministry of Foreign Affairs), *Gazdaságpolitikai osztály* (Gazd. pol. oszt.) [Economic Policy Department] pcl 3. item A/4. 21596/1919.

4. *Ibid.*

5. *Ibid.,* pcl 11. item A/5. 611/1918.

6. *OL, Minisztertanács (MT)* [Council of Ministers] minutes, January 13, 1919, points 8.

7. Papers Relating to the Foreign Relations of the United States. The Paris Peace Conference 1919. Vol. I–XIII. (Washington, 1942–1947), [Papers PPC] Vol XII, p. 383–86.

8. *OL Küm. Bécsi követség iratai* [Papers of the Vienna Legation] pcl 4. 513/1919.

9. *Österreichisches Staatsarchiv (ÖSA)* [Austrian State Record Office]; *Neues Politisches Archiv (NPA)* [New Political Archive] Fasc. 990. Liasse Ungarn (LU) 9/1. 836/1.

10. See, Katalin Soós, *Burgenland az európai politikában* [1918–1921] (Budapest, 1971); Mrs. Sándor Gábor, *Ausztria és a Magyarországi Tanácsköztársaság.* (Budapest, 1969), pp. 46–59; 121–46.

11. *ÖSA,* NPA Fasc. 887. LU 2/3. 2611/4. 22 March 1919. Alfred D. Low, "The first Austrian Republic and Soviet Hungary," *Journal of Central European Affairs,* (1960), 2, p. 178.

12. *Párttörténeti Intézet* (PI) *Archívum* [Archives of the Institute of Party History of the Hungarian Socialist Workers' Party] f. 601. pcl 3. 29 March 1919.

13. *Ibid.,* April 1, 1919.

14. *Ibid.,* f. 606.

15. *Ibid.,* f. 601. pcl 3, March 25 and 28, 1919.

16. *ÖSA* Abt. *Verwaltungsarchiv (VA) Bundesministerium des Innern (BI)* 22/NÖ 5066. 17598/1919. May 14.

17. *ÖSA* NPA Fasc. 881. LU I/6. 3180/1919.; *Ibid.,* Präsidialakten 6. Ungarn. 4. 1641/1919.;*Ibid.,* Abt. VA BI 22/NÖ 5067. 25208/1919.

18. Bauer, *Die österreichische Revolution,* p. 138.

19. Protokoll der Konstituierenden Nationalversammlung. Session 25. July 26, 1919. p. 225. 126/I.

20. Sir Thomas Montgomery-Cuninghame: *Dusty Measure. A Record of Troubled Times* (London, 1941), p. 332.

21. *ÖSA* Abt. VA BI 22/NÖ 5066. 14185. and 14359/1919, April 18.

22. According to another source, there were 28, but really 60 dead and more than 200 wounded. *Die Kommunistische Internationale (1919),* 7–8, p. 1212. Police superintendent Schober writes in his report of 17 June about 18 dead. [*ÖSA* ABt. VA BI 22/NÖ 506. 23062/1919.]

23. PI Archivum f. 501. guarding unit 1/6, June 22, 1919.
24. *ÖSA* K. 262. Ungarn Varia. *Präsidialakten des Staatssekretärs* Dr. Otto Bauer, June 16, 1919.
25. *ÖSA* K. 261. *Präsidialakten des Staatssekretärs* Dr. Otto Bauer. II/b. 2170.

# ROMANIA AND SOVIET HUNGARY, 1919

Dinu C. Giurescu

"In Hungary, the proletariat headed by Comrade Béla Kun had seized power and set up a Soviet Republic. The new government got into touch with the Russian Socialist Republic. It was a great event which fell like a thunderbolt on the Entente imperialists...". That is how *Lupta socialistă* [the Socialist Struggle], a paper of the trade-union movement in Prahova county (Ploiesti), announced revolution in Hungary to its readers on March 24, 1919.[1] From late March to September 1919, Romania's workers repeatedly took a stand in favor of the Hungarian revolution; they did it unequivocally and firmly.

The expressed it in many and sundry ways. To begin with, news items were regularly inserted in the workers' press. *Socialismul* [Socialism], the official paper of the Socialist Party of Romania, printed "The Declaration and the Call of the Hungarian Soviet Government..." on March.[2] Reprinting news from *Der Abend,* it pointed out that on the day after the seizure of power —that is, on 22 March—there was "perfect peace and order" in Budapest and that "throughout that morning, telegrams from all over the country had made it known that there was complete order everywhere."[3]

There is no point in giving a full account of the news that continued to be published about the favorable course of the revolution in Hungary. Romanian readers, thus, came to know about the new constitution and electoral law,[4] Béla Kun's personality,[5] and the interview he gave to *Excelsior*[6]; the proceedings of the Hungarian Socialist-Communist Congress (July 1919);[7] the struggle of the revolutionary government in Budapest against internal reaction; and the Communist International's appeal for the defense of the Hungarian Soviet Republic.[8]

Favorable prospects were opening up to the European proletariat—especially in Austria and Germany—owing to the success of the revolution in Russia and Hungary; that was the comment of the Bucharest *Socialismul* July 11, 1919.[9]

There were naturally a number of moves to make common cause with the revolution. In the directives given by the leadership of the Socialist Party of Romania for the May Day celebrations, stress was laid on the following: "...Pay heed to the army as well. The military power of the bourgeoisie must be broken up. Leaflets for the soldiers. Demand non-interference of the army against socialism in Hungary and Russia. The soldiers are not to fire on their brothers...."[10] Support and approval of the Russian and Hungarian revolutions were voiced at various meetings, such as those of the railwaymen at the Giuleşti Workshops on 1 April;[11] at Galatz;[12] at the Paşcani railway dépot—the latter meeting was commented on as follows in a note sent by the State Security Service to the General Army Headquarters (on 29 June): "... Mr Zaharia Tănase-Iasi and Dragomir Ioan, the trade union secretary, made an incendiary speech, impugning the government, the policy, the army and the gendarmes, inciting to rebellion and bolshevism, and stigmatizing the measures taken against the bolsheviks in Russia and Hungary."[13] Similar feelings were also voiced at Mureş Uioara (Marosújvár),[14] at Tulcea and Sibiu,[15] Ploieşti, Cîmpina, Baicoi, Moreni, and Tintea,[16] and also by a delegation of the Executive Committee of the Socialist Party of Romania and of the General Trade Union Commission, at an audience with the Minister of Home Affairs, Gh. Mârzescu.[17]

There were also strikes in protest. In April in Bucharest (the Vulcan metal workers and the printers of the *Universul* newspaper); in June, the railwaymen of Bucharest, Craiova, Turnu Severin, Cluj (Kolozsvár), Iassy, Galatz, Contantza, Brăila...[18] Then the general strike of July 21, 1919 following the call of the leadership of the Third International in support of Soviet Russia and of Soviet Hungary.[19]

It was effective in Bucharest, where it involved 17 metalworking plants, 10 woodworking plants, and 12 units of various types (the Army Workshops included)[20] and also at Ploieşti,[21] Cîmpina, Galatz, Brăila, and Buzău.[22]

The strikes gave rise to confidence, which was euphorically expressed in the July 23, 1919 editorial of *Socialismul*:

What power resides in the workers of the world, who are not divided into camps, but are all swooping upon an enemy who will arrest the progress of the world to serve their interests, upon capitalism!

A formidable force but not a destructive one; it is a force creating social contentment!

It is plain that this force is now on the march. Its first call on 21 July, which sounded the alarm, has been heard. Nothing can be imagined or devised to prevent the other bugles from being heard and followed, for the slogan—liberation—already pulsates in the hearts of all.[23]

It is significant to note the conclusions drawn by the Ministry of Home Affairs in Bucharest on the day following the sympathy strike: "... the constant unrest kept up among the workers by the red trade unions and the demonstrations of an international nature of the socialist party, especially those aiming to paralyze the policy of the Romanian state and to promote the progress of the communists in Hungary and in Russia, with whom we are at war, makes it obvious that the Marxist current still prevails in the Central Committee of the Socialist Party... ."[24] In sum state security concluded that a pro-Communist (Bolshevik) trend was prevalent in the Socialist leadership.

In order to complete the picture we have sketched here, we should also mention the Romanian volunteers who fought in the Hungarian Red Army, whether organized in separate battalions,[25] or as part of Magyar political units.[26] The volunteers printed leaflets for "their suffering brothers in the Romanian army"[27] and for their "Romanian brothers," urging them to turn their weapons "against the Romanian boyars, the Hungarian nobility and the moneyed people, against the capitalist rascals and imperialists."[28]

The protests of the Socialists and Communists in Romania against the intervention in Hungary (August 1919) should likewise be mentioned, as should also their vehement condemnation of the repressions unleashed by the new Hungarian authorities against Communists and their sympathizers. A year after the collapse of the Béla Kun government, the Congress of the Socialist Party of Transylvania and Banat passed (on August 15–16, 1920) a motion of solidarity with the Russian Revolution and the Soviet Republic in Hungary, while *Socialismul* (August 8, 1920), pointed out when commenting on the aforementioned events: "But in view of the interests of the Romanian people, it was, and still is, more important to have on our borders a proletarian state showing no chauvinism, no conquering lust... and only taking up arms when capitalist enemies, whether national or international, seek to overwhelm them."[29]

When examined in the light of class interests, the relations between the Romanian workers and their political parties on the one hand, and the Hungarian workers and Soviet Hungary on the other hand, show the solidarity of the workers of the two nations in striving to defeat a common enemy: the bourgeoisie and national and international capitalism. Considered from this standpoint, aims, feelings and activities were very similar.

Nevertheless, in order to outline the evolution *in 1919* of the relations between Romania and Soviet Hungary and between the Romanian and the Hungarian nations as a whole, two other fundamental facts should be considered:

a) the social and political forces in the two countries, which declared for private ownership of the means of production, for capitalism, and for a pluralistic parliamentary system within a bourgeois democracy;
b) the new territorial configuration is Southeast Europe as a result of the exercise, in 1918, of the right to self-determination of the nationalities in the Austro–Hungarian monarchy.

In 1919—a year of great, manifold strains—the three predominant realities—the workers, the middle class and the unitary national state—conditioned one other while evolving under the circumstances characteristic of that stage of history, interacted with the relations between the great powers.

In this brief paper, I have so far given an account of the concepts and actions of the Romanian proletariat toward Soviet Hungary, on strict class interests.

I will now take the liberty of dealing with the other two fundamental realities, with their essential motivations, and mandatory requirements.

For the Romanian middle class (as well as for the Hungarian middle class), and for all the political forces supporting a plural parliamentary democracy in all the countries of Europe, the proclamation of the Hungarian Soviet Republic and its possible consolidation—occurring after the victory of the Socialist Revolution in Russia—was a most serious threat. Under the special conditions prevailing during the first half of 1919, more precisely during the first months after the hostilities had come to an end on the western front, the confrontation between the working class and the middle class took place, with various degrees of intensity, on a national as well as a European scale. It was an antagonistic confrontation which became a direct clash after the Hungarian Communists had assumed power.

The response of the Bucharest government—headed by Ion I. C. Brătianu—was prompt: all the more so as the country was confronted with Soviet Russia to the east, and now with Soviet Hungary to the west, both of them promoting a political, social, and economic system totally opposed to the one existing in Romania.

Consequently, it is not surprising that a fair number of the Romanian publications of those days should have described the government and the administration established in Budapest on March 21 in the darkest colors, for they were considered as a direct threat to European peace and stability. Even a brief survey will show the similarity—if not the identity—of the analyses and the positions adopted by the forces opposed to Communism in Romania as well as in Hungary (and in the other countries of the continent, irrespective of the confrontations or the divergencies existing between the various states).

This was the situation in which the talks between the Supreme Allied Council and the Béla Kun-headed government took place. Contacts were made at the time between the Entente countries to decide on the organization of a collective military move against the Budapest regime (the talks, which remained in an exploratory stage, are irrelevant here).[30]

The third fundamental reality—the territorial configuration that resulted after the exercise of the right to self-determination—a right which was stated and recognized in 1917 and in 1918 by the new Soviet Russian government as well as by the main Entente powers. This third reality was at work simultaneously with the former two and was above the class interests and objectives in 1919.

Without going into such details as the proposals and counterproposals made and the provisional decisions envisaged for the lining up of the troops, this survey will try to outline the essential objects of the two governments—in Bucharest and Budapest—with regard to the territorial configuration in Southeast Europe.

On various occasions, as well as in a special report on the foreign policy of the Hungarian Soviet Republic (submitted on 19 June, 1919), Béla Kun set forth the views of his government.

He saw the new Hungarian frontiers proposed by the Entente powers during the March—June 1919 interval as being unacceptable: "...the territories bounded by those frontiers are such as to make it impossible for us ever to ensure decent means of existence to the proletariat even if the resources offered by modern international trade were to be made the maximum use of."[31]

Kun also stated that in 1919, the right to self-determination actually amounted to an annexation policy. An official statement on the foreign policy of Soviet Hungary went on to specify:

In actual fact, the right of the nations to self-determination only achieves a distribution of the controversial territories by authority.... The best example is the territory of ancient Hungary; the Entente imperialism has interpreted the right of the nations to self-determination in such a manner that it has merely had its armed forces occupy the controversial territories and moreover regions which from its own point of view would not give rise to any disputes.... This only amounts to an annexation policy.[32]

States made up of, or rounded off to include, territories belonging to what had been the Austro—Hungarian monarchy were described by the Hungarian Communists as "so-called national states and so-called new national republics..." These states were identified as being under the suzerainty of the Entente. Béla Kun added that they:

are carrying on an imperialistic policy. ...the armed intervention of the states under the suzerainty of the Entente, whose imperialism was hungering after more voracious-ly than any one else.[33]

The first Congress of the Soviets in Hungary stated the Soviet Republic not only refuses to adopt a position in support of territorial integrity" but that it has put an end to the oppression of national minorities and "pro-claims the right to self-determination for the workers of all nations."[34]

*Socialismul* made most favorable comments on Kun's proposals in the note transmitted to the Czechoslovak, Yugoslav, and Romanian govern-ments on May 1. The note stated the following: "We unreservedly recognize all your national-territorial claims." In exchange, the Budapest government demanded immediate cessation of hostilities, noninterference in domestic affairs, and the conclusion of suitable economic conventions.[35]

When the military situation on the "northern" front—in Slovakia—evolved in favor of the Hungarian Soviet Republic, with the Slovak Socialist Republic being proclaimed on June 16, Béla Kun again officially voiced his desire to conclude peace with the neighboring states.[36]

The kind of peace he envisaged, however, was stated in the report on his foreign policy, which was read on June 19: "From our standpoint, it could indeed be no other peace than one of the kind similar to that of Brest—Litovsk or of Bucharest, that is a peace which would inevitably be unsettled and cancelled by a revolution...."[37]

In 1919 the politicians and public opinion well knew that the Brest—Litovsk peace signed by the Russian Soviet Federative Socialist Republic with the Central Powers on March 3, 1918, had been cancelled eight months later, in November 1918, when Germany and Austria—Hungary had ended hostilities. The idea of a provisional peace similar to the one signed at Brest—Litovsk, had been put forward by Béla Kun on other occasions as well.[38]

Soviet Hungary's relation with her neighbors was shaped according to the view that "the watchword of the proletariat was not the creation of small states but the grouping of the proletariat in a federation that was to be as extensive as possible."[39]

Until that aim was attained, until a more comprehensive federation was established (naturally under the aegis of the dictatorship of the proleta-riate), a peace might possibly be negotiated, with stress laid more particular-ly on mutual economic interests. "Let us consequently build up a new eco-nomic life on the ruins of the late Austro—Hungarian monarchy and on those of the Balkans...." This was all the more possible as trade relations, according to the views of the Hungarian revolutionary government, should be developed primarily with the neighboring countries, "with the countries which formerly made up an economic community with us."[40]

These notions on the 1918–19 events and those put forward by the Romanians relating to the same events were poles apart. In 1918, the Romanian nation had exercised its right to self-determination by its accredited deputies at widely representatitve assemblies which voiced the will and the interests of the main social classes and categories, workers included. From September to November 1918, the Romanian nation in Transylvania, Banat, Körös (Crişana) and Máramaros (Maramures) had of its own accord, without the support of the Romanian army from the Romanian kingdom, shown its bent, and on December 1, 1918, had decided for the Great Union.[41]

The Brătianu government made it its primary aim to achieve a unitary national state, to consolidate the Great Union achieved in 1918 and to have it recognized by the international treaties. The government opposed the formation of an economic community incorporating several states. With these objectives in view, the government had the unconditional support of the whole Romanian nation, including the working class.

The Congress of the Social-Democratic Party of Transylvania and Banat held at Sibiu (Nagyszeben) on January 19–20, 1919, passed a special resolution declaring its full agreement with the activities and the decisions of its representatives at the Alba Iulia National Assembly. The following statement is made in the resolution: "The Congress avers that the union of the Romanian people in a single independent state is a historic necessity based on the right of all the peoples to free self-determination—and Romanian social-democracy did not in any way diverge from the principles established by the international socialist congresses..."[42]

On February 17, March 2, 1919, the Socialist Party and the Trade-Union Association in their turn published in *Socialismul* a declaration stating among other things:

In accordance with the right of the nations to self-determination—a principle recognized by international socialism as a whole—the Romanians of the subjugated territories, in the decisions of their national assemblies, voiced their will to be united to Romania on the basis of the resolutions that had been passed.

In our capacity as internationalist Romanian socialists, we joyfully greet the national liberation of the Romanian people in the provinces that had been subjected up till now and will observe the conventions decided by the union.

The Socialist Party of Romania—the representative of the working class—pledges to militate together with the workers in the territories united to Romania, for the observance of the freedom and of the rights that have been won, and considers it a point of honour to observe the rights of the minorities of other nationalities in every field, whether economic, political or cultural.

"Today's new Romania must become tomorrow's socialist Romania."[43]

The Declaration we have quoted from was passed by the same Socialist Party of Romania which from April to July 1919, was most resolutely to support Soviet Hungary, as we have already pointed out.

A comparison between the relevant documents, therefore, unequivocally shows that the concepts and interpretation of the events which occurred in 1918 were poles apart in Romania and in Hungary as regards the right to national self-determination and the formation of unitary national states in Southeast Eurpe. There was no conciliation possible at the time. This essential fact, with the territorial changes it involved, went beyond class trends, inspiring the nations as a whole. With antecedents stretching over many centuries, it determined the decisions made and the steps taken from March to July 1919 by the two sides, with the results well-known to all.

What is left today of the feelings and activities of solidarity voiced and carried out in 1919 with revolutionary enthusiasm by the workers of the two nations? Due consideration being given to the developments and transformations that have taken place in the intervening 66 years, we might conclude that the message of cooperation, friendship, and mutual support sent out in 1919 is of present-day interest.

The history of the two nations—the Romanian and the Hungarian—spreading over more than a thousand years, cannot be separated, whether one or the other should want to recognize the fact or not. Nevertheless, the history of the two nations remains unchanged, even though a number of interpretations are too much imbued with resentment.

History repeatedly offers occasions to make a choice. For the better or the worse. With trends impelling toward drawing apart from one another or, on the contrary, for drawing nearer, for cooperation. The appeals launched in 1919, despite their romantic strain, preserve their significance to this day. They prompt us to act accordingly.

## NOTES

1. *In Support of the Hungarian Soviet Republic. Solidarity of the Working People of Romania with the Hungarian Soviet Republic, 1919. Documents and Recollections* (Bucharest, 1969), p. 55. Hereafter cited as *1919, Documents.*
2. *1919. Documents,* pp. 56–57.
3. *1919. Documents,* p. 58.
4. *1919. Documents,* pp. 76, 63–64, 114–15.
5. *1919. Documents,* p. 77.
6. *1919. Documents,* p. 94.
7. *1919. Documents,* pp. 108–109.
8. *1919. Documents,* pp. p. 110, p. 113.
9. *1919. Documents,* pp. 110, 113, 118, 120–23.
10. *1919. Documents,* p. 78.
11. *1919. Documents,* p. 65.
12. *1919. Documents, p. 79.*
13. *1919. Documents,* p. 111.
14. On June 19, 1919; see the note of July 10 by the General of State Security of Sibiu. At a restricted meeting of mechanics and miners, Marian Drăghici enjoined: "...no one is to serve in the army or fight against the Budapest workers, for they are our brothers, and why should we shed our blood for the capitalists?," in *1919. Documents,* p. 117.
15. *1919. Documents,* pp. 240–43, 286–88.
16. *1919. Documents,* pp. 263–64.
17. *1919. Documents,* p. 93.
18. *1919. Documents,* p. 25.
19. *1919. Documents,* pp. 119, 26, 124–25.
20. *1919, Documents,* pp. p. 129.
21. At a meeting attended by 1200 in the courtyard of the Trade Union, V. Iordăchescu, a metal worker, demanded that "no one should interfere where the comrades had awakened an hour earlier than we did, for example in Russia and in Hungary...." He continued that "These two countries must be allowed to rule themselves, as requested by Béla Kun, president of the soviets in Hungary, and a fair peace should be concluded with all countries...," in *1919. Documents,* pp. 131–32.
22. *1919, Documents,* p. 136.
23. *1919. Documents,* pp. 113–35.
24. *1919. Documents,* p. 36.
25. *1919. Documents,* pp. 36–37, 70–72, 75, 99–100.
27. *1919. Documents.* For example, the manifesto published by the Romanian Communist Party in Hungary, April 1, 1919 and another on May 1, 1919, in *1919. Documents,* pp. 66–67, 82.
28. *1919. Documents,* pp. 83–86.
29. *1919. Documents,* p. 197.
30. See Constantin Kiritescu, *Istoria războiului pentru întregirea României* (Bucharest, ?), III, 396–428, 430–37; Geoghe Unc and Vladimir Zaharescu, "Din cronica relatiilor romano–ungare în anii 1918–1920," *Analele de istorie,* Vol. XXVII, (1981), No. 5, 105–26; Mircea Musat, Ion Ardeleanu, *De la statul geto-dacic la statul român unitar* (Bucharest, 1983), pp. 644–55.

31. Béla Kun, *La République Hongroise des Conseils. Discours et articles choisis* (Budapest, 1962), p. 197.

32. Kun, *La République Hongroise*, p. 19.

33. Kun, *La République Hongroise*, pp. 191, 197–98.

34. Kun, *La République Hongroise*, p. 204, 129.

35. Kun, *La République Hongroise*, pp. 87–89.

36. Kun, *La République Hongroise*, pp. 197–98.

37. Kun, *La République Hongorise*, p. 198; The Peace Treaty of Bucharest was forced on Romania by the Central Powers on May 7, 1918. On November 10, 1918, a day before Germany signed the Armistice at Compiègne, Romania declared war on Germany.

38. Kun, *La République Hongroise*, p. 204.

39. Kun, *La République Hongroise*, p. 202.

40. Kun, *La République Hongroise*, p. 202.

41. For details, see Stefan Pascu, *Făurirea Statului national unitar român 1918* (Bucharest, 1983), Vol. II, 131–270; Musat and Ardelenau, *De la statul geto-dacic*, pp. 654–99.

42. *Documente din istoria mişcării muncitoreşti din România 1916–1921* (Bucharest, 1966), p. 157.

43. *Documente*, pp. 166–67.

# THE YUGOSLAV GOVERNMENT
# AND THE COUNTERREVOLUTION IN HUNGARY, 1919–1920

Vujica Kovačev

News of the proclamation of the Soviet Republic in Hungary on March 21, 1919 was received in Yugoslavia with surprise not only in official political circles but also by the Social Democratic parties which were at the time busy trying to unite into a single party. As a preventive measure against the events in Hungary, the Serb Supreme Military Command organized greater control along the demarcation line. They even went so far as to dismantle railway lines between Yugoslavia and Hungary and to sever all telephone and telegraph communication between the two states.

Matters became clearer only at the end of March after the arrival of Lieutenant-Colonel Fernand Vix and the Allied Military Mission in Belgrade and Vix's statement about the situation in Hungary. The proclamation of a Soviet Republic in a neighboring country posed new problems for the Yugoslav government which had, a little earlier on, at the beginning of January 1919, sent a representative delegation to Paris backed by a group of the country's most distinguished economists, lawyers, historians, ethnologists, geographers, and others, to prepare Yugoslavia's demands and to hold negotiations on Yugoslavia's future definite frontiers. What had now happened was that a new danger had appeared in her immediate vicinity—that of Bolshevism, which threatened to spread to Yugoslavia. Although the proclamation of the Soviet Republic meant less danger of a restoration of the Habsburg monarchy in Hungary, something that Yugoslavia's politicians had been fervently fighting against after the war, the danger of Communist propaganda was also present because the ideas from Russia were also popular with Yugoslavian workers.

The newly created situation in Hungary led to numerous crossings across the demarcation line by sympathizers of the *ancien régime* who rallied in Serb-occupied Baranya county and particularly in the town of Pécs which was something that the Yugoslav military authorities did not take kindly to; in fact, they tried to have them transferred as quickly as possible to Arad or Szeged where the French military command took them under its wing. Some French military circles directly encouraged their efforts to rally and organize, hoping that they would be useful to them for the intervention in Hungary. And so, under the protection of these officers, a counterrevolutionary government under Count Gyula Károlyi was formed in Arad on May 5, with direct encouragement and assistance from General Henri Léopold Gondrecourt and Captain Saint Laumer.[1] The number-one task in the government's program was the overthrow of Soviet rule in Hungary along with help from the Entente and the formation of a national army. At the end of May, this government had transfered its headquarters to the town of Szeged where it intensified its action to rally reactionary officers and to create its own military detachments. But, the French command was also made up of officers like General Paul de Lobit who did not foster any particular sympathies for the Hungarian aristocracy and counterrevolutionaries, and although they did not allow them to hold their military demonstrations along the demarkation line, they did not directly prevent them from rallying in the town of Szeged.[2]

After the proclamation of the Hungarian Soviet Republic, the Yugoslav government did not wish to have any contacts, not even diplomatic ties, with the Hungarians, and to begin with, it only had an unofficial representative in Budapest who was in charge of consular affairs. It was not until the beginning of May that Mirko Petrović was sent to Hungary. His prime task was to follow the work of the Yugoslav Communist organization in Hungary and to report back to the responsible organs in Yugoslavia on their activites.[3]

At the time, the statements made by Commissar for Foreign Affairs, Béla Kun, that Hungary recognized the existing borders and had no territorial pretensions on Yugoslavia, had a soothing effect on the Yugoslav government. An attempt was made by the Hungarian side to establish closer relations between the two countries. Wishing to ensure lasting peace on the southern demarkation line, Kun sent his envoy, József Diner-Dénes, to Belgrade at the beginning of April 1919. He had already been to Belgrade several times as the confident of Count Mihály Károlyi, and Aleksandar Jovanović, a state Official of high rank, in Soviet Hungary. Prime Minister Stojan Protić did not wish to meet them but they were received by an official in the Foreign Affairs Ministry by the name of Mihailo Gavrilović with whom they discussed relations between the two countries. The talks were not particularly successful but they were informed of Protić's message that the Yugoslav army would not intervene in Hungary. This surprise visit was recorded in the

Yugoslav press and was also known in the diplomatic circles. Fontenay, the French envoy, reported it to the French government, assessing it as Hungarian tactics to stall matters until military aid was forthcoming from Soviet Russia.[4] Henry Percival Dodge, the American envoy, also informed his government about the matter.[5]

Meanwhile, there was a great deal more traffic by the emissaries of various Hungarian counterrevolutionary political circles who sought contacts with the Yugoslav government and its military organs. The majority of these envoys were armed with recommendations from high-ranking French officers, the most active among them being Louis Franchet d'Esperey, although none of these missions had any visible success in negotiating with the Yugoslav authorities. Archduke József himself wanted to make a personal appearance in Belgrade to negotiate joint action for the restoration of the old order in Hungary but the Yugoslav government most emphatically rejected the offer. Hence, Captain Gyula Gömbös, his plenipotentiary, arrived in Belgrade at the beginning of April and was followed by the representative of the Viennese Anti-Bolshevik Committee, Count György Pallavicini. Both conducted talks on the possibility of organizing White units in Baranya. The proposal was, however, categorically rejected by the Yugoslav side because the formation of the units would present a latent danger to Yugoslavia itself. The negotiations were subsequently conducted in Szeged.[6]

At the end of April, Archduke József made another attempt to come into contact with the Yugoslav government by sending two of his officers to Belgrade where nobody wanted to talk to them. The military authorities were thus ordered to escort them, as officers, to a prisoners of war camp in Požarevac.

Count István Bethlen also decided to send someone from Vienna to Belgrade in April. His choice was Viktor Balás, an engineer, who went to the Foreign Affairs Ministry for talks on the formation of White Hungarian detachments in the town of Baja and Baranya, in return offering political concessions once the old regime had been restored in Hungary. He too fared no better and was quickly banished to Austria.[7]

At the beginning of June, two representatives were sent, by the Szeged government, to Belgrade for negotiations. Their mission was also connected with the formation of counterrevolutionary units in the territory of Yugoslavia. And since they too achieved nothing, Miklós Horthy and Count Pál Teleki were sent to Belgrade from June 20–25 for talks on the same issue but Prime Minister Protić categorically rejected their demands.

During June, a large number of Hungarian officers fled to Yugoslavia. On this occasion, the Yugoslav military authorities made a concession and instead of dispatching them to a prisoner of war camp as they had done on previous occasions, they conducted them to Szeged and handed them over to the Hungarian authorities there.

At the end of July, Count Teleki made another attempt at convincing the Yugoslav government to allow the mobilization of the Hungarian population in Szabadka (Subotica) Baja, and Baranya, and asked that military equipment be supplied for the units.. All these demands were once again turned down and the Supreme Command of the Yugoslav Army forbade the arrival of White officers for the purpose of soliciting soldiers.[8]

Because the attitude of the Yugoslav government and the military mission towards the Hungarian White emigrés in their endeavors to become militarily organized in the town of Szeged was not particularly friendly, contacts between the counterrevolutionaries from Soviet Hungary and those in Szeged had to pass along illegal channels across Yugoslav-controlled territory. The courier service was usually operated by young officers.[9]

The initiative to collect the military materiel necessary to overthrow the revolutionary government in Hungary was taken by French politicians and military commanders. It did not, however, meet with enthusiastic support from the governments of the United States and Great Britain which were reluctant to engage their armies and were in favor of having matters solved peacefully. Similarly, the government of Italy was itself not prepared to allow its soldiers to take part in the expedition.

Yugoslavia which was engaged in a struggle to establish definitive state boundaries did not want its soldiers, who were poorly equipped and exhausted from a long war, to enter into the adventure of intervention. It was, in fact, satisfied with the territory it had grasped; it also had numerous problems to contend with, both of an internal nature and threats from outside from the Italians, Bulgarians, and Romanians who wanted to appropriate some of the territories that had come under Belgrade's control. Thus, the Yugoslav government was ready to engage in an intervention provided the big powers made certain concessions in return and gave guarantees that there would be no attacks from neighboring states.

The first initiative at rallying the interventionist forces came from the French politicians as early as the beginning of April and was furthered by the Greek Foreign Minister Nikola Politis who made a proposal in Paris to the representatives of Yugoslavia, Romania, Czechoslovakia, and Poland, to launch a broader drive against Soviet Hungary.[10] A few days later, a meeting of these representatives took place at which the details of a military intervention were discussed. Under pressure from France, the Yugoslav government sanctioned the participation of its Danube Division which numbered 16,000 men, but it did its best, at the same time, to prevent these units from actually taking part in the operations.[11] Chief-of-Staff of the Supreme Command Živojin Mišić informed General, de Lobit of the conditions of such an involvement and asked that the units be used only for the purpose of an offensive and not for that of holding Hungarian territory under occupation. He also asked for the necessary military equipment in order to prepare for battle.[12]

In the midst of preparations for the offensive, bad feelings were fanned by a statement made by General Franchet d'Esperey who believed that once the *Commune* was overthrown, Archduke József should assume the throne. This set off a wave of sharp protest. His statement led to anxiety in Belgrade, and the Yugoslav representatives at the Peace Conference in Paris lodged a sharp protest note with the French government on April 19, lamenting the combinations that were being made to bring a Habsburg to the Hungarian throne.[13]

In the meantime, on April 16, a full-scale offensive had been launched by the Romanian army on the Eastern Front in which the Romanians managed to break down the Hungarian defense and to advance unhampered towards Tisza. Taking advantage of the confusion in Hungary, the Czech offensive on the Northern Front started on April 27, and it too was successful. As the Romanian and Czech troops achieved what they had set out to do by their offensive, there was no need for the French, Yugoslav, and other troops to engage in battle.

However, the great successes scored by the reorganized Hungarian Red Army in the operations against the Czechoslovak army in the May–June offensive obliged Entente forces to undertake more serious preparations for the final overthrow of Soviet Hungary, which, in June, was feeling the effects of counterrevolutionary plots and revolts. Moreover, after Georges Clemenceau's notes and the withdrawal of the Red Army from Slovakia, the fighting spirit of Hungarian soldiers suffered a serious blow which led to a general decline in their fighting power.

A top-level conference was called in Paris on July 11, to discuss the intervention in Hungary. It was attended by the representatives of Romania, Czechoslovakia, and Yugoslavia, with the participation of the French. Its aim was to reach an agreement over the collection of military materiél. Clemenceau expressly asked the participants in the conference to prevail upon their governments to determine what men and equipment they could spare to place at the disposal of the Allied command for an offensive to be launched. Marshal Ferdinand Foch was assigned the task of elaborating and submitting a plan of operation.

Fully conscious of the fact that there was no more room for stalling, Yugoslav Foreign Minister Ante Trumbić telegraphed Belgrade to inform it of the seriousness of the situation and asked the government to take a decision in the matter and to designate the units which would be taking part in the operations.[14] The government gave its permission without further ado, and the Supreme Command informed the allies that its troops would be taking part in the intervention in the following composition: one infantry regiment, one mounted brigade, and artillery.[15]

While the preparations for the operations were in full swing, along with a lot of bargaining over how many troops would be taking part, the Hungarian Red Army lauched a desperate offensive, on July 20, on the Eastern Front against Romania. After a good start, the offensive gradually began to lose steam. As the pressure let up, the Romanian forces organized a counter-offensive and began to repulse the Red Army units in the direction of Budapest.

Meanwhile, in Paris, a decision had been reached to cede a part of Banat with Temesvár to Romania which was met with protest in Yugoslavia. The decision, however, was irreversible, and Yugoslav troops withdrew from Temesvár on July 27.

This was one of the reasons why the Yugoslav army did not take part in the intervention in Hungary. The decision not to participate was also in part due to the fact that the Yugoslav workers had launched a successful general strike on July 20–21, against intervention in Soviet Russia and Hungary.[16]

At the end of July, under pressure from the Romanian troops, the Eastern Front fell. The troops marched undisturbed on Budapest, where, on August 1, the Soviet government was compelled to resign, and power was turned over to a "trade union government" with Gyula Peidl at the head. The same day, a large number of Soviet government members and other fighters of the revolution left the country to become emigrés. Romanian troops entered Budapest on August 4.

Victory over Hungary caused great jubilation in Bucharest and the whole of Romania. Yugoslavia's military envoy in Bucharest was able to report, on August 9, on the general enthusiasm of the people while in Bucharest the popular masses were delirious in greeting their king and queen with cries of "Long live the emperor and empress!." In Romanian military circles, the completed operations against the Red Army and the occupation of Budapest were assessed as the greatest military feat in the history of the entire World War I.[17]

After these victories, Romania's territorial appetite was further whetted. Romania now wanted the whole of Banat, Dobrudja, Transylvania, and Besarabia for itself, a demand which necessarily put it in conflict with Yugo-slavia. Having been informed from Paris by Minister Trumbić of the danger of a Romanian attack on Banat, the Yugoslav government met on August 21 and decided to send army reinforcements.[18] At a subsequent meeting, on September 21, the government decided to enforce a number of repressive measures, the result being a complete ban on exports to Romania.[19]

After the fall of the Hungarian Soviet Republic, most of the members of the Soviet government, as prominent Social Democrats and Communists, crossed over to Austria where they were granted political asylum. A considerable portion of those who had taken part in the events in Hungary, however, fled to Yugoslavia. The demarkation line saw the mass crossings of former Red Army members who carried their arms and other military equipment with them and gave themselves up to the Yugoslav military authorities rather than fall into the hands of the Hungarian counterrevolutionaries. According to the press cuttings from those days, some 4000 people crossed over into Baranya; all were granted political asylum in Yugoslavia. Among them, were many miners from Baranya who had gone to Hungary after the proclamation of the Soviet regime and who had fought in the ranks of the Red Army. Their homecoming was enthusiastically received in view of the fact that their departure had caused a great labor shortage in the Baranya mines which were all important to the Yugoslav railways.

In Budapest on August 6, the trade union government was overthrown with the help of White detachments under András Csillery. This led to the immediate formation of a civilian government under István Friedrich. But Archduke József Habsburg then put his finger in the pie, desiring to take advantage of the situation to further his own ends. Claiming hereditary rights, he announced that he would be assuming power in Hungary. His statement was met with a wave of protest from the governments of neighboring countries. The Yugoslav delegation in Paris took steps to prevent this and presented a protest note to the Supreme Council on August 15, while Pašić paid the head of the US delegation Frank Polk a visit and told him of the danger that would arise with a Habsburg in power in Hungary. Polk agreed with him.[20] The Yugoslav government met again on August 18, and decided to draw up an agreement with the Czechoslovak government on launching a joint struggle against all attempts by any member of the Habsburg dyansty to usurp power, be it in Austria, Hungary, or Germany.[21]

Edvard Beneš himself lodged a protest with the Supreme Council on August 14, concerning the same issue in the name of the Czechoslovak government. The constant threat of a restoration of the Habsburg monarchy led to greater rapprochement between Czechoslovakia and Yugoslavia, and later on, Romania joined the process. The situation was so explosive that on August 23, the Supreme Council compelled Archduke József to renounce his claims to the Hungarian crown.[22]

But, despite these misunderstandings, the Yugoslav government wanted to establish diplomatic relations with Hungary, and at its session of August 18th, it decided to send its representative to Budapest. For his part, the Minister For the Interior Svetozar Pribičević offered to cooperate with the Hungarian side in waging a struggle against Communism and in questioning the Communist participants in the Hungarian revolution. As a gesture of good will, Pribičević offered to extradite a group of Hungarian Communists who were in jail in Baja. He also sent his emissary, Gligorire Popović, to Budapest to question Communists of Yugoslav origin.[23]

In September 1919, via the Yugoslav embassy in Budapest, Pribičević sent a letter to his Hungarian colleague, Ödön Beniczki, proposing an agreement on the extradition of Communists on the basis of reciprocity and in groups of ten at the demarcation line between Szeged and Baja.[24] In its reply, the Hungarian Ministry referred to the 1911 Accord on Extradition signed between Hungary and Serbia which stipulated that the proceedings for the extradition of persons required an arrest warrant and a bill of indictment.[25] This insistence upon formalities was probably why very few political prisoners were extradited between the end of 1919 and the beginning of 1920. Later on, there were more because the system enabled both sides to rid themselves of revolutionaries who were a threat to the regime.

The Romanian troops which had crossed into Hungary routing the Red Army units were followed by an officers' detachment under Miklós Horthy led by fanatic counterrevolutionaries thirsty for revenge, such as Pál Prónay, István Héjjas, Antal Lehár, and others, who, with tacit agreement from their Supreme Commander, went around Hungary venting their rage and bringing terrible misery and death to many revolutionaries, Red Army fighters, members of the directorate or sympathizers of the erstwhile Soviet Republic. News of their butchery spread throughout Europe and word got round to Yugoslavia, too. A report on their dealings was sent to the foreign ministry by the Yugoslav envoy in Budapest.[26]

After the capitalist order was restored in Hungary, Yugoslav authorities in Baranya could not longer rely on the old civil-servant apparatus and the bourgeois politicians because they were, body and soul, supporters of the Irredentist policy of the Hungarian government. All power in Baranya was thus handed over to the Pécs—Baranya Socialist party which had a large number of Communists in its ranks. The Yugoslav authorities turned a blind eye to their activities because they were fervent opponents of Horthy's White terror and did not want to see Baranya fall into Hungary's hands.

There was a short-lived improvement of relations between Yugoslavia and Hungary at the end of 1919 and the beginning of 1920. So much so, in fact, that at the insistence of the English and French, an agreement was signed on the export of Yugoslav foodstuffs and other articles to Hungary.[27] But, the truce was only superficial. Yugoslavia knew full well that Hungary would never give up its territorial claims to the lands that had fallen to Yugoslavia. It was precisely at this time that plans were being made for a rapproachement with Czechoslovakia and the creation of a corridor which would be a territorial link between the two countries.[28]

At the beginning of January 1920, a Hungarian delegation arrived in Paris led by Count Albert Apponyi. Its task was to negotiate a peace treaty. The event was an occasion to sound the alarm and call another meeting of the representatives of Yugoslavia, Czechoslovakia, and Romania, to prepare their joint defense should the Hungarian delegation prove successful in altering some of the provisions of the peace treaty.[29]

And, while a tactical war was being fought in Paris over the drawing up of a peace treaty, elections were held in Hungary on January 25–26, 1920, at which the representatives of the Anti-Habsburg party of small-scale landowners secured the majority vote. But, during the preparations for the election of head of state, a group of influential monarchist magnates were busy plotting to install their pretender, Karl Habsburg, as the country's new head of state. This led to a fresh wave of protest at the Paris Peace Conference.[30]

Getting wind of the situation, the Yugoslav government convened a meeting for February 4, 1920. There were sharp protests and the Minister of Interior Svetozar Pribičević and the Minister of Social Welfare Vitomir Korać, a Social-Democrat, went so far as to demand a military intervention in order to prevent a restoration and the return of a Habsburg to the Hungarian throne. The meeting finally decided that negotiations be held with the representatives of Austria, Czechoslovakia, and Romania, on a joint protest action.[31]

Soon afterward, on February 10, on orders from their governments, the delegates of Yugoslavia, Romania, and Czechoslovakia met in Paris and decided to write a protest note without delay banning the return of a Habsburg to the throne of any one of their countries.[32] The note was submitted to the Supreme Council at the Peace Conference.

With the election of Miklós Horthy as Regent of Hungary, on March 1, 1920 the battle for the throne of Hungary was struck off the agenda for the time being. The governments of neighboring states, were partially appeased. However, Horthy's appearance at the helm of Hungary fanned the flames of irredentist policy, and after the Trianon Peace Treaty had been signed on June 4th, 1920, it took the form of preparations for revenge and the revival of a Greater Hungary.

## NOTES

1. Service historique de l'Armée de Terre, Vincennes, Paris (hereafter AS: *Service historique*). Armée française d'Orient, 20 N 527.

2. Vinaver dr Vuk, *Jugoslavija i Madjarska 1918–1933* (Belgrade, 1971), p. 70.

3. Diplomatski archiv Saveznog sekretarijata za inostrane poslove. Belgrade, (hereafter: *DA-SSIP*), Poslanstvo Kraljevine SHS u Budimpešti, F 1–1919.

4. *Service historique,* Attachés militaire-Hongrie, 7 N. 1357.

5. Živojinović R. Dragan, *Sovjetska republika u Madjarskoj i politika Sjedinjenih američkih država u Jugoistočnoj Evropi 1919. godine. Zbornik Filozofskog fakulteta* XII–1 (Belgrade, 1974), p. 555.

6. Vinaver, *Jugoslavija,* p. 69.

7. *Ibid.,* 71.

8. *Ibid.,* 72–73.

9. Párttörténeti Intézet Archívuma, Budapest. Tagyob II/15, 1–20, pp. 35–37.

10. Krizman Bogdan–Hrabak Bogumil, *Zapisnici sa sednica Delegacije Kraljevine SHS na Mirovnoj konferenciji u Parizu 1919–1920* (Belgrade, 1960), p. 101; Vinaver, 55

11. Vinaver, *Jugoslavija,* p. 56.

12. *Service historique,* Armée francaise d'Orient, 20 N. 527.

13. Vinaver, *Jugoslavija,*, 69.

14. Archiv Vojnoistorijskog instituta, Belgrade, Operacijski dnevnici Operativnog odeljenja Vrhovne komande. Box 28, 219.

15. *Ibid.,*

16. Vinaver, *Jugoslavija,* p. 75–76.

17. *DA-SSIP.* Delegacija na Mirovnoj konferenciji u Parizu. Fasc. 5.

18. Archiv Centralnog komiteta Saveza komunista Jugoslavije, Beograd, (hereafter *A-CK SKJ*), Političke stranke i organi Kraljevine Jugoslavije, Zapisnici sa sednica Ministarskog sastanka. Sednica od August 21, 1919.

19. *Ibid.,* Sednica, September 1, 1919.

20. Krizman–Hrabak, *Zapisnici,* p. 174; Vinaver, *Jugoslavija,* p. 84.

21. *A-CK SKJ,* Političke stranke i organi Kraljevine Jugoslavije. Zapisnici sa sednica Ministarskog saveta, Sednica, August 18, 1919.

22. Boros Ferenc, *Magyar–csehszlovák kapcsolatok 1918–1921-ben.* (Budapest, 1970), p. 109–11.

23. *DA-SSIP,* Poslanstvo Kraljevine SHS u Budimpešti, F–1.

24. *Ibid.,*

25. *Ibid.,*

26. *Ibid.,* F–2.

27. Vinaver, *Jugoslavija,* p. 102.

28. Boros, *A magyar–csehszlovák,* p. 137.

29. Krizman–Hrabak, *Zapisnici,* p. 211.

30. Boros, *Magyar–csehszlovák,* p. 152.

31. *A-CK SKJ,* Političke stranek i organi Kraljevine Jogoslavije, Zapisnici sednica Ministarskog saveta. Sednica, February 4, 1920.

32. Krizman–Hrabak, *Zepisnici,* p. 264.

# THE HUNGARIAN COMMUNIST REVOLUTION
# AND THE PARTITO SOCIALISTA ITALIANO

Frank J. Coppa

The October Revolution, which spawned a Bolshevik regime in Russia, aroused interest throughout Europe.[1] In Italy, the *Partito Socialista Italiano* (PSI) the first modern political party there, was particularly vulnerable because it had long been divided into a reformist and a revolutionary wing, and this division was exacerbated by Lenin's triumph.[2] The influence of the Russian Revolution on Italy is well documented in a series of works.[3] Less is known about the Italian response to the formation of the Communist government of Béla Kun in March 1919. This essay focuses upon the reaction of Italian Socialists to Kun's brief, but intense attempt to radicalize the Magyar state and the impact this had on the *Partito Socialista Italiano* and politics in the peninsula.

Italians were frightened and fascinated by Lenin's prediction that the Russian proletariat would serve as the stimulus for a world-wide upheaval.[4] By February 1917, *L'Avanti!*, the Socialist party's national organ, began to concentrate on the snowballing developments in Russia.[5] It reminded readers what Lev Davidovich Trotskii had promised. "To us internationalism is not an abstract idea existing only to be betrayed on every opportune occasion... but is a real guiding and wholly practical principle. A lasting decisive success is inconceivable for us without a revolution in Europe."[6] Lenin and Trotskii proved true to their word for the revolution in Russia was followed by steps to abet and incite rebellion elsewhere. The dominoes were beginning to fall.

As early as 1918, Moscow feverishly planned to provoke additional revolutions and created a Federation of Foreign Groups of the Russian Communist Party, formed mainly from prisoners of war converts, and containing German, Hungarian, and Austrian cells, among others. This was the basis of the Communist International, the "International of Deeds" in the words of Béla Kun, the leader of the Hungarian contingent. The son of a Jewish village notary,

Kun had served as a minor labor-union official before he had been captured by the Russians during the war and converted to Communism. His loyalty daring, and enthusiasm led the Russians to encourage him to spark a Communist coup in his native Hungary, which was in turmoil.[7]

*L'Avanti!* welcomed the transformation of Russia and the prospect of a wider upheaval, acting as the optimistic herald of the day of reckoning. All of the disorders and the threats of revolution were dutifully recorded, especially those that erupted in the lands of the former Austro–Hungarian empire. The proletariat had assumed the offensive on all fronts, and *L'Avanti!* hailed each new victory.[8]

In October 1918, the PSI enthusiastically received the Proclamation of the Hungarian Socialists to the Workers of the World, asking for assistance in their attainment of the basics of democracy. *L'Avanti!* seconded both the Hungarian call for social justice and the prospect for an International Socialist Conference.[9] Although the Italian party was troubled by tensions within its ranks, and confronted right-wing violence at home, it supported the Hungarian demand for liberty and independence, and rejoiced at the appearance of the Hungarian Republic in November 1918.[10] Radicals in the party claimed that the role of International Socialism was to facilitate a just peace.[11]

As part of their European-wide perspective, Italian Socialists monitored developments in Budapest closely, noting the formation of the government of Count Mihály Károlyi at the beginning of 1918, and its attempts to provide national and social reforms.[12] *L'Avanti!* approved the move of the Catholic bishops to transfer their lands to the government in order to facilitate agrarian reform.[13] To be sure, the Italian Socialist daily saw difficulties in the path of meaningful reform in Hungary, as in Italy, but it was convinced that with courage and determination the workers would triumph. Thus, *L'Avanti!* supported the measures taken by the Hungarian government against the wealthy landowners, who sought to flee the country to avoid taxation. Confiscation of their estates, the editors judged, was warranted under the circumstances.[14] Many Hungarians and Italians disagreed.

The Károlyi government was attacked by both the right and the left, receiving little sympathy from the Allied Powers. The Soviets, on the east, were clearly bent on subversion as their disciple Kun called for the liberation of the enslaved.[15] Kun attacked the Social Democratic press, and in February, led an armed attack on the Social Democratic daily, *Népszava,* in which seven were killed and some 80 wounded. "Social Democracy is our Number One Enemy," he bellowed. "We must destroy it to clear the road to communism."[16] The Communist leader opposed participation in any bourgeois government placing his trust in the workers' organizations which he stressed would act as agents for the workers, soldiers, and peasants' councils. Calling for the army and police formations to be disbanded, and the creation of "a class army of the armed proletariat," he insisted that the Hungarian Revolution would soon pass from "Its general and national phase into the era of ...social revolution"[17]

Károlyi understood the danger and his government responded energetically by arresting the Communist leader. However, the republic's stability was undermined the following month when Colonel Fernand Vix, head of the French Military Mission in Budapest, transmitted the Peace Conference's order for Hungarian troops withdrawn from an earlier demarcation line, and in the process, allowed the Romanians to occupy a large chunk of Hungarian territory. In a note of March 21, Count Károlyi protested the decision as contrary to the Belgrade Armistice of November 13, 1918, and announced he would not assume the responsibility for its implementation. The Hungarian government therefore resigned.[18]

Following the collapse of the Károlyi regime, patriots looked to the extremists to resist the demands. This prompted the formation of a Socialist/Communist coalition under Kun's leadership.[19] Sándor Garbai, the stonemason, union leader, and chief spokesman for the Social Democratic Party of Hungary, explained his position:

From the West we can expect nothing but a dictated peace, which forces us to abandon free elections. There is no alternative to the acceptance of a new form of dictatorship. The Entente has driven us into adopting a new course which will secure for us from the East what the West has denied us...[20]

The Italian Socialist Party, which adhered immediately to the Third International (Comintern) formed at the Moscow Conference of March 1919 allied itself with the Bolsheviks and looked at the Russian and Hungarian revolutions as models other parties should follow.[21] The party organ, *L'Avanti!*, under the direction of Giacino Menotti Serrati, who had succeeded Benito Mussolini in 1914, found itself torn between loyalty to the traditions of Italian Socialism and the position of the Third International.[22] Pleased by the success of the revolution in Hungary, *L'Avanti!* nonetheless reported that nationalist rather than internationalist aims had led to the creation of a Communist government, the dictatorship of the proletariat, and the appeal to Soviet Russia for assistance.[23] It had been formed to combat the Czechs and Romanians as well as the capitalists.[24] It was a solution which smacked of nationalism.[25] *L'Avanti!*'s immediate interpretation of the Communist revolution in Hungary was later sustained by others.[26]

Mussolini, the ex-Socialist, wrote that if the French head of the military mission had not transmitted the Allies' decision concerning Hungary's frontiers with Czechoslovakia and Romania, the Soviet regime in Hungary would not have materialized. The transformation, in Mussolini's words, was effected not by the proletariat but by the bourgeoisie, not by a Socialist, but by a conservative republican. Károlyi's gesture was inspired by nationalist rather than Socialist sentiments. Hungarian Communism, he concluded, was a trick to deceive the allies and defend Magyar territorial aspirations, even to the point of waging a new war.[27] Thus Mussolini's newspaper *Il Popolo d'Italia* shared *L'Avanti!s* initial interpretation of the origins of the Hungarian Revolution, but appreciated, as did the Socialist daily, that it could evolve into a bolshevism in the style of Lenin.[28] The Allies, for their part, refused to accept any responsibility for developments in Budapest, placing the blame on German machinations and Russian intrigue. *L'Avanti!* deemed the allied accusations groundless, insisting that the revolution was provoked by allied insensitivity to developments in Hungary.[29]

If the allies saw the revolution in Budapest arranged by the Russians, and reported that all foreigners were either harrassed or arrested during the turmoil, in Moscow Vladimir Ilich Lenin sought assurances that the new government was really Communist and not bourgeois-Socialist.[30] At first there was considerable confusion about the situation in Budapest. London, among other capitals, received contradictary reports of what was happening in Budapest.[31] The coalition of Socialists and Communists in Hungary sougth to clear the air in its appeal to the proletariat of the world.[32] The new government indicated that the revolution was precipitated by two causes: the determination of workers, soldiers, and peasants not to remain subservient to the capitalists, and the excessive territorial demands of the Czechs and Romanians.[33] It sought to prove its mettle by immediately abolishing private property.[34] Meanwhile a radio telegram from Budapest announced that elections for a National Assembly had been abandoned, martial law had been decreed, revolutionary tribunals created, and steps taken to have businesses, services, and even homes, socialized.[35]

These measures were implemented on March 22, when the Council of Peoples' Commissars, in which Béla Kun was the guiding force, voted the abolition of titles and privileges, the separation of church and state, produced plans for Workers', Soldiers', and Peasants' Councils, and drafted proposals for a wide range of socialization.[36] All branches of government now fell under the scrutiny of the Peoples' Commissars while revolutionary tribunals replaced the existing judicial system and a Red army was contemplated.[37] The frenzied pace of socialization aroused fear of a bolshevization of Europe in the west, but pleased Trotskii who promised that the Red Army would sustain the Hungarian regime against its imperialist enemies.[38]

Antonio Gramsci, one of the angry young men of the PSI who rejected the gradualism of the reformists as well as the rhetoric of the maximalists, was influenced by developments in Hungary. Already in his 1917 article, "The Revolution against *Kapital*," he argued that Marx's *Kapital* was misused to demonstrate that revolution had necessarily to await the evolution of bourgeois capitalism. The revolution first in Russia, and then in Hungary, confirmed Gramsci's thesis that the war had made it possible to usher in proletarian governments. The Sardinian intellectual attacked the complacency of the Socialist party in Italy as well as the policies of the unions, urging them to learn from the Russian and Hungarian examples.[39] A figure who looked to the factory councils in Italy to lead the revolution, he appreciated the fact that in Hungary Béla Kun had exhorted the masses to transform their labor unions into Soviets embracing all workers.[40]

Gramsci was not alone in the PSI in recognizing the importance of the Hungarian revolution. Writers for the party organ had first seen Budapest's Soviet regime as a stratagem employed by Magyar nationalists to undermine the obnoxious peace treaty. While acknowledging the connection between the revolution and resentment over the solution of the nationality problem in the treaties, which *L'Avanti!* had early noted, the editors now insisted that the Hungarian revolution, like the Russian was effectively the work of the proletariat.[41] Thus, *L'Avanti!* writers did not find it strange that a Communist regime intially inspired by national goals should turn its attention to social and economic questions.[42] Italian Socialists praised the Hungarians for their reforms and their energetic organization of production.[43] Likewise they praised the Communist-led government for transferring control of agriculture to the proletariat.[44] The religious issue, too, had been well handled according to the *L'Avanti!* Although some claimed that the Communists interfered with the beliefs of individuals and prohibited religious functions, the journal reported that the regime had simply withdraw state support, considering faith a private matter.[45]

By April 1919, the majority party position dispelled any and all reservations concerning the Hungarian revolution and praised both the internal and foreign policy of the regime. The writers of *L'Avanti!* stressed that, while the bourgeois powers sought new and brutal means to resolve the frontier questions, the Hungarian government had shown moderation and good sense. "Regarding Hungary's occupied territory," Béla Kun was quoted as saying, "I am personally for their continued union with Hungary, but I do not insist on this because we are apostles of universal frontiers. We are disposed to let the populations of the occupied provinces decide upon their own political future."[46] Moderation was also perceived in Kun's call for a federation of Soviet Republics.[47] The danger, in the view of Italian Socialists, came not from Hungary but from abroad and was reflected in the English and French threats against the Magyar state.[48] Bourgeois Europe, they claimed, was frightened by the gains made by Communism and sought to block its extension to the rest of Europe.[49] This prompted the great capitalist counteroffensive against the Hungarian proletariat.[50] It also explained their attempt to incite counterrevolution inside Hungary.[51]

The harshness of the proposed treaties which sparked the Bolshevik revolution in Hungary also worked to discredit Wilsonianism and to undermine moderate socialism throughout Europe, and Italy in particular. By the end of April 1919, independent Socialists throughout the continent were abandoning Wilson, concluding that only the proletariat could create a new international order. By this time the American president could no longer count upon the support of Serrati, Lazzari, and Nenni, and even Turati and Leonida Bissolati refused to champion Wilson's internationalism.[52] L'Avanti! expressed this new insurgency by proclaiming that only through socialism could peace be attained.[53] The worldwide proletariat revolution seemed imminent to the radicals who controlled the journal.[54] In turn they predicted that bourgeois Europe would do all within its means to snuff out the proletariat's success.[55]

L'Avanti!'s fear of western intervention against the Soviet regimes was not without foundation. When the American Minister in Berne suggested military intervention, a view some of the allies shared, Allen Dulles proposed measures to isolate the Hungarian revolution from Russia and prevent its spread to neighboring countries. Dulles specified that:

a) The Czechs and Rumanians should be allowed to occupy the passes of the Carpathian Mountains and the railway connecting Czechoslovakia with Rumania, south of the passes.

b) The Servians or the French should be permitted to occupy a strip of territory to connect the Slovene territory with the Danube near Pressburg, now held by the Czechs.

c) The Czechs should be granted the necessary railway connections along their present line of occupation in Slovakia.[56]

The English, French, and Italians, even more than the Americans, feared that the triumph of revolution in Hungary meant that Bolshevism was no longer isolated and contained in Russia, and threatened to overturn the whole of Europe. At the end of March 1919, Vittorio Emanuele Orlando, prime minister of Italy since October 1917, sparked a discussion of the problem in the Council of Four.[57] The new Italian Minister to Yugoslavia, Prince Borghese, in passing through Budapest, was asked by Béla Kun to transmit a note to the Peace Conference. In his memorandum, Kun explained that his agreement with Russia was simply an *"entente cordiale"* without any aggressive aims. Furthermore, the Hungarian government was willing to negotiate territorial matters on the basis of the principle of national self-determination and asked the powers to send a mission to Budapest. While Wilson and Lloyd George were receptive, Clemenceau balked at the notion of a "regular mission" but agreed to send "an investigator." This led to the abortive Smuts mission of April 4–5, to Budapest.[58]

By mid-April 1919, the regime of Béla Kun, surrounded by three hostile powers ready to increase their encroachment, was in serious difficulty. It proved unable to negotiate with the West, lift the blockade, or acquire military assistance from Lenin's Russia. Romanian troops assumed the offensive along the western front and by May were deep in Magyar territory, while the Czech army, led by French officers, advanced southward into the rich mineral basin of Salgótarján. The Socialists of *L'Avanti!* perceived these forces as the vanguard of capitalist reaction.[59] While it praised the Hungarian attempts to stop the invasion and end the counterrevolution,[60] it deemed the future of the regime uncertain.[61] As rumors reached Italian Socialists that the Romanians had occupied Budapest, *L'Avanti!* criticized the capitalist powers, their lackeys, and the bourgeoisie.[62] The allies were seen to conduct a vendetta against the Hungarians, refusing to lift their blockade until the Soviet government had been toppled.[63]

Although the Big Four had not sent infantry units to fight alongside the Romanians, they certainly encouraged them and sought the fall of the Béla Kun government, as the Italian Socialists reported. Early in May, in an address to the Workers' and Soldiers' Council in Budapest, Béla Kun issued a call for the nation to arm, which led to the creation of the continent's second Red Army and the adoption of radical measures at home. The Communist leader vowed that the capitalist attempt to overturn his regime would be resisted by the masses in his country.[64] In fact, on May 19, a successful counteroffensive was launched, creating a rift between the Czech and Romanian forces, and momentarily relieving the military pressure. The Italian Socialists applauded this turn of events, pronouncing it a triumph for the proletariat everywhere.[65]

While *L'Avanti!* acclaimed the mobilization of the Hungarian proletariat and their resolve to defend their Soviet republic,[66] other Italians were less than enthusiastic. In fact, the Hungarian Revolution soon became a dividing sword in Italian politics as reports reached Rome that the Kun government wished to establish relations with Italy, and sought an Italian military and economic mission in Budapest.[67] Conservative elements in the peninsula did not share the conviction of the radical Socialists that revolution was inevitable when its hour has come.[68] These forces sought to convince the masses that there would be no red revolution in the West, and planned to use the failure of the Hungarian Revolution to prove their point.

Mussolini, who formally founded the Fascist movement in Milan in March 1919, also believed that the Italians could learn important lessons from events in Budapest. Embittered by the pacifism of the Italian Socialist party, which had provoked his ejection from its ranks in 1914, he reminded his former colleagues that the Hungarian party they praised had organized an army and was waging war. When faced by three menacing forces in 1919, the Council of Commissars might have adopted the Italian Socialist policy of nonresistance maintained during the course of World War I. Fortunately, Mussolini continued, the Hungarian Communists had more sense, and opted for war, not hesitating to send their proletariat to battle the proletariat of other nations. The very victories which L'Avanti! hailed in its headlines, would not have materialized if the Hungarian regime had foolishly pursued the pacifism of the PSI.[67]

Mussolini was also quick to point out that the Soviet regime in Hungary had combined Socialist with nationalist aspirations,[68] precisely what he hoped to accomplish in Italy.[69]

The Hungarian Communists have broken the antithesis between socialism and war —when it is a matter of defending the Patria, which has installed a socialist regime, then war is holy... . If, today, the Hungarian Soviet Republic appears vital, it is not only because it has avoided internal havoc by shying away from the bolshevik brutality displayed in Russia, but because it has the courage to wage war.[70]

The Duce and his followers did not accept Béla Kun's assertions that he was not concerned with national questions. Dismissing with disdain his call for the emergence of an international soviet government.[71]

Whatever Kun's motivation, by mid-May it appeared that the Hungarians had managed to halt the advance on their capital, and had momentarily saved the revolution.[72] By this time, Italian Socialists felt that all Marxists, Bolshevik or not, had to make some effort on behalf of the revolutions in Russia and Hungary, to show by actions and not simply by words, that they championed the cause of the workers of the world. On May 19, L'Avanti! proposed that rather than issuing empty protests against allied policies towards the revolutions, European Socialists should make their voice heard by calling a general strike.[73] In this fashion the organized proletariat could actively and openly combat the new "Holy Alliance" and the lies of bourgeoisie, behind it.[74] Such a protest was in the interest of the working class worldwide for the Italians feared that the defeat of Lenin and Béla Kun would be followed by the strangulation of Socialism throughout the continent. These sentiments were soon echoed by the French Socialist Party, the *Confédération General du Travail,* and the British Triple Alliance.[75]

While the Italian Socialists and unions were prepared to call for a complete work stoppage, to protest allied policy toward Russia and Hungary, James Ramsay MacDonald cited the difficulty in persuading the British trade unions to strike for a political cause—even for only 24 hours. The French proved more receptive to the Italian suggestion, but only on condition that the Italians, French, and English act jointly, and the protest include economic as well as political objectives. Eventually a compromise formula was ironed out among the Italians, French, and English, stipulating that the workers in their respective countries would hold their own demonstration by the means they found most suitable, and in accordance with their unique modes of operation. Their joint announcement made it clear that in addition to protesting allied intervention in Russia and Hungary, the demonstrations sought economic and political objectives at home. Finally, it was decided that while the English would hold massive demonstrations on Sunday, July 20, the Italians and French would call for a 24-hour strike on Monday, July 21.[76] The Hungarian Communists welcomed the effort on their behalf, believing that only such international action could save their revolution.[77]

Anticipating the general strike, *L'Avanti!* sought to galvanize opinion at home and abroad. It published the appeal of the Hungarian proletariat to the proletariat of the allied powers, seconding their call for action against the bourgeoisie and the counterrevolution.[78] Determined to pressure Italian Socialists to take a stronger stand in favor of the Soviet regimes, *L'Avanti!* observed that rather than being intimidated by the pressure of the Allies, the Hungarian Socialists meeting in Congress, June 12–13, 1919, had announced their adherence to the Third International and supported the dictatorship of the proletariat.[79] The Italian Socialists daily defended their action finding the dictatorship of the proletariat far more broad-minded and generous than the dictatorship of the bourgeoise, and preferable to democracy which *L'Avanti!* denounced as the greatest enemy of Socialism.[80] In fact, the dictatorship of the proletariat in Hungary was perceived as a transition towards socialism and the classless society.[81]

According to *L'Avanti!* the Italian press had been neither accurate nor fair in its treatment of developments in the Magyar state.[82] Socialist journaists who ventured to Hungary returned home impressed with Béla Kun and his transformation of Hungary.[83] Angelica Balabanoff, a leading maximalist in the PSI, was one of the few who remained singularly unimpressed with the Communist leader.[84] Most other writers proclaimed that a new spirit had been kindled in that ancient nation, where crime and violence had diminished.[85] The masses, they wrote endorsed the regime. Thus, the Hungarian revolution was seen to provide an important example for the workers in the West, both as regards internal as well as foreign affairs. Only by abandoning secret diplomacy, as had Béla Kun, could nationalist oppression be eliminated and world peace, assured.[86]

The Hungarian problem stemmed from the Western powers rather than the Soviet regime, according to L'Avanti! The Communist government had made a number of conciliatory overtures; the allies had proved inflexible.[87] England, France, Italy, and the United States had from the first been hostile to the regime and had not dealt with it in a forthright manner. Italian Socialists complained that Georges Clemenceau had pressured the Hungarians to withdraw from Czech territory, promising that in turn the Romanians would leave Hungarian soil. The Hungarians had complied, but not the Romanians, and the Allies were little inclined to have them abide by the commitment.[88] To make matters worse, Western powers were seen to scheme with and encourage counterrevolutionary forces in Hungary.[89]

To combat the hostile bourgeoisie which threatened the very existence of the Soviet regime in Hungary, Italian Socialists called upon the workers of the world to pose a countervailing force.[90] The allies should not be allowed to strangle liberty.[91] In the words of Antonio Gramsci, the massive and complex formation of capitalism had to be opposed by the equally massive organization of the international proletariat, whose interest it was to prevent the destruction of the Communist governments of Russia and Hungary.[92]

As the Socialists became increasingly shrill about the prospect of a hostile intervention, Francesco Saverio Nitti, the new Italian prime minister, promised in the Chamber of Deputies that Italian troops would not intervene in either Hungary or Russia.[93] His words did not reassure the Left. Italian Socialists no more trusted their government than that of the other powers and called upon the workers to assure that there would not be an intervention. Only firm action on the part of the workers could prevent the allied liquidation of these Soviet regimes.[94]

L'Avanti!, organ of the Bolshevik party direction of the PSI called for the unity of the proletariat worldwide to defend the Soviet regimes against the forces of the counter revolution.[95] The accord reached by the CGT and the CGL, respectively the major unions of France and Italy, had paved the way for the defense of the Russian and Hungarian revolutionary governments.[96] French workers, it seems, had finally opened their eyes to reality, and now agreed with the Congress of Soviets in Hungary, that the triumph of the reactionary allied policy would be a defeat for them as well as the Hungarian proletariat.[97] While some Italian Socialists seemed to indicate that their support for Béla Kun was conditional, L'Avanti! insisted that the majority position of the party was favorable without reservation of any sort to the dictatorship of the proletariat in Budapest. It wanted the entire world to see the complete solidarity of the French, English, and Italian proletariat in defense of the Hungarian Revolution.[98]

Actually there were considerable differences among the Italians, French, and English, on the question of the best means of defending the dictatorship of the proletariat in Hungary. Indeed, there were deep divisions within the PSI intself, with the reformist Turati, who had originally founded the party, suspicious of the emphasis on violence and the dictatorship of the proletariat, warning his fellow Italians not to become the tools of the Bolsheviks.[99] Unlike those Italian Socialists who saw a possible prototype in the Hungarian Revolution, Turati was not encouraged by the Hungarian example.[100] Turati's doubts, and those of the other reformists in the party, distressed Gramsci. The Hungarian Revolution as well as the Russian, contributed to his conclusion that the PSI, to which he belonged, could not serve as the revolutionary agent of the Italian working class.[101]

The PSI's reaction to Hungarian developments aggravated the deep divisions which long plagued it. Already at the end of 1918, the maximalists within its ranks had in an order of the day called for the institution of a Socialist republic directed by a dictatorship of the proletariat, with the aim of socializing the means of production. This had been opposed by the parliamentary faction of the party, dominated by the reformists, which denied that a Socialist republic could be formed by a minority by means of a *coup d'état*. Socialism could only be instituted by the gradual conquest of power by the working class masses of the country.[102] Despite these differences, the two factions sought to cooperate and maintain the semblance of unity during what was clearly a dangerous period.

As July 20–21 and the general strike approached, there were a series of articles in L'Avanti! which were increasingly hostile to the policies of the Allies and the actions of the bourgeoisie.[103] Turati, who opposed the use of violence and was pessimistic about the possibility of assuring the happiness of man even by peaceful means, shied away from the Bolshevik direction the party was taking. Above all, he feared that the barrage of Socialist threats would provoke a ferocious reaction and ruin the Socialist movement for half a century. This concern was shared by Leonida Bissolati, Ivanoe Bonomi, Claudio Treves, and Giuseppe Emanuele Modigliani, among others. These men believed that socialism was not a matter of popular will, but of economic maturation.[104]

The Secretary of the Party, Costantino Lazzari, thought otherwise, convinced that the strike on behalf of the Soviet regimes would reveal the proletariat of the world united for the first time, in an effort to initiate their own foreign policy.[105] Broad Italian participation would invigorate the party and provide visible proof of their support for the revolution. Gramsci wrote that to belong to the Communist International meant linking one's institutions organically to the Russian and Hungarian proletariat states. Only in this manner could the workers win the class struggle both nationally and internationally.[106]

The agitation of the Italian Socialists on behalf of the Hungarian Revolution was not without impact for it led the Italian government to dismiss any thought of intervention against either the Hungarian or Russian regimes as its representatives claimed that a recourse to military intervention would provoke a strike by its own Bolsheviks.[107] Both Béla Kun and Lenin appreciated the Italian effort. It is not surprising that of all the Socialist movements, the Russians prized the Italian the most for it had saved the Bolsheviks from virtual isolation in Western Europe.[108] There were limits to its influence, however, and of course its actions would have internal as well as international consequences. Some in Italy feared that the strike on July 21, was merely a pretext to overturn the Nitti government. Mussolini was not frightened, convinced that the Socialists had neither the will nor the means to bring down the liberal state. The Italian Railroad workers, whose participation he deemed essential, would not strike, Mussolini predicted in his *Popolo d'Italia*.[109] Nonetheless Mussolini decided to exploit Socialist support for the Hungarian Revolution to demonstrate the recklessness of the party and undermine its position at home.

On July 17, 1919, Mussolini once again focused his attention on the proposed strike in the columns of his *Popolo d'Italia*. He branded the projected strike pseudo-international, for at best it would be a Franco-Italian effort, and would not be a general strike even in Italy. In the view of the Fascist leader the plan was confused from the start and he not only doubted its success, but also questioned its objectives.[110] Others were not so sure of its outcome, and to allay fears and mitigate its impact, the Italian prime minister took steps to contain the strike. He again affirmed that the Italian government would not intervene against either the Hungarian or Russian regime. Then he threatened state employees, such as railway workers, who joined the strike with the loss of their jobs. These measures proved successful, for, on July 16, the Executive Committee of the Railway Union urged its workers to foresake the strike and merely endorse the manifesto against allied intervention against the Soviet regimes.[111]

Mussolini was among the first to applaud the railway workers in Italy for refusing to participate in a strike for the Soviet regimes of Hungary and Russia.[112] The *Duce* claimed that the Italian Socialists had overestimated their influence and sought to achieve objectives well beyond their grasp. We have always had faith in the sound national instinct of the Italian proletariat," Mussolini wrote, "there will be a strike, but it will be neither international nor general."[113] Italy would never become a "slave barracks" as had occurred in the "glorious" republics of Moscow and Budapest.[114]

Mussolini's analysis proved accurate for the strike of July 21, 1919, was far from global even though in Italy the work stoppage was nearly total in the country's industrial and urban economy. It exposed the illusions of Lenin and the other Bolshevik leaders who believed in the power of revolutionary developments abroad. The strike showed that only in Italy was there wholehearted support for the Bolsheviks among organized workers, and that, in the other Western nations, the anti-interventionist position did not necessarily reflect acceptance of Bolshevik aims.[115] This led *L'Avanti!* to claim that the Italian proletariat alone had responded to the appeal of the besieged proletariat of the Soviet republic of Hungary.[116] Italian support had not been sufficient to prevent the fall of the Béla Kun regime on August 1, precipitated by the counteroffensive launched by the Romanians and the Allies' refusal to negotiate with a government with Communist members.

Filippo Turati, the man who more than anyone else was responsible for the formation of the Italian Socialist party, believed the "international strike had failed because there was no international."[117] On this occasion the radicals in the party who controlled *L'Avanti!* concurred with him. The Hungarian regime had counted on the support of the worldwide proletariat, and this did not materialize.[118] This was to influence not only the future of Turati, but of Mussolini and Gramsci as well. Mussolini ridiculed the "decisive" and "universal" strike in the columns of *Il Popolo d'Italia.*[119]

> Was the strike universal? No.
> Were there strikes in England? No.
> Were there strikes in France? No.
> Were there strikes in the other countries? Almost universally, no.
> Was the strike general in Italy? No.
> Did Italian railway and postal workers strike? No.
> Was life in Italy's great cities disturbed? No.[120]

In a sense this was the beginning of the end of the Socialist myth of revolution. The collapse of Hungarian Communism seemed to substantiate the Fascist contentions and provided inspiration for those who determined to wage war on Socialism in Italy.[121]

Antonio Gramsci, one of the figures who organized the Italian Communist party in Leghorn in January 1921, was not surprised by the failure of the Socialist general strike. Gramsci argued that where the proletariat was still organized along parliamentary and bureaucratic lines, rather than on the Soviet model, there was the potential for revolutionary ferment but this could not be channeled into the sort of effort needed to accomplish meaningful goals.

> An action of this sort cannot be carried out by the Socialist Party and craft federations: only the workers and peasants themselves can carry it out on a sustained basis, in the factories, the railway stations, the mines, the ports, on the steamships and the farms. And if it is to be carried out successfully, the proletariat organs that emerged during the war must be further developed and systematized on a national and international basis: the anti-State must be organized.[122]

Gramsci's repudiation of democratic ideology and absenteeism from parliamentary politics was influenced by the failure of the Hungarian revolution and the International's interpretation of the reasons for the fiasco. According to this interpretation, the Hungarian defeat was not so much the result of poor preparation on the part of the party as it was the fusion of the Communists with the Social Democrats.[123] The way the Allies triumphed by getting rid of Béla Kun, who did not receive the support and solidarity of the international proletariat organized in Socialist parties and traditional trade unions, led the followers of Gramsci to uphold Lenin's position against the formation of Communist/Social Democratic governments.[124] In this fashion, first the outbreak of the Hungarian Revolution of 1919, and then its suppression, frustrated the radical Left on the Italian peninsula that found itself unable to alter the march of events. It thus contributed to the splintering of the Italian Left, the encouragement of the Right which became more aggressive, and played a part in the triumph of Fascism in 1922.

## NOTES

1. John Reed, *Ten Days that Shook the World* (New York, 1919).
2. *Il Partito Socialista Italiano nei suoi Congressi.* Volume III: 1917–1926, ed. Franco Pedona (Milan, 1963), pp. 23–46; Franco Catalano, *Storia dei Partiti Politici Italiani* (Turin, 1965; Lelio Baso, *Il Partito Socialista Italiano* (Milan, 1958), pp. 41–53.
3. See, for example, Stefano Caretti, *La Rvioluzione Russa e il Socialismo Italiano (1917–1921)* (Pisa, 1974); E. Ragionieri, "Il Socialismo Italiano e il movimento di Zimmerwald," *Balfagor* II (1973), 129–60.
4. Stanley W. Page, *Lenin and World Revolution* (New York, 1959), pp. 143–46.
5. Gaetano Arfè, *Storia del Socialismo Italiano,* 1892–1926 (Turin, 1965), p.146.
6. Leon Trotsky, *My Life* (New York, 1970), p. 332.
7. David Mitchell, *1919: Red Mirage* (New York, 1970), pp. 42–43, 60; Peter Pastor, "One Step Forward, Two Steps Back: The Rise and Fall of the First Hungarian Communist Party, 1918–1922)," in Ivo Banac, ed., *The Effects of World War I: The Rise of Communist Parties (New York, 1983), p. 87.*
8. Gaetano Arfè ed., *Storia dell' Avanti!* (Milan, 1956), p. 158.
9. *L'Avanti!* November 13, 1918.
10. *L'Avanti!* October 18 and 19, 1918; November 19, 1918.
11. "La funzione internazionale dei Socialisti," *L'Avanti!,* November 20, 1918.
12. "Reforme sociali in Ungheria," *L'Avanti!,* December 14, 1918.
13. "Il 4 Agosto della Chiesa in Ungheria, "*L'Avanti!,* December 4, 1918.
14. "Nella nuova Ungheria," *L'Avanti!,* March 14, 1919.
15. Although there is a broad spectrum of interpretations on the social and economic casues of communism in Hungary, there is a general consensus that the Hungarian Communist Party was Russian inspired. Pastor, "One Step Forward," p. 87.
16. *Mitchell, 1919* pp. 117–18.
17. Arno J. Mayer, *Politics and Diplomacy of Peacemaking: Containment and Counterrevolution at Versailles 1918–1919* (New York; Vintage Books, 1969), p. 540.
18. Francis Deák, *Hungary at the Paris Peace Conference: The Diplomatic History of the Treaty of Trianon* (New York, 1971), p. 57; C. A. Macartney, *Hungary and her Successors: The Treaty of Trianon and its Consequences, 1919–1937* (London, 1937), pp. 38–39; "Le dimissioni del Gabinetto Ungherese," *L'Avanti!,* March 24, 1919.
19. Sándor Garbai, a trade union leader, was made president, although Kun, who was commisar for Foreign Affairs, was the real head of the regime. Twenty-five of the 36 commissars were Jewish which led the London *Times* to brand it "the Jewish mafia." Mitchell, p.119.
20. Mayer, *Politics and Diplomacy* p. 552.
21. For the formation of the Third International see *Il Congresso della Terza Internazionale* (Rome; Edizioni Samona, 1970).
22. Arfè, *Storia del Socialismo Italiano,* pp. 204–12.
23. Mayer, *Politics and Diplomacy,* p. 555; "I proclami di Károlyi e del nuovo governo rivoluzionario," *L'Avanti!,* March 24, 1919.
24. "L'Ungheria si mette sotto la protezione delle truppe russe", *L'Avanti!,* March 24, 1919.
25. "La situazione internazionale in Ungheria "*L'Avanti!* March 25, 1919.
26. Pastor, "One Step Forward," pp. 85–87.

27. Benito Mussolini, "Il Ricatto dei Vinti, *Opera Omnia di Benito Mussolini. Dal discorso di Piazza San Sepolcro alla Marcia di Ronchi (24 Marzo 1919–13 Settembre 1919)*, ed Edoaro and Duilio Susmel (Florence, 1954), XIII, 10–11.

28. *Ibid.*

29. "L'Imprevisto ungherese. Manovra bolsevisca?" *L'Avanti!*, March 27, 1919.

30. Mitchell, *1919.* p. 195; "La Situazione," *L'Avanti!*, March 27, 1919.

31. "Notizie contradittorie dell'Ungheria," *L'Avanti!*, March 28, 1919.

32. For the text of Béla Kun's first official proclamation in English, see, Baron Albert Kass and Fedo De Lazarovics, *Bolshevism in Hungary: The Béla Kun Period* (London, 1931), pp. 327–328.

33. "Un appello al proletariato," *L'Avanti!*, March 27, 1919.

34. Melina Insolera, *Il Socialismo e il movimento operaio* (Messina, 1973), p. 14.

35. "Nell 'Ungheria dei Soviets," *L'Avanti!*, March 28, 1919.

36. Mayer, *Politics and Diplomacy.* p. 555; "Come si sciolse L'Assemblea," *L'Avanti!*, March 29, 1919.

37. "Nell'Ungheria dei Soviets. La Socializzazione continue," *L'Avanti!*, March 31, 1919; "La Socializzazione delle industrie," *L'Avanti!*, April 1, 1919.

38. "Il Saluto di Trotsky," *L'Avanti!*, March 28, 1919.

39. Alastir Davidson, *Antonio Gramsci: Towards an Intellectual Biography* (London, 1977), p. 117.

40. Joseph V. Fermia, *Gramsci's Political Thought* (Oxford, 1981) p. 143.

41. "I Soviet in Ungheria," *L'Avanti!* April 5, 1919.

42. "In Ungheria,' *L'Avanti!*, April 7, 1919.

43. "Il Comunisimo in Ungheria," *L'Avanti!*, April 7, 1919.

44. "In Ungheria,"*L'Avanti!,* April 4, 1919.

45. "La Politica religiosa dei Soviet Ungheresi," *L'Avanti!*, April 22, 1919.

46. "I Socialisti al governo e le questioni territoriali,"*L'Avanti!*, March 31, 1919.

47. "Per una Federazione delle Repubbliche dei Soviets," *L'Avanti!*, April 5, 1919.

48. "Minacce inglesi all'Ungheria," *L'Avanti!*, April 20. 1919.

49. "Un Grido d'allarme," *L'Avanti!*, April 17, 1919.

50. "La grande offensiva capitalistica contro L'Ungheria," *L'Avanti!*, April 28, 1919.

51. "Le borghesie s'affrettano alla loro pace," *L'Avanti!*, April 18. 1919.

52. Mayer, *Politics and Diplomacy*, pp. 564–65.

53. "Solo nel socialismo la pace," *L'Avanti!*, April 26, 1919.

54. "Il Proletario ascende," *L'Avanti!*, April 10, 1919.

55. "Un grido d'allarme," *L'Avanti!*, April 17, 1919.

56. Mayer, *Politics and Diplomacy,* p. 577.

57. For the minutes of the March 29, 1919 session see Paul Mantoux, *Les Délibérations du conseil des quatres* (Paris, 1955), I, 80–82.

58. Mayer, *Politics and Diplomacy*, pp. 724–29.

59. "La grande offensiva capitalista contro L'Ungherisa proletaria," *L'Avanti!*, April 28, 1919; "L'Intensa impone all'Ungheria sovietisa di restaurare la proprieta privata," *ibid.*, April 27, 1919.

60. "I Communisti ungherisi si preparano alla lotta," *L'Avanti!*, April 28, 1919; "I Rivoluzionari ungherisi per la difesa della repubblica sovietista," *L'Avanti!*, May 7, 1919.

61. "La incerta situazione della repubblica ungherese," *L'Avanti!*, April 27, 1919.

62. "Czechi e Rumeni contro L'Ungheria," *L'Avanti!*, May 4, 1919; "Gli operai rumeni contro l'invasione dell'Ungheria," *L'Avanti!*, April 30, 1919.

63. "Avviso all'Ungheria," *L'Avanti!*, May 27, 1919.

64. "Un intervista di Béla Kun," *L'Avanti!*, May 3, 1919.

65. "Le Vittorie ungherese," *L'Avanti!*, May 25, 1919.

66. "La mobilizatione del proletariato in Ungheria," *L'Avanti!*, May 6, 1919; "Le truppe ungheresi difendono la repubblica," *L'Avanti!*, May 11, 1919.

67. "La situazione nell'Ungheria e i suoi rapporti con L'Italia," *L'Avanti!*, May 12, 1919.

68. "La rivoluzione nel momento storico attuale," *L'Avanti!*, May 14, 1919.

69. Benito Mussolini, "La Lezione Magiara," *Opera Omnia di Benito Mussolini*, XIII, 188–189.

70. *Ibid.*, XIII, 189.

71. "Un importante discorso di Béla Kun,"*L'Avanti!*, May 18, 1919.

72. "Il governo ungherese rimane, " *L'Avanti!*, May 15, 1919.

73. Mayer, *Politics and Diplomacy*, p. 856.

74. "La rivoluzione contro la Santa Alleanza,"*L'Avanti!*, May 24, 1919; "Le menzogne della borghesia sulla situazione ungherese," *L'Avanti!*, May 24, 1919.

75. "I Socialisti francesi contro l'intervento in Russia e Ungheria," *L'Avanti!*, June 5, 1919.

76. Mayer, *Politics and Diplomacy*, pp. 857–63.

77. "Un discorso di Béla Kun. La rivoluzione mondiale e la nostra salvezza," *L'Avanti!*, July 5, 1919.

78. "I Fratelli ungheresi al proletariato dell'Intesa," *L'Avanti!*, May 30, 1919.

79. "Il congresso dei socialisti ungheresi," *L'Avanti!*, June 20, 1919.

80. "La dittatura del proletariato," *L'Avanti!*, June 27, 1919.

81. "Nei paesi della rivoluzione," *L'Avanti!*, June 27, 1919.

82. "Il comunismo nella vita ungherese," *L'Avanti!*, June 24, 1919.

83. "Nostra intervista con Béla Kun sulla rivoluzione ungherese," *L'Avanti!*, June 10, 1919.

84. Angelica Balabanoff, *My Life as a Rebel* (Bloomigton, 1938), p. 224.

85. "La diminuzione della criminalità nell'Ungheria rivoluzionaria," *L'Avanti!*, June 4, 1919.

86. "Béla Kun parla al congresso socialista ungherese," *L'Avanti!*, June 15, 1919; "Il congresso dei Soviet. La politica estera," *L'Avanti!*, June 24, 1919.

87. "Béla Kun non ha fiducia nella durata della pace," *L'Avanti!*, June 23, 1919.

88. "La repubblica ungherese dei soviet di fronte alla mala fede dell'Intesa," *L'Avanti!*, July 15, 1919.

89. "L'Intesa continua nella sua azione contro le repubbliche dei soviet," *L'Avanti!*, July 12, 1919.

90. "Il discorso dell' On. Claudio Treves alla Camera." *L'Avanti!*, June 25, 1919.

91. "L'Intesa non deve strongolare la liberta." *L'Avanti!*, July 19, 1919.

92. Antonio Gramsci, *Selections from Political Writings (1910–1920)* ed. Quintin Hoare, trans. John Mathews (London, 1977), p. 81.

93. *L'Avanti!*, July 16, 1919.

94. "Partito Socialista Italiano per lo sciopero generale internazionale," *L'Avanti!*, July 16, 1919.

95. "Inquadramento della difesa proletaria," *L'Avanti!*, July 2, 1919.

96. "Un movimento internazionale per la smobilizzazione, l'amnestia, e la pace con La Russia e L'Ungheria," *L'Avanti!*, June 17, 1919.

97. "La situazione dell'Ungheria al Congresso dei Soviet," *L'Avanti!*, June 21, 1919.

98. "Partito Socialista Italiano. Mentre si prepara l'azione internazionale," *L'Avanti!*, June 28, 1919.

99. Spencer di Scala, *Dilemmas of Italian Socialism: The Politics of Filippo Turati* (Amherst, 1980), p. 95.

100. W. Hilton-Young, *The Italian Left: A Short History of Political Socialism in Italy* (Westport, Conn, 1975), p. 96.

101. Simon Serfaty and Lawrence Gray (eds.), *The Italian Communist Party, Yesterday, Today, and Tomorrow* (Westport, Conn, 1980), p. 5.

102. Franco Catalano, *Storia dei partiti politici italiani* (Turin, 1965), pp. 274–75; Lelio Basso, "Turati, il riformismo e la via democratica," *Problemi del Socialismo* I (February, 1858). pp. 95–110.

103. "Lo sciopero generale internazionale del 20–21 luglio," *L'Avanti!*, July 13, 1919; "Verso so sciopero generale internazionale," *L'Avanti!*, July 15, 1919; "Il proletariato contro ogni insidia borghese," *L'Avanti!*, July 18, 1919.

104. Di Scala, p. 148; Ivanoe Bonomi, *Leonida Bissolati e il movimento socialista in Italia* (Rome, 1945), pp. 229–30; Leo Valiani, *Questioni di storia del Socialismo* (Turin, 1958), p. 426.

105. "Per lo sciopero generale del 20 e 21," *L'Avanti!*, July 17, 1919.

106. "La direzione del partito per lo sciopero internazionale del 20 e 21 corr." *L'Avanti!*, July 9, 1919; Gramsci, *Selections from Political Writings*, pp. 80–81.

107. Mayer, *Politics and Diplomacy*, p. 835.

108. Balabanoff, *My Life*, p. 268.

109. Benito Mussolini, "Lo Scioperissimo," *Opera Omnia di Benito Mussolini*, XIII, 234–35.

110. Benito Mussolini, "Caporettismo," *Opera Omnia di Benito Mussolini*, XII, 240–42.

111. Mayer, *Politics and Diplomacy*, pp. 865–66.

112. Benito Mussolini, "Aurora!" *Opera Omnia di Benito Mussolini*, XIII, 243–44.

113. Benito Mussolini, "L'Incantesimo," *Opera Omnia di Benito Mussolini*, XIII, 246–47.

114. Benito Mussolini, "Menzogna e Impudenza," *Opera Omnia di Benito Mussolini*, XIII, 257.

115. Balabanoff, *My Life*, p. 187.

116. "L'Italia proletaria ha risposta all'appello. Lo sciopero generale e stato completo frai gli operai dell'industria," *L'Avanti!*, July 22, 1919.

117. Mayer, *Politics and Diplomacy*, p. 870.

118. "Lo scioglimento del governo dei Soviet," *L'Avanti!*, August 4, 1919.

119. Benito Mussolini, "La seconda disfatta," *Opera Omnia di Benito Mussolini*, XII, 259–61.

120. Benito Mussolini, "Colmo D'Impudenza!" *Opera Omnia di Benito Mussolini*, XIII, 263.

121. Benito Mussolini, "Se Tornano I Re," *Opera Omnia di Benito Mussolini*, XIII, 292.

122. Gramsci, *Selections from Political Writings, 1910–1920*, p. 80.

123. Paul Piccone, *Italian Marxism* (Berkeley, 1983), p. 136.

124. "Le dimissioni di Béla Kun," *L'Avanti!*, August 3, 1919.

# IV
# INTERVENTIONS AGAINST REVOLUTIONS

# THE FRENCH MILITARY MISSION IN HUNGARY, 1918–1919

Peter Pastor

A year after the rise of the short-lived Hungarian Soviet Republic of 1919. Oszkár Jászi, prominent sociologist and minister of nationalities in the 1918 Károlyi cabinet, wrote in his memoirs, that, for those who see the shaping of history in acts of individuals, the father of Bolshevism was István Tisza, and its godfather—Lieutenant-Colonel Fernand Vix. It was István Tisza who, as prime minister of Hungary in 1914, went on to support the Austro–Hungarian declaration of war on Serbia. This led to the outbreak of World War I and to the eventual collapse of the Habsburg monarchy as a result of military defeat and revolutions in the closing days of the war.[1]

In Hungary, the revolution of October 31, 1918, brought to power the liberal democratic government headed by Mihály Károlyi. It was this government that negotiated a military convention with the commander of the Allied armies of the Balkans, General Louis Franchet d'Esperey. Consequently, a French Military Mission was sent to Budapest, headed by Lieutenant-Colonel Fernand Vix. Vix was to see to it that the terms of the convention were carried out by defeated Hungary. As it turned out, however, it was not the Hungarians, but France and her allies, Czechoslovakia, Serbia, and most of all Romania that appeared to be the treaty breakers in the eyes of the Hungarians. Economic hardship, exacerbated by the continuing allied blockade, apparent French hostility and its support of the territorial appetites exhibited by Hungary's neighbors at Hungary's expense—all led to conditions in Hungary where Bolshevism appeared to be not only a panacea from economic ills, but also protection against what seemed to be Entente imperialism. On March 21, 1919, the Károlyi regime gave way to Béla Kun's Communist republic. The immediate cause for this new revolutionary act was Lt.-Col. Vix's ultimatum, which demanded additional Hungarian lands, thus making it appear that Romania would reach the Tisza River boundaries accorded to her in the 1916

Secret Treaty of Bucharest.[2] Hence Vix entered into Hungarian historical conscousness as an examplary *bête noire,* and for Jászi and most of the Hungarian leaders of the liberal-democratic revolution—the godfather of Communism.

The opening of the French archives for this period, in 1969 and in 1972, however, shed new light on the activities of the French Military Mission in Hungary, and in a broader perspective on the role of the Allied Army of the Orient in East Central Europe and in Russia as an instrument of French foreign policy. The examination of documents from the above-mentioned sources indicates that the French Military Mission in Hungary had a great deal of sympathy toward the plight of the Hungarians. Vix often complained to his superiors about the way agreements were observed by Hungary's neighbors. Furthermore, the Allied commander of the *Armée d'Orient,* General Louis Franchet d'Esperey, also attempted to be even-handed with the Hungarians. Orders from Paris, however, seemed always to work against Hungarian interests. For this reason, the rise of Communism in Hungary was not the result of French military mismanagement in the field, but was due to foreign policy considerations made in Paris. The establishment of the Soviet regime in Hungary represented the first failure of French foreign policy in the region.

As the war was coming to its conclusion, French foreign policy goals toward Eastern Europe reached Napoleonic proportions. As recent publications based on French archival sources demonstrate, French foreign policy toward Russia and Eastern Europe were based on the same two-pronged strategy. It aimed to stop the spread of Bolshevism to the west, which could have helped to link Soviet Russia with Germany. Secondly, France intended to use Russian resources to help her recover from a crippling war, which, unlike the German effort, was financed by foreign, rather than domestic loans. This required the replacement of the Bolshevik government with one that would have been willing to toe the French line.[3]

French foreign policy desires toward Eastern Europe were influenced by their policy toward Russia. East Central Europe was to serve as a *barrière de l'est,* in separating Russia from Germany with a band of anti-German states. At the same time these states were to form a *cordon sanitaire,* keeping Bolshevism from reaching Germany while contributing to Bolshevism's destruction in Russia.[4] East Central Europe, just like Russia, was also envisioned as being in the French sphere of economic interest, helping Paris' economic recovery. This was the reason why the French desired some kind of economic unity among the successor states of the Austro—Hungarian empire.[5]

Thus, in the closing days of the war, France found itself shaping a post-war grand strategy that stretched from the Rhine to the Urals, and was based on the principle of a weakened France exploiting even weaker states in the East to make France strong again. In this process, Germany and Russia—two potential great powers—had to be kept in perpetual submission. Czechoslovakia was to be enlisted in this effort vis-à-vis Germany, Poland was to serve a similar role with respect to both Germany and Russia, while Romania was to provide aid in the control of Russia.[6] Serbia was perceived as fulfilling similar responsibilities, but its quarrels with its earstwhile ally, Italy, lessened such expectations. Hungary had even less significance in French calculations. Rather, its geopolitical situation—that is, its defeated status and its geographical separation from both Germany and Russia—made it possible for the French policy makers to acquiesce to a piecemeal loss of Hungarian territories to its neighbors between the months of November 1918 and March 1919. This was the price that France was willing to pay for the successor states to accept French policy.

French foreign-policy design was to be realized with the assistance of the Allied Army of the Orient, which, in fact, was a French army in the Balkans under the command of General Franchet d'Esperey. The Military Convention of Belgrade of November 13, 1918, between the representatives of France acting in the name of the Entente, and Hungary, were drawn with French goals in mind. The demarcation lines between Hungary and Romania, and Hungary and Serbia, did not follow the old frontiers of Hungary. Although these detached territories coming under Allied control, were ostensibly under Hungarian administration, they were soon annexed by Serbia and Romania.

The Belgrade Convention did not establish demarcation lines in northern Hungary. This should have allowed Hungary to administer Slovakia, which was an integral part of Hungary, but which was claimed by the the newly recognized state and ally of the Entente powers: Czechoslovakia. According to the Belgrade Convention, the French Army of the Orient had the right to occupy strategic points in Hungary, if it was so decided. Hungary's final frontiers were to be decided by the Peace Conference.[7] Evidently, General Franchet d'Esperey expected that Budapest would be occupied and that the Peace Conference would meet quickly and decide on the new frontiers of Hungary. This assumption was reinforced by the fact that the French commander had a very low opinion of the morale of the French army in the Balkans, and for this reason their quick demobilization was expected. Intervention in the Ukraine and southern Russia, however, lengthened the stay of the army, making the troops claim that the acronym AO *(Armée d'Orient)* stood for *Armée Oubliée.*[8] Frontier-making also streched out beyond his expectations and decisions were not made until mid-March.

The slow pace of preparations for the peace conference and peacemaking offered the opportunity to Hungary's neighbors to occupy Hungarian territories with the support of Paris. Thus, the French Military Mission, whose job was to oversee Hungarian compliance to the Armistice and the Belgrade Convention, faced the problem of seeing Hungary's neighbors—France's allies—changing the terms of the treaties. The French Military Mission, representing the Allies, arrived to Budapest on November 26, 1918, and it was soon inundated by Hungarian complaints of aggression.

On November 30, the Hungarian government requested the occupation of Hungary by French troops in order to protect the erosion of Hungarian imperium and to put an end to clashes in northern Hungary between Hungarian and Czechoslovak troops claiming Slovakia. The Hungarians assumed that as signatory of the Belgrade Convention, France would prevent the occupation of Hungarian lands by the "small allies," Hungary's neighbors.

Neither the Hungarians, nor the local French commanders were aware, that on November 28, Stephen Pichon, the French foreign minister, at the urging of Edvard Beneš, his Czechoslovak counterpart in Paris, pushed through the Allied Supreme Council an order calling on the Hungarians to withdraw to the historical boundaries of the Czechoslovak state. That such a state had no historical precedents did not matter to Pichon. What was the important issue was the sustenance of French foreign policy goals that the Czechoslovaks seemed to serve well. Pichon's action, in fact, indicated French disregard of Article 17 of the Belgrade Convention, stipulating Hungarian administration of all former Hungarian lands, until the Peace Conference decided otherwise.[9]

The order for the Hungarian withdrawal from Slovakia was transmitted to Vix on December 2. With this order, Vix also recived directives from the Ministry of Foreign Affairs informing him of the French government's refusal to recognize the Hungarian People's Republic and its government, headed by Károlyi. Another communiqué to Vix ordered him to treat the Károlyi government as a local authority without international status.[10]

After Vix delivered the French order for Hungarian withdrawal from Slovakia, Hungarian public opinion turned against Colonel Vix and the French Military Mission. The Hungarian leaders came to regard Vix as a heartless tyrant. In contrast to these perceptions, Vix, in communication with his immediate superior, General Paul-Prosper Henrys in Belgrade, complained that the Belgrade Convention was unilaterally broken over the Czechoslovak question. He also had difficulty in understanding the Ministry of Foreign Affairs' refusal to deal with a government which in fact had signed a treaty with the French, representing the Allies. Henrys and his superior,

General Franchet d'Esperey, shared Vix's concern, since they believed that the ability of the Károlyi government to rule was related to the temporary respect of the status quo.[11]

If the Czechoslovak affair put the French Mission in an uncomfortable position, Romanian incursions into Transylvania caused further difficulties for the French guardians of the Convention. On December 16, 1918, Vix was informed that General Henri Berthelot, commander of the Allied forces in Romania and southern Russia, had given the green light to the Romanian troops to cross the line of demarcation and to take up positions at a new line that cut further into Transylvania. In fact, it also cut into the non-Transylvanian part of Hungary. This order came two days before French intervention began in Russia with the landing of 1800 French troops in Odessa. Since Romania was expected to participate in the intervention, Berthelot's anti-Hungarian policy was tied to the Russian situation.[12]

Since General Berthelot was not Colonel Vix's superior and since Vix perceived Romanian advances as threatening the stability of Hungary, he protested to General Henrys and Franchet d'Esperey. He proposed that the French Military Mission be withdrawn since the Belgrade Convention had been destroyed, and the treaty had become a scrap of paper [chiffon de papier]. Berthelot's actions, which were taken without orders from Paris and certainly without his orders, infuriated Franchet d'Esperey, Berthelot's commanding officer. He went on to complain to Paris in January that General Berthelot's action would facilitate the spread of Bolshevism in Hungary.[13]

Franchet d'Esperey's warning of Bolshevism in Hungary was especially significant, since in his summary reports on the events of November, he stressed that Bolshevism was not a threat in East Central Europe, and that the Hungarian government's warning about the destructive potential of Bolshevism was merely a ruse to solicit favorable treatment from the Allies.[14] Yet by January Bolshevik agitation in Hungary was taken seriously enough to warrant Colonel Vix's pressure on the Hungarian government to take action against the Soviet Russian Red Cross mission in Budapest. This delegation was ostensibly in Hungary to arrange for the repatriation of Russian prisoners of war.[15]

This French pressure on the Hungarians was significant as the French Military Mission had strict orders not to interfere in the political affairs of Hungary. The French, however, saw a connection between the Russian Red Cross Committee and Béla Kun, who was sent back from Russia to organize a communist party in Hungary. Kun in the party's paper, Vörös Ujság [Red News], had attacked the Vix mission and assailed what was called "Entente imperialism." Finally, the Hungarian government, bending to French pressure, arrested the Red Cross Mission and handed its member over to the French military police who took them to Szeged for interment.[16]

In his report to Paris, Franchet d'Esperey noted that most members of the Russian Red Cross Mission were Jewish, and that in addition to the large sums they found on them earmarked for agitation, there were indications that the Russians were readying a propaganda campaign directed at the French troops who were expected to occupy Budapest. According to Franchet d'Esperey, this propaganda aimed not only to reject French anti-Bolshevik propaganda, but it also called on the French soldiers to destroy capitalist society. The French general concluded his reports by noting that the need of all revolutions to expand·was graver in this case as the urge was combined with a particular kind of Russian mysticism that desired to have the rest of the world share in the joy brought about by Communism.[17]

Franchet d'Esperey's fear of the impact of Bolshevik agitation on French troops was misplaced. The appeal of Bolshevism to French soldiers of the *Armée d'Orient* was negligible. Indeed, most looked upon this ideology as a special brand of Russian mysticism that was not for French consumption. On the other hand, the perception that Bolshevism presented a threat to the men was seriously believed by their officers. This suspicion was fanned by frustration caused by the low troop morale, since the soldiers wanted to be sent home and demobilized. Additional causes for this state of mind were the lack of supplies, and the ravages of the Spanish influenza, which killed 3224 troops, or nearly 15 percent of the 21,683 men who came down with the disease. Thus, Bolshevism in the eyes of the officers came to be the catch all that replaced Germany as the enemy.[18] Consequently, even Franchet d'Esperey, who was against intervention in Russia, came to perceive Bolshevism as a paramount threat.[19]

Franchet d'Esperey's frustration was further exacerbated by General Berthelot, who as commander of the *Army of the Danube* was his subaltern in Romania, but who also commanded the troops in the Ukraine and southern Russia on orders coming directly from Paris. Franchet d'Esperey, who was still responsible for the logistical support of the troops in Russia, felt slighted by the command structure. Furthermore, Berthelot overstepping his responsibilities, also tended to interfere in the Hungarian situation, much to the annoyance of his commander-in-chief, who feared that these actions would further undermine the Hungarian government.

Yet in spite of all this, he accepted and conveyed to Paris a Romanian canard, fanned by Berthelot, that the Hungarian government was encouraging the spread of Bolshevik agitation into Transylvania. This baseless charge was used as the justification by Berthelot to encourage Romanian expansionism that had as its goal the acquisition of lands accorded to her in the Secret Treaty of Bucharest, 1916.[20]

Most who saw Bolshevism as a danger also seemed to consider it being of Jewish making. Thus, the use in the Ukraine of some African troops from Algeria was questioned by some intelligence officers. It was assumed that they would become easy targets for subversive ideology spread by their Russian coreligionists.[21]

The Jewish-Bolshevik nexus was also seen in existence in Hungary, whose capital, according to the French ambassador in Bucharest, Count Charles Saint-Aulaire, was called *Jewdapest.*[22] Franchet d'Esperey was also aware of the supposed Jewish connection, as evidenced by his report to Paris on the Jewish make up of the Russian Red Cross Mission in Hungary. No doubt the Jewish background of many of the Hungarian Communist leaders, including Béla Kun, spelled Kuhn in Franchet d'Esperey's report, reinforced his suspicions. Hence the arrest of the Red Cross Mission was incorrectly seen in a salutory light, leading to the decline of Bolshevik agitation in Budapest.[23]

On February 26, 1919, the Peace Conference decided to adopt a recommendation of the Supreme Council that aimed at eliminating the almost daily flare-ups in Transylvania between Hungarian and Romanians. The new line of demarcation called for further Romanian advances that surpassed the Belgrade Convention line by 45 miles. Furthermore, a neutral zone was to be created between the Romanians and the Hungarians that was to be occupied by non-Romanian troops.

The "Temporary frontier" of Arad–Nagykároly–Szatmárnémeti, fitted into the strategy of Marshal Ferdinand Foch, who was bent on an all-out intervention in Russia. On February 25, Foch informed the Council of Ten that he planned to establish a united front against the Russian Bolsheviks stretching from Finland to the Crimea. For the assault, he planned to use Finnish, Polish, Czechoslovak, Romanian, and Greek troops. Direct rail connections through Hungarian territory were imperative for the campaign, and the revised demarcation lines in Hungary put the essential railways under Allied control. Foch's plan for an all-out war was rejected, but the tactical "temporary frontier" was not modified. It was not taken into consideration that in the absence of war in Russia, Allied control of the railways was not needed.[24]

Having seen Romania's unauthorized advances legitimized in Paris, Franchet d'Esperey began to assume that Transylvania would be awarded to Romania. He also expected that Romanian advances would bring Hungarian military resistance. Romania, therefore, needed to field eight divisons to face six Hungarian divisions. Franchet d'Esperey, however, wanted to make sure that these troops did not come from Bessarabia and Dobrudja, where a clash with the Red Army was a possibility. For this reason Franchet d'Esperey decided not to transmit to the Hungarians the Peace Conference decision until this problem was resolved.

While Franchet d'Esperey sought to find an opportune situation for the transmission of the *démarche* to the Hungarians, French intervention in Russia took a turn for the worse. On March 10, the pro-Bolshevik forces of Ataman Grigoriev took Kherson; by March 14 Nikolaev fell, and the Reds were advancing on Odessa. Ordered to hold the city by Clemenceau, the French declared a state of siege there.[25] In response to the crisis, Berthelot was relived of his command in Southern Russia and the whole East European theater came under Franchet d'Esperey's control.[26]

The new emergency in Russia gave the Romanians a fresh opportunity to press the French for concessions in Hungary. On March 14, on the day French intervention reached a crisis point, Victor Antonescu, a Romanian delegate at the Peace Conference, sent a memorandum to Premier Georges Clemenceau. He asserted that the Hungarians reached an accord with the Bolsheviks in the Ukraine to launch a concerted attack. This claim was without foundations, but during the days when French defeat put panic in the hearts of the French leaders, Antonescu's argument found receptive ears.

On the same day, Clemenceau, using almost the same wording of the Antonescu memorandum in justifying his order, commanded Franchet d'Esperey not to delay any further the establishment of the neutral zone. Clemenceau, like Antonescu, claimed that the Hungarians were using a scorched earth policy in Transylvania.

Having received his orders from Paris, Franchet d'Esperey ordered General De Lobit, the replacement of General Henrys in Belgrade, to transmit the order for delivery to the Hungarians. On March 20, Colonel Vix contacted the Hungarian President, Mihály Károlyi, and his Prime Minister, Dénes Berinkey. He handed them the February 26 decision of the Paris Peace Conference that called on the Hungarians to withdraw to the new demarcation line. The Hungarians were given 36 hours to reply. In Hungarian history, the Vix *démarche* became the well-known Vix Ultimatum[27]

Rather than accepting the ultimatum, which was seen as bringing about economic disaster, Károlyi and the Berinkey government's ministers resigned. Power was given to the Social Democrats, who dominated the Berinkey cabinet and who were counting on the formation of a purely Socialist government following the scheduled elections coming up in April. Károlyi hoped that the Socialists could muster Western support from the Socialist International.

Károlyi also proposed to the Socialists that they mend fences with the Communists, so that the Russian Bolsheviks on the offensive in the Ukraine would not attack Hungary in the rear, while its army would be resisting the Romanians. To improve relations with the Communists, who numbered approximately 2500 members, the government had to release the Communist party leadership from prison, where they had been incarcerated since the end of February for instigating riots.

The Socialist decision, however, was to fuse with the Communists and follow a policy which was based on Soviet Russian, rather than on Western help in fighting against exactions that were demanded by Colonel Vix. The Hungarian population, moved by national resentment, went on to provide, if only temporarily, support for the Communist-dominated government.

The Hungarian Soviet Republic was born on March 21, 1919. Two days later the Vix Mission left Budapest. The resistance of the Hungarians to French demands, represented the beginning of the unravelling of French grand strategy in Eastern Europe and Russia. The withdrawal of the French forces from Russia in April represented the final blow to French plans. This made it all the more evident that the unqualified support France gave to the territorial demands of Hungary's neighbors, leading to sizable Hungarian irredenta, was misdirected. France's partiality made rapprochement between Hungary and the successor states virtually impossible, and the unresolved tension in the Danube basin facilitated Nazi Germany's domination of the area 20 years later.

## NOTES

1. Oszkár Jászi, *Magyar Kálvária, magyar feltámadás* (München, 1969), p. 109.

2. Peter Pastor, *Hungary between Wilson and Lenin: The Hungarian Revolution of 1918–1919 and the Big Three* (Boulder, 1976), pp. 139–40.

3. Michael Jabara Carley, *Revolution and Intervention, The French Government and the Russian Civil War 1917–1919* (Toronto, 1983), p. 133; Anne Hogenhuis-Seliverstoff, *Les relations franco-soviétigques 1917–1924* (Paris, 1981), p. 91; D. Stevenson, *French War Aims against Germany* (Oxford. 1982), pp. 133–136.

4. Kalervo Hovi, *Cordon Sanitaire, or Barriére de l'Est? The Emergence of the New French Eastern European Alliance Policy 1917–1919* (Turku, 1975), p. 216; Philippe Masson, *La Marine française et la Mer Noire–1918–1919* (Paris, 1982), p. 95.

5. Maria Ormos, *Padovától Trianonig, 1918–1920* (Budapest, 1983), p. 55; Kovi, *Cordon Sanitaire*, p. 177.

6. Hogenhuis-Seliverstoff, *Les relations franco-soviétiques*, p. 108.

7. For the terms of the Belgrade Convention, see Francis Deak, *Hungary at the Paris Peace Conference* (New York, 1942), pp. 359–61.

8. Patrick Facon, *Soldat français de l'Armée d'Orient 1915–1919. Recherches sur le moral et approche des mentalités.* (Ph. D. diss. , Paris, 1978), p. 379.

9. Pastor, *Hungary between Wilson and Lenin*, p. 69; György Litván, ed.,"Documents des relations Franco–Hongroises des années 1917–1919." *Acta Historica Academiae Scientiarum Hungaricae*, No. 21, 1975, p. 194.

10. Pastor, *Hungary between Wilson and Lenin*, p. 83.

11. Ormos, *Padovától Trianonig*, pp. 104–108.

12. Peter Pastor, "Franco–Rumanian Intervention in Russia and the *Vix Ultimatum:* Background to Hungary's Loss of Transylvania," *The Canadian–American Review of Hungarian Studies*, I, 1974, 21; Ormos, *Padovától Trianonig*, p. 114.

13. Pastor, *Hungary between Wilson and Lenin*, p. 89.

14. Jean Bernachot, ed., *Les Armées Alliées en Orient aprés l'Armistice de 1918. Comptes-rendus mensuels adressés par le General Commandant en Chef des Armées Alliées en Orient, a l'Etat Major de l'Armée à Paris, de décembre 1918 á octobre 1920* (Paris, 1972) Vol. I, p. 24.

15. Pastor, *Hungary between Wilson and Lenin*, pp. 114–15.

16. Bernachot, *Les Armées Alliées*, I, 154.

17. Bernachot, *Les Armées Alliées*, I, 138.

18. Facon, *Soldat français*, pp. 437–43.

19. Facon, *Soldat français*, p. 443.

20. Peter Pastor, "Hungarian Territorial Losses During the Liberal-Democratic Revolution of 1918–1919," in Béla K. Király, Peter Pastor and Ivan Sanders, eds., *Essays on World War I: Total War and Peacemaking, A Case Study on Trianon* (New York, 1982), p. 265.

21. Facon, *Soldat français*, p. 419.

22. Comte de Saint-Aulaire, *Confession d'un vieux diplomate* Paris, 1953), p. 483.

23. Bernachot, *Les Armées Alliées*, I. 137.

24. Pastor, *Hungary between Wilson and Lenin*, pp. 122–23; Ormos, *Padovától Trianonig*, pp. 172–73.

25. Claude Paillat, *Dossiers secrets de la France contemporaine*, Vol. I. *1919: les illusions de la gloire* (Paris, 1979), p. 141.

26. Masson, *La Marine française*, p. 186.

27. Pastor, *Hungary between Wilson and Lenin*, pp. 134–35.

# THE HUNGARIAN DEMOCRATIC REPUBLIC
# AND THE PARIS PEACE CONFERENCE, 1918–1919

Zsuzsa L. Nagy

The military defeat of the Austro–Hungarian monarchy, the collapse of the Dual Monarchy opened the way to power for the democratic tendencies in Hungary. On October 31, 1918, the revolution brought a liberal democratic government to power and the monarchy was replaced by a republic. A coalition of the middle class left-wing [liberal, democratic independent, and bourgeois radical] and of the Social Democratic party politicians formed a government; Mihály Károlyi became prime minister and later, from January 1919, president of the republic. He represented modernization and the will to catch up with Western Europe. On the other hand, he symbolized the hope that the Allies would treat the country benevolently as Hungary fundamentally broke with the Habsburgs' domestic and foreign policies.[1]

The Hungarian Democratic Republic attempted to consolidate its situation among far less favorable circumstances than the majority of its neighboring countries did. Prague, Bucharest, and Belgrade enjoyed the status of minor allies of the victorious Entente. Austria, too. received much more of the Great Powers' attention, and they paid more than adequate attention to Austria than they did to Hungary.[2] The defeat and the success or failure of the attempts to establish contacts with the Entente, to break out of complete isolation, all had primary importance in the consolidation and future of liberal democracy in Hungary.

The Károlyi administration declared a pro-Entente policy. This was neither a tactical measure nor simply a reorientation of foreign policy but an internal political program, for the new regime identified its political ideals with those of Western liberal democracies,[3] and Wilson's standards served as the basis of this pro-Entente policy.

In December 1918, Károlyi declared, at the meeting of his party: "I base our foreign policy on Wilson's principles. We have only one maxim: Wilson,

Wilson and Wilson.... I am absolutely confident of Wilson conquering Europe as well as he conquered America before. Now America is facing the task to remodel all Europe, to clear the thought of revenge out of it and to create a peace that would not leave the thorn of bitterness in the heart of any single people."[4]

Károlyi's and the new political leaders' sympathy for the Entente–already well-known for the past several years–provided the main basis of the prime minister's personal appeal and of the confidence in the new regime. Illusions, however, surrounded Károlyi's personality and possiblitites just as belief in Wilsonianism was an illusion in itself. But was there any other possibility than to trust in Wilson? The answer is a clear-cut no, as the well-known Fourteen Points were the only program for them to cling to in their complete isolation and defenselessness. The special standing of the United States was the only source of any hope when facing other Great Powers. President Wilson's message of November 5, 1918 reinforced the Hungarian government's hopes. In it, he expressed his faith that "nothing would contaminate" the beginning of the new postwar era, and that the peace system would really be brought into being in a peaceful way.[5] When answering this appeal, Károlyi asked the President of the United States to come to the help of the young Hungarian democracy, "The Fourteen Points mean the only firm and just basis of legal and sensible political conditions for the Hungarian government. They offer the only solution for the internal problems already present in our country for a long period"[6]

In January 1918, in his tenth point, Wilson promised autonomous development to the peoples of the Habsburg monarchy, on the peoples and basis of the right of self-determination.[7] However, the wording of the message and the situation were ambiguous: Hungarians could base their demand for the preservation of the country's integrity on it, while non-Hungarian nationalities could also interpret it as their right to secession and creation of their own independent homelands.

Hence the fundamentally different nature in standing of Hungarians and non-Hungarians resulted from this fact. But, at the same time, Budapest, Prague, Bucharest and Belgrade possessed treaties and commitments to bolster their claims; Hungary's lot was determined by defeat and by the treaties and promises concluded in 1915–16,[8] which contained the partition of historical Hungary. The war aims of the Entente Powers as finalized and settled in 1918, were similar to the earlier goals: the creation of Czecho-slovakia and the re-establishment of Poland's national integrity and independence. The Entente promised not only territories inhabited clearly or dominantly by the nationalities of the future Czechoslovakia, Yugoslavia, or Romania but a considerable share of territories inhabited completely by Hungarians. From the many examples, suffice it to mention the region on the east of the Tisza which is to the east of the Debrecen line including Szeged as well.

The instance of the Banat can serve as an appropriate illustration of this fact that, first of all, military purposes and interests motivated the background of these pacts and promises instead of some carefully thought out cept for the territorial rearrangement of this region. In 1915, the Banat was promised to Romania. Then, at war's end, in the autumn of 1918, the two "small allies" tried to claim their rights by force of arms. French troops separated them and both occupied the town of Szeged, almost as a second thought.[9]

The United States—joining the Entente Alliance only in 1917—did not sign the treaties concluded during the war, and in this way, they had no formal obligations to abide by. Anyway, when the Great Powers gathered in Paris, the Fourteen Points had already been brought up to date by American experts, and were harmonized with the aspirations of the other Allies. The tenth point was declared invalid by the Inquiry which was an American committe of specialists: The committee also favored detaching upper northern Hungary [Slovakia], which would become part of the Czechoslovakian state. Transylvania would go to Romania.[10]

As far as Hungary's fate and that of liberal democracy was concerned, it did not matter too much whether the government was Wilsonian or not. Absolutely different factors decided the future.

The realization of these treaties and promises would have meant a serious shock for the Hungarian society even if it took place as a result of the Peace Conference's decisions, after the peace treaty had been signed, and if the territories concerned changed hands in a peaceful and ordinary way. It is clear and well known that it did not happen this way. Beside the partition of old Hungary, the manner of its execution played an equally important part in the forming of a deep and serious crisis of Hungarian society and consciousness. It also became the key factor in the lack of confidence in the Károlyi regime and its speedy loss of popularity. The same reason can be found for the extremely quick strengthening of the regime's right-wing opposition and to an even greater extent, for that of its left-wing opposition. To say the least, Hungarian society was not all prepared for the events to come. Although the Dual Monarchy's Social Democratic, Radical, and Liberal opposition often attacked the government's policy toward nationalities, they never meant to solve the social and national conflicts by the partition of historical Hungary. Oszkár Jászi had outlined a system of alliance for the democratic transformation of the Danube-basin as a whole, in which Hungarians, Czech-Moravians, Croatians, etc., could have taken part as equal partners, and in which, at the same time, Hungary could have preserved its integrity while offering her nationalities the widest autonomy possible.[11]

The joint Austro–Hungarian Army laid down its arms before the Italian army on November 3, 1918 while Germany was still actively waging war. This armistice pact fixed a demarcation line favorable from the Hungarian viewpoint: beyond the sphere of the Adriatic the then-existing borders of state were accepted.[12] However, Louis Franchet d'Esperey, the commander of the Allied Balkan Army, which was advancing in force at that moment, did not accept this line as valid for his part of the front. For this reason the Hungarian government was forced to sign a Military Convention on November 13, 1918. In the south, it already drew the demarcation line within the territory of historical Hungary, but it left the line unaltered in the north, as that territory had no military significance in that given moment.[13]

There were, and even today there are, hot debates on the necessity of the Military Convention, on the justification of the course taken by Károlyi and his companions. Those who attack them forget the very thing Jászi has formulated in his book, published in 1923, namely, that the mistake lay not in the conclusion of the Belgrade convention but in the fact that the Entente did not observe it.[14] On November 7, Károlyi and his entourage traveled to Belgrade, to negotiate with Franchet d'Esperey. The Serb Army already crossed the Dráva on the very same day. Next day, on November 8, the Czech Army penetrated the demarcation line which was identical with the border, although the Military Convention of November 13, did not permit it. Anyway, soon Paris gave its approval. The Bucharest government also gained approval for its advance in Transylvania. This way, while the Great Powers preoccupied with their preparations for the Peace Conference, the occupation of the majority of those territories took place, which were deemed their own by the neighboring countries on the basis of wartime pacts and promises.[15]

The occupation and the conflicts resulting from it, the flood of Hungarian refugees from the occupied territories, only added to the difficulties of the Károlyi government and to Hungary's consternation. One of the outcomes of occupation was that food and coal supplies were also lost, when the already poverty-stricken population would have needed them the most. In the winter of 1918–19, this became but yet another source of dissatisfaction against the regime.[16]

The greatest dilemma was to find the proper government reaction for the violation of the Armistice, for the occupation. Larger and smaller Hungarian forces, among them groups recruited by local Social Democratic organizations, tried to put up some resistance. The government itself financed actions of this sort with quite significant sums. On the other hand, they did not undertake general and centrally controlled armed resistance. Károlyi and his coalition cabinet were afraid of getting into wide-spread armed conflict with the protegés of the Great Powers as they thought it could have made the chances of Hungary fatally worse at the Peace Conference. At that time, no politician could admit that local military actions would influence, or determine, high-level diplomatic and political decisions. The Hungarian government did not give up the principle of territorial integrity, although Oszkár Jászi, as the minister responsible for matters concerning nationalities, was prepared to disclaim counties inhabited clearly, or in majority, by national minorities when negotiating with Slovakian and Romanian politicians.[17] The administration turned against Habsburg nationalistic policy, and because of its principles, it was also unable to follow the nationalist policy based on territorial gains. This cast a very dark shadow on the national minorities' aspirations for independent states. Károlyi and his companions did not want to take part in the struggle for the territories of the monarchy and of historical Hungary, as they trusted the principle of democracy and the right of self-determination. On the other hand, as the Communist daily newspaper pointed out, the non-Hungarian "national bourgeoisie did not intend to share the prey with the Hungarian bourgeoisie... ."[18]

However, let us suppose the Károlyi government wanted to take part in this struggle, and let us see if they had the means to achieve at least some minimal success? My answer to this question is a firm no. The country hardly could have been able to meet military resistance on three fronts. Reorganization of the scattered army had just begun, and was making very little headway. The bulk of its officers opposed the government from a nationalist and conservative position; the rank and file opposed it because the regime was not revolutionary enough. The soldiers, who came mostly from the peasantry, were mainly occupied with the question of land distribution and with the showdown with their old masters. In autumn 1918, returning soldiers and prisoners of war organized and directed actions like raiding manor houses, food and goods stocks of domains and city shops, expelling officials of the old administration, and lynching on more than one occasion. In only five weeks, 5000 men volunteered in a recruiting appeal—instead of 70,000 planned previously.[19]

Entente policy carried the government toward a crisis internally. For, militant enthusiasts of integrity, conservatives opposing, liberal democracy as well as left-wing radicals and Communists turned against the government simultaneously for quite different reasons and purposes. In autumn 1918, the League for the Protection of Hungary's Territorial Integrity was established under the lead of Lajos Lóczy, to express general dissatisfaction. Prominent members of the coalition cabinet were present among its founders, among them the Social Democrats Dezső Bokányi, Manó Buchinger, and Sándor Garbai. The slogan "No, no, never!"[20] was, in fact, born then, but it remained for the Horthy regime which followed the revolutions to make real use of it in its irredentist propaganda.

Nonetheless, Károlyi and his followers were conscious of the seriousness of an ever-worsening situation. In the middle of December, Károlyi declared at a cabinet session: "Vix must be informed of the Hungarian government being firmly resolved to resign if the matters will not be put right and they keep on paying so little attention to agreements. Then the French will have to take over the country and they will have to govern it by military dictatorship. What the French government is doing is a hotbed for Bolshevism."[21] Barna Buza, minister of agriculture, emphasized: "It would be a crime to stay in office and to make the country believe that any policy at all can be carried out here."[22] He proposed Allied control instead.

This idea, which resulted from the defenselessness and despair of the Hungarian administration, emerged several times, and quite seriously among the Great Powers in autumn 1918. Mainly the French—Henrys, Franchet d'Esperey, and Foch—kept on urging dismemberment, but the political leaders partly as a matter of principle and partly because they did not want the French positional advantages to grow further,[23] kept rejecting it.

Although Károlyi—via eager Swedish mediators—had already asked for an Entente mission to be sent to Budapest in November, the Peace Conference turned its attention toward Hungary only when they wanted to gather information on the general situation in East-Central Europe. Anyway, even this bore great significance; for until that time the government could contact the Entente only through Lieutenant-Colonel Fernand Vix.[24] Very understandably this link could not be sufficient for the Hungarian democratic regime struggling for its very existence and for the country.[25]

Two problems attracted the attention of the Peace Conference: the stability and ability of resistence of various governments facing Bolshevism spreading out of Soviet-Russia, and economic conditions, the misery of the populations, as sources of revolutionary unrest.

As a result of the position of the United States Herbert Clark Hoover gained a dominant role in the Supreme Economic Council while he was also the European head of the American Relief Administration. A number of committees were established, such as the Inter-Allied Food Council, Railway Mission, and the Coal, the Supreme Economic Council. These played prominant roles in the economic reorganization of Europe and the former Habsburg Monarchy. The Communication Section working for the Supreme Economic Council constructed telephone and telegraph services for Hoover, and his staff established contact with Hungary.[26]

In Switzerland, Hoover established a committee under the leadership of Alonzo Englebert Taylor for the analysis of the economic situation of the former monarchy and so this soon moved to Vienna.[27] Another mission was organized headed by Archibald Carry Coolidge to measure the political situation of the area, to collect information suitable to draw borders [the distribution of the population by natonality and by religion, employment structure, etc.] and this also settled in Vienna.[28] The very fact that these important missions worked in Vienna was favorable for the Hungarian administration as well. The Austrian government – in quite an unparallelled way–was willing to accept the Hungarian administration's representative with the standing of an ambassador, and what is more, they also delegated an ambassador to Budapest.[29] The reason for this is clear: independence produced a lot of problems needing solution in all aspects of life for the two former ruling nations of the empire. On the other hand, the democratic Austrian administration felt sympathy for the Károlyi regime. For these reasons, the Hungarian embassy in Vienna could obtain precious and most needed information on the activities of the Entente mission, and Hungary pinned high hopes on it.

At the beginning Károlyi and his colleagues found it prejudicial that the economic problems of Hungary were not treated by a separate commission; hence, they wanted the Taylor mission to move its residence from Vienna to Budapest.[30] This attempt failed. However, they managed to establish contact with Taylor as well as with Coolidge well before they arrived at Budapest and even before they arrived at Vienna. In late November, early December 1918, the emissary of the Hungarian government in Switzerland, Róza Bédy-Schwimmer, had several negotiations with Taylor; she explained to him the difficulties of food supply in Hungary.[31] Talks took place with Coolidge in Switzerland, too. Count Antal Sigray, special representative of the Hungarian cabinet, informed Coolidge that Hungary favored plebiscite to decide the future status of Slovakia, the Banat, and Transylvania. He stressed that Hungary needed a seaport on the Adriatic, and protested against the one-sided violation of the Belgrade Military Convention which put the Károlyi regime in a very grave situation.[32]

In January 1919, the Taylor and Coolidge missions visited Budapest one after another.[33] At the same time, a cabinet crisis broke out. The question emerged, could the coalition cabinet be maintained or was it to hand power over to a purely middle class or to a purely Social Democratic cabinet!

Both missions had talks with many public figures besides Károlyi and his cabinet. Their manner of information gathering was characterized by goodwill and understanding and they referred to Hungarian conditions in the same manner to their superiors.

Taylor and his staff were correct when they stated that food supply was not so very critical in Hungary as it was in Austria. At the same time, they pointed out the importance of the lack of coal, which paralyzed industry, thereby creating unemployment, and hence increasing the appeal of Bolshevik propaganda. Taylor and Coolidge both concluded that it was necessary to supply food aid to Hungary, in the spirit of the views expressed by Hoover. It was Hoover, who declared: "The whole problem of building a bulwark against encroaching Bolshevism from Russia revolves around larger and larger food supplies to the bordering states."[34] The well-informed embassy of Vienna wrote the following to Károlyi, before the Coolidge mission arrived in Budapest: "our position is considerably strengthened by the quite visibly demonstrated fear of not only the Entente Powers but of America itself. This fear is generated by the spreading of victorious Bolshevism and they recognize their only chance to stop it in supplying food and consumers' goods to the Central European states which are in critical situation."[35]

Coolidge's and his colleagues' mission saw the violation of the Armistice, the country's occupation, and the breaking up of its economic unity as factors which really shattered the cabinet's position. They noticed that the left-wing opposition utilized it for in its own interests when demanding a Soviet orientation instead of the unsuccessful Wilsonian policy of Károlyi and his followers.

Coolidge and some members of his mission expressly supported certain territorial demands of the Károlyi government, as they found them justifiable from economic and political aspects,—not to mention ethnical.[36]

In their reports to the Paris Peace Conference,[37] both missions urged the strengthening of the position of Károlyi and the regime, to make it possible for them to face internal left-wing pressure. At the same time, they requested clear-cut and determined measures to be taken against the Communist movement. Sir Thomas Cuninghame, head of the British military mission in Vienna, propounded it even more categorically. In January he also had talks in Budapest.[38]

In spite of these reports, the efforts of the American Relief Administration and the personal efforts of Hoover as well, as in spite of some American business agreements (as the relief transports were far form being free of charge), the Hungarian liberal democratic system received no economic support deserving mention. The refusal of Prague and Belgrade to transport coal and foodstuff proved to be stronger than the intentions of the American experts.[39]

Any support of Hungarian democracy was opposed in the most determined manner by the French, and the hands of the American and the British were tied by the economic blockade effective since the start of the war, and brought to bear on Hungary as well. That is why Hoover, a more far-sighted man with a clearer concept, had already urged the raising of the blockade from the end of 1918. On March 12, 1919 he really managed to get the Supreme Economic Council to agree to raising of the blockade and to propose it formally before the Council of Ten for an ultimate decision on the matter. However, it was placed on the agenda only after March 21, 1919, and by then the proletarian dictatorship had come to power in Hungary.[40] As a final conclusion, we may state that the economic blockade remained effective against the liberal democratic regime to the same extent as it a did against the dictatorship of the proletariat. Hungary received no more than 633 out of the 27 million metric tons of foodstuff which arrived in Europe from overseas according to American Relief Administration statistics for the period December 1, 1918 to June 30, 1919. It is also true however, that it was all given to the Károlyi government.[41] Anyway, the very limited amount of food transport could not influence events in Hungary according to the desires of the Entente, the more so as it was not able to alter the root of all unrest, the occupation and territorial dismemberment.

Chiefly from economic aspects, primarily American experts suggested the necessity of a closer cooperation among the nations of the former monarchy on more than one occasion. The Inquiry when re-evaluating President Wilsons' Fourteen Points raised the issue of the forming of a democratic alliance system. The experts of the American Relief Administration, of the Supreme Economic Council, and of other organizations considered the destruction of a working economic organism irrational, including the blocking of transport routes. There were also some French politicians who agreed with the forming of some sort of alliance, and what is more, they intended Hungary to play a central role in it.[42] Anyway, at the end the Great Powers realized a quite different concept for this region: they did not enforce the founding of some closer cooperation in the least degree. For that matter it hd only two supporters in the Danube basin: Austria and Hungary. This fact alone made the whole idea suspicious to other countries.

The Hungarian administration had to admit that the visits of the Entente missions to Budapest did not change the behavior of the Great Powers toward Hungary. The country's disadvantagous, and discriminated, position remained the same. However, its isolation lessened somewhat, and a certain kind of interest in Hungarian matters began to present itself. Károlyi and his colleagues tried to profit from the conflicting interests of various powers and the still fluid conditions in the area.

Of the Great Powers only Italy showed readiness to establish some relations with Hungary. As backround for this, two motives could be discerned: one, the desire to turn the Danube basin into an Italian sphere of influence: the other, to weaken and to isolate Yugoslavia, Italy's rival in the Adriatic. That is why intense talks were initiated by the Italians with Hungarian diplomats. These continued not only during the dictatorship of the proletariat but also resulted in various food, manufactured goods, and war materiél transports.[43]

Of the neighboring countries, allies of the Entente, Czechoslovakia and Romania were not willing at all to cooperate with the Károlyi regime. Yugoslavia and Poland, however, showed willingness to cooperate, and this was considered as being very important by Budapest. Yugoslavia had only minimal territorial demands and Poland had none at all. As far as Yugoslavia was concerned, the future of Fiume had great significance for Hungary and arrangements were being worked out to secure the use of this Adriatic port. Warsaw and Budapest were brought close to each other by the fact that both regimes had serious conflicts with Prague concerning the possession of certain territories. Traditional Hungarian–Polish sympathies and historical relations also played their part in this. The good relationship with Yugoslavia and Poland offered reason to hope for the easing of French hostility toward Hungary. That is why Károlyi judged it more useful to cooperate with Yugoslavia although he continued negotiations with Italy as well.[44] After some initial probing in Trieste and Vienna, more serious talks were started in neutral Switzerland. Returning from Paris, Kosta Stojanović, a member of the Yugoslavian Peace delegation spent some time in Switzerland where he consulted László Szilassy. Stojanović proposed the following to the Hungarian government—with the knowledge and consent of Foreign Minister Ante Trumbić: Yugoslavia would offer a special status and some advantages for Hungary in Fiume if the Hungarian regime supported the Yugoslavian claim for the port (formally this was still under Hungarian sovereignty). They would also accept some border corrections favorable for Hungary if the rights of the Southern-Slav inhabitants of the territories in question were guaranteed in advance. Stojanović also hinted at the fact that they would have found it more favorable if Hungary obtained those territories (the Banat) which Yugoslavia proved to be unable to get from Romania. Yugoslavia was prepared to establish an economic alliance or a customs union with Hungary.[45]

At the end of February 1919, Károlyi naturally gave a positive answer to Stojanović's most favorable offer. He was even willing to establish the customs union before the bilateral settlement of territorial problems. In March, the negotiations showed the most favorable prospects.[46]

In the development of Polish-Hungarian relations the efforts of the Károlyi government to coordinate its conduct with the anti-Soviet policy of the Great Powers played a prominent part—beside the factors already mentioned. Prague gave no permission for the transport of arms for the Polish army through Czechoslovakian territories because of existing border debates with Poland, although France intended to support the Poles with most means in their fight against the Red Army.[47] For this reason, the Hungarian government —at the request of Vix—routed war materièl destined for the Ukraine in exchange for gasoline, to Poland.[48] The Poles, however, had already regularly delivered coal to Hungary before this, as Czechoslovakia was not inclined to do it. At the end, on March 4, 1919, the Hungarian and Polish partners signed a formal transport contract.[49]

Károlyi, as well as the Polish regime, considered close cooperation a vitally important matter. Establishment of a common border also emerged in accordance with historical traditions. The slightest hint of a common Hungarian—Polish border provoked the most vehement protests of Prague.[50] Direct contact between the two countries by the way of state frontiers held significance for Károlyi, first of all, from the aspect of an over-all plan. The favorably developing Hungarian—Yugoslav and Hungarian—Polish relations and the demand from various sides to look for the possibilities of cooperation with those countries which had no essential conflicts with Hungary also had a part in the development of Károlyi's concept. At the end, it took the shape of a proposed alliance of Poland, Hungary, and Yugoslavia. Károlyi wanted to draw Austria into this system from the outset; he also wanted Czechoslovakia and Romania to take part after resolving outstanding conflicts.[51]

Károlyi's alliance system would not have excluded any state of the region. In this form, it could have been just the opposite of the later Little Entente as that meant the alliance for winners only.

These promising contacts, however led nowhere: one of the Peace Conference's well-known decisions brought about the fall of the liberal democratic regime. In the last days of February 1919, the establishment of a neutral zone was proposed on the Hungarian—Romanian demarcation line by André Tardieu, to satisfy Romanian territorial claims and by Marshal Foch as a preliminary measure of a planned large-scale anti-Soviet military campaign. On February 26, 1919, military experts of the Council of Ten consented to this proposal and worked out its details. Although it had opponents—as the French general Antoine Charpy—it was passed as a resolution in the absence of the leaders of the Big Four after it was declared that the decision was a simple military measure taken for the maintenance of order in this region. The establishment of the neutral region wuld have meant the loss of sovereignty over towns like Debrecen and Szeged, with purely Hungarian population.[52]

News of this decision reached Budapest in February. However the cabinet did not pay it any more attention than it did to any other rumors and information originating in Paris.[53]

About a month later, the situation took a tragic turn. On March 20, 1919, Lieutenant-Colonel Vix and the American Captain Nicholas Roosevelt handed over a note signed by French General Paul de Lobit to Károlyi. In it, the borders of the neutral zone were clearly outlined. The Hungarian government was obliged to withdraw its troops, but as the note stated: "The peace conference empowered the Romanian troops to push their lines forward to the Eastern border of the neutral zone." The note, dated March 19, prescribed the giving of an answer of acceptance until 6 pm on the 21st.[54]

This memorandum was another and last evidence of the fact that the Entente did not attach any importance to the survival of Hungarian liberal democracy, to the fate of Hungary. This disregard was also expressed by the procedure followed, because, although the decision dated back to February 26, the Hungarian government was informed of it only on March 20, and an answer was demanded within 24 hours.

It is indisputable that more radical and quickly executed internal reforms could have improved the government's position. However, there can be no doubt that the Great Powers sealed the fate of the Hungarian People's Republic from the very beginning when they practically excluded Hungary from their aid program, and when they made territorial gains possible before the official decision of the Peace Conference. No Hungarian government could give up still more territory in spring 1919. For President Mihály Károlyi and Prime Minister Dénes Berinkey had no choice but to state "the government is not in the position to accept the decision of the Peace Conference and to cooperate in its execution".[55]

The policy of the Great Powers, as a determining factor, made the consolidation of liberal democracy impossible in Hungary and had a primary role in a peaceful Communist takeover. The dictatorship of the proletariat, the Soviet type of regime, did not come to power by armed force. The Peace Conference not only did not prevent the creation of the political system it wanted to avoid, but directly caused its establishment. Dezső Bokányi, one of the leading figures of the Social Democratic party, aptly characterized the general situation and the mood of the masses: "So here we recognized that we were simply disillusioned with this whole appeal (namely Wilson's 14 Points) and I harangued about the British and the French all in vain—by then only the Russian star shone bright."[56]

## NOTES

1. For a general outline of the history of the democratic republic, see, Tibor Hajdu, *Az 1918-as magyarországi polgári demokratikus forradalom*[The bourgeois democratic revolution of Hungary in 1918] (Budapest, 1968); for its international situation and foreign policy Zsuzsa L. Nagy, *A párizsi békekonferencia és Magyarország 1918–1919* [The Paris Peace Conference and Hungary, 1918–1919] (Budapest, 1965); Zsuzsa L. Nagy "Magyar határviták a párizsi békekonferencián 1919-ben" [Debates on the Hungarian Frontier Question at the Paris Peace Conference], *Történelmi Szemle* 21, 3–4, (1978); Peter Pastor, *Hungary between Wilson and Lenin: the Hungarian Revolution of 1918–1919 and the Big Three (New-York-Boulder, 1976);* Mária Ormos; *Pádovától Trianonig 1918–1920* [From Padova to Trianon] (Budapest, 1983).

2. See the activity of the American Relief Administration and the case of west-Hungary (Burgenland). Suda Lorena Bane and Ralph Haswell Lutz, eds., *Organization of American Relief in Europe 1918–1919,* (Stanford, 1943); Katalin Soós; *A nyugat-magyarországi kérdés 1918–1919* (Budapest, 1962).

3. Oszkár Jászi and the radical intellectuals worked out the program of Hungary's modernization on this basis at the beginning of our century. György Litván, János F. Varga, eds., *Jászi Oszkár publicisztikája. Válogatás* (Budapest, 1982); Oszkár Jászi, *Uj Magyarország felé. Beszélgetések a szocializmusról* [Toward a New Hungary. Conversations on Socialism] (Budapest, 1970).

4. *Pesti Hírlap* Dec. 31, 1918.

5. *Papers Relating to the Foreign Relations of the United States. 1918.* Supplement I. *The World War* Washington 1933), Vol. 1. 470 (henceforth *Papers*).

6. *Papers Relating to the Foreign Relations of the United States. The Paris Peace Conference* (henceforth Papers PPC) (Washington, 1942) II, 193–195.

7. *Papers* pp. 15–16, 270, 319.

8. See, H. W. Temperley; *A History of the Peace Conference of Paris.* (London, 1921) IV, 516–17. F. J. Vondarcek, *The Foreign Policy of Czechoslovakia 1918–1935. (New York, 1937)* 24 ff. Ivo J. Lederer, *Yugoslavia at the Paris Peace Conference* (New Haven–London, 1963) 12 ff., Piotr S. Wandycz; *France and Her Eastern Allies 1919–1925.* (Minneapolis, 1962). pp. 10, 14–15.

9. József Breit, *A magyar 1918–19. évi forradalmi mozgalmak és a vörös háború története.* [The History of the Revolutions of 1918–1919 and the Red War] I–II (Budapest, 1925), vol. I. 133.

10. *Papers PPC* I (Washington, 1942) pp. 34, 41, 85.

11. Jászi Oszkár, *Uj Magyarország.*

12. *Papers* p. 430. ff. Ferenc Nyékhegyi, *A Diaz-féle fegyverszüneti szerződés* [The Diaz Armistice Treaty] (Budapest, 1922), p. 5 ff.

13. *Memoirs of Michael Károlyi: Faith without Illusions.* (London, 1956), pp. 130–137; *Papers PPC* II. pp. 183–85.

14. Oscar Jászi: *Magyariens Schuld Ungarns Sühne. Revolution und Gegenrevolution in Ungarn* (München, 1923), pp. 56–57.

15. *Papers PPC* IVII (Washington, 1946), p. 179 ff; XII (1947), p. 373; Peter Pastor; "Hungarian Territorial Losses During the Liberal-Democratic Revolution of 1918–1919," in, Béla K. Király, Peter Pastor and Ivan Sanders, eds., *War and Society in East Central Europe.* VI. *Essays on World War I: Total War and Peacemakin, A Case Study on Trianon..* (New York, 1982).

16. Országos Levéltár, Budapest (National Archives) K 27 MT Jkv (Minutes of the Council of Minister) Dec. 3., 1918. and K 63 KÜM Gazd. pol. (Ministry of Foreign Affairs, Department of Economic Policy) Bundle 1 item A/16. 1222/1918; *Organization of American Relief* p. 193; *Papers PPC* XII pp. 373–74.

17. Országos Levéltár K 27 MT Jkv Dec. 3, 17, 1918. Jan. 21, 1919, and K 40 A Magyarországon élő nemzetek önrendelkezési joga előkészítésével megbízott tárca nélküli miniszter (Jászi Oszkár) iratai (The Minister in Charge of the Preparation of the Right of Self-determination of the Nations Living in Hungary) 1918–1919; C. A. Macartney: *Hungary and Her Successors. The Treaty of Trianon and its Consequences* 1917–1937 (London–New-York–Toronto, 1937). pp. 23, 49–51, 103 ff, 213–14, 218.

18. *Vörös Ujság* Dec. 14, 1918.

19. Sándor Juhász Nagy: *A magyar októberi forradalom története* [The History of the Hungarian October Revolution] (Budapest, 1945), p. 453.

20. Országos Levéltár K 27 MT KJkv Jan. 30. 1919.

21. *Ibid.*, Dec. 17. 1918.

22. *Ibid.*, Dec. 18, 1918.

23. See, for example, *Papers PPC* II. pp. 214–15. V. S. Mamatey, *The United States and East Central Europe 1914–1918. A Study in Wilsonian Diplomacy and Propaganda* (Princeton, 1957), p. 347.

24. *Papers PPC* II. pp. 204–205.

25. Sándor Vadász: "Vix és Károlyi," *Hadtörténlmi Közlemények* XVI, 2, (1969). Peter Pastor, "The Vix Mission in Hungary 1918–1919: A Re-examination," *Slavic Review* (1970) 3.

26. *Organization of American Relief* pp. 306–307, 383, 455, 459, 461, 485, 666 ff. *Papers PPC* X. 44–45, 131, 399. *The Memoirs of Herbert Hoover,* I–III. (New York, 1951–52)

27. Bane and Lutz, *Organization of American Relief,* pp. 65, 91, 11–112, 127, 221–22.

28. Harold Jefferson Coolidge and Robert Howard Lord, eds., *Archibald Carry Coolidge. Life and Letters.* (Boston–New York, 1932); *Papers PPC* I. p. 194. ff. *Papers PPC* II pp. 209–210, 219.

29. Országos Levéltár K 27 MT Jkv Nov. 12, 13. Dec. 6, 1918 and K 64 KÜM A bécsi magyar követség iratai (Papers of the Hungarian Embassy in Vienna). There was another state—the neutral Switzerland—the government of which accredited the diplomatic representative of the Károlyi regime. See, Országos Levéltár K 27 MT Jkv Nov. 18, Dec. 29, 1918. Jan. 18, 1919; K 63 KÜM A bécsi magyar követség iratai, 1918/88. The first Hungarian representative in Bern was Róza Bédy-Schwimmer. (Her papers can be found in the New York Public Library.) Her successor was Baron László Szilassy, the only diplomat of the old monarchy who accepted the representation of the Károlyi regime. Ladislaus Szilassy, *Der Untergang der Donau-Monarchie* (Berlin, 1921).

30. Országos Levéltár K 63 KÜM Gazd. polg. Bundle 5, item a/24. 1919/20 659

31. Ibid. Bundle 11, item H/15, 258/1918, 979/1918, 20 338/1918, 2320/1918 Bundle 1, item A/16. 132/1918; Bane and Lutz, *Organization of American Relief* p. 1 119.

32. Országos Levéltár K 27 MT Jkv Dec. 28, 1918. *Papers PPC* ii. pp. 221, 224. Coolidge and Lord, *Archibald Carry Coolidge*, p. 210.

33. For negotiations of the two missions in Budapest, see, Zsuzsa L. Nagy; *A párizsi békekonferencia*, pp. 31–78; Zsuzsa L. Nagy, "Az antant segélyprogramja és az 1918–1919. évi forradalmak," [The Aid Program of the Entente Powers and the Revolutions of 1918–1919] *Párttörténeti Közlemények* IX., 3 (1963), pp. 48–52.

34. Bane and Lutz, *Organization of American Relief* p. 258.

35. Országos Levéltár K 63 KÜM Gazd. pol. Bundle 5, item A/16. 20 298/1919.

36. The American peace delegation warned Coolidge on Feb. 26, 1919, because he had dealt too much with the territorial problems of the late Monarchy. *Papers PPC* XII. p. 522; Coolidge, and Lord *Archibald Carry Coolidge*, pp. 205, 212.

37. The reports of the Taylor mission: *Papers PPC* XII. p. 232. ff; Bane and Lutz, *Organization of American Relief* pp. 381–84; Coolidge's reports, *Papers PPC* II, pp. 221, 224; XII, 232 ff, 266 ff, 372 ff, 395 ff.

38. Sir Thomas Cuninghame. "Between the War and the Peace Treaties. A Contemporary Narrative," *Hungarian Quarterly* 5. (1939).

39. Bane and Lutz, *Organization of American Relief* p. 225; *Papers PPC* XII, pp. 237–39.

40. *Papers PPC* IV, pp. 204, 469, 522. X. (Washington, 1947) p. 66.

41. Bane and Lutz *Organization of American Relief*, p. 651, Table II.

42. *Papers*, p. 411; *Papers PPC* XII, pp. 241, 331. Mamatey, p. *The United States*, p. 381. On the French conceptions, see, Wandycz, *France*, p. 187 ff.

43. Zsuzsa L. Nagy, "Italian National Interests and Hungary in 1918–1919," in Király, Pastor and Sanders, eds., *War and Society in East Central Europe*, pp. 201–26.

44. Országos Levéltár K 63 KÜM Res. pol. 1919/982.

45. *Ibid.*, 1919/996, 1919/1 133, 1919/1 601, 1919/1661.

46. *Ibid.*, 1919/1133.

47. *Ibid.*, Gazd. pol. Bundle 10, item H/9. 1919/20 460.

48. *Ibid.*, the papers of bundle 1, item A/7. 1918.

49. *A magyar munkásmozgalom történetének válogatott dokumentumai* (Budapest, 1956) Vol. V. 1917 november 7–1919. március 21. (Budapest, 1955) p. 488.

50. *Papers PPC* XII pp. 275, 323. Wandycz *France*, pp. 92–83.

51. Országos Levéltár K 63 KÜM Res pol. 1919/996. Rome also had backed the idea of such confederacy of state if instead of Yugoslavia Italy was the member of it. Wandycz, *France*, p. 94.

52. *Papers PPC IV*, pp. 59–61, 145–46. VII., p. 180.

53. Juhász Nagy, *A magyar októberi forradalom*. p. 422.

54. *Papers PPC* XII, p. 413 ff.

55. *Ibid.*, p. 417.

56. PI Archívum Budapest [Archives of the Institute of the History of the Party] fond. 704. Károlyi-per [Trial of Károlyi] Box 1. Dezső Bokányi's confession.

# GENERAL HENRI BERTHELOT
# AND THE ARMY OF THE DANUBE,
# 1918–1919*

Glenn E. Torrey

The *Allied Army of the Orient (AAO)* at Salonika dramatically improved its military position in autumn 1918. A political and military football since its creation in 1915,[1] it carried out a successful offensive in mid-September under the leadership of the energetic General Louis Franchet d'Esperey, knocking Bulgaria out of the war and endangering the entire Austro–German position in southeastern Europe.[2] The army's advance brought Romania back into the center of Allied plans. Forced to leave the war almost a year before by the Russian Revolution, the Romanians occupied a strategic position and possessed a militaty potential the French were determined to utilize. Their army, reorganized and proven in 1917 under General Henri Berthelot, was counted on heavily in Paris for assistance in subduing the strong Austro–German forces in southeastern Europe and south Russia, and as cadre for the creation of an effective anti-Bolshevik coalition. As Kalervo Hovi and others have pointed out, Romania was re-emerging as an indispensible link in the French alliance system in Eastern Europe, whether that be interpreted as a *cordon sanitaire* or a *barrière de l'est*.[3]

The logical person to rouse Romania to action and to coordinate her contribution to the Allied cause was General Henri Berthelot. His first mission (October 1916–March 1918) had given him acceptance and authority among the Romanians that went beyond respect and bordered on worship. The king and the army leadership trusted him implicitly and the masses had made him the object of a veritable cult, some peasants even placing a picture of "Papa Berthelot" among their sacred icons.[4] Two days after Bulgaria surrendered (September 29), Berthelot was called to Paris from his command of the *Fifth Army* on the Western Front to be briefed by Premier Georges Clemenceau for a second mission in Romania. He was surprised that his tasks were much political as military: one, to work for the dismissal of the collaborationist Marghiloman government in Iasi and the organization of resistance to the Austro–German occupation; two, to organize Allied military action to liberate Romania and bring about her re-entry into the war at the side of the allies; three, to organize the Romanian army for cooperation with the *AAO* and with Russian forces favorable to the Allies.[5]

Berthelot's second mission has been praised by Romanians as an important contribution to the creation of Greater Romania, but it has been criticized by others. The latter regret his Romanophile policies and deprecate his role in the unsuccessful French military expedition in south Russia. This study utilizing Berthelot's unpublished "Mémoires" and personal correspondence, will not resolve these controversies but, one hopes, will contribute to an understanding of the general's thinking and his stewardship as commander of the *Army of the Danube*.[6]

Berthelot departed Paris for Salonika on October 8 by special train, taking with him his personal staff and hand-carrying orders for General Louis Franchet d'Esperey outlining his mission. The commander of the *Armées Alliées d'Orient (AAO)*, who had no advance warning of what Paris had planned, gave Berthelot a cool reception.[7] Franchet d'Esperey had fought long and hard for permission to launch his offensive and now that it was succeeding he believed his contribution was not being properly recognized.[8] Furthermore, Franchet d'Esperey had ambitions to continue his advance to Budapest, Vienna, and possibly even Berlin. Berthelot's arrival and the orders he carried meant the cancellation of these plans and the transfer to Berthelot of an appreciable portion of his forces to create a new *"Army of the Danube."* Although Berthelot's activity in the Balkans remained under Franchet d'Esperey's supervision, for operations in South Russia he was answerable directly to Paris.[9]

Franchet d'Esperey interpreted Berthelot's appointment as a deliberate move to restrict his authority by Clemenceau and by Chief-of-Staff Ferdinand Foch "who could only conceive of and desire victory on the front he commanded."[10] Although Franchet d'Esperey was vain, intolerant, and quarrelsome by nature,[11] the hostility and unfair evaluations of Berthelot which pervade his writings appear related to his view of the latter as the instrument of his enemies in Paris. Franchet d'Esperey's hostility, which Berthelot soon reciprocated, is an essential key to understanding what later transpired.

Nevertheless Franchet d'Esperey, following his new orders, had given Berthelot a military force by the end of October. The *Army of the Danube* consisted of three French divisions, one British division, and various smaller units. Franchet d'Esperey charged Berthelot with organizing his forces in

Bulgaria, advancing to the Danube, liberating Romania and then joining with the Romanian army in routing the Austro–German forces.[12]

By November 8, Berthelot and units of the *Army of the Danube* were poised on the right bank of the river anxious to intercept the army of General August von Mackensen, which had already begun to withdraw from Romania. On that day Berthelot telegraphed to Iasi "I earnestly request the Romanian army be mobilized immediately. Any later will be too late."[13] King Ferdinand, who had already brought in a government favorable to the Entente, ordered the army to reenter the war on November 10.[14] During the night of November 9–10, the *Army of the Danube* crossed onto Romanian soil near Giurgiu, 35 miles south of Bucharest. Simultaneously French aircraft dropped Berthelot's famous "call to arms" on the capital, a document which reveals an intimate knowledge of the Romanian spirit, ending with the stirring appeal, "Wake Up Romanian brothers and throw yourselves on the enemy."[15] Berthelot's diary and private correspondence reveal how important this moment was to him emotionally, fulfilling as it did his promise to the Romanian people that his forced departure several months previously was "not goodbye but 'til we meet again, soon, after victory."[16] His behavior was carefully planned. As he confided to his nephew, Georges, he intended by "a sensational entry into Romania" to pass "into Romanian posterity"[17] During the victory parade down the Calea Victoriei some weeks later, he rode at the right hand of the king, amid the adulation of the populace. Berthelot's sharing with the Romanian people their exaltation in victory, as he had already shared in the agony of their defeat, strengthened his identification with the Romanian cause and gave him immense pleasure. "Here one honors me on all sides." he wrote to his sister-in-law Louise, "and people recognize me as nothing less than the liberator of Romania. I confess to you that it pleases me."[18] The depth of Berthelot's identification with the Romanian people and his participation in their euphoria at the prospect of a Greater Romania is another essential key to understanding his tenure as commander of the *Army of the Danube*.

The Austro–Hungarian surrender on November 4, followed by that of Germany on November 11, eliminated for Berthelot and the *Army of the Danube* the necessity of conducting a military campaign against the strong forces of General August von Mackensen. That aspect of Berthelot's original orders had been reduced to the supervision of their withdrawal and the maintenance of stability in the territory destined for Romanian sovereignty.[19] The delineation of this sovereignty seemed simple to the Romanians, and to Berthelot: the restoration of the frontiers of 1916, augmented by Bessarabia, plus the Austro–Hungarian territories promised in the Treaty of 1916.[20]

To the Hungarians, seeking to save as much as possible of historic Hungary, to the Serbs, claiming portions of the Banat promised Romania, and even to certain Allied leaders themselves, the Romanian claims appeared excessive. The major Allied powers, embarrassed by their own often conflicting promises, sought to defer a final solution until the deliberations of the peace conference. The interplay of nationalist feelings and ideological ferment, together with the breakdown of authority accompanying the end of the war, made an orderly interim difficult if not impossible. It was into this situation that Berthelot and the *Army of the Danube* were thrust.

Buoyed by euphoria over victory and his own natural optimism, Berthelot oversimplified his tasks as he established his headquarters on Romanian soil. "I have three principle problems to liquidate," he wrote Louise, "Dobrudja with the Bulgars, Transylvania with the Hungarians, and South Russia with the Bolsheviks. I hope that this will not take too long."[21] This study will consider briefly the role of Berthelot and the *Army of the Danube* in each of these three questions.

The Bulgarians had claimed the entire Dobrudja as a reward for their contribution to the defeat of Romania in 1916 but their German allies had restricted them in the Treaty of Bucharest (May, 1918) to the territory south of the line, Cernavoda-Constanta. The Treaty of Bucharest was voided by the armistice of November 11, but as the German army evacuated Dobrudja at the beginning of November the Bulgarians extended their occupation northward. Franchet d'Esperey ordered the Bulgarians to withdraw all their forces from Dobrudja, replacing them with Allied troops (British) but permitting Bulgarian administration to remain and assuring the Bulgars this action would not prejudice the decisions of the peace conference.[22] The Romanians, nervous about rumors of Allied hedging concerning the future of Dobrudja, were determined to reclaim immediately what had been theirs in 1916 and demanded that Romanian administration replace the Bulgarian.[23] Berthelot, believing he had the authority, obliged. As he wrote his nephew Georges: "I have secured also from the Allied governments that one treat the Bulgars as they deserve and that one obligate them to evacuate the Romanian Dobrudja. I have given them until December 3 to go home, failing that, it is by cannon shots that one will force them."[24] Franchet d'Esperey, however, reiterated to Berthelot on November 26 his orders that Bulgarian administrators be left in place. Berthelot, believing it "strange that we would tolerate this expropriation by those people who have been our enemies to the detriment of the Romanians who have been our friends,"[25] termed Franchet d'Esperey's position "inadmissible" and went over his head to Clemenceau, arguing that to deny the Romanians full rights to their own territory would gravely compromise French influence. Paris agreed and during December the transfer of administration began.[26] This incident heightened the tension between Berthelot and Franchet d'Esperey.[27]

With the question of Dobrudja seemingly resolved, Berthelot now turned his attention to Transylvania. The Romanians were anxious to occupy this province promised to them in the Treaty of 1916, together with the Banat and additional Hungarian counties east of the Tisza. Arguing that "this province is full of Bolshevism and we would be guilty if we remained indifferent,"[28] they began to send their military forces across the Carpathians the day they re-entered the war. Although impeded by bad weather and difficulties in mobilization, the Romanian army reached Tîrgu Mureş on November 25.[29] Encouraged by Berthelot, by the end of the month they had advanced to the demarcation line set up by the Belgrade Convention negotiated previously between Franchet d'Esperey and the Hungarian government, but were not satisfied as it prevented them from occupying all that had been promised under the Treaty of 1916.[30] At this point, on December 1, the urge for a realization of Greater Romania was given a powerful emotional boost by two events. One, the triumpal reentry of the Romanian government into Bucharest; the other the massive assembly of Romanians at Gyulfehérvár (Alba Iulia) which declared Transylvania's autonomy and called for union with Romania. Beginning on December 5, the Romanian Consiliul Dirigeant of Transylvania repeatedly asked for the protection of the Romanian army.[31]

The Hungarians, desperately hoping that the Peace Conference might preserve some semblance of historic Hungary, clung to the Belgrade Convention which not only limited Romanian occupation but permitted Hungarian administration to continue in the areas surrendered. Romanians supported by Berthelot, pressed for an immediate extension of the demarcation line, basing their claim on two points. First, they denied the applicability of the Belgrade Convention negotiated without reference to Romania or to the Treaty of 1916. Second, they stressed the need to introduce Romanian authority to counter the disorder resulting from the retreat of the Austro–German army, the alleged misconduct of Hungarians toward Romanians, and, as Berthelot put, because Hungarian emissaries were promoting Bolshevism in the province.[32]

On December 9, during a visit to Bucharest by Franchet d'Esperey, the issue was discussed and the Romanian Chief-of-the-General-Staff, Constantin Prezan, outlined in the presence of both Franchet d'Esperey and Berthelot Romanian plans to extend their occupation. According to Berthelot's "recollection", Franchet d'Esperey raised no objections to the Romanian advance and also approved Berthelot's proposal for the *Army of the Danube* to occupy portions of the Banat and certain Hungarian countries to the north which were also in contention.[33] On December 14, Berthelot authorized the advance of the Romanian army and called for French troops to occupy contested areas in the Banat and to the north, including Arad and Nagyvárad. He justified the move on the basis of the armistice by which Austria–Hungary had surrendered and which authorized allied armies to occupy "strategic" points.[34] Although Berthelot had not acted unilaterally but in concert with Franchet d'Esperey, Clemenceau vetoed the involvement of the *Army of the Danube* in the occupation of "the contested points in Hungary and the Banat," reserving these for French forces directly under Franchet d'Esperey and ordered Berthelot to defer to Franchet d'Esperey in applying the armistice with Hungary.[35] Berthelot commented in his diary: "This is total incoherence."[36] The Romanian Army was not affected and made a limited advance during the last half of December to a line which encompassed Kolozsvár (Cluj), Gyulafehérvár (Alba Iulia), Vajdahunyad (Hunedoara), and Petrozsény (Petroseni), but still far east of Arad and Nagyvárad (Oradea) [37]

Although the *Army of the Danube* and Berthelot were now officially excluded from direct control of developments in Transylvania, the latter did not back off in his advocacy of Romania's full claims. Late in December he undertook, as he told Louise, "a tour of peacemaking between Romania, Serbia and Hungary relative to the Banat of Temesvár and Transylvania." Everywhere he visited he discovered reasons to justify Romanians' claims. The eastern frontier of the Banat was "completely artificial as the population of this region is purely Romanian, although the Serbs express the intention of seizing it."[38] Crowds besieged his train and he received delegations of all nationalities, although he accused the Serbs of hindering Romanian visitors.[39] After meeting with Serbian officials in Belgrade and French officers of the Budapest control commission in Szeged he proceeded to Arad.[40] "We were received by an immense crowd," he wrote Louise, "all the people of Romanian nationality coming together and in a fashion carried us in triumph. It appears that after our departure some Bolsheviks made some disorders."[41] In his diary, Berthelot mentions "over-excited spirits.... even gunshots."[42] In a memorandum written much later, he elaborated his account, placing the blame for the disorders on the Hungarians whom, he had remarked in his diary: "Still do not realize that they have been beaten!"[43] "... I verified myself, the 29th of December at Arad, and the 30th at Carei Mare, that the violence came clearly from the Hungarians. In the railroad station, also at Arad, a train, armored and armed, came as if to defy me, stopping alongside my car. Such are the facts which provoked the Romanian advance and, in all conscience, I have only been able to approve the decision."[44]

At Kolozsvár (Cluj), he wrote Louise, there was "delirium" and it was the same at Nagybánya (Baia Mare), Szatmárnémeti (Satu Mare), Des (Dej), Beszterce (Bistriţa), Nagyszeben (Sibiu), Mediaş, Segesvár (Sigişoara), and Brasso (Braşov). He was especially impressed by the huge numbers of peasants who came "out of the mountains" at many stops "bowing religiously" before *"le Grand Général Français."*[45] While at Kolozsvár (Cluj), he met with the Hungarian General Commissioner of Transylvania István Apáthy and secured his cooperation in the extension of the Romanian occupation slightly farther to the west.[46] Returning to Bucharest, after a trip of nine days which covered rather completely the disputed areas to which Romania laid claim, he visited King Ferdinand to share   his experience. "Unforgettable" was the way he summed it up.[47]

The emotional impact of this trip on Berthelot is another key for understanding his policy. His diary and private correspondence reveal his suspicions of the Hungarians, his commitment to Romania and his belief that the French government was neglecting its own self interest. By failing to give complete support to the Romanian cause, he wrote his nephew on January 7: "I cannot but recall with pleasure the few days of my tour in the midst of people completely sympathetic, who hope in France for their deliverance forever from the Magyar yoke. I fear that in Paris one does not grasp completely the importance of the question. It is not necessary to disillusion those who like us to the benefit of the Hungarians who would not show us any kindness..."[48] To Louise four days later: "We are really in process of losing the war from the diplomatic point of view after having won by arms."[49] He expressed himself similarly to one of his former staff: "We would work then for the Hungarians who do not like us, who have been our enemies... when we have in Greater Romania the best French colony that there is in the world. When one has made the tour that I have just finished, one is absolutely convinced."[50]

Berthelot urged his superiors to implement his point of view. He suggested to Franchet d'Esperey that he denounce the Belgrade armistice and allow the advance of the Romanians to the Tisza. Franchet d'Esperey refused.[51] Berthelot also sent a strongly worded telegram to Clemenceau, highly critical of French policy, and advocating Romania's claims on the basis of the Treaty of 1916.[52] Clemenceau, involved at that time in an extremely disagreeable dispute with Romanian Premier Ion Brátianu over Romania's role and claims at the Peace Conference,[53] had little patience for Berthelot. In telegrams of January 15 and 24, he rebuffed Berthelot's arguments, reemphasizing that his competence did not extend to either the

Banat or Transylvania and inviting Berthelot's resignation if the did not agree with the government's policy.[54] Privately, Berthelot fumed. He found Clemenceau's words "disagreeable, which I cannot accept" and the telegraphed a request for recall.[55] But in his dealings with the Romanians, Berthelot adopted a more reserved attitude and, as the Allied situation in south Russia was deteriorating, he turned his attention from Transylvania to the defense of Romania's eastern frontier. Although the change in Berthelot's command did not lessen his influence in Bucharest or upon the subsequent advance of the Romanian troops in Transylvania, he did advise more restraint upon the Romanian General Staff first in January[56] and again in February.[57] It appears as if Berthelot's advice was taken. Clemenceau also backed off. His anger passed and he did not accept Berthelot's resignation possibly because the French ambassador to Bucharest, Charles Saint-Aulaire had warned of the "disastrous effect" the departure of Berthelot would produce and because events in Hungary and Russia made it expedient to avoid estranging Bucharest.[58] By the end of February the Paris Peace Conference awarded Romania a substantial portion of her claims, and the identity of interests between Paris and Bucharest which Berthelot advocated was emerging.[59]

Berthelot's banishment from policy making regarding Transylvania freed him to devote his attention to the third area of his mandate, south Russia. In discussing his role and that of the *Army of the Danube* in south Russia, it is unnecessary to recount the story so ably told and interpreted by Philippe Masson, Michael Jabara Carley, and J. Kim Munholland.[60] Rather, the concluding portion of this study will emphasize some of Berthelot's personal responses to this operation and the role it played in his relations with Paris, with Franchet d'Esperey and with the Romanians.

For almost two months after leaving Paris, Berthelot remained without substantial instructions concerning his mission in South Russia. On November 21, Paris instructed him to organize a wide-ranging operation in the Ukraine far exceeding the occupation of Odessa which he had envisioned.[61] He was alloted three French divisions and three Greek divisons with the prospect of Romanian contingents later. Berthelot, believing he would be completely independent of Franchet d'Esperey, was at first pleased, noting in his diary that he had received a *"carte blanche"* from Clemenceau.[62] But he insisted from the the beginning that the resources alloted were insufficient. Consequently he proposed that the six divisions initially authorized be supplemented by fifteen Romanian regiments, formed into seven to nine mixed Franco–Romanian divisions under French leadership. These mixed units would have required seven to nine additional French infantry regiments plus artillery and other support troops. All the expense, even for the Romanian elements, would be borne by France.[63] In December, he warned again that if the operations were attempted with insufficient forces, the consequences would be disastrous. Saint-Aulaire and Franchet d'Esperey agreed.[64] Franchet d'Esperey, well aware of the war weariness of French troops and their susceptibility to Bolshevik propaganda, opposed sending any large number of French troops at all and proposed instead to rely primarily on indigenous, anti-Bolshevik forces guided by a much smaller French force of advisors.[65] Berthelot, from his experience of the previous year, had little faith in the Russians. As it turned out, Berthelot failed to get the forces he requested. The French government, hard pressed by demobilization and far-flung commitments failed to authorize the mixed divisions and in the end only portions of one French division plus some Greek units actually landed in the Ukraine.[66] As Saint-Aulaire quipped, the "free hand" Berthelot believed he had received from Clemenceau turned out to be an "empty hand."[67]

Almost immediately after units of the *Army of the Danube* landed in Odessa on December 17, the operation began to go awry. As Franchet d'Esperey had accurately predicted, the French troops suffered from lack of equipment, missing cadres, poor morale, and susceptibility to Bolshevik propaganda. In addition, the local population was often hostile, and effective indigenous anti-Bolshevik forces failed to materialize. Almost immediately the offensive action of the expeditionary force had to be abandoned in favor of a defensive stance and in a few weeks its very existence was threatened by resurgent Bolshevik units.[68]

Among other reasons most often given for the French failure in south Russia is a failure of command and Berthelot has received his share of the blame.[69] During his three-month tenure in overall charge of the operations, he made only one visit to south Russia. He was absorbed primarily in Romanian affairs and was headquartered in Bucharest. Here, because of the poor communications,[70] he was out of touch with events in Odessa and without proper liason with his immediate superiors, Franchet d'Esperey in Constantinople and the government in Paris. Lack of Paris—Bucharest train service and technical problems with wireless-telegraphy were partly to blame,[71] but the causes of this command weakness go deeper and eventually lead to Clemenceau and the French High Command. Whatever their reasons, they persistently, one might say perversely, maintained an unworkable dual command structure. Berthelot was placed in charge of operations in Romania, Transylvania, and south Russia, and was directly responsible to Paris, while Franchet d'Esperey was responsible for the Balkans south of the Danube, Hungary, and Turkey. Yet Franchet d'Esperey retained a measure of control over the *Army of the Danube* because Paris made him responsible for its supply and for the "coordination of all operations in the East."[72] Although this unworkable command structure between the *Army of the Danube* and the *AAO* contributed to several crises which dictated its overhaul, on each occasion Paris reaffirmed this duality until just before the decision to evacuate south Russia.[73] Paris compounded its folly by leaving Franchet d'Esperey and Berthelot without precise instructions for weeks on end.[74]

Franchet d'Esperey was profoundly dissatisfied with the duality of command and sought to have it changed. As he wrote a friend "...from the general point of view it is absurd. It has been made by the Foch general staff, which knows nothing about foreign questions and leads to the most extraordinary confusion."[75] He traveled to Paris in January to enlighten the government on the situation in the East. He met twice with Clemenceau, with the Chief of Staff and with other leading personalities.[76] Exactly what Franchet d'Esperey said in Paris is not clear. The duality of command was not basically changed but it is interesting that Clemenceau's eruption against Berthelot coincided with Franchet d'Esperey's visit.

A threat by a Bolshevik force on the Bessarabian frontier and the mutiny of French troops ordered to engage them coincided with Berthelot's first visit to his command in south Russia and may have triggered it.[77] Spending February 12–15 in Odessa, he not only counseled with his military commanders but received many of the Russian, Ukranian, and emigré community, both military and civilian. He was disturbed by the reports given him concerning the army's morale.[78] He was also disturbed about the prospects of success of Paris's attempt to unite all the representatives of the "phantoms" of government in south Russia. As he had written Louise: "For some one who knows a little about the Russians this is a pure utopia. And this is for us a waste of time, and the Bolsheviks will profit in order to carry out some more crimes. Such will be the most tangible result."[79] Again, "I have heard only whining from people to whom war and revolution have taught nothing and who are not able to achieve an agreement among themselves. What a race. Proud of that, as those can be who contemplate the navel all day. They think only of leaving us to do their work and of having a good time while we pull their chestnuts out of the fire. I left that place with pleasure and I will return only unwillingly."[80]

Berthelot also returned from Odessa determined to press for his recall, for which he had been preparing his family and friends since late December.[81] He was thoroughly frustrated by the lack of support he had received from Paris and angered by its failure to back Romania wholeheartedly. Clemenceau, responding to his formal request for recall early in March, hesitated at first to grant it, probably because the worsening of the situation in south Russia and in Hungary made the closer cooperation of Romania essential and Berthelot clearly was the best person to insure this.[82]

Meanwhile, however, Franchet d'Esperey had launched a bitter campaign against Berthelot, blaming him unfairly for the fiasco in south Russia and suggesting to Paris that he might be relieved of his command. As might be expected, Franchet d'Esperey's actions, some of which Berthelot was aware of, embittered the relationship between the two men. Franchet d'Esperey's assessment of Berthelot's personality and character was slanderous: "intelligent, learned, active, vigorous, well-spoken but megalomaniac and deceitful."[83] His evaluation of Berthelot's policies were uniformly unfair and sometimes knowingly false. His charge that Berthelot rushed into intervention in south Russia incautiously ignores Berthelot's warning to Paris as early as November 28, a copy of which was sent to Franchet d'Esperey, and Berthelot's subsequent reservations.[84]

At the beginning of March and several times thereafter, d'Esperey suggested that Berthelot be replaced, because as he told Clemenceau, Berthelot was "tired and discouraged."[85] He was much less charitable in private latters: "I have informed Clemenceau that I do not have any confidence in Berthelot, despite his fine intelligence which permitted him, in time of peace, to do remarkable things on the map..."[86] Clemenceau, already in possession of Berthelot's formal request for recall decided to relieve Berthelot of his command in south Russia and to limit his authority to Romania, including the defense of its Dniester frontier. Orders went out March 14 appointing Franchet d'Esperey to command the Allied forces in south Russia.[87]

Berthelot and d'Esperey met at Odessa on March 21, to survey the situation and to coordinate the change in command. Although Berthelot remained outwardly calm, his diary entries then and later reveal the degree of resentment he was experiencing. March 21: "I found Franchet d'Esperey boorish as always and playing Napoleon." April 1: "I have searched for the characteristics of Fr. d'Esperey. Crass ignorance; lack of intelligence; conceit and infatuation 'über alles.'" He was especially critical of Franchet d'Esperey's visit to Bucharest in April and his allged intermixing in the command structure there, which of course was closest to Berthelot's heart: "Franchet d'Esperey plays at proconsul commanding kings..."[88] To have Franchet d'Esperey exercising influence where he had been supreme for so long appears to have been especially difficult for Berthelot.

Although Berthelot remained in Romania until early May, the relinquishment of his command in south Russia was the preliminary to his return to

France. But before he left, he received the statisfaction of seeing Paris shift its policy toward the close entente with Romania he had long advocated. During the first half of March he sent a series of messages to Clemenceau and Foch which outlined "a remarkably lucid and precise picture of the political and military situation in all of southeastern Europe."[89]

Berthelot proposed that "the Russians be abandoned to themselves" and a defensive front be organized "from the Baltic Sea to the Black Sea... confined to the two powers most directly interested, Poland and Romania... ."[90] Although the concept of a *cordon sanitaire* or *barrière de l'est* had been mentioned before, it appears that Berthelot's recommendation directly influenced its adoption. The French general staff immediately took steps in this direction.[91] and on March 24, the Allied Council of Four decided to evacuate Odessa and divert to Romania aid designated for the anti-Bolsheviks in south Russia.[92] Strengthening Romania economically and militarily to resist the Bolshevik threat on the Dniester, now advocated by voices more influential than Berthelot's, became a priority in French policy.

This. shift was also influenced by another Bolshevik threat when on March 21, Béla Kun came to power in Hungary. Berthelot, while he could hardly be pleased with this development, saw it as justifying his criticism of "our policy of temporizing and caution."[93] He (and Franchet d'Esperey also) were anxious to unleash the Romanian army to march on Budapest, an event which did take place several weeks later.[94] When Berthelot's formal telegram of recall arrived on April 11, he could leave with a measure of satisfaction that the broad outlines of his Romanian policy had been achieved. As he rode to the station on the day he departed, crowds thronged the streets, and he was attended by the cabinet, the diplomatic corps, the army high command and the crown prince. His last words, "Long live Greater Romania," represented a cause which he, himself, had done much to advance.[95]

## NOTES

*The preparation of this study has been assisted by grants from the International Research and Exchanges Board, the U.S. Department of Education, the American Philosophical Society, and the Faculty Research and Creativity Committee of Emporia State University.

1. For a recent, informed account of the problems of the Allied *Army of the Orient* (hereafter *AAO*), see Jan Tanenbaum, *General Maurice Sarrail 1856–1924* (Chapel Hill, 1974).

2. On Franchet d'Esperey, see the partisan biography of Paul Azan, *Franchet d'Esperey* Paris, 1949).

3. Kalervo Hovi, *Cordon Sanitaire or Barrière de l'Est: The Emergence of the New French Eastern European Alliance Policy 1917–1919* (Turku, 1975), especially pp. 176–80.

4. There is little published on Berthelot except anecdotal references. See, N. Cerbulescu, *Generalul Henri Berthelot* (Sibiu, 1931), Compte Auguste de Saint-Aulaire, *Confession d'un vieux diplomate* (Paris, 1953); Saint-Aulaire's eulogy for Berthelot in *Figaro* (Paris), January 31, 1931.

5. Henri Matthias Berthelot, "Mémoires," entries October 1–8, 1918. These "Mémoires" are the unpublished diaries of General Berthelot, with annexes, and together, with his unpublished correspondence, form the primary source for this study. The "Mémoires," whose publication was forbidden for 30 years, passed to his nephew M. Henri Dubois upon the general's death. I am grateful to Madame Dubois and her son Jean-Claude for their permission to use this material to prepare portions of it for publication. A Xerox copy of the "Mémoires" is deposited at the Hoover Archives, Stanford, California.

6. For Romanian evaluations, see, Aurel Cosma, jr., *General Berthelot şi dezrobirea Românilor* [Generalul Berthelot and the Emancipation of the Romanians] (Bucharest, 1932); Cerbulescu, *Berthelot.* For critical views, see, Peter Pastor, *Hungary Between Wilson and Lenin; The Hungarian Revolution of 1918–1919 and the Big Three* (New York, 1976), pp. 12–24, 132–34; especially Azan, *Franchet d.Esperey,* pp. 244–46.

7. "Note du général Berthelot sur sa deuxième mission en Roumanie," Ministère de la Guerre, Etat-Major de l'Armée, Archives de la Guerre, Vincennes, Fonds Berthelot, 1 K 77, Carton 118.

8. Azan, *Franchet d'Esperey,* pp. 201–204.

9. *Ibid.,* pp. 211–15, 232. A copy of the orders Berthelot bore are in: France, Ministère des Affaires Entragères, Archives Diplomatiques, Correspondance des Affairs Politiques, Europe 1918–1929, Roumanie Vol. 19 (hereafter, *AD Roumanie* followed by volume number

10. Azan, *Franchet d'Esperey,* pp. 216, 237–38.

11. Franchet d'Esperey was hypersensitive about challenges to his authority. See, for example, Francesco Guida, "La politica Italiana nei confronti della Bulgaria dopo la prima Guerra Mondiale (La questione della Dobrugia)," *Etudes Balkaniques,* XIX, No. 1 (1983), 51.

12. Jean Bernachot, *Les armées françaises en Orient après l'armistice de 1918: L'armée du Danube, L'armée française d'Orient, 28 octobre 1918–25 janvier 1920* (Paris, 1970), pp. 18–20.

13. *Ibid.,* p. 27.

14. Victor Atanasiu, *et al.*, *România in primul război mondial* [Romania in the First World War] (Bucharest, 1979), pp. 418–19; Eliza Campus, "La Roumanie rentre en guerre (Novembre, 1918)," *Revue roumanie d'historie*, X, No. 6 (1971), 133–52.

15. Bernachot, *L'armée du Danube*, pp. 30–32; Cosma, *Berthelot*, p. 17.

16. Cerbulescu, *Berthelot*, p. 18.

17. Berthelot–Georges, October 18.

18. Berthelot–Louise, December 2, Saint-Aulaire to Ministère des Affaires Entrangères (MAE), December 3, 1918, Franchet d'Esperey to Ministère de la Guerre, December 4, 1918 *AD Roumanie* Vol. 32.

19. The handling of von Mackensen and his army is a major story in its own right. See, Jean Bernachot, *Les armées françaises en Orient après l'armistice de 1918: L'armée française d'Orient, l'armée de Hongrie 11 novembre 1918–19 septembre 1919* (Paris, 1970), pp. 34–41; Max Luyken, *Generalfeldmarschall von Mackensen, Von Bukarest bis Saloniki* (Munich, 1920); V. A. Varga, "Retragerea armatei germane din România la sfîrșitul anului 1918 *"Studii,"* XIV, No. 4 (1961), 873–96.

20. On the Treaty of 1916, see, Atanasiu, *România în primul război mondial*, pp. 114–29.

21. Berthelot to Louise, December 2.

22. Bernachot, *L'armée du Danube*, pp. 34–38.

23. "Note du General Berthelot ...;" Saint-Aulaire to M.A.E., November 23, 1918 *AD Roumanie* Vol. 31.

24. Berthelot to Georges, November 24.

25. Berthelot Rapport No. 1, November 20, 1918 *AD Roumanie* Vol. 31.

26. Bernachot, *L'armée du Danube*, pp. 42–43.

27. "Mémoires," December 2.

28. General Coanda to General Erimie, November 22, 1918. România, Ministerul Afacerilor de Externe (Bucharest), Fondul Primul Războiul Mondial 71/1914, E 2, Vol. 177.

29. Prezan to Coanda, November 13, 1918; *ibid.*, Atanasiu, *România în primul razboi mondial*, pp. 419–20.

30. Berthelot said that he encouraged their advance as a means of cutting off the retreat of General Mackensen's forces. (See footnote 25.) For a discussion of the negotiation of the Belgrade Convention, see, Pastor, *Hungary Between Wilson and Lenin*, pp. 63–66.

31. Berthelot to Ministère de la Guerre, August 22, 1923. Archives de la Guerre, Vincennes. Fond Berthelot. (A memorandum requested by Foch, which clarifies some of Berthelot's actions in 1918–1919.) Saint-Aulaire maintains that Franchet d'Esperey "proposed" the Romanian participation in the occupation of the Banat. Saint-Aulaire to M.A.E., December 21, 1918, *AD Roumanie* Vol. 32.

32. Bernachot, *L'armée du Danube*, p. 48; Gheroghe Unc and Vladimir Zaharescu, "Romanian–Hungarian Relations in 1918–1920" in *Romania: Pages of History*, Vol. VII, No. 3 (1982), 24.

33. See footnote 31.

34. Diaz (or Padua) Armistica, November 4, which predated the Belgrade Convention, November 13. Bernachot, *L'armée de hongrie*, pp. 32–33.

35. *Ibid.*, p. 32; Bernachot, *L'armée du Danube*, p. 48.

36. "Mémoires," December 23.

37. G. D. Mărdărescu, *Campania pentru desrobirea Ardealului și ocuparea Budapestei (1918–1920)* (Bucharest, 1921), pp. 17–21. General Mărdărescu assumed command of the Romanian troops later.

38. Berthelot to Louise, December 26.

39. "Mémoires," December 26.

40. "Mémoires," December 27. Berthelot did not visit Budapest then or later.

41. Berthelot to Louise, December 30.

42. "Mémoires," December 29.

43. Berthelot to Louise, January 3.

44. See footnote 31. Colonel Victor Petin, Berthelot's longtime associate, charged that irregular Hungarian guards fired, killing eight and wounding fifteen. Memorandum-Colonel Petin, January 11, 1919. *AD Roumanie* Vol. 32.

45. *Ibid.*, Berthelot to Louise, January 3; "Mémoires," December 31.

46. The so-called Berthelot-Apáthy Agreement was verbal, no final written document was produced. (See footnote 31.)

47. "Mémoires," January 5.

48. Berthelot to Louise, January 11.

50. Berthelot to Marchal, January 7, Archives de la Guerre, Vincennes, Papiers Charles Marchal, 1 K 175, Carton 3.

51. Bernachot, *L'armée de hongrie,* pp. 59–60; Franchet d'Esperey to Ministère de la Guerre, January 15, 1919. *AD Roumanie* Vol. 47.

52. Berthelot to Clemenceau, January 9.

53. Sherman D. Spector, *Rumania at the Paris Peace Conference* (New York, 1962), chapter II.

54. Clemenceau to Berthelot, January 15. *AD Roumanie* Vol. 32; Clemenceau to Berthelot, January 24, Archives de la Guerre, Carton 16N3027.

55. "Mémoires," January 18, 19.

56. "Mémoires," January 26.

57. "Mémories," February 19.

58. Saint-Aulaire to M.A.E., January 22, *AD Roumanie* Vol. 19.

59. Pichon (M.A.E.) to Bucharest, February 13, A.D. Roumanie Vol. 32. Pastor, *Hungary Between Wilson and Lenin,* p. 121 ff.

60. Philippe Masson, *La marine française et la mer Noir* (1918–1919) (Paris, 1982); Michael Jabara Carley, *Revolution and Intervention: The French Government and the Russian Civil War 1917–1919* (Montreal, 1983); J. Kim Munholland, "The French Army and Intervention in Southern Russia 1918–1919," *Cahiers du Monde russe et soviétique,* XXII, No. 1 (January–March, 1981), 43–66.

61. Bernachot, *L'armée du Danube,* pp. 66–67.

62. "Mémoires," November 26.

63. Bernachot, *L'armée du Danube,* pp. 69–70.

64. Carley, *Revolution and Intervention,* pp. 112–14. To Louise on December 18, Berthelot stated that intervention in Russia "must be treated with caution. It would require a rather great quantity of troops and above all a lot of resources. Lacking that it would be better to abstain and let the Russians shift for themselves all alone. But I will not be sorry, if one decides on it, in order to know what I have to do."

65. *Ibid.,* pp. 112–13.

66. As late as January 9. Franchet d'Esperey was pressing Paris for an answer to Berthelot's request to form mixed divisions. D'Esperey to Ministère de la Guerre, January 9, *AD Roumanie* Vol. 11.

67. Saint-Aulaire, *Confession*, p. 482.

68. For a good, short survey, see Munholland, "French Army and Intervention," pp. 46–50. For more detailed coverage, see, Carley, *Revolution and Intervention*, pp. 105–121, 142–58; Masson, *La marine française*, pp. 69–98.

69. Bernachot, *L'armée du Danube*, p. 170.

70. Masson (*La marine française*, p. 55) calls them "detestable."

71. Berthelot's diary and correspondence are replete with examples of these communication problems.

72. Bernachot, *L'armée du Danube*, pp. 109, 170; Masson, *La marine fraçaise*, pp. 54–55; Carley, *Revolution and Intervention*, pp. 151–153; Munholland, "French Army and Intervention," p. 45.

73. Etat-Major to d'Esperey and Berthelot, January 21, *AD Roumanie* Vol. 19.

74. Masson, *La marine française*, p. 40.

75. Azan D Esperey, *p. 242.*

76. *Ibid.*, p. 243.

77. "Mémoires," January 26, Frebruary 5; Berthelot to Louise, January 27.

78. "Mémoires," February 12.

79. Berthelot to Louise, January 27.

80. Berthelot to Louise, February 16.

81. Berthelot to Louise, December 26, February 11, 14, 19, 31; Berthelot to Marchal, January 25. To Marchal, a former subordinate, he indicated that he would step down when peace had been signed. It is my opinion that frustration over his government's Romanian policy, as well as the situation in South Russia, influenced Berthelot's desire to give up his command.

82. Pastor, *Hungary Between Wilson and Lenin*, pp. 132–33.

83. Azan, *d'Esperey*, p. 241.

84. *Ibid.*, pp. 244–45.

85. Bernachot, *L'armée du Danube*, pp. 119–120; d'Esperey to Clemenceau, March 1, *AD Roumanie* Vol. 19.

86. Azan, *d'Esperey*, p. 247.

87. Bernachot, *L'armée du Danube*, p. 150.

88. "Mémoires," April 20.

89. Masson, *La marine française*, p. 183.

90. Carley, *Revolution and Intervention*, p. 165.

91. Ibid., p. 165; Hovi, *Cordon Sanitaire or Barrière de l'Est?* p. 177 ff.

92. Bernachot, *L'armée du Danube*, pp. 138–139.

93. "Mémoires," March 23.

94. "Mémoires," April 3; Azan, *d'Esperey*, p. 249.

95. Saint-Aulaire to M.A.E., May 9., *AD Roumanie* Vol. 19.

# THE IMPACT OF THE RUSSIAN REVOLUTIONS
## OF 1917 ON ROMANIA

Stephen Fischer-Galati

The impact of the Russian revolutions of 1917 on Romania has been variously assessed, normally in terms of individual historians' ideological or political obligations or commitments. Paradoxically, perhaps, the consensus—albeit for different reasons—is that the impact was favorable from several points of view.[1]

Almost every writer on Romanian affairs agrees that the events of 1917 in Russia greatly facilitated the establishment of Greater Romania in 1918. There is also agreement on the impetus which those events gave to agrarian reform in postwar Romania. The politicizing of the working class and of the peasantry, another partial consequence of the revolutions of 1917, has been generally acknowledged as beneficial depending, of course, on whether it was beneficial for the course of Romanian Nationalism or that of Socialism and Communism. Such potentially negative consequences as the rise of anti-Semitism, chauvinism, revisionism, and political and economic instability —while often recognized—have been either rationalized or subordinated to interpretations which stress the positive effects, both in the short and in the long run, on Romanian history since 1917.

It is not the purpose of this paper to analyze the reasons for historic divergency; rather, it is concerned with a review of the principal contentions regarding the impact of the revolutions of 1917 on Romania from spring 1917 to the realization of the territorial goals of the leaders of the Old Romanian kingdom at the end of World War I. Nor does this paper intend to restate shopworn data or arguments since the basic facts are well known to historians of the war.[2]

The Convention of August 1916 whereby the four Allied Powers secured Romania's intervention in the war against Austria—Hungary did guarantee not only the territorial integrity of the Kingdom of Romania "in all the extent of her present frontiers," but also recognized Romania's right to annex Habsburg territories to the maximum extent desired by the ruling Brătianu government, including Bukovina as far north as the Prut River and Czernowitz. It did not, of course, promise the reincorporation of Bessarabia into the Romanian body politic.[3]

But, it is also true that by March 1917 Romania's contribution to the allied cause and her expectations regarding territorial aggrandizement at Austria–Hungary's expense were minimal given the military debacle in Transylvania and the ensuing enemy occupation of Wallachia. The dire circumstances, even before the March Revolution, were at least in part related to factors pertaining to Russia. Such were the indecent haste with which the Romanians sought to secure Transylvania before the Russians could do so themselves, and to Russia's inability, or perhaps reticence, to support the Romanian forces in the Transylvanian campaign. Ioan I. C. Brătianu's attempts—which antedate the Revolution—to salvage Romania's aspirations and guarantees provided by the Convention of August 1916 were inconclusive. After the Revolution they seemed futile as neither the Provisional Government nor the Petrograd Soviet were interested in supporting territorial annexations by Romania. Brătianu's worst fears were, of course, realized in November when the Bolsheviks first decreed the abolition of all Tsarist commitments to the Allies, and then renounced all secret treaties. To avoid a total military defeat by the Central Powers in the face of the rapid dissolution of the Russian armies but, even more so, to avoid the negating of Romania's territorial aspirations through the bolshevization of Russia's armies in areas coveted by Brătianu, the Romanian government sought to gain time and "sauve que peut" by concluding the Armistice of December 9 with the Germans.[4] The rationalization of this move was to a large extent based on Brătianu's perception that an anti-Bolshevik position could secure the attainment of at least some of Romania's ultimate territorial goals no matter who would emerge victorious. With the Bolsheviks becoming his primary target, Romanian troops were sent into Bessarabia in January 1918 to prevent a Bolshevik takeover of that province following a decision by the pro-Romanian leaders of Bessarabia to become part of Romania.

Bessarabia did, indeed, become the trump card in Romania's strategy as the Germans, following the conclusion of the Treaty of Brest–Litovsk in March 1918, were prepared to accept Romania's position on Bessarabia in return for Romanian cooperation with Germany's plans for occupation of the Ukraine.[5] Thus, as the Romanians, following Russia's withdrawal from the war, had no other option than to conclude a separate peace treaty with the Central Powers in May 1918, the Germans recognized the Romanian annexation of Bessarabia in April 1918 as a *fait accompli*. In fact, the validity of Romania's contention that she was threatened by Bolshevism and was, therefore, at the forefront of the resistance to that perceived threat was gaining acceptance among most combatants in the war.

Exploitation of anti-Bolshevik sentiments became the essence of Romanian policies during the last few months of World War I on the assumption that no matter how the war would end Romania, as Russia's immediate neighbor, would benefit from her location and posture. The main thrust of Romania's political efforts was directed toward the Allied Powers which, if victorious, would be able to satisfy Romanian aspirations to Transylvania and Bukovina. No stone was, in fact, left unturned, and so source of support, no matter how diverse, failed to be quoted or used. The message, whether delivered by Romanian immigrants in Geneva, by French statesmen or intellectuals such as Albert Thomas, Henri Franklin-Bouillon, Emil Picard, Charles Seignobos, or Ernest Lavisse, by British publicists or journalists, such as R. W. Seton-Watson or Henry Wickham Steed, or even by anti-Bolshevik Socialists, including George D. Herron, was, however, only partially persuasive and, as such, in need of reinforcement through dramatic action.[6] It is fair to say that the Romanian decision to re-enter the war on the side of the Allied Powers on November 10, the day before the signing of the Armistice with Germany in the West, was expressly designed to secure Romania's territorial claims in the face of division in the allied camp over fulfilment of the terms of the Convention of August 1916 and over territorial adjustments in East Central Europe.

The bickering, maneuvering, and manipulations of the various parties involved in the peace negotiations need not detain us in detail. What matters in this instance is the systematic and skillful exploitation of the Bolshevik threat by the architect of Greater Romania, Ioan I. C. Brătianu, a policy which ultimately prevailed over the threatening, frequently anti-Romanian positions, adopted originally by Woodrow Wilson, Vittorio Orlando, and David Lloyd George.

It is certain that had it not been for Béla Kun's extremism and the Russian Bolsheviks' inability to stage any sort of relief action on his behalf to check the activities and movements of the Romanian armed forces in Hungary, the disposition of the skeptics at the Peace Conference—not to mention that of Transylvania—would not have been to Brătianu's liking.[7] When, however, Kun's true colors were exposed and the potential magnitude of the Bolshevik Revolution was realized by the peace makers, the Romanians were able to secure everything they had hoped for in terms of territorial aggrandizement and even more than envisaged by the Convention of 1916. And that would have been impossible had it not been for the Bolshevik Revolution of 1917 and its aftermath in Hungary.

Another effect of the Russian revolutions of 1917 was the resolution, at times partial and uneven, of the agrarian question. There is still substantial controversy over whether the decision of the Romanian parliament to enact the vast agrarian and electoral reforms, initially promised in 1914, in June 1917 was directly caused by the radical propaganda emanating from Russia after the March Revolution or whether it was prompted by other, more or less altruistic, motives such as influencing Allies critical of Romanian internal policies or by King Ferdinand's determination to show the country's appreciation for the heroic efforts of the Romanian peasant soldier.[8]

There can be little doubt that the events in Russia were decisive in the action of June 1917 and that they were clearly related to events in Bessarabia. The distabilization of Bessarabia promoted by the anti-Romanian agrarian revolutionary forces which threatened the forcible expropriation of all non-peasant owned lands and opposed the attempts of the nationalist, prounionist Romanians of the province was well known to King Ferdinand and the government. The actual seizure of land by the peasantry, which was assuming major proportions by June 1917, shaped not only the agrarian policies of the Old Kingdom but also the political course of both Brătianu and the Romanian leaders in Bessarabia. In Bessarabia, the agrarian reforms forced upon the unionists by the events of 1917, determined their political actions which foreclosed repudiation of the reforms after the Romanian armed forces occupied the province in January 1918, and for that matter, even after the formal union of Bessarabia and Romania decreed by the unionists in April 1918.[9]

More problematic is the relationship between the enunciation of the principle of radical agrarian reform in the "Act of Union of Transylvania and the Old Kingdom" of December 1, 1918 and the Bolshevik Revolution. In fact, the entire relationship between the evolution of the Romanian unionist movement in Transylvania from the March Revolution to December 1918 is worthy of careful evaluation not only in the context of agrarian reform proposals, but also, and all-the-more so, in the context of the general impact of the Russian revolutions on the politicizing of the working class and of the peasantry in Transylvania, the Old Kingdom, and the other territories which were incorporated into Greater Romania after World War I.

Recently formulated theses and theories which could attribute a decisive role to the impact of the Russian revolutions on Transylvania's Romanian workers', peasants', and progressive intellectuals' role in staging the "revolution" which led to the Act of Union must be taken *cum grano salis*. [10] True, peasant agitations and workers' strikes, such as those staged by miners in the Zsil valley in May 1917 or by iron workers in Vajdahunyad (Hunedoara) in October, or even the general strikes of January and June 1918, were partially inspired by Russian developments and Bolshevik propaganda. But, also true, both the Romanian section of the Social Democratic Party of Hungary and the majority of the Romanian unionist leaders in Transylvania encouraged such manifestations, and in the last analysis, the social and political programs enunciated and advocated by the unionist leaders were basically compatible with those emanating from Russia and propagated by her sympathizers, supporters, spokesmen, and representatives in Transylvania. It is indeed questionable whether the Act of Union would have been different in any significant way had there been no political and ideological input from Russia. This is not however, to say, that the military consequences of Russia's withdrawal from the war were not of capital importance for the evolution of the history of the Austro–Hungarian monarchy in general and of Transylvania, in particular, in 1918. Nor is it to deny the fact that the political consciousness, and corollary activism, of workers and peasants in Transylvania was clearly enhanced by events in revolutionary Russia. But even then, nationalism remained the dominant factor in determining political attitudes and actions.

On the other hand, the politicization of the masses was probably greater in the Old Kingdom given the traditionally bad conditions of the proletariat and the peasantry, the resentment of the population at large toward the German occupation, and the organized offerts of Romanian Bolsheviks or pro-Bolshevik Romanians, operating largely out of Russia, to exploit the "objective conditions" of 1917 and 1918 for the benefit of their cause. The strikes, labor disturbances, and the mass demonstration led by Constantin Ivănuş following the withdrawal of the German troops from Bucharest in November 1918, significant as they were as political manifestations, affected, however, only a minority of the workers since the Social Democrats had no revolutionary intentions and were more closely identified with the workers' political and socio-economic interests than were the Communists at that time. [11] And, as previously noted, the restless peasantry—whether in Wallachia, Moldavia, or Bessarabia—although a beneficiary of the revolutions of 1917 did generally identify with agrarian or nationalist parties rather than with Socialist political organizations and ideologies.

Whereas this paper has so far "accentuated the positive," it cannot avoid assessing the negative consequences of the revolutions of 1917.

The most obvious and direct was the Russo–Romanian dispute over Bessarabia which colored not only the adversary Russo–Romanian relations of the years following the Bolshevik Revolution but was pivotal in all external relations related to revisionism.[12] And it was the linkage between the Bolshevik Revolution and that of Béla Kun which led, as is well known, to actions and reactions that were to determine the character of Romanian–Hungarian relations, and exacerbated tensions, after World War I.[13]

Significant as these consequences turned out to be in the realm of international affairs, they were to assume even greater importance in Romanian internal affairs. The assuption by Brătianu of the posture of champion of anti-Bolshevism and of Romania, of that of the first line of defense against the spread of Communism, although initially designed to secure the attainment of the territorial goals of the Old Kingdom became, as a result of identification of Bolshevism with anti-Romanianism and with Judaism, the cornerstone of radical Romanian nationalism. The association of Judaism with Bolshevism was rooted in the actions of Bolsheviks and Jews in Bessarabia in 1917 and became the legitimizing formula for Moldavian nationalists and anti-Semites, most notably for Corneliu Zelea Codreanu whose political beginning was connected with fighting Communists in the border town of Huși. And this association could be, and was, exploited not only by Codreanu but by anti-Bolshevik political leaders who would ignore the existence of autochthonous Communists in Romania and point out the Jewish and/or otherwise non-Romanian origins of the Communist leadership.[14]

It may, of course, be argued that the international consequences of World War I would have been the same regardless of whether the Bolshevik Revolution would have succeeded or whether someone other than Béla Kun would have secured power in Hungary. Indeed, territorial revisionism was an inevitable consequence of the peace treaties. It may likewise be argued that Romanian nationalism had been characterized historically by anti-Magyarism, anti-Russianism, and anti-Semitism. Nevertheless, it was the anti-Bolshevik part of all equations which legitimized Romanian policies in the eyes of anti-Communists abroad, of nationalists politicians at home, and last but not least, of ordinary Romanians who expressed their frustrations and prejudices by accepting, albeit in varying degrees and with varying conviction, the tenets of the anti-Bolshevik and anti-Semitic propaganda expounded by those committed to fighting a national Christian crusade against the "Judeo-Communist conspiracy."

Thus, no matter how biased and exaggerated the theses and antitheses connected with the impact of the Russian revolutions of 1917 on Romania may be, there can be no doubt that the impact was profound in both the short and the long run after 1917. It may even be further said that the impact of the Bolshevik Revolution on Romania was more decisive than any other factor in shaping the course of Romanian history during and after World War I.

## NOTES

1. The most comprehensive discussion of these issues is contained in Nicholas Dima, *Bessarabia and Bukovina: The Soviet-Romanian Territorial Dispute* (Boulder, East European Monographs, 1982), pp. 17 ff., 161–68.

2. An excellent account is to be found in Sherman David Spector, *Rumania at the Paris Peace Conference* (New York, Bookman Associates, 1962), pp. 15–66.

3. The terms of the Convention are listed in Spector, *Rumanian*, pp. 35–36.

4. James Brown Scott, ed., *Official Statements of War Aims and Peace Proposals* (Washington, Carnegie Endowment for International Peace, 1921), pp. 203–204.

5. Spector, *Rumania*, pp. 51 ff.

6. *Ibid.*, pp. 56–58.

7. *Ibid.*, pp. 113 ff.

8. On these issues consult the two fundamtneal woorks by Henry L. Roberts, *Rumania: Political Problems of an Agrarian State* (New Haven, Yale University Press, 1951); David Mitrany, *The Land and the Peasant in Rumania: The War and Agrarian Reform, 1917–1921* (London, Oxford University Press, 1930).

9. Roberts, *Romania*, pp. 32 ff. See also, Stephen Fischer-Galati, "The Moldavian Soviet Republic in Soviet Domestic and Foreign Policy," in Roman Szporluk, ed., *The Influence of East Europe and the Soviet West on the USSR* (New York, Praeger Publishers, 1976), pp. 231 ff.

10. See, for instance, Ion Popescu Puţuri and Augustin Deak, eds., *Unirea Transilvaniei cu România* (Bucharest, Editura Politica, 1970), pp. 424 ff.

11. A good discussion is to be found in Ghita Ionescu, *Communism in Rumania, 1944–1962* (London, Oxford University Press, 1962), pp. 10 ff.

12. Dima, *Bessarabia and Bukovina*, pp. 19 ff.

13. See, John F. Cadzow *et al.*, eds., *Transylvania: The Roots of Ethnic Conflict* (Kent, Kent State University Press, 1983), pp. 161 ff.

14. See, in particular, Eugen Weber, "Romania," in Hans Rogger and Eugen Weber, eds., *The European Right. A Historical Profile* (Berkeley, University of California Press, 1965), pp. 501–74.

# THE ROMANIAN INTERVENTION IN HUNGARY, 1919*

Glenn E. Torrey

Romania's intervention in Hungary in 1919 represents a landmark in the history of both nations. For Romanians, it crowned the creation of Greater Romania. For Hungarians, it crowned the destruction of historical Hungary. Many recent studies by distinguished specialists, some in this series, touch on this theme from the vantage point of Hungarian, British, American, or French documentation. Consequently, the primary focus of this study will be upon the genesis and execution of the Romanian action, emphasizing Romanian sources.

Romanian intervention, which began the day after Romania reentered the war on November 10, unfolded in four successive phases: one, the military occupation of Transylvania, November 1918–March 1919; two, the Apuseni Campaign (from the) Erdélyi-szigethegység [Apuseni] Mountains to the Tisza River, April–June; three, the Tisza Campaign (from the Tisza River to Budapest), July–August: and four, the occupation of Budapest, August–November.

On November 10, the Central Romanian National Council in Transylvania sent a representative to the Romanian government requesting military aid "to check Bolshevism."[1] General Constantin Coanda, the Romanian premier agreed: "This province is full of Bolshevism and we would be guilty if we remained indifferent."[2] Simultaneously the French were urging the Romanians to hasten their mobilization so as to intercept the retreating Austro–German armies and to provide the principal occupation forces for Transylvania.[3] Furthermore, the Romanians, especially Ion Brătianu who returned as premier on November 29, realized that Romania's full territorial *desiderata* as outlined in the 1916 treaty with the Entente would be challenged and the only sure guarantee of achieving it would be the occupation of the areas in question.[4]

The Romanian General Staff (MCG) ordered its troop commanders to move as quickly as possible.[5] But, as the only organized and equipped Romanian forces were in Bessarabia at that time, the initial advance of the Romanian army was slow and the Maros (Mureş) river, the demarcation line set forth in the Belgrade Convention,[6] was not completely reached until late December. Reports of the unopposed advance of the Romanian forces was received with "indescribable enthusiasm" in the Old Kingdom. One editorial called it the greatest national event since Michael the Brave's conquest of Transylvania in 1599. "It is ours," exalted another.[7] The formal return of King Ferdinand and Queen Marie to Bucharest on December 1, coincided with the proclamation by the Romanian National Assembly at Gyulafehérvár (Alba Iulia) of the unification of Transylvania with Romania. For the Romanians, this settled the issue. Greater Romania had come into existence. All that remained now was to occupy their legacy and to save their Transylvanian "brothers" whom they believed were in jeopardy from Hungarian chauvinism, violence, and Socialist-Bolshevik agitation.

Romanian military reports as well as the press proclaimed this belief with hundreds of examples of "disorders," "devastation," "massacres," "hostile manifestos," and "revolutionary ideas" in Transylvania. No evaluation of all of these charges (as well as Hungarian countercharges) will ever be satisfactory to all. But it is undeniable that the province was in ferment. As Habsburg authority disintegrated, armed bands including Hungarian, Saxon, Szekler, Ukrainian, and Romanian "guards," remanants of Austro–Hungarian military forces, and other irregular units held sway. Zealous advocates (both Romanian and Hungarian) of Nationalism, Republicanism, Socialism, and Communism excited the population. Local and personal grievances were exploited. That there should have been tension, conflict, and even violence was natural and predictable. Regrettable as this may be, it should not be exaggerated nor allowed to obscure the responsible behavior of many Romanians and Hungarians.

The MCG was not unmindful of the delicate situation into which the Romanian army was moving and was especially concerned to win over the Romanian and Saxon populations. Chief-of-the-General-Staff Constantin Prezan and his operations officer Colonel Ion Antonescu gave their commanders specific instructions for cooperating with the Consiliul Dirigent[8] and the Romanian population toward whom they should act not as "occupying troops but as brothers come to aid them... so they will be satisfied in our midst." The Saxons "an element of order and work, having peaceful sentiments ... will be treated as Romanians... ." Alongside the Romanian military commandant there was to be a representative of the local administration be it Romanian or Saxon. Local Romanian legions or national guards formed earlier under the aegis of the Local Romanian national councils, were allowed to continue, as were the Saxon guards. Romanian troops were told that armed conflict with them must be avoided.[9] Requisitions were to be paid for in cash (not worthless vouchers) and under no circumstances were they to involve food necessary for the population. Violators were to be severely punished.[10]

These last instructions bring up an often overlooked reason for the Romanian advance in Transylvania and for close cooperation with the Consiliul Dirigent, the economic. For the Old Kingdom, especially Bucharest, 1919 was the year of hunger and cold. "Give us food. Give us wood," demanded one headline. High level delegations crossed the Carpathians several times to arrange imports, and the arrival of the first trainloads of provisioning from Transylvania were occasions of rejoicing.[11]

The Romanian population in Transylvania received the advancing troops with great enthusiasm according to both military intelligence and press reports: "All Romanian residents of the county are enthusiastic for the national ideal" (Fagaras); "All the Romanian population ... are very excited for union with Romania and await with impatience the arrival of Romanian troops..." (Apuseni Mountains)[12] Delegations from outlying areas traveled to MCG asking that troops be sent to their area.[13] Saxon leaders adhered to the Alba Iulia declaration of union in December and January.[14]

While the occupation forces sought to court the Romanian and Saxon populations, the "foreign population" (i.e., Hungarians, Serbs, Ukrainians, and Szeklers) were viewed with suspicion, and their "guards" were disarmed as soon as possible.[15] Because organized Hungarian military units generally retreated without fighting, "no military operations of note" occured before April. Distracted by their own revolution and political infighting, the Hungarians allowed the Romanians to occupy Transylvania with a relatively small force, three weak divisions.[16] Nevertheless, the Romanians had a number of concerns, one being "disorder and crime" by various irregular Hungarian, Ukrainian, and Szekler groups.[17] Another was Hungarian bureaucrats left in place by the Belgrade Convention. Except in the predominately Hungarian regions, this was unacceptable to the Romanians, and they were gradually replaced, especially gendarmes and prefects.[18] Apprehension about hostile propaganda also occupied a prominent role in Romanian military reports. A Romanian military official claims that at the beginning of December "Károlyi sent in a clandestine manner throughout Transylvania, 3000 agents with 30 million crowns ... and millions of manifestos" into Romanian villages to work against the idea of union."[19] The Commander of Troops in Transylvania (CTT) claimed that there were "4000 well organized socialists who make propaganda to demoralize the Romanian army ... Many women are used to spread revolutionary ideas."[20] Socialist, Communist, Republican, and Hungarian Nationalist ideas were all viewed as equally dangerous. While, in most instances, the Hungarian population seems to have received the Romanian army with resignation, submission or, in the case of some isolated families, flight, in the larger Hungarian urban centers more of a spirit of resistance was manifest.[21]

Citing "alarming" reports from Kolozsvár (Cluj), the MCG ordered its troops to cross the demarcation line at the Maros (Mureş) river on December 14 and advance to the line Kolozsvár–Torda–Nagyenyed–Gyulafehérvár (Cluj–Turda–Aud–Alba Iulia).[22] But this move was not the result of a quick decision but the consequence of a fundamental conviction that the Romanian occupation must be advanced. The Romanians had not been a party to the Belgrade Convention and they rejected the demarcation line it established. In their minds the treaty of 1916 and the proclamation at Gyulafehérvár (Alba Iulia) were their only guidelines. A week before the Romanians advanced, they revealed their intention to General Franchet d'Esperey,[23] commander of the Allied *Army of the East;* they received specific approval from General Henri Berthelot, commander of the French *Army of the Danube.*[24]

The importance of this first modification of the demarcation line and General Berthelot's approval of it should not be exaggerated. The Romanian advance was inevitable unless prevented by military force. But, the Hungarians were too weak and the Allies were unwilling or unable. The British resisted commitments north of Salonika and the French, overextended and with war-weariness growing both in their army and civilian population, were unable to maintain an effective presence in the area.[25] Furthermore, both short-range and long-range French interests dictated support of Romania's claims. She was a vital link in the emerging *cordon sanitaire* and the most promising base for French political, economic, and cultural influence in southeastern Europe, "the best French colony in the world" as General Berthelot put it.[26] But this first alteration of the demarcation line *did* establish a pattern for subsequent Romanian advances: a perceived threat from Hungarian chauvinism or Bolshevism and French encouragement, on the spot if not from Paris.

After the first Romanian advance, General Berthelot decided to investigate the situation himself. His two-week trip (December 25–January 3) took him to the Banat and Belgrade as well as to Transylvania on both sides of the demarcation line. It occasioned a great outpouring of Romanian national feeling and confirmed his belief in Romania's claims and in Hungary's perversity. "Now you are free," he had told the adoring Romanian crowds that besieged him.[27] While in Kolozsvár (Cluj) he met Dr. István Apáthy, the Hungarian commissioner for Transylvania, who agreed to yet another extension of the demarcation line.[28] Berthelot gave direct orders to the local Romanian commander to advance his forces 20 kilometers north and west of Kolozsvár (Cluj).[29] The unfortunate Apáthy pleased no one. His government repudiated him, and the Romanians soon arrested him on a variety of charges including the dissemination of "bolshevik tracts."[30]

Meanwhile, the Romanian authorities were confronted with another problem, a series of strikes. A planned work stoppage in the coal mines of Petrozsény (Petroşeni), in December, had been thwarted by force,[31] but the trouble broke out again in January among the miners, a half of whom were Romanians. A battalion of Romanian troops quickly ended the strike but arrest and interrogations lasted two months. Romanian investigators linked the unrest to Hungarian or "Hungarianized" Romanian Socialists, "working in common accord with the government in Budapest"[32] At the same time, and reportedly in support of the miners, the railroad and postal telegraph workers at Kolozsvár (Cluj), Marosvásárhely (Tirgu-Mureş), Nagyszeben (Sibiu), and other localities refused to work.[33] There was angry nationalistic rhetoric and the Romanians saw the strike as an attempt to impede the occupation of Transylvania (most of these functionaries being Hungarians), but a more immediate issue seems to have been salary and job security. Tension was high in Kolozsvár (Cluj) and Marosvásárhely (Tirgu–Mureş) especially.[34]

Simultaneously with the strikes, more serious military incidents between the Romanian army and Hungarian units occurred at Zám (Zam) and Zilah (Zălau), which triggered a new Romanian advance, again with Berthelot's approval, to the line Máramarossziget–Nagybánya–Zilah–Zám,[35] (Sighet-Baia Mere–Zălau–Zam). This move put the Romanians in the Erdélyi-szigethegység, (Apuseni) Mountains overlooking the plain of the Tisza. Here, the military occupation of Transylvania, strictly defined,[36] was completed. There was no significant additional advance until the opening of full-scale hostilities between Romania and Hungary in April.

The Romanian pause during February–March in their occupation of Hungarian territory they claimed was not due to a lessening of tension. To the contrary, reports of Hungarian "atrocities" continued to fill the press, and Professor Iorga's newspaper called for military action on behalf of "the unfortunate terrorized Romanians of Banat and 'Transylvania,"[37] but there were other voices urging restraint. General Berthelot, heretofore an important catalyst for the Romanian advance, now seems to have been instrumental in restraining it. First, he had been sharply rebuked by Clemenceau in mid-January for his militant advocacy of the Romanian cause and Transylvania had been stripped from his command.[38] Second, he was increasingly concerned about the unfavorable turn of events in south Russia and the consequent threat to Romania on the Dniester. On January 26, Berthelot mentioned the Soviet threat to Prezan and spoke of the "necessity" of halting in Transylvania.[39] Shortly thereafter, the MCG ordered the CTT: "Stop troops on line where they now stand ... avoid armed conflict. But, if attacked, counterattack. Provocateurs will be exterminated without consideration."[40] Two weeks later when Prezan informed him that the Romanian government had decided to advance again, this time to the Arad–Nagyvárad–Szatmárnémeti (Arad–Oradea Mare-Satu Mare) line, Berthelot advised against it.[41]

On the other hand, this pause witnessed a decisive turn of events which gave a powerful boost to Romanian claims. Several French investigators visited Transylvania and gave resounding support to the Romanians. General Patey, the subject of Romanian praise but the object of Hungarian protest in Kolozsvár (Cluj), spoke out strongly for the Romanians and even recommended that Colonel Fernand Vix, head of the French Military Mission in Budapest, be dismissed for his alleged pro-Hungarian attitude.[42] An emmisary from Franchet d'Esperey, Colonel Eugene Trousson received Romanian adulation in Nagyszeben (Sibiu) and responded with a speech expressing compassion for the Romanian "martyrs" and promising that the demarcation line would be changed until it extended to all the Romanian homeland.[43] The Romanians also received strong encouragement from the allied diplomatic and military representatives in Bucharest who likewise advocated the extension of Romanian sovereignty to include the promises of 1916.[44]

The Romanians were pleased also with developments in Paris where the French led the Peace Conference in establishing an entirely new demarcation line. This arrangement called for the Hungarians to withdraw behind the line assigned to Romania in the treaty of 1916 and allowed the Romanians to advance to a line just short of what later became the final settlement. It involved a wide neutral zone which included the major population centers of Arad, Nagyvárad (Oradea Mare), and Szatmárnémeti (Satu Mare) on its eastern edge. This concept was conceived by Berthelot, approved by Franchet d'Esperey who lamented that the Romanians would not obey his orders anyway, and recommended to the Allied Supreme Council by its Romanian Commission. Lacking sufficient troops to occupy Nagyvárad (Oradea Mare), Nagykároly (Carei Mare), and Szatmárnémeti (Satu Mare), the French general staff recommended these important population and communications centers be alloted to Romania. The Supreme Council compromised, and while forbidding "military occupation," allowed these cities and the connecting railway to be utilized by the Romanian army and the inhabitants for economic needs. Approved on February 26, its implementation was to begin a month later.[45]

Although there were Allied disclaimers that the decision of February 26 would prejudice the final delineation of the frontier, Romanians and Hungarians both believed otherwise. Already on February 27, the Bucharest press, with some understanding of French plans for Romania in a *cordon sanitaire* and a hint of the recent decision in Paris, proclaimed that Romanian policy had triumphed. "At first the conference appeared to favor our antagonists but now it has changed the axis of its policy toward us," an editorial stated. Romania was seen as the "Gendarme of the Entente on the Danube."[46] The Romanian press also stepped up its condemnation of "Hungarian horrors," the "bandits of Budapest," "terror and massacres in Transylvania," and Károlyi's "policy of extermination pure and simple."[47]

The Romanian government expected Hungarian armed resistance and was encouraged to prepare for it by Franchet d'Esperey.[48] This assumption proved correct. Károlyi, aware that developments in Paris were unfavorable to Hungary, made preparations to rally his people in opposition.[49] The official delivery of the Council's decision by Colonel Vix on March 20, precipitated the resignation of Károlyi and the advent of a new government dominated by the Communist Béla Kun, which promised armed resistance and an alliance with Bolshevik Russia.[50] The Romanian press, at first, saw little difference between Kun and Károlyi, dismissing the "revolution" as a "bluff," a "comic opera" of Magyar chauvinism, planned by the Hungarian "magnates down to the smallest detail."[51] But Kun's open courting of Lenin heightened fears that the allied defeat in south Russia and a possible "Bulgarian–Hungarian plot" would result in an attack on Romania from three directions.[52]

The Romanians, with vision of being "submerged" as they had been in 1917, asked the "urgent cooperation of the allies, in order to liquidate the situation in Hungary" before a Russian attack on Dniester.[53] The council had already decided to strengthen Romania on both fronts yet was not ready to sanction a march on Budapest. But apparently Clemenceau or Foch ordered Franchet d'Esperey to prepare such plans.[54] Franchet d'Esperey, who had been obsessed with a march up the Danube since summer 1918, wholeheartedly agreed and traveled to Bucharest early in April to organize the expedition to Budapest.[55] Berthelot's journal puts it succinctly: "April 6. Long conference with him [d'Esperey], Prezan ... Antonescu; decision to settle immediately the Hungarian question."[56] That evening Charles St.

Aulaire the French ambassador, quoted King Ferdinand as calling for the occupation of Budapest without delay, promising that the Romanian troops would march "at the first signal under our command." The rationale for this action, though put in the king's mouth, sounded like Franchet d'Esperey's or Berthelot's[57]

Franchet d'Esperey, accompanied by Antonescu, traveled to Belgrade to arrange Serbian participation. While there, he received word of the Smuts Mission and Clemenceau's telegram relating the Council's decision forbidding an immediate march on Budapest. Franchet d'Esperey "furious at not being able to act against Hungary" returned to Bucharest where he learned that the Romanians had decided to attack alone.[58] Although Franchet d'Esperey appears to have had some doubts that they could succeed,[59] Berthelot told an American that he could guarantee the occupation of Hungary in nine days.[60]

Berthelot was correct. On the night of April 15–16, while General Gheorghe Mărdărescu, the new CTT, was preparing his offensive, the Hungarians attacked. The Romanians quickly repulsed them and advanced to the new demarcation line Nagyvárad–Nagykároly–Szatmárnémeti (Oredea Mare –Carei Mare–Satu Mare).[61] Clemenceau's instructions to halt here read more like an invitation to continue, and the French general staff tacitly approved a continuation of the Romanian's advance.[62] And so they did, to the Tisza whose entire east bank was in Romanian hands by May 1. The French military were surprised and pleased with the showing of the Romanian army.[63]

The march to the Tisza touched off a national rejoicing in Romania which bordered on delirium. Celebrating the crossing of the "blasphemous" line of demarcation, the press cried "On to Budapest! On to Budapest!"[64] A *Te Deum* was prescribed on Sunday May 4 for all Romanian churches from the Dniester to the Tisza.[65] Later in the month, Ferdinand and Marie made a triumphal tour of Transylvania with hundreds of thousands lining the rail lines over which they traveled, as far as Debrecen. It was reported that even delegations of Hungarians came to thank them for deliverance from Bolshevism, although in some cities there were Hungarian demonstrations. The royal couple banqueted in the Károlyi palace at Nagykároly (Carei Mare). For Marie, the trip was "the ultimate realization of a great dream."[66]

The march to the Tisza greatly inflated Romania's national pride and spirit of independence. General Victor Petin, French military attaché in Bucharest, warned Paris that this change must now be taken into account.[67] Its most immediate impact seems to have been upon the situation in the Banat where a stiffening Romanian attitude caused the Serbs and some Frenchmen to fear a military confrontation there also.[68] There was much friction in Arad where the French occupation authorities continued to use Hungarian administrators.[69] In an attempted compromise Franchet d'Esperey ordered the installation of a Romanian prefect in Arad county but kept the status quo in the city until July.[70]

Once installed on the Tisza, the Romanians were forced to weight their options. Their first inclination was to continue on to Budapest, take care of the Bolshevik menace, and then turn to the defense of the east. Indeed, such orders were issued to General Mărdărescu on May 5.[71] This was also the advice of French representatives in Bucharest. General Petin creatively promoted the march on Budapest as "a good object lesson" [to Germany] of allied determination "to enforce their will on an enemy state that rebels against their decisions."[72] Franchet d'Esperey as usual continued to press the Romanians to act.[73]

But the Romanians were beginning to have second thoughts. First, they feared that to move without at least token Allied participation would open them to the charge of imperialism. "One French regiment would suffice," the king told St. Aulaire.[74] But the Allied leaders in Paris could not agree on joint action and Clemenceau was unwilling to act alone.[75] Secondly, Brătianu recognized that it would be politically unwise to contribute to the stabilization of Hungary and to the emergence of a strong government in Budapest before the final determination of the Romanian frontier.[76] Last, and most decisive, was the fact that Romanians were worried about the situation on the Dniester where the renegade Romanian Socialist Christian Rakovskii, now Bolshevik Commissar for the Ukraine, had issued an utlimatum demanding Romanian evacuation of Bessarabia and Bukovina.[77] The Romanian military feared that the sole responsibility for occupying Budapest (and with it much of Hungary) would overextend Romani's resources whereas the Tisza offered a highly defensible position. Consequently, the orders to advance were cancelled and part of the Romanian army transferred to the east.[78]

That the Romanian's prime concern was for security rather than further conquest was reflected in their attitude to Kun's request for armistice terms on May 2. The Romanian's primary concern was the Hungarian military threat rather than the occupation of territory.[79] Kun rejected their terms, continued to reorganize his forces, and on May 20, launched an attack on the Czechs who, like the Romanians, had occupied Hungarian territory.[80] The Romanians, concerned about a possible Hungarian—Soviet linkup, took the initiative in making contact with the Poles in Galicia, thus erecting a barrier on the most likely avenue of contact between Soviet Hungary and Soviet Russia.[81]

During May and June, as the situation in Hungary became more volatile and threatening, the Romanians found Allied policy shifting and contradictory. Modern commentators agree.[82] On the one hand, the French military, including Franchet d'Esperey and Foch, continued to advocate a march on Budapest. Other influential Allied figures agreed, including Herbert Hoover, Robert W. Seton-Watson, and, somewhat later, Arthur Balfour.[83] On the other hand, in the council, there was considerable anger toward Romania on a variety of issues and little concern for Romania's demand for security vis-à-vis Hungary. On May 30, Clemenceau informed Franchet d'Esperey that the council had expressly forbidden a march on Budapest.[84]

Nevertheless, worried by Hungarian success against the Czechs, the council went along with Clemenceau's suggestion that the Allied military prepare plans for such an eventuality. Eagerly Franchet d'Esperey hurried to Romania and worked out details for military operations according to which he would go to Arad to lead the operations personally.[85] With plans for a Romanian-dominated punitive expedition well underway, the council endorsed and sent to Budapest on June 15 an ultimatum conceived by Clemenceau which demanded that the Hungarians cease hostilities and withdraw from Czechoslovakia, and promised in return that the Romanian army would withdraw behind the frontiers established by the conference.[86] The Romanians were puzzled by the council's actions, taken without consulting them and in direct contradiction to Franchet d'Esperey's initiative. More importantly, it would require them to give up their strong defensive position on the Tisza before the Hungarian threat was ended. Brătianu flatly refused, but in Bucharest the king offered to withdraw if the council would guarantee Romania against Hungarian aggression. This offer was repeated several times.[87] The Romanian resistance to withdrawal drew immediate support from British and French military leaders. Foch pointed out how the holding of the Tisza line would allow release of Romanian troops for the east.[88] The head of the British military mission in Bucharest also argued against a Romanian withdrawal, after a personal tour to the Tisza. Even the Hungarian population wanted Romanian occupation to continue lest Kun's return bring terrorist reprisals, he reported. In fact "everybody hopes the allies will march on Budapest as the only measure which will allow Hungary to get rid of the communists and choose a government which represents the people."[89]

Meanwhile, Franchet d'Esperey again visited the Romanian capital and once again King Ferdinand called for a military operation "to liquidate the Hungarian question," stressing the military danger to Romania.[90] In Paris, Foch pointed out a justification for action in that Hungary's armaments exceeded those allowed by the armistice.[91] Balfour agreed and took the lead in urging before the council the disarmament of Hungary, by military means if necessary.[92] Clemenceau was not unwilling but, as previously, hesitated to commit French resources unless the other Great Powers were ready to do likewise.[93] None were. Therefore, even Foch was hesitant to take responsibility for military action with the forces available but he was favorable to *fait accompli* by the smaller powers. Among the Czechs, Serbs, and Romanians, only the latter exhibited "a very willing spirit" and a firm commitment of troops.[94]

Kun himself resolved the council's indecision by attacking the Romanian forces on July 21. Clemenceau and other allied leaders were fearful at first that the Romanians would not be able to hold.[95] And, indeed, the Hungarians did cross the Tisza and push the Romanians back some 60 kilometers on a front 80 kilometers wide.[96] But there was no panic in the Romanian army and the retreat was always in order. In fact, although the two armies were approximately equal in numbers, the Romanians were vastly superior in almost every category especially in organization, training, morale, and leadership. In both smaller and larger units there was homogeneity and discipline born in the long hard months of fighting in 1917. Newly formed Transylvanian units, which included veterans of the Austro–Hungarian army, made remarkable progess, motivated by a common patriotism for the new Romania and a common hostility toward Hungary.[97] A French observer labeled the morale of Romanian soldiers "comparable to the best in Europe,"[98] and a British officer called them the most loyal in Europe, perhaps in the world, except for the Japanese army.[99] Their armament and equipment were sufficient and a deficiency in horse had been corrected by the good sources available in occupied Hungary. In appearance, however, they were described as "miserable, clad in an melange of uniforms: Romanian, French, Austrian and even civilian dress, their shoes were especially lamentable."[100] The problem of inexperienced leadership, the disgrace of the disastrous campaign of 1916, had been corrected. Able leaders had emerged during the wartime campaigns and these had been augmented by recruitment from Habsburg veterans of Romanian descent.[101]

On July 24, after three days of retreat, the Romanian army, which had kept only two divisons on the Tisza, now brought up its strategic reserves and counterattacked. Within two days they had dealt the Hungarians a disastrous defeat which not only threw them back across the Tisza but opened the road to Budapest.[102] This time there was no doubt on the part of the Romanians about pushing on.[103] However, thorough preparations were made of crossing the Tisza and King Ferdinand and Queen Marie came to observe the event which began on July 30.[104] Little resistance was encountered, the biggest Romanian problem being: "Where is the enemy?"[105] On August 4, the Romanian army ceremoniously entered Budapest.

For the Romanians, the occupation of Budapest began like a dream come true. Their troops paraded down the grand avenues, they gazed like tourists at the famous buildings, and set up occupation headquarters in the famous Hotel Gellért. Back in Romania, Marie was jubilant and even the taciturn Brătianu could exalt that the Romanian victory "refreshed my soul ... these seven days have been the best in my political life."[106] Believing they had acted at the expressed wish of their allies and in their common interest, the Romanians expected to be showered with gratitude. Instead, from the very beginning, their behavior was severely criticised by Allied authorities both in Paris and Budapest and they were accused of a wide variety of crimes and misconduct: installing a reactionary government, engaging in widespread violence and pillaging, systematically stripping Hungary of private and state property, especially railroad rolling stock, creating famine by requisitions and by impeding imports, and prolonging the occupation for the above purposes. These charges have been repeated over the years almost without question.[107] Recent research has cast doubt on the first charge, direct Romanian involvement in the coup of August.[108] Future access to archival materials one hopes, will make possible an equally dispassionate evaluation of the others.[109] In the space of this study, the only contribution I can make is to draw attention to several aspects of the context in which the Romanian occupation took place.

First, the Romanians entered Budapest fervently believing that the preceding 1000 years of Romanian—Hungarian relations were essentially years of humiliation, oppression, and denationalization.[110] Added to this emotional historical heritage were more recent events: the long, bloody months of combat during 1916—17, the suffering of the besieged population in Moldavia, the harsh Austro—German occupation of Wallachia, the rapacious Treaty of Bucharest (1918), and the real or alleged Hungarian acts of mistreatment of Romanians after Armistice. Like the French in regard to Germany, the Romanians felt their experience with Hungary justified weakening their enemy and making her pay.[111]

Secondly, Romanians could balance off their requisitions in Hungary against the food, petroleum, and rolling stock looted from their own country by the Germans. Dissatisfied with the handling of their reparation claims in Paris, they felt justified in collecting their share immediately. With their own people hungry, the Romanians believed they were more than generous in their attempts to feed their former enemies, especially since it was the Kun regime that had created economic chaos in Hungary.[112] Certainly, there was a measure of hypocrisy in the Allies' criticism of Romania when they themselves starved Germany.

Thirdly, one must keep in mind that the occupation of Budapest occurred at the height of a larger controversy between Romania and the Great Powers. At Paris there were bitter arguments over Romania's role at the Peace Conference, over reparations, frontiers, the minority clauses, all exacerbated by the obstreperous behaviour of Brătianu. The Romanians felt hurt and were suspicious of the intentions of the Allies. The latter were exasperated almost beyond measure and tended to treat the Romanians as erring children.[113] From the moment the Romanians entered Budapest the Allies began to upbraid them and the Romanians became uncooperative. Hostile personal relations between Romanian officers and Allied representatives in Budapest exacerbated a lack of mutual trust and understanding. The failure to include a Romanian representative on the Inter-Allied Military Mission, which sought to supervise the occupation, was a serious mistake and the behaviour of the four Allied generals and their soubordinates compounded this error. Also, there was rivalry among these officers personally and between their conflicting national interests. The Italians pursued their own policies and Lieutenant-Colonel Guido Romanelli was especially hostile to Romania. The French tended to support the Romanians while the British and American missions tended to be overly critical of them. The tactless, and at times contemptuous, attitude of the American General Harry Bandholtz, who dominated the reporting of the mission, was especially regrettable. He appears to have acted largely on impulse wihout investigating all facets of the problems that arose, treating the Romanians like subalterns in the process.[114]

As a result, the input of the Inter-Allied Military Mission not only clouded the view from Paris, but also confused the Romanians and encouraged them to be even more defensive and resentful. The prolongation of the Romanian occupation is a point is question. The Romanian government has been repeatedly accused of bad faith in this issue but as early as September 7 it gave its representatives in Budapest, a *carte blanche* to arrange evacuation of "all territory west of the Tisza", "in order to put an end to the difficulties which the Peace Conference makes for us in Hungary." The only condition was that there be a Hungarian authority to insure order—a condition on which everyone agreed. But the selection and empowering of such an authority by the Allies was slow and difficult. Also, the Allies themselves were not in agreement, some wanting the Romanians to delay their departure until stability was assured.[115]

Sir George Clerk, who was sent to Budapest in October and November, to promote the formation of a representative coalition government, eventually decided that the Romanian army should leave even though a new government had not yet been agreed on and elections held. But the Allies were unable to agree on replacing the Romanians with their own troops, thus allowing Admiral Horthy and his forces to move in on the heels of the Romanians.[116] This gave Hungarian history a direction which almost everyone regrets. Although counterfactual speculation cannot change that past, one wonders what the outcome might have been if there had been more good will and cooperation between Romania and the Allies in their handling of the Hungarian question in 1919.

## NOTES

*The preparation of this study has been assisted by grants from the International Research and Exchanges Board, the U.S. Department of Education, the American Philosophical Society, and the Faculty Research and Creativity Committee of Emporia State University.

1. Nicolae Iorga, *Memorii: Insemnări zilnice mai-martie 1920*, 2 vols., II (Bucharest, 1931), 105, 112–15.

2. General Coanda to General Erimie, November 22. Romania, Ministerul Afacerilor de Externe (Bucharest), Fondul Primul Războiul Mondial 71/1914, E 2. Vol. 177.

3. Jean Bernachot, *Les armées françaises on Orient après l'armistice de 1918: L'armée du Danube, L'armée française d'Orient, 28 Octobre 1918–25 Janvier 1920* (Paris, 1970), p. 21.

4. Under the terms by which Romania entered the war, the Entente had promised her the Banat and Transylvania, plus other Hungarian counties to the west, as well as Bukovina. The validity of this treaty was in question because of Romania's separate peace (March, 1918). See, Gheorghe I. Brătianu, *Actiunea politică și militară a României in 1919* (Bucharest, 1939), pp. 25 ff.; Viorica Moisuc, ed., *România și conferința de pace de la Paris 1918–1920* (Cluj, 1982), especially chapter VI.

5. M.C.G. to Comandant Trupelor din Transilvania (C.T.T.), November 18, 1918. Arhiva Militara (Bucharest), Transilvania Dosar Nr. 15. (hereafter as A.M. followed by dossier number.)

6. Armistice with Hungary negotiated by Franchet d'Esperey on November 13 to regulate Allied occupation of Hungarian territory. The demarcation line between Allied and Hungarian authority in Transylvania was the Maros (Mureș), which allowed Romania to occupy only a small portion of her claims. For an account of the Romanian advance, see, Dumitru Tuțu "Les actions de l'armée roumaine en Transylvanie au cours des années 1918–1919," in *Revue Roumaine d'Historie*, XXIV, No. 1–2, pp. 101–23.

7. *Steagul* (Iași), November 15, 20.

8. The "Directing Council" or executive for the Transylvanian government established at Gyulafehérvár (Alba Iulia) December 1.

9. M.C.G. to C.T.T., December 17. *A.M.* Dosar Nr. 15. On the Romanian national guards, see, Miron Constantinescu, *et al.*, *Unification of the Romanian State* (Bucharest, 1971), p. 241.

10. MC.G. to C.T.T., November 15, December 14. *A.M.* Dosar Nr. 15, *Ibid.*, December 25; *A.M.* Dosar Nr. 50.

11. *Steagul*, December 10, 11, 18.

12. Buletin de Informare, C.T.T., December 28. *A.M.* Dosar Nr. 17. (hereafter *Buletin de Informare* with date.)

13. *Steagul* December 30.

14. Constantinescu, *Unification* pp. 304 ff; *Steagul*, December 10.

15. *Buletin de Informare*, December 28, 19.

16. Gheorghe D. Mărdărescu, *Campania pentru desrobirea Ardealului și ocupare Budapestei 1919–1920* (Bucharest, 1921), p. 37; Radu Cosmin, *Românii la Budapesta. Vol. I. Desrobitorii* (Bucharest, 1920), p. 28.

17. *Buletin de Informare*, December 26, 28, 29.

18. Cosmin, *Romanii*, pp. 30–31.

19. *Ibid.*, p. 30.

20. *Buletin de Informare*, January 18.

21. *Ibid.*, December 27, 28, 29.

22. M.C.G. to C.T.T., December 14, *A.M.* Dosar 15.

23. Berthelot to Ministère de la Guerre, August 22, 1923. Ministère de la Guerre, Archives de la Guerre, Vincennes. Fonds Berthelot 1 K 77; Victor Atanasiu, *et al.*,

*România în Primul Război Mondial* (Bucharest, 1979), p. 442. Franchet d'Esperey told the Romanians that if he had known of the existence of the treaty of 1916, he would not have established the demarcation line on the Maros (Mureș) in the first place. I. Gheorghe Duca, *Amintiri politica*, III (Munich, 1982), 176.

24. Berthelot's service as head of the French military mission in Romania during her darkest hour (1916–18) had given him enormous influence with the King, the army, and the populace.

25. L. Arday, "The Question of an Armistice and of the Military Occupation of Austria–Hungary in October–November 1918 Traced in the Relevant British Documents," *Acta Historica*, 26, Nr. 1–2 (1980), 171–78.

26. Berthelot to Marchal, January 7. Archives de la Guerre, Papiers Charles Marchal, 1 K 175. On the *cordon sanitaire*, see Kalervo Hovi, *Cordon Sanitaire or Barrière de l'Est; The Emergence of the New French Eastern Alliance Policy 1917–1919* (Turku, 1975).

27. Henri Berthelot, *Memoires* (manuscript. Hoover Institution, Stanford California) entries December 25–January 3. The M.C.G. had seen to it that his itinerary was widely publicized. This and Berthelot's partiality was questioned by the Saxon and Hungarian press. M.C.G. to C.T.T. December 24, A.M. Dosar Nr. 5; *Buletin de Informare*, December 31, January 2, 3, 4.

28. See footnote 23. Included was a 15-kilometer "neutral zone" to be occupied by French troops, but none were available.

29. *Buletin de Informare*, January 8.

30. Captaine Amiel to Lt.-Colonel Vix, February 4. Ministere de Affaires Extrangères, Archives Diplomatiques, Correspondence des Affairs Politiques, Europe 1918–1929, Roumanie, Vol. 47. (Hereafter *A.D. Roumanie* followed by volume number.) Amiel, a representative of Colonel Vix, head of the French military mission in Budapest, essentially absolved Apáthy of these charges.

31. *Buletin de Informare*, December 29.

32. *Ibid.*, January 20; Cosmin, *Romanii*, pp. 31–33.

33. General Holban (Division VI) to C.T.T., January 23, *A.M.* Dosar Nr. 5.

34. *Ibid.*, C.T.T. to M.C.G. January 22. *A.M.* Doar Nr. 17. *Buletin de Informare*, January 22, February 1.

35. General Holban to C.T.T., January 23. *A.M.* Dosar Nr. 5. These towns fell within the neutral zone proposed by Berthelot but his request for French occupation troops had not been fulfilled so there was no supervision. A French investigator blamed the incident at Zilah (Zălau) about equally on both parties (footnote 30).

36. These cities lay just beyond the traditional confines of Transylvania. *Cf.* the map in R.W. Seton-Watson, *A History of the Roumanians* (Cambridge, 1934), p. 568.

37. Great Britain, War Office, *Allied Press Supplement to the Daily Review of the Foreign Press*, p. 506. (Hereafter *Allied Press Supplement.)*

38. Peter Pastor, *Hungary Between Wilson and Lenin: The Hungarian Revolution of 1918–1919 and the Big Three* (New York, 1976), pp. 88–90.

39. Berthelot, *Memoires*, January 26.

40. C.T.T. to Holban, February 2. A.M. Dosar Nr. 15.

41. Berthelot, *Memoires*, February 18.

42. *Buletin de Informare*, January 25. The report of General Patey is referred to in Pichon to Clemenceau, March 19. *A.D. Roumanie* Nr. 47. The Romanians believed that Vix was "completely bought" having been wined and dined by the Hungarians. *Buletin de Informare*, January 26.

43. *Rumânia* (Bucharest), Februaary 16.

44. See, for example, the report of Sir George Barclay in Great Britain, Public Record Office, Cabinet Office Papers 24;150, February 19. Hereafter *C.A.B.* with file number and date.)

45. Franchet d'Esperey to Clemenceau, February 14, 15; Commission des Affaires Roumaines to Conseil Supreme, February 17; Note Lue du General Alby, February 19; Clemenceau to Franchet d'Esperey, March 1. *A.D. Roumanie* Nr. 47.

46. The change in the Allied attitude was explained as due to Queen Marie's visit to Paris, *România,* February 28.

47. *Ibid.,* March 2, 4; Delegation Roumaine a la Conference de la Paix, March 6. *A.D. Roumanie* Nr. 47.

48. *România,* March 13, 20; Pastor, *Hungary* p. 124; *Tradiţii de solidaritate revoluţionara româno–ungară* (Bucharest, 1979), p. 56.

49. Reports of the Council's decision appeared in the press almost immediately. *România,* March 6.

50. Pastor, *Hungary,* pp. 142–45.

51. *România,* March 27, 30.

52. *Ibid.,* March 30, 31. These reports circulated much earlier. See Robert de Fleurs (chargé-Bucharest) to Pichon, February 27. *A.D. Roumanie* Nr. 47.

53. Romanian Delegation to General Alby, April 3. *A.D. Roumanie* Nr. 11.

54. Maria Ormos, "The Hungarian Soviet Republic and Intervention by the Entente," in Béla Király, ed., *War and Society in East Central Europe,* VI (New York, 1982), 134–35. Huge quantities of supplies were diverted from South Russia to Romania, *ibid.,* p. 133.

55. Paul Azan, *Franchet d'Esperey* (Paris, 1949), p. 250.

56. Berthelot, "Memoires," *April 6.*

57. Saint-Aulaire to Pichon, April 6. *A.D. Roumanie* Nr. 47.

58. M.C.G. to C.T.T., April 10. *A.M.* Dosar Nr. 15; Berthelot, "Memoires," April 6, 11; Azan, *d'Esperey,* p. 250; on the Smuts mission, see, Gyula Juhász, *Hungarian Foreign Policy 1918–1945* (Budapest, 1979), pp. 21–22.

59. Franchet d'Esperey to Clemenceau and Foch, April 12, *A.D. Roumanie* Nr. 47.

60. Green to Hoover, April 11. Cited in John Thompson, *Russia, Bolshevism and the Versailles Peace* (Princeton, 1966), p. 200.

61. Mărdărescu, *Campania,* pp. 40–50.

62. Clemenceau to Franchet d'Esperey, April 14, *A.D. Roumanie* Nr. 47; Ormos, "Intervention," p. 136.

63. *Ibid.,* p. 136.

64. *România,* April 16.

65. *Ibid.,* May 5.

66. *Ibid.,* May 13, 15, 25, 28, 30; Hanah Pekula, *The Last Romantic* (Simon and Shuster, 1984), p. 290. This new biography utilizes Marie's unpublished diary and corespondence.

67. Petin to Clemenceau, May 19. *A.D. Roumanie* Nr. 47.

68. *România,* May 18, 25, 26, 29; d'Esperey to Foch and Clemenceau, May 24; Saint-Aulaire to Pichon, June 12, *A.D. Roumanie* No. 47. The scope of this study has not permitted dicussion of the Banat.

69. The Romanians believed certain French generals were biased because of their "scandalous" cohabitation with Hungarian women. Duca, *Amintiri,* III, 177; Saint-Aulaire to Pichon, June 18, *A.D. Roumanie* Nr. 47.

70. D'Esperey to Foch, May 5; Clemenceau to Pichon, July 3. *A.D. Roumanie* Nr. 47.

71. M.C.G. to C.T.T., May 5, A.M. Dosar Nr. 15; Petin explains the fluctuation of Romanian plans. Petin to Clemenceau, May 6. *A.D. Roumanie*, Nr. 47.

72. *Ibid.*

73. Bratianu, *Acţiunea*, p. 58.

74. Saint-Aulaire to Pichon, May 9. *A.D. Roumanie* Nr. 47.

75. Thompson, *Russia*, pp. 209–210.

76. Bratianu, *Actiunea*, p. 59.

77. *Romania*, May 6; *Les Armées alliées en orient après l'armistice de 1918. Comptes-rendus ... de decembre 1918 à octobre 1920 tome III (Mai, 1919)* (Paris, 1972), pp. 50, 98, 118; Saint-Aulaire to Pichon, May 6, *A.D. Roumanie*, Nr. 47.

78. Petin to Clemenceau, May 6. *A.D. Roumanie* Nr. 47; Mardarescu, *Campania*, p. 71; the French general Staff appears to have been of the same opinion. Ormos, "Intervention," p. 137.

79. Gheorghe Unc and Vladimir Zaharescu, "Din cronica relaţiilor româno–ungare în anii 1918–1920," in *Din cronica relaţiilor poporului român cu poporale vecine* (Bucharest, 1984), p. 272. St. Aulaire to Pichon, May 6. *A.D. Roumanie* Nr. 47; Tuţu, "Les actions de l'armée roumaine," p. 118–19.

80. Josef Kalvoda, "The Czechoslovak–Hungarian Dispute," in Király, *War and Society*, pp. 286–87.

81. Constantin Kiriţescu, *Istoria războiului pentru întregirea României 1916–1919*, III (Bucharest, n.d.), 430 ff; Mărdărescu, *Campania*, pp. 77–78.

82. Alfred D. Low, "Soviet Hungary and the Paris Peace Conference," in Ivan Volgyes, ed., *Hungary in Revolution 1918–1919* (Lincoln, 1971), p. 116.

83. Hugh and Christopher Seton-Watson, *The Making of a New Europe* (Seattle, 1981), pp. 374, 379–380; Thompson, *Russia*, pp. 209–210.

84. Bratianu, *Acţiunea*, pp. 59–60, 75–77, 90–99; Sherman D. Spector, *Rumania at the Paris Peace Conference* (New York, 1962), pp. 137–149. Clemenceau to d'Esperey, May 30. *A.D. Roumanie Nr. 47.*

85. Ormos, "Intervention," p. 137; d'Esperey to Foch, June 11. *A.D. Roumanie* Nr. 47.

86. Juhász, *Hungarian Foreign Policy*, pp. 24–25; Ormos, "Intervention," p. 137, argues that Clemenceau never expected the ultimatum to be accepted. Clemenceau later admitted the obligation put on Romania was a mistake. Great Britain, Foreign Office, *Documents on British Foreign Policy. 1919–1939. First Series*, I, 87. (Hereafter D B.F.P. followed by volume and page.)

87. Bratianu, *Acţiunea*, pp. 106–107; Saint-Aulaire to Pichon, June 20. *A.D. Roumanie* Nr. 47; *D.B.F.P.* I, 17; VI. 83.

88. Franchet d'Esperey to Clemenceau, June 22; Foch to Clemenceau, June 25, *A.D. Roumanie* Nr. 47.

89. *D.B.F.P.* VI, 15. C.A.B 24;150, July 16. The French military attache, after a ten day visit to the Tisza, had the same impression. Petin to Clemenceau, May 23, July 2. *A.D. Roumanie* Nr. 47.

90. Saint-Aulaire to Pichon, June 25. *A.D. Roumanie* Nr. 47. The phrases attributed to the King are suspiciously similar to those used by Franchet d'Esperey in a private letter. Azan, *Franchet d'Esperey*, p. 252.

91. Foch to Clemenceau, June 25. *A.D. Roumanie Nr. 47.*

92. Seton-Watson, *New Europe*, p. 380; *D.B.F.P.* I, 82–83, VI, 64–65.

93. Ormos, "Intervention," pp. 138–139.

94. D.B.F.P., I, 72–73; Atanasiu, *România*, p. 446.

95. D.B.F.P., I, 163; Franchet d'Esperey to Foch, July 21, *A.D. Roumanie* Nr. 47.

96. Kirițescu, *Istoria Războiului*, p. 464; Mărdărescu, *Campania*, p. 120.

97. *Ibid.*, pp. 110–112; Brătianu, *Acțiunea*, p. 117.

98. Petin to Clemenceau, May 23, *A.D. Roumanie* Nr. 47.

99. Appreciation de l'attache Militaire Anglais sur l'Armée Roumaine, Saint-Aulaire to Pichon, September 3, *A.D. Roumanie*, Nr. 11.

100. Petin to Clemenceau, May 23, *A.D. Roumanie* Nr. 47; Rapport du Capt. Selves sur son voyage à Bucharest du 11–19 March, *A.D. Roumanie* Nr. 11.

101. Allied Press Supplement, p. 506. Probably the most prominent example was General Danila Papp, commander of a Romanian division in the Tisza Campaign, who had been a member of the Austro–Hungarian General Staff and a professor in the military academy at Wiener Neutstadt. Luchian Predescu, *Enciclopedie Cugetarea* (Bucharest, 1941), p. 633.

102. Mărdărescu, *Campania*, pp. 135. ff.

103. Brătianu, *Acțiunea*, p. 119; Roumanian Delegation to Clemenceau, July 31, *A.D. Roumanie* Nr. 47; Kiritescu, *Istoria Războiului*, p. 474. However, socialist strikes in opposition occured in several Romanian cities. Unc and Zaharescu, "Din Cronica," p. 279.

104. Mărdărescu, *Campania*, p. 149.

105. Mărdărescu, *Campania*, p.147.

106. Marie exclaimed "We have strengthened ourselves more with that move on our own hook than with all the so called help that was being grudgingly given us by our so called friends," Pekula, *Last Romantic*, p. 291; Brătianu, *Acțiunea*, p. 131.

107. See, for example, Spector, *Roumanie*, pp. 167–96.

108. Eva S. Balogh, "Romanian and Allied Involvement in the Hungarian *Coup d'Etat* of 1919," in *Eastern European Quarterly*, IX, Nr. 3 (Fall, 1975), 297–313.

109. Perhaps the best assessment presently available can be found in the reports of Frank Rattigan, British chargé in Bucharest, who also visited Budapest, and of Sir George Clerk, the special envoy of the Peace Conference. *D.B.F.P.* VI, 138, 170, 236, 268, 280, 288, 341, 357, 389.

110. Kirițescu, *Istoria Războiului*, p. 385; Cosmin, *Românii*, p. 7; *România* April 16. For a well-informed summary of the status of Romanian–Hungarian relations on the eve of the war, see, Keith Hitchins, "The Nationality Problem in Hungary; István Tisza and the Rumanian National Party, 19190–1914" in *Journal of Modern History*, 53, Nr. 4 (December 1981), pp. 619–51.

111. *România*, January 16. Saint-Aulaire was quoted as saying in a speech in Bucharest that "the difficult times for Romania were over and that the time had now come for the recompense of the sacrifices make in the triumph of Romanianism." *Ibid.*, January 18.

112. *D.B.F.P.* I, 337, 340; Brătianu, *Acțiunea*, p. 139; Atanasiu, *România*, pp. 456–460; Mardarescu, *Campania*, pp. 170–182.

113. Spector, *Rumania*, documents this in vivid detail.

114. *D.B.F.P.* VI 268–70. Guido Romanelli, *Nel'ungheria de Béla Kun e Durante L'Occupazione Militare Romena* (Udine, 1964); Zsuzsa L. Nagy, "Italian National Interests and Hungary in 1918–1919," in Király, *War and Society*, pp. 201–26; Harry Hill Bandholtz, *An Undiplomatic Diary* (New York, 1933). Bandholtz's diary speaks for itself, but the editor has compounded its distortions. For example, the Introduction

(p. 3) states that General Holban, the Romanian military governor of Budapest, committed suicide on the eve of an investigation by the Romanian government. As a matter of fact, Holban was decorated for his service, later served as minister of war, and died in 1939. (Predescu, *Enciclopedia,* p. 39. 9.)

115. M.C.G. to C.T.T., September 7, October 7, 9. *A.M.* Doser Nr. 15; *D.B.F.P.* VI, 268, 309, 372.

116. Juhász, *Hungarian Foreign Policy* (pp. 31–35) has a good short summary of the negotiations in Budapest that led to Horthy's assumption of power.

# GREEK PARTICIPATION AND THE FRENCH ARMY
# INTERVENTION IN THE UKRAINE

Theofanis G. Stavrou

The title of this paper reflects the traditional approach by politicians and historians in treating Greek participation in the Ukraine during a brief period of civil war and intervention, as an aspect, and a small one at that, of the French Expeditionary Force in the are. Even Lenin, for reasons of his own, in several speeches during 1919 and 1920 referring to the Allied intervention in the south, talks about the French presence but makes no reference whatsoever to the Greek units who fought not only against Bolsheviks but who even clashed with French sailors sympathetic to the Soviet cause.[1] Admittedly, Greek participation in what in usually referred to as the Ukrainian or Southern Russian Expedition was under French command, and most likely the Greeks would not have participated in the conflict at all had it not been for the Entente, and especially the French connection. Still, the Greek presence was a sizable one, and according to some, a significant one. And, if for a moment we allow ourselves the belief that one of the main concerns of history is what happens to human beings, then the Greek participation merits some discussion. Out of an estimated 70,000 men who constituted the anti-Bolshevik forces in the south, (French, Poles, White Russian volunteers, and various other small groups), 23,351 were Greeks.[2] The French contribution during this entire involvement never exceeded 15,000. Equally noteworthy for our consideration is the fact that the Greeks were the only ones among the foreign participants who could identify with a sizable ethnic group inside Russia. Ninety percent of the 600,000–700,000 Greeks residing in Russia at the time lived in the south, the Crimea, and the Caucasus, and the fate of the majority of them was decidedly affected by the outcome of the Allied intervention. The objective of this paper, then, is partly not only to remind us of the Greek presence in the Allied Expedition, but also to encourage us to take another glance at this familiar story, this time through the Greek prism or perceptions of the situation.

By way of parenthetic introduction, I should point out that whereas little has been written in Western languages, especially English, on the subject and that usually cursory and sometimes uncomplimentary,[3] there is a great deal of unexamined material available in Greek. This material, published and unpublished, deserves systematic investigation and the findings could very well illuminate or at least corroborate our knowledge about certain aspects of this period. The most important of these sources, some of them utilized for this paper, are first of all the accounts of participants, especially military officers, some of which were published immediately after the war and some of which saw publication only recently.[4] Then there is the large "official version" of the expedition prepared by the History Divison of the Army General Staff published in 1955.[5] Interestingly enough, during the preparation of this volume, the Greek compilers sought to supplement their findings with pertinent information from the French military archives. When they wrote to their counterparts in Paris who were then working on their version of the History of the First World War, the French were not very cooperative. Finally, they explained that their project terminated with the end of the war in 1918 and that subsequent events did not preoccupy them and neither would they preoccupy them in the future.[6] The eagerness of the Greeks and the reluctance of the French to preoccupy themselves with the records of this expedition may well suggest something about their respective appraisal of their role in the enterprise. Especially significant are the reports prepared by the heads of the various Greek communities in southern Russia who at one point had welcomed the Expeditionary Force, and subsequently, had to be evacuated by Allied ships. Finally, there are the reports of Greek consuls, special government envoys, and the Greek Ambassadors in Petrograd and Paris, which are available in the Archives of the Ministry of Foreign Affairs in Athens.[7]

The testimony from this material reinforces the conventional story of confusion, misery, and sense of futility of this expedition which, from the Greek point of view, is succinctly expressed by a contemporary student of the problems as follows: "If the Entente were not serious about fighting alongside the White Russians against the Bolsheviks, why did they send our children to the frozen steppes of Russia? To what purpose then the nine-day heroic resistance of Constantine Vlachos in Kherson and the Ukrainian *epopée,* since the French planned to evacuate Odessa last week?" And in a more condemning statement she added: "But they will keep quiet, the Allies, and they will busy the Ukrainian expedition with its battles, and retreat of our army which even a matter of glory for us, is nevertheless disgrace for them who have treated us like mercenaries, not like Allies, who ignored human material because it was Greek and gave all their attention to commercial interests representing their investments."[8] This angry statement reflects the feelings of most Greek participants and observers, and it summarizes, among other things, the lack of singleness of purpose among the Allies and the absence of any meaningful communication.

It is now generally accepted that the involvement of the Greeks in southern Russia was chiefly the result of the pressure from French politicians, especially Georges Clemenceau, who viewed the whole operation as a continuation of the Entente's commitment to World-War-I objectives and as an opportunity to extinguish Bolshevism. Warned by the French military of the exhaustion and low morale of the French army, Clemenceau sought to man his operation in Russia with Allied troops. The Greeks looked like good fighting material. They enjoyed a good reputation among French military officers who had observed them in action in the Balkans. Furthermore, they were relatively rested, and Greek politicians could be pressured into participating with promises of favorable consideration at the Paris Peace Conference on Greek claims in eastern Thrace and possibly Smyrna in Asia Minor.[9]

Once the Greeks accepted the Allied "suggestion," they agreed to put at their disposal a fighting force of 42,000 men, constituting the three divisions of their *I Army Corps,* under the command of Constantine Nider and the Chief of Staff, Alexander Othonaios. Of the three divisions, only two reached the Ukraine—the *2nd* and the *13th.* A third remained at Karalla and was later used for the capture of Smyrna. The entire Allied Force under Major General Philippe Henri d'Anselme was supported by a mixed naval force consisting of units from the French, British, and Greek fleet, It was a motley crew, to be sure. Many among the French disapproved intervention and in fact some of them viewed sympathetically the young Bolshevik regime. In this context, the Greek troops, devoid of many of the political or ideolgoical problems plaguing the French, turned out to be the most worthwhile fighting force. Instead of dejection, the Greek troops, in the beginning at least, were characterized by enthusiasm and a messianic euphoria that they were lending a hand to threatened Orthodox Russia who had been their "protector" during the last two centuries as well as providing assistance and moral support to their fellow Greeks in southern Russia. Finally, the appeal of the "Great Idea" of creating a greater Greece with the blessings of the Allies, linked the Crimean campaign to an immediate national objective.[10]

On the other hand, the Greek expedition in southern Russia was the first such overseas undertaking by Greece since becoming an independent state. At home it generated both criticism and excitement. Even proponents, such as Venizelos himself and some members of the military, had reservations about the whole affair. They ran the risk of spreading themselves too thin, some argued, for the units committed to southern Russian could be employed in areas recently acquired by the Greeks in Macedonia. Then there was the fear of ideological infection, of Greek troops becoming carriers of Bolshevik ideas and propaganda upon their return home. Finally, there was the serious consideration of the repercussions that it could have for the flourishing Greek communities in southern Russia whose numbers had recently increased because of massive migrations from the Pontus area. With all these problems in mind, Venizelos insisted, before making his final commitment, that the Greek contribution should be part of a general Allied decision and plan, not just French, and more importantly that the Greek troops would be treated with dignity and provided with all necessary equipment including food and clothing. There is no doubt, however, that supreme in Venizelos' view was the need to acquire abundant credit to be used with the Allies at the Peace Conference. Clemenceau's threat that, "if you Greeks abandon us, I will abandon you," was taken seriously by Venizelos, who hastened to assure the Allies that the Greek army was at their disposal.[11] The commitment once made, the Greeks displayed unusual enthusiasm, and even though they talked a great deal about their mission as championing universal values, what loomed large before their eyes was the relationship of the expedition to the question of eastern Thrace and Asia Minor with the approval of the Allies. As a matter of fact, Greek historians like to compare the diplomatic activities of Venizelos in this regard with those of Cavour during the Crimean War when the participation of Sardinia against the Russians ensured a favorable attitude of the British and the French in Italy's struggle for unification.[12]

The episodic Greek odyssey in southern Russia began with the transportation of the *I Army Corps* from northern Greece in early January, 1919, a process which continued until March 21, and ended with the evacuation of Odessa and Sevastopol and the retreat of the Greek troops to Bessarabia by the end of April 1919. The main theaters of operation for the Greeks included the Kherson area (January 17–February 25), where the Greek infantry distinguished itself by freeing the Allied garrison surrounded by Soviet units and then turned with it to Odessa. Soon thereafter, the same regiment, (the *1st of the 2nd Divison*) participated effectively in the defense of Berezovka north of Odessa. On February 25, another regiment (the *7th of the 2nd Divison*) participated in the defense of Nikolaiev and during the period of March 5–24, held the main defense line of Odessa which served as the headquarters of the Allied Force as well as of the Greek *I Army Corps.* The *34th Regiment* of the *2nd Division* participated in the battles of Bere-zovka and Kremmydovka as well as the defense of Odessa. Then there were the activities of the *13th Division,* some of whose regiments were described as being among the most significant of the Allied detachments. This was especially true of the *2nd Regiment* under the command of Neokosmos Grigoriadis, which was transferred to Sevastopol on March 10. They par-ticipated in the defense of Sevastopol itself, but one of their major accom-plishments was to bring under control the "outbreaks" of the workers in the city, the workers being supported by French soldiers who had mutinied. Two other regiments of the *13th Divison* (the *3rd* under G. Kondilis, and the *5/42* consisting of Evzones under N. Plastiras) participated in the long battle of Sermka and the surrounding area (March 8–21) and covered the retreat of the Allies from Odessa to Bessarabia. After the decision of the Allies to evacuate Odessa on March 20, the Greek units, with the exception of the *2nd Regiment* which was in Sevastopol, left for Romania where they arrived by mid-April. The retreat was orderly. They crossed the Dniester and were stationed in the west bank for the defense of Bessarabia in the event of at-tack by the Red Army. The *I Army Corps* with headquarters in Galatz, remained in Romania until June 19 when, replaced by Romanian troops for the defense of the Dniester, were gradually transferred to Smyrna by July 4.[13]

The picture that emerges from this sketchy chronicle of the major mili-tary conflicts, involving the Greeks, confim the one reflected in the various communiquès and memoires that the strategic objective of the Allies was to protect the southern part of the Ukraine and the Crimea from the threaten-ing Soviet forces and provide enough material for the Russian volunteer ar-mies under Denikin to deal with the Bolsheviks further up north and drive toward Moscow. In the beginning, at least, there was optimism that this was a feasible plan if the Allies responded with alacrity to the needs of the *Volun-teer Army.* Yet despite some heroic fighting, the Allied expedition was almost from the start transformed into a series of retreats. This was partly because of the numerical superiority of the Bolsheviks, especially after January, 1919, when they crushed the Ukrainian autonomous movement, set up headquarters in Kharkov, Kiev, and Vinnitsa and started moving south in the direction of the Crimea and Odessa. It was also the result of the inefficiency, indecision, and inability of the Allies to appraise the situation accurately and utilize local conditions to further the expedition's cause. Thus, the Greek military units found themselves in a helpless situation to influence events dramatically despite their readiness to fight. It is important to keep in mind that among them there were no desertions, mutinies, or reported converts to Bolshevik ideas during their stay in Russia.[14] Their role in the conflict was determined as much by local conditions as it was by the overall policy of the Entente powers and their own political leaders, especially Eleutherios Venizelos.

The Greek detachments did not share the reservations of the French military about the success of the proposed expedition. They rather felt that the Crimea and southern Russia as a whole was defensible with relatively few units if properly equipped, replenished, and supplied. With the support of the Allied fleet, they could transform the area into a formidable base of operations affecting communications and supplies northward. Control of key cities such as Kherson, Odessa, Nikolaiev, and Sevastopol was, therefore, crucial. The failure of the Allied intervention to achieve its objectives disappointed and disillusioned the Greeks and what follows represents some of their views of what influenced the outcome.

According to Greek perceptions of developments, the enterprise failed because the expeditionary force was ill-conceived and poorly executed. A "lame expedition," they called it.[15] Besides the complexity of French politics, several factors contributed to this malaise. First of all, the Greek testimony supports the view that the Entente Powers, especially the French, were badly informed about Russian local conditions, especially the alleged strength and potential of the *Volunteer Army* under Denikin. Despite deep sympathy with the volunteers and admiration for Denikin and Kolchak (the latter fared better than the former), the Greeks were almost immediately convinced of the sad condition of the anti-Bolshevik forces: deprivation, exhaustion, selfishness, irritability, lethargy, and desertions. This was true even in areas where Denikin was directly in charge.[16] The Greek record also reveals in no uncertain terms that the crude behavior of French officers and soldiers contributed to humiliation and poor morale among the volunteers.[17] As the war progressed, the *Volunteer Army* was losing whatever respect or popularity it had enjoyed in the beginning and on occasion likened Denikin's behavior with that of his opponents. By contrast, the Bolsheviks projected a more energetic, organized, and confident image; they also enjoyed greater following among the workers than was generally acknowledged. The Allies were equally misinformed about the opportunistic mood and rivalries of the various ethnic groups in the region, especially Greeks, Tartars, Armenians, Jews, and Ukrainian nationalists, all of whom were competing for favors to protect their interests during this volatile period when political authority was shifting rapidly between Reds, Whites, nationalists, and foreign interventionists. By and large, the Allies were the losers in this confusion of loyalties; the Bolsheviks, the beneficiaries. This theme of not keeping up with the realities or tempo of a "revolutionary situation" runs through most of the Greek reports.

Probably more serious than poor information, however, was the fact that because of poor planning and the nature of the war, never once did the Allied Force display its full might against the Bolsheviks. At best, they amounted to dispersed units usually dispatched to unfamiliar posts soon after disembarkation.[18] And soon the Greeks came to resent the fact that they were assigned the heaviest part of the fighting. In fact the makeup of the fighting units in many local conflicts gave the impressions that the expeditionary force was manned entirely by Greeks. The lengthy telegraphic conversation between Hetman Nikolai Aleksandrovich Grigoriev and a Greek captain Matthios during which the former asked the latter, "What the hell are you Greeks doing in the Ukraine?" illustrates the point.[19] And, the Greek troops were not properly reinforced. Suffice it to point out that of the 42,000 men committed to the cause by Venizelos, only slightly over half of that number were transported to Russia. The rest stayed at Kavally because of lack of transportation facilities. Worse than that, those who were transported did not receive the supplies promised by the French: ammunitions, food, and clothing; not even beds, I should add.[20] This not only reduced the performance of the soldiers, who were often sent to the front without basic equipment, but it had its adverse effects on the population already feeling the shortage of Ukrainian food supplies which had been directed to Berlin the previous year. The Greek view is that the Allies could have been more successful if they had dispatched fewer, but better, equipped units. As one of the participants put it, "What reached Russia was not an army but many soldiers." This was in direct contrast to the plan suggested to the Allied Council by Marshal Ferdinand Foch who insisted that what was needed for a successful intervention in Russia was quantity of soldiers, not quality.[21]

Finally, there was the increasing tension among the Allies, natural under such conditions but nevertheless pernicious. The Greeks felt that the French withheld from them badly needed supplies but worse than that information about overall objectives as well as specific operations. They would usually inform the Greeks about operations at the last minute and still expect them to move immediately without consideration as to whether this was logistically or humanly possible. Frequently, the Greek commanders were not informed of the whereabouts of Greek contingents under French orders. The report of one such Greek commander, Colonel Tsolakopoulos-Rebelos, the well-known hero of the Macedonian War, conveys the pathetic conditions under which they operated and the increasing disillusionment with French behavior:

I can already say that they have destroyed my regiment and no regiment is left here to impose order and protect the town of Odessa. We are, at any moment, at the discretion of the Russian hordes who massacre anybody who is not a bandit or insane... The different armies and the police often surpass the criminal elements whom they support in a contemptible way. Not a single civil or military court functions. Total anarchy. Once more I protest and ask for measures to be taken for our army, which does not deserve such fate. I have reached the point where I will have to think if it is worth obeying blindly any longer the vague, dangerous and suspect order of people who are ignorant of what they do and what they want. I will now think how those whom I was entrusted with and myself will have to die.... If this is the result of a policy (which I do not believe), it is infamous and I will never understand it....I am fully aware of the national interests, for which I have often bled, and for this reason I have suffered this lamentable situation. But I cannot endure it any longer. If no reinforcements are sent, I ask you to replace me for I fear I might do some harm...[22]

The above indictment is especially telling when one keeps in mind that when he arrived in Odessa at the beginning of January, Colonel Tsolakopoulos-Rebelos, at a reception given in his honor by the local Greek community, praised the French extravagantly.[23]

Invariably, reinforcements arrived too late, and this aided the Bolsheviks in their drive toward Odessa after they had captured Kherson, Nikolaiev, Berezovka, and Mariopol (March 10–24). Even though Odessa had not as yet "participated in the Revolution," there were several disturbances there because of the presence of many Bolsheviks especially among workers at the port. The tension in the city is well illustrated in the words of I. Dragoumis: "personally, I have the impression that I live on top of a volcano ready to explode at any moment.... We recently apprehended two Bolsheviks who were about to blow us up... with bombs.[24] Odessa's population had swollen to over 1,500,000, including refugees from all over Russia as well as members of the Allied forces. Many of the inhabitants were armed with equipment abandoned by the Germans. Bolshevik propaganda, aimed at all sections of the population, was carried on incessantly. There even existed an association calling itself "The Greek Communist Group of Odessa" which strove to influence the Greek troops and enlighten them about the revolutionary cause and the futility of the intervention. In fact, a lengthy proclamation in Greek, interestingly enough signed also by Jacques Sadoul, was distributed to the Greeks of Odessa by the committee.[25] The local authorities and the Allies were unable or unwilling to disarm the population. Food supplies were scarce and the advancing Red forces convinced the French authorities that civil and military evacuation was the wisest course they should take.

The handling of the defense and evacuation of Odessa is symbolic of the policy enunciated in Paris by French and Greek politicans and translated into action by the military command in Southern Russia. The decision to abandon the city was depressing enough but to undertake it without sufficient warning led to frustration and fury, especially in view of the fact that two days earlier General Louis Franchet d'Esperey who had impressed upon Paris the need for evacuation was assuring the inhabitants that the Allies were not going to abandon Odessa.[26] The evacuation was accomplished in two days under the protection of French and Greek ships and the relative tolerance or cooperation of the Bolsheviks. Among the refugees from this, the first evacuation of Odessa, were 12,000 Greeks. The Greek troops retreated toward Ackerman on their way to Bessarabia.

For the Greeks, the evacuation of Odessa highlighted an explosive issue which among interventionists was unique to them. That was the fate of the Russian Greeks. The Greek authorities were compelled to come to their rescue, but they also realized that they could not accommodate all of them in the small Greek state which was transformed by the impact of the war into a major recipient of refugees. Besides, many Russian Greeks might have chosen to stay in their adopted homeland. This new dimension forced the Greek authorities to encourage their troops to pursue a prudent policy in regions of mixed population where the Greeks were in control, and also, to strive for an understanding or an agreement with the Soviet authorities about the future status of such Greeks. The Greek authorities had several official and unofficial warnings by the Bolsheviks to abandon their interventionist allies or face the consequences. The most serious warning came on February 20, 1919, by Christian Rakovskii, chairman of the Provisional Workers' and Peasants' Governments of the Ukraine and foreign commissar.[27]

The safety of the Russian Greeks was especially critical in the Crimea, after it had become evident that the Perekop Isthmus could no longer be defended without 2000 additional new troops. As usual, these new troops arrived late, on March 23. In the meantime a new idea was being entertained seriously and suggested to General Nider, commander of the Greek forces, by Franchet d'Esperey—the recruitment of local Greek civilians to meet some of the needs of the Allied army. Denikin had actually tried this possibility also. It was further suggested by the French that the new recruits would fight under the Greek flag. After considerable deliberation, the Greeks agreed to the first suggestion but declined the second, the main reason being their concern that the Bolsheviks might use this as a pretext to initiate reprisals against the Greeks. Nothing came of this movement to recruit local Greeks which in the opinion of some could have raised, within two months,

200,000 Greek volunteers for the defense of the Crimea.[28] In fact, any attempt to reinforce the Perekop Isthmus or even Sevastopol after April 8 was abandoned because, as Venizelos informed them the following day, the whole campaign was abandoned by the French. From then on, it was a matter of negotiating the evacuation from the towns of the Crimean coastline. Attention was focused on Sevastopol. Despite the French sailors' mutiny in the city, thanks to a special truce, evacuation was completed rather uneventfully by the middle of April. The Greek troops were again directed toward Bessarabia. During their three-month sojourn in southern Russia, their casualties amounted to 1055 (398 dead and 657 wounded), including 48 officers (18 dead and 30 wounded).[29] Those Greeks who stayed behind, despite promises to the contrary by the Soviets at the time of evacuation and before,[30] faced severe consequences as did most of the other nationalities which at some point had opposed the Bolsheviks. But that's another story which cannot be developed here because of limitations of space.

Unfortunately space does not allow us to consider another important question which resulted from Greece's participation in the expedition in southern Russia—the question of the Greeks from Pontus. These Pontic Greeks who lived primarily in the northern coast of Asia Minor were forced to emigrate into Russia, especially the Caucasus toward the end of the war.[31] As political control of this region changed frequently, they became wanderers victimized by Turks and Bolsheviks, and creating a strange swell in this sea of ethnic claims and counterclaims. Many of them, approximately 100,000 were transferred to Greece as part of a special project sponsored by the Greek government and under the supervision of writer Nikos Kazantzakis, who had been recently appointed minister of public welfare by Venizelos.[32] But the latter wanted most of them to return to the Pontic areas from where they had fled. Their return to Pontus created a demographic imbalance between them and the Armenians. Representatives of both groups were trying to get the support of the Allies in Paris for the creation of an independent Armenian or Pontic-Armenian state. Pontic Greeks were even advocating union of the new state with Greece. Venizelos, skeptical of their claims, knew that the Allies would not support such a scheme anyway. He advocated instead an independent Armenian state with an autonomous status of the Pontic Greeks residing in it.

For purposes of this paper, the Pontus Question is relevant in that it is one of the many problems bequeathed to the Greeks by the legacy of the expedition in southern Russia alongside the French Army. It deserves greater investigation as does the whole question of the presence of the Greeks in southern Russia, and I hope that this paper, schematic as it is, may serve as a step in that direction. Furthermore, investigation on the subject may help us realize that whereas occasionally intervention may be a crucial necessity for great powers, smaller states can ill afford such luxury.

## NOTES

1. For a sample of Lenin's speeches in this regard, see, V. I. Lenin, *Collected Works*, vol. xxix, pp. 315, 320, 513–14; vol. xxx, pp. 303, 384–85, 484. Sporadic references are also to be found in A. Gukovsky, *Frantsuskaia Interventsia na Iuge Rossii: 1918– 1919* [The French Intervention in Southern Russia: 1918–1919] (Moscow, 1928). See the work by Jean Xydias, *L'intervention française en Russie, 1918–1919: Souvenirs d'un temoin* (Paris, 1927), and the more recent study by Michael Jabara Carley, *Revolution and Intervention: The French Government and the Russian Civil War 1917–1919* (Kingston and Montreal, 1983).

2. Genikon Epitelion Stratou (Army General Staff), *To Ellinikon Ekstratevtikon Soma is Mesivrinin Rossian* [The Greek Expeditionary Corps in Southern Russia] (Athens, 1955), p. 34. See also, E. Bujac. *Les Campagnes de l'Armée Hellenique 1918– 1922* (Paris, 1930)

3. Representative examples of this cursory treatment are, on the positive side, George A. Brinkley, *The Volunteer Army and Allied Intervention in Southern Russia 1917–1921* (University of Notre Dame Press, 1966), pp. 86, 132–33; to a lesser extent Richard Ullman, *Anglo–Soviet Relations, 1917–1921 Vol. II Britain and the Russian Civil War November 1918–February 1920* (Princeton University Press, 1968), p. 137. On the negative side, see, John Bradley, *Allied Intervention in Russia* (London, 1968), p. 150. A recent study by Andrew L. Zapantis, *Greek-Soviet Relations, 1917–1941* (Boulder, East European Monograph Series,1982), pp. 46–53, devotes more attention to the subject. Finally, there is the article by N. Diomidis–Petsalis, "Hellenism in Southern Russia and the Ukrainian Campaign: Their Effect on the Pontus Question." *Balkan Studies,* Vol 13, Number 2, 1972, pp. 221–63.

4. The most important among these relatively unknown accounts are: Petrou Karakassoni (Major General). *Istoria tis is Oukranian ke Krimean Yperpontiou Ekstratias to 1919* [History of the Overseas Expedition in the Ukraine and the Crimea in 1919] (Athens, 1934)–probably the most comprehensive treatment undertaken by any of the participants; Neokosmou [Grigoriadi], *O Stratos mas sta Xena: Rossia-Roumania* [Our Army Abroad: Russia-Romania] (Smyrna, 1919), and his *Sta opla i Ellas* [Greece in Arms] (Constantiople, 1920); and, of course, C. Nider, "I Ekstratia tis Oukranias" [The Ukraine Expedition] in *Megali Stratiotiki ke Naftiki Egkylopedia* [Great Military and Naval Encyclopedia] Vol. I, Numbers 6–63 (Athens, 1927–1928). There is a supplement to Neokosmos Grigoriadis' earlier works, prepared at the request of Penelope Delta in volume IV of the *Archive of P. S. Delta* under the title *Ekstratia sti Mesimvrini Rossia, 1919* [Expedition in Southern Russia, 1919], edited by P. A. Zannas (Athens, 1982). The volume includes other important texts by participants in the expedition which were kept in Delta's archive. These are by Iankos Dragoumis, Konstantinos Manetas, and Konstantinos Vlahos. Zannas has also edited Nikolaos Plastiras, *Ekstratia Oukranias, 1919* [Expedition to the Ukraine, 91919], which appeared as volume II of *Archive of P. S. Delta* (Athens, 1979).

5. Genikon Epitelion Stratou (Army General Staff), Diefthinsis Istorias Stratou (Army History Divison), *To Ellinikon Ekstratevtikon Soma is Mesimvrini Rossian, 1919* [The Greek Expeditionary Corps in Southern Russia, 1919], (henceforht *GES*).

6. *Ibid.,* p xiii

7. See especially the account by the head of the Odessa Greek community, Eleftherios Pavlidis, *O Ellinismos tis Rossias ke ta 33 hronia tou en Athines Somatiou ton*

*ek Rossias Ellinon* [Hellenism in Russia and the 33 Years of the Athens Society of Greeks From Russia] (Athens, 1953); E. G. Kapsambeli, *Anamnisis Diplomatou* [A Diplomat's Reminiscences] (Athens, 1939; 1940): the same's, *Ti Ofili i Rossia stin Ellada* [What Russia Owes to Greece] (Althens, 1947), which does not dwell on the subject at hand but which chronicles the activities of successful Greeks in pre-revolutionary Russia.

8. The student is the well-known novelist and historian, Penelope Delta (1874–1949), and these comments appear in her unpublished novel, *Romiopoules* [Greek Girls], which was inspired by the expedition in southern Russia. I am grateful to Mr. P. Zannas for discussing with me Delta's archive which is in his possession and whose publication he is now supervising. The above excerpts are quoted by Zannas in the introduction of Vol. IV, *Expedition in Southern Russia,* pp. 7–8.

9. M. S. Margulies, *God interventsii* [Year of Intervention] (Berlin, 1923), Vol. II, p. 10.

10. Almost all accounts I consulted are permeated by this spirit. The Greek troops enjoyed warm reception when they arrived in Russian cities where there was a sizable Greek population. E Pavlidis, *O Ellinismos tis Rossias,* pp. 61–62. They also felt very much loved by the Russian people. Iankos Dragoumis, *Ekstratia sti Mesivrini Rossia,* p. 41.

11. N. Diomidis-Petsalis, 221–63, discusses the diplomatic aspects of the decision to intervene.

12. *Istoria tou Ellinikou Ethnous. Neoteros Ellinismos apo to 1913 os to 1914* [History of the Greek Nation. Modern Hellenism From 1913 to 1914], Vol. XV (Athens, 1978), pp. 112–13.

13. *GES,* p. 28ff. The area of the Uraine in which the Greeks fought was between the Dnieper and the Dniester and was about 220 kilometers wide between Kherson and Bender. Toward the north it was extended from 80 to 100 kilometers from the Black Sea to the cities of Kherson, Nikolaiev, Vasilinovo, Berezovka and Tiraspol. In addition, there was the Crimean theater.

14. The Greek high command, especially General K. Nider, pointed this out repeatedly. K. Nider, pp. 207, 310, 319, 327; Karakassoni, p. 233. Because of this record, the French preferred to put the security of some towns in the hands of the Greeks. *Ibid.,* 231.

15. Neokosmos Grigoriadis, *Sta Opla i Ellas,* p. 149; K. Manetas, in *Ekstratia sti Mesimvrini Rossia (P. S. Delta Archiees IV),* pp. 81–82.

16. Karakassoni, pp. 228–29; K. Nider, *op. cit.*

17. The crude behavior of the French toward the Greeks as well as toward the Russians is reported by Neokosmos Grigoriadis, who observed them in action in the Crimea. *Ekstratia stin Mesimvrini Rossia,* pp. 143–44; Iankos Dragoumis, p. 41; also, consult *GES,* pp. 357–59.

18. *Ekstratia stin Mesimvrini Rossia,* p. 144.

19. This long, charming dialogue was quoted extensively in several Greek accounts. The entire text was published in P. A. Zannas, (ed.), *Ekstratia stin Mesimvrini Rossia,* pp. 165–88. See. p. 166 for the above question.

20. *GES,* pp. 361.

21. Neokosmos Grigoriadis, *Sta Opla i Ellas,* p. 145ff; Richard H. Ullman, *Anglo–Soviet Relations,* p. 137.

22. Quoted in N. Diomidis–Petsalis, pp. 238–39.

23. E. Pavlidis, *Ellinismos tis Rossias,* pp. 64–65.

24. Iankos Dragoumis in *Ekstratia sti Mesimvrini Rossia,* p. 146.

25. E. Pavlidis, pp. 57–60.

26. *Ibid.,* p. 64.

27. Petsalis-Diomidis, p. 240.

28. This project is discussed in a memorandum by a journalist, Kepetzis, who was sent to the region by the Greek Foreign Ministry. J. Kepetzis, "The Fate of Hellenism in Russia and Its Salvation." 'The report was received in April 1919,, and is found in the Ministry of Foreign Affairs in Athens (YE-A/SVI)

29. *GES,* pp. 91, 261. The number of casualties became a controversial issue in later Greek politics, with supporters of the Expedition suggesting the minimum figure and critics exaggerating the casualties list.

30. During the truce offered by the Bolsheviks for the evacuation of Sevastopol, a delegation of Bolsheviks visited the Greek naval commander, Admiral Kakoulidis on board the Greek battleship *Kilkis.* The Bolsheviks expressed friendly feelings toward Greece, promised that the Greek communities in Russia would not be harmed and the Greek army evacuation would not be hindered. Subsequently, a Greek diplomat, Stavridakis, met with Pavel Dybenko, the commander-in-chief of the Bolshevik forces in the Crimea and other Bolshevik representatives at Yalta. The Bolsheviks handed Stavridakis a signed statement promising to respect the civil and property rights of the Greek communities. The Bolsheviks also expressed the desire to establish good relations with Greece and asked that no more Greek troops be sent against them. Diomidis-Petsalis, pp. 245–47; Zapantis, p. 51; and the interesting observations on the sensitivity of the interaction of the Greeks in Sevastopol by Neokosmos Grigoriadis, *O Stratos mas,* pp. 30–31.

31. On the Pontic question, see, D. Apostolidou, *I Megali Tragodia tou Pontou* [The Great Tragedy of Pontus] (Athens, 1919); De. Ikonomidou, *O Pontos ke ta dikea tou en afto Ellinismou* [Pontus and the Rights of Hellenism There] (Athens, 1920); Gr. Tilikidou, *I Kafkasii Ellines pro ke meta tin Rossikin Epanastasi* [The Caucasian Greeks Before and After the Russian Revolution] (Athens, 1921)

32. The Greek Marxist historian, Yannis Kordatos, makes an unconvincing attempt to link the mission of Kazantzakis with a well-financed spy conspiracy to undermine the Bolsheviks. See his *Istoria tis Noeteras Elladas* [History of Modern Greece], Vol. V. (Athens, 1958), p. 523. It might be of some interest to the reader to note that during this mission when Kazantzakis observed the uprooting of thousands of people, he was inspired to write his famous work, *The Greek Passion (or Christ Recrucified).* For a literary person's appreciation of the drama of the Pontus Greeks, read Kazantzakis' *Report to Greco* (New York, 1965), pp. 510–23. Kazantzakis also prepared a report about his expedition which he sent to Venizelos but the latter received both Kazantzakis and the report coldly. I am indebted for this detail to Kazantzakis' closest friend, Pandelis Prevelakis, whom I interviewed on the subject in Ekali (Summer, 1984).

# THE FRENCH ARMY AND INTERVENTION IN THE UKRAINE

Kim Munholland

In the twentieth century military interventions into another nation's internal conflicts, or civil wars, have seldom produced results that were satisfactory to the intervening power. The term "failure" is often employed to describe such actions. To a considerable extent these frequent failures may reflect the inherent difficulties of the assignment and the particular and frequently complex conditions of civil wars. On the surface, a decision to intervene would seem to follow the Clausewitzian precept that war is the extension of policy by other means. The decision to go to war — or to intervene — is a political one, and the army's assignment is to achieve the stated objectives, or war aims, by defeating the opposition through the application of superior force. Yet in the conditions of a civil war, victory or defeat in a classical military sense, may be hard to define. The notion of battlefield victory over one's opponent, or enemy, becomes blurred when the opposition includes irregular forces and even the involvement of civilian populations. The battlefields or "fronts" in civil wars are difficult to locate or limit as opposition may be found wherever the intervention occurs. In this sense, wars of intervention bear a greater resemblance to the colonial wars of the late nineteenth century than they do to the more traditional battlefield conflicts of the Napoleonic era or to eastern or western fronts of World War I. In the circumstances of intervention, a military solution to the fulfillment of political goals may be difficult or even impossible to attain, producing a sense of frustration and impatience among the officers and soldiers who are called upon to fulfill these goals. Certainly, the experience of the French Army's intervention in the Ukraine at the time of the Russian civil war illustrates the nature of this problem in twentieth-century military history.

There are four general areas that can be considered in assessing the role of the French Army during the intervention in the Ukraine. One might be called the *problem of the French army's assignment:* what were the goals of French policy, and what were the means that the army had to attain them? A second and closely related issue had to do with the attitude of the army, officers and soldiers alike, whose morale and reaction to the situation that they confronted were of crucial importance in determining to course and direction of the military intervention. A third problem arises from what might be termed the *environment* of intervention, or the local conditions that the army faced as an outside force intruding into a bitter and divisive domestic quarrel. In this instance, the French army contended with the hostile attitude of the local population and the divisions among the various factions and interests operating in the Ukraine, ranging from the Ukrainian nationalists to the *Volunteer Army* of General Anton Ivanovich Denikin. Finally, there was the difficulty of fighting a coalition war in alliance with not only France's Entente partner, Great Britain, but also with the Greeks, who supplied a sizable military force, and with the border states of Poland and Romania.

Before turning to the goals of French intervention and an assessment of the army as an instrument toward their fulfillment, we might remind ourselves that the French army and the French people had just been through a long struggle in which an initial political consensus – *union sacrée* – gave way in 1917 to a sharp division over war aims. French Socialists began questioning fighting for a victory that appeared difficult, or even impossible, to attain and was meanwhile bleeding the country to death. Even if the war was won, the Socialists argued, this would only benefit the ruling political and economic elites. At the same time, soldiers challenged the deadly, unimaginative military tactics that produced little gain at the price of unbearably onerous casualty figures. Doubts about war aims and resentment over the bloody conditions of warfare led to the French military mutinies of 1917. While the army eventually recovered from this shock and claimed a French share in the triumph over Germany, the scars of mutiny remained as a legacy of the war. Moreover, the effort had left the army victorious but drained. This sense of exhaustion was expressed in a French newspaper headline that proclaimed the end of the war with a simple exclamation: "Ouf!" The war was over at last... or was it?

Before an armistice had even been signed, Premier Georges Clemenceau had decided to intervene militarily in the Ukraine. On October 23, he proposed a broadly based Allied intervention that was to take place throughout Russia from Siberia to the Baltic. Allied action was to strangle Bolshevism, "this new and monstrous form of imperialism," that menaced all of Europe. Intervention was necessary to prevent any recovery of German influence in Eastern Europe and to permit healthy elements of Russian society to restore order and form a national government that would take its rightful place in a Europe "regenerated" by the peace. As for the Ukraine, France would assume a leading role in this region, which had been designated a French sphere of influence in agreement with the British government six weeks after the Bolshevik's seizure of power.[1] Occupation of this valuable wheat-producing area and control of the industrial resources of the Donetz basin were considered potential compensation for the losses that French investors had suffered when the Soviets renounced Czarist debts. Thus, Clemenceau elaborated an ambitious plan for achieving certain political and economic goals that would benefit France.[2] The French army was to have a central role in their fulfillment.

French and Allied troops would soon be available. The capitulation of Bulgaria and the anticipated collapse of the Ottoman empire would free units then operating in the Balkan theater as part of General Louis Franchet d'Esperey's *Army of the Orient,* and British forces in the Levant could also be tapped to serve in the Black Sea region once the Dardenelles were opened to Allied warships. Clemenceau was confident that the "several divisions" required for intervention could "easily" be found among these forces. They would provide "the nucleus for Allied forces around which the healthy elements of Russia will be able to organize themselves in preparation for the renovation of their country under the aegis of the Entente."[3] By its action, the French army's task was to assist anti-Bolshevik forces in establishing a stable government that would be sympathetic to the political and economic interests of the Entente. This was a large assignment. Whether or not it could be fulfilled depended upon the condition of the French and Allied forces and the material resources available to them.

The decision to intervene in the Black Sea was not the first occasion that the French army had been involved in the political turmoil of the Russian Revolution. A large French military mission had witnessed the two upheavals that shook the Russian empire and ultimately led to the Soviet withdrawal from the war at Brest-Litovsk in March 1918. This mission originally had been sent to coordinate supply and to serve as observers with the Russian army's General Staff before the February revolution. With the establishment of the Provisional Government, the military mission became involved in assessing prospects for maintaining the Eastern Front against Germany. Even before summer 1917 and the disastrous Kornilov offensive, the French military mission had become pessimistic about conditions in the Russian army. French military leaders hoped that the army would be able to hold out through the year, but they realized that such hopes were fading with the rapid deterioration of morale among Russian soldiers.[4] The disintegration of the army seemed inevitable just before the Bolsheviks seized power, and in October, the French High Command in Paris considered a plan of military intervention to stem the collapse of Russia and prevent areas of vital economic importance from falling into German hands.[5]

With the Bolshevik revolution and Lenin's decision to negotiate a peace settlement with the Central Powers at Brest-Litovsk, fears of a Russian defection from the Allied cause became a reality. In the absence of formal French diplomatic recognition of the new regime, representatives of the military mission became important spokesmen for French interests in Russia, although the *Quai d'Orsay* continued to exercise its influence through Ambassador Joseph Noulens, who remained in the country until early summer 1918. In an effort to minimize the effect of the Soviet decision to leave the war, French representatives groped for a policy in the aftermath of the Brest-Litovsk peace that the Bolsheviks signed on March 3, 1918. A divergence of view appeared briefly as Noulens and the *Quai d'Orsay* urged a complete break with the Bolheviks. The diplomats favored Allied intervention to overthrow Lenin's government and install pro-Allied leaders, who would oppose the extension of German influence into Russia and the Ukraine. By contrast, after Brest-Litovsk, the French military mission initially argued for accommodation with the Soviets as the only disciplined force in Russia that was capable of resisting German pressure. Military proposals for assistance to Trotskii and the new Red Army were rejected by Noulens and the *Quai d'Orsay*, however, in favor of a complete break and support for the various anti-Bolshevik movements that had appeared in Siberia, the Ukraine, and northern Russia. By late summer 1918, French policy was one of active hostility to the Soviets, and the diplomatic and military missions were withdrawn. Temporary divergence of views between the hard line of the *Quai d'Orsay* and the somewhat more flexible approach of the military mission had been resolved in favor of the foreign ministry. Clemenceau's decision to send a military expedition to the Ukraine represented an extension of French wartime policy, but it should be noted that several French military commanders doubted prospects for a successful military intervention against the Bolsheviks.

As his commander of the expeditionary force, Clemenceau selected General Henri Berthelot, who had previously served as head of the French military mission to the Romanian army. Berthelot had considerable experience on the Eastern Front, but he was sympathetic to Romanian claims to Bessarabia. His appointment was regarded with some concern by advocates of a "Great Russia," who feared that he would condone Romania's annexation of what they considered to be Russian land. Nevertheless, Berthelot was optimistic about the intervention and was convinced that it would occur on a large scale. Clemenceau preferred Berthelot to the more pessimistic Franchet d'Esperey, toward whom Clemenceau harbored a personal antipathy.

Although the primary mission of the French army was to replace the occupation forces of the Central Powers, quite clearly Clemenceau intended to use the intervention to extend French economic and political influence in the Ukraine. Instructions to Berthelot made this clear. He was to provide military support to local governments and organizations in their struggle against the Bolsheviks. Technical advisors were assigned to the armed forces so that they might, "contribute to the economic rebuilding of the country by extending its [the army's] action into the industrial and commercial area."[6] In addition to its peacekeeping role, the French army's assignment included the advancement of French economic and political interests. Recent scholarship, drawing upon diplomatic and military archives, has stressed this aspect of French policy, which was downplayed in previous Western accounts.[7] From the outset, French military intervention had the appearance of a colonial expedition in which the army's role was to assure political and economic gains in return for a limited investment of military resources.

Since the French Army would confront a "colonial" situation during its intervention in the Ukraine, certain conditions were essential for success. To overcome resistance, the army's experience in the French empire before 1914, had demonstrated the crucial importance of obtaining the collaboration, or at least the passive acquiesence, of the local population during the intervention; secondly, the intervention had to be sufficiently powerful to convince the population that the French forces and their allies represented the principal source of order and stability. In short, it was essential to overawe the opposition and gain the collaboration and support of elements that were already active in the region.

From Clemenceau's initial proposal, it is not clear how many troops would be assigned to the intervention. Initially, there was some discussion of eighteen to twenty Allied divisions to be provided by the French, the British, and the Romanians.[8] Rather quickly the proposed force was reduced to more modest dimensions. Two days after Armistice, the War Ministry called for an Allied army corps of twelve divisions, five of them French, two British, two Italian, and three Greek.[9] This proposal apparently was the basis for the promise that General Berthelot made in mid-November to General Dmitrii Grigoievich Scherbachev, General A. I. Denikin's representative to Allies, that there would be a sizable intervention of twelve divisions.[10] No sooner had this promise been made than Clemenceau further reduced the size of the expedition to three French and three Greek divisions, with "eventual" participation of Romanian troops. Possible British and Italian participation would depend upon governmental approval in London and Rome. Supplies and equipment were to come from the *Army of the Orient*.[11] Moreover, one French division (the *16th*) scheduled for the Ukraine had been weakened as the result of the flu, so that some companies in that division were at half strength. Volunteers, however, were under the comforting illusion that the French and their allies intended to intervene on a massive scale and restore them to power in Russia. As a British liaison officer with Denikin observed, "General Denikin's staff had prepared a beautiful paper scheme for the re-conquest of Russia which required eighteen Allied Divisions and munitions, etc. for half a million Russian troops whom they proposed to mobilize under the cover of the Allied

Divisions."[12] Here was the basis for the misunderstanding between the Russians and the French over the scale of the French intervention.

Decimated by the effects of the flu epidemic and scattered throughout the Balkans, the resources of the *Army of the Orient* were less impressive than their recent victories over the Central Powers might have indicated. Franchet d'Esperey was well aware of these limitations. Further misunderstanding over the size of the French intervention resulted from the activities of the self-appointed French consul, Emile Henno, whose enthusiasm for the cause of Great Russia far exceeded his authority. The promises made by Henno and by Charles Saint Aulaire at the Jassy Conference in late November and early December, went beyond the army's ability to deliver, and these commitments were neither officially sanctioned by Clemenceau nor reflected the intentions of the *Quai d'Orsay*. The hopes raised by Henno and General Berthelot subsequently provoked bitter expressions of disappointment among Denikin's Volunteers.

When informed of this reduced force, Berthelot began protesting that he lacked enough toops to hold the Ukraine.[13] Clemenceau's response was to further limit the intervention to the principal ports of the Black Sea — Odessa, Nikolaev, and Sebastopol — as well as Tagenrog on the Sea of Azov. Any extension of this limited occupation would await the arrival of reinforcements, but additional, fresh troops could not be expected before early February, and they were slow to arrive.[14] Difficulties in finding sufficient transportation delayed the first Greek units, who often appeared without the clothing and equipment that had been promised to them. Further, increased domestic criticism of the intervention caused Foreign Minister Stephen Pichon to accept the French Chamber of Deputies' insistance that reserves not be called to serve in Russia. This political condition limited the French army's manpower resources for the Ukrainian expedition, but the French command agreed that draftees should not be called upon for service in the Black Sea. Although Berthelot insisted that the intervention would succeed only if it were conducted on a massive scale, he also was convinced that he had to have "reliable" troops who would volunteer for service in Russia. He continued to press for a large Allied force of twenty divisions, including a substantial Romanian contingent, but Clemenceau steadfastly opposed the employment of Romanian troops on Russian soil. When the expected reinforcements failed to appear on the scale that Berthelot felt was necessary, it became obvious that the intervention was going to be something less than massive, and Berthelot asked to be recalled.

Other French officers shared Berthelot's belief that any successful intervention would have to be made on a large scale. General Lavergne, who had assumed command of the French military mission in Moscow in April, 1918, had warned Paris that the overthrow of Bolshevism would require an army of at least five hundred thousand. Lavergne had argued that the Allies had either to intervene in force or come to terms with the Soviets.[15] The intervention that Clemenceau contemplated would be nowhere near the 500,000 troops that General Lavergne had recommended for the defeat of Bolshevism, nor the half-million troops of the Central Powers that had held the Ukraine in 1918.

Berthelot's growing doubts about the French government's commitment to intervention were shared by his military rival, General Franchet d'Esperey. From the outset Franchet d'Esperey had been skeptical of the intervention, and his fears seemed to be confirmed as promised reinforcements failed to appear. Franchet d'Esperey had resented Berthelot's appointment, rightly suspecting that it was Clemenceau's way of getting around his command and avoiding his resistance to an extension of the *Army of the Orient's* activities. He had warned Paris that the intervention was unlikely to succeed, since the expedition would have to include at least 10,000 more troops than the six Allied divisions scheduled for the Ukraine. Otherwise, the promises of the French government could not be fulfilled. These troops would have to be fresh. Many of the troops under his command had seen long service in the East and were anxiously awaiting demobilization. Franchet d'Esperey's doubts found echoes within the French military command in the Black Sea region. General Philippe Henri d'Anselme, who assumed command of the French forces in the Ukraine in January, expressed his reservations at the outset about the wisdom of intervention on a small scale with exhausted troops, and he argued that in the absence of large numbers of reliable troops, the only alternative was to withdraw. In March Franchet d'Esperey sent Lieutenant-Colonel Huntziger on an inspection tour of Odessa, and his recommendation was blunt: if the government was not prepared to make the necessary sacrifices for a large scale intervention, then it should, "Contemplate the rapid withdrawal of all our forces, whatever might be the immediate psychological consequences."[16] Thus, from the very early moments of the intervention down to the decision to withdraw, there was a serious conflict between the views of the military and political leadership over what was necessary for a successful intervention in pursuit of French interests in the Ukraine.

As the reality of the numbers actually available for service in Russia became apparent, the French government was compelled to trim its policy, and the French army's assignment was reduced. By the time Clemenceau issued his order of 18 December 1918, the army was instructed to act as a peacekeeping force that would assure order and stability while Russian, anti-Bolshevik forces organized themselves and prepared to overthrow the revolutionary regime. Clearly, the French and Greek divisions could not bring about the downfall of Bolshevism unaided, nor were they prepared to play a leading role in fighting against the Soviet forces. The original goal of French policy had been an ambitious one, but, as Peter Kenez notes, that policy had not been thought through and exceeded the means available to it.[17] The French army lacked the resources to fulfill its assignment, at least as originally conceived in Paris, and it remained to be seen whether or not these six depleted divisions would be adequate even to hold the port cities of the Black Sea against an attack by Soviet forces.

The shortage of troops led the French officers in the Ukraine to improvise policy and try to find accommodation with the various elements in the region. When the first French units reached Odessa on December 17, they discovered that the city was effectively dominated by forces loyal to Simyon Vasilevich Petliura and the Ukrainian Directorate, which recently had been established in Kiev. An uneasy truce existed between Petliura and the handful of Volunteers in the city. Each side regarded the other with suspicion, reflecting profound differences over the future Russian state. Ukranian desires for national identity, or at least considerable autonomy within a federated system, clashed with the Volunteers' insistence upon a great and unified Russia. After initial skirmishes with Petliura's forces, the French commander, General Albert Borius, arranged for the withdrawal of the Petliurians and announced that Odessa was henceforth under French protection. He designated a Volunteer officer, General Grishin-Almazov, military governor of the city. Knowing that their own resources were thin, the French officers were compelled to make the most favorable arrangments possible with little regard for the intense differences that existed among the local rivals for power in Odessa.

As French and Greek reinforcements trickled in during the next six weeks, the Allied expedition occupied Nikolaev, Kherson, Tiraspol, and Sebastopol in the Crimea. In extending the sphere of French occupation, General d'Anselme reached a series of agreements with Petliura for a peaceful transfer of power in Nikolaev and Kherson. He justified these arrangements on military grounds, arguing that Petliura's forces effectively controlled land communications with Odessa, but his dealing with a representative of the Ukrainian Directorate infuriated Denikin and the Volunteers. In defending his action, d'Anselme maintained that his instructions required that he cooperate with all patriotic elements who opposed the Bolsheviks.[18] Whereas the Volunteers had anticipated a massive intervention by the French army, victorious over the Germans, the French high command was driven to improvise policy with limited resources in an environment that was more hostile than had been expected. The uneasiness of the French commanders quickly became apparent as rumors of approaching Bolshevik forces reached the command posts at Kherson and Nikolaev and were reported to the French headquarters in Odessa.

The immediate threat to Kherson and Nikolaev came from a large force, estimated to be between 10–12,000 troops commanded by the flamboyant Ataman Nikolai Aleksandrovich Grigorev, who at this point was allied with the Bolsheviks. As Grigorev's troops approached Kherson, he called upon the small garrison of French and Greek forces to withdraw. At the time, there were no more than 150 French and 700 Greek soldiers in Kherson. The Greek captain in charge of the railway station rejected Grigoriev's ultimatum, and instead, prepared to defend the city. Reinforced by two additional companies of Greek soldiers, the Allied force was able to hold out for over a week, but faced hopeless odds. Under cover of a French naval barrage, they evacuated the city after Greek reinforcements liberated a contingent of French and Greek soldiers who had been surrounded in the citadel in the center of Kherson. They had fought desperately, but were overwhelmed by the superior numbers of Grigoriev's army.[19]

Grigoriev quickly moved on to Nikolaev, where Allied defenses were even less impressive. There were only 500 Greek troops in the city alongside two depleted French companies. The 12,000 German troops still in Nikolaev were suspected of being sympathetic to Grigoriev and the Bolshevik cause. In any event, the Germans had no intention of joining the Greek and French forces in a crusade against Bolshevism. Since the loss of Kherson made any defense of Nikolaev untenable, the two senior French commanders in the region, Admiral Gustave Lelay and Rear Admiral Louis Antoine Exelmans, decided to evacuate the city and negotiated a temporary truce with a Latvian named Ego on behalf of the Ukrainian Communist Directorate. By March 16, French, Greek, and German troops in the city had been withdrawn.[20] An absence of reinforcements and the overwhelming numerical superiority of the opposition were cited as reasons for the defeat at Kherson and the precipitate withdrawal from Nikolaev.

With the loss of these two cities, the Allies began to consolidate their forces within a perimeter around Odessa, a city that was becoming swollen by refugees. The loss of the hinterland in the western Ukraine meant that the base for support and feeding the population in Odessa had become increasingly restricted. These conditions added to French anxieties. Although some reinforcements had reached the city, the French commander feared that an internal uprising might coincide with an expected attack upon the city's defenders. By this time, General Berthelot had become so disheartened with the situation that he asked to be relieved. In explaining the events at Kherson and Nikolaev, Berthelot noted that the Allies faced an armed opposition that was ten times larger than their forces, and repeated his argument that the situation could be salvaged only with the prompt arrival of massive reinforcements.[21] In the absence of such reinforcements, Berthelot recommended that Russia be left to its own internal disorders, and that France support strong Polish and Romanian states as barriers against Bolshevism.[22] Franchet d'Esperey, d'Anselme and the other French commanders fully shared Berthelot's pessimism.

When Franchet d'Esperey arrived in Odessa on March 20, d'Anselme reported that the outnumbered Allies had been defeated, and they now faced the prospect of an internal uprising within the city. Chances for holding Odessa dimmed as news of skirmishes reached French headquarters. On March 18, pro-Soviet troops overran Berezovka, 40 miles northeast of Odessa. This Bolshevik army, which French intelligence estimated to be between 10–17,000, overwhelmed a small and dispirited force of Greeks and Algerians, who fled in panic and left much of their equipment behind them. They had received little support from the Volunteer troops in the area, who refused to fight, according to accounts by disgusted French officers. A few days later the Bolshevik forces, this time reported to be no more than a few armed peasants, routed the Volunteers at Ochakov.[23] Given the poor performance by these thin forces, d'Anselme concluded that he lacked the manpower to hold the perimeter around Odessa and to secure the city itself; he recommended an evacuation before the French army and its Allies experienced another debacle on an even greater scale than Kherson. Franchet d'Esperey quickly agreed and secretly ordered that preparations be made.[24] He pressed his views upon Paris, and on March 29, he received a reluctant consent from Clemenceau and Foch, both strong advocates of intervention, to proceed with the evacuation.[25]

In accounts of the French intervention, the decision to evacuate Odessa has evoked strong criticism, particularly from the Volunteers and on the part of historians who have been sympathetic to the Volunteer cause. Neither the Volunteers nor the Greek commanders were informed of French intentions until the operation began, and the hasty withdrawal produced a panicked confusion at the docks. Given this chaotic departure, which was marked by many human tragedies, it is not surprising that bitter recriminations should have been levied against the French. Among the charges, the French military command has been accused of an unnecessary retreat. From the point of view of the French officers, however, the decision to pull out of Odessa reflected an unfavorable situation. They believed that there were no more than ten days' supplies of food available and were uncertain of any future shipments. Above all, the military situation looked bleak. Therefore, d'Anselme recommended evacuation.

Another charge against the French is that Odessa was in fact defensible but the army fled in unnecessary panic. On paper, the defense of Odessa looked possible. Defensive works had been built around the city, and an estimated 30,000 Allied troops were in Odessa itself. This force, critics have argued, was sufficient to hold off the advancing Bolsheviks. Since the French command declined to fight, the argument cannot be settled one way or another. The French commanders believed, however, that Odessa might become a military defeat like Kherson, only on a greater scale. General d'Anselme was convinced that even if the city could have been provisioned, the military situation was hopeless, as the allied troops were outnumbered, morale was low, and French intelligence reported that an estimated 50,000 armed workers were prepared to rise up upon the approach of the Bolshevik forces.[26] French officers vividly remembered that in the streets of Kherson the local population had engaged in guerrilla-style sniping at the French and Greek soldiers. Already rumors of uprisings to the southwest of Odessa raised fears that the Allied line of retreat might be cut. D'Anselme was harsh in his judgment of the French withdrawal. "We have fled a military debacle," he later reported to Paris.[27]

Not only were the numbers of troops insufficient for a successful intervention, but their morale, as General Berthelot put it, was also "frankly bad."[28] Many soldiers had served eighteen months or two years without relief. Their enthusiasm for continuing to fight and risk their lives in Russia was understandably limited, and the French commanders were well aware of these sentiments. For this reason, both Berthelot and Franchet d'Esperey had insisted that only volunteers or otherwise politically trustworthy troops be selected for service in the Black Sea intervention. Franchet d'Esperey also warned that the Senegalese colonial soldiers who were scheduled for the Ukrainian expedition would find the climate intolerable.[29] And, as noted previously, the ravages of the flu epidemic also had a negative impact upon morale, as the troops complained that sanitary conditions were inadequate.

Under these circumstances, French officers feared that Bolshevik propaganda would find a sympathetic hearing within the ranks. Shortly after the Allied forces landed in Odessa, the Soviet government sent a propaganda mission to Kiev, headed by Jacques Sadoul, a French officer who had rallied to the Bolshevik cause. Sadoul's pamphlet, *"Vive la République des Soviets,"* and other materials from the French Communist group in Kiev were discovered in the hands of French soldiers and sailors serving in the Black Sea.[30] French officers complained that the Bolsheviks in Odessa used not only propaganda but also money and women to incite mutiny. One report observed that in the absence of any news from home, "Our soldiers, subjected to an intense Bolshevik propaganda, think only of their return to France and consider, in general, that they have no reason to fight against a country with which France is not officially in a state of war."[31] Under these circumstances, another officer wrote, "...our soldiers do not wish to fight the Bolsheviks, not because they are Bolsheviks themselves, but simply because they find it stupid to fight."[32] Not only did the rank and file resent having to serve in the Ukraine, but, too, French officers were less than enthusiastic for intervention. General Berthelot noted on his inspection tour of Odessa in February, "Our men and even the officers show a great reluctance to go any further into Russia," and concluded that morale for the entire expeditionary corps "is far from satisfactory."[33] At most, Allied troops were willing to occupy territory, but they were reluctant to risk their lives in battle since they considered the war to be over.[34] Soviet pamphleteers, officers complained, played upon a general disaffection with service in a distant land for apparently no reason other than, as a French officer sourly observed, to save the gold of the capitalists.[35] This comment suggests that even officers found some logic in the arguments of the Bolshevik propaganda, although they could hardly be seen as sympathetic to the idea of revolution. Complaints about poor food, the climate, lack of leave time, and the isolation of service in the Ukraine added to the overall discouragement for officers and soldiers alike. Certainly, the reluctance of the French troops to continue the conflict created an unfavorable impression among the local population and with the Volunteers.

To a considerable extent, the French army's disenchantment with intervention stemmed from what proved to be false assumptions about what awaited them upon arrival in the Ukraine. Clemenceau's order of November 21 indicated that the army was intervening at the request of local officials. Much to their surprise, French soldiers were not warmly welcomed when they stepped ashore in Odessa in mid-December. Instead, they faced a political environment of great complexity, marked by intense rivalries and hatreds, and the local population looked on sullenly as the French troops took up positions in the city. As the French and Allied forces occupied Kherson and Nikolaev, they reacted with uneasy nervousness to the obvious hostility around them. This hostility became overt when women and children supported partisans who attacked French troops in the streets of Kherson as Grigoriev's army reached the outskirts of the city. Faced with this local hostility, French morale began to crumble. Two companies of French reinforcements had refused to disembark when they arrived at Kherson; Algerian units had refused to embark at Costanze when ordered to Odessa. The threat of mutiny once more raised itself within the ranks of the French army and could not be ignored.

Not only did the soldiers resent risking their lives in a hostile civilian environment, but also the commanders were convinced that the population was strongly pro-Soviet in its sympathies. In explaining the defeats at Kherson and Nikolaev, General d'Anselme claimed that the entire city and surrounding countryside had risen up, had enthusiastically welcomed Grigoriev, and had rallied to the Bolsheviks. Moreover, the French Commanders were impressed with the discipline of the Bolshevik troops, who appeared to be very effectively commanded.[36] The local population's willingness to aid the Bolshevik forces made the situation of the outnumbered French forces untenable. In his report to Clemenceau, Franchet d'Esperey subsequently explained the withdrawal from Odessa as due to the overwhelming numbers of the opposition and the hostility of the local population.[37] Following the Kherson and Nikolaev defeats, the French military leaders argued that since their soldiers wanted no more of combat on alien soil amid a population that sympathized with the opposition, the government should come to terms with the Bolsheviks and withdraw from a hopeless situation.[38] The French government, they concluded, had promised more than could be achieved.

The political situation in the Ukraine tried the patience of French officers, who displayed little symphathy and even less tact in dealing with the intricacies of local rivalries. French commanders had been assured that they were to seek the assistance and support of all elements who might be engaged in the struggle against the Bolsheviks. This meant that they were prepared to deal with both the Volunteers and their political rivals, hoping to encourage the development of a unified front. Much to their disgust, the local factions refused to set aside their political differences for a common cause. On this score, Berthelot wrote Paris, the Russians had learned nothing, "neither from the war, nor from their revolution."[39]

Even more, the Volunteers were, as Franchet d'Esperey cabled in exasperation, more of a liability than an asset.[40] This negative assessment of the Volunteers and their behavior was widespread. The Volunteers showed little interest in fighting the Bolsheviks, the French complained. "They play, drink and amuse themselves as in the past."[41] Furthermore, the arrogant behavior of the Volunteers had heightened their alienation from the people and exacerbated old class hatreds. Colonel Henri Freydenberg, who was d'Anselme's chief of staff, noted that the *Volunteer Army* was 90 percent officers and had absolutely no ties with the people.[42] The Ukrainian peasantry identified them with the old order, and, as a result, "Between the volunteers and the people," d'Anselme reported, "there is a truly savage hatred."[43] French officers argued that the failure of the intervention was due in part to the French army's ties with these reactionaries.[44]

On the other hand, the Volunteers complained of the arrogant behavior of the French, who seemed to act as if they were occupying colonial territory. There is something to the charge. French impatience with the internal divisions among the anti-Bolsheviks and disgust with the behavior of the Volunteers led the French commanders to take matters into their own hands. As one historian has noted, French officers behaved toward the Russians as they would toward a "protectorate" and were astonished not to receive the marks of deference they felt were due to the representatives of the protecting power.[45] Furthermore, many of the officers serving in the Ukraine had previous experience in the French empire, and nearly a half of the French units were from the colonies or from Algeria, having been drawn from the disparate elements that made up the *Army of the Orient*. This background provided the military with certain views of how "pacification" could be accomplished. In circumstances that bore some resemblance to colonical warfare, the French army looked to support from the local population and expected that the Volunteers would provide this link. When it became obvious that not only were the Volunteers incapable of providing a bridge to the local population but also were in fact an obstacle to any support or even sympathy from the Ukrainian population, the French command concluded that the situation could not be saved. Officers throughout the hierarchy of command came to believe that the intervention was on behalf of a lost cause and certainly would not succeed until the base of support for the Volunteers was broadened, but among the people of the Ukraine and among the other potential elements opposed to the Bolsheviks.

Once the French commanders in the Ukraine reached the conclusion that they faced the prospect of a military defeat at Odessa, they began preparations without consulting either the Volunteers or their Greek allies. On March 21, one day after his arrival in Odessa, Franchet d'Esperey and d'Anselme drew up plans for an evacuation. Two days later, he cabled Paris that a "liquidation" of the Ukrainian intervention was necessary; he repeated his warning to Clemenceau and Foch three days later that the situation was rapidly deteriorating.[46] On the 25, before receiving orders from Paris, d'Anselme gave detailed orders to his French officers on how the evacuation would be accomplished. Not until the 30, over a week after Franchet d'Esperey's initial decision to withdraw, did the cable approving this action arrive from Clemenceau.[47] Two days later, d'Anselme began the evacuation in stages, which were not fully completed until the morning of April 7.

The French command, fearing a panic in the event that news of the evacuation leaked out, refused to confide in either the Volunteers or the Greek officers commanding the large contingent of Greek troops in Odessa. News of the withdrawal had in fact led to a panic at the docks on April 2, as desperate refugees sought places on French ships in the harbor. The haste and secrecy of the French evacuation left a legacy of bitterness. The Greek commander was informed only at the last minute, and Denikin was not informed of the evacuation until after it had taken place. This high-handed action by the French touched off an angry communiqué from Denikin's taff, which accused the French of cowardice and an unnecessary retreat.

The French army's relationship with the Volunteers was not, however, the only friction created by the intervention and the precipitate withdrawal from Odessa. What is usually described as a French intervention in the Ukraine was in fact an Allied effort. Polish, Czech, and Romanian detachments participated in a minor way in the intervention. The largest contribution of troops came from Greece where Prime Minister Eleutherios Venizelos, under pressure from Clemenceau, had agreed to send an army corps of three divisions. Clemenceau promised Venizelos that the French would provide transportation for the Greeks and supply them with clothing, ammunition, and equipment that would be of the same quantity and quality as the material available to French units, although the Greeks justifiably complained that deliveries were slow and inadequate. Since nearly a half of the troops in Odessa were Greeks, this contribution was important and represented a major element in the intervention.[48] At the time of the evacuation the French forces constituted only one-third of the troops in Odessa, but the French high command did not confide in its most important ally. The Greek commander was not informed of the French decision to evacuate until the order had been given, although the Greek commander in Odessa, General Constantine Nider, shared French pessimism concerning prospects for defending and supplying the besieged city. When General Nider first expressed his concern to d'Anselme on March 26, the French officer gave no indication that preparations for withdrawal were under way or that the orders had been drawn up and only awaited confirmation from Paris before being executed.[49] Moreover, the Greeks were given the difficult assignment of covering the retreat of the Allied forces that withdrew overland to positions west of the Dniester. Although they carried out their assignment successfully, the Greeks understandably complained at a lack of consultation on the part of the French command. The refusal of French officers to take their allies into their confidence left a bitter taste that carried over into the Crimean episode three weeks later, when the Greeks openly resented having to fight when the French had clearly lost enthusiasm for intervention.[50] Coalition warfare is often a difficult task; the Ukrainian intervention fully demonstrated the dominant partner's tendency to pursue its own interests and policy with little regard for the concerns or sensibilities of its allies.

Even with Great Britain, France's wartime partner, relations were marked by distrust, for French officers suspected, with some justification, that their old colonial rival had designs upon the French "sphere of influence" in the Ukraine and the Crimea, despite the Anglo–French agreement of December 23, 1917 that had assigned this area to French interests. British officers at Denikin's headquarters quickly and successfully exploited Volunteer resentment at the way in which the French Army had behaved in Odessa.

Finally, the presence of some 3000 Polish and 2500 Romanian troops as part of the intervention created problems for the French army. Again, French officers appreciated the fighting qualities of these units, but their presence alarmed Ukrainian separatists and Great Russian nationalists alike, since it appeared that the French favored Romanian and Polish claims to territory that was considered either Ukrainian or Russian, depending upon the national perspective. Furthermore, the intrusion of troops from smaller powers wounded both Ukrainian and Russian pride. As Admiral Lejay reported, the Russians and Ukrainians both regarded the presence of Romanian and Greek troops to be a humiliation.[51] In short, crosscurrents of local politics and national sentiment, whether Ukrainian or Russian, dashed whatever hopes the French army may have had for popular, unified support in the Ukraine, and the lack of tact in dealing with erstwhile Allies produced a common front that was less than harmonious. Colonel Freydenberg summarized the feelings of many

French military commanders when he reported that the French-led expedition had come to the Ukraine on three false assumptions: that the Volunteers were a "national army" representing a majority of the population; that the Russian people would welcome an Allied intervention against Bolshevik brigands; and that the fighting would be done by the Volunteers, which would require only technical assistance from the French. Instead, he glumly observed, the local population preferred the Bolsheviks to the reactionary Volunteers; the Ukrainians resented Allied presence; and the Volunteers had little desire to fight.[52]

Although the French and allied forces had evacuated Odessa, there was still a military intervention in the Crimea, where Allied troops had gone ashore shortly after the landings in Odessa in December. Clemenceau saw the Crimea as a stronghold against a complete Bolshevik control of the Ukraine; he urged that the French Army maintain its occupation of Sebastopol, supported by units of the French Navy.[53] Reinforcements that had been scheduled for Odessa were diverted to Sebastopol. For a while, the political situation in the Crimea seemed more promising for a successful intervention. The government of the Ukraine was relatively liberal and tried to work with the various political factions. However, the government depended militarily upon support from the Volunteers, who appeared to be backed by the French armed forces. Increasingly, Volunteer influences within the Crimean government began to prevail, and their reactionary policies elicited the same hostility that had occurred in the western Ukraine. A combination of local antagonism and internal conflicts between the Volunteers and other political groups evoked a familiar pattern. Moreover, the morale of the Allied units had further deteriorated in the aftermath of the Odessa evacuation. By mid-April there were 5000 Allied troops in and around Sebastopol, but French reports indicated that two thousand of them were "unenthusiastic" Greek units.[54] The French showed no desire to continue the intervention in the Crimea, and again the prospect of disobedience appeared within the French ranks when Algerian troops at Costanza refused to embark for Sebastopol. Over half the French troops in the Crimea were colonial soldiers who lacked sufficient noncommissioned officers to command them. Their discipline was poor, and the metropolitan French units in the city were described as weak and demoralized.[55]

When Volunteer resistance collapsed on the Perekop Isthmus on April 3, the French commanders feared another Kherson and decided to repeat the action they had taken at Odessa. The Bolshevik forces reached the outskirts of Sebastopol on April 16, but were temporarily checked by a bombardment from French warships.[56] The following day a truce was signed that was to last until the 25. The French agreed to turn the governance of Sebastopol over to the local Soviets on the 19 and evacuate their forces from the city.[57] From the French perspective conditions in the Crimea resembled those in Odessa.

Admiral Jean-François Amet reported that the Volunteers had been completely defeated and could offer no defense, and panic had broken out among the wealthier citizens, who feared an uprising in the city. Daily demonstrations filled the streets of Sebastopol, and workers refused to obey the orders of either the local government or French officers. Amet warned Franchet d'Esperey that the population hated the bourgeoisie and their French protectors.[58] On April 13, he requested permission to evacuate Sebastopol, citing problems in provisioning the city and expressing his concern over the hostility of the local population. Above all, morale within the French units was at an ebb. Franchet d'Esperey cabled Paris that the situation in the Crimea was serious; he again urged an evacuation before the Allies faced a catastrophe. Clemenceau yielded and gave Franchet d'Esperey permission to evacuate whenever it was necessary to do so.[59]

As the military command was preparing to evacuate Sebastopol, mutinies broke out on two French warships in the harbor, *Jean Bart* and *France,* and soon spread to other ships. The following day, April 20, a delegation of sailors went ashore and participated in a large demonstration of support for the local Soviets. Fighting erupted between the demonstrators and a detachment of French marines and Greek soldiers, who had been ordered to disperse the crowd. Two civilians were killed and ten demonstrators were wounded, including four French sailors. These Black Sea mutinies were the most serious display of disaffection and even revolutionary sentiment that had yet occurred. They brought to a climax a tendency toward indiscipline that had existed from the early stages of the intervention. Certainly the French soldiers and sailors in the Black Sea had reached the limits of their tolerance for what was seen as an impossible task. The French command negotiated with representatives of the sailors and agreed to depart. On April 23, *France* sailed away, and by April 28, the evacuation of Sebastopol had been completed.

Although the French government continued its interest in the affairs of the Ukraine, and more broadly, in southern Russia during the next several months, particularly as the military fortunes of Denikin and the Volunteers improved dramatically in summer 1919, the idea of a direct military intervention by French troops was never again considered. Military intervention in the Ukraine was a failed policy that may be attributed to many factors. The initial goals of the intervention were impossibly ambitious and exceeded the resources that the French government was prepared to make available. An Allied force of eighteen to twenty divisions meant sacrifices that no one was prepared to make. When the size of the intervention was scaled down to three French and three Greek divisions, aided by a smattering of troops from the states of Eastern Europe, and the assignment was reduced to a "peacekeeping" mission, the intervention faced intractable problems. Outnumbered in every encounter, French and Allied forces absorbed a series of military defeats. Hostile attitudes of the local population, combined with the intramural political conflicts of the various anti-Bolshevik factions, meant that a unified front was impossible to attain. Rather than risk further catastrophies and perhaps suffer from a complete disintegration of the army, French officers preferred to cut their losses and depart. The intervention in the Ukraine was, to say the least, a less than glorious page in French military history. It had, however, rather profound effects upon French military and political policies in Eastern Europe in the interwar period.

The sudden evacuations of Odessa and Sebastopol provoked a stinging denunciation of French behavior on the part of Denikin's staff. This "secret" yellow book, which was soon printed and circulated, was a partisan document that reflected a deep hostility toward the French government and its military representatives in the Ukraine. The anger and sense of betrayal on the Volunteer side is understandable, but the account of events is scarcely balanced and reveals little insight into the problems that the French Army faced. Moreover, this yellow book and the subsequent memoirs and records of the White opposition have colored interpretations of the French intervention until recent access to French archives has enabled a fuller picture to be drawn. The evidence does not necessarily excuse French actions, but it does suggest that the French Army confronted what might be termed an unwinnable situation in the Ukraine.

In an effort to smooth over relations with the Volunteers, a meeting was held with Volunteer representatives at the *Quai d'Orsay* on April 4, to regulate matters between General Denikin and the French command in the Ukraine.[60] This attempt to mollify Volunteer sensibilities came, however, before the Sebastopol episode and the publication of the Volunteers' yellow book. A further effort to improve French-Volunteer ties, inspired in part by French fears of growing British influence at Denikin's headquarters, came in late summer 1919 with the appointment of General Charles Mangin, a well-known commander of French forces during the war, to head a mission to General Denikin that offered French material assistance and advisors to the Volunteers. Still, a legacy of bitterness toward the French remained, despite the fact that France became a home of refuge for many Russians and Ukrainians who were forced to flee after General Wrangel's last stand in the Crimea in 1920. This resentment indicated that the wounds opened by the manner of French intervention never really healed, and the Whites would continue to blame the French for the failures of 1918—19. Efforts to repair relations with Denikin and his followers were too little and too late.

At the same time, the military had to judge soberly the costs and prospect for a successful intervention. Given a nearly impossible assignment, combined with a refusal to meet the army's demands for support, the military leadership became disenchanted with the approach of the French political leadership.

From the experience in the Black Sea, the army learned that a strictly "military" solution to the problems of a revolutionary age was difficult. They understood, perhaps better than Clemenceau or the *Quai d'Orsay*, the risks of intervention into another nation's strife with neither adequate military nor the support of local forces. Furthermore, the experience of intervention in a civil war presented the French army with a situation that was as much political in character as strictly military. By the very act of intervention, in the choice of allies, and in seeking local support, the army discovered that it could not be simply a neutral, peacekeeping force behind which an orderly government and indigenous force could organize and assume control. The line between technical military operations and political action became blurred. Much as in conditions of colonial warfare during the late nineteenth century, political, economic, strategic, and purely military motives and objectives became mixed. Choices of a political character had to be made on the spot, even if justified on military grounds. The officers leading the French intervention understood this dilemma and warned of the dangers in becoming involved without adequate preparation or clearly defined and potentially attainable goals. The prescription of political neutrality and the injunction against military involvement in politics that had guided the French army began to erode in the conditions of revolutionary civil warfare that were to become increasingly familiar in the twentieth century, particulary with the wars of decolonization that would draw the French Army into politics later in the century. The failure of the French army's intervention in the Ukraine held a lesson that unfortunately was not heeded.

Finally, the intervention in the Ukraine revealed the relative military weakness of France, despite its celebrated victory of 1918, and a reluctance of French policy makers to trim their ambitions to fit the realities of French power in Eastern Europe. The creation of a *cordon sanitaire* was a substitute for a French inability to intervene directly with military force and meant an inevitable contradiction between the reality of French power and the ambitions of a French foreign ministry, which made commitments in Eastern Europe that served French security interests but could not offer a reciprocal security to those states that were allied with France during the interwar years. The failure of the Ukrainian intervention indicated that even against a relatively weak Soviet state the French government lacked the means to assure the advancement of its political and economic interests in that part of the world. The economic, political, and psychological "costs" of intervention had greatly increased, and the era of relatively "inexpensive" colonial-style interventions of the late nineteenth century was coming to an end.

## NOTES

1. "Convention entre la France et l'Angleterre au sujet de l'action dans la Russie Méridionale," 23 December 1917, Archives de la ministère de la Guerre, Chateau de Vincennes, Service Historique de l'Armée (henceforth *SHA*), carton 7N 800.

2. Pres. council and war min. to for. min. 23 Oct. 1918, *SHA* 4N 49, 17N 581.

3. *Ibid.*

4. Michael Jabara Carley, *Revolution and Intervention: The French Government and the Russian Civil War 1917–1919* (Montreal, 1983), 7.

5. *Ibid.*, p. 15.

6. Min. for. aff. to pres. council and war min., Dec. 7, 1918, Archives du ministère des Affaires étrangères français (henceforth *AMAEF*), Europe 1918–1919, Russie 56.

7. Both Carley, *Revolution, passim,* and Anne Hogenhuis-Seliverstoff, *Les Relations Franco–Soviétiques 1917–1924* (Paris, 1981) give emphasis to the economic considerations behind the French intervention. Hogenhuis-Seliverstoff states (p. 127) "La mise en valeur des richesses ukrainiennes inspire beaucoup plus le gouvernement français que la cause des Volontaires."

8. Although the source is unclear, this is the figure given by Carley, *Revolution,* 111 and 224, fn. 25.

9. *Ibid.*, citing, "Note sur le plan d'action militaire de l'Entente," 13 Nov, 1918, *SHA* 16N 3172.

10. George A. Brinkley, *The Volunteer Army and Allied Intervention in South Russia, 1917–1921* (Notre Dame, 1966), 79.

11. Pres. council and war min. to commander, Allied Armies of the Orient, 21 Nov. 1918, *SHA* 16N 3172.

12. Memorandum by Major Keyes on his Russian experiences, India Office Library (London), Keyes Collection, Mss. Eur. F 131/12a.

13. Gen. Berthelot to war min., 4 and 5 Dec. 1918, *SHA* 16N 3172.

14. Pres. council telegr. to Cdr. Army of Orient, 18 Dec. 1918, *SHA* 7N 800.

15. Carley, *Revolution,* 107, 117.

16. "Rapport du Lt. Col. Huntziger de l'état-major de M. le Général Franchet d'Esperey sur le tour d'inspection du 8 au 9 mars," March 19, 1919, *AMAEF*, Eur. 1918–1929, Russie 228.

17. Peter Kenez, *Civil War in Southern Russia 1919–1920* (Berkeley, 1977), 178.

18. "Minute sur les relations entre le Général Denikin et le Général Berthelot," March 20, 1919, *AMAEF*, Eur. 1918–1929, Russie 228; "Rapport sur les relations du commandant militaire français à Odessa avec les gouvernements locaux du 14 janv. au 6 avr. 1918," 20 mai 1919, *AMAEF* Eur. 1918–1929, Russie 230.

19. Général Jean Bernachot, *Les Armées françaises en Orient après l'arministice de 1918* (Paris, 1970), 2: 102.

20. *Ibid.*, 103; Contre-Amiral Exelmans to M. le Vice-Amiral de la deuxième escadre (Amet), 18 March 1919, *SHA* 6N 231 (Fonds Clemenceau); *AMAEF*, Eur. 1918–1929, Russie 230.

21. Gén. Berthelot to war min., 12 March 1919, *SHA* 20N 273; Gén. Franchet d'Esperey to pres. council and war min., 16 March 1919, *AMAEF*, Eur. 1918–1929, Russie 228.

22. Gén. Berthelot to war min., 12 March 1919, *SHA* 20N 273.

23. Same to same, 19 March 1919, *ibid.*

24. "Note sur la situation en Odessa," 20 March 1919, *SHA* 6N 233.

25. Pres. council and war min. telegr. to Gén. Franchet d'Esperey, 29 March 1919, *SHA* 20N 273, *AMAEF,* Eur. 1918–1929, Russie 228.

26. Bernachot, *Armées françaises,* 2: 125.

27. M. Chevilly (Constantinople). to for. min., 14 April 1919, *AMAEF,* Eur. 1918–1929 Russie 229, citing d'Anselme.

28. Gén. Berthelot to war min., 19 Feb. 1919, *SHA* 20N 273.

29. Bernachot, *Armées françaises,* 2: 68–69.

30. "Compte-rendu hebdomadaire," 2<sup>e</sup> Bureau, 22 June 1919, *SHA* 20N 753-3.

31. "Note sur la question d'Odessa," 20 March 1919, *AMAEF,* Eur. 1918–1929 Russie 229.

32. "Note sure la situation en la Russie du Sud," 19 April 1919, *AMAEF,* Eur. 1918–1929 Russie 229.

33. Gén. Berthelot to war min., 19 Feb. 1919, *SHA* 20N 273.

34. "Intelligence Bulletin," Supreme command, Constantinople (Franchet d'Esperey) to war min., 21 March 1919, *ibid.*

35. Philippe Masson, *La Marine française et la Mer Noire, 1918–1919* (Paris, 1982): 80.

36. Arthur E. Adams, *Bolsheviks in the Ukraine: the Second Campaign, 1918–1919* (New Haven, 1963): 177.

37. Gén. Franchet d'Esperey to pres. council and war min., 18 March 1919, *AMAEF,* Eur. 1918–1929 Russie 821.

38. Contre-Amiral Exelmans to Vice-Amerial de la deuxième escadre (Amet), 18 March 1919, *SHA* 6N 231; Gén. Franchet d'Esperey to Gén. Foch, 19 March 1919, *AMAEF,* Eur. 1918–1929 Russie 228.

39. Gén. Berthelot to pres. council and war min., 17 Feb. 1919, *SHA* 20N 273.

40. Bernachot, *Les Armées françaises,* 2: 109–10.

41. "Situation en Russie du sud vu par l'état-major du Général Berthelot," 17 March 1919, *AMAEF,* Eur. 1918–1929, Russie 228.

42. Report of Lt. Col. Freydenberg, "Renseignements: évacuation d'Odessa et pays ukrainies," 22 April 1919, *SHA* 7N 651.

43. "Rapport sur les relations du commandant militaire français à Odessa avec les gouvernements locaux du 14 janv. au 6 avr. 1918," 20 May 1919, *AMAEF,* Eur. 1919–1929 Russie 230.

44. "Note de renseignements sur l'évacuation d'Odessa," *S. S. Justice* Intelligence Service, 12 April 1919, and Gén. Franchet d'Esperey to Gén. Foch, 29 March 1919, *AMAEF,* Eur. 1918–1929 Russie 229.

45. Hogenhuis-Seliverstoff, *Les Relations Franco–Soviétiques,* 154.

46. "Note sur la question d'Odessa," 20 March 1919, *AMAEF,* Eur. 1918–1929 Russie 229.

47. Pres. council and war min. to Gén. Franchet d'Esperey, 29 March 1919, *SHA* 20N 273.

48. "Note sur la situation en Odessa," 20 March 1919, *SHA* 6N 233.

49. Général K. X. Nider report from Odessa, 26 and 29 March 1919, in Ghenikan Epiteleiou Stratou, Thieuthensis Istorias-Stratou, *To Ellinikon ekstrateutikon soma eis mesimvirinin Rosiea* (Athens, 1955): 331, 335.

50. Gén. Berthelot to war min., 19 March 1919, *SHA* 20N 273.

51. Contre-Amiral Lejay to Gén. Berthelot, 17 March 1919, *AMAEF,* Eur. 1918–1929 Russie 228.

52. Report of Lt. Col. Freydenberg, "Renseignements," 22 April 1919, *SHA* 7N 651.

53. Pres. council and war min. to Gén. Franchet d'Esperey, 2 April 1919, *AMAEF,* Eur. 1918–1929 Russie 229.

54. Vice-Am. Amet to navy min., April 1919, *AMAEF,* Eur. 1918–1929 Russie 230.

55. Gén. Franchet d'Esperey to Gén. Foch, 15 April 1919, *AMAEF,* Eur. 1918–1929 Russie 229.

56. "Note pour le ministre: évacuation de Sébastopol" (n. d.), *AMAEF,* Eur. 1918–1929 Russie 230.

57. Gén. Franchet d'Esperey (telegr.) to Gén. Foch, 20 April 1919, and "Compte rendu de l'entretien entre Col Trousson et le délégué bolchevique sur l'évacuation de Sébastopol," 16 April 1919, *AMAEF,* Eur. 1918–1929 Russie 822.

58. Vice-Am. Amet to navy min., 10 April 1919, *AMAEF,* Eur. 1918–1929 Russie 821; M. Defrance (Constantinople), "Rapport sur l'évacuation de la Crimée," 3 May 1919, *AMAEF,* Eur. 1918–1929 Russie 230.

59. Gén. Franchet d'Esperey to pres council and war min., 14 April 1919, *AMAEF,* Eur. 1918–1929 Russie 229.

60. Brinkey, *The Volunteer Army,* 139.

# THE FOREIGN POLICY OF THE HUNGARIAN SOVIET REPUBLIC

Mária Ormos

To begin with, the first question bound to arise in connection with the foreign policy of the Hungarian Soviet Republic is to what extent, and in what sense, can we talk about foreign affairs?

Clearly, several factors contributed to limiting the scope of such policies. Among these, we can list the short duration of the regime, the state of war which prevailed during most of this brief period of 119 days, and the general curtailment of the normal network of foreign relations. Among the limiting factors, we should also mention that Béla Kun, the man in charge of the commissariat of foreign affairs, had no background in international relations, nor did he have an established apparatus at his disposal. Under the circumstances it seems more proper and justified to speak here of foreign policy as a set of basic assumptions and as a tendency manifesting itself during the life of the Soviet Republic.

In formulating basic assumption, the leaders of the Soviet Republic including Béla Kun, found themselves in a charged field on one end, a negative pole of argumentation fueled by conditions prevailing in the country, and on the other, with a set of arguments, which formed the positive pole. Both Social Democratic and Communist leaders started from the basic premise that the country's position could not possibly get any worse than it had been up to March 1919. Thus, Hungary could be hurt neither by a break in diplomatic ties, nor by economic blockade, nor even by military intervention, inasmuch as the Károlyi regime had not succeeded in resuming diplomatic contacts, and its foreign policy proved a fiasco. The economic blockade continued, and the Peace Conference took no steps to end it. As regards the demarcation line, the armed forces of neighboring countries had already crossed it several times at various spots.

It was no secret that Social Democratic leaders had deliberately provoked cabinet crisis primarily because they wanted to substitute a different orientation to the hopeless foreign-policy moves of the Károlyi regime. The new government made it abundantly clear in its first official statements, that, in addition to solving social problems, its basic aim was to stop the military advance of the "Imperialist" government forces, the outcome of which threatened to deprive Hungary of its means of economic survival. As to the blockade itself, several political leaders pointed out that, at the beginning of 1919, the choice facing the country was between "two types of starvation."

Hungary's international "outlaw" status, which lasted for several months, and the continuous draining of its energies, provided the ethical grounds for the country's leaders to attempt to realize their own alternative. This entailed immediate diplomatic and military contacts with revolutionary Soviet Russia, particularly with the Ukraine and the area then referred to as Eastern Galicia; in a somewhat more distant future this augured tremendous potential support.[1]

Expectation of a so-called world revolution was another stimulant for daring enterprise. On the basis of rhetorical references to this "world revolution," or to the flames of revolution spreading like wildfire to the borders of France, this expectation can be dismissed as rank illusion of idle day-dreaming, but a closer examination of the documents and the practical measures taken by the Soviet Republic reveals, however, that the expectation was not worldwide revolution but of a revolutionary upheaval in Central Europe, and for Hungary, a mini-Central European revolution.

Considering the conditions for stabilization and survival, Hungarian leaders counted primarily on the Ukrainian connection, and moreover, on revolutions in Vienna and Prague. They were most active in promoting such a turn of events in Austria, where the circumstances seemed propitious: personal contacts, illusions regarding the Social Democratic leadership, the initially friendly attitude and promises of the Austrian leaders. Revolution was "in the air" in Vienna until April 17, and undoubtedly expected, in the hope that it would set off a chain reaction.[2]

It is worth noting that in April 1919 there was not a single Entente politician or military leader in Europe who was not convinced that a swing to the left in Austria was but a matter of days, if not hours, away. Nor was there any doubt that such an occurrence would not only stabilize the position of the Hungarian Soviet Republic vis-à-vis the West, but would also become the starting point for further revolutionary action in the area, and for all practical purposes, throughout the former Austro—Hungarian monarchy. Furthermore, the signs indicated that, to the east, the Hungarian leadership had no other plan than resisting Romanian penetration and further territorial expansion through the use of arms. This was the reason why diplomatic and military collaboration with the Red Ukraine and leftist forces seemed so essential at this time.

The basic assumption of the Hungarian Soviet Republic was, in part, founding theory regarding a new Central European order. Although, as far as I know, this theory was never given systematic formulation, its outlines can be reconstructed from scattered elements of foreign and nationalities policies. On several occasions Kun made proposals concerning the organization of a meeting or conference to discuss common problems of, particularly economic cooperation among, the small states of Central Europe—indicating thereby, among other things, that he was bent on forestalling the economic disintegration of the area. The measures he took and the declarations he made on the issue of nationalities show even more clearly and explicitly his intentions in this regard. On one hand, the Republic recognized unreservedly, and with immediate effect, the cultural as well as political autonomy of the nationalities living under its jurisdiction; on the other hand, it insisted on economic unity and postponed the formation of a system of economic relations to a future date. And, Kun himself made no secret of the fact that he had in mind a federation, consisting of autonomous parts, which would preserve its unity from an economic point of view. Should revolutionary expectations be realized in Austria and in the Czechoslovak area, and even more so, should Germany join this nucleus, a Central European federation might come about, and thus, would its economic survival be assured.[3]

The history of the foreign relations or the international history of the Hungarian Soviet Republic of Councils is the history of debates surrounding this basic assumption, the gradual diminution of the concept, and its ultimate failure.

The formulation of the theory outlined above remained valid in its entirety during the first period of the Soviet Republic—until April 17, if we must seek precise dividing lines of time. Indefinite postponement of the long-awaited Viennese turn to the left had a serious shock effect on Budapest, and became one of the most important ingredients of the political crisis in late April and early May. Another factor contributed to this diplomatic tremor: Soviet Russia's help fell short of Hungarian leaders expectations, and some of it never materialized. Although news was regularly exchanged by cable between Budapest and Moscow, institutionalized personal and diplomatic relations were never established.[4] As for myself, I am not able to assess the reasons why the Bolshevik leaders did not dispatch a permanent high-ranking representative to Hungary; but it is quite clear that the internal military and political predicament of Soviet Russia prevented military cooperation or indirect support.

It was a peculiar and unfortunate convergence of circumstances that precisely when military support by Soviet Russia was about to happen—the May 1 ultimatum directed to Romania and the plans of an offensive along the Dniester—political crisis was the order of the day in Budapest. I do not know whether the news of the ultimatum helped overcome the crisis, but it is certain that its effect could not be lasting, inasmuch as the offensive never got off the ground, for reasons internal to Soviet Russia as well as to increasing foreign intervention in Hungary.

Thus it was the expectation of revolutions in neighboring countries and of Soviet aid that stamped the character of the first period of the Hungarian Soviet Republic; furthermore, the period was also characterized by the fact that the government came up with dilatory proposals to gain a grace period from the Entente pressure. If we accept the latter assumption, and I am quite convinced it is correct, we must not wonder at Kun's proposals to the Peace Conference at Paris that indicate a considerable degree of readiness to compromise, even though these proposals were somewhat divergent.[5]

The text of the note handed to Livio Borghese and to Colonel Fernand Vix, after the takeover of power in Budapest, was identical, with but different from, the message Kun dispatched to the Entente powers by way of his delegate, Otto Roth, and later via Professor Philip Marshall Brown; additionally, the stand adopted by the revolutionary governing council and by Kun himself during negotiations with General Christiaan Smuts was again rather different. Kun went, it seems, further along the path of compromise when he was able to avail himself of secret channels, but did not go as far as he could when his stand was to be made public. All the signs, without execption, however, point to the fact that he did not consider any of the variations as final, but merely as a tactical measure to gain time for him and for the Soviet Republic. It is no accident then that, in the course of a debate on his tactics, he referred to Lenin's skilful maneuvering at Brest—Litovsk, by way of example.[6]

After the disappointment of April 17 and the postponement of the Soviet offensive, new solutions and new tactics had be found. The only course that could make it possible to gain time, and even await revolution in neighboring countries, or the arrival of Soviet help, was to hold out militarily: in May the Hungarian Soviet Republic endeavored to do just that. It was clear however, that it was no longer possible to slow down Entente interventionist designs by voicing readiness to compromise on territorial issues.

This time demonstration of force and, it was hoped, military success would serve as a compromise which would ensure the republic's survival.[7]

Chances of success were enhanced by the fact that shortly after launching the Czechoslovakian offensive, the Romanian front stabilized. Although government circles in Romania resented the Czechoslovakian move, and some among them advocated a march directly onto Budapest but, because of the intervention of the Romanian military leadership, Bucharest's troops halted at the line on the Tisza, declaring that Romania had no claims against Hungary beyond this river. Since the Yugoslav leadership was hesitant in those times to participate in intervention, and especially to pull the chestnuts out of the fire for others, the Soviet Republic found itself fighting a war on a single front for the time being.

Nevertheless, it had no choice regarding the Northern Campaign. The Hungarian Red Army would never have stepped over the northern demarcation line had the Czechoslovaks not done so first. For, the logical and purposeful direction of advance was to the east and northeast. Such an advance was dictated by the necessity of establishing contact with Soviet Russia, as well as by worsening food shortages, as a result of which the reconquest of the plains became an utmost necessity. Moreover, there was a valid demarcation line in the east, and at least theoretically, there were no obstacles to reaching it.

Although such a move was forced upon Budapest, the Northern Campaign offered some advantages. In addition to making it possible to concentrate considerable forces against a basically weak Czechoslovakian army struggling with serious problems of leadership, it gave the Red Army opportunities to achieve quick victories.[8] Consequently, a new basis for compromise did indeed come about. In this framework, the Soviet Republic succeeded in hastening, on June 11, the Peace Conference's finalization of its northern and eastern boundaries, theoretically (and practically as well) excluding the possibility of effecting further modifications in territory at Hungary's expense to satisfy Czechoslovakian and Romanian appetites.[9] This was important, since under the ideological cloak of anti-Bolshevik intervention, further territorial demands had been discussed.

But we do know that Béla Kun did not succeed in obtaining concessions for a tie-in between the northern and eastern boundaries. He did make such a request, and the Peace Conference, by way a memorandum from Georges Clemenceau, did make a promise to the effect that after Hungary withdrew to the northern boundary line, Romanian troops would likewise occupy only the areas designated for them. Kun did ask for guarantees. It is likely that no one in Paris would have wanted to go that far, but, for the sake of objectivity, we must note that once Romanian Prime Minister Ioan Brătianu refused to accept the Peace Conference's boundary line, the conferees could not have given such guarantees even if they had been inclined to do so.

The Republic of Councils accepted the compromise offered without the guarantees. This meant, on the basis of the line drawn in the north, that the Red Army would surrender some Hungarian towns it liberated, but would retain still more towns which the Czechoslovak forces had occupied in the course of their attack in late April. Moreover, it would thus have legal grounds for the reoccupation of the plains, where the harvest was in the offing, and where the inhabitants were strictly ethnic Hungarians. This assessment of the situation also undoubtedly influenced Deputy Commissar of Foreign Affairs Péter Ágoston who noted in his diary: "Pest was literally without food."[10] By withdrawal from the north and by acceptance of the boundary lines, the Soviet Republic placed itself on a firm legal footing and therefore could now demand the withdrawal of the Romanian forces to the line designated by the Peace Conference. In fact, it even had a legal basis for resorting to force to recover this area. Nor, if it succeeded in so doing could the Peace Conference oppose it. It was therefore no accident that British Foreign Minister Arthur Balfour began to harp on Hungary's exceeding the number of military effectives prescribed in the armistice agreement and to demand immediate Hungarian demobilization, precisely in order to eviscerate this *de jure* position.[11]

The Soviet Republic and Béla Kun attained unquestionable moral superiority vis-à-vis the representatives of the Entente powers. This superiority was confirmed by Clemenceau who, when Kun asked in what way had Hungary offended against the armistice agreement, was forced to declare that justice was on the side of Béla Kun: Hungary had carried out the demands of the Entente, whereas Romania had not.[12]

At the end of June and in July, the government was hard pressed by the *de facto* situation, the continuation of the blockade, and food shortages. Additionally news had just arrived that the peace treaty drafted for Austria would deprive Hungary of Burgenland. Meanwhile Paris was the scene of feverish negotiations regarding the organization of mass intervention.

In these days Kun—much as at the end of April—tried at the same time to obtain military aid from Soviet Russia, and to force the Entente to take positive steps partly by way of concessions, partly by threats. He sent desperate telegrams requesting, even demanding, that the Soviet Red Army provide help.[13] Yet, he must have known, there were serious physical obstacles to so doing: the distance between the territories under Soviet control and Hungary had become enormous.

As in April, discussions were once again initiated in Vienna to reshape the governing council in a way which would render peace negotiations and the cessation of the blockade possible. In the course of these discussions, however, Vilmos Bőhm and his companions went further than Kun deemed imaginable; hence, the commissar for foreign affairs awaited positive results from the offensive along the Tisza launched on July 20: i.e., from renewed military pressure. The Great Powers and, the smaller powers as well, except for Romania, watched the proceedings with arms folded. This time the Peace Conference took no measures, not even those for the organization of defense. Balfour's outburst is understandable: he declared it inadmissible that an insignificant army of a tiny country should paralyze the alliance of all powers. Actually, this was but a part of the story. The Allied camp proved impotent to launch a massive intervention, but many felt that the Romanian army would, on it own, be an able substitute for the Allies as a whole.[14]

The Hungarian attack of July 20 entailed enormous risks. Still we must assert that it was not a measure taken lightly, or the consequences of panic; it constituted a last chance for a solution to Hungary's dilemma. A victorious battle would provide the occasion for improving the morale of the army, especially since on this particular battlefied, the troops were fighting literally for their homes and their daily bread. The attack was also the logical outcome of policies pursued by Kun since the acceptance of the Clemenceau Memorandum: this was the only way to justify the evacuation of the northern areas. Finally, the attack was unavoidable as a matter arising from the very nature of the revolution: a revolution pursued to its logical conclusion, to avoid creating the appearance of retreat and surrender.

The attack collapsed. A number of factors played a part in this, such as economic difficulties, internal issues, exhaustion, the Northen Compaign's mixed results, lack of enthusiasm on the part of the officer corps, military blunders, so on and so forth. But a single factor accounts for the defeat better than any other: the Hungarian forces crossing the Tisza met with a force that exceeded their own three- to fourfold.

Thus, the Hungarian Soviet Republic did not succeed in bringing its basic concept of foreign policy to fruition. It remains a fact, however, that the Soviet Republic had formulated this concept as a Hungarian and Central European alternative. It was a broad concept of a socialist federation, capable of further expansion, in which every constituent nation and nationality would have enjoyed autonomy, but one which would ensure overall economic cohesion. This vision was indeed neither a nationalist one, nor was it tantamount to an "integral Hungary," It entertained no notion of a Hungarian state that would attempt to centralize again, nor, on the other hand, of any nation, including the Hungarian, being subject to foreign control. This is the reason why we may consider the strategy advocated by Kun—a man who joined the international revolution and was counting on this revolution—both a Central European and a national alternative, without tacking on the label of natonalism in any sense.

## NOTES

1. Mária Ormos, *Padovától Trianonig 1918–1920* (Budapest: 1983), p. 211,
2. Sándorné Gábor, *Ausztria és a Magyarországi Tanácsköztársaság* (Budapest: 1969), pp. 36–46; 61–116.
3. László Kővágó, *A magyar kommunisták és a nemzetiségi kérdés* (Budapest: 1985), pp. 63–65.
4. Magda Imre and Imre Szerényi, eds., *Budapest–Moszkva. Szovjet–Oroszország és a Magyar Tanácsköztársaság kapcsolatai táviratok tükrében* (Budapest: 1979), p. 9; György Borsányi, *Kun Béla. Politikai életrajz* (Budapest: 1979), p. 170.
5. Zsuzsa L. Nagy, *A békekonferencia és Magyarország 1918–1919* (Budapest: 1965), p. 85.
6. Borsányi, *Kun Béla*, p. 181.
7. Mária Ormos, "The Hungarian Soviet Republic and Intervention by the Entente," in Béla K. Király, Peter Pastor, Ivan Sanders, eds., *Essays on World War I: Total War and Peacemaking, A Case Study on Trianon* (New York: 1982), pp. 140–41.
8. Tibor Hajdu, *A Magyarországi Tanácsköztársaság* (Budapest: 1969), pp. 235–45.
9. Archives diplomatiques, Paris. *Tchechoslovaquie*, T 44 ff. 81–83, June 11, 1919; US Department of State, *Papers Relating to the Foreign Relations of the United States, 1919. The Paris Peace Conference*, IV (Washington: 1943), 803–14.
10. Párttörténeti Intézet, "Ágoston napló," PI 689 f.
11. E. E. Woodward and Rohan Butler, eds., *Documents on British Foreign Policy 1919–1939*, First Series, Vol VI (london: 1956), 76–77.
12. Ormos, *Padovától Trianonig*, p. 320.
13. Imre and Szerényi, *Budapest–Moszkva*, pp. 176–77,
14. Ormos, *Padovától Trianonig*, p. 326.

# PLANS OF STRATEGIC COOPERATION BETWEEN THE RUSSIAN AND HUNGARIAN RED ARMIES

Tibor Hajdu

Victorious revolutions always give birth to big dreams, exaggerated hopes which create optimism among the people and influence their leaders. However, dreams usually disappear and cruel awakening inevitably leads to tragic turns in the mood of the masses, and in the fate of the revolution.

The Hungarian Soviet Republic was born from resentment against the Western powers who abandoned Hungary for the sake of their Central European allies. The country naturally turned towards Soviet Russia. As early as its first proclamation, the new revolutionary government declared the Hungarian Soviet Republic to be allied to Soviet Russia. On the evening of March 21, at the revolutionary session of the Budapest Workers' Soviet, Sándor Garbai, a leader of the left-wing Social Democrats, accounted for the sudden shift of his party to the left with these words:

> We must find a new orientation in order to obtain from the East what has been denied to us by the West. We must join the stream of new events. The army of the Russian proletariat is approaching rapidly.[1]

One day earlier, President Mihály Károlyi informed his cabinet that in the judgment of his military experts, Colonels Aurél Stromfeld and Jenő Tombor, "its is only a matter of weeks for the Russian Red Army to break through the Romanian lines and to reach the Eastern boundaries of Hungary." Béla Kun himself maintained "that immediate military assistance would be forthcoming from the Russian Red Army, which is presently at the foothills of the Carpathians."[2]

But was it indeed there? "According to Budapest newspapers, the Red Army captured Tarnopol on March 18, and the cannonade in Galicia could be heard even at our side of the Carpathians."[3] Actually the attacking division of Shchors reached Zhmerinka on March 20. Zhmerinka is less than 250 km to the Carpathians and some 160 km to the east of Tarnopol.

The fighting went on, mainly against the Ukrainian White Army of Semyon Petliura which neither had ties with the Hungarian army, nor had hostile intentions against it. The Russian offensive, therefore, could not yet possibly influence Hungary's position. By mid-April, Ukrainian Red troops, formerly incorporated in the Ukrainian Red Army under the command of Vladimir Aleksandrovich Antonov-Ovseenko, reached the line of Ovrutsh – Novograd Volinski – Shepetovka – Staro Konstantionovo – Proskurov – Kamenets Podolski – Mohilev Podolski,[4] and were, thus, standing as far as 100 km from the Carpathians.

On April 12, in the village of Pálfalva near Szatmár the airplane of the Soviet pilot Todorovich landed. He was accompanied by a former Hungarian POW, G. Fodor, as his navigator and interpeter. Todorovich was the first to cross the Carpathians by air between Vinnitsa and Hungary, and therefore, was awarded with the Order of the Red Banner.

We do not know what exactly Todorovich told Kun about the plans of the Ukrainian Red Army, but this newborn army surely had very ambitious plans. The head of the Ukrainian Soviet government, Christian Rakovskii, had previously been the leader of the Romanian left Socialists. Most certainly, he regarded the overthrow of the Romanian kingdom as a natural aim of the Ukrainian revolution. Commander-in-Chief of the Ukrainian Red Army Antonov-Ovseenko continued to maintain, in his memoirs, many years later, that the aim of crushing the Romanian army with a coordinated Ukrainian – Hungarian offensive was thoroughly realistic.[5] In the first days of March, that is, three weeks before the Socialist revolution in Hungary, the Ukrainian CP included in its message to the First Congress of the Comintern the following evaluation:

> Undoubtedly, the masses of Hungary are impatiently waiting the moment when they'll be able to free themselves of chains of the capitalists, with the help they'll get from the East and they will become the point of junction, joining the Social revolution of the both halves of Europe.[6]

No wonder, after March 21, the Kiev leadership considered its basic strategic aim to reach the Carpathians and Hungary. According to their plan of campaign:

> Our task is: crossing the Romanian border, with our right wing leaning on Hungary to press the Romanians to the [Black] Sea... When we performed our manoeuvre and thus captured Northern Moldavia and the main parts of the Russian Bessarabia, we'll have to unite with the troops of Soviet Hungary, which by then will have to reach Suceava, through Carlibaba and Compulung and then be united with our Suceava–Botosani group.

The other Ukrainian column had to link up with the Hungarian Red Army in the South, about Ploesti.[7]

According to these plans, the Kiev leaders overestimated the Hungarian army to the same extent as the Hungarians overestimated the possibilities of the Ukrainian Red Army.[8] Ukrainian Red troops were practically partisan units, tied to their homeland. They were undefeatable because of their flexibility and closeness to the local population. But for the same reason they were not capable of leaving behind Ukrainian territory for more than a few days. Rakovskii, obviously obsessed with the idea of extending the revolution to Romania and other neighboring countries, was easily convinced of ambitious plans, in spite of the warnings from Moscow.

As soon as March 25, 1919, Ioahim Ioahimovich Vatsetis, commander-in-chief of the Russian Red Army on the Western Front, gave an order to Antonov, forbidding further operations towards the Black Sea and Romania:

> You must transfer from there all dispensable troops to the Petliura front, as your immediate task is the final liquidation of the attacks of Petliura; you must at the same time reach in the Western direction the borders of South-Eastern Galicia and Bukovina, what is sufficient for getting a solid and immediate connection with the Hungarian soviet troops.[9]

However, the Ukrainian Red Army went on with its attack toward Odessa, and on April 6, the Entente troops were driven out of the city. Now the Ukrainian Red Army stood along the Dniestr, that is, along the border of Bessarabia.

In the proclamation issued by the Rakovskii government after Odessa had been taken, they declared:

> New perspectives are developing for the victors of Odessa: our help is being asked by the revolting workers and peasants of Bessarabia, Bukovina, and Galicia. The hands of the Red Army of the Hungarian Socialist Soviet Republic are reaching out towards us through the Carpathians...[10]

As for the last sentence, the Hungarian Red Army inherited the disorganized troops of the Károlyi regime among whom only a few were capable to stand for the defense of the country. They were far from being able to attack the quite strong Romanian army. The northeast Carpathians facing eastern Galicia, were held only by weak border guard units, as the Károlyi government did not plan any operations toward Galicia. Therefore, it was evident that had the Red Ukrainians reached the Carpathians, there they would not have found anything to join forces with.

However, Antonov gave the following command on April 13, to the First Ukrainian Army:

You must concentrate all units in Bessarabia on the fringe of the right wing, waiting for my special command: a. help the group of comrade Nikolai Akimovich Hodiakov which is to attack Romania; b. attack through Bukovina and along the Carpathians to establish contact with Soviet Hungary.[11]

In these days the events in Eastern Galicia seemed to justify the optimism of Antonov. The approach of the Red Army promoted the strengthening of the left in Galicia and provoked a number of workers' and peasants' actions which culminated around April 14–15, in the insurrections of the workers of Drogobich and Stanislau. A number of previously anti-Bolshevist partisan groups joined the Red Army, and this in turn, had a significant effect on Stanislau government politics.

Earlier, on February 9, the Socialist Vinnichenko government resigned to comply with the demand of the French General Berthelmy who stated: "they should not count on any aid until the leftist elements of the Stanislau government are chased out like dogs."[12] Although Petliura did continue to fight the Polish army, he stopped, in order to win French support, the talks with Moscow which had been begun by the Vinnichenko government.

By April Kun realized the importance of the changing western Ukrainian situation for Hungary, for the advent of peace between Moscow, Kiev, and Stanislau would have opened up the road between Budapest and Kiev, although railway connections could only have been established after the seizure and occupation of Lemberg, which was held sturdily by strong Polish forces. Therefore, he made an offer to Vladimir Akimovich Vinnichenko who had fled to Vienna, to mediate between him and Lenin. In the beginning of April Kun repeatedly requested Vladimir Ilich Lenin to consider a compromise with Vinnichenko, which meant a pluralist government for the whole Ukraine, formed by the left Socialist parties that accepted the platform of Soviet dictatorship and alliance with Soviet Russia and her army.[13]

In the end, Kun's suggestion was rejected; that this rejection had been a realistic one, was acknowledged even by the emigré Ukrainian historical literature.[14] Any agreement with Vinnichenko in Vienna would have been in vain as long as power was in the Petliura's hands. However, some real steps toward the agreement were taken. Although following the 1918 insurrection of the Social Revolutionary Party (SR), Lenin decided against pluralism in the Soviet government, on April 18 he made an exception for Rakovskii, and allowed no more than Social Revolutionaries into the Kiev government, who were indeed coopted in a few days.[15] About May 1, Rakovskii sent a note to the Stanislau government, proposing a ceasefire and a pact of alliance of the two Ukraines.[16]

Kun in his diplomatic efforts with Soviet Russia made the Soviet leaders aware of the weakness of his own army especially in the northeastern direction. This may seem strange in the light of his announcements placing high hopes on establishing connection with the Russian Red Army. However, he well knew of the dangers which threatened Hungary especially from the Romanian front, but also from the south.

On the other hand, the Allied commands were no less cognizant of the danger which the above-mentioned connection meant for them. Therefore, Foreign Secretary of Czechoslovakia Edvard Beneš, as early as on March 25, asked Georges Clemenceau, the French premier "... to stem the way by which the bolshevists may pass through towards Hungary... We are asking you for the sake of our common case, allow us to block this passage-way as switftly as possible." On the same day, Colonel Dimitriu, Romanian Liaison Officer in Belgrade, reported to Bucharest: "the French are asking the Romanians and Czechoslovaks to do all in their power to make impossible a direct connection between the Hungarians and Ukrainians."[17] But, owing to differences within the Entente and among its allies, the Czechoslovak and Romanian troops only met on May 2, and blocked the gap in the Carpathians from then on.[18] The weak Hungarian troops around Csap couldn't do anything against them. After this *cordon sanitaire* had been set up no possibility remained to connect Budapest with Kiev — at any rate, not with such weak military forces, railway, and other supplies with which Hungary was left.

The Romanian attack against Hungary was started on April 16, and at the same time in the eastern Ukraine, the concentration of White units under the command of general Anton Ivanovich Denikin and the revolt of the Don-Cossacks created a dangerous situation. Therefore, between April 18–23, the Red Army Supreme Command, and Lenin himself, gave a series of warnings asking Antonov-Ovseenko to give more help for the Donets basin and the Don and to stop bigger operations westward except securing the establishment of railway connection with Budapest. At the same time, impressed by the grave Hungary's situation and the Kun's messages asking for help, Rakovskii and Antonov-Ovseenko decided to attack instantly the main enemy of Soviet Hungary — even without the hope of real cooperation with the threatened Hungarian army.

They seemingly had the consent of Commissar of Foreign Affairs, Georgii V. Chicherin, who telegraphed to Kun on April 28: "The behavior of the Romanians is strange indeed. Step by step, they abandon Bessarabia sending [troops] against Hungary, as if they were forgetting that there is no peace between them and Soviet Ukraine or Soviet Russia... If they don't understand this, it is all the worse for them."[19]

On May 1, Chicherin and Rakovskii addressed an ultimatum to Romania demanding that she vacate Bessarabia and Bukovina. They made no secret of the fact that, quoting Nikolai Ilich Podvoiskii the Ukrainian War Commissar, attempts by the Romanians to "throttle the young Hungarian Soviet Republic" influenced their decision.[20] After the ultimatun had expired, the attack was started on the Dniester line, and the main forces of the Ukrainian Red Army [the First and Third Armies] were concentrated there. On Podvoiskii's orders they began to organize an "internationalist division" consisting largely of POW's from Hungary.

Already on May 5, Rakovskii was seriously warned by Lenin that the "turn towards Romania" was to be temporarily suspended in order to overcome Denikin.[21] The Ukrainian Soviet government nevertheless ordered their Third Army on May 7 to break through the Romanian line on the Dniester. Next day, the division led by the Hetman Nikolai Aleksandrovich Grigoriev, who had recently joined the Red Army with his hitherto anti-Bolshevik troops and made a name for himself by first riding into Odessa, instead of carrying out the decisive blow, mutinied against the Soviet government. In fact, soldiers did not want to fight outside the frontiers of Ukraine, they considered the support for the Hungarian revolution a foreign cause; this was a major contributing factor in their revolt. The fight against the mutineers tied up the major forces of the Ukrainian Red Army for two weeks, and by the time they supressed it entirely, at the end of May, Denikin's offensive put them on the defensive. True, Petliura's army had largely fallen apart by then, and by the end of May, the Red Army advanced as far as Brody [less than 100 km from the Lemberg end of the Budapest—Lemberg railway line], but the Poles quickly occupied the line of the Stryj, and thus any possibility of aid via Galicia was out of question since such attempt would have meant war against Poland as well.

All the same, the Ukrainian Red Army had crossed the Romanian plans about forcing the Tisza at the decisive moment, early in May allowing the Hungarian Red Army time to regroup. "Apparently the Romanians have stopped their advance at the Theiss owing to the situation in Bessarabia," a Foreign Office official noted in the margin of the May 6 despatch from Bucharest on May 8.[22] [Among other reasons for the suspension of the Romania offensive was a call by the Paris Peace Conference prohibiting the crossing of the Tisza.]

The Hungarian Red Army started its successful Northern Campaign against the Czechoslovak Army on May 30. During the preparation of the offensive and at the selection of its direction the expectation of a simultaneous Russian breakthrough through the Carpathians toward Stryj-Csap obviously had a decisive part.[23] Kun and Stromfeld should have been better informed: in the last days of May the Polish Army attacked toward Stanislau and blocked the way of the Red Army to the west more effectively than Petliura. We might wonder whether the over-optimistic telegrams of Chicherin or the voluntarism of Kun were to blame. But from May 31, Kun and Stromfeld surely became well-informed: this was the day when Tibor Szamuely flew back from Vinnitsa. Szamuely, one of the best-known Hungarian Communist leaders, visited Lenin and Nikolai Ivanovich Bukharin in Moscow, and Rakov-skii in Kiev; and for all his optimistic public speeches, he undoubtedly informed Kun about the hard facts. The news was not only about the advance of Deni-kin and Jozef Pilsudski, but also about the resolution of the Russian Supreme Command to remove Antonov-Ovseenko from command for his adventurous "westward orientation." If after May 31, Kun still did not cease dreaming about a Russian breakthrough toward Hungary, this was exclusively his own fault. On June 16, the Hungarian army reached the northeastern Carpathians but without a hope of establishing a railway connection with the Soviet troops [following Antonov's removal the Ukrainian Red Army was integrated into the Russian Red Army], which until that time tried to keep Kharkov against the attacks of Denikin, thus, having no possibility for an offensive manoeuvre westward.

The fact that Kun withdrew the Hungarian units from the north and north-eastern Carpathians in the end of June, after Clemenceau, as President of the Paris Peace Conference, had twice demanded it, showed that the Hungarian Soviet leadership did no longer attach such decisive importance to keeping the Carpathian passes as it did a few weeks earlier.

The Hungarian Soviet government tried to maintain not only telegraphic but also air connection with Soviet Ukraine. As Hungary had an air force, quite significant by World War I standards, the Hungarian envoy in Moscow, Endre Rudnyánszky signed agreements with the Russian Supreme Command on establishing regular air traffic between Budapest and Kiev, providing technical know-how, and building long distance aircraft in the Hungarian factories for the Red Army.[24]

Its military possibilities reduced, the Kiev government sought new ways to help Hungary. From May, they recruited units out of the numerous Hungarian POWs who remained in Ukraine and in European Russia.[25] While in Kiev, Szamuely visited this division and gained good impressions. The Hungarian Internationalist POW Division fought in south Ukraine and was preparing to pass the Carpathians at the next propitious moment, with the slogan: "we go home, carrying our weapons." Meanwhile, fighting along the Dniestr con-tinued, with occasional Soviet success, but the main aim of these battles could only be but to tie down Romanian forces.

At the moment of the Hungarian attack against the Tisza line of the Ro-manian Army on July 20, Soviet troops fighting along the Dniestr faced the danger of becoming encircled; after the fall of Kharkov and Poltava, Denikin was less than 500 km from the revived army of Petliura and successfully attack-ed toward the northwest [Kiev had fallen on August 30].[26] Thus, Kun must have had an overoptimistic view of the situation in the Ukraine, when, while crossing the Tisza, he asked Lenin and Rakovskii for a new offensive on the Dniestr. There was no such possibility, but Kun and Rudnyánszky blamed

Rakovskii for that. "I consider the complete lack of cooperation as the reason for our coming defeat by the Romanian forces moved here from Bessarabia" Kun telegraphed to Lenin on July 28.[27]

When Lenin, defending Rakovskii, answered: "We know the difficult and dangerous situation of Hungary and we do all we can,"[28] he meant the counter-attack against Denikin, ordered to be launched on August 1; but the counter-attack failed this time, and that very same day the Hungarian Soviet Republic fell.

## NOTES

1. *Népszava*, March 22, 1919.
2. Cited after Rudolf L. Tőkés, *Béla Kun and the Hungarian Soviet Republic* (New York, 1967), pp. 133–35.
3. Ervin Liptai, *"Adalékok a Magyar Tanácsköztársaság és Szovjet-Oroszország fegyveres szövetségének kérdéséhez,"* in *Hadtörténeti Közlemények* (1958), 1–2, p. 73.
4. Liptai, pp. 74–77.
5. V. Antonov-Ovseenko, *Zametki o grazhdanskoj vojne* I–IV. (Moscow, 1924–1933).
6. *Izvestiia* (Moscow), March 12, 1919, see also, the March 5 and 6 Issues [Statements of N. Skripnik, Home secretary of the Rakovskii-government and others]; For similar official statements, see the articles of L. Nezhinskii in *Voprosi Istorii* (1959), 2; "A Magyar Tanácsköztársaság történelmi jelentősége és nemzetközi hatása" (Budapest, 1960).
7. Antonov, *Zametki,* IV. p. 30.
8. Liptai,*Adalékok,* and T. Hajdu, *"Adatok a Tanácsköztársaság és Szovjet-Oroszország kapcsolatainak történetéhez,"* in *Párttörténeti Közlemények* (1961), 3.
9. Antonov, *Zametki,* III. p. 324.
10. Antonov, *Zametki,* III. p. 249.
11. Antonov, *Zametki,* IV. p. 35.; also Hajdu, p. 106.
12. V. Vinnichenko, *Vidroshdennia Nacii* (Kiev–Wien,1920); see also, T. Hajdu, *The Hungarian Soviet Republic* (Budapest, 1979), p. 29.
13. M. Imre and I. Szerényi, eds., *Budapest–Moszkva* (Budapest, 1979), pp. 39, 79–82, 96–97, 99, etc.; Vinnichenko *Vidroshdennia;· Lenin Magyarországról,* 2nd edition (Budapest, 1965).
14. Vinnichenko *Vidroshdennia,* and W. Kutschabsky,*Die Westukraine im Kampfe mit Polen und dem Bolschewismus in den Jahren 1918–1923* (Berlin, 1934); also, A. Liholat, *Razgrom natsionalistitseskoi kontrrevoljutsii na Ukraine* (Moscow, 1954).
15. *Leninskii Sbornik* XXXVI. (Moscow 1959), p. 74, *Budapest–Moszkva,* pp. 81–82, [Chicherin's telegram to Kun on April 28].
16. *Budapest–Moszkva,* p. 96.
17. Liptai *op. cit.;* József Breit, *A Magyarországi 1918/19. évi forradalmi mozgalmak és a vörös háború története* (Budapest, 1925) II., p. 41.
18. Maria Ormos, *Padovától Trianonig 1918–1920* (Budapest, 1983), p. 232.
19. *Budapest–Moszkva,* pp. 81–82.
20. *Izvestiia,* May 6, 1919; Hajdu,*Adatok.* On their motives, see, Chicherin's April 28 telegram to Rakovskii cited by S. Halász, *Adatok a szovjet–magyar kapcsolatok történetéhez 1917–1919* in *Századok* (Budapest, 1967) 5.
21. V. I. Lenin, *Collected Works,* 4th edition, 35. and 44.
22. Public Record Office (London), FO 371, Vol. 3515.
23. Liptai*Adatok,* p. 82.
24. Hajdu, *Adatok,* p. 119.
25. *Essays on World War I: Origins and Prisoners of War,* edited by Samuel R. Williamson and Peter Pastor (New York, 1983), p. 157; G. Obitshkin, P. Zhilin, H. Vass, G. Milei et al., *A magyar internacionalisták a Nagy Októberi Szocialista Forradalomban és a polgárháborúban,* I, II (Budapest, 1967).
26. S. Shiskin et al.,*Istoria Grazhdanskoi Vojni v SSSR* (Moscow, 1959), chapter 6.
27. *Budapest–Moszkva,* p. 192.
28. *Leninskii Sbornik,* p. 79.

# THE FRENCH ARMY AND THE RIGHTIST RESTORATION
# IN HUNGARY, 1918–1919.[1]

Leslie C. Tihany

The Belgrade Military Convention authorized the Allied armies to occupy certain strategic points in Hungary without reference to the line of military demarcation. The city of Szeged on the Tisza, about 160 kilometers southeast of Budapest was one such strategic point. The Belgrade line of demarcation crossed the south-flowing Tisza below Szeged. Here two bridges, one, a railroad bridge, spanned the Tisza. The city was a strategically important bridgehead because it controlled the principal route of communication with General Henri Berthelot's *Army of the Danube* in Romania; marshalled railroad traffic toward France; and dominated fluvial transportation vertically from the Balkans almost to the Polish border and laterally across Transylvania. It was also the gateway to the Budapest region both from the Batchka plain bounded by the Danube and the Tisza, and from the former Banat of Temesvár, bordered by the Tisza, the Maros, and the east-flowing Danube. It was one of the main entry points from Transylvania into the Danube-Tisza mesopotamian area. At the end of World War I, Szeged had a population of 130,000. By occupying it, the French army could protect the zones of occupation to the south, and at the same time, maintain a springboard for resuming an offensive in a northwesterly direction.

The first French military unit entered Szeged on December 10, 1918. By mid-December, a French army command post was functioning at the suburban Rókus railroad station. On December 30, under the command of Colonel Boblet of the *76th Infantry Division,* 50 officers and 600 men of the *157th Infantry Regiment* arrived. On January 3, 1919, two battalions of the *210th Infantry Regiment,* of the same division, made their entry, followed by reinforcements in short order. Command headquarters was first set up in a privately owned residence in *Szentháromság utca,* but after a few weeks it moved into the Hungarian army's military district command building, where the enemy French and Hungarian flags flew side-by-side for some time. On January

2, Colonel Boblet made a courtesy call on the mayor and assured him that, as long as order prevailed in the city, the French army would not interfere in internal affairs. Indeed, the French scrupulously adhered to Articles 42–56 of the Hague Regulations regarding military occupation, which specify that an occupying military authority has no right to make changes in the laws or in civil administration except for security purposes.[2]

Compliance with these requirements was not easy. By winter 1918–19, ideological factionalism in Szeged had developed into press polemics, mass demonstrations, and political rivalry. According to a Socialist observer, the Communists had won over to their side the army barracks, and on one recorded occasion, a battalion of soldiers had to be sent from Budapest to maintain order. The Social Democrats were more numerous, writes the observer, but the smaller Communist group was more determined and ready for action.[3] A Communist participant in the events notes that at this time the French occupiers did not try to influence the struggle between the two Marxist factions. The same participant confirms the Socialist eyewitness's assertion of military reinforcements being dispatched from the capital, but claims that this was done at the invitation of right-wing Social Democrats, and that consequently the local Communist leaders had to go into hiding.[4]

Although the city was already rent by ideological strife, even more vehemently between Marxists and anti-Marxists than among Marxists, the main problem during the tenure of the Károlyi regime (October 31, 1918–March 21, 1919) was resupplying the city cut off by foreign occupation from its traditional hinterland. During December, while General Berthelot was visiting Szeged, a government delegation was sent to the city from the capital to plead with him for coal from the Transylvanian mines. By the end of December, the economic, social, and cultural repercussions of the occupiers' presence became quite noticeable. The French archival materials contain recurrent references to the "xenophobic Magyar mentality" noted for having denied to non-Magyar nationalities the freedom felt to be a Hungarian birthright. It was also commonly known to the French that, at least partially, the cordial reception they were receiving in Szeged was due to the Hungarian realization that the French military presence meant an escape from dreaded Serb or Romanian occupation. French officers were eagerly sought as tenants by bourgeois landlords, whose premises would be exempt from requisitioning by their own government if rented or occupied by the French military. Thanks to the French officers on occupation duty in or near Szeged, hotels, restaurants, and cabarets in the city were doing a land-office business. With the exception of Hungarians of extreme leftist or far rightist sympathies, the people of Szeged reacted enthusiastically to French military parades and surrounded with charisma such respected French generals as Charles Antonine Charpy, Paul de Lobit, and Henri Leopold de Gondrecourt. Press reports, except in the leftist papers, showed fascination with the colorful appearance of colonial troops. Staged Spahi cavalry charges drew thousands of spectators, who were told by their naively provincial press that the onrushing horsemen were commemorating their Prophet's speedy departure from Mecca to Medina![5]

The life of the French garrison in Szeged evolved under the influence of countervailing factors. During the first four months of occupation, Hungary was ruled by a weak, but pro-Entente, government. Still the country was enemy territory, most of it claimed by France's eastern allies. The culture was of the familiar Latin and not of the unfamiliar Byzantine Christianity of the Greeks, the Serbs, and the Romanians; but the language seen and heard was an unintelligible and unpronounceable Finno-Ugrian idiom. Social contacts were restricted to Francophone intellectuals and merchants but even these persons began to cool off and turn argumentative when it was gradually realized that, under French auspices, multinational Hungary was about to suffer drastic territorial dismemberment. The population insufficiently understood that the French army was in Hungary not to make, but to carry out, policy made in Paris and Versailles. During winter 1918–19, Hungarian hosts would engage their French guests in passionate arguments designed to prove their patriotic conviction that Hungary should not be punished for Germany's sins, that it should not lose provinces the Hungarian census of 1910 showed to be heavily Magyar-inhabited. Posters protesting the pending amputation of Hungary's peripheral regions began to appear on the walls, posing in French the rhetorical question to the soldiers of the Republic: *"Voulez Vous Quatre Alsaces?"*[6] There were also other controversial grievances felt by the local population that tended to poision military–civilian relations, as the winter of defeat was receding before the Red spring of 1919 already in the offing.

First, there was the matter of inflation, which was popularly blamed on the French military. In December 1918 the exchange rate between the French franc and the Hungarian crown was one to three. By the end of 1919, a franc would bring 18 or 20 crowns. The steady rise in prices through 1919 was laid at the door of the occupying foreign power. French officers, it was claimed, were on a spending spree in the city's hotels and restaurants. In the market places, it was charged, housekeepers, cooks, and other locals employed by French military households, drove up the prices of victuals by their willingness to pay any price, no matter how high, for foodstuff brought into the city by farmers.

Then came unemployment as the city's industries were being more and more cut off from their accustomed sources of raw materials in the Bácska and in the Bánát now under Entente occupation. During the first winter of occupation, in the city of Szeged alone, about 25,000-30,000 out of a total population of 130,000 were said to be on some form of Hungarian-government dole and relief. The French military command offered its cooperation to the City Council in creating jobs and work opportunities. But prospects continued getting darker rather than brighter. It was whispered among the population that certain French officers were making profits on a developing black market. The French military police, commanded by a Lieutenant Gertoux, became increasingly unpopular because it allegedly maintained paid informers in the industrial plants, in the barracks of the Hungarian soldiers, and even at City Hall. Some French officers began losing their social acceptability to middle-class hostesses because of their reported tendency to respond to invitations in the company of women frowned upon by Szeged bourgeois society.[7]

By the end of December 1918, the task of feeding the occupied city entered a crisis stage. Tempers rose to a breaking point. Partly to blame, the population well knew, were the Hungarian "national councils" which, in the absence of civil government, had taken upon themselves the functions of administrative authority. In the matter of provisioning and in the control of supplies, these national councils were prone to behave as governments of petty republics concerned only with their own regional welfare. Rural communes on the peripheries of Szeged prohibited the transportation of lard and hogs beyond their boundaries. Faced with a shortage of bread during the Christmas season, the mayor of Szeged was compelled to requisition for the needy 40 wagonloads of flour from one of the city's larger mills. In retaliation for this flagrant and unauthorized interference with private enterprise, the Ministry of Food Supply in Budapest placed Szeged under a ban for food and coal allotments.[8] When on January 2, 1919, Colonel Boblet routinely called at City Hall, the mayor appealed to him to make possible the provisioning of the city from Serb-occupied territory to the south. Boblet began issuing French military passes to Szeged merchants to travel and to buy foodstuff for their city in the occupied hinterland. This remedial measure petered out, however, before the end of the month. On January 24, the Yugoslav command in Szabadka informed Colonel Boblet that, in accordance with instructions received from Belgrade, it was to allow bearers of French military passes to purchase victuals only to satisfy the needs of French troops stationed in Szeged.[9] Caught between the sanctions of its own national government and the Yugoslav occupiers in the south, the Szeged city government, in spite of French benevolence, could feed its population only by resorting to illicit business deals with unethical members of the occupying forces.

A strike of the workers of the Hungarian State Railroads (MÁV) that started on February 2 and lasted until March 18, made the civilian supply situation still worse. The strike affected the running of the trains both east and west of the Danube, from the Slovene border to the Bácska-Bánát area. Striking workers blamed "economic misery" for their walkout, which was gravely interfering with the nodal function of Szeged in east-west transportation. The extent of the strike was due to the increasing ability of secret Communist cells in MÁV unions to stimulate revolutionary action by transmitting coded telegraphic signals all along the peripheral lines from Szabadka eastward to Temesvár and westward to Szentgotthárd.[10] In Transdanubia (west of the Danube), in the exclusively Serb zone of occupation, the occupying military authorities did not refrain from drastic measures, which included cavalry charges against strike demonstrators in city streets. In Cisdanubia (east of the Danube and west of the Tisza), the French commandment discreetly stood by and awaited further developments. On February 22, strikers and their sympathizers were dispersed by Serb soldiers using rifle butts in Szabadka though the crowd was acclaiming France.[11] The Serb military took hostages and threatened them with firing squads unless work resumed at once. Bowing before superior force, MÁV workers started returning to their trains, switches, and roundhouses toward the middle of March. The troubled interlude of the railroad strike was, however, only a curtain raiser to more serious political events which were to alter radically the execution of the French military mission in Hungary.

During the night of March 21, 1919 — while advance units of the Red Army were approaching the outskirts of French-occupied Black Sea ports and the isthmian defenses of the Crimea — wireless monitors of the French *Army of Hungary* intercepted a message from Budapest addressed to Lenin in Moscow.[12] The communication informed the Bolshevik leader that a proletarian dictatorship had been established in the Hungarian capital, whose new rulers were asking for Russia's protection and alliance. In Szeged, telephone connections with Budapest had been cut off on the evening of March 21. On the morning of March 22, the morning papers printed no news from the capital. On the other hand, the press contained three proclamations by an unknown "City Commander" calling for the registration of automobiles and convoking a morning meeting of the Workers' Council and an evening assembly of the Grand Workers' Council.[13] Not published in the press was a collective warrant of arrest, also signed by the self-styled City Commander and sent to every Hungarian military unit in the city, ordering the seizure of all French military officers.[14] At 5 am, the Hungarian garrison began distributing arms among the workers, who were told by NCOs that an attack on the French army was impending.

On learning of the Communist takeover in the Hungarian capital, the French command began posting military guards in some public places, at the two railroad stations, the Central Post Office, the Gas Works, and in front of the formidable Csillag Prison. At 10:30 am on March 22, two of these posts — the suburban Rókus railroad station and the Prison — were attacked. The French guard at the railroad station, including three officers, were captured, disarmed, and later released. The detachment at the prison resisted. The sound of rifle fire prompted the intervention of the Hungarian military from the nearby Mars-tér barracks. Shortly after 11, machine-gun posts manned by steel-helmeted French troops were set up in front of all important public buildings and at strategic thoroughfares. A modern Hungarian historian writes that, in a surprise attack, the workers and soldiers of Szeged disarmed the French guard at the Rókus railroad station, assaulted the French troops guarding political prisoners in the Csillag Prison, but failed.[15] The French threw back the Hungarian attackers with machine-gun fire. The armed clash claimed one civilian victim: a housewife on her way to the marketplace. Bloody street-fighting now marred the hitherto peaceful occupation.

On March 23 a Colonel Jean-Joseph Bétrix arrived in Szeged from the *11th Colonial Infantry Division* in Temesvár, and took command of the French garrison. His first action was to summon both the pre-Communist civil administrative body and the new three-member Directorate, which claimed to govern the city in the name of the Hungarian Soviet Republic (HSR). Bétrix dutifully recognized the latter as the lawful civil administration and stated that, in accordance with international law, the French military command would not interfere with the performance of its functions, provided that they stayed within the framework of the following stipulations:

1. Delivery, to the occupational authority, of 1500 rifles and 15 machine guns hidden in the city; 2. no more than 1300 officers and men of the Hungarian army could remain in the city; 3. no other troops could enter Szeged without notifying the French command; 4. armed assemblies were to be dispersed; 5. unarmed assemblies in the streets and city squares were to be held only with the permission of the French command; in public meeting halls no French permission was necessary; 6. every armed Hungarian soldier found detached from his unit was to be fired upon; 7. every distributor of printed material inciting either French or Hungarian soldiers was to be imprisoned; and 8. observation of French troop movements was strictly forbidden.[16]

The Directorate accepted these eight conditions and resumed its newly-acquired administrative functions. For the French military, the occupation of Szeged, a city under a Soviet national government, would be a new experience, especially at a time when relations between occupied and occupiers had been deteriorating. Accordingly, early in March, a Captain de Lamaze of the French *Army of Hungary* received orders to prepare a report on the political and military situation in Szeged for the commanding general. His report,[17] although it mirrored the spirit of the times, fairly accurately presented a picture of a city with sharp class differences, in which Colonel Bétrix, who received a copy, would have to safeguard French security interests. Would coexistence be possible between soldiers of the Third Republic and the urban population of a city acknowledged as part of a Soviet republic? The test period would last for 133 days, during which the Béla Kun Soviet regime was to retain power in Budapest.

In his report, de Lamaze expressed the opinion that Szeged had a middle-class majority hostile to Bolshevism, which did not dare react to its proletarian government nor side openly with the Entente forces for fear of retaliation. A French information service was being performed by one sole officer assisted by a corporal-interpreter. An additional Hungarian-speaking officer with staff should be assigned. The French command was also short on interpreters and was employing for this task Hungarian laison officers. These were said to have a tendency to favor their side and may not at times act as faithful translators.[18]

It is in knowledge of the foregoing facts that Colonel Bétrix, an "officer with a democratic reputation," took command in seething Szeged. His administrative baptism of fire came during his first week in office. The HRS Directorate triumvirs did not long remain within the framework of the colonel's eight governing conditions. In accordance with orders received from Budapest, they began making preparations to remove Hungarian war matériel from the city and to flee to one of the neighboring unoccupied villages, where they would be free to operate without French-imposed restrictions. During the night of March 26, they were able to have MÁV boxcars shunted onto the city's trolley tracks and to begin loading them. A French patrol arrived and quickly dispersed the loaders, whereupon the three members of the HSR Directorate and eleven members of the Workers' Council fled the city accompanied by a handful of Hungarian military personnel. According to the modern Hungarian historian Endre Gaál, the Directorate's flight was a response to Bétrix's unacceptable eight-point ultimatum. The Marxist leaders "came to the conclusion that, in view of the local situation, they were unable to carry out the instructions of the Governing Council [in Budapest] and for this reason decided to leave the city." In face of tremendous French superiority, the Szeged working class and soldiers could not engage in "open and effective resistance," insisted Gaál.[19]

A Revolutionary Action Committee was left behind to represent the HSR Directorate during its absence. The following day the committee was summoned before Bétrix, who told the three members that, on higher instructions, he would no longer deal with a provisional civil administration but would himself appoint the members of the municipal leadership. He did so by recalling to their offices the pre-Communist prefect and mayor and by naming a new chief of police who had been sworn in during the days of the Károlyi government. The same eight conditions prescribed for the vanished HRS Directorate were to be binding on the restored bourgeois city administrators. The French, for their part, would continue their policy of noninterference in civil government and would take additional measures to facilitate the city's provisioning.

However, postal, telephone, and telegraph services between Budapest and Szeged would be prohibited; the railroad stations and the main post office would be occupied by the French military.[20] On April 3, Bétrix began signing himself as "Governor of the City of Szeged."

His task was to govern a city in a state of latent class warfare, insulated from its sovietizing political and economic environment only by the presence of the French army. The security requirements, as well as the mission of this army, had to be assured without violating the Hague Regulations, without interfering with the local civil administration. Bétrix began to handle this difficult task adroitly. Early during his administration, he assembled the city's leading employers in his office and asked for their support in steering a middle course between extremes by refraining from any exploitation of the workers. Employees, he said, should be paid decent wages and have a say in management. If this were done, he promised, he would in return not allow implementation of HSR decress in Szeged.[21] He carried out his part of the bargain by banning the implementation of HSR decrees ordering socialization of apartment buildings and industrial plants.[22] He told leftist newspapers to drop ideological qualifiers such as "Proletarian" and "Red" from their mastheads.[23] He ordered his military censor to delete from the press all ideologically tendentious articles.[24] He placed the middle-class administration under the same obligations he had prescribed for the former working-class rulers but, in view of the changed circumstances, "intensified" the nature of the military occupation by posting military guards at key strategic points in the city. In addition, he threw a cordon of military outposts around Szeged and its satellite villages for a double purpose: to seal off the occupied area from its sovietizing physical environment and to create a viable economic unit of urban consumers and rural suppliers. The cordon could be crossed only by bearers of French passes, between 7 am and 7 pm. Travelers arriving from the unoccupied zone were vetted by French military intelligence. Postal, telephone, and telegraphic communications into and out of Szeged were not only prohibited but strictly surveyed as well. Bétrix also maneuvered the transfer from Szeged a controversial Hungarian colonel[25] commanding both the police and the local garrison, to whom violent exception had been taken by his right-wing fellow officers.

On the other hand, to please the workers, he did his best to bring food into the city at affordable, low prices.[26] When waiters went on strike against restaurateurs, he sided with them.[27] He arranged for the return of objects below a certain value left at pawnshops.[28] When, during early May the bourgeois city prosecutor made use of the local police to arrest five Communist leaders, Bétrix ordered their immediate release. He followed up without delay and had the five persons handed over to HSR authorities at the military cordon.[29] He prevailed on the nationalist commander of the Hungarian garrison to free 250 imprisoned Soviet-sympathizing infantrymen.[30] He proposed and tried, though unsuccessfully, the establishment in the city of a "People's Committee" consisting of both middle-class and worker representatives.[31] He strongly upbraided prominent nationalists when provocative posters of a newly formed Anti-Bolshevik Committee were plastered on city walls without his previous permission.[32] The unpopularity Bétrix earned on the Right by such measures, outweighed the popularity he gained on the Left. For eleven weeks, however, he continued to rule over a private-enterprise island surrounded by a Communist sea. His regime was dubbed *denatured Communism.*

On April 17 General Charles Antonine Charpy — formerly General Louis Franchet d'Espèrey's chief of staff at Salonika and now in command of the *76th Division* — arrived, set up headquarters in the Serb-occupied Ujszeged suburb, and told the Szeged administrators that "wherever the French are, there is no Communism!"[33] This aphorism became a slogan of encouragement for the Right during the rest of the occupation.

Part of Bétrix's endeavor to insulate Szeged from the HSR was directed at the local court system. In a military government decree he issued on April 25,[34] he ordered the continued functioning of the old, pre-Communist courts. Parallel with these traditional Hungarian tribunals functioned the French military courts of the *76th Division,* with their jurisdiction limited to security cases, such as the unlicensed bearing of arms, resistance offered to the French military, unauthorized crossings of the cordon, smuggling, and the like. Fines assessed by the French military courts were turned over to the municipality for the use of Hungarian charities or for Franco–Hungarian cultural projects. In political cases resulting in the loss of liberty exceeding three months, Hungarian convicts were occasionally deported to Albania, Algeria, or Tunisia. The most severe sentence passed during Colonel Bétrix's administration was pronounced on May 21, in a case of espionage against the French armed forces on behalf of the HSR. Of five Hungarian defendants, one was sentenced to death, another to life imprisonment, two to 20 years each, the fifth was acquitted.[35] The fact that the primary defendant managed to escape before the sentence of death could be carried out, was ascribed by the indignant Right to Colonel Bétrix's alleged secret sympathy for the Communists.

By mid-May, the growing dislike between the military governor and right-wing leaders led to an impasse. Bétrix was blamed by White intelligentsia for not following in the footsteps of General Cavaignac in 1848 and Marshal MacMahon in 1871,[36] who had drowned in blood the pretensions of the Paris workers. As for Bétrix, he was growing weary of it all, and on May 11, told the commander of the Hungarian garrison that he had reached the end of his tether as far as the Hungarian military in the city was concerned. He said he was proposing to General Charpy a division of his responsibilities with another French officer.[37] Charpy agreed. Under the new arrangement, Colonel Rondenay, the Szeged bridgehead commander, took over from Bétrix supervision of the Hungarian garrison. On May 14, representatives of the local industrialists called on General Henri-Léopold de Gondrecourt, ostensibly to inquire about French intentions to march on Budapest, but actually to complain about Bétrix's way of governing Szeged. According to them, Bétrix was responsible for the fact that the working classes had been able to establish a "reign" over the occupied city.[38] On May 29, several newspapers of the Right attacked the Military Governor for his preference for the workers over the middle class.[39] On June 15, a general strike broke out, during which General de Gondrecourt replaced Bétrix as military governor. In his new capacity the General ordered the arrest of the strike leaders, which Bétrix apparently had been reluctant to do. When the strike ended, de Gondrecourt proposed the establishment of labor management arbitration committees and warned against vengeful treatment of workers willing to return to their jobs. But, the breaking of the strike marked the final defeat of the Left in Szeged. From this time on, forces of the rightist restoration would face the future more confidently. Colonel Bétrix had tried, but failed, in his attempt for Left-Right coexistence in the Szeged microcosm.

Having policed Hungary's peripheral partitioning in the south and in the east, the French armies under Franchet d'Espèrey and Berthelot had one remaining, urgent task to perform. The *Army of Hungary* was scheduled for dissolution on September 10; general demobilization in France was set to be completed by October 4; the political climate in the metropole was becoming increasingly anti-interventionist. There was little time left in Hungary to hatch out of several counterrevolutionary eggs a post-occupation government that would be "Francophile" as well as "democratic" and "anti-Bolshevik." The unoccupied parts of the country were still ruled by a Communist government, but there were counterrevolutionary stirrings in various parts of the country in Transdanubia and in the Bánát; also, in the Styrian town of Feldbach and in Vienna, where dispossessed Magyar aristocrats and commandless officers of a defeated army were sitting out the Red interlude in Budapest. Which one of these regional groups could eventually prove itself capable of serving as a kernel for a post-occupation government that fulfilled the French criteria? A Captain Saint-Laumer,[40] intelligence officer on the staff of General de Lobit in Belgrade, took an interest in anti-Communist Hungarian groups in the nearby Bánát, who made their political existence known on May 6 in a proclamation issued in the Romanian-occupied town of Arad. The Aradists claimed to include representatives of all prewar parliamentary parties in Hungary. They were headed by a Count Gyula Károlyi, conservative country cousin of the liberal Mihály Károlyi. The program announced by the Aradists was fourfold:[41] it called for a crushing of Bolshevism; for reestablishing order by the abolition of revolutionary constitutions since 1918; for settling differences with the neighboring states of Romania, Yugoslavia, and Czechoslovakia; and for giving Hungary a nationalist government responsive to the democratic aspirations of the Western Powers.

The Gyula Károlyi group did not feel at operational ease in the half-Romanian town of Arad. Consequently, on May 9, it decided to transfer to the purely Magyar Szeged, where under French occupation its freedom of action would be less restricted. Károlyi and his colleagues arrived there on May 28. The same day, the new anti-Communist leader made known to General Charpy that, with French permission, he and his friends were anxious to recruit a Hungarian military force for a march on Red Budapest. He thought that 300 armed Hungarians would be able to break through the HSR line north of Szeged and could then be followed by the entire French *Army of Hungary* up to the gates of the capital.[42]

Until May 14, the Vienna Hungarians had only vague and incomplete information regarding the gathering of anti-Bolshevik forces in Arad, and had thought of the Red-held area between Vienna and Budapest as a base for military action against Béla Kun. A Vienna representative, former General Staff Captain Gyula Gömbös, had been in Szeged since late April to reconnoiter the situation and to maintain some form of liaison with Vienna via Belgrade. In the meantime, however, a monarchist committee member had approached Henri Allizé, the French minister in Vienna, to sound him out about the possibilities of Entente recognition for his counterrevolutionaries as a Hungarian government.[43] The Hungarian interlocutor reported that Allizé showed himself quite reserved, was critical of the predominance of "reactionaries" in the Hungarian anti-Communist groupings, and squarely stated that French support was out of the question as long as men known to be "Germanophiles" were playing leading roles in the movements. As far as the Szegedists were concerned, the French diplomat held out the hope that the French Government might consent to *de facto* contacts with it, provided that it managed to wield power in an area of Hungarian territory, no matter how small. Under such conditions, Allizé said, he would be prepared to recommend to his government *de facto* recognition for the Szeged group.[44]

Allizé clearly established the *quid pro quo* for a merger between Vienna and Szeged: the latter would supply the required territorial base; the former, the experienced and acceptable leadership. Accordingly, a rush toward Szeged began from Vienna, and on May 29, Count Károlyi announced a new cabinet with himself as premier, the learned Transylvanian Count Pál Teleki as foreign minister, and Captain Gömbös from Vienna as undersecretary under a yet unnamed minister of war. Within a few days this still vacant post was also filled by the newly arrived Admiral Miklós Horthy, a former adjutant to the Emperor Francis Joseph and last Commander of the Austro–Hungarian Navy. In its proclamation of May 31, the Szeged Provisional Government pledged the holding of parliamentary elections on the basis of universal suffrage and the subsequent establishment of a constitutional government.[45] The French tolerated, but did not trust, the new cabinet, because in their eyes it showed "reactionary tendencies" and contained "Germanophile elements." In a heated exchange between General de Lobit and Count Károlyi on June 6, the general took exception to the presence of "pro-Germans" among the Ministers. He did not, however, totally reject Károlyi's request for release of requisitioned Hungarian war materiél to equip a budding force of four battalions, one company of Hussars, one armored train, and a small corps of engineers.[46] On June 15, the miniscule kernel of the new Hungarian army was set on foot, a company consisting exclusively of former officers under the command of the Right-extremist Captain Pál Prónay.

On June 25, Franchet d'Esperey arrived in Szeged to have a look at the new Hungarian provisional government. The generalissimo showed himself considerably mellowed since the November day, after the victorious dash to the Danube, when in Belgrade he imperiously faced Gyula Károlyi's radical cousin Mihály. He treated the provisional premier with great courtesy and promised him permission for the recruitment of a new national army, to be equipped "within limits" by the French, but not allowed to march out of Szeged into Transdanubia.[47] After his conversation with Count Károlyi, the generalissimo also received in audience Sylvester Somogyi, the Szeged mayor.[48] First of all, he asked, how was the city getting along? Then: how could Bolshevism be defeated in Hungary? When the mayor suggested that if the French command should permit an increase of the national army from 1300 to 10,000 men, return and supplement its equipment, an offensive could begin with only artillery support needed from the French *Army of Hungary*. Franchet d'Espèrey replied: how could the mayor think that French blood would be shed for setting things aright in Hungary? "The *canaille*, the scum does at times get the upper hand, but only in defeated countries!" he opined. "How strong was the Hungarian Red army?" he asked. The mayor gave an estimate of 150,000. "Your army of 10,000 could take on a force of 150,000 men?" commented ironically the generalissimo. There would be desertions to our side, replied Dr. Somogyi. Looking at a map, Franchet d'Espèrey pensively remarked that as he saw it, the military phase of the counter-revolution would have to start in the Transdanubian region, west of the Danube.[49] Still examining the map, Franchet d'Esperey asked about the size of territory the mayor would consider necessary for the provisioning of Szeged. He smiled at the sight of the large area Somogyi indicated on the map in reply. Then he reassured his visitor that the Hungarians had nothing to fear for the French nation was just. Magyar-inhabited areas would not be placed under foreign rule, nor would Hungary retain control of regions populated by non-Magyars. Still taking notes, Franchet d'Espèrey returned to the problem of provisioning, and promised to write a letter to the Romanian commander in

Temesvár who was blocking the arrival in Szeged of two trainloads of lumber. He ended the conversation by walking the mayor to the door, where he took "very cordial" leave of him, remarking in parting that he would want to meet him again because he considered him "a good and honest man."[50]

Franchet d'Espèrey's subordinates knew and no doubt reported to their chief that the Hungarian counterrevolutionaries were split into hostile factions, working against one another. Gyula Kàrolyi's partisans were venting their spleen on the Vienna committee, which was financing them, but whose representative, Captain Gömbös, they classed with other "adventurers" from the former Habsburg capital.[51] General Charpy said that he never knew with what Hungarian group he was dealing, because one faction's claims were constantly repudiated by another. As long as such dissension existed, the general said, it would be impossible for the French command to assist in the establishment of a provisional government. When the interlocutor expressed confidence in the ability of Gyula Károlyi to end factionalism among his followers, Charpy remarked: "If that is the case, they can rely on my unconditional support to restore order. They will have food and arms and a free hand in the town to do what they please." The French in Hungary, he said, had only one aim: to eliminate Bolshevism from the country.[52]

Indeed, other than anti-Bolshevism, there was no common ground between the Szeged government and the French generals. Károlyi and most of his men could never convince their French protectors that they were democratic, Francophile anti-Bolsheviks. British Admiral Troubridge, visiting Szeged on June 28, "quasiofficially" informed Károlyi that not only the French authorities but his Majesty's Government as well considered the Szeged government "reactionary," because its premier was a count and its minister of war a former aide-de-camp of Emperor Francis Joseph.[53]

On July 1, Károlyi made one more attempt to gain General Charpy's support. The French general cautiously expressed confidence in the person of the Premier but remained silent about his cabinet.[54] When subsequently Károlyi called on General de Lobit at his headquarters in Nagykikinda, he was given assurance only of French neutrality but not of support.[55] This was the final blow. On July, 5 Károlyi resigned in favor of a minor figure of the 1918 bourgeois revolution, a P. Dezső Ábrahám, who could by no stretch of the imagination be dubbed either "reactionary" or "Germanophile." Admiral Horthy stayed out of the new cabinet, although he assumed the powerful post of army commander-in-chief. On July 12, the Ábrahám cabinet served notice in a proclamation that it would perform its duties in a "democratic and Francophile" spirit.

About this time an embarrassing incident took place, probably in the presence of French invitees, at a regatta party given on a large raft floating on the Tisza. One of the numerous corpses which at that time were beginning to float downstream from a wooded area north of the city, where the Prónay officers' detachment was carrying out secret executions, got caught in the understructure of the raft and started swamping it.[56] The body was acknowledged in Prónay's diary as that of a French courier of Russian nationality, allegedly employed by the occupiers to communicate with the HSR Directorate beyond the military cordon.[57] French military intelligence was quite disturbed by the disappearance of the person they were assumed to be expecting to arrive with a message. They never found out what happened to him. He was tortured, killed, and thrown in the river by the Prónay detachment.

The top Szeged leaders dissociated themselves from the atrocities of the incipient White Terror but were powerless to control it. It was only on November 20, 1920, after the French departure, that Premier Pál Teleki was able to liquidate the last of the terrorist officers' detachments. The French historian Jean Bérenger disgustedly demurs from "the complicity of the French forces of occupation"[58] in the establishment of an interwar regime conceived in the White Terror.

On July 20, with the resumption of Hungaro–Romanian hostilities east of the Tisza, the chances of a rightist restoration in Hungary brightened. The French military remained inactive during the operations, although General de Gondrecourt maintained intelligence liaison with the Romanian left wing.[59] On July 23, the Romanians launched a counteroffensive, and Szeged was abuzz with semi-official information from Paris that the Peace Conference had approved a military march on Budapest.[60] This time, the long-awaited march did indeed materialize but by the Romanian and not by the French Army. On August 4, Budapest fell to the Romanians, the members of the Hungarian Soviet government having fled to Vienna. With the disappearance of the Béla Kun regime, a governmental vacuum opened up in the capital, which only the French-backed Szegedists could fill. The rest of it is macrohistory: the entry of Admiral Horthy's National Army into Budapest on November 16, 1919; a restored monarchy in name but kingless in fact, with Horthy serving as regent until his deposition by the Germans on October 16, 1944.

A detachment of the disbanded French *Army of Hungary* was kept in the Szeged area until February 18, 1920. As a last, parting gesture, the French made a gift of their weapons and equipment to the allied Serbs. And, to the Szeged library and museum, they presented sets of French literary classics.[61]

The last French military governor of Szeged was General Charles Louis de Tournadre, who succeeded General de Gondrecourt on August 12. On September 8 Franchet d'Espèrey paid a final visit to the city. He paid tribute to his two generals for a job well done in difficult circumstances. De Gondrecourt was noted for his attempts to impress on the Szegedists the necessity of an *union sacrée*[62] in Hungary among all parties and classes. In the eyes of the Hungarian conservatives, de Gondrecourt was the most pro-Hungarian of all the French city governors. When he was called to other duties after only 19 days in office, Hungarian rightists were convinced that the general was replaced because he had exceeded the limits of French High Command policy in backing the Szeged Provisional Government.[63]

We can almost visualize General de Tournadre, the last of the military governors. He ruled the occupied city from August 12, 1919 until its final evacuation. He is described as slow-spoken, suffering from some kind of nervous facial tick, wearing a monocle. He was highly cultured, spoke German and English. A prisoner during the war in Germany, he hated "the *Boche*," of whom he gave an unflattering account in a book he published about his captivity. A devout Catholic, he went to mass daily and to confession weekly. He loved music and insisted on having a piano in his quarters. He familiarized himself with local antiquities; visited simple folk in their homes; studied at first hand the harvesting and industrial processing of the famous Szeged paprika; and was interested in developing commercial relations between France and Hungary.[64]

The French armies in Hungary did not accomplish their mission to provide this ex-enemy country with a goverment either "democratic" or "Francophile," although they did succeed in sheltering for national leadership an unquestionably anti-Bolshevik team. The authoritarian-parliamentary regime they left behind was subsequently enticed by frontier revisions and forced by irresistible German pressures into the Axis camp, and so to new defeat in 1944. Szeged was, and today remains, a name unrecognized by the average Frenchman. Nevertheless, the French tricolor that flew over Szeged for fourteen months in 1918–1920 gave proof to the thitherto-unrecognized fact of German vincibility and served as a cultural reminder for the local inhabitants of the existence of a great Western civilization other than of the Teutonic variety.

## NOTES

1. The present essay and the larger work from which it was extracted and digested were made possible by a travel grant from the National Endowment for the Humanities for research begun in French state archives and continued, through interlibrary loans obtained by the Kenton County (Kentucky) Public Library from the holdings of the Library of Congress, the National Széchenyi Library of Budapest, and the Municipal Somogyi Library of Szeged. The author wishes to thank all the foregoing.

2. Lauterpacht, H., ed., *Oppenheim's International Law* (London and New York, 1944–1947), II, 335–49.

3. Csongor, G. (ed.) *A forradalmak szegedi szemtanúi* [Szeged Eyewitnesses of the Revolutions] (Szeged, 1959), 57–59. (Henceforth *Cson.*)

4. *Cson*, 39–40.

5. Tonelli, S. *A franciák Szegeden* [The French in Szeged] (Szeged, 1939), 51–52. (Henceforth *Ton.*)

6. *Ton*, 53.

7. *Ton*, 55.

8. *Ton*, 35.

9. *Ibid.*

10. Hajdu, G., *Harcban a megszállók ellen* [Fighting the Occupiers] (Pécs, 1957), 238–39.

11. Bernachot, J., *L'Armée Française d'Orient: L'Armée de Hongrie* (Paris, 1970), 51. (Henceforth *Bern.*)

12. Vincennes Army Archives: Commanding General, Allied Armies in the East to Commanding General, Army of Hungary, March 22, 1919 (printed in *Bern.* 107).

13. Kelemen, B., *Adatok a szegedi ellenforradalom és a szegedi kormány történetéhez* [Data for the History of the Szeged Counterrevolution and of the Szeged Government] (Szeged, 1923), 40–42. (Henceforth *Kel.*)

14. *Ibid.*

15. Gaál, Endre, *A szegedi munkásság harca a Tanácsköztársaságért* [The Struggle of the Szeged Working Class for the Republic of Councils] (Budapest, 1956), 102–103 (Henceforth *Gaál.*)

16. *Bern*, 120; *Kel*, 44.

17. Vincennes Army Archives: Report of Cap. de Lamaze to Commanding General, Army of Hungary, March 31, 1919 (printed in *Bern.*, 279–82).

18. *Ibid.*

19. *Gaál*, 118–19.

20. *Kel*, 45–46.

21. *Kel*, 64, 83.

22. *Ibid.*, 50.

23. *Ibid.*, 44.

24. *Ibid.*, 163.

25. *Ibid.*, 186.

26. *Ibid.*, 133–34.

27. *Ibid.*

28. *Ibid.*

29. *Ibid.*, 138.

30. *Ibid.*

31. *Ibid.*

32. *Ibid.*, 163.

33. *Ton*, 12; *Kel*, 164.

34. *Ton*, 29.

35. *Ton*, 31; *Kel*, 190.

36. *Kel*, 164.

37. *Ibid.*, 139.

38. *Ibid.*, 145.

39. *Ibid.*, 164.

40. *Bern*, 181; for a cabinet list see *ibid.*, 323–24 and *Kel*, 137, 185.

41. *Kel*, 137.

42. *Ibid.*, 161.

43. Gratz, C., *A forradalmak kora* [The Age of the Revolutions] (Budapest, 1935), 206–207.

44. *Ibid.*

45. *Ibid.*, 209.

46. *Ibid.*, 215.

47. *Kel*, 302 ff.

48. *Ibid.*, 21 n., 163.

49. *Kel*, 302 ff.

50. *Ibid.*

51 Ashmead-Bartlett, Ellis, *The Tragedy of Central Europe* (London, 1923), 191. (Henceforth *Ash*), Varjassy, Louis, *Révolution, Bolchevisme, Réaction* (Paris, 1934), 77.

52. *Ash*, 159.

53. *Gratz*, 216.

54. *Ibid.*, 217.

55. *Ibid.*,

56. Ágnes Szabó and Ervin Pamlényi eds., *A határban a halál kaszál...* [Death Reaps in the Meadows...] (Budapest, 1963), 66–67. (It was impossible for the author to check on the editorial accuracy of these memoir-fragments by the White Terrorist Pál Prónay.)

57. *Ibid.*, 84.

58. Jean Bérenger, *L'Europe danubienne de 1848 à nos jours* (Paris, 1976), 120.

59. *Ton*, 57.

60. *Kel*, 145, 153, 163; *Ton*, 13.

61. *Ton*, 13–14.

62. *Kel*, 534.

63. *Ton*, 13–14.

64. *Kel*, 534.

# V
# REVOLUTION NORTH AND SOUTH OF HUNGARY

# EAST CENTRAL EUROPE 1918:
## WAR AND PEACE, CZECHOSLOVAKIA AND POLAND

Piotr S. Wandycz

The year 1918 stands, of course, for the rebirth or birth of Poland and Czechoslovakia, although their consolidation as states was completed only in 1920. The two countries reappeared on the political map of Europe through war, and assumed their final shape through peace: the treaties of Versailles, St. Germain, Trianon, and Riga. Yet, paradoxically, the greatest military effort Poland made was only after the signature of the Treaty of Versailles, and Czechoslovakia engaged only in serious fighting when World War I was actually over. If we remember the Clausewitz dictum about war being "a mere continuation of policy by other means," so we can speak here also of *peace* as a continuation of war by other methods.

Independence of Poland and Czechoslovakia was achieved by a combination of military and political-diplomatic efforts, and we need to look closer at the ingredients of this combination. The range of interpretations of the main causes of the birth of an independent East Central Europe is considerable, and the connection between these interpretations and ideology close. Since a victory of the Entente over the Central Powers was a prerequisite for Czecho-slovak and also largely Polish independence, the latter could be, and was re-presented as, a gift of the Entente. Western statesmen were more than willing to use this argument for political purposes. As Britain's Prime Minister David Lloyd George asserted at the Paris Peace Conference, "the Poles had not the slightest hope of getting freedom, and have only got their freedom because there are a million and a half Frenchmen dead, very nearly a million British, half a million Italians, and I forget how many Americans. That has given the Poles their freedom..."[1] The implication that the Allies had sacrificed all these lives specifically for the cause of Poland's freedom cannot, of course, be accepted. Georges Clemenceau did not hesitate to admit that "our programme when we entered the war was not one of liberation... We had started as allies of the Russian oppressors of Poland," and only when "all over Europe

oppressed people raised their heads... our war of national defense was transformed by force of events into a war of liberation."[2]

The thesis that the victorious Entente had brought freedom to Czechoslovakia corresponded to the generally accepted interpretation according to
which Tomáš Garrigue Masaryk and Edvard Beneš — the "President Liberator" and the perennial foreign minister — succeeded in persuading the Allies
to become champions of the Czechoslovak cause. The argument ran as follows:
Allied policies culminating with President Wilson's note of October 18, 1918
— which rejected negotiations with Austria on the basis of the Fourteen Points
— gave the final push toward the collapse of the monarchy and made possible
the proclamation of Czechoslovak independence on October 28. The Allied
action was a direct result of the efforts of the Czechoslovak National Council
in the West, supported by volunteer troops organized in Russia, Italy, and
France. Hence, Masaryk's concept developed in late 1914 of an independent
Czechoslovakia was realized with small correctives by 1918; the delay being
due to the hesitations of the Western powers, finally overcome by the Masaryk—
Beneš diplomacy as supported by various Czech and Slovak groups.[3]

There is no doubt that the Entente did change its attitude toward Czechoslovakia, actually between May and September–October 1918, but the
question remains whether it did so as a result of successful Masaryk–Beneš
diplomacy or other equally or even more important factors.

Surely, the collapse of separate talks with Austria, as well as the Italian
defeat at Caporetto, must not be forgotten, nor was the disintegration of the
Habsburg monarchy itself artificially caused by the Allies, but occurred when
internal conditions were ripe.[4]

The dominant thesis ascribing Czechoslovak independence to the Entente
as affected by the efforts of the Masaryk–Beneš camp abroad — the so-called
zahraniční odboj — was early challenged mainly on political grounds, both
from the Right and the Left. A prominent representative of the Left, Lev
Borský, claimed that independence had been won by the military and political
acts of the Czechoslovaks in Siberia and the domestic takeover in Prague followed by a successful military defense of gains. To the zahraniční odboj of Masaryk and Beneš, he opposed the domácí odboj (domestic struggle) led by Kramář
and the men of October 28. If the dominant thesis may be called Western-
oriented, and closely connected with Wilsonian ideology, that of Borský,
followed and developed in a major work by Antonín Kalina, is rather pro-
Russian. Kalina's important book, characteristically entitled Through Blood
and Iron, ascribed the change of American attitude toward Czechoslovakia to
the role played by the Legion in Russia, a role which Masaryk did not anti-
cipate in his plans, and which he failed to use fully to destroy the Bolsheviks
and restore a "true Russia."[5]

The criticism of the dominant thesis coming from the extreme Left shared

— as the historian Pichlík noted — with that of the Right an emphasis on Russia and the domestic front as the most important factors. Except that the heroes of the conservatives, Kramář and the men of October 28, became replaced in the leftist writings by the people, and the Russians now meant the Bolsheviks. Wilsonian myth made room for the October Revolution. Political motivation which was stronger than detached historical analysis in the official thesis, its rightist criticism became completely unrestrained. This was particularly true during the Stalinist period, when Klement Gottwald's dogma — "without the Great October Revolution there would have been no independent Czechoslovakia" — was echoed among others by such historians as Říha, Křížek, and Král.[6] After the Twentieth Party Congress in Moscow, a new kind of polemics began among the Czechoslovak historians: the issue of independence was being approached now as a bourgeois-national solution used as an instrument against the revolution. If this was another blow at the "Wilson legend" — a favorite target of an earlier period — it also signified a departure from the former ground shared with the rightist critics.[7] Finally, by the late 1960s, a more balanced synthesis of the factors responsible for the 1918 independence began to emerge, less influenced by political assumptions, and taking all the concrete elements into consideration. The notion of freedom being a gift of the Entente was definitely rejected by an historian like Pichlík. He would see in the establishment of sovereign state, a logical denouement of the development of modern-type Czech nation,[8] and in the international recognition of Czechoslovakia a demonstration of the nonviability of the Habsburg empire as a separate factor in the balance of power.

As in Czechoslovakia so in Poland, a debate on the elements decisive for the recovery of independence was also affected by political divisions. With the ascendancy of Piłsudski after 1926, the official line glorified the "armed deed" (*czyn zbrojny*) of Piłsudski's legionnaires, seeing in it the single most important reason for Poland's rebirth. Only active national efforts involving sacrifices, the argument ran, could have exploited the favorable international constellation. Most historians connected in one way or another with the legions subscribed to this interpretation.[9] By contrast, the national democratic camp, which during World War I had concentrated its efforts on winning over the Entente to the cause of Polish independence, stressed the collapse of Germany and the Allied victory.[10] To Piłsudski, the "savior of the country," the Right sought to oppose Roman Dmowski, Ignacy Paderewski, and such generals as Józef Haller, the commander of the Polish army in France. Insisting on the decisive contribution of the pro-Allied Dmowski Line, Piłsudski's tactical cooperation with the Central Powers was denounced with an even greater bitterness than in a comparable case of the Masaryk—Kramář dichotomy. The latter operated after all *within* one and the same Allied camp. An attempt to represent the two Polish trends as really complementary, and in that sense necessary for the recovery of independence, was made by the great historian, Michał Bobrzyński. After World War II, the thesis of compatibility and "a division of roles" would be reflected in Titus Komarnicki's work.[11] Other historians placed special emphasis on the role of Woodrow Wilson as combined with native Polish effort (Paderewski), on internal developments as assisted by the Entente, and on various variants thereof.[12]

According to the Communist interpretation from Julian Marchlewski to Henryk Jabłoński, Leon Grossfeld, and Norbert Michta, a victory by neither of the belligerents in the "imperialist war" could have brought Poland independence. Only a class struggle culminating in the October Revolution could have achieved that result; hence the crucially important place of the latter.[13] This thesis, advanced in a somewhat crude and dogmatic way in the 1950s and early 1960s, made room for genuine scholarly discussions. In the course of such debates, more sophisticated presentations of the complexity of causes of Poland's rebirth became possible.[14] By and large, the gap between the opposite theses has been considerably reduced, and my own point of view, expressed a few years ago, may no longer be regarded as controversial. I wrote then:

> As in the case of every great historical event, multiple factors combined to bring about Poland's resuscitation. The war and the complex sociopolitical upheavals that accompained it, the collapse of the partitioning powers, the Russian revolutions, and the emergence of a new diplomacy – each had its share in the final outcome. And yet, all the favorable circumstances notwithstanding, Poland might not have reappeared on the map of Europe had it not been for the stamina, patriotism, and determination of the Polish nation, which had never fully accepted the verdict of the partitions.[15]

This brief reminder of the principal theses as to the recovery of independence in 1918, indicates the presence of the "military-effort" approach versus the "diplomatic-political" argument. In the Czechoslovak case, it was the Right which put a particular stress on the struggle of the legion in Russia; Lev Borský even invoked a "legionary messianism" and contrasted the Žižka-Hussite martial tradition with the corrupting pacifist ideals of the old Unity of the Czech Brethren.[16] Masaryk, although he disliked the stereotype of the good old Soldier Švejk, and was no pacifist, would still place himself and be placed in the essentially anti-militarist tradition of Hus–Komenský–Palacký. In the Polish case, if the Right criticized – in the name of political realism – the "Romantic heroic" approach of the Piłsudski camp, it did not, and could not oppose the martial tradition which pervaded the Polish national outlook. Were the Švejk and Kozietulski clichés – allegedly epitomizing the nonheroic (Czech) versus the heroic (Polish) Weltanschauung – useful in a debate on Czech and Polish roads toward independence?[17]

Let us now look closer at the military component of the plans and policies of Czechoslovak leaders during the war. The initial stages of the conflict witnessed Czech hopes for a liberation of their country by the advancing Russian armies. A certain passivity accompanied this wait-and-see attitude, but one should mention instances of desertion to the Russians as well as the formation of a detachment (*Družina*) composed of Czechs living in Russia. This small unit would grow later into a brigade, but had no real military or political significance in the first years of the war. By 1916, the appearance of larger groups of Czech and Slovak prisoners of war in France, however, made it possible for the Czecho-Slovak National Council operating in the West, to demand a special treatment of those prisoners in anticipation of forming autonomous Czechoslovak detachments in France and Italy. Thus far, only a couple of hundred Czech and Slovak volunteers had fought in the ranks of the French Foreign Legion.

The February Revolution in Russia created a climate for both the build up of Czechoslovak armed units in the East — in June 1917 the Russian-based brigade fought its most famous battle at Zborów — and for the transports of these troops to France. Masaryk became a strong advocate of a large Czechoslovak army, and his associate, Milan Štefánik explored the possibility of mass recruitment in the United States. Benes simultaneously sought to gain over Rome to the idea of Czechoslovak units in Italy. A Czechoslovak army in the West was not only to demonstrate the participation of the Czechs and Slovaks in the war on the Allied side, but lead to a political recognition of the emigré council as a representative of an Allied-belligerent nation. The chances of a sizable army were numerically the best in Russia, but politically it was most difficult to agitate for a warlike effort within a country which was speedily moving toward peace. Thus, successes came first in the West. The decree of President Poincaré of December 16, 1917 established an autonomous Czechoslovak army on the French soil, and a few months later, an agreement between Premier Vittorio Emmanuele Orlando and Štefánik provided for the creation of a similar military force in Italy. In Masaryk's words these armies were "a military foundation of a future, free and independent Czechoslovak state."[18]

Obviously, the Czechoslovak military contribution could not be of decisive importance from the Allied point of view. But the psychological effect was significant, and in the fourth year of the war, no new reservoir of manpower could be ignored. Masaryk's over optimistic references to 100,000 even 120,000 troops on the Western Front in the near future were helpful for the Allied morale severely tested by the long years of carnage. As far as the Czechoslovak troops in Russia were concerned, they became, almost accidentally, a trump card, played with great artistry by Benes and Masaryk. The magnitude of the tasks expected of the legion in Russia was disproportionate to its actual size (probably between 40,000 and 60,000); the nature of the tasks evolved as the situation was changing. Appreciated because of the relief it could bring on the Western Front, the legion then became a significant element in the bolstering and rebuilding of the Eastern Front against the Germans. Finally, when the legion embarked on its Anabasis and came into conflict with the Bolsheviks, it appeared as the God-sent force to control Siberia and the trans-Siberian railroad. The Czech rightists blamed Masaryk for not using the legion to destroy the Bolsheviks. Indeed, the Czechoslovak leadership was trying hard to keep the legion neutral and then extricate it from the Russian cauldron. Thus, paradoxically, the deeds of the legion and their exploitation by Czechoslovak diplomacy followed no previously set plan but resulted from a series of largely unforeseen developments.

The actual contribution of Czechoslovak troops to the Allied war effort was rather small – in a struggle of millions it could hardly have been otherwise. The takeover of October 28 – involving the proclamation of an independent Czechoslovakia – was a bloodless coup. There were, of course, no regular Czech troops in the homeland when the event occurred. Similarly in the October–November establishment of Prague's control over the Sudeten German area, which had claimed their right of self-determination and separation, regular armed forces played no role. Slight German resistance was overcome by improvised military detachments. Slovakia was evacuated by Hungary as a result of pressure by French and not Czech might. It was only in mid-December that some 20,000 Czechoslovak troops returned from Italy, and in January 1919, around 10,000 from France. Transports of the Czechoslovak legionaries from Russia were spread out between December 1919 and September 1920. Thus, the Czechoslovak government found itself in control over most of the territories it claimed without having to use an armed force. There were exceptions. In the contested area of Teschen (Ciesayn, Těšín) a Czechoslovak advance on January 23, 1919 led to a clash with Polish troops and a number of engagements. The other instance, on a grand scale, of an actual use of force occurred over Slovakia, culminating in spring 1919 with an offensive by Béla Kun's Hungarian Soviet Republic, which drove the Italian-commanded Czechoslovak units out of the eastern part of the province. Allied intervention stopped the hostilities. Whatever the exact figure of Czech and Slovak losses during the fighting in the last stages of World War I, and in the operations which resulted in a final territorial consolidation of the republic, it is likely that they were greatly inferior to those suffered in the imperial-royal uniform between 1914 and 1918.

Except for the battle of Zborów, of which General Jan Syrový was the acknowledged hero, and the somewhat mixed heritage of the Siberian Anabasis, Czechoslovak wartime armed effort left no visible imprint on the people's mentality. Far from being cultivated, militarism was looked down upon; the sole foray into politics by a high-ranking Czechoslovak general Radolo (Rudolf) Gajda, only helped to discredit such ambitions.

The military component occupied a much more important place in Poland's rebirth in 1918, and her subsequent evolution. To Józef Piłsudski who from a leader of the PPS, evolved, well before World War I, into a military figure, independent Polish participation in the approaching war was imperative for several reasons. The Polish nation could not remain a passive spectator in a war fought on its territory: even a small Polish force could effectively throw its weight on the scale when the major combatants would be exhausted by the struggle. Piłsudski did mention as the best possible solution from the Polish viewpoint, a defeat of Russia overwhelmed by the German might, and followed by a defeat of the Central Powers unable to withstand the superiority of the West.[19] But, pragmatic as he was, he did not rule out other developments.

A Polish military effort, prepared for several years in tactical cooperation with Austria, was thus important on moral grounds – the Poles had to demonstrate their will to fight for their independence – and for practical strategic reasons – stepping into a power vacuum likely to appear toward the end of a long and bloody war between the partitioning powers. To identify Piłsudski's line with a military effort, while undoubtedly correct, must not result, however, in an oversimplified interpretation. The connection with politics was inseparable, and at moments when a military effort might undermine political objectives, the former had to be curtailed. Thus, for instance, Piłsudski parted company with some of his collaborators who wished to utilize fully the manpower of the Congress Kingdom (conquered by the German and Austrian troops by 1915) to expand the Polish armed forces. Piłsudski preferred a "poker game" with Berlin and Vienna, bluffing with the potential Polish manpower to demand political concessions and raising the antes. Simultaneously, he was building up an underground military organization (POW) which owed allegiance directly to him. Nor did Piłsudski hesitate in 1917 to provoke an open conflict with the occupying German–Austrian authorities which resulted in a disbanding of a major part of the legions, interment of many soldiers, and finally his own arrest. Accusations of Piłsudski having destroyed with his own hands the painstakingly built Polish army were widespread at the time.

The Polish legions, which enhanced the legend of the armed effort and Piłsudski's own contribution, were obviously numerically small. It has been calculated that about 30,000 men had passed through the three brigades of the legions – Piłsudski formally commanded only the first brigade – during their entire existence. The POWs, which were the only armed force at the disposal of the Polish government, as it emerged in 1918, comprised about 30,000 a year earlier. The so-called *Polnische Wehrmacht,* composed of legionnaires who took an oath of allegiance to the Central Powers and who were subsequently joined by some volunteers, reached a figure of 9000 by

1918.[20] But, as Piłsudski had rightly foreseen, in the chaotic situation which developed in the Polish lands with the breakdown of the partitioning powers, even this small force was of importance, and it could serve as a cadre for a rapid build up. If there were only five infantry battalions and three cavalry squadrons in Poland in November 1918, ten months later the respective figures were 110 battalions, 70 squadrons, and 85 batteries.[21]

The armed force, thus, played a central but not an exclusive role in Pilsudski's political strategy of rebuilding Poland. Similarly, the reliance of his chief opponent, Roman Dmowski, on diplomacy must not be oversimplified. To offset the popular appeal of the legions on the Austrian side, attempts were made to create the so-called Puławski Legion under Russian auspices. The tsarist regime went along halfheartedly, and when by 1915 the legion was integrated into a Polish rifle brigade, the only thing Polish about it was the official language of command. It was only with the fall of tsardom that a Polish Division of some 18,000 men came into existence together with a huge reserve regiment which became "neutralized" and revolutionized by Bolshevik propaganda. The creation of the Polish army in Russia during the revolutionary period — composed of three army corps, less than 40,000 men in all — cannot be credited to a single Polish political "orientation." Largely by force of circumstances the national democratic pro-Entente camp of Dmowski achieved a greater influence over the corps than the Piłsudski trend. In contrast to the Czechoslovak development, however, the Polish troops in Russia did not become a real political trump which the pro-Entente Polish National Committee of Dmowski could have exploited for Poland's benefit.

Numerically the largest Polish army came into existence on French soil (although it comprised mostly American Poles) and was formally called in existence by President Poincaré's decree of June 4, 1917. Again, it was not a Dmowski-inspired move, although his committee subsequently succeeded in obtaining political control over this army, better known as the Haller Army. In view of a dualism between the Piłsudski-led government, which emerged in Warsaw in 1918, and the National Committee in Paris, which the French viewed as the rightful representation of Poland, the question of the return of the Haller Army to the homeland raised difficulties. International problems also caused delays. The seven divisions (some 40,000 men) began to return to Poland only in April 1919. By that time a good deal of fighting had already taken place in the country. Since November 1918, Poles and Ukrainians were struggling for the control of eastern Galicia; there had been a successful Polish uprising against the Germans in Poznania; in January, as mentioned, the Poles had fought against the Czechs in Teschen; from February 1919 in there was a virtual war between Poland and Bolshevik Russia in the east. The latter conflict assumed eventually proportions not comparable with any of the border struggles fought by the reborn Czechoslovakia. The Eastern Front involved a million men and had a very important impact on Polish economic life.[12]

In the case of the Polish–Soviet war, once again, Piłsudski's emphasis on military force – a settlement being possible only after a major victory – conflicted with the policies of his opponents afraid of taking military risks. In the final analysis, if the victory on the battlefield at Warsaw in August 1920 was Piłsudski's, the compromise peace of Riga which followed was mainly the work of the national democrats, and a political defeat of the marshal.

What was Piłsudski's vision of Poland in postwar Europe? He and Dmowski did not feel it necessary to justify the re-emergence of Poland in universalist terms. Her right to exist was derived from the status of a great, historic nation of Europe. With the crime of partitions obliterated, the Polish nation was to resume her rightful place in international society. Piłsudski and Dmowski also agreed that there was no room for a small Polish state between Germany and Russia. Where they disagreed was whether Poland should be great as part of a bloc – federated, confederated, or linked by some other ties – that would push Russia back to her strictly ethnic frontiers, and be strong enough to deal with Germany, or whether the country should be a centralized state, absorbing only those non-Polish fringes it could assimilate and integrate. In the contest between Piłsudski's "federalist" versus Dmowski's "centralist" or "incorporationist" line, by 1921, the latter prevailed. Reborn Poland was a state which was strong enough to have great power aspirations, but not powerful enough to play a dominant role in East Central Europe.

In the Czechoslovak case, in order to justify national independence Masaryk and Beneš had first to demonstrate convincingly that the Habsburg monarchy was a pillar of Pan-Germanism – and ideological – Austria-Hungary was a bastion of reaction. Czechoslovak leaders advocated the replacement of the monarchy by a belt of free national states in East Central Europe – Bohemia with Slovakia, Serbia with Slovenia and Croatia, and Poland – which would not only serve as a barrier against German expansion, but represent a natural completion of the process of national emancipation and democracy going back to the French Revolution. Here Masarykian philosophy shared common ground with Wilsonianism. The anticipated cooperation of the three states implied a limitation of Polish territorial aspirations in the east which clashed with those of Russia. Czechoslovakia, seen as the center of the new East Central Europe, would in turn need a connection with Russia through eastern Galicia, and it was even hoped, with Yugoslavia through a "corridor", a landstrip carved out from Hungary. This Czechoslovak vision of East Central Europe which was virtually irreconcilable with the Polish concept of a great Poland, failed to materialize. Czechoslovakia remained somewhat isolated, and had to fall back on a more restricted combination known as the *Little Entente*.[23]

If neither the Piłsudski nor the Masaryk—Beneš program was fully realized, its impact on the First Czechoslovak and the Second Polish Republic was undeniable. Military effort became part of the Piłsudski legend, seen indeed as epitomizing the Polish national character; Masaryk's famous dictum "Christ not Caesar" gave a special ideological coloring to the heritage of the reborn Czechoslovakia. Should we conclude then with a banality by saying that peace and war are inseparable as parts of human experience? Or should we rather point to the complexities of East Central Europe in 1918 which the historian tries to ellucidate without succumbing to the contrasting black and white colors?

## NOTES

1. David Lloyd George, *The Truth about the Peace Treaties* (London, 1938), Vol. I, p. 997.

2. Georges Clemenceau, *Grandeur and Misery of Victory* (New York, 1930), pp. 190–92.

3. See comments in Karel Pichlík, *Zahraniční odboj 1914–1918 bez legend* [Independence Action Abroad 1914–1918 without Legends] (Prague, 1968), pp. 6–7, and the same author's "Zur Kritik der Legenden um das Jahr 1918," in Karl Bosl, ed., *Aktuelle Forschungsprobleme um die Erste Tschechoslowakische Republik* (Munich, Vienna, 1969), p. 79. The thesis is exemplified by such works as Zdenek Tobolka, *Politické dějiny československého národa* [Political History of the Czechoslovak Nation] (Prague, 1937), Vol. IV, and Emil Strauss, *Die Entstehung der Tschechoslowakischen Republik* (Prague, 1935).

4. A Czechoslovak historian connects the birth of Czechoslovakia with the democratic transformation of Europe resulting from the war and the victory of the national principle as applied to Central and Eastern Europe; both were accelerated by the Bolshevik Revolution. See, Radko Břach, "To the Origins and the Beginnings of Czechoslovak Foreign Policy", *Problems of Contemporary History* I (1968), 25–27. For the change in American policy, see, the classic of Victor S. Mamatey, *The United States and East Central Europe 1914–1918: A Study in Wilsonian Diplomacy and Propaganda* (Princeton, 1957); for the Rome Congress see the recent Michał Pulaski, *Z Dziejów genezy 'Europy wersalskiej': współpraca Słowian zachodnich i południowych w ostatnim etapie I wojny światowej* [On the History of the Origins of 'Versailles Europe': Cooperation of Western and Southern Slavs in the last Stage of World War I] (Wrocław, 1974).

5. Lev Borský, *Znovudobytí samostátnosti* [Recovery of Independence] (Prague, 1928), and Antonín Kalina, *Krví a železem* [With Blood and Iron] (Prague, 1938).

6. J. Křížek, O. Říha, *Bez Velké říjnové socialistické revoluce by nebylo Československa* [Without the Great October Socialist Revolution there would have been no Czechoslovakia].

7. See, Karel Pomaizl, *Vznik ČSR 1918: problém marxistické vědecké interpretace* [Emergence of Czechoslovakia 1918: The Problem of Marxist Scientific Interpretation] (Prague, 1965) viewed by Pichlík as typical for the late 1950s. For the example of a crude attack on Wilson see J. S. Hájek, *Wilsonovská legenda v dějinach ČSR* [The Wilson Legend in the History of Czechoslovakia] (Prague, 1953).

8. "Die Gründung eines souveränen Staates war die logische Folge der tschechischen nationalen Entwicklung, der Existenz einer modernen tschechischen Nation", Pichlík, "Zur Kritik...", 88.

9. For instance, Michał Sokolnicki, Wacław Lipiński, Marian Kukiel or Władysław Poból-Malinowski.

10. For example, see, the writings of Roman Dmowski, Marian Seyda or Stanisław Kozicki.

11. See respectively Michal Bobrzyński, *Wskrzeszenie państwa polskiego* [The Resuscitation of the Polish State] (Cracow, 1920); Titus Komarnicki, *Rebirth of the Polish Republic: A Study in the Diplomatic History of Europe 1914–1920* (Melbourne–London, 1957). The effects of this dualism on Polish efforts are stressed by Kay Lundgreen-Nielsen, *The Polish Problem at the Paris Peace Conference: A Study of the Policies of the Great Powers and the Poles 1918–1919* (Odense, 1979).

12. See, among others, the contributions of Adam Szelągowski and Stanisław Kutrzeba.

13. See, Henryk Jabłónski, *Narodziny Drugiej Rzeczypospolitej* [The Birth of the Second Republic] (Warsaw, 1962); also, his "Miedzynarodowe warunki odbudowy niepodległósci Polski" [International Conditions of Reconstruction of Independent Poland] and Leon Grosfeld, "Sprawa polska w pierwszej wojnie światowej", both in *Ruch robotniczy i ludowy w Polsce w latach 1914–1923* [The Workers' and Peasants' Movement in Poland in the Years 1914–1923] (Warsaw, 1980).

14. See, Tadeusz Jedruszczak, "Spory o geneze II Rzeczypospolitej" [Controversies about the Origins of the Second Republic] and Czesław Madajczyk, "Odrodzenie Polski w 1918 roku" [Poland's Rebirth in 1918] in *Droga przez półwiecze: o Polsce lat 1918–1968* (Referaty z sesji naukowych Polskiej Akademii Nauk i Uniwersytetu Warszawskiego poświecone 50 rocznicy odzyskania niepodległości, Warsaw, 1969) [A Half-Century Road: About Poland 1918–1968, papers from a session of the Polish Academy of Sciences and Warsaw university on the 50th Anniversary of the recovery of independence]. Compare a survey of the divergent interpretations in Janusz Pajewski, *Odbudowa państwa polskiego 1914–1918* [The Rebuilding of the Polish State 1914–1918] (Poznań, 1978), pp. 9–14, also, a thought-provoking collection of articles: Krzysztof Kozłowski (ed.), *Drogi do niepodległości* [Roads toward Independence] (Cracow, 1979).

15. Piotr S. Wandycz, *The Lands of Partitioned Poland 1795–1918* ("A History of East Central Europe," edited by Peter F. Sugar and Donald W. Treadgold, Vol. VII [Seattle, 1974]), pp. 369–70.

16. Interesting remarks on this score by Bedrich Loewenstein, "Český pravicový radicalismus a první světová válka" [Czech Rightist Radicalism and the First World War] in *Naše živá i mrtvá minulost* [Our Living and Dead Past] (Prague, 1968), pp. 169–71.

17. Kozietulski, the commander of a squadron of Napoleon's chevaux-légers of the guard, became famous for leading a bold charge at Somosierra. His name was made symbolic for recklessness and senseless sacrifice of life, in clear disregard for actual facts. See the interesting "Zwietrzałe stereotypy: Szwejk i Kozietulski" [Arid Stereotypes: Szwejk and Kozietulski] in *Polityka* March 7, 1964.

18. Cited in Pichlík, *Zahraniční odboj* [Independence Action], p. 251.

19. Piłsudski's interview, January 13 and his lecture in Paris, February 1914 in Waclaw Jedrzejewicz, *Kronika życia Józefa Piłsudskiego 1867–1935* [The Chronicle of Józef Piłsudski's Life 1867–1935] (London, 1977), Vol. I, 251, 264. Compare Victor M. Chernov, *Pered burei* [Before the Storm] (New York, 1953), 295–306.

20. Figures and brief characterization of different formations in a glossary in Jerzy Holzer, Jan Molenda, *Polska w pierwszej wojnie światowej* [Poland in the First World War] (Warsaw, 1963).

21. See interesting comments by Eugeniusz Kwiatkowski in Kozłowski (ed.), *Drogi do niepodległości* [Roads toward Independence], p. 87.

22. See the useful survey: Tadeusz Jedruszczak, "Powstanie II Rzeczypospolitej: rzady i terytorium" [Emergence of the II Republic: governments and territory], *Dzieje Najnowsze* [Newest History], X, no. 4 (1978), 41–58. The impact of the Polish–Soviet war on Poland's industrial development is discussed by Zbigniew Landau and Jerzy Tomaszewski, *Gospodarka Polski miedzywojennej: w dobie inflacji 1918–1923* [Economy of Interwar Poland: the Period of Inflation 1918–1923] (Warsaw, 1967), Vol. I, 84–89.

23. On Czechoslovak international isolation see the concluding remarks in D. Perman, *The Shaping of the Czechoslovak State: Diplomatic History of the Boundaries of Czechoslovakia, 1914–1920* (Leiden, 1962), pp. 274–75. Compare the treatment in Alena Gajanová, "Entstehung und Entwicklung der internationalen Beziehungen der ČSR", in *Die Entstehung der Tschechoslowakischen Republik und ihre international-politische Stellung: zum 50 Jährigen Grundsjubiläum der ČSR* (Acta Universitatis Carolinae, Philosophica et Historica 2–3, 1968, Studia Historica I–II, Prague, 1968), pp. 135–61.

# BULGARIA, THE BALKANS, AND THE PEACE OF 1919

Khristo A. Khristov

The history of the Balkan peoples contains periods when they helped each other in solving important political, social, and cultural problems, and in waging a common struggle against external enemies. Such a period was the National Revival in the eighteenth and nineteenth centuries when the Balkan nations were formed, when their progressive material and spiritual culture was built, and when a struggle was conducted for national and antifeudal liberation. It was then that was formed, and gained in popularity, the idea of setting up a Balkan democratic federation which was shared by generations of progressive politicians and cultural figures.

There were, however, also periods of confrontation in the history of the Balkan peoples. They led to sharp ideological and propaganda collisions and to wars that destroyed the traditions of good-neighborliness and mutual help along the road of historical progress. Such were the years of the Second Balkan War and World War I into which were dragged the Balkan countries. These two wars ended in unjust peace treaties which dealt a heavy blow on the understanding and cooperation of the Balkan peoples, and served as a prerequisite for their involvement in World War II.

The 1919 peace treaties were a turning point in the confrontation of the Balkan countries for a long period of time. They confirmed the results of World War I and gave a new direction to the internal development of the Balkan and southeast European states along the line of eroding and doing away with the bourgeois democracies by Fascism and the intensification of imperialist penetration in the Balkans.

The peace treaties affecting the Balkan countries are usually connected with the realization of two basic goals of the victorious Balkan states: *first*, political liberation and unification of states formerly under Austro–Hungarian rule and the territorial expansion of the Greek state in the Balkans and Asia Minor, and *second*, punishment of Bulgaria and Hungary for their participation in world war on the side of Germany.

In point of fact, however, other important circumstances and goals should be taken into account for the correct definition of the causes, the working out, and the character of the peace treaties. These were the aspirations of the victorious Great Powers to expand and consolidate their economic penetration in the Balkans, to win as their ally one or other Balkan country and to help the Balkan middle classes in their struggle against the revolutionary wave that was rising in the Balkans after the end of the war. An important place was taken also by the striving of the Entente states and the USA to make use of the Balkan countries for intervention in Soviet Russia and for overthrowing the Soviet rule in Hungary.

The national liberation and unification of the Southern Slavs and the Romanians who were under Austro—Hungarian rule was a just and progressive cause. But this in itself is not sufficient to evaluate correctly the peace treaties of 1919 which sanctioned this cause. The winning of national unification and freedom is not the only criterion of historical progress. An important condition for this is in whose hands the power falls after winning freedom, and for the attainment of what aims it is used.

In the Kingdom of Serbians, Croats, and Slovenes, newly established after the war, and in Romania, which obtained national unification, and Greece, which achieved territorial expansion, the deprivation of rights of a national minority was replaced by depriving of rights of another national minority. Typical examples in this respect were the position of the Hungarians and Ukrainians in Romania, of the Albanians and Hungarians in the Kingdom of Serbs, Croats, and Slovenes, and of the Bulgarians in that same Kingdom and in Greece and Romania. There was something else of particular importance which should be taken into consideration in characterizing the peace treaties of the Versailles system affecting the Balkans. This was the circumstance that the realization of the national liberation and unification of the Southern Slavs and the ceding of foreign territories to the Kingdom of Serbs, Croats, and Slovenes, as well as the formation of a Great Romania and a Great Greece were connected with the plans of the Entente and the USA to involve these countries in the implementation of their anti-Soviet and counterrevolutionary plans. A few examples may be adduced as proof.

Turkey's leaving the war with the Armistice of Mudros (October 30, 1918) made it possible for the Entente to proceed with the implementation of extensive anti-Soviet plans. At the beginning of November, Entente naval units sailed through the Dardanelles and occupied Constantinople. In a report of Colonel Petrov, the Bulgarian liaison officer with the Command of the Eastern Army of the Entente, of November 27, 1918, it is said that French and British divisions in the Balkans, Asia Minor, and Mesopotamia were moving toward Russia's southern frontiers. The main route of these divisions passed through the straits. The objective was, together with the White guards in the Caucasus, to overthrow the "Bolshevik regime" and restore the Russian bourgeois-land-owner state.[1]

Greek troops jointed Entente forces designed for anti-Soviet intervention. After the end of the war, the Venizelos Government proceeded to increase its military forces. They were intended for intervention in Soviet Russia, for the occupation of Thrace and anterior Asia Minor, and for exercizing pressure on and threatening Bulgaria. In January 1919, together with the troops of the Entente that landed in the ports of the Ukraine, were three Greek divisions.[2]

Lacking enough troops to conduct the anti-Soviet intervention and with the reluctance of their forces to fight against the Soviet rule, the principal states of the Entente — Britain and France — supported the Greek territorial claims against Bulgaria and Turkey and encouraged the Greek government in conducting hostile operations against Soviet rule. They supplied the Greek army with arms, ammunition, clothing, and other war materials, and granted it considerable funds.[3]

But Greece was not the only state in the Balkans that the Entente was trying to drag into the anti-Soviet intervention. The Entente interventionists also paid considerable attention to Romania for this purpose. In February 1919, British General Greenly sent a report to his government in which he emphasized the need for promptly giving Romania military, technical, and food assistance, so that "the peasants and the army may stand up to Bolshevik propaganda" which attacked them from three sides: Soviet Russia, Hungary, and Bulgaria. Romania, in Greenly's view, was very suitable for the investment of British capital. The Romanian peasants could be an "ideal bastion" against Bolshevism. The army was made up of "excellent material" and if it was fed and clad, it could oppose Bolshevism.[4]

In reply to this and other similar reports, in March 1919, the British government decided to send urgent help to the Romanian rulers, so as to assist and encourage them in the struggle against Bolshevism. Meanwhile, Soviet rule was established in Hungary and the British aid was designed chiefly for helping Romanian intervention against the Hungarian Soviet Republic. It was expressed in granting a big financial loan and in sending military equipment. Canada also promised to give assistance in funds and military equipment to the Romanian government. The size of Allied aid may be judged from the fact that the clothing given alone amounted to 150,000 sets.[5]

The Romanian government, like the Greek, was well aware of the importance of its participation in the struggle against the Soviet rule in Russia and Hungary, and also, against the threat of the breaking out of a revolution in Bulgaria, and was trying to extract the maximum profit from that. In May 1919, it put forward a demand to the participants in the Paris Peace Conference for the inclusion within its boundaries the lands extending to the west up to the Tisza, Bukovina, Bessarabia, and the whole of Dobrudja. Only in such a case — according to the Romanian prime minister — and also after granting bigger material aid, could Romania "block the road of invading Bolshevism."[6]

The Entente and the USA made efforts to also drag the military forces of the Kingdom of Serbs, Croats, and Slovenes in the struggle against the revolutionary movement in the Balkans and in Hungary. On March 25, 1919, British General Plunkett sent to the High Command of the British Army a report significantly entitled "The Serbian Army as a Weapon against Bolshevism." In it, he reported that he had met Minister Mišić and the Prince Regent and had a talk with them on the participation of Serbian troops in suppressing the Hungarian revolution. In his report, Plunkett pointed out that the Serbian army was "the only effective reliable force capable [of fighting] against the Hungarians." The persons whom he visited declared that they were agreeable to the use of Serbian troops against Soviet Hungary, but the army suffered from lack of food and clothes. The Romanians, in the opinion of Mišić and the prince regent, were to defend the northern frontiers of the Kingdom of Serbs, Croats, and Slovenes from the Bolsheviks, and the Serbian army could immediately advance towards Budapest and stifle the "Bolshevik movement."[7]

The leaders of the Kingdom of Serbs, Croats, and Slovenes, which was torn by acute internal national and class contradictions and struggles and was in strained relations with all its neighbors owing to territorial disputes, of course did not miss the opportunity to gain benefits from its possible participation in the counterrevolutionary struggle. They told Plunkett that they were ready to join the struggle against Bolshevism provided pressure was exercised on the Italians for compliance (concerning the dispute for lands on the Eastern Adriatic coast), on the Romanians (concerning Bánát), and on the Bulgarians (concerning Macedonia and the Western outlying parts), and provided they were assisted with funds, arms, clothing and military equipment.[8]

To the Kingdom of Serbs, Croats, and Slovenes, as well as to Greece and Romania, were granted loans, and large quantities of war materials were supplied by the British, French, and American governments. Since Greece and Romania, according to the plans of the Entente and the USA, had to take part in the struggle against the Soviet rule in the lands along the Black Sea, Bessarabia and Bukovina, chiefly the Serbian army was envisaged for the struggle against the Hungarian revolution of March 1919. Provided it was supplied with arms, clothing, and food, according to Plunkett, it would be turned into a "first-class force for combating Bolshevism."[9]

The internal confusion in the Kingdom of Serbs, Croats, and Slovenes and sharp national and class contradictions and struggles prevented the Serbian army from taking an active part in suppressing the Hungarian revolution. Entente troops and the Romanian army were then entrusted with this task.

The information provided about the anti-Sovietism of the Entente and the

USA and their striving to suppress the revolutionary wave in Central and southeastern Europe show that this was one of the reasons for the support which they gave to their Balkan allies in the territorial and other claims in preparing the peace treaties. It was not only this, admittedly, that determined their policy toward the Balkans at the Peace Conference. Other motives and causes were in operation here, above all their strategic, political, and economic interests.

After the victory of the Great October Socialist Revolution in tsarist Russia, bourgeois France lost her strong ally against Wilhelminian Germany. The loss had to be compensated for since Germany could restore her economic and military potential after the defeat in the imperialist wars. This compensation could be achieved through the establishment of a bloc of Central and southeast European states: Poland, Czechoslovakia, Romania, and the Kingdom of Serbs, Croats, and Slovenes to move in her orbit. This made the French diplomats at the Paris Conference give full and most resolute support to the delegation of the Kingdom of Serbs, Croats, and Slovenes in all its demands toward all neighboring countries, and mostly toward Bulgaria and Albania. Particularly categorical was France's support in discussing and solving the so-called Macedonian question in preparing the Peace Treaty of Neuilly. And it was France that had the last word at the Peace Conference.

Britain's role in preparing the Treaty of Neuilly was the second in importance. After the defeat of Germany and Austria—Hungary, she was interested in expanding her economic penetration and political influence in the Balkans. Besides this, she was interested in keeping the sea route across the Mediterranean and the Suez Canal to the Middle and Far East. For this reason, she supported Greece's territorial claims to the full and tried to settle in the non-Turkish territories of the disintegrated Ottoman empire. With respect to Macedonia, the British delegation differed from the French. It proposed the sending of an "Inspector General" with advisory rights on minority and other questions to Vardar Macedonia. This position was, however, weakly defended and was rejected under French pressure by the Peace Conference.

Firmer, but inconsistent with respect to the peace treaty with Bulgaria, was the stand of the American delegation. With his declaration at the beginning of 1918, President Wilson pledged himself to defend the principle of self-determination of the peoples and their right to political freedom. This position was soon abandoned. At the Peace Conference at first the US delegation declared itself against the territorial claims of the Kingdom of Serbs, Croats, and Slovenes on the west Bulgarian lands. Based on accurate statistical data and information of American missionaries about the national composition of the population in Macedonia, it declared itself in favor of insuring minority rights for the Bulgarian population there. This, however, did not lead to a positive result, owing to the resistance of France and the Kingdom of Serbs, Croats, and Slovenes and the lack of insistence from the American side. The same happened also in connection with the disagreement of the American delegation with the ceding of southern Dobrudja to Romania. The American delegation did not agree to the taking away of western Thrace from Bulgaria and the introduction in it of an occupation regime of the Entente. Its position came up against the resistance of the British, Italian, and French delegations. The American proposal for ceding to Bulgaria part of eastern Thrace up to the Midia-Enos line, delineated by the Peace of London of 1913, was also rejected.

The position of the American delegation on the above questions was connected with the idea of setting up a state in Constaninople as an American protectorate. It was envisaged besides Constantinople and its environs to include eastern Thrace, anterior Asia Minor, and some Aegean islands as well. After the successful development of the Turkish national liberation revolution, headed by Kemal Ataturk, however, this idea was abandoned. By this the American position on the Bulgarian national question was also abandoned.

As far as Italy was concerned, her delegation emerged as the most interested in solving the so-called Macedonian question. This is most explainable when one takes into consideration her disputes with the Kingdom of Serbs, Croats, and Slovenes on territories on the eastern Adriatic coast. At one of the sessions of the Commission on the New States and Minorities, the Italian delegation proposed the introduction of administrative autonomy in Vardar Macedonia in view of the fact that the population living there was not Serbian. The same proposal was made with respect to Kosovo and Metohija. Both proposals were rejected. The French delegation declared itself decisively against, while the suggestion of the British was to find out what were the intentions of the Kingdom of the Serbs, Croats, and Slovenes for granting a "certain form of self-government" to the non-Serbian population in these two regions. Its intentions were revealed in a letter of Nicole Pašić, the leader of the delegation of the Kingdom of Serbs, Croats, and Slovenes, to President of the Peace Conference Georges Clemenceau, in which it was said that the population in Macedonia had always been regarded by the Serbian state as Serbian. After the war, it enjoyed the same rights which the other citizens of the kingdom had. What they were like is shown by the fact that in 1919 of the 17,000 policemen in the kingdom 12,000 were in Vardar Macedonia.[10]

Space limitations do not allow the discussion in detail of the subject in which we are interested. But what has so far been said is sufficient to understand some of the most important causes and factors which determined the character of the "peaceful settlement" of relations between the Balkan states by the Paris Conference. By the totality of its inequitable decisions on a number of territorial and other questions concerning the Balkan countries, the conference dealt a blow to the noble idea of understanding and cooperation between the Balkan peoples and states which was the only alternative to the policy of division and enmity pursued by the victorious countries. This idea now again, after World War II, is the sole alternative to the policy of distrust and hostility conducted by some alleged well-wishers of the Balkan peoples. Let us hope that, instructed by experience and inspired by the progressive ideas of the past generations, the Balkan peoples will follow the true road of their relations, the road of mutual understanding, progress and peace.

## NOTES

1.   Centralen durzshaven istoricheski arkhiv, f. 176, op. 3, a. e. 1171, 1. 1.
2.   Public Records Office, London, FO. 371, 3586.
3.   *Ibid.*, 3592.
4.   *Ibid.*, 3586.
5.   *Ibid.*, 3586.
6.   *Ibid.*, 3587.
7.   *Ibid.*, 3583.
8.   *Ibid.*, 3583.
9.   *Ibid.*, Khristo Khristov, "Bulgariia na Parizhkata konferentsiia za mir priev 1919 g.," *Voenno-Istoricheski Sbornik*, kn. 1, 56.

# STAMBOLIISKI'S BULGARIA
# AND REVOLUTIONARY CHANGE, 1918-1923

John R. Lampe

"Revolution" is an ill-defined word, ironically overused by Western liberals to describe economic change and by East European Marxists for political upheaval. Most scholarly definitions would demand major structural changes in the factors of production and a decisive transfer of political power, revising the existing social structure, in order to apply the word. Such revolutions have been rare, and their replication outside the original location rarer still. The American historian Ivo Banac has rightly called the Russian Revolution a unique phenomenon which could not have been duplicated elsewhere in Eastern Europe after World War I.[1]

The Bulgarian experience after World War I has rarely been seen by scholars as revolutionary. Even the title of the present paper could be taken to mean that between the Communist failure to seize power in 1919 and the violent overthrow of Stamboliiski's Agrarian regime in 1923, by a counter-revolutionary coalition, nothing had occurred of a revolutionary nature in this long interim period. The thrust of this paper will be to argue that it had, not in the sense of a full-scale political and economic revolution but in ways that would inadvertently prepare some of the way for the full-scale Communist revolution of 1944-47 and beyond. These ways were the rise of political intolerance and party programs for unilateral rights to impose change, on the one hand, and the emergence of powerful state leverage and initiative in the economy, on the other.

In order to understand why the Bulgarian Agrarian National Union (BZNS) would be the focus for these changes, we must look beyond the charismatic abilities of its leader, Aleksandur Stamboliiski. And these were formidable personal qualities, they played a major part in the Agrarian pluralities in the several multi-party elections during 1919-23 and in the Agrarian formation of a coalition government in 1919 and a single-party regime the following year. Yet, we must also examine the revolutionary setting of 1917-19 and pay brief attention to why the Narrow Socialist, later Communist, party failed to take the lead as they did in Russia and Hungary. We may then better understand the political and economic initiatives which the Agrarian undertook from 1919 forward.

A useful, comparative approach to Bulgaria's revolutionary turmoil from 1917 to 1919 is to consider why this Balkan country whose experience at the end of the World War I was most like Hungary's and whose Communist party was proportionally larger would fail to follow in the footsteps of the short-lived Hungarian Soviet Republic. Here was the only Balkan state on the Central Powers' losing side as the war came to an end. The civilian and military privations of the last wartime years would, thus, like Hungary's, seem to have been suffered in vain.

Privations reached even the Bulgarian countryside by summer 1918. Urban food shortages had appeared by 1917, prompted by the absence of peasant men at the front, the effectiveness of the army's new directorate in obtaining needed supplies, and the drain of German requisitions, authorized and un-authorized. Housewives demonstrating in the streets and children begging in front of Sofia restaurants led some military units to demand guarantees that their families would be fed before they fought any more.[2] The government's new, more systematic requisitions in the countryside in spring and summer 1918 alienated much of the peasantry, but failed to bring enough food, or even leather for shoes, into the towns. Inflation pushed prices to more than ten times their prewar level. The black market spread, and more housewives' demonstrations followed. On top of everything, bad weather damaged the fall harvest. Only an expensive, emergency purchase of American wheat would prevent widespread starvation in 1919.[3]

Before then, the war had ended for Bulgaria as bitterly as it had for Hungary. By summer 1918, rumors had spread throughout the Bulgarian army, war weary after nearly three years on the Salonika Front, that the terms of the German alliance which kept them in the war would end on September 15.[4] When that date brought only a renewed Allied offensive, the army fell back and began to fall apart. Within a week some 15,000 troops had converged on the rail junction at Radomir, west of Sofia, in hopes of seizing supplies from general staff storehouses. Sentiment for a march on the capital grew spontaneously. This was the well-known Radomir Rebellion, or Soldier's Uprising in current terminology.[5] King Ferdinand released Stamboliiski from prison to quell the uprising, but he, or more accurately his associate Daskalov, was soon leading an advance on Sofia with the proclamation of a republic in hand. Better-armed units of the remaining royal army and several German detachments repulsed the clumsy attack on the capital, but within another week Ferdinand had fled the country. The potential for military soviets on the Russian or Hungarian pattern seemed to have been established. Then an armistice was signed on September 30. The largely peasant army split up, and men returned to their villages as quickly as possible.

Several more enduring similarities to Hungary's experience in the immediate postwar period are nonetheless evident. After the signing of an armistice and Tsar Ferdinand's abdication, the first coalition governments tried to reach over the heads of their victorious neighbors to the Western allies but met with no more success than had Hungary's Count Mihály Károlyi.[6] The Treaty of Neuilly (November 1919), denied Bulgaria not only Macedonia and northern Thrace, as might have been expected, but also most of Dobrudja, and with it one-quarter of the country's prewar wheat acreage. Refugees poured in from these lost territories, totalling over 100,000 by 1920, and 220,000 a few years later. Less territory was lost than in the Hungarian case, but the refugee total was proportionally just as large, 5 percent of the postwar population. Refugees from Macedonia were the largest contingent, they concentrated in the Pirin region near the western border or in the shanty town that sprang up on the western outskirts of Sofia, now swollen to twice its prewar size.[7]

Joining their discontented ranks, often in equally menial occupations, were some 6500 officers of the wartime army.[8] The treaty had reduced all ranks to 20,000 volunteers. Stamboliiski's regime forced out still more officers for political reasons, some from the prewar officer corps who were of Macedonian origin. Hence, the cadre for a nationalistic counterrevolution was already in place at the start of Agrarian rule. Frustration with Stamboliiski's foreign policy would culminate when he signed the Treaty of Nis with Yugoslavia, thereby ratifying Bulgaria's western border in May 1923. Barely one month later, his Macedonian assassins would begin their bloody work by cutting off the hand that had signed the treaty.

The cohesiveness of these counterrevolutionary forces should not be over-estimated. The connections of former junior officers, and still less of the refugees from Macedonia, with the Germanophile generals around the new tsar were limited and uncomfortable, especially in the initial postwar years. (The young Boris was 24 years old in 1918.) Divisions among the irridentist refugees from Macedonia were still deeper and more bitter.[9] "Another Macedonian murder" quickly became a common headline in the Sofia newspapers. In addition to these divisions, the ultranationalist ranks lacked the sanctuary entirely outside the control of the ruling Agrarian regime which southern Hungary, under Yugoslav occupation (read the Serbian army) until 1921, had furnished to the opponents of Béla Kun's Soviet Republic. There would be no Serbian sanctuary for any Bulgarian group seeking to re-acquire Macedonia.

The Bulgarian Communist party (BKP) would face no significant internal divisions and attracted members in most major towns. Its Narrow Socialist predecessor had adopted that name at its May congress in 1919 at least partly in response to the proclamation of the Hungarian Soviet Republic. Its membership had risen past 21,000 by that time and would peak at 39,000 in 1923, a larger proportion of the population than the Hungarian party had ever achieved.[10] Its trade-union membership fell short of half of the Hungarian party's but amounted to 32,000. A majority of these union members, if not of the party itself, belonged to an industrial proletariat which had more than tripled since 1911 to reach 55,000 by 1921. Perhaps one-third of that number was concentrated in Sofia itself.[11]

Despite larger in size than its Hungarian counterpart and far longer in existence as a party espousing Bolshevik principles, the BKP would labor under several handicaps during the early postwar period. No cache of abandoned German arms would fall into its hands, like the 35,000 rifles which Kun's followers had acquired with Bolshevik financial aid during the withdrawal of German General August von Mackensen's army through Hungarian territory in late 1918. The only significant quantity of foreign weapons brought to Bulgarian territory would come with some 20,000 men of the White Russian General Piotr Nikaleievich Wrangel's forces after the Red Army had expelled them from the Crimea in late 1920. They would retain their 25,000 rifles, in the face of repeated Communist protests, until April 1922. Then Stamboliiski himself decided that these displaced units constituted a threat to his own Agrarian regime and largely disarmed them. The reaction of the Communist leadership, however, was overconfidence. They drew a dubious parallel to the Russian Revolution and comforted themselves until late 1922 with the notion that Bulgaria's "Aleksandr Kerenskii" (i. e. Stamboliiski) had barely prevented a Kornilov-like *coup d'état*.[12] He would thereafter, they thought, have to make concessions to them as did Kerenski to the Bolsheviks. But Stamboliiski never considered allowing Red Guards to be formed, let alone to rival his Orange Guards.

In addition to periods of overconfidence and a continuing lack of its own arms, the BKP leadership suffered from what Bulgarian party historians now call *excessive caution*. Western historians have joined them in criticizing the aging party leader Dimitur Blagoev for his reluctance either to push ahead toward a seizure of power, on the one hand, or to conclude some sort of alliance with Stamboliiski's Agrarians, on the other.[13] He had already declined, correctly as it turned out, to support the sort-lived Radomir Rebellion of Bulgarian troops which clumsy leadership and the armistice of September 30, 1918 brought to an end. Let me suggest several other constraints beyond Blagoev himself.

First, the Bolshevik strategy and tactics before the seizure of power in October appear to have had more effect than the seizure itself on the Bulgarian Communists after the war. The Canadian scholar Lucien Karchmar has even suggested that the 1917 February Revolution had a greater impact on the Bulgarian party than did the October Revolution; Bulgarian scholars, however, can point to a post-October upsurge in party confidence and in the effectiveness of Bolshevik propaganda with Bulgarian troops on the Romanian front.[14] This interim period *between* the two revolutions probably made the greatest impact on the Bulgarian party. The Bolshevik leadership itself, less Leninist than others, pursued cautious tactics through the summer of 1917, while maintaining an intransigent strategy against any cooperation with the regime or the other political parties.

In any case, the war's end did not leave Russian POWs inside Bulgaria to spread the faith, as did some of the 124,000 prisoners left from the tsarist armies in Hungary. Nor, more importantly, were there any significant numbers of Bulgarian POWs returning from revolutionary Russia in the fashion which had brought Béla Kun and his strongest supporters into Hungary. The only large number of Bulgarian POWs, by late 1918, found themselves in Serbian camps in southern Hungary. Some did escape but to the north, where they joined Kun's short-lived regime in 1919. Inside Bulgaria, the BKP announced plans to send volunteers to Budapest to join an International Red Army, but nothing came of it by the time Kun and his inner circle were forced to flee the country.[15]

The much-discussed demise of the Hungarian Soviet Republic made its own contribution to subsequent caution by the BKP. The republic's disintegration in late July, 1919 coincided with the long-planned climax of the BKP's spring and summer demonstrations in the major Bulgarian towns. The demonstrations of July 27 were supposed to be the largest and to lead to the formation of worker's soviets, the prospects for military councils having ended after the Radomir Rebellion and the rapid dissolution of the Bulgarian army. The failure of Kun's fusion with the Socialists and the violent suppression of these Bulgarian demonstrations by the militia of Stamboliiski's Broad Socialist Minister of the Interior Khrustiu Pastukhov, were not so important for the blow they dealt to the BKP disposition to form a coalition with the Broads or the Agrarians, as John Bell has argued.[16] Its disposition was already insufficient. More important was the BKP's turn back to traditional party tactics which the defeat of Kun's apparently well-armed revolution indicated as more prudent.

This turn to more moderate tactics followed not just from the Bolshevik example of caution in mid-1917, but also from the relatively greater experience with legal party politics and openly operating institutions in Bulgaria than in Russia, and perhaps, in Hungary, too, if prewar Socialist activity is considered. The brief, perilous existence of Russia's prewar parties, the limits on their legal publications, and the obstacles to formal trade unions are well known, if never explicitly compared by Bulgarian scholars to their own experience with more open activity. The major Narrow Socialist leaders had after all remained members of the *Subranie* throughout the war years. The lack of legal experience for all parties would make it easier for the Bolsheviks to attract supporters across party lines and in unparliamentary institutions like the Soviets in 1917.[17] The new BKP continued, after 1918, to think in Narrow-Socialist terms of approaching power by expanding party membership and the local party organizations and of attracting more members to the party's trade unions.

The growth in these numbers and in the number of legal party newspapers sold were impressive but were not signs of impending victory through becoming the largest of the competing parties. The revolutionary rhetoric and the red newsprint used in party papers in BKP's renewed propaganda offense in fall 1919 obscure the fact that the party was not reaching out for mass support beyond those who were ready to be incorporated as full members. Like the Bolshevik leadership during the workers' demonstrations demanding revolutionary action during the "July days" of 1917 in Petrograd, the party leadership was taken by surprise at the wildcat strike of transport workers in late December. The leaders at first declined to join the strike committee because a majority of railway unionists were not party members, and then, called a general strike which they abandoned within one week.[18] They made no noticeable efforts to form soviets or any other extra-party organizations at the time.

The substantial Bulgarian experience with party organization did not, however, include any constructive tradition of coalitions with, or even tolerance, of opposing parties. Tsar Ferdinand's various coalition governments of ruling party leaders before the war had been in part designed to split and weaken their own parties. In large measure, these tactics had succeeded.[19] The three radical parties, the Agrarian and the Broad and Narrow Socialists, had abhorred coalitions from the start. The emotionally charged atmosphere in postwar Bulgaria only fed their intolerance for one other, was well as for the old parties. Any of them that might have won the initial postwar elections, held in the old multiparty framework, would have wanted one party government. Stamboliiski used his chance to begin making revolutionary political changes, from above if with an electoral mandate.

Before turning to the several revolutionary initiatives of the Agrarian regime, let us set aside any notion that Stamboliiski enjoyed a serious opporunity to form a coalition with the BKP or the Broad Socialists in 1919 or afterward, on the pattern that would predominate in the Scandinavian countries. Joseph Rothschild has joined many postwar Bulgarian historians in lamenting the failure of the BKP to combine forces with the Agrarians.[20] John Bell has expressed similar regret over the inability of the Broads and the Agrarians to form a coalition government. Both these American historians place most of the blame on the Socialist side. The present writer finds the Agrarians equally intractable. Bell's biography of Stamboliiski rightly identifies his famous offer of a partnership to the BKP following the August, 1919 election as an offer designed to be refused. Refusal would win support from the hostile Western Powers, and thereby make a solely Agrarian regime more palatable to some of its Bulgarian opponents. The Agrarians subsequent offer to the Broads may have been more genuine, as Bell argues, but the three ministries offered and refused (war, commerce, and finance) lacked any political leverage.[21] Most powerful politically was the Interior Ministry, already held by the Broad leader Pastukhov, and the Ministry of Railway and Communications. Stamboliiski turned instead to two much smaller, more moderate parties to form his first government.

An increase in the Agrarian share of the vote from 28 to 38 percent combined with Stamboliiski's invalidation of 13 of the 229 deputies elected to the *Subranie* in late March 1920, to allow the formation of a one-party government. Stamboliiski himself was war and finance minister, as well as prime minister. He was 41, and the average age of his fellow Agrarian cabinet members was about the same. Although not as young as Béla Kun and his Hungarian associates, they did represent a new generation in Bulgarian politics. And their accession to one-party rule in 1920 marked the first of two decisive transfers of power in the political history of modern Bulgaria.

Marxist historians writing in postwar Bulgaria, in the wake of the second transfer, the Communist accession to power, were initially reluctant to recognize the Agrarians' revolutionary initiatives. Only the so-called left-wing Agrarians led by Raiko Daskalov were credited with plans to transfer power away from the urban bourgeoisie and bureaucracy. Blagoev's old suspicions of Stamboliiski as the representative of a small peasant minority of large property owners lived on, but not forever. Recent Bulgarian scholarship now gives Stamboliiski and the main stream of his party much more credit.[22] These works, nonetheless, continue to neglect the precedents for one-party rule set under Stamboliiski. They were his primary political legacy to Bulgaria since World War II.

What were these precedents? The first was virtually his first act in power in fall 1919: the arrest of members of the last long-term wartime cabinet under Tsar Ferdinand. Stamboliiski was at the same time compelled to sign the punitive Allied peace treaty of Neuilly, so the arrests afforded some political compensation. For a number of weeks, however, Stamboliiski also entertained the idea, strongly put forward by the BKP, of trying these men before "peoples' courts," especially convened outside the existing legal system.[23] The Agrarian regime rejected this last approach in November, leaving it to the post-1944 Communist regime to implement with a vengence.

The Agrarians did, however, go ahead with plans to restructure the country's educational system. The greatest permanent accomplishments of Minister of Education Stoian Omarchevski, were probably the construction of some 1100 new rural schools, 800 of them for the extra three years of compulsory primary education now added to the already existing four of instruction,, and the emphasis on practical, especially agricultural education from the primary through the university level. Faculties of agronomy and veterinary medicine were initiated at Sofia University. More important politically were Omarchevski's efforts to purge leading political figures from the university's faculties if they held public office. Several opposition members were actually dismissed. These measures plus a proposed spelling reform infuriated much of the existing academic community, even leading to a student and faculty strike at Sofia University in 1922.[24] But, the idea of a regime's right to enlist the educational system in implementing its political program had been introduced.

Stamboliiski also took advantage of Tsar Ferdinand's departure and the young Boris' initial weakness to place the army under the direct control of the civilian government, rather than under the tsar. The Minister of War was now a civilian loyal to the prime minister of the elected regime rather than an army general loyal to the tsar. Indeed, as already noted, Stamboliiski was his own minister of war from 1920 forward. The army was in any case limited by the Treaty of Neuilly to 20,000 volunteers, a modest figure not even met during the Agrarian era. The Agrarians' Orange Guards, although armed only with clubs, formed a paramilitary body larger than the 10,000-man state militia also authorized by the treaty.[25] Todor Alexandrov's armed irregulars – the IMRO – exceeded 9000. Other IMRO factions and the Communist and Broad trade unions also established their versions of paramilitary organizations. By 1922, the gathering opposition of the right to Stamboliiski sent some of its youth to Mussolini's Italy for counterrevoltionary training. Even before then, the Bulgarian army had lost its military monopoly to a variety of groups ready to use their militias to defend themselves if out of power and to advance the regime's interests if in power. The army would regain its monopoly in the 1930s only by becoming the same sort of political instrument.

What the Agrarian Union had launched, more than any other group because they alone were actually in power between 1919 and 1923, was a series of measures to substitute its own authority for that of the *Subranie* or the state bureaucracy. Its attraction to the "unity of state power" may be seen in Stamboliiski's several efforts to bypass established channels and checks on executive authority.[26] These involved the supervision of local schools by parents (read local Agrarian members), the creation of the Orange Guard through the BZNS local organizations, and the implementation of land and agricultural reforms through Agrarians' cooperative network.

The internal opposition generated by a number of Stamboliiski's domestic and foreign policies did not subside, but rather increased, in intensity from 1919 to 1923. Such opposition only encouraged Stamboliiski to expand his regime's unchecked executive authority wherever possible. The same perception of dangerous internal opposition after 1944 would allow the Communist regime to build on a precedent already established by Stamboliiski in Bulgarian political culture. That was to replace the previous parliamentary and legal framework, not fully honored by previous regimes since 1934 anyway, with a new one built around a single party's right to represent the national interest.

Stamboliiski's economic policies strengthened the place of the state, however structured, and in a more permanent way. These policies were more fully implemented than any changes in political structure while the Agrarians were in power and remained largely in force under the anti-Agrarian regimes which succeeded them. The subsequent, avidly counterrevolutionary regimes would pretend that the Stamboliiski era had never occurred. Interwar-Bulgarian scholarship would say relatively little about the Agrarians' economic initiatives. Although they remained in place or were soon revived, these initiatives generally represented control from above rather than reform from below. Such direction from the central government downward has hardly been alien to the revolutionary experience of Eastern Europe.

The Agrarians' economic policies were more carefully prepared and systematically implemented than Western observers used to appreciate. John Bell has identified the political bias of long-standard Western sources on the land reform of 1920. Whereas such sources called the reform hasty, ill-prepared, and irrationally ruthless, Bell has offered convincing evidence that the redistribution of those relatively few properties over 30 hectares was carefully prepared over a six month period.[27] The final measure provided a number of exceptions to the 30 hectare maximum where export crops were concerned and afforded former private owners partial compensation. The state was, in fact, the owner of two-thirds of the land redistributed (and that was only 4 percent of the cultivated total). In partial response to the reform, peasants increased their cultivation of crops. Fallowland fell back to the prewar proportion of the cultivated total.[28] The consolidation of separate strips into continuous fields, desired as a consequence of the reform, however, did not occur. This rational economic aim had nonetheless been important to Stamboliiski, perhaps as much as the notion of limiting holdings to "labor property", that is, to what land one family could work. It was this commitment to the preservation of private property for all peasant smallholders for which Stamboliiski's agricultural policy is most widely remembered. The commitment to improving agricultural productivity and tying those gains to exports and industry is often forgotten. Yet, it is there to see, not only in the desire for consolidation but also in the already noted commitment to modern agricultural education.

Unlike his land and educational reforms, Stamboliiski's other economic policies rested on enduring, institutionalized state controls, not on legislative initiatives which would then allow private smallholders and local school boards to lead the way.   The first of these other policies was the abortive Grain Consortium of 1920–21.[29] The Agrarian regime established the consortium in November 1919, with funds from the major state banks. It was to collect subsequent grain harvests in "centrals" of the sort set up during World War I. Now, however, the state price would exceed that offered by the private market. The consortium would then act as an export monopoly to recapture Bulgaria's prewar markets at prices more favorable than the glutted postwar market would otherwise afford. Profits were initially intended to go mainly toward the state's construction of elevators needed for grain storage. Pressure on the Allied Reparations Commission by private grain traders and the continuing wheat surplus on world markets combined to force Stamboliiski to abandon the consortium by the end of 1921. Yet, the precedent had been set for *Hranoiznos*, the export and eventually sales monopoly for grain and then other foodstuffs. Founded in 1930, its major growth during the war years left *Hranoiznos* in place by 1944 to facilitate rapid control of agricultural trade.[30]

Another precedent for the interwar and post-1944 periods followed from the institution of compulsory labor service. From 1920 forward, all males reaching 20 years old were drafted as *trudovaki* into uniformed labor battalions for one year's service. Some 30,000 were assembled for 1921. Viewed by contemporary Western observers as merely a device to circumvent the treaty limits on a standing army, the service was something else to Stamboliiski. He saw it as a way to instill public-spirited discipline and as an institution to provide agricultural or industrial training.[31] Although its members were cut by one-third after Stamboliiski's overthrow, the service continued to build bridges, roads, railway lines, and even factories into the 1930s. Since 1944, its activities and emphasis on training have been taken over by the army and by high school student obligations for summer service.

The third institution crucial to Stamboliiski's economic policy was neither established by his Agrarian regime nor would it be much used by the Communist government since 1944. This was the credit network composed of largely rural cooperatives but headed by the *Bulgarska Zemedelska Banka*, the Bulgarian Agricultural Bank. This bank had been founded in 1903 as an autonomous state institution from a series of existing rural savings banks. It was already the second largest Bulgarian bank in terms of assets before the war.[32] But afterward, under the auspices of the Agrarian regime, it became the largest. Its loans soon tripled the amount of credit extended by the central bank. Stamboliiski's prewar leadership had already pushed the number of Agrarian credit cooperatives past 800 by 1912. By 1922, the total reached 1200. Some 40 percent of the Agricultural Bank loans funneled to peasants through these cooperatives were directed toward better seed selection, use of artificial fertilizer, and irrigation.[33] The construction of several electric power plants received some long-term credit. Otherwise, mortgage loans from this network remained scarce. Loans to the cooperatives were not coordinated by the Agricultural Bank to pursue any policy of planned development.

The network was nonetheless the most impressive in southeastern Europe and continued to grow throughout the interwar period. By the 1930s, its leverage in granting what credit was available during the depression pushed more and more peasants into the cooperatives. Perhaps 50 producers cooperatives had also grown up by the outbreak of World War II. The postwar Communist regime would use the existing cooperative network only briefly to facilitate control of agricultural trade, and discard the Agricultural Bank in creating its own network of collective farms on the Soviet model.

A final word should be said about Stamboliiski's policy toward modern industrial development. Bulgarian industry would not of course receive enough capital and labor from the country's largely agricultural economy to begin modern development until the Communist era. Stamboliiski himself could not have foreseen the numbers of the Bulgarian peasantry falling behind the total for industrial workers. According to his notion of class-based parties (or more accurately parties based on occupational strata) would make the Agrarians a minority party. But, he did not object to a Communist party representing existing industrial workers as long as its leadership came from the workers' ranks. Nor did he oppose modern industry *per se*.

His brief regime promoted not only industrial cooperatives, but also other manufacturing, especially if food or other agricultural processing were involved.[34] Prewar legislation affording tax and import tariff exemptions to manufacturers beyond a minimum size was renewed under Agrarian auspices. The peace treaty banned any new protective tariffs, but Stamboliiski instituted coefficients of currency depreciation which at least maintained prewar tariffs at their original *ad-valorem* levels in postwar leva.

Although Bulgaria's Industrial Revolution would come later, the relatively rapid growth of the country's small industrial sector throughout the interwar period did begin during the Agrarian regime. Stamboliiski approved of such growth and even of the phenomenon of cartels, as he had before World War I, as long as state control was sufficient. Here, as in all other areas of economic policy except land and some educational reforms, his inclination was to rely on the power of the central government rather than private self-interest to solve economic problems and to reshape society. In this and in its unwillingness to collaborate with other political parties, Stamboliiski's postwar regime set neglected precedents for the more sweeping and enduring set of revolutionary changes which the BKP would implement when Bulgaria faced the turmoil of a second postwar period in a generation.

## NOTES

1. Ivo Banac, "The Emergence of Communism in East Central Europe, 1918–1921," in Banac, ed., *The Effects of World War I: The Class War after the Great War: The Rise of Communist Parties in East Central Europe, 1918–1921*, vol. XIII in *War and Society in East Central Europe* (New York, 1983), p. 3.

2. On the economic privations of the later war years, see, Richard J. Crampton, *Bulgaria, 1878–1918 A History* (New York, 1983), pp. 457–67, 500–503.

3. John R. Lampe and Marvin R. Jackson, *Balkan Economic History, 1550–1950: From Imperial Borderlands to Developing Nations* (Bloomington, Indiana, 1982), pp. 377–82.

4. Khristo Khristov, *Revolutsionnata kriza v Bulgariia prez 1918–1919* (Sofia, 1957), pp. 217–32, describes the various mutinies below the division level which broke out during 1918. Most were led by Agrarian or Narrow Socialist party members.

5. For brief accounts, see John W. Bell, *Peasants in Power: Alexander Stamboliski and the Bulgarian Agrarian National Union: 1899–1923* (Princeton, N. J., 1977), pp. 130–39; Joseph Rothschild, *The Communist Party of Bulgaria: Origins and Development, 1883–1936,* (New York, 1959), pp. 78–82, a longer, Bulgarian account is Khristov, *Revolutsionnata kriza*, pp. 250–323.

6. Milen Kumanov, "On the Problem of the Balkan Policy of Bulgaria, October 1918–October, 1919", *Études historiques*, X (1980), 229–42.

7. A satisfactory monograph on the refugee population in postwar Sofia remains to be written. On postwar Budapest, see, István Mócsy, *The Effects of World War I. The Uprooted: Hungarian Refugees and their Impact on Hungary's Domestic Policies, 1918–1921* (New York, 1984).

8. Bell, *Peasants in Power*, p. 208.

9. The IMRO guerilla units of Todor Alexandrov, numbering some 9,000 men by 1923, held sway in the Pirin region, but in Sofia the Internal Macedonian Revolutionary Organization was divided into several factions. On Alexandrov, see, Ivo Banac, *The National Question in Yugoslavia. Origins, History, Politics* (Ithaca, N. Y., 1984), pp. 321–25.

10. Rothschild, *Communist Party of Bulgaria*, pp. 81, 101; Joseph Rothschild, *East Central Europe Between the Two Wars* (Seattle, Wash., 1974), p. 143.

11. John R. Lampe, "Interwar Sofia versus the Nazi-style Garden City: The Struggle over the Muesmann Plan", *Journal of Urban History*, vol. 11, no. 1 (Nov., 1984), 40–46.

12. Rothschild, *Communist Party of Bulgaria*, p. 103.

13. *Ibid.*, p. 108.

14. Lucien Karchmar, "Communism in Bulgaria, 1918–1921", in Banac, ed., *Rise of Communist Parties*, pp. 237–39; Stoiko Kolev, "bulgarskata istoricheska nauka za otnoshenieto na BZNS kum Februarskata i Oktomvriiskata revolutsiia", *Izvestiia na instituta po istoriia na BKP*, 50 (1983), 107–110; Aleksandur Velev, "Idei velikoi oktiabrskoi sotsialisticheskoi revolutsii i BZNS (1917–1923)", *Études Historiques*, X (1980), 197–228.

15. Stela Dimitrova, "Otzvukut na ungarskata revolutsiia ot 1919g. sred bulgarskata revolutsionno dvizhenie", *Izvestiia na instituta po istoriia na BKP*, 6 (1959), 282–89.

16. Bell, *Peasants in Power*, pp. 148–150.

17. For a brief, balanced overview on the Bolsheviks and the role of the Russian Soviets in 1917, see, Sheila Fitzpatrick, *The Russian Revolution, 1917–1932* (New York, 1984), pp. 34–60. For a detailed study, see Alexander Rabinowitch, *The Bolsheviks Come to Power: The Revolution of 1917 in Petrograd* (New York, 1976).

18. Karchmar, "Bulgarian Communist Party", pp. 249–257; Dr. Kodzheikov *et al.*, *Organizatsiia i borbi na transpornite rabotnitsi v Bulgariia, 1878–1944* (Sofia, 1962), pp. 158–207.

19. See, Crampton, *Bulgaria, 1878–1918*, and Stephen Constant, *Foxy Ferdinand, Tsar of Bulgaria* (New York, 1980).

20. "Lenin would have seized the chance" of a coalition with agrarians, posits Rothschild, *Communist Party of Bulgaria*, pp. 82–83.

21. Bell, *Peasants in Power*, pp. 143–46. The latter regime would indeed have brought into the government a number of state employees, bureaucrats as well as railway workers who belonged to the Broads.

22. See the collection of commemorative essays, *Aleksandur Stamboliiski. Zhivot, delo i zaveti* (Sofia, 1980), especially Khristo Khristov, "Aleksandur Stamboliiski v novata i nai-novata istoriia na Bulgariia", pp. 21–63.

23. Bell, *Peasants in Power*, p. 147.

24. *Ibid.*, pp. 176–80; Efrem Karanfilov, "Aleksandur Stamboliiski i kulturata", *Aleksandur Stamboliiski*, pp. 154–68.

25. Bell, *Peasants in Power*, pp. 149, 161, 213.

26. *Ibid.*, pp. 181–183; Aleksandur Velev, *Glavni reformi na zemedelskoto pravitelstvo* (Sofia, 1977).

27. Bell, *Peasants in Power*, pp. 162–67.

28. On postwar agricultural conditions, see Louis G. Michael, *The Cereal Crop Situation in Bulgaria*, T. B. no. 25, U. S. Dept. of Agriculture (Wash., D. C., 1923), pp. 7–10; Michael, *Agricultural Survey of Europe, Danubian Basin*, Part 2, T. B. no. 126, U. S. Dept. of Agriculture (Wash., D. C., 1929), pp. 93–98.

29. The following account is drawn largely from John R. Lampe, *The Bulgarian Economy in the 20th Century*, forthcoming from Croom-Helm Ltd. (London, 1985), chapter 2.

30. See, *ibid.*, chapters 3–5.

31. The standard source remains Max Lazard, *Compulsory Labor Service in Bulgaria* (Geneva, 1922), also see, Bell, *Peasants in Power*, pp. 171–76.

32. Lampe and Jackson, *Balkan Economic History, 1550–1950*, pp. 197–200.

33. *Ibid.*, pp. 351–74, 396–97; J. S. Moloff, "Bulgarian Agriculture", in O. S. Morgan, ed., *Agricultural Systems of Europe* (1933), (New York, 1969), pp. 69–79.

34. Nikolai Todorov *et al.*, *Stopanska istoriia na Bulgariia, 681–1981* (Sofia, 1981), p. 328.

# THE SIGNIFICANCE AND PLACE OF
# THE SLOVAK SOVIET REPUBLIC IN THE HISTORY
# OF CZECHOSLOVAKIA*

Martin Vietor

The authority of the Hungarian state had declined to a large extent by the beginning of 1919. Peasants turned soldiers had returned to their fields. The Károlyi government had decided to disperse the army; the corps of generals and staff officers were forced to resign; and, beginning in March, the bulk of the officer corps was dismissed. The noncoms and troops could remain within the ranks of the army only if they volunteered for guard duty, the essential function of which was to maintain law and order and repress the Communist movement. No longer were there any combat worthy, larger units. Thus, the Hungarian government was not in a position to organize serious armed resistance to Serbian, Romanian, and Czechoslovakian troops advancing along the demarcation lines.

Hence, without arms the Hungarian government had to confront the political and military pressures applied by the successor states, moreover, it was forced to carry out instructions handed down by the head of the Entente mission, Lt.-Col. Fernand Vix, who more than once threatened to occupy Hungary with Serbian and Czechoslovak troops. Károlyi miscalculated when he counted on France's political support. In fact, for all practical purposes, it was the French who became Hungary's political overlords. From Paris' point of view, it was to its advantage that the Hungarian liberal-democratic revolution should drift increasingly leftward, because the promised land reform, persecution of monarchists, censorship of the press, and especially, the rapid disintegration of the army served only to strengthen the position of the French army, whose goal was to occupy Hungary with four to five divisions. In spite

* Copyright © Martin Vietor. Reprinted from László Kővágó, ed., *A Tanácsköztársaság és szomszédaink* (Budapest, 1979), 195–245, with the permission of Slovenská Literárna Agentúra.

of this, only a single brigade appeared in Budapest,while the rest of the French troops were stationed in Belgrade. Thus, the Hungarian liberal-democratic revolution and its attendant political consequences bolstered the interests of already exhausted French forces rather well. For the unexpectedly smooth acceptance of the armistice conditions on the part of the Hungarians, in Belgrade, enabled the French army command to occupy with its troops the border regions of Romania, Serbia, and Hungary, and thereby control the isolated Mackensen army.[1]

The Hungarian government covered up its own weakness by adopting a ruthless stand against the newly formed Communist Party of Hungary, and by exacerbating irredentist propaganda in Slovakia.[2] Police measures initiated against the workers in Hungary, however, were doomed to failure from the start, as were the activities in Slovakia, which were intended to defend the integrity of historical Hungary.

The Czechoslovakian government and its Slovak representative, Dr. Vavro Šrobar, meant to thwart the "Bolshevik peril" and Hungarian irredentism by means of countermeasures. Whether these, outside influence notwithstanding, were appropriate or not is another issue here. The political system introduced in Slovakia in February 1919 had to carry out the following goals, mainly with the help of gendarmes and through its own agencies: one, keep an eye on the Bolsheviks and the workers' movement in general in other words, on strikes, social demands, and "the causes of all these phenomena"; two, put under surveillance the leaders and officials of workers' organizations; three, monitor the general mood of the population, with special regard to the availability of basic commodities and to the consequences of a deficient system of supplies; four, keep track of the activities and connections of politically unreliable elements, furthermore, investigate the sources of illegal leaflets and the underground press; five, assess the reliability of civil servants and railroadmen who remained in the service of the Czechoslovak state, from a national point of view – particularly the reliability of the police agencies.[3]

Thus, activities of the revolutionary workers' movement were of top priority, difficulties in supplies and the growing dissatisfaction among the people came next, and impact of Hungarian irredentism from within and-out was last. Undoubtedly, the flyers printed by the Communist Party of Hungary were smuggled into Slovakia and distributed in large numbers.[4] Also obvious, the number of strikes was on the increase.[5] Šrobar applied the same measures that the former minister initiated in Slovakia. Those Hungarians and Slovaks suspected of the "Bolshevik way of thinking," were interned in camps. These measures were to assume greater importance after the introduction of the military dictatorship and the formation of the Hungarian Soviet Republic.[6] Yet, in spite of this, the spontaneous workers movement continued to grow. And, after the halt of traffic over the Danube bridges[7] and the occupation by several military units of the demarcation line, acts of sabotage in the rear of the Czech army, and in all of southern Slovakia, became increasingly frequent.[8]

The Hungarian national movement gathered momentum, too. Leaflets were distributed, demonstrations organized, by word of mouth propaganda spread.[9] In the course of interning representatives of the Hungarian professional class — the carriers of irredentist ideas — large numbers of Jewish citizens were imprisoned as well, often merely as victims of anti-Semitism, but also because of their national unreliability.[10] Those Hungarian officials not accepted into Czechoslovak state service were barred from entering the cities of Slovakia by the military and by the gendarmery.[11]

Dissatisfaction also spread among Slovak peasants and middle class. In addition to the deficiencies in the supply of basic goods, and the lack of welfare, insensitive "Czechoslovakianism" and crude Czech chauvinism exhibited by inadequately trained Czech officials, civil servants, and noncommissioned officers, who, under the guise of struggle against the "pro-Magyars and Bolsheviks," grossly underestimated, or blatantly disregarded, Slovak national interests. The use of Slovak in official transactions was paternally conceded by the Council of Ministers on the grounds that "the Slovak language must be considered a dialect of the Czech."[12] In short the state administration had not yet been stabilized. In some sectors, it woefully lacked competent specialists, and as the Slovak applicants did not meet the expectations of the Czech bureaucrats, personnel from Bohemia, who did not have the prescribed training, were transferred to Slovakia, a fact which naturally elicited opposition and disappointment among the Slovaks. Frequent clashes in jurisdiction, lack of coordination between the areas of competence of civil and military authorities further complicated matters, and thereby, enhanced the distrust and bitterness of the Slovak population.[13]

Hence the situation in Slovakia at the time of the proclamation of the Hungarian Soviet Republic evolved in conflicting ways. Dissatisfaction was instinctive among the workers, the unemployed, and the soldiers, and political considerations played no part. The peasants were awaiting the implementation of the land reform. The Hungarian population, including the peasants, followed events in Hungary with increasing interest and sanguine hopes. The dissatisfaction of the Slovak nation as a whole derived from the fact that the official agencies neglected Slovak national demands. If we want to assess whether the situation was objectively ripe for the liberal-democratic revolution to turn into a Socialist revolution, we must take the following into consideration: the urban proletariat, which formed the Social Democratic party, was numerically not very strong, could not have resolved the tasks of the revolution without the support of the peasantry, even if it had been able to liberate itself from the Social Democratic influence and form a revolutionary party with a revolutionary program. The potentially revolutionary forces of the peasantry were paralyzed throughout Slovakia by promises of land reform. Even if the workers had been adequately armed (of course, the arms at the disposal of the workers' councils were insufficient), they would have needed to win over the army in order to carry out a successful uprising. But such an opportunity arose only when the Czech army launched an interventionist attack against the Hungarian Soviet Republic and the Hungarian Red Army went on the counteroffensive. Yet, dissatisfaction was not directed against the Czechoslovakian state. Its manifestations and symptoms derived from the domestic policy strictures of the postwar period, and awaited internal solutions. Its consequences were mitigated by the positive stand public opinion took as to the independence of Czechoslovakia.

The "Vix note" of March 20, 1919 which led to the proclamation of the Hungarian Soviet Republic, came about as a result of the Romanian military situation. The Ukraine and Bessarabia were in the hands of the Russian Red Army, and heavy fighting was taking place in Bukovina and Moldavia. Romanian villages were opposed to the government, Communist groups were gaining in strength, the reliability of the troops was highly questionable. The French intended to occupy a new strip of territory along the Tisza, which the Hungarians were expected to evacuate; by assuming these new positions, the Entente troops would prevent an eventual junction of Hungary with the "Bolshevized" East.[14]

The note's repercussions came as a surprise, first and foremost, to Vix himself. For, he, as well as the representatives of the Entente powers in Budapest, understood too late that Károlyi and his cabinet had used the new Entente demands to resign voluntarily, out of patriotism, and to be absolved from any further responsibility, once power had been transferred into the hands of the Hungarian proletarian government, without bloodshed. In March 1919, the situation of the Károlyi government had become untenable. The recently formed Communist party had been able to win the trust of the majority of workers, even in the provinces, where peasants confronted landlords, and agricultural workers kulaks. The Vix note, offensive to Hungarian national sentiment, elicited great bitterness and patriotic resistance. This bitterness was sufficient in itself to make the majority of Hungarians temporarily enthusiastic about joint struggle for Hungarian national interests. Hence, the revolutionary governing council of the Hungarian Soviet Republic assessed the situation very optimistically. It deemed the Entente impotent. There were even rumors to the effect that Vix himself had offered to retract his note in exchange for "re-establishing the status quo"— something the proletarian government rejected, of course. For, Budapest felt the situation in the successor states was likewise favorable, from its own point of view. It assumed that Slovakia had been so permeated by Bolshevism that the Czech bourgeoisie would not be able to maintain control. Moreover, it felt Romania was threatened by the Russian Red Army; that the country was internally debilitated by Bolshevism, and furthermore, that Yugoslavia was preoccupied by its conflict with Italy and the disgruntled Croatians, whereas the Entente was reluctant to send its troops into the Danubian basin.[15]

The Hungarian Soviet Republic's foreign policy was determined by the proletarian character of the state. Its basic element was alliance with Soviet Russia and solidarity with the international workers' movement, including collaboration with the working classes of neighboring states. This collaboration should have taken the form of support for the Communist movements in the successor states. The Hungarian revolutionary government wanted to meet Hungarian national interests and discard the traditional Hungarian policy of territorial integrity at the same time. It intended to live in peace with the Entente powers, primarily for the sake of gaining time to consolidate its power. The latter political concept was realistic as long as the revolutionary council remained aware of the fact that the very existence of the Hungarian Soviet Republic was inseparable from the global evolution of Socialist revolution. Its assessment of the international balance of forces was less realistic, however: particularly the opinion of the Soviet Russian government that the Socialist revolution would soon spread to Germany, Austria, and Czechoslovakia as well.

On March 24, 1919, Béla Kun, in the name of the revolutionary government, addressed a note to the Entente, based on these very same principles. This note was debated at the Peace Conference on March 29, 1919. Béla Kun informed the Entente that the Hungarian proletarian government had no intention of breaking diplomatic relations with them, that it was willing to discuss territorial issues on the basis of the principle of "self-determination of nations," and that it viewed the matter of "territorial integrity strictly from this point of view."[16] It is true that the successor states did not take this declaration seriously, if only because it referred to the right of self-determination of "the people" rather than that of the "nation."

But how did the Entente react? Public opinion in the United States greeted the news of the formation of the Hungarian Soviet Republic with surprise, because the average American man on the street could not conceive of Bolshevism spreading to Central Europe. It felt that the situation could be remedied only by the dispatch of food packages, although the opportunity for so doing had been missed. It was now the general conviction that only a part of Western Europe could still be saved, and that there was little hope of preventing the spread of Bolshevism from countries like Czechoslovakia, Yugoslavia, Poland, and Romania. Washington demanded that the liberal forces at the Peace Conference support the Americans in their endeavor to "arrive at a liberal peace, and thus save the world from reactionary as well as from Bolshevik forces," because the one like the other threatened the world with destruction by "the terror of protracted class struggle." Thus, the American government felt that the Hungarian Soviet regime would have a positive impact on the outcome of the Peace Conference by speeding up its work. American diplomats even expressed views that the events in Hungary were brought about by the joint effort of Germany and Russia. All these were fed by fear, to wit, partly by fear of a Germany that had not surrendered as yet, and partly by the fear of the revolutionary power of Russia, which they were unable to confront effectively. The American army was not sufficiently disciplined and combatworthy. In the United Kingdom, domestic conditions were deteriorating, discontent of the workers and soldiers was on the rise. Americans and British agreed that military moves against Hungary could not be contemplated, or even mentioned, as long as Germany had not accepted the terms of peace.[17]

The French generals reacted differently. Generals Pau and Pétain were of the opinion that the Bolshevik danger was so considerable as to warrant support for the White Guard against Bolshevism. For instance, the French government should supply Denikin's army with German weapons, and should make Germany pay for these weapons.[18] Hence, the fear of Bolshevism was great among the French as well.

Italy pursued yet another set of objectives. After the signing of the Armistice, only French troops were stationed in Hungary (in Budapest and at Szeged), apart from the Danube Control Commission on which England was represented through its own fleet. After the proclamation of the Hungarian Soviet Republic, the English and French military missions left Budapest, and Italy intended to take their place.[19]

In spite of the contradictory interests of the Entente powers, a unified stand evolved at the Peace Conference as to the need to isolate the smoldering fire of revolution in Hungary. While the British and Italians sought economic and political means to achieve this end, the French opted for military intervention, and were supported in this, of course, by the governments of the successor states, intent as they were on securing their territorial demands in a most advantageous manner. Anglo-American endeavors were promoted by a few instances of diplomatic negotiations conducted with the Hungarian revolutionary government.[20]

The Germans expected revolutionary movements in Poland and Czechoslovakia as well, especially if the Entente should fail to meet their demands. For them, Bolshevism was "born out of anger and discontent." They were aware of the vulnerability of Slovakia, namely, the discontent of the Slovaks, the resistance of the large Hungarian minority, as well as of the attraction the working class in Slovakia felt toward the Hungarian Communist regime.[21] The Austrian Social Democratic government endeavored to remain neutral. It rejected the requests of revolutionary Hungary for the transportation of arms on the grounds that Austria was dependent on food supplies from the

Entente, and thus, could not antagonize them. On the other hand, it feared that Budapest would support the Communist movement in Austria, or even foment an uprising there.[22]

Soviet Russia, as we know, welcomed the Hungarian Soviet Republic, which it regarded as the signal for world revolution. The Soviet press intimated that Romania must "transform itself into a Soviet republic," that Poland as an independent state was but an illusion because "the Polish working class will erase the border separating Poland from Russia," and that the Baltic states were also in sympathy with Russia. In late March, the principal Soviet dailies published articles to the effect that the Entente was unable to destroy the revolutionary regime in Hungary by force, because occupation troops were "infected with Bolshevism."

Toward the end of July 1919, Petrograd newspapers were saying that the workers "the world over are convinced of the rightness of the Communist cause," and considered imperialist rule unbearable. The Entente, it alleged, was contributing to the revolutionary movement by "strangling Germany with one arm, threatening Russia with the other" – thus bringing worldwide revolution a step closer. Both Germany and Austria were well along the road of "following the Czech and Slovaks," who were on the verge of splitting up, whereas Slovakia was about to play its role as an "independent Slovak republic." They assessed the position of Soviet Hungary with rose-colored glasses, as if Hungary had the prospect of successfully concluding negotiations with the Entente in the matter of the war with Czechoslovakia and Romania.[23] Such, and similar, news reports served first of all internal ends, but, at the same time, reflected the official position of the Soviet government and thus, had an influence on political decisions in Hungary.

What was the situation in Slovakia? Šrobar described it as favorable. At a conference (April 11–15, 1919), with the participation of the under secretaries of the Ministry of Slovakia, provincial governors and the representatives of the central government, he referred to the main duty of his office and of the governors as taking forceful measures "against that segment of the population which does not want to reconcile itself to the new relations" – although he explicitly mentioned neither Hungarians nor Communists; moreover, duty impelled them to "undertake the purification of the country from disturbing elements." He threatened the Hungarian worker activists and irredentists with internment and expulsion; he addressed a warning to disgruntled Slovak workers and peasants as well. He spoke in these terms: "The Slovak nation must get accustomed to thinking and acting in a Slovak spirit, and must shed Hungarian feelings completely." This was only the beginning of the myth so often referred to in the future, according to which all Slovak national or social demands had to be stamped as pro-Magyar if they were in opposition to "Czechoslovakism," or to the idea of Czech centralization.

Šrobar saw the way out "in putting an end to unemployment, and in the painstaking cultivation of land to ensure an adequate food supply." Moreover he required the governors to "watch the people, go among the people, and instruct the people." Thus, the situation was not so favorable even among the Slovak population. Slovak dissatisfaction increased not only as a result of inadequate supplies, but also because of the chaotic conditions in the administration. Provincial government offices were not functioning for the most part; in fact, often they had not even been set up, for lack of competent personnel. The means of mass communication so important for the administration of a modern state, such as the postal services, were not functioning either. The aversion to the new government's antidemocratic methods was very strong among the Slovak population, and it only increased as a consequence of the extraordinary measures introduced when the Hungarian Soviet Republic came into being, such as statutory judgments and mobilization, to such an extent that the state did not even dare to hold elections on Slovak territory.

The following was the situation in some branches of the state administration, according to the pertinent government spokesmen:[24]

There was a dire lack of supplies. It was assumed at the beginning, in Bohemia, that Slovakia would export foodstuffs; but it proved most difficult to obtain even the most basic commodities. By the end of April and the beginning of May, wheat had to be requisitioned from the peasants by military force, which resulted in considerable resentment on the part of the village population; all the more so, because even the villages had no hidden reserves, and because a large part of the fields were left fallow. Potatoes were left rotting in the ground because there were no railroad wagons to cart them away. Distribution of gasoline had come to a complete halt.

Hungarian civil servants who had been dismissed were replaced by supervisors brought from Bohemia to administer agriculture. Agricultural workers were awaiting the regulation wages. Lack of veterinarians, unresolved problems of grazing were stumbling blocks to animal husbandry. Land requirements of the legionaires did nothing to curtail the impatience of the peasants, who were awaiting the execution of the already enacted land reform.

Industrial production stagnated for lack of raw materials and fuel. Commodities disappeared from the shops only to reappear on the black market. The numbers of unemployed grew.

The administration worked feebly, if at all. Slovak professionals were lacking, particularly those who could also speak Hungarian. Salaries, given the continuous inflation, were completely inadequate. Some specialists did come from the historical lands (Bohemia and Hungary), but not in sufficient numbers. Only in the counties of Pozsony and Trencsén, Liptó, Sáros, and Turóc did the authorities function effectively. Conditions were the worst in Zemplén, Ung, Hont, and Gömör. In fact in Gömör no one could be appointed to an official post, and even if the governor was able to appoint somebody, the appointee did not receive his official papers and pay. High-level top functionaries were demoralized. The prefect had no vehicle at his disposal, hence he could not visit the districts under his supervision. At the same time, while the counties were being purified of unreliable officials, Hungarian aristocrat landowners and industrialists escaped to Slovakia after the proclamation of the Soviet Republic. Unlike Jewish professionals, who were interned, the Slovak Ministry issued residence permits to these individuals, on the grounds that "they had offered their services against Bolshevism."

The judicial system was also in shambles. Ninety-nine percent of the judges were declared unreliable from a national point of view, yet there was no one to replace them. In this period, Derer was able to appoint 16 Czech judges in all. Only five of the courts were functioning.

The postal services were hampered by the resistance of the Hungarian postal officers, and the fact that the Czech mailmen had no knowledge of the local geography. Railroads to the east of Kassa (Košice) were under military administration because of the military operations in the area of the Carpatho-Ukraine.

The school year ended on May 3, 1919, in those Hungarian schools that had not been taken over, and everywhere there were no Slovak teachers available. Since Hungarian teachers resisted the regime more actively, schools in the southern part of Slovakia were closed down. In theory, the Hungarian teachers were neither certified, nor transferable into Czech state service. Prefects were instructed to encourage them to leave the republic.[25] The solution of the education problem of the Hungarian and German minorities was delayed time and again in Pozsony (Bratislava), Kassa (Košice), and throughout southern Slovakia. The most burning issue was the inadmissibly inadequate pay of Slovak teachers. They received far less than their counterparts in Bohemia and Moravia. Moreover, there was a complete lack of textbooks in Slovak language. Under these extraordinarily difficult circumstances, there could be no question of the flowering of Slovak cultural life.

The health-care situation was likewise not rosy. The supply of drugs broke down. Nor were there enough public hospitals.

Consolidation in Slovakia was most promising in the area of Catholic church reorganization. The bishops of Nitra (Nyitra) and Banská Bystrica (Besztercebánya) had left the republic. Church lands were administered by the curatorium of the diocese. The majority of the priests were willing to take the oath of loyalty.

The prefects rounded out situation reports with their own data, they emphasized that unemployment was on the rise because the factories were not supplied with coal, the main Communist and Hungarian agitators had been removed, interned, or expelled from Czechoslovakia. In spite of this, Micura, the prefect of the county of Bars, reported that at the meeting of the Slovak members of the Hungarian Communist Party held in Budapest on March 27, 1919, there were some participants from Lučenec (Losonc), Nyitra (Nitra), Zsolna (Žilina), and Považska Bystrica (Végbeszterce) – altogether seventeen; these would be expelled from the republic should they attempt to return. The prefects also reported that, as a consequence of the Hungarian events, there were meetings and uprising in the area of Rimavská Sobota (Rimaszombat), especially at Hňúšt'a (Nyustya), where small armed groups were formed for the purpose of carrying out sabotage in the rear of the Czech army. Telephone wires along the railroad line were cut at several points; gendarmes had taken five persons into custody in this connection.[26] Not only Hungarians, but Slovaks as well, were in sympathy with the events of Hungary. This was demonstrated by the above-mentioned incident at Nyustya; moreover, on April 25, after the first counterattack of the Hungarian Red Army in the direction of Rimaszombat, which was beaten back by the Czech forces, the workers gathered in the area of Nyustya with the objective of lending a hand to the Red Army; in fact, the most active Slovak workers had gone over to the Red Army. Prefect Daxner expressed the view that the revolutionary mood of the Slovak population should not be condemned in general nor could it be interpreted simply as a manifestation of a "Hungarian way of thinking." In this connection he wrote to Ivánka; "These people have suffered a lot for their Slovakism; yet now they are abandoned, deprived of everything they need for survival, and at the same time cut off from the world. Neither the transportation system nor the postal services are functioning." Without generalizing, it must be noted that the situation was similar in other Slovak villages, counties, and towns, especially in the ethnically heterogeneous belt, but even elsewhere: for instance, in Krompachy (Korompa), Vrútky (Ruttka), so on and so forth.[27]

When the proletarian government was formed in Hungary, and the broad strata of the nationalistically inclined Hungarian population were imbued with certain expectations, which later found an outlet in strongly nationalist sentiments, this elicited a favorable reaction among the Hungarian minority living in Slovakia, including, of course, the Hungarian workers; but the workers' social and political demands reflected the dissatisfaction of the Slovak workers and unemployed as well, although, to be sure, this dissatisfaction did not assume an antistate character.

The revolutionary government, immediately upon taking power, embarked on the rapid Socialist transformation of the relations of production, of the state apparatus, and of all aspects of social life; under the concentrated pressure of the dictatorship of proletariat based on the Russian model, the wave of nationalism began to subside, as did widespread public support given to the government.

Nationalist forces in Hungary soon realized that the proletarian government had no intention of reoccupying the territories of the successor states; rather, that government meant to lend support to the world revolution, particularly in the neighboring countries, by its ideological impact and by the construction of Socialism. By so doing, it was acting in the spirit of Soviet Russian and of the recently formed Comintern, the goals of which became increasingly manifest even in Hungary's foreign policy at the time. At the beginning of April, Commissar József Pogány expressed this idea at a meeting of the steelworkers: "We must carry the revolution beyond our borders, because the socialist revolution has to be a world revolution." It was in this spirit that the Hungarian revolutionary government was bent, with all its might, on consolidating the regime within the country as quickly as possible, by taking over the means of production in industry, in commerce, and in transportation, and by introducing Soviet-type institutions in all aspects of social life. As regards the neighboring successor states, the revolutionary governing council gave up the demands regarding territorial integrity, while endeavoring to foster closer relations, first of all at the commercial level, in order to contribute to revolutionizing the proletariat of the neighboring countries, thanks to its propaganda. It was intent on avoiding any armed conflict with the Entente powers. By extending diplomatic privileges (the representatives of the Entente enjoyed privileged positions in the Hungarian Soviet Republic), it was temporarily able to thwart direct outside intervention in the domestic affairs of the country, and to parry the constant threat of military intervention. This foreign policy manifested itself, in practice, in an emphasis on friendly relations with Austria and Germany; the Hungarian government, at the same time, took up contact with revolutionary groups – the enemies of the regime – in these very same countries. The diplomatic representatives of the Hungarian Soviet Republic supported the propaganda activities of these groups. The Hungarian press also supported the workers' movement in these countries and sharply criticized the bourgeois regimes in power.

We may assert, in contrast to the one-sided negative assessment to which it has been subjected until now, that the Hungarian revolutionary government did not follow a straight policy line. The Hungarian Communists, particilarly Béla Kun, began deliberately to brake the initial outburst of national enthusiasm, a consequence of the increasingly uncompromising dictates of the Entente, and a key element in the peaceful takeover of power, which Social Democrats and bourgeois circles supported Béla Kun meant to use the Hungarian revolution, in conformity with Lenin's intentions, primarily to construct a proletarian state and a Socialist society, as well as to promote world revolution.

Therefore, Kun strove to convince the representatives of the Entente powers in Budapest that the revolutionary government had no aggressive intentions, and that, moreover, it would be advisable to call a conference of the successor states for the purpose of reaching an agreement on economic and border issues under debate. He wanted to gain time to consolidate the workers' state and establish contact with neighboring countries. The Hungarian Communists laid emphasis on securing the proletarian dictatorship within the country, and on supporting those Communist groups abroad who were set on lighting the torch of revolution. Béla Kun and his companions were Communist internationalists first of all, not Hungarian nationalists. They saw their main duty in adopting Lenin's revolutionary tactics and carrying out, under the prevailing circumstances, the Communist International's resolutions. It remains true, of course, that this position did not exclude in the least conflict with the successor states; on the contrary, it hastened the process.

Hungary's foreign policy was made possible by the Entente decision not to dispatch military units against the Communist regime for the time being. For, as we noted, the Entente did not have combatworthy troops in sufficient numbers at its disposal. For instance, even the American forces refused to assume occupation assignments.[29]

Soviet Russia agreed with the Hungarian revolutionary government that it should concentrate on solving domestic tasks first and thereby secure for itself the time needed for Socialist construction through diplomatic moves. On several occasions, Lenin inquired of Béla Kun whether he had been proceeding according to the Soviet example, and emphasized that this issue was crucial. Kun was undoubtedly aware of Lenin's views regarding the methods of takeover by the proletariat and its initial activities. Before his return from Russia he had the opportunity to become acquainted with these methods first-hand.

Leninist guidelines made allowance for local circumstances.[30] Hence, they applied to Hungary also where the problems of the peasantry were seriously neglected, and the Communist party's leading role even more so. But basic measures, that is, realization of the goals of the proletarian dictatorship in a manner almost identical with the Russian model, began to be realized in the Slovak Republic as well. Under the influence of the Hungarian propaganda, sympathy for the Soviet system grew, especially in southern Slovakia.[31]

The Hungarian revolutionary government's hopes that, after the failure of Western troops in Russia (at Odessa), they would refrain from attacking the Hungarian Soviet Republic proved unwarranted. Nor did the expected world revolution take place. By the end of April the situation at the Peace Conference had become so exacerbated that Wilson was prepared to leave. Hungary ceased to be the focus of attention, and this was precisely the moment to launch a war against the Soviet Republic. The plans of Marshal Ferdinand Foch were realized after April 7, 1919, that is, after Wilson had departed from Paris. Although it is true that the Romanian troops intervention, on

April 16, 1919, was directed by the French general staff, the other Entente powers had tacitly acquiesced.[32] Hence, the Hungarian revolutionary government had misjudged the international situation, and had deluded itself as to the prospects of the proletarian regime in Hungary as well. The sudden attack took it by surprise.

The interventionists counted on the Romanian and Czech armies jointly to encircle the Hungarian Soviet Republic, thereby isolating it from Soviet Russia, and thus pressuring it to surrender. At the end of April, Béla Kun addressed another appeal to Wilson, requesting the American president to "take measures in order to put an immediate halt to all belligerent actions against us." At the same time, he addressed a diplomatic note to the Czechoslovak, Romanian, and Yugoslav governments, stressing that he recognized without reservations their territorial and national claims, that he did not stand fast on the issue of territorial integrity. But, if they should continue the war in spite of this, they would be waging it strictly for alien, imperialist interests, and "primarily in the interest of the Hungarian ruling class."[33] The notes were handed over with some delay, and therefore, had no impact on the course on the war. Both the Romanians and the Czechs stood firm; the issue of the borders belonged within the competence of the Peace Conference, but they sought to occupy the territories awarded them and protect them from Bolshevism until the borders were finally defined.[34]

Once war broke out, the situation of the Hungarian Soviet Republic deteriorated rapidly. Economic difficulties rendered the already critical political situation even more acute. The population was no longer supplied with essential goods; the peasants, squeezed by requisitions, turned against the government. The depots were already empty, and aid from abroad was held up by the blockade. Those plants still in operation produced exclusively for the military. Money had lost all value. The rights of the unions were curtailed. In practice, Communist organizations were fused into Social Democratic institutions. Communists could let their weight be felt only within the governing council where they were outnumbered. The domestic crisis was solved solely by the great, unexpected triumphs of the Hungarian Red Army. Certain foreign policy factors also affected the military situation favorably for Hungary: conflicts between Serbians and Romanians; between Yugoslavia and Italy; the Communist movement in Germany tied down the Entente's forces there. When the Entente rejected the proposal to establish a corridor linking Yugoslavia and Czechoslovakia, the Yugoslav and Czechoslovakian general staffs' war fever began to flag as well. Discipline was particularly lax among Czechoslovak troops, and it was further loosened by Communist propaganda. And in the ranks of the French army stationed along the southern border of Hungary, there were rebellions and a high incidence of absences without leave, so that the Hungarian Red Army had little to worry about an attack from the southern flank. Temporarily, the Hungarian Red Army had the advantage. Its opponents were weak, exhausted, and committed mistakes. But, the advantage was only temporary, because, in spite of the fact that it was better disciplined, and thanks to the reactivation of the officers of the K. u. K., it was also better led, the Red Army could not resist an offensive threatening from three sides. Therefore, it had to break through the front of the interventionists, preferably at its weakest point.[35]

It was only during the first period of the interventionist attack, when the attempt to dislodge the revolutionary government failed, when the Romanian offensive came to a halt, because the Russian Red Army had launched its own offensive in Bessarabia, and when the Czech forces' advance ground to a halt, that the Entente powers once again took up the subject of Hungary. The Hungarian Red Army's unexpected success caused consternation in Paris, the more especially since Italian arms shipments had broken the Entente's blockade. After war broke out, the Entente's military and diplomatic missions left Budapest; a reinforced Italian mission intended to take their place. The Italians offered help in the form of ammunition and food, originally destined for Czechoslovakia, within the framework of an Austro–Czechoslovak agreement, which were then rerouted by the Italian military mission in Vienna to Hungary.[36]

The Czech army's campaign did not unfold as planned. Its mission was to make it impossible for Soviet Hungary to influence the Czech workers' movement, to make good the territorial claims of the bourgeoisie. Already by the end of March, plans for war had been drawn up at the French army's headquarters in Belgrade but, on account of negotiations conducted by Entente representative Christiaan Smuts in Budapest,[37] the timing of the attack was postponed to April 6. When the first Czech attack was held up, scapegoats had to be found. Hungarian–Italian negotiations had been monitored closely by Prague; thus, the Czech government found out about the shipments to Hungary, and about their origin in particular. So it was primarily the Italian military mission in Czechoslovakia that was blamed for defeat at the front.[38]

Looking for sacrifical lambs, however, did not suffice to hold up the impending Hungarian Red Army's counterattack. Civilian and military authorities in Slovakia made efforts to reinforce the hinterland and to preserve law and order in the Czech army's rear. They continued to intern all potential pro-Hungarians and "Bolsheviks." In spite of martial law and strict censorship, spontaneous support for the Red Army kept growing in the southern part of Slovakia, and likewise in some purely Slovak counties, where, because of the mass internment of Communists, disorganized political administration could not contain such sentiment even at the local level.

The prefects dismissed summarily all county officials who had refused to take the oath of allegiance. In the county of Gömör–Kishont, Prefect

Jesensky even went so far as to remove mayors and local judges if he felt they were pro-Hungarian. They searched the homes of those interned for weapons, they introduced registration of a change in address. The prison at Il'ava (Illava) was emptied and transferred to Terezín. Activities of lawful Social Democratic organizations were curtailed in the counties inhabited by Hungarians, while measures against the workers were also introduced in the purely Slovak communities, on the grounds they harbored pro-Hungarian feelings (in Korompa, Trebišov (Tőketerebes), etc.).

Consequently, tension between the Slovak population and the Czech civil service increased. At Nove Mesto (Vágújhely) nad Vahom, the local judge deemed the local Slovak guard unreliable and requested that it be replaced by a Czech unit. In Hont county, it was requested that the Czech police be dispatched to several communities (Lantov (Lontó), Bočovice (Bácsfalu), Pliešovce (Tótpelsőc), Senohradz (Szénavár), etc.) to maintain order. At Zsolna, there were clashes between the Czech troops and the Slovak municipal employees.

Slovak worker opinion found expression in the left-wing press of Bohemia (*Sociálni Demokrat, Sloboda, Rovnost*). In spite of the strict controls imposed by the government, the Communist newspapers (*Vörös Újság, Červené noviny, Armáda Proletařů*) and flyers (in Pieštány (Pöstény), Nyitra, and all over southern and eastern Slovakia) published in Hungary, were illegally disseminated in Slovakia. The mood against intervention spread to the army as well. As we know, there were uprisings of various dimensions in the southwestern areas of Bohemia, in Slovakia, and the Carpatho-Ukraine (Losonc, Levice (Léva), Nové Zamky (Érsekújvár), Komárno (Komárom), Užhorod). Workers' organizations carried on active agitation in Nyitra, Topolčany (Nagytapolcsány), Kežmarok (Késmárk), and Bratislava. More and more telegraph and telephone lines were cut in the army's rear. Acts of sabotage of greater significance were carried out at Érsekújvár, Šurany (Nagysurány), Bajč (Bajcs), and the Komarno area, particularly along railroad lines. These same applied to the areas of Rožňava (Rozsnyó), Dobšiná (Dobsina), Plešivec (Pelsőc), and Tornal'a (Tornallya).[39]

Tension in Slovakia reached its climax when the Red Army penetrated Slovak territory as a result of a counterattack. The retreating Czech army was disintegrating, because, apart from the legionnaires, neither Czech nor Slovak soldiers wanted to fight against the Hungarian proletarian army. The civilian population, primarily the Hungarians of course, but the Slovak workers as well in some instances, turned against the bourgeois government, particularly in areas occupied by the Hungarian Red Army (Érsekújvár, Zvolen (Zólyom), Detva (Gyetva), Prešov (Eperjes), Kassa, Sátoraljaújhely).[40]

The Hungarian Communist' Socialist revolutionary program was proletarian internationalism in the name of which the Hungarian Red Army intended to lend a hand to the proletariat of Slovakia, so that, following the example of the Great October Socialist Revolution and of the Hungarian Soviet Republic, it should seize power for itself. This potential force of attraction was, of course, but one side of the coin. The other side *renewed fire of Hungarian nationalism,* a powerful source of energy, increased manifold the strength of the Red Army with the banner of "liberation of the Hungarian territories," in spite of the internal crisis of the regime.

Yet, the difficulties experienced by the Hungarian proletarian government reached their zenith. At the beginning of June, cables arrived from the president of the Peace Conference, the French Prime-minister Clemenceau. Although the Red Army had fought valiantly, the public supply system fell apart, and the blockade surrounding the country tightened. Famine threatened workers, peasant resistance was on the rise, counterrevolutionary activity became more and more frequent. Hungarian Communists, namely Béla Kun, tried to turn back the tide of national chauvinism, stressing proletarian internationalism instead.[41] The Communists, however, continued to remain a minority in the cabinet, and the Red Army's successes were the sole argument the government was able to muster vis-à-vis the Entente.

But, military successes were not enough to improve a difficult situation. The Entente had succeeded in forcing Germany to sign the peace treaty, and thereby, vanished the ray of hope of Socialist revolution there. Soviet Russia was unable to lend assistance to the Hungarian Red Army. The only item that seemed obtainable in the governments' plan to break through in eastern Slovakia and unite with the advancing Russian Red Army in Galicia was that the Hungarian troops might reach Bártfa (Bardiov), and thereby cut the liaison between the Czechoslovakian and Romanian armies for the time being.

Therefore, circumstances on the whole, favored the Czechoslovaks, on the other hand, the Hungarian Red Army's presence in southern and eastern Slovakia, the tense atmosphere in other parts of Slovakia, moreover the uncertainty regarding the further objectives of the Red Army, finally the protracted diplomatic intervention of the Entente, did contribute neither to overcoming the impotence of the administration in Slovakia nor to halting the disintegration of the state apparatus at all. Further military units were directed from Bohemia and Moravia to the Slovak front; further shipments of weapons and ammunition from Austria were urged; the Ministry of Administration of Slovakia was getting ready to leave Bratislava.[42] The county officials of Zolyom and Nógrád (Markovic, Bazovsky, Fajnor) left for Turčiansky Svätý Martin (Turócszentmárton) with the prefects in the lead.[43] The prefect from Ipoly transferred his seat to Krupina (Korpona) together with the civil servants from Léva. General Šnejdárek ordered the evacuation of the area spreading from Besztercebánya and Zólyom, all the way to Tisovec (Tiszolc). County officials left in the direction of Ružomberok (Rózsahegy), authorities escaped from Zemplén and Abaúj-Torna, as well as from Gömör and Kassa to Liptó and the Szepes area. The evacuation of Spíšská Nová Ves (Igló) was excepted, too, so that civil servants and their families tried to go as far west as possible, all the way to Bratislava and Moravia by way of Zsolna. Refugees scattered in Turóc, Árva, and Trencsén, as well as Moravia, were to be gathered at Uherské Hradišté.

And, the internment of "Bolshevik agents" continued.[44] This, however, did not contribute to an improvement in conditions in the army. The Ministry of Slovakia received alarming news from Czech and Slovak officials. For in the area of Leva, the troops of the 26th reserve infantry battalion "fled en masse," and the Czech police and fiscal agents evacuated the commune of Bátovce (Bát) prematurely. Even the railroadmen were "escaping in panic" from Leva. The commander left Bañská St'avnica (Selmecbánya) along with his troops, without having received orders to that effect; soldiers likewise left Nová Baña (Újbánya). During skirmishes in the vicinity of Pukanec (Bakabánya) a Slovak enlisted man was shot to death: he was "probably an intellectual." Even the legionnaires ran away from Bakabánya. Troops complained about inadequate weapons, the officers about the cowardice of gendarmes. Zlaté Moravce (Aranyosmarót) was defended only by the members of the gymnastic Sokol organization, whereas the military had retreated. The Slovak population of Hronský Sväty Beňadik (Garamszentbenedek) fled into the woods, while the corps of Czech officials, numbering about 60, left the town in the direction of Nagytapolcsány, under the cover of darkness, so that the "population would not prevent them from leaving." Allegedly it was a priest, a certain Buzalka, who obtained vehicles for them at a high price. The Red Army was welcomed only by the Hungarianized population, which belonged largely to the "propertyless strata." Well-to-do Hungarians, as can be expected, "were not enthusiastic." The Slovak population was "depressed and submissive," but only the activists of the "national movement were getting ready to leave." At Ipel'ské Sahy (Ipolyság), civilians shot at the 34th Legionnaire Regiment. The Czech officials departed, alongside the legionnaires, in the direction of Bratislava. The gendarmes had left Slovenská L'upča (Zólyomlipcse) already at the beginning of June. At the approach of the Red Army, they left the communes of Očová (Nagyócsa) and Dobrá Niva (Labonya), as well as the towns of Selmecbánya and Hronská Breznica (Garamberzence). Elsewhere, in Zólyom for instance, they were terrorizing the population: nine male hostages were shot to death or hanged. The miners and workers of Dobsina were armed, would not allow the gendarmes units to cross, and attacked even the soldiers. At Rozsnyó, it was the miners who shot at the departing Czech officials and soldiers. The railroadmen at Érsekújvár, Tardošked (Tardoskedd) and Slovenský Meder (Tótmegyer) went over to the Reds and organized an assault on the Czech troops; the inhabitants of Selmecbánya also shot at Czech soldiers. Civil servants abandoned their posts even where the advance of the Red Army did not represent an immediate threat.[45]

The Ministry of Slovakia, in collaboration with army headquarters, resorted to draconian measures to maintain order in areas that were not under occupation. As long as it disposed of reliable gendarmes units, it dispatched these to the exposed areas, especially in Gömör and elsewhere.[46] On the basis of the Law LXVIII of 1912, Šrobar authorized the gendarmery and military commanders to carry out necessary measures in connection with the military operations in the manner they deemed fit. Communes were entrusted with protection of bridges, railroad lines, telephone wires. The military held the whole commune responsible for damages if the guilty party could not be found, and handed down fines. They also collected hostages. Cases of weapons concealment were judged in statutory court. Prefects and other officials were given orders to remain at their post. Members of the Sokol organizations were armed as volunteers and assigned to gendarme units. The Ministry issued prohibitions against meeting and assembly. The means of communication and transportation lines were under constant guard. The statutory courts became more severe. In early June, Šrobar described the situation as "showing general improvement," and added "that significant military reinforcements had been thrown in, and further reinforcements were on the way." This information was not altogether accurate, of course, and was designed mainly to calm the fears of the population. For this reason, he also directed prefects not to allow the civil servants to leave their post as long as evacuation had not been ordered by the military commander. He demanded that statutury measures be taken against those "who spread rumors and against agitators." The field gendarmes were thrown into the fray at the Csallóköz–Aranyos–Vág River–Galgóc–Nagytapolcsány–Zólyom line, and at the railroad junctions.[47]

In the areas of Slovakia under Hungarian occupation, the regime that evolved was the direct opposite. As a result of the counterattack, the Slovak section of the Communist Party in Hungary expected that the workers of Slovakia and Bohemia would also "embark on the only correct road, which leads to the final victory in which the Slovak and Czech proletariats are freed from the yoke of the Czechoslovak capitalists." Its organization and measures taken in Slovak territory were all directed to this end. Office holders and rank-and-file members of the section, in collaboration with the agencies of the Hungarian revolutionary government, and with the help of the local union leaders, disbanded the civilian administration and replaced it with revolutionary organs of the proletariat. As directorates and councils were set up, unions were also formed in all areas of production and administration. The help provided by the Hungarian Communists accounts to a large extent for the rapid formation of the regime of Soviets. The achievements of the Slovak Soviet Republic in a period of less than three weeks, by introducing a good many measures worthy of attention, may be explained, naturally, only by the intense activity stimulated by the organizations brought about by the rapid development of the Soviet system.[48]

In the areas of Slovakia under the Hungarian occupation, the revolutionary activity of the workers was not limited to support and assistance for the fighting troops. At the people's assembly in Losonc, Léva, Eperjes, and Kassa, miners, railroadmen, and industrial workers manifested their desire to follow the examples of the Russian and Hungarian workers. The background of the proclamation of the Slovak Soviet Republic was, nevertheless, not quite so simple as we have traditionally been led to believe. Not that the proletariat of southern and eastern Slovakia was free to decide and express its will; but neither was it simply a matter of the "invasion of Hungarian Bolsheviks."

Hungarian nationalist feeling, as we have shown, played an important part in the formation of the Hungarian Soviet Republic. Under the impact of Entente dictates the Hungarian population, easily offended in its national sentiments, welcomed any kind of regime inclined to reduce the military and political pressures exerted by the Entente and the neighboring states. Precisely for this reason, those elements of Hungarian society which could not be described as proletarian in the least, and middle-class elements also, gave their support to the proletarian government in the beginning. Communists who lined up alongside Béla Kun, as we have noted, saw their main goal as contributing to the victory of the dictatorship of the proletariat and of Socialist revolution; they were intent on avoiding an all-out armed conflict, and on influencing the workers of the successor states by the example of socialist construction in their own country. Propertied classes were soon to adopt a negative attitude toward the proletarian regime. Industrial capital, the landed estates, and even the antagonistic attitudes of the peasantry and of the lower middle class jeopardized the existence of proletarian power, especially during the first phase of military intervention.

As Czech troops lined up in front of Salgótarján, Béla Kun once again turned to the Hungarian people and called upon them to defend their country. In his view, the most pressing matter was to save Socialist Hungary. Hence, the government recalled the old officer corps into active service, tightened discipline, and, with the slogan of "war of national liberation," launched a massive offensive, as a result of which the focus of military operations shifted to southern and eastern Slovakia. The successes gained by the Hungarian Red Army, which nobody had expected at the beginning, and which were due not only to the spirit of sacrifice of the armed workers, but also the enthusiasm of the troops and of the officer corps, fed by a spirit of nationalism, undoubtedly influenced the tactical considerations of the Hungarian Communists. Although the revolution remained the principal objective, some ideological consessions could be allowed, if only to continue to hold a broad line of defense.[49] Kun and his companions regarded the proclamation of the Slovak Soviet Republic not only as the creation of a fresh revolutionary nucleus in southern and eastern Slovakia, but expected, first of all, that the proclamation of Eperjes would mobilize revolutionary forces in other parts of Slovakia, and, even in Bohemia, that the Republic would become the starting point of the spread of proletarian power all over Czechoslovakia. They equally counted on a revolutionary explosion in Austria, particularly in Vienna. In their view, successor states' governments would be prompted to sit down and negotiate with the representative of the Hungarian Soviet Republic as a result of the fresh successes, in the class struggle, of the Slovak or Czech proletariat's international solidarity in the spirit of the Communist International! Still more, they counted on the possibility of signing a peace with the new proletarian governments of the successor states, behind the back of the Entente. Béla Kun and other Hungarian Communists truly believed in what they proclaimed: the love of peace of the armed proletariat, the mission of the workers in fighting the "final battle," the power of the example of the Hungarian Soviet Republic, the power of that proletarian inernationalism which would enhance the strength of Czech and Slovak proletarians in their struggle against their own bourgeoisie.

Such expectations were not obtained, though. The reaction to national enthusiasm came not at the front, but within the country. The middle-class strata soon realized that the *national spirit, to Kun, was nothing more than a tool for the preservation of the proletarian regime.* The village once again refused to supply the capital and the army with food. Counterrevolutionary groups became dangerously active. Representatives of right-wing Social Democracy, the majority within the government, did not share the illusions of the Communists. Under the given conditions, they had a more objective assessment of the chances of nationalism and internationalism. They would have liked to take advantage of the Hungarian Red Army stationed on Slovak territory to exacerbate the contradictions between Czechs and Slovaks, and support the separatist tendencies among the Slovaks, which they considerably overestimated. At the ceremony on the occasion of the Red Army's march into Kassa, Commissar Vilmos Böhm, a right-wing Social Democrat, confidentially informed the diplomatic observers that the government was in favor of an independent Slovak Republic, to be proclaimed in Zólyom within a few days. He expressed the view that with the proclamation of the Soviet Republic the contradictions between Czechs and Slovaks would sharpen to the point where separation becomes unavoidable. Nevertheless, Böhm did not have the reintegration of Slovakia with Hungary in mind. He did expect, of course, that strong bonds of alliance would develop between the Hungarian and Slovak republics.[50]

The news of the proclamation of the Slovak Soviet Republic caused confusion and unease in the ranks of Entente diplomats. Cecil Gosling, British ambassador to Prague, was convinced that after this event even French help would not suffice to save Czechoslovakia. In Vienna, the revolution, it was expected would also break out in Austria, and British diplomats there urged the Entente to intervene.[51] The Great Powers at the Peace Conference blamed the governments of the successor states for the failure of military intervention. The leash of anti-Hungarian policy slipped entirely into the hands of Clemenceau, thus leading to the diplomatic steps of June 7 and 13, 1919. The choice of the manner of intervention was influenced in part by David Lloyd George's formulation "that we should not do the same thing in Hungary as we had done in Russia − one Russia is quite enough;" in part by the fact that in early June Germany had not yet accepted the peace conditions, and thereby, was tying down all the Entente's military power.[52]

Soviet-Russia was not in a position to lend military assistance to Hungary. It welcomed the proclamation of the Slovak Soviet Republic, but, under the circumstances, could do no better than lend moral support.

Interventionist opportunities improved when, on June 28, 1919, Germany accepted the peace conditions. From then on, the Americans refused to get involved in European problems, and the British no longer participated in the negotiations at the Peace Conference. Thus did Clémenceau become master of the situation and could threaten to transfer the entire French army to the Hungarian front.

Béla Kun reassessed his political chances. He rejected the Entente's first note of June 7, but the second note offered, in exchange for the evacuation of Slovak territories, conditions which the Hungarian Soviet Republic could well accept. Clemenceau promised rectification of borders and withdrawal of Romanian troops from Hungarian territory the moment Hungarian troops left Czechoslovakia. The majority of Hungarian Communists were of the view, already after the second note, that the continuation of the struggle was an internationalist obligation, inasmuch as it would check anti-Soviet intervention and help the young Slovak Soviet Republic. They had no faith in Entente promises, and in this, they were correct. On the other hand, they failed to examine why the proclamation of the Slovak Soviet Republic did not elicit the expected echo in other parts of Slovakia and Bohemia. Therefore, in reply to the second note, the Hungarian government declared that it was willing to halt military operations, which, in any case, it had not initiated. Nevertheless, it stressed that the borders as established rendered normal economic life impossible for Hungary; furthermore, that though the note made no claim to the principle of territorial integrity, Hungarian-inhabited  areas should not be attached to Slovakia.[53] Béla Kun was willing to accept General Pellé's third ultimatum only after the peace with Germany had been signed. The Hungarian Soviet government was reorganized. The Communists received the majority of cabinet posts, whereas right-wing Social Democrats began to abandon the sinking ship. After the evacuation of the Slovak territories and the disintegration of the Red Army, Budapest had grass roots support – in addition to the workers – only from the unemployed.

The situation in Slovakia was no less complex. After the Czech army's retreat, Slovak soldiers deserted left and right, and on occasion joined the Red Army as a unit. There were Czech soldiers among them as well. (A revolution among the Sudeten Germans was also a possibility.) The Czech government was equally worried that Poland, too, might take advantage of the difficult situation in which the republic found itself. The meeting of Tomáš G. Masaryk with Ignacy Paderewski proved abortive. The Polish attack took place on Slovakian soil, on the excuse that Czech "bands had penetrated into Polish territory"; thus, Poles occupied the country of Árva and the northern sector of the Szepes area; there were clashes in the area of Ostrava as well. The very existence of the Republic of Czechoslovakia was in the balance. Organization of armed defense was slow. While the Hungarian Red Army was improving, day by day, in discipline and combatworthiness, the Czech army had no reserves which it could have transferred to the zones in jeopardy. At certain spots of tactical importance, there were but a few hundred troops confronting the overwhelming superiority of the Red Army. Even internally, the balance of power shifted to the left. The Marxist left wing constituted by the Muna group had already serious political weight. The expectation during the upcoming Bohemian and Moravian elections was that the Social Democrats would gain a decisive victory, which, in Masaryk's opinion, should be used to consolidate the bourgeois regime. After a few critical weeks, the situation suddenly changed as a result of Germany's acceptance of the peace proposals. Béla Kun, as already mentioned, accepted the ultimatum of General Pellé on June 24, 1919, and the military operations in Czechoslovakia came to a halt. The Czech government could now breathe easily and began a deliberate campaign blaming the "Hungarian Bolsheviks" for the military defeat and for the Slovak Soviet Republic. It wisely kept quiet about having itself launched the offensive.[54] Nevertheless, the fact remains that the proclamation of the Slovak Soviet Republic did not have the expected repercussions in other parts of the Czechoslovak Republic, which gave credibility to the bourgeois interpretation that it was the "Hungarian Bolsheviks" who had broken into the Republic. Therefore, let us examine the Slovak situation.

On June 7, 1919, the minister in charge of the administration of Slovakia issued fresh instructions regarding evacuation in the case of "further enemy thrusts." On June 20, 1919, he proclaimed a military dictatorship throughout

Slovakia, placing all troops in western Slovakia under the command of French General Mittelhauser, whereas the jurisdiction of the governors, along with the entire state apparatus, was transferred to the government representative, Dr. Milan Ivánka. In eastern Slovakia, the French General Hennoque was appointed military dictator, and Dr. Juraj Slávik was Prague's representative.[55] Yet, a month before, on May 19, 1919, an internment camp was opened at Moravská Třebova and Choč to contain Hungarians unreliable from a political point of view. Several hundred citizens from Gömör and Korompa were, thus, placed behind barbed wire; communists were interned at Terezin. The Ministry of Slovakia, according to its directive of June 20, 1919, had to purge all those men "between the ages of 18 and 45," especially workers, railroadmen, peasants, and mailmen who had been "coopted by the Bolshevik government." According to data that remain incomplete, about 2500 were incarcerated in compliance with these guidelines, under inhuman conditions.[56] Interment of the most active members of the working class explains why the workers remained so passive in unoccupied Slovakia, where, after the agitators had been purged, the influence of the bourgeois and Social Democratic parties prevailed.

Because further Czech officials abandoned their posts, even at places which were not directly threatened by the advance of the Hungarian Red Army, state administration became paralyzed, although ethnic contradictions became more moderate for the time being.[57] Official propaganda blamed the Hungarian Bolsheviks and their supporters in Hungary for all difficulties. But this interpretation was, of course, one-sided, and could not fully account for the facts.

As we have outlined the motivations, intentions, and goals of the Communists and right-wing Social Democrats in the Hungarian revolutionary government, so now we must also make distinctions in the attitudes of the Hungarian, Slovak, and Czech members participating in the Slovak Soviet Republic. Although the Slovak republic did come about on the initiative of the Hungarian revolutionary government, members of the central council, directorates, commissariats, and other organizations of the proletarian revolution were able to operate according to *their own* concepts – plans, policies and immediate goals. These concepts did not have to be in harmony with right-wing Hungarian Social Democracy and the objectives of the Hungarian nationalists. In fact, they were not.

The Slovak Soviet Republic survived for a few weeks only, hence it could not realize its various plans and goals. If we are to judge from the official records and the published programs, we must conclude without hesitation that the Slovak and Czech members of the revolutionary governing council did not intend to separate Slovakia from Czechoslovakia. On the contrary. In the cable which the Chairman of the Revolutionary Council, Antonín Janoušek, addressed to the Czech government on June 16, 1919, it stated, "in the name of the proletariat of Slovakia," that "our innermost yearning is to live in close and indivisible bonds of friendship with the Czech proletariat, who are blood of our blood" and that "we want to work along with them in indivisible state alliance for the sake of general peace and for the promotion of proletarian power among all nations." At a meeting of the workers of Kassa on June 22, 1919, Janoušek had the following to say: "We can defeat the capitalist Czechoslovak government and its army only with the help of the revolutionary Czech proletariat... Every proletarian and Communist of Slovakia, whether he be Czech, Hungarian, Slovak, German, or Ruthene, has but a single interest: to keep Slovakia for the working people, and that can happen only and exclusively with the help of the revolutionary proletariat of Bohemia. And the way to do it is to bring down the Czech bourgeoisie, with our help..." Such was the thinking of the Czech and Slovak section of Budapest. Even at the time of the Hungarian Red Army's counterattack, the idea was "to realize proletarian power on the territory of the Czechoslovak Republic as defined by the Alliance of the Four." The representative of the section spoke along these lines at a congress of the Socialist—Communist Workers Party in Hungary: "The liberation of the proletarians of Slovakia is but a step towards the liberation of the proletarians of Bohemia and Moravia, moreover, of the proletariat of other western countries." We find the same idea embodied in the program of the Slovak section: "The Slovak section of Hungary is of the opinion that all power in the Czechoslovak state should be transferred to the proletariat, through the proclamation of the dictatorship of the proletariat, with the help of the victorious Russian and Hungarian proletariats, with the help of the workers belonging to all the ethnic groups living in Bohemia, Moravia and Silesia, with the help of the internationally united proletarians of the whole world, along its revolutionary class program." The point here was to bring the next stage of the world revolution to the lands of the Czechoslovakian republic, and to link the proletarian Czechoslovak state with the "international republic of soviets" as outlined by Lenin. Furthermore, the Slovak section adopted, as part of its program: "The proletarian Soviet republic will form a federation consisting of individual international proletarian bodies, in which there will be no national or religious contradictions, in which there will be no national boundaries to elicit arguments and wars. Common matters will be referred to the soviets of the federated republic of proletarians."[58]

The right of self-determination, the right to an independent state was, thus, accorded to the proletariat rather than to the nation; at the same time, they unrealistically underestimated the problem of national boundaries. Further evidence of this is found in the following document, little known until now: On June 18, 1919 the Petrine  wireless telegraph bureau in Prague received a cable signed by Janoušek and addressed to the government of the Austrian republic:

> The workers power and its armed proletarian might, the Red Army, declare Slovakia a Soviet Republic and, as representatives of this republic, we, the government of the Republic, assume power over your German brothers oppressed and detained by Czech imperialism, insofar as they live in the areas defined by the military agreement of November 13, 1918. We solemnly declare that we want to live in friendship with the Czechoslovak Republic, because our objective is to put an end once and for all to national conflicts unleashed by the war and instigated by Czech imperialism, so that the working classes, which had brought the greatest sacrifices on the battlefield, may from now on enjoy a happier life. With this liberation of our working people your brothers' freedom has likewise come, hence it would be desirable to enter into close commercial relations and negotiate the necessary measures and issues. We do not take a negative stand with regard to the allegiance of your brothers [i. e. allegiance to Austria] because we firmly profess the right of nations to self-determination. Our Soviet Republic has but one goal: to carry out the sacred principles of the international proletariat.[59]

In spite of all their mistakes and shortcomings, in spite of the fact that the right of self-determination was limited to a single class, and in spite of the one-sided approach to the importance of the nation-state and of national boundaries, it must be conceded that the subjective intentions of Slovak and Czech Communists participating in the government were good. After national liberation, they also meant eventually to carry out the social liberation of the Czech and Slovak nations. From this angle, Janousek's cable to Prague is rather important: "Beginning today in proletarian Slovakia, in the areas determined by the military agreement of November 13, we have proclaimed the Soviet Republic of Councils. We have assumed power, leaning on the workers and the armed proletariat, and have authorized the appointed commissars to take up their administrative duties. We explicitly state that from this day Slovakia belongs exclusively to the Slovak working people." Without any doubt this was the first attempt at Slovak Socialist statehood.[60] Indeed, it is quite a different matter whether this subjective goal was realistic and realizable.

Hungarian workers of Slovakia took it for granted that in this "international Soviet republic," in which there would be no frontiers, they would be able to join up with their own nation. At protest meetings in Kassa, Eperjes, Losonc, when it became certain that the Hungarian Red Army would leave Slovakian territory, where the workers showed their determination and willingness to even fight for a proletarian government, the workers of Hungarian ethnic background also let their will become manifest; they, too, were determined to participate in the defense of the Slovak Soviet Republic, they stressed that the Hungarian workers "want to live together with the Slovak workers in the Slovak Soviet Republic... that they want to join their Slovak brothers in the struggle waged against Imperialism," and that they want to fight even after the departure of the Hungarian Red Army.[61] Apart from the fact that the Hungarian Red Army's departure rendered all further resistance illusory, even this resolution elicited uncertainty in Czech government circles, worried as they were that the common front of revolutionary workers without regard to nationality might yet come about, and whether the government would be able to repress the disturbances in Slovakia resulting from such joint action. These worries proved unwarranted, but that depended little on the Czechoslovak government's actions.

After the end of the Slovak Soviet Republic, Entente diplomatic and military design shifted completely to crushing proletarian power on Hungarian territory. On June 30, as the Red Army was retreating toward the demarcation line, Béla Kun requested the Entente to order the promised retreat of the Romanian troops. Clemenceau's negative reply was an indication of the trend of affairs. Impelled by an internal crisis, the Hungarian revolutionary government reported to Paris, on July 20, that the Hungarian Red Army had launched an offensive against the Romanians. (It was an open secret in Viennese diplomatic circles that one of the Hungarian Social Democratic commissars, Vilmos Böhm, made statements to the effect that he was willing to break with the Communists and prepare a *coup d'état* with the help of the Hungarian labor unions.)[62]

But, the offensive against the Romanians collapsed. The final ultimatum from Paris (July 27, 1919) demanded the nomination of a new government, and, in exchange, offered to lift the blockade against Hungary. The Hungarian Communists put up a bitter defense, but the disintegration of the regime could not be halted. The government lost control of the administration, particularly in the provinces. Chauvinist, nationalist, and anti-Communist propaganda spread in ever-widening circles and pointed in the direction, and toward objectives, of counterrevolution White terror.[63]

Although the Entente had made promises not to intervene in Hungary's internal affairs, nevertheless, it demanded the formation of a new government; it opted in favor of the Social Democrats, because they had become wary of their own working-class. Hungarian public opinion, which fell prey to counterrevolutionary forces, rejected the notion of a Social Democratic government, because Social Democracy had been "compromised" by collaboration with the Bolsheviks. Thus was prepared the road to Horthy's seizure of power.

State administration was in the process of consolidation in Slovakia. Even by the end of July 1919, however, no work was carried out in the county offices of Gömör, postal services did not function, and not a single official had received an appointment. Yet, there was a complete dearth of trained officials in the eastern counties of Slovakia. Those liable for military service did not report for duty: draft notices simply went undelivered, courts relegated matters under their jurisdiction to notary publics, and temporary residence permits were issued en masse, without any legal basis. The draftees did not report for duty, especially in the southern and eastern counties, where the proletarian government had been in power.[64] Lack of trained officials became particularly felt as a consequence of the dismissal of everyone suspected of having collaborated with the organs of the Slovak Soviet Republic, or with the Hungarian Red Army.[65] Lack of understanding and the contradictions between Czech officials and the Slovak population increased and multipled. Czech officials, gendarmes, and soldiers, at least those who bothered to return to their stations after the departure of the Red Army, were intent on restoring their prestige, damaged as a result of their cowardice, by finding a single culprit behind every mistake, including their own: they blamed the pro-Hungarian, the Communist, or the usual scapegoat, the Jew. They claimed that it was only because of these antagonistic elements that the Czechoslovak troops had failed at the front: they were the ones who had chased the "old state-building" persons out of Slovakia. The office of the plenipotentiary minister in charge of the administration of Slovakia was swamped with denunciations coming from Czech gendarmes and soldiers accusing Slovaks in search of work or of a job of being "too Slovak," that is, pro-Hungarian. Should a Slovak apply for some post he was accused of "attempting to chase out the Czech officials." They claimed that the Czech officials were the only ones who had defended the interests of the republic, that the "Jews and the priests" were anti-republican, that "they are the ones to incite the good Slovak people against the state, and these people have allowed themselves to be seduced" and turned against the Czech patriots who have not been able to win the sympathies of the population until now.

Untrained personnel from Bohemia, to salvage their well-paid jobs in face of the justified pressure of Slovak candidates, deliberately distorted the activities of the "pro-Hungarians." This designation was aimed not only at the dismissed officials of Hungarian descent, but at the unemployed Slovak professionals as well. Those untrained and unprepared individuals who could not obtain a post in Bohemia referred to the justified claims of the Slovaks, that the vacated posts be filled by Slovak candidates, "as merely hatred of everything Czech" or "hatred of the Czechoslovak government."

Of course, this was not true. If anyone had harmed the Czech idea of the state, it was primarily that stratum of gold-diggers and profiteers from Bohemia who regarded Slovakia as their private colony. The untrained Czech official — according to the prevailing rumor — could be bribed for less than the Hungarian gentry. The population was aware of this and took advantage; this was one of the reasons why Czech officials considered the posts in Slovakia as attractive from a financial point of view. And, it was precisely those who filled these well-paid posts who spread alarming rumors "regarding the terror regime of the Bolsheviks," the anti-Czech mood in Slovakia, in order to further demonstrate their "patriotic devotion."[67] Of course, Slovak public opinion resented this deeply.

Roots of dissatisfaction in Slovakia have to be sought elsewhere. Requisitions, more aggressive than any the peasants had known under the Hungarian regime, trampling underfoot the religious feelings of the Slovak people, highhanded manners of the Czech soldiers, difficulties in supplying the population with basic goods, the black market, military service, unemployment, etc. — these were the real causes which gave rise to dissatisfaction after the fall of the Slovak Soviet Republic. Czech officials, we should add, as is well known, enjoyed all kinds of financial advantages, whereas even the modest daily wages of those Slovak officials who had been transferred to south Slovakia in summer 1919, were left forgotten and undisbursed on more than one occasion. Under such circumstances, the prestige of state agencies was bound to diminish.

All this does not imply in the least that the Hungarian irredentists remained inactive in Slovakia. The Hungarian counterrevolutionary regime represented a constant danger for Czechoslovakia. Hungarian irredentist organizations smuggled not only flyers into Slovakia, but agents as well. Nineteen-nineteen was only the beginning of antagonistic acts by the Hungarian government; at the time the counterrevolutionary regime came to power the danger was not yet realistic. Yet, the propaganda of the Horthy regime, even at its inception, was intense enough to influence public opinion, so that it was once again the Czechs who had come to rescue Slovakia from the Bolshevik menace, and that the Czechs are the only ones to defend the country against the pro-Hungarians. Still, public opinion in Slovakia remained united, even without this kind of propaganda, on the issue of the defense of the Czech state.

The October Revolution in Russia had considerable impact on the pace and form of the construction of the Czech state. Its impact derived not only from the fact that Soviet Russia appeared as the political and ideological center of gravity of all oppressed people, but also from the fact that bourgeois states, old and new, felt threatened by social revolution; moreover, its impact elicited political and social crises in the aftermath of the war. According to the plans of the Russian Bolsheviks, Communist groups were supposed to spread the Socialist revolution in Europe, particularly in the defeated countries.

The duty awaiting the Communists was to wage further struggles for the liberation of the masses oppressed by imperialism, and for promoting proletarian dictatorships on the Soviet model. The uniform character of this process had altered already during a first phase, when Soviet regimes came to power in Hungary, Bavaria, and Slovakia. National traditions, cultural heritage, political ambitions, and economic factors in these countries all contributed to various ways of departure from the Soviet model. It was clear, already in 1919, that the road to socialism had its own peculiar features in every single country.

The possibility of transforming the bourgeois democratic revolution in Czechoslovakia into a Socialist one in 1919 cannot be studied in isolation; we cannot analyze it strictly from a domestic point of view. The consequences of the Socialist revolution in Russia were so evident in 1919 that their effect could be felt not only in the successor states but at the Paris Peace Conference as well. The examples provided by the proletarian governments in Hungary and Bavaria, the agitation carried out by soldiers who were former POWs and by Communists, the problems of supply, inflation, unemployment, all this together resulted in a revolutionary mood in Czechoslovakia, but particularly in Slovakia; and this, following the proclamation of the Slovak Soviet Republic, and while the Hungarian Red Army was present in Slovakia, represented an acute danger from the point of view of the bourgeois system. But, in spite of all this, the immediate echo of the Slovak Soviet Republic in other parts of the country was not loud enough, for reasons already enumerated. Nevertheless, there was an echo. Witness the workers' councils in Bohemia (*Kladno*), and the demand of these councils that Czechoslovakia be converted into a Socialist state, finally the events of the year 1920 until the December general strike which marked an end to the Soviet movement within our country. Within the framework of the revolutionary events between 1918 and 1920, the Slovak Soviet Republic was the first attempt to realize a Slovak Socialist state.

Such are the factors that determine the place of the Slovak Soviet Republic in the context of Czechoslovak history.

Undoubtedly, as the special forms of Czech parliamentary and bourgeois democracy evolved, the workers movement and the Slovak Soviet Republic had as much of an impact as the national past, the geographical position of the country, the way of thinking of Czechs and Slovaks, democratic traditions, etc. It is, for certain, furthermore, that the Czechoslovakian liberal democratic government could weather the crisis of 1919—20 not only because it received decisive help from the Entente, but also because it enjoyed significant prestige: prestige in the political sense, that is, the capacity to carry out its will not so much by resorting to a display of power, but rather with the consensus and voluntary support of the population. The program of the Czech government, the principal motto of which was the consolidation of the nation-state, was able to neutralize not only the growing strength of the young Communist movement, but also the increasing dissatisfaction and disappointment of the entire Slovak nation, and even irredentist resistance among Hungarians and Germans.

The main reasons of the failure of the Slovak Soviet Republic are to be sought in its leaders who did not recognize the importance of the organic development of society; who mechanically transferred the idea of revolutionary proletarian power, and by-passed certain stages of natural evolution — all of which contradict the principles of Marxism.[69] Recent Czechoslovak Marxist historiography has also committed errors in contrasting the events of 1918—19 with the events of the 1950s without sufficient distinctions and comparisons. The results, even in the case of this author, were one-sided generalizations, which did not take into consideration the historical uniqueness of the period under examination, or the lack of repetition. We forget something that Max Weber had noted long ago — the more general judgments or assertions regarding laws governing society and history, the more meaningless they become.

Reappraisal of the significance of the Slovak Soviet Republic in the history of the Slovak nation and of Czechoslovakia, while avoiding the same mistake, ascribes a more modest role to this event. Still, it expresses the fact that its relevance remains considerable to this day: moreover, the lessons to be learnt from it are of interest and timely indeed.

## NOTES

1. West Germany. *Deutsches Hauptarchiv des Auswärtiges Amts.* Political Archives. (Hereafter PA AA.) Österreich f. No. 92., No. Bd. 27, A 7192, "Report of the German Consulate from Budapest,"Feb. 28, 1919.

2. *Ibid;* Martin Vietor, *Slovenská sovietska republika* (Bratislava, 1954), pp. 84–85.

3. Czechoslovakia. *Státny slovenský ústredny archiv.* Slovakian Ministry of Justice (hereafter ŠSÚA, MPS.), f. 270/1919 fasc., no. 860/19, Feb. 19, 1919.

4. Vietor, p. 103.

5. ŠSÚA, MPS f. 270/1919. fasc., no. 933/19 (The list of the victims of the Bratislava demonstration, no. 973/19, no. 1185/19); Vietor, pp. 60–61.

6. ŠSÚA, MPS f. 271/1919. fasc., no. 1506/19, no. 1524/19.

7. Bratislava(Pozsony), Komárom (Komárno), Stúrovo(Párkány) from March 25, 1919.

8. Vietor, pp. 85–86.

9. ŠSUA, MPS f. 281/1919. fasc., 1512/19. (Demonstration in Špišské Vlachy (Szépolaszi) in support of the Hungarians), 269/1919. fasc., no. 86/19, no. 87/19.

10. ŠSÚA, MPS f. 269/1919. fasc., no. 16/19 (The National Council of Tapolčany (Nagytapolcsány) interns the Jewish intelligentsia of Tapolčany, Chynorany (Kinorány) and Bánovce (Bán) to the camp at Uherské Hradišstěi), no. 79/19 (The National Council issues them security clearances, whereupon Dr. Ivánka orders their liberation); no. 49/19. (The Jews of Trnava (Nagyszombat), were interned as hostages in Brno); no. 37/19. (The list of the 107 persons, mostly Jews, interned in Brno, but who were allowed to go Žilina (Zsolna).

11. ŠSÚA, MPS f. 269/1919. fasc., no. 0909/19. (Expulsions from Košice (Kassa), no. 1073/19. (Expulsion from Turčianský Svätý Martin (Túrócszentmárton), no. 1150/19. (The guiding ideas of Dr. Srobar on this topic.)

12. ŠSÚA, MPS f. 269/1919. fasc., no. 56/19.

13. ŠSÚA, MPS f. 269/1919. fasc., no. 56/19. (The offer for the available positions in Slovakia by the "The United Alliance of the Administrators in Brno of the Autonomous Countries of the Czech Crown".) 272/1919. fasc., no. 2235/1919. (March 30, 1919 report to the Slovakian Ministry of Justice: the civilian authorities interfere in the affairs of the military authorities, they issue military deferments, etc.)

14. PA AA, Österreich No. 92, No. 1, Bd. 28, no. 1881, the report of the German military representative, March 23, 1919.

15. PA AA, Österreich No. 92, No. 1, Bd. 27, no. 9658, the report of the German ambassador in Vienna, April 23, 1919, report of the same, March 23, 1919.

16. *Vörös Újság,* March 30, 1919; Béla Kun, *Válogatott írások és beszédek I.* (Budapest, 1966), 214; Zsuzsa L. Nagy, *A párizsi békekonferencia és Magyarország 1918–1919* (Budapest, 1965), p. 103.

17. PA AA, Österreich No. 92, No. 1, Bd. 27, Reports from Lyon to New Brunswick, March 24, 1919; Telegram no. 10064 from Madrid, March 29, 1919.

18. PA AA, Österreich No. 92, No. 1, Bd. 27, No. 10769, report from Paris, April 17, 1919; PA AA, Internationale Angelegenheiten, No. 2, Bolschevismus Bd. 6, No. 12402, report of the German ambassador in Vienna, April 22, 1919.

19. Sándorné (Mrs.) Gábor, "Dokumentumok Szovjet-Oroszország és a Tanácsköztársaság kapcsolatairól," *Párttörténeti Közlemények* (1), 1961, 211.

20. Especially the Smuts Mission, see, Zsuzsa L. Nagy, *A párizsi békekonferencia.*

21. PA AA, Internationale Angelegenheiten, No. 2, Bolschevismus Bd. 6, No. 11020 report of the German ambassador in Vienna, April 6, 1919.

22. PA AA, Österreich No. 92, No. 1, Bd. 27, No. 19446 report on the speech of State Secretary Bauer.

23. PA AA, Internationale Angelegenheiten, No. 2, Bolschevismus Bd. 6, No. 10671/19 Press Reports, no. 5–6; No. 19977/19 Press Reports of the German Embassy in Helsingfors on the issues of the *Pravda* of Petrograd, June 15–22, 1919.

24. ŠSÚA, MPS f. 255/1919. fasc., no. 663/19.

25. In April 1919, there were nineteen gymnasia, four commercial high schools, and five teachers' training schools in Slovakia. Furthermore, there were trade schools in carpentry, textiles, and metallurgy; three training institutions for the deaf and mute, and the blind; three trade schools, and three girls high schools. All together there were some 31 schools of higher learning and 20 junior high schools for 5700 students.

26. The arrested were: Jozef Kucúr, 50, metalworker; Adolf Matula, 65, clerk in Likier (Liker), Anton Valko, notary of Klenoc, and two teachers of the Likier orphanage. According to Daxner, a police official, Anton Valko was reliable on national issues. ŠSÚA, 255/1919. fasc., no. 370/19, Report of the Slovak National Gendarmery, Rimovská Sobota (Rimaszombat), April 25, 1919.

27. Vietor, pp. 94–95; M. Dzvonik, *Ohlas VOSR na Slovensku* (Bratislava, 1957), pp. 118–19.

28. PA AA Österreich No. 92, No. 1, Bd. 27. No. 10256, report from Vienna, March 29, 1919; No. 10899, report from Vienna, April 8, 1919; No. 11549, report from Budapest, April 8, 1919.

29. PA AA Österreich No. 92, No. 1, Bd. 27. No. 10926, report from Copenhagen, April 8, 1919.

30. Hans Beyer, "Die Bayerische Räterrepublik 1919," *Zeitschrift für Geschichtswissenschaft*, 2 (1954) 205.

31. Vietor, pp. 94–95.

32. C. A. Macartney, *Hungary and Her Successors* (Oxford, 1937), p. 39.

33. Zsuzsa L. Nagy, p. 127.

34. Louis Fischer, *The Soviets in World Affairs. A History of the Relations Between the Soviet Union and the Rest of the World, 1917–1922* (Princeton, 1951), p. 177–78.

35. PA AA, Österreich No. 92, No. 1, Bd. 27, no. 16369, report from Budapest, May 29, 1919; no. 8020, report from Vienna, May 20, 1919.

36. Czechoslovakia, Archiv Ministerstva zahraničnich veči (AMZV), Praha. Pařižsky archiv, Pa 48. k. no. 4880, 72. k. no. 69823; Zsuzsa L. Nagy, p. 268.

37. Zsuzsa L. Nagy, "Smuts tábornok budapesti küldetése 1919 áprilisában," *Történelmi Szemle,* 2 (1963) 255; Smuts had also conducted negotations with Masaryk concerning the Czechoslovak–Yugoslav corridor. See, S. S. Millin, *Samuel Smuts* (London, 1936), p. 206; Macartney, pp. 51–52.

38. *Prager Tagblatt*, April 29, 1919, May 30, 1919; *Der Demokrat*, July 4, 1919, *Bohemia*, July 14 and 29, 1919; Leo Valiani, "La politika estera del governi rivoluzionari ungheresi del 1918–19," *Rivista Storica Italiana*, 78: 2 (1966), 850–51.

39. Vietor, pp. 38–39.

40. PA AA, Österreich No. 92, No. 1, Bd. 27, no. 16907, report from Vienna, July 9, 1919; no. 8027/I, report of the German military attaché in Vienna, July 9, 1919.

41. The position of the Governing Council was expressed by Béla Kun in his first telegram to Clemenceau: "We did not attack them, they attacked us... We do not recognize any frontiers. The home of the proletariat is the whole world. We want to make the whole world into the home of the proletariat, but in the period of transition, while world revolution does not spread from the east to the west, and does not win the whole world, we want to live in peace with the working people of every country." Quoted by Kaas and Lazarovics, *Der Bolschevismus in Ungarn* (Münster, 1930), pp. 145–56.

42. PA AA, Österreich No. 92, No. 1, Bd. 27, no. 17338, report from Vienna, June 13, 1919; ŠSÚA, MPS f. 255/1919. fasc., no. 663/19.

43. ŠSÚA, MPS f. 256/1919. fasc., no. 1268/19.

44. ŠSÚA, MPS f. 256/1919. fasc., no. 1317/19.

45. Vietor, pp. 47–48.

46. ŠSÚA, MPS f. 271/1919. fasc., no. 1639/19.

47. ŠSÚA, MPS f. 272/1919. fasc., no. 2548/19, no. 2178/19, no. 3127/19, no. 3255/19, no. 3256/19.

48. Vietor, pp. 52–64.

49. PA AA Österreich No. 92, No. 1, Bd. 27, no. 19424, report of the general staff, "Fremde Heere–Ost," July 1, 1919: Osterreich no. 101, Bd. 45, no. 16525, report of the ambassador in Vienna, June 4, 1919.

50. PA AA, Österreich No. 92, No. 1, Bd. 27, no. 17182, report from Budapest, June 14, 1919.

51. Zsuzsa L. Nagy, pp. 165–66.

52. Paul Mauntoux, *Les délibérations du Counseil du Quatres (24 Mars–28 Juin 1919)* (Paris, 1955), I, 18–19; Paul Birdsall, *Versailles Twenty Years After* (New York, 1941), 184–85.

53. Párttörténeti Intézet, *A magyar munkásmozgalom történetének válogatott dodokumentumai* (Budapest, 1959) VI/b, 157–72.

54. PA AA, Österreich No. 101, Bd. 53., no. 16526, report of June 4, 1919, from Vienna; no. 17774, report of the German Consul in Brno on June 13, 1919. It was claimed that French General Hennocque gave a very embarassing report about the Czech soldiers: "The Czech are dirty swine, they run like rabbits," Österreich No. 1010, Bd. 54, no. 19399 general staff report, "Fremde Heere-Ost," Berlin, July 1, 1919.

55. ŠSÚA, MPS f. 259/1919. fasc., no. 6326/19; 277/1919. fasc., no. 3299/19.

56. ŠSÚA, MPS f. 260/1919. fasc., M. V. no. 5695/IV–1919.

57. Martin Vietor, *K pročiatkom buržoazhného sudnictva v ČSR* (Bratislava, 1960).

58. Martin Vietor, *Slovenska sovietská republika* (Bratislava, 1955), pp. 351, 368; Martin Vietor, pp. 70–72.

59. *Prager Tagblatt*, June 19, 1919; PA AA Österreich No. 101, Bd. 54, no. 19399.

60. Dzvonik, *Ohlas VOSR*, p. 166; Vietor, p. 351.

61. Vietor, *Slovenská sovietská republika* (Bratislava, 1955), pp. 100–101.

62. PA AA, Österreich No. 92, No. 1, no. 20480, report of the German embassy in Vienna of July 13, 1919 containing the discussions of Colonel Thomas Cuninghame with State Secretary Bauer. It was at this time that Ernő Czóbel, the Hungarian envoy was replaced by Péter Ágoston. It is known that Ágoston belonged to the group opposing Kun.

63. It was typical of the situation that Henrik Kalmár, commissar of the German Nationalities, resigned. He reported to the government that when in accordance with the Constitution of the Soviet Republic he attempted to carry out the right of self determi-

nation of the Germans, he did not enjoy the support of the local authorities. Rather, he faced all kinds of obstacles. He was not allowed to set the borders of the German-inhabited areas, and German schools were not allowed to open. Public opinion was hostile and looked upon his office as the center of Pan-German activities. He claimed that in place of the liberties enshrined in the Constitution, in the counties Hungarian chauvinism was dominant. PA AA Österreich No. 92, No. 1, Bd. 29, no. 206663, telegram from Budapest, August 23, 1919.

64.  ŠSÚA, MPS f. 256/1919. fasc., no. 2189; 257/1919. fasc., no. 1922/19; 258/1919. fasc., no. 2975/19.

65.  ŠSÚA, MPS f. 256/1919. fasc., no. 807/19, no. 1346/19.

66.  ŠSÚA, MPS f. 257/1919. fasc., no. 1919/19, "Situation in Slovakia." Reports from July 22, 1919 to May 10, 1920.

67.  *Tagesbrote*, Brno, July 25, 1919.

68.  ŠSÚA, MPS f. 257/1919. fasc., no. 6509/19; Nespokojenost' na Slovensku," *Venkov,* October 21, 1919.

69.  Marx wrote in the Preface of the first volume of *Das Capital:* "A society even if it found its laws of movement..., could not jump its natural phases, nor could it abolish them by law. It could, however, shorten and ease the birth pangs." In, *Marx—Engels Mŭvei* (Budapest, 1967), 23: 9.

# VI
# HISTORIOGRAPHY

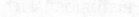

# RECENT PUBLICATIONS ON THE HISTORY OF THE HUNGARIAN SOVIET REPUBLIC AND BÉLA KUN

Peter Pastor

On a popular Hungarian radio program on history broadcast in March, 1980, the moderator, the well-known Hungarian historian Péter Hanák, observed:

An historiography of the Hungarians Soviet Republic would be exciting reading. It would be the history of a drama. The most exciting chapter would probably be the post-1945 rehabilitations process carried out in several stages. First, the rehabilitation of the spirit of the revolution and the revolution itself. Then the rehabilitation of its leaders, and finally the re-evaluation of the Communist Republic's international and national role. Regardless of the stress and subjectivity that accompained this historical search, the fact is that the Soviet Republic, the organic part of our history, became the subject of scientific research. Through this process, a rapprochement is being brought about between justice and truth.[1]

One exciting chapter of this historical literature of the revolution is the recent appearance of three publications which indeed come close to the truth.[2] These authors present neither the Soviet Republic nor its leader, Béla Kun, in a favorable light. To the contrary, the judgement of these historians comes close to the critical appraisals of Western scholars.[3]

The authors of the publications under discussion approach the subject of the Communist revolution from three different perspectives. One author is a biographer, the second a local historian, and the third an economic historian. György Borsányi examines the life of Béla Kun, covering not only the Soviet Republic of Hungary, but the whole revolutionary epoch beginning with 1905 and ending with Stalin's bloody purges. Ignác Romsics focuses on the Danube and Tisza. György Péteri turns his attention to the industrial policies of the Soviet Republic.

Borsányi's monograph, *Kun Béla,* the most noteworthy, was withdrawn from the bookstores soon after its appearance in 1979. It is presently available only to scholars through research libraries.

The controversial Béla Kun has been maligned not only by Hungarian historians acceptable to the interwar Horthy regime, but also by such prominent Russian revolutionaries as the Marxist Lev Trotskii and the anarchist Victor Serge. Both considered him an incompetent fool.[4] The victim of Stalin's purges, Kun became a "non-person" soon after his arrest in 1937. His posthumous rehabilitation started after Khrushchev's secret speech denouncing Stalin in February 1956. His rehabilitation was concluded in 1964, although only in 1979 did a full length scholarly biography appear in Hungary, however briefly.

Borsányi's image of Kun differs little from those drawn by Kun's earlier detractors. He is depicted as an opportunist, a *bon vivant,* and petty thief. He is seen as a mediocre and dogmatic thinker, an irresponsible organizer, foolhardy, arrogant, intolerant, a coward who denounced his opponents on false charges. If anything positive is said about Kun, it is that he was a good soldier with an aptitude for foreign languages.

Borsányi's work deflates the acclaim heaped on Kun in works published during the previous decade. These include a book written by Tamás Dersi about Kun's career as a publicist, as well as a book of recollections by Kun's widow.[5] For Borsányi, Kun was a mediocre writer who sold his pen to the highest bidder. A 1905 article of Kun, which appeared in a Kolozsvár paper, "Let there be revolution then," has been viewed by Dersi and others as an early sign of the young Kun's revolutionary belief. Borsányi dismisses this assertion with the claim that in 1905 public opinion was revolting against the high-handed behavior of the Vienna court. Consequently, Kun's writing is viewed as an attempt to please the public and not as a sign of personal conviction.

Borsányi emphasizes the fact that during those days Kun was influenced by the chauvinistic gentry world; his coffee-house lifestyle had little in common with the workers whose cause he later embraced. Kun's later claim that he was a radical within the Social Democratic party is also rejected. Borsányi indicates that even during the Great War, Kun was a "defensist," rather than a Zimmerwaldist.

Kun was captured on the Galician Front during spring 1916. In the Russian prisoner-of-war camp, he joined the Socialist prisoners-of-war. For this, he received reprobation from the conservative officers, who boycotted the Socialists.

Following the outbreak of the March 1917 revolution, Kun and the other Socialists in Tomsk made contact with the Russian revolutionaries in town. Although it has been claimed in Mrs. Kun's book and elsewhere that Kun soon became a Bolshevik,[6] Borsányi casts doubt on this. In Siberia Mensheviks and Bolsheviks shared similar views and the same Socialist organization (p. 50). The author is equally skeptical about the claim that following the Bolshevik revolution in November, 1917, Kun went to Petrograd, to the Bolshevik Central Committee. Borsányi suggests that Kun went to the Russian capital because he believed it to be the fastest way home, given that the foreign missions in charge of repatriating prisoners of war were headquartered there. In summary, Borsányi sees Kun as a reluctant revolutionary who turned to Bolshevism not out of conviction, but in order to make the best of a bad situation.

In Borsányi's view, Kun was not the only one motivated to become a Communist out of opportunism. Many in Russia joined the movement in order to avoid famine. When Lenin wanted them to return to Hungary to spread world revolution, these new converts were reluctant to embark on such a mission, even in the closing days of the war. As is Borsányi's style, he is a determinist in his defense of their hesitation. The damning behavior of one Communist or another is explained away by the claim that under the circumstances, little else could have been done. For example, for the former prisoner-of-war revolutionaries, a return to Hungary would have meant isolation, court martial, or reassignment to the Italian Front, and not a return home to loved ones. Therefore, hesitation to be repatriated was justified.

This type of hesitation from supposedly dedicated revolutionaries, however, pales by comparison with Kun's cowardly behavior during the days of the Hungarian Soviet Republic (March 21 to August 1, 1919). At the end of April, when the military situation looked bleak for the Hungarian Soviet government, Kun, ready to flee, arranged asylum for himself in Austria. Borsányi rationalizes Kun's behavior by claiming that Kun wanted to save his life in order to be ready for the next revolutionary action (p. 156). The author seems only slightly more critical of Kun's conduct during the closing days of Soviet power. At that time, he arranged exile for the leading participants of the revolution, but failed to arrange an escape for the "Lenin boys," the revolutionary terror squads, who in turn fell victim to the counterrevolutionary White Terror.

Romsics' book also deals with the cowardice of the Communist leadership. During the local peasant revolutions against Communist authorities, Communist officials took to their heels at the first news of an uprising, thereby creating a power vacuum which was quickly filled by malcontents.

In addition to depicting Kun as a coward during the revolutionary days in Hungary, Borsányi also charges him with incompetence. Kun returned to Hungary with Lenin's blessings early in November, 1918. His task was to form a Hungarian Communist party which, in fact, had already been formed in Moscow on November 4.

Traditional Marxist historiography explains that Kun managed to form the party in Hungary by bringing together several Socialist factions.[7] Borsányi proposes that there were no clear factions, only individuals with different views (p. 81). By prematurely pressing for the organization of the Communist party, Kun had, in fact, prevented the possibility of winning over a large number of Social Democrats who may have also differed with the Socialist leadership (p. 81).

As a party historian, however, Borsányi rejects the opinion of Western scholars that the party was established in Hungary by "Moscow's agents." He claims that only seven of the sixteen leaders had been prisoners of war. This may be true, but if one argues that Kun was too hasty in setting up the party, then it also implies that the "home communists" would have been satisfied with staying in the Social Democratic party had Kun not forced the premature formation of the Communist party. Hence, without the Muscovites there would have been no party organized in November.

One positive achievement of Kun during the early days of the party was the establishment of the party journal *Vörös Újság* (Red News). It embarked at once to agitate for revolution. According to Borsányi, *Vörös Újság* dealt with a topic that was taboo for the Social Democratic party journal *Népszava* – the Jewish question. The Communist paper frequently referred to the Jewish identity of the majority of Hungary's capitalists.

The author underplays the journal's anti-Semitic overtones. He claims that the repeated attacks by *Vörös Újság* on the Jewish bourgeoisie were not a concession to anti-Semitic strains in public opinion, they were, instead, a way to unmask the chauvinism of the Jews, who tried to outdo the gentry-Christian right wing (p. 92).

The defense of *Vörös Újság*'s Jew-baiting seems to be especially weak in the light of Romsics' analysis of anti-Semitism. Romsics sees anti-Semitism in 1919 as the "uneducated public's quest for justice" (p. 147). For these impoverished people, wealth and Jewishness were synonymous. For this reason, Romsics perceives that even some proletarian leaders were imbued with this kind of anti-Semitism. As an extreme example of this tendency, Romsics brings up the case of the leader of proletarian women of Kalocsa whose favorite slogan was: "down with the Jew Archbiship of Kalocsa!" (p. 148) It is evident from Romsics's book, therefore, that *Vörös Újság* could reinforce incipient anti-Semitism among the poor.

The achievements of the Soviet Republic come under fire by all three authors. As indicated by these scholars, the Communists had no electoral support nor organization when they fused with the Social Democrats in a united party and established a Soviet government in Budapest on March 21, 1919. This government embarked on a disastrous agrarian policy, recognized as such even by the Communist leaders soon after the collapse of the Soviet Republic.

Romsics's regional study clearly details the rise of peasant dissatisfaction resulting from the ineptitude of the Communist leadership. Policies such as forced draft at harvest time, collectivization, nationalization, and forced requisitioning created a great deal of resentment. They led to local uprisings, which in a chain reaction spread throughout the region and resulted in a temporary collapse of Soviet power and authority between June 18 and 23 (p. 137). These uprisings have been seen by Marxist historians, including Borsányi, as being coordinated by refugees from Vienna, or from French-occupied Szeged, and by conspirators from Budapest. Contrary to this view, Romsics sees a mass basis for the local revolutions against Soviet power. He views the revotions as being free from ideology, spurred on by simple slogans such as "liberation from the yoke of the thieving Communists!" (p. 146) The peasants were generally satisfied with merely chasing away their Communist oppressors. When Communist authority was reestablished, however, punishment was harsh.

Reprisals were often taken against proletarian and agrar-proletarian elements, which Romsics considers as "destructive to the working class movement" in the long run (p. 162). The implication here is that it was not Horthy's terror that prevented the rebirth of the Communist movement in interwar Hungary, but the Communist policies, which, during the Soviet Republic, had alienated the proletariat from its representatives. This was already noticeable during May and June, 1919. Romsics states that is was during these months that "within the class basis of the dictatorship of the proletariat signs of listlessness and dissatisfaction were noticeable" (p. 142).

György Péteri concludes that the management of industries during the Soviet period was as incompetent as the management of the agrarian sector. His thesis is significant because historians have not as yet scrutinized industrial policies of the Soviet government in a thorough fashion. Communist exiles of the Soviet period never admitted to industrial mismanagement in the way admitted to faulty agrarian policies.

In fact, the Hungarian Soviet government turned the already shaky industrial sector of the economy it inherited into a shambles. The lot of the workers, who had expected to benefit from the revolution, worsened during the four months of Soviet power. Industrial output declined during this period and Péteri blames this on nationalization and on the creation of industrial "sectoral centers." Thus, the doctrinaire Hungarian leaders replaced a market-oriented system with an ineptly-centralized industrial management model.

The result was scarcity and shortages. Centralized distribution of commodities was done haphazardly and without priorities. Key industries were idle and unemployment increased. The neglect of effective cost accounting led to financing of production through the printing press. Consequently, money lost its value and barter was practiced. As in Russia, this phenomenon was hailed by Marxist ideologues who saw money as a capitalist tool. In reality, this loss of the means of exchange undermined centralized coordination of production of industry and led to obstructive autonomous decision making by individual enterprises.

Péteri suggests that industrial mismanagement would have led to the collapse of the Soviet Republic; only its military defeat pre-empted such an eventuality.

The Soviet Republic's military defeat is closely tied to the failure of its foreign policy. It was assumed that only with Soviet Russian help could Hungary maintain its integrity. Therefore, Béla Kun and the Communists were invited to fuse with the Socialists and to form a government. Kun, as the commissar of foreign affairs, was expected to deliver Bolshevik help to the Hungarians. As Borsányi indicates, he failed in this most conspicuously.

From the very first report of Soviet power in Hungary, Lenin expressed reservations and suspicions about the Socialist–Communist fusion into a united Marxist party. Kun tried to allay Lenin's fears by stressing that the Communist minority had a firm grip over the Socialist majority. Surprisingly, Kun's rebuttal did not lead to further criticism. Instead, seeing the revolution in Hungary shifting into Communist tracks, Lenin responded with praise. Borsányi, however, doubts that Lenin was sincere in his assessment since he saw the Social Democrats as the enemy of Communists everywhere (p. 145). Charging the apostle of Communism with duplicity is a significant departure from the norms by a Hungarian Marxist–Leninist.

Although Lenin eventually praised the Hungarian revolution, he was reluctant to provide the kind of help Kun and the Hungarians expected. On April 21, Kun fired an impatient message to Lenin questioning the wisdom of the Russian world revolutionary and asking him why the Soviet leadership only paid attention to Russia and the Ukraine and not to Hungary (p. 155).

Reverting to a familiar approach, Borsányi goes on to explain why Lenin was more correct in stressing the conquest of the Donets basin in the Ukraine instead of following Khristian Rakovskii's plan of linking the Russian Red Army with the Hungarian through Romania. Borsányi points out that by mid-May, Khristian Rakovskii's plans had become unrealistic; the pro-Bolshevik Hetman N. Grigoriev and his troops had risen in rebellion, making Rakovskii's project against Romania impossible. The uprising also facilitated the counter-attack of the White Denikin forces in southern Russia.

A reader versed in Russian history knows that Grigoriev rose against his Red allies in protest against the very exactions and terror deemed unnecessary in Hungary by Borsányi and Romsics. It can be concluded, therefore, that had Lenin and the Russian Communists been more conciliatory toward the Ukrainian peasants, Grigoriev's army and the troops used to crush Grigoriev could have provided help for the Hungarian cause. The price for unconditional victory over the Ukranian peasant was the defeat of revolution in Hungary.

If the Bolshevik failure to deliver military help could be explained away, no such rationale exists for its failure to deliver a less tangible, more symbolic aid, sorely needed by the Hungarian Soviet government. Borsányi mentions, for example, that in spite of repeated requests, the Soviet Russian government never sent an official ambassador to Soviet Hungary. Nor was Bukharin sent to the party congress as a morale booster, as was requested of Lenin by Béla Kun. What comes out of Borsányi's text is that Lenin was preoccupied with the Russian revolution at the expense of world revolution.

In light of this conclusion, Borsányi's attack on Kun's unflinching internationalism becomes even more glaring. Borsányi criticises Kun for his rigid internationalism at a time when Hungary was fighting against its neighbors, the Romanians and the Czecho-Slovaks. He believes that Kun, for the sake of Communist victory, should have been more pragmatic and should have appealed to the ideology of Hungarian nationalism. Instead, Kun was opposed even to such symbolic acts as the show of the Hungarian tricolor among the troops instead of the red flag.

In the past, Kun has been criticised by Marxist historians for following the Bukharinist concept of "proletarian self-determination" instead of the Leninist concept of "national self-determination." Borsányi recognizes that as an internationalist, Kun, like Bukharin, believed in the assimilation of the proletariat of different nations. In practice, however, as the author points out, Kun followed Lenin's precepts. This resulted in the creation of the Slovak Soviet Republic in the area which was liberated by the Hungarian Red Army in July, 1919.

Although Kun's nationalities policy is defended, he is held responsible for the poorly organized and ill-fated Communist putsch in Vienna of June 15, 1919. As usual, Borsányi marshals the mitigating circumstance: at that time the "International labor movement was saturated by putschist tendencies" (p. 178). As an example, he refers to a similar trend in the Bolshevik party during July 1917 which was opposed by Lenin. The reader, however, could also think of the November revolution. It, too, could be considered a putsch.

Borsányi is less forgiving of Kun's failure to build a Marxist–Leninist party in Hungary. In the author's view, it should have been the *raison d'être* of the dictatorship of the proletariat (p. 169). It is difficult to understand his criticism since elsewhere in his book he indicates that there were simply not enough cadres. Romsics' book underscores the fact that there were very few people who were party members before the fusion. After the two Marxist parties united, most members gravitated toward the erstwhile Socialist leaders.

Two important myths were created after the fall of the Soviet Republic. Both of these are convincingly demolished in the book. The first, favored by

Marxist historians, speaks of the mobilization of the working class against the first offensive of the Romanians. Workers are regaled because they stopped the threat to Budapest when they did not allow the Romanians to cross the Tisza. Borsányi suggests that on May 2–3, the Romanians were stopped not by the Red Army, but by pressure from the conferees of the Paris Peace Conference and by Romanian troop redeployments in which some troops were transferred from Hungary to Bessarabia.

The second myth is favored by nationalistically-minded historians, who attribute final military collapse to Kun's acceptance of the second Clemenceau memorandum, which arrived in Budapest on June 15, 1919. This demanded the withdrawal of Hungarian troops from Slovakia. Kun's adherence to the terms of the memorandum immediately after victory against the Czechs has been perceived as a cause for disillusionment among the patriotic troops in the army. Kun's submission has been judged as a grave mistake even by the authoritative *Magyar forradalmi munkásmozgalom története* (first printing, 1966).[8]

Borsányi believes that facing Allied pressure, Kun had little choice and looked upon the agreement as another Treaty of Brest-Litovsk, ready to be broken even before the ink on the signatures was dry. Borsányi demonstrates that the troops were not withdrawn immediately; Kun used the excuse of Czech hostility in order to slow withdrawal (p. 181).

Romsics also shares the view that Kun had no choice but to withdraw. He stresses the fact that draft evasion and the revolts taking place in the countryside forced the hand of Kun to accept Clemenceau's dictate (p. 164).

The collapse of the Hungarian Soviet Republic on August 1, 1919, led to the prearranged departure of the Communist leaders for Vienna. Borsányi charges Kun with committing a significant error in not preparing an underground party to function under adverse conditions (p. 192). This failure is attributed, in part, to Kun's belief in an imminent second Communist revolution. Kun's unrealistic expectation is mitigated, however, by the fact that Lenin expected the same. To muster proof, Borsányi refers to Kun's theoretical work of the period, *From Revolution to Revolution,* which was criticized by Lenin only for its lack of detail, but not for its unrealistic thesis.

Following a brief stay in Vienna, Kun was allowed to go to Russia. On October 1, 1920, Kun, the former Red Internationalist and revolutionary leader, was appointed to the Military Council of the Southern Front, commanded by Mikhail Frunze. Frunze's troops were in the process of clearing the last obstacle to Soviet power in Russia, the army of General Piotr Wrangel. The last stand of Wrangel took place on the Crimean peninsula, from where it was dislodged by a surprise Red Army attack.

The Red Army offensive started on November 8, 1920 through the Perekop Isthmus, across an ice-clogged lake. A surprise attack through such an inhospitable area cost the lives of tens of thousands of Red troops. Borsányi terms this attack as close to senseless slaughter. Yet, again, it is explained away on the basis that it shortened the civil war by at least a half-year, the period significant to the consolidation of Soviet power (p. 228). This Machiavellian justification, however, is again weak. By the end of November 1920, there was no question that Soviet power was firmly established in Russia. Borsányi's startling evaluation of the offensive as senseless because of the slaughter of Red Army troops is a view unlikely to be found in any contemporary Soviet publication.

Following the defeat of Wrangel's forces, Kun, Sergei Ivanovich Gusev, and Rozaliya Smoylovna Zemlyachka then embarked on the pacification of the Crimea. The bloodbath conducted by Kun has been widely known among the students of Russian history. Borsányi's aim is to clear Kun, the head of the Revolutionary Council of the Crimea, of charges that he was the instigator of the "bloodbath," which, according to Serge and Borkenau, brought the ire of Lenin against Béla Kun.[9]

Consequently, the Red Terror in the Crimea is seen by the author as a necessary and common practice of pacification. Kun's participation in the terror is also excused on psychological grounds; Kun vented his anger against the Whites in Russia because the White Terror raged in Hungary. Kun, like many revolutionaries, saw their action in global terms. Therefore, he saw no difference between Russian and Hungarian counterrrevolutionaries.

The last line of Borsányi's defense is the dismissal of claims that Lenin and the Soviet government had a negative view of Kun's activities. He reverses Borkenau's argument that Kun was sent to Germany on a Comintern assignment because Lenin wanted him out of Russia following his misdeed in the Crimea.[10] Instead, Borsányi claims that Lenin approved what Kun was doing and hence rewarded him with another important mission.

This debate could be decided by the examination of Soviet sources which obviously were not provided to Borsányi, as they had not been made available to Borkenau almost 50 years earlier. It is significant, however, that in the case of Borsányi, the right to research was denied to a trusted cadre. Since Kun spent almost twenty years, over half of his adult life, in Russian positions of leadership, inaccessability to Soviet documentation indicates that this important biography of Kun is hardly a definitive one.

In Borsányi's argument concerning Lenin's orders to Kun, there is also an implicit admission that the Comintern was a tool of Soviet Russian policy as early as 1921. Kun's activities on behalf of the Comintern, however, were disastrous. This view of western historians is shared by Borsányi.

Borsányi is also critical of Kun's activities on behalf of the faction-torn Hungarian Communist Party in exile. For example, Kun was unable to recognize oppressive conditions in Hungary; he favored the repatriation of party workers to Hungary "unprepared for the Hungarian situation." (p. 256) Furthermore, Kun did not pay sufficient attention to the infiltration of the party, which led to the repeated elimination of the fledgling underground. One such action by the Hungarian police is blamed directly on Kun's incompetence. In December 1926, Kun visited Vienna. His contact at the railway station had with him a briefcase full of documents concerning underground members in Hungary and their activities. The conference on party activities took place in a taxicab. When the cab reached its destination the briefcase and the compromising documents were accidentally left in the cab. The unsuspecting cabbie turned the documents over to the Hungarian Embassy. At the embassy the documents were copied and, according to Borsányi, returned to Kun in a roundabout way an in effort to allay suspicions that they had been seen by unfriendly eyes (p. 288). Borsányi faults Kun not for losing the briefcase, which was not his, but for taking it back without the slightest suspicion of foul play, which might have prompted him to take precautionary measures.

Borsányi's account, however, omits one significant detail that does appear in a monograph that he identifies as a source. In Ervinné Liptai's work, the disappearance of the briefcase was not tied in with Kun. In her book, she merely mentioned that lost party documents were found by a cabbie and turned over to the Hungarian Embassy by the Austrian Political Police. To throw off suspicions, the photographed, though seemingly untouched documents in the briefcase were then turned over by the paid-off cab driver to the Soviet Embassy.[11] This combination of sources indicates, therefore, that if Kun was incompetent, the Soviet officials were also inept; they should have alerted Kun of possible mischief. If Mrs. Liptai did not wish to tarnish Kun's name, Borsányi, too, presented only part of the truth. This may indicate his desire to avoid adverse reaction from political authorities. In any case, both Borsányi and Mrs. Liptai believe that the purloined documents had catastrophic consequences for the underground and for the Hungarian Socialist Workers party, a legal organization that was now exposed in Hungary as a cover for the illegal Communist party.

Some of Kun's other party activities are also criticized by Borsányi. He is held responsible for not recognizing the Fascist threat and for regarding the Hungarian Socialists as "social Fascists." In this, he, of course, shares the views of Stalin and the official Soviet position. Yet nowhere in the book is there an explanation or analysis of the Stalin—Kun nexus, which Trotskii stressed in the early thirties.[12]

No doubt, it is this nexus that led Kun to engage in those despicable actions in 1929 which are brought to the reader's attention. That year, Kun denounced his factional opponents living in Russia as Trotskyites. These people were temporarily imprisoned, and then released. One only wonders how many of these men were later rearrested and killed during the purges on the same charges that had been proven as falsifications earlier.

In spite of the outcome of Kun's denunciations, he had Comintern support against the home Communists who disagreed with his views on the Socialists. Some of these men came to Russia in 1932 to clarify some disagreements, only to be arrested on Kun's urgings as agents of the Hungarian Regent Admiral Miklós Horthy.

The influence of Béla Kun began to eclipse following a shift in Soviet foreign policy in 1935. The success of Nazism forced Stalin to recognize that the Fascists and not the Social Democrats were the real enemies of the Soviet Union. The Comintern, which Borsányi depicts as an independent organization, in fact followed Stalin's cue. It introduced the Popular Front policy. Béla Kun, compromised by the old course, fell into disfavor as a "sectarian."

Kun was not the only Hungarian in disgrace. The whole Hungarian Communist party was dissolved in 1936 by the Comintern, being charged with "sectarianism" and "factionalism." Appearing as thinly veiled criticism of the Soviet policy, Borsányi questions why the Comintern dissolved the Party. Factionalism had always been a pervasive problem; it was no more factional in 1936 than it had been earlier.

The final change in the status of Béla Kun came in the midst of the ongoing purges. During the night of June 29, 1937, the fallen leader of the Hungarian Communist exiles and of the Comintern was arrested and was not seen by his family again. According to the rehabilitation papers of the Military College of the Soviet Supreme Court, he died on November 30, 1939. Borsányi notes that the circumstances of his death were not revealed in this document.

If the circumstances of Kun's death are still shrouded in mystery, the reasons for banning the Kun biography may also remain an enigma for some time to come. It is unlikely that it was banned for criticizing Kun's leadership of the revolution. Romsics' and Péteri's book did not suffer a similar fate, despite their negative evaluation of the Hungarian Soviet regime.

For this reason, reports from Hungarian academic sources that the book was withdrawn upon Soviet pressure, seems convincing. The demythification of Kun also demythified the Soviet government, aspects of the Bolshevik Revolution, and Lenin. In Russia, this could have been done only through samizdat, leading to charges of anti-Soviet slander, imprisonment, or at best expulsion of the monograph's author.

The long hand of the KGB could not reach Borsányi in a similar fashion. Therefore, only his book was banned. Since several thousand copies of the book had been sold before it was withdrawn, its "weaknesses" had to be publicly aired. Apparently, this chore was left to the then Politburo member Dezső Nemes who had first read the work in its manuscript form, criticized it, but obviously had not objected to its publication. The official attack of this

Hungarian Pooh-Bah appeared in *Párttörténeti Közlemények* (Party History Review). From the introduction to the article, the uninitiated reader would hardly know that the book had been withdrawn. The impression given is that *Kun Béla* was published for the research libraries, and that inadvertently several thousand had reached the reading public.

The nearly 80 pages of Nemes' text, or one-fifth the size of Borsányi's entire book, was the purported prepublication evaluation of Borsányi's manuscript. Nemes now claimed that the changes he proposed had been disregarded by the author. In his criticism, Nemes objected to Borsányi's one-sided view of Kun throughout the book. This, Nemes charged, provided ammunition "for those who attempted and will attempt to soil the revolutionary past of the Hungarian Communist Party and to prove the right of the renegades, the liquidators and different anti-party factions" (p. 88). For this and other reasons, Nemes concluded in italics, "the picture of the Communist Party of Hungary drawn by the author is often far from the truth" (p. 94).

Nemes also criticized Borsányi's view of Lenin and his perception of the Comintern. Nemes claimed that Borsányi's analysis is similar to the fairy tales of "anti-communist propaganda" (p. 80). He also criticized Borsányi for including unnecessary information in this book. Among these is Borsányi's explanation of the "Comintern bureaucracy," which Nemes claimed had little relevance to Kun's biography. Since Kun was a Comintern leader, Nemes' criticism is unjustified. What must have grieved Nemes and the others behind the scenes is that through Borsányi's narrative the reader could see the extent of Soviet control over the Comintern. This is exactly what Nemes considered the fairy tale of the anti-Communists.

Curously, Borsányi is chastised for "detached reporting," generally considered a prerequisite for any historian. Nemes wanted Borsányi to omit the truth as in the case of Endre Rudnyánszky's letter to Grigorii Zinoviev. The letter was found in the Hungarian party archives, a collection which is open only to a few party historians. In his book, Borsányi had revealed the contents of the letter in which the Hungarian Comintern activist in his resignation letter of 1921 wrote Zinoviev that there was no true historical basis for Soviet power in Hungary in 1919.

In addition to omitting the truth, Nemes also wanted Borsányi to falsify history. An example of this relates to Borsányi's criticism of Kun for equating the political goals of Western democracies with that of the Fascists. He stated that Kun was right. Nemes claimed that the conservative leaders in England allowed German rearmament in the 1930s in order to make it easier for Germany to attack Russia and that the French bourgeoisie supported the British goal at Munich (p. 102). For seeing history differently, Nemes branded Borsányi as a man with limited intellectual abilities.

In essence, Kun's biographer was criticized for exposing a number of compromising truths that undermine the myths set down by the authoritative *History of the Hungarian Revolutionary Labor Movement,* edited by the late Dezső Nemes. For this reason, Nemes criticized Borsányi for not including this work among the sources he had used for his manuscript. Nemes accused Borsányi of symbolic defiance through this omission:

... in spite of the fact that the evaluations of this book are more firmly established than the ones found in other works on which the author relies as sources for his own interpretation. Naturally, we do not desire the 'canonization' of the *History of the Hungarian Revolutionary Labor Movement,* although its text was approved by an editorial committee set up by the Central Committee of the Party following extensive debates. This is well known to the author. Reliance on this work could not only have helped his way through complicated questions, but could also have helped him to avoid confusion and the exaggeration of certain events.[13]

Evidently, Borsányi came under Nemes' scathing attack for deviating from the official party line on its history.

In Hungary, however, historians had been able to deviate from the official party line for some time. In this sense, Borsányi's book fits into trends of contemporary Hungarian historiography. This fact is borne out by Péteri's and Romsics' publication. The latter was published almost three years after Borsányi's. In a review in *Könyvvilág,* the Hungarian book review journal, the reviewer expressed satisfaction at learning the views of Romsics and Péteri on the Soviet Republic of Hungary. These, she claimed, "help us to overcome our one-sided views."[14] This indicates that most Hungarian historians intend to continue to be fairly unrestrained about their examination of history. They will, however, have to conform to official party standards if they want to write about party history or Soviet affairs.

Evidence for this is the more recently-published book co-authored by György Borsányi and János Kende. The monograph is recommended by the publisher to "students of party schools and of the history of the labor movement." It lacks all the objectivity of Borsányi's *Kun Béla,* or the monographs of Romsics and Péteri.

Thus, whereas Kun's role in the prewar movement was dismissed in Borsányi's biography, he is identified as an active member of the Social Democratic party since 1902 in the Borsányi–Kende monograph.[15] This date is especially significant as Kun was born only in 1886! In contradiction to the biography, Kun is also identified as a "prominent and militant leader of the pre-war Transylvanian labor movement (p. 47)."

The Soviet Republic is depicted without blemishes. Even its fatal agrarian policy is seen in a favorable light (p. 75). The myth of the heroic stand of the Hungarian workers at the Tisza, deflated in *Kun Béla,* is also resuscitated in this book. Lastly, the uprisings in the Danube-Tisza area are considered as part of the coordinated counterrevolutionary movement (p. 106).

On the post-1919 events, the book omits the discussion of the factional conflicts, although it admits that "at the end of the 1920s and early 1930s the Hungarian Communist Party was held back by sectarian mistakes in the Comintern." These were, however, "recognized and corrected by the Comintern itself." (p. 124) The text passes over the fate of Kun and the other Hungarian communists; nor is it mentioned that the Comintern dissolved the party.

The return to an uncritical evaluation of Béla Kun has been further demonstrated by publications on the occasion of the centennial of Béla Kun's birth. Dezső Nemes's book, written just before his death is most illustrative of this trend.[16] The book's conclusion reflects the tone of its content:

Béla Kun was with his entire work, revolutionary activities a *generally recognized great man of the Hungarian and international labor movement*. With his activities of 1918–1919, and with his work as the leading figure of proletarian power, he became *one of the greatest figures of the Hungarian people*. [Italics in the original] (186)

Nemes's swan song only refers to Borsányi's earlier biography when he questions the latter's evaluation of Kun's role in the Crimea and in his activities in Germany as Comintern representative in 1921. Nemes's attack on Borsányi's analysis of Frunze's campaign in the Crimea and Kun's role supports the claim that *Kun Béla* was withdrawn on Soviet orders.[17] Nemes takes Borsányi to account not only for blackening Kun's reputation but also for reinforcing anti-Soviet propaganda. (p. 136)[18]

Nemes's whitewashing the Soviet Union also comes through in his description of the circumstances of Kun's death:

His health deterioriated even before his arrest, as he suffered from diabetes. Evidently his health was further undermined by his arrest and the unjust criminal charges which discredited his revolutionary past, and he died in prison. (186)

Thus, Borsányi claimed that the way Kun died has not been revealed by the Soviets as yet; Nemes unequivocally stated that he died in prison, but not as a result of deprivation and mistreatment, which was known to have been the fate of the purge victims. Rather, he died of an illness, which would have killed him anyhow!

The return to the cult of Béla Kun characteristic of the 1960s represents serious setback for scholarship. Historicist pretenses dictated by political exigences will, however, only confuse the collective memory of Hungarians, contributing to a negative perception of the revolutionary era of 1919.

## NOTES

1. Péter Hanák, ed., *A Dunántúl, Történelmi figyelő* [By the Danube, Historical Observer] (Budapest, 1982), 176.

2. György Borsányi, *Kun Béla, Politikai életrajz* [Béla Kun, Political Biography] (Budapest, 1979); Ignác Romsics, *A Duna–Tisza köze hatalmi–politikai viszonyai 1918–1919-ben* [The Power–Politics of the Danube and Tisza Region in 1918–1919] (Budapest, 1982); György Péteri, *A Magyar Tanácsköztársaság iparirányítási rendszere* [The Industrial Management System of the Hungarian Soviet Republic] (Budapest, 1979).

3. For some examples, see, Rudolf L. Tőkés, *Béla Kun and the Hungarian Soviet Republic: The Origins and Role of the Communist Party of Hungary in the Revolutions of 1918–1919* (New York, 1967); Andrew C. János and William B. Slottman, eds., *Revolution in Perspective* (Berkeley, 1971); Iván Völgyes, ed., *Hungary in Revolution, 1918–1919* (Lincoln, 1981); Branko Lazitch and Milorad M. Drachkovitch, *Lenin and the Comintern* (Stanford, 1974); Bennett Kovrig, *Communism in Hungary from Kun to Kádár* (Stanford, 1979); Peter Pastor, "One Step Forward, Two Steps Back: The Rise and Fall of the Hungarian Communist Party, 1918–1922," in Ivo Banac, ed., *Effects of World War I: The Class War After the Great War: The Rise of the Communist Parties in East Central Europe, 1918–1921* (New York, 1983).

4. Albert Kaas and Fedor de Lazarovics, *Bolshevism in Hungary* (London, 1931); Elemér Mályusz, *The Fugitive Bolsheviks* (London, 1931); George Breitman and Sarah Lovell, eds., *Writings of Leon Trotsky [1932]* (New York, 1973), 307–309; Victor Serge, *Memoirs of a Revolutionary 1901–1941* (New York, 1963), 139.

5. Tamás Dersi, *A publicista Kun Béla, Pályakezdő korszak* [The Publicist Béla Kun, The Start of a Career] (Budapest, 1973); Béláné Kun, *Kun Béla. (Emlékezések)* [Béla Kun (Recollections)] (Budapest, 1966).

6. Béláné Kun, *Kun Béla,* 59–61; I. M. Gramchak and M. F. Lebovich, *Béla Kun – Vidaiuschiisia deiatel' vengerskogo i revoliutsionnogo dvizheniia* (Moscow, 1975), 22.

7. Dr. Tibor Szamuely, *A Kommunisták Magyarországi Pártjának megalakulása és harca a proletárdiktatúráért* [The Formation and Struggle of the Hungarian Communist Party for the Dictatorship of the Proletariat] (Budapest, 1964), 196–97; Ervin Liptai, *A Magyar Tanácsköztársaság* [The Hungarian Soviet Republic] (Budapest, 1965); 43–44; János Kende, *Forradalomról forradalomra* [From Revolution to Revolution] (Budapest, 1979), 79–80.

8. Dezső Nemes, ed., *A Magyar forradalmi munkásmozgalom története* [The History of the Hungarian Revolutionary Labor Movement] (Budapest, 1979), 187, 191.

9. Serge, *Memoirs,* 140; Franz Borkenau, *World Communism, A History of the Communist International* (Ann Arbor, 1962), 115; Lazitch and Drachkovitch, *Lenin and the Comintern,* 488.

10. Borkenau, *World Communism,* 115; Lazitch and Drachkovitch incorrectly claim that, at first, the angry Lenin sent Kun away to Turkestan. Lazitch and Drachkovitch, *Lenin and the Comintern,* 488.

11. Ervinné Liptai, *A Magyarországi Szocialista Munkáspárt, 1925–1928* [The Hungarian Socialist Workers Party, 1925–1928] (Budapest, 1971), 236.

12. George Breitman and Bev Scott, eds., *Writings of Leon Trotsky [1934–1935]* (New York, 1971), 155, 341 n. 161.

482    REVOLUTIONS AND INTERVENTIONS

13. Dezső Nemes, "Észrevételek Borsányi György: Kun Béla politikai életrajza című munkájához" [Observations on György Borsányi, Béla Kun's Political Biography], *Párttörténeti Közlemények* [Reports on Party History] 25, no. 3 (1979): 109.

14. Katalin Fenyves, "A Duna összeköt bennünket" [The Danube Ties us Together], *Könyvvilág* [Book World] 28 no. 2 (1983): 4.

15. György Borsányi and János Kende, *Magyarországi munkásmozgalom 1867–1980* [The Hungarian Labor Movement 1867–1980] (Budapest, 1982); for an earlier version used as a textbook at party schools, see, János Kende, György Borsányi et al., *Előadások a magyar forradalmi munkásmozgalom történetéből* [Lectures on the History of the Hungarian Revolutionary Labor Movement] (Budapest, 1976).

16. Dezső Nemes, *Kun Béla politikai életútjáról* [About the Political Life of Béla Kun] (Budapest, 1985). For other publications praising Kun, see, Lajos Arokay, *Kun Béla* (Budapest, 1986), Katalin Petrák, ed., *Kun Béla a kortársak szemével* [Béla Kun with the eyes of contemporaries] (Budapest, 1986).

17. Timothy Garton Ash, "The Hungarian Lesson," *The New York Review of Books,* Vol. XXXII, No. 19 (Dec. 5, 1985), p. 5.

18. For a positive Soviet interpretation of Kun's activities in the Crimea see, Nikolai Derzhaluk, "Kun Béla a Krimben," *Historia,* Vol. VIII, no. 1, (1986), 24–26.

# 1918–1919: THE CHANGING IMAGE
# OF TWO REVOLUTIONS

Tibor Hajdu

It would indeed be impossible to hand down an unequivocal judgment on the revolutions of 1918–19 as reflected in the Hungarian "national consciousness." We cannot even speak of a single-minded national consciousness once the feudal concept of a nation, which had prevailed until 1848, became outdated. Such a concept only began to emerge again more recently, after the old orders ceased to exist, around the turn of the 1860s. Even presently, however, under the conditions which prevail in our press and in our public life, it would be difficult to define that concept, let alone to define it in relation to certain events of the past.

If we resort to the subtleties of legal jargon and declare that "we shall suppose, without actually allowing" the existence of such a national or public consciousness, and we nevertheless attempt to give it a general formulation, there is only one way to do it in my opinion: that is in a relative way. And since the object of comparison can only be the revolution of 1848, we must ask ourselves the question: why did the revolutions of 1918–19 not exert such a determining influence on consciousness and on the future path of the nation as 1848–49 had seventy years earlier? The question, indeed, is a legitimate one, for it is not academic in the least: this is actually how we meet with the problem in the press, in literature, in the schools.

Moreover, it is a legitimate question because, although the views of different circles show some variations, it has been phrased and rephrased as a question every year since 1919. Again, therefore, why did not the revolutions exert a deeper influence?

Those who do not think of 1918 and 1919 as true or national revolutions, but merely as the side effects of a collapse which had taken an alien turn from the straight path of the history of the Hungarian nation, or which had stumbled along that road, etc., may answer the question more easily. The question becomes far more difficult for the person who accepts the events of

1918–19 as a true revolution, and who accepts the views presented by contemporary historiography and by the public schools today, namely that 1918 and 1919 were, one, national revolutions; two, represented a higher stage in the evolution of the history of the nation and of society as compared to 1848; and three, the progenitor of our present social system, essentially as Socialist as 1919 had been – in other words, its continuator, in the long run. If this be our opinion then we must ask: why is 1918–19 not a constant theme – something to celebrate – in today's Socialist brigades, in discotheques, at house parties, as 1848 had been in among the nationalist circles and the hayrides in the 1860s?

First of all, possibly, because public opinion does not concern itself with the goal, but rather the results; the revolutions of 1918–19 had failed. In spite of the military defeat of 1848–49, that revolution continued to determine to a large extent the course of the following 70 years. After all, the demands of March 15, 1848, were met in 1867. Secondly, and equally fundamentally, the national program of 1918 and 1919 represents a Danubian confederation on a Wilsonian, and later on a Communist and internationalist basis. It seems utopian for the time being, and even a harmful utopia according to many, a utopia which blunted the determination of the nation to fight precisely at a moment when there was the greatest need for it. The victory of the Socialist system in the successor states, which did not bring about a substantial improvement in the situation of the Hungarian nation, tends to support such an appraisal.

The other aspect of the revolutions, namely democracy and socialism, met a more favorable evaluation. The democracy of the liberal October Revolution has been judged more generally, whereas the judgment on the dictatorship of the proletariat has always been along class lines. Even the nature of the latter tradition is not without its problems. Only when the building of Socialism is completed in Hungary will it become possible to tell for sure how much relationship there is – beyond the slogans they share – between Socialist concepts then and now. In a paradoxial manner, Hungary was closest to 1919 in the practical realization of Socialism during the so-called fifties (before 1956), when 1919 was regarded as a collection of errors, although the government managed to commit the selfsame errors in economic and domestic policies (land reforms and collectivization, nationalization of small entreprises, a Communistic housing policy, absorption of the vanguard into a mass-party of millions, etc., etc.). From the end of the fifties on, the official evaluation of 1919 has become more favorable. In fact, there was a time when attempts were made to play it up as the counterpart of the "nationalist" 1848; yet, nevertheless, the practical realization of socialism diverges more and more from this "model."

The popularity of 1919 had always been hampered, to a greater or lesser extent, by the exaggerated, yet constantly sounded charge of "un-Hungarianism" presented by counterpropaganda, as opposed to the incontrovertibly Hungarian nature (and therefore unpopular only among the minority nationalities) of 1848. The elements of this un-Hungarianism included the dominant role of the Jewish intelligentsia among the political and cultural leaders, the pro-Russian orientation, the internationalist character of the Red Army which was manifest even in its outward appearance, the policies pursued for the sake of winning over the minority nationalities. It can be added here that these two revolutions increasingly neglected the tenet of territorial integrity which had formed the basis of the programs of all Hungarian regimes until that time. That there was no other way for the revolutions cannot be demonstrated in retrospect. The utopian nationalities policies also contributed to the fact that the majority of Hungarian intellectuals from Transylvania, as well as the railroadmen, the postal employees, etc., became homeless. Even the phraseology of the revolution was "cosmopolitan" and by-passed popular, Hungarian-style motives.

Part and parcel of the above, of course, is the problem area of the Treaty of Trianon, into which I shall not enter, because Zsuzsa L. Nagy has already done that in her outstanding contribution.[1] I only wish to mention that there is an indirect, yet important, relationship between the Horthy regime, the interpretation of the World War II, and the allocation of responsibilities for Trianon. The point of view which used to judge the Horty regime and its participants mainly on the basis of their actions and statements in fall 1919, prevailed during the fifties, and has survived to some extent to this day; what is more, that point of view has occasionally even extended to the Social Democratic party (the Gyula Peidl cabinet and the pact it signed with István Bethlen). But this interpretation has been rejected effectively by an opposing interpretation which takes as its criterion Horthy's attitude in 1944, and thus absolves even Horthy from his former sins, not to mention his less well-known props, from General Kálmán Shvoy to General Szilárd Bakay. The study by Gyula Juhász deals with this phenomenon in detail — here I am merely making a reference to the relationship.[2]

I deliberately mention in last place the role of counterpropaganda, for that is characteristic of certain periods only. It was quite natural that the cultural policy of the Horthy era should include a deliberate and organized campaign of slander directed against the two revolutions, and the effect of this campaign on the older generation can still be felt. The circumstance that the different political groups of the revolution blamed each other for its failure has had a more lasting impact; indeed, subsequent observations and recollections also consist largely of mutual recriminations. Indirectly, this effect has lasted to our day. For instance, the reason a number of instructive and interesting memoirs by Communist and Socialist participants in the revolutions have not been published is because they are filled with mutual accusations. But to a lesser extent this attitude can also be found in those contemporary works that have been published. The general impression gathered by the reader may be that the consensus is: the defeat of the revolutions resulted from their failures, and the only thing left to debate among the participants of the revolutions is who was responsible for those failures? Although there had been similar manifestations after 1848 as well, from the work *Forradalom után* [After the Revolution][3] to János Arany's *A nagyidai cigányok* [Gypsies of Nagyida][4], or the controversy surrounding General Artúr Görgey,[5] nevertheless a clearer picture of that revolution began to emerge after the 1860's.

The reader may rightly regard what has been said in the preceding paragraphs as generalizations, but as I had stressed from the beginning, there is no chance for more than that unless we focus on specific periods, tendencies, or classes. I will attempt to do just that below.

The first period, the aftermath of the revolutions, is characterized, on one hand, by the fact that literature (whether in favor or against the revolution) was dominated by passions and political motives that were still fresh. On the other hand, a decisive segment of the population had lived through the revolutions, and they naturally started from their personal experiences. By the same token, this signifies that in its evaluation of the revolutions "public opinion" is divided sharply along class lines. Although it is easier to express such an opinion than to find documentary support for it, I will, nevertheless, make a schematic attempt at proving it.

The main carrier and grassroots support of the revolutions were the organized workers. Although these workers became disappointed in the two revolutions — because of their defeat and because of the utopianism of the dictatorship of the proletariat — their disappointment was manifested in the fact that they no longer were available for any further revolutionary activity, rather than that they rejected the spirit and goals of 1919. The first part of the above thesis has become undeniable fact by today, yet it was misunderstood by both workers' parties: by the Communist party inasmuch as its slogan during this era was the "second Hungarian dictatorship of the proletariat!" and by the Social Democratic party, inasmuch as the guiding principle of its official propaganda was the rejection of that dictatorship. This dichotomy merges nicely in the attitude of those, on either side, who rejected most categorically the union of the two parties, and shifted the responsibility for it on each other; whereas those who had submitted to the fact of the union passively, the organized workers, greeted the renewed split with a certain degree of incomprehension and indecision. What *facts* can we muster to support the argument that the organized workers held out in favor of the ideology of dictatorship, in favor of the revolution?

In the first half of the 1920s, the membership in unions, in spite of persecutions and mass emigration, and in spite of a considerable decrease in the total population of the country, grew from an average of 100,000 in the years preceding the war to around 150,000 to 200,000. After this, a slow decline set in; nevertheless, the non-Socialist unions still did not constitute a serious force in the twenties, except in some state enterprises. In those regions of the successor states which had belonged to Hungary the Communist movement was in general far stronger than the Social Democratic one, as indicated by the election results among other evidence.

The revolution even brought new strata to the side of the workers' movement. Thus, for instance, the miners' union, which had been weak and semilegal before the war, became one of the mainstays of the workers' movement toward the end of the war, during the revolutions, and after. Organized private employees who had joined Socialist organizations amounted to no more than a thousand or two, but during the revolutions their membership reached the 15,000 level, where it remained.

The peasant policy of the revolutions, generally described as misguided, contributed largely to the fact that not a single Socialist or democratic organization was able to find a serious footing among any stratum of the peasantry in the twenties. The revolutions had been able to stir up the landless peasants only momentarily. It was the economic and social rise of the well-to-do peasant that marked the twentieth-century village in Hungary. Already in the last months of the Hungarian Soviet Republic, however, this broad stratum was tuned against the revolution because of economic mistakes, confiscation of the goods of the churches, a contemplated elimination of the church schools, etc. The defense policy of the revolution made but a limited impression on the peasants in the areas west of the Danube and between the Tisza and the Danube, areas which were not directly threatened by enemy action. Peasants remained partly under the influence of the churches, and some joined the various smallholder parties which tried to make the public forget the role they had played under the Károlyi regime. Even those segments of the peasantry which had participated in the revolutions of 1918–19 preferred to adopt the attitude that a renewed revolutionary movement could only bring them trouble.

It is worth referring to the results of the 1922 elections, in which the Social Democratic party achieved a signal success, whereas the various candidates who were openly or covertly in favor of the October movement achieved more modest results. During the following elections, when the revolutionary generation had grown too old, the votes for the Social Democratic party declined slowly but surely. During the 1922 elections in Budapest, the "sinful city" of the revolution, the Social Democrats received close to 40 percent of the votes cast, and had the absolute majority if we add the octoberists. Gyula Peidl, the only one among the Social Democratic ministers of the Károlyi cabinet who had not emigrated, was a delegate in the parliament for several terms.

The influence exerted by the revolution, or rather by its failure, on the intelligentsia, was much more complex. The mostly Jewish professionals of the capital, or the self-employed who, before the war, had supported the Social Democrats, the Radicals, the Vázsonyi Party or the Munkáspárt [the Party of Work] now sought refuge among the Social Democrats, if only because of the persecutions. Another segment of the intelligentsia, however, under the pretext that the middle strata had been persecuted even under the Soviet Republic, tried to give tokens of good behavior by retreating from public life, becoming passive. For the progressive arts ("compromised" in the revolution) this meant the loss of a significant portion of its earlier supporters.[6]

The gentry stratum of civil servants, who had been members of the Party of Work for the most part, reached the conclusion — as a result of the lesson taught by the revolution and by Trianon — which Gyula Szekfű summarized in *Három nemzedék* [Three Generation][7]: the principal weakness of the Tisza period[8] was its excessive permissivenes and tolerance with regard to the "aliens."

The most valuable stratum of the progressive, democratic intelligentsia reacted to the events in a rather sensitive manner. After the defeat of the Soviet Republic, and even during the last months of its existence, the journal of the Intelligentsia, *Nyugat* (West) and its readership turned against what in their opinion was the excessive radicalism of the revolution. The basic tone was one of disenchantment, and it found a variety of justifications. The first issue of the *Nyugat* after the revolution opened with poems by Mihály Babits which, not only condemned Red terror, but went so far as to condemn the defensive campaigns of the Soviet Republic; yet, at the same time, these poems perceptibly disassociated themselves from the counterrevolution. Other writers, like Dezső Szabó or Gyula Krúdy, who welcomed Horthy and the counterrevolution, expressed the mood of a wider circle.[9] But Krúdy, and those who thought like him, were soon disappointed by Horthy as well, and resolved to stay away from politics once and for all.

The stand of the stratum of the intelligentsia which oscillated between democracy and nationalism was defined by the attacks from the extreme right: official circles did not even accept this point from Zsigmond Móricz or Mihály Babits, and even sent Dezső Kosztolányi packing in the spring of 1920: how can he figure that "in the morning in the radical Christian and nationalist daily *Új nemzedék* (The New Generation) he strikes at those very writers he embraces in the afternoon at the *Nyugat...*" wrote the *Magyar Múzsa*, edited by Gyula Pekár. They were willing to tolerate "the poor poetasters who seek their living wherever they can. But such a person should not hop around and act spoilt..."

The same process took place in the control committees at the schools and offices — even those who themselves considered their revolutionary roles as a misstep were condemned. Thus, even among the old "Latin scholar" stratum there evolved an "inner emigration" which read liberal newspapers and, although they did not identify with the revolutions, they did not reject them either, because even that did not pay off. Until about 1923 they expressed their opinions rather freely, but from then on preferred to retreat into the ivory tower of passive silence.

Their disenchantment, their critique of the revolution found its most beautiful expression in Zsigmond Móricz' well-known novel *Légy jó mindhalálig* [Be Good Unto Death][10] which, although based on childhood experiences allowed the contemporary reader to perceive that the lottery ticket had been thrown away, in reality, by Béla Kun; or that the intransigent grownups and teachers, who never forgave, were very much like the control committees of the regime.

This stratum was mostly silent until the late twenties, as were the worker and peasant victims of the regime's campaigns of vengeance. Not until the beginning of the thirties do they reach such a peak of hopelessness that they begin to fight rearguard action; the teacher and the clerk wrote petitons to be reinstated; enthusiastic supporters of the revolution like József Révay wrote the biography of the right-wing politician Gyula Gömbös,[11] whereas Géza Lackó, who had been forced to retire for the sins he had committeed in the revolutions, wrote *Szent Iván tüze* [Fire of Saint Ivan],[12] slandering the revolution:

We would give up an armchair for a six-person steak, and all we had in our pantry was an unripe squash and stale oatmeal; with sadly rumbling stomach Professor Lányi looked out the window of his studio at the revolting row of workers leaving the factory next door each with a sizable duckling tucked under his armpit...

It is worth noting that the author of these lines was the kind of person against whom one of the main accusations was that, after the victory of the counterrevolution, he had refused to authorize the removal of the red star from the school building of which he was the principal. It is no less noteworthy, however, that relatively few progressive writers or journalists followed this path — because, although their bitterness toward the revolution that failed was growing from year to year, their honest opinions were nevertheless not palatable to the counterrevolutionary regime. Even a writer like Dezső Szabó soon metamorphosed from one who had only negative things to say about the revolutions to a vitriolic critic of the existing regime. Thus, the creation of the official image of the revolution was left up to the old-time conservatives: Cecil Tormay,[13] Ferencz Herczeg[14] (*Bújdosó könyv* [Book from the Underground], *Északi fény* [Northern Light]). Their bestsellers, written often in a style from the gutter, built on ignorance, backward thinking, and xenophobia — along with similar works that were not quite so successful — exercised increasing influence particularly on the younger generation and the narrow-minded elements among the white-collar workers.

At least emigrant memoirs and other political works smuggled in from abroad constituted a significant competition to the official propaganda in the first half of the twenties, even here at home. Their impact, however, was muted from the beginning by the mutual charges, unparalleled even in the history of lost revolutions, between the various parties and platforms, and even within the same parties. Not only did those Social Democratic memoirists dissociate themselves from the Soviet Republic who, on March 21, 1919, had turned their backs on the revolution, but even those who had participated in it at high level positions. The most important product in the latter category was the work of Vilmos Böhm, former commander-in-chief of the Red Army (*Két forradalom tüzében* [In the Crossfire of Two Revolutions])[15] which, though rich in data, and though he accepts the Soviet Republic, takes a partisan point of view. As András Siklós pointed out in his historiography of the 1918—19 revolutions: "The chapters dealing with the Soviet Republic give credit to the Social Democratic leaders and, by the same token, to the author himself, for everything that was well done during those famous 133 days, whereas the Communists were held responsible for all the faults and troubles."

The same thing however, can be said about the Communist memoirs. As the party's official poet of the time, Aladár Komját,[16] wrote on the fifth anniversary of the Commune:

We dared to do great things, /only stupidly/, in a cowardly way,/ lazily/. We had faith in lying "comrades"/ We were protesting on account of our stomach/ We were not united even amongst ourselves/ We did not beat the bourgeois to death./ We did not beat the Social Democrats to death...

Although in a less poetic vein, the same basic tendency found expression in the most authentic source, the writings of Béla Kun himself, especially after the mid-twenties. Others writing on behalf of the Landler faction, however, made it appear as if the Communist party's fusion with the Social Democrats on March 21, 1919, and other actual or imagined weakness of the Soviet Republic were all Kun's personal mistakes, which, moreover, he had committeed in spite of the will of his comrades, or behind their backs. Incidentally, Böhm's book was what launched the "Görgey myth" of 1919, cut to the size of Ferenc Julier. This myth had a stongly personal bias, for it was basically directed against Landler: Julier had been his chief-of-staff. Responsibility for giving away the secrets of the Red Army rests, however, on Döme Sztójay among others, rather than on Julier – but Böhm devised the story so well that it stuck with public opinion and historiography which, in any case, thrive on myths.

Independently from who was right, to what extent, and when in the mutual recriminations, what remained in public consciousness was that the revolutions were a collection of errors, even according to the participants themselves; the only thing left to argue about was what was more harmful—adventurism or opportunism.

Among the various social groups, the refugees from the confiscated territories and the officer corps went through the fastest transformation. These two strata were the most prestigious, key elements in the armies of the two revolutions; a goodly number among them expected revolution to make good for world war and the national catastrophe after the Habsburgs' collapse. Nevertheless, after the victory of the counterrevolution, they soon rallied to form its most reliable social base, antirevolutionary and anti-Habsburg at the same time. This rapid change derived from their social position.

The following period stretched by and large from 1933 to 1944, and it was undoubtedly in this period that the most unfavorable picture of the 1918–19 revolutions emerged. Reasons for this are obvious. The camp of supporters of the revolution diminished in numbers as a result of emigration, or simply, of old age. Besides the natural process of aging, certain social movements also played a part.

Skilled workers, although small in numbers, but thoroughly competent, comradely and internationalist, were the principal guardians of the memory of the revolution; but they gradually blend, from the beginning of the twenties, into the indifferent mass of trained labor, the male and female semi-skilled workers who exhibited an altogether different spirit. As the advantage of the position of the skilled workers vis-à-vis the latter group decreased, they also lost the leading role among the workers which had gone unchallenged in 1918–19. The revolution's other mainstay strata, the railroadmen and the teachers, had been paralyzed by the counterrevolution with its ban on organization, which more exactly, had forced them into official, state-dominated unions. By the early forties, the revolutionary tradition of the large enterprises was mostly empty words.

Counterrevolutionary propaganda became more and more effective as time passed. After the pamphlets of the twenties, there appeared, in 1935, a work which could be read even by the thoughtful reader: Gusztáv Gratz' *A forradalmak kora* [Age of Revolutions].[17] The new generations, however, who had no direct experience of the revolutions, continued to be influenced by the pamphlets. For example, the history textbooks used in secondary schools generally dealt with the events of 1867 briefly and drily; but during the war the army had obtained the introduction of a separate subject called "Military Science" and in the textbooks pertaining to this course considerable space was devoted to World War I and to a detailed history of the revolutions in a provocative, extreme right-wing, and anti-Semitic style. Moreover, in the years of the World War II, a number of books with a similar tone were published as part and parcel of the ideological campaign waged against the Soviet Union.

The propaganda of the Horthy era and its application by the state exhibited a curious dichotomy in the appraisal of the revolutions. While law-enforcement agencies did not consider participation in the Liberal Democratic Revolution a punishable offense, and the main object of disciplinary proceedings was behavior during the time of the Soviet Republic, nevertheless, the very part of the propaganda that was truly effective lumped the two revolutions together. In fact, the *Bújdosó könyv*, which ran through so many editions, had Mihály Károlyi as its "negative hero." All this only enhanced the tendency of those who had participated in the revolutions to attempt to set themselves apart from the other revolution: the exception being the two volumes of Lajos Kassák's autobiography, *Egy ember élete* [One Man's Life],[18] which dealt with the revolutions and which appeared in the mid-thirties, for which Kassák was sentenced to a month in jail, under the charge of "agitation."

From the mid-thirties the changed policies of the Comintern, and in part, of the Social Democrats (the Popular Front) in connection with the striving for unity contributed to a decrease in mutual recriminations. It would be a mistake, however, to assume that the Popular Front policy provided a more favorable basis for a better understanding of the revolutions. Quite to the contrary. The Social Democratic party continued to identify itself exclusively with the Liberal Democratic Revolution (see Manó Buchinger's *Tanúvallomás* [I Testify[ ).[19] The Hungarian Communist party, partly to contribute to the Popular Front policy, partly as a consequence of the tragic end of Béla Kun and a number of other former commissars, fell into the opposite extreme of advocating a "second Hungarian Soviet Republic"; it also contributed to spreading fantastic accusations against the "traitor" Kun – to the consternation of the survivors of 1919 – but on the whole preferred to avoid the topic of 1918–19 altogether. Hardly a word was dropped about it in Communist historiography and ideological debates in the years between 1935 and 1950. The fear that the youth, brought up in the midst of a period of slander, would be impervious to any favorable reference to the revolutions played a part in this silence, which must be described as in bad taste – for it does not become anyone to deny the passions of his youth. Moreover, the consideration that for some older politicians and other strata who had to be won over – like Endre Bajcsy-Zsilinszky – even the Liberal Democratic Revolution would be a turn-off also played a part. Official propaganda on the other hand, terrorized those who may still have hesitated, in March 1944 (the 25th anniversary of the Soviet Republic, and the beginning of the German occupation) with what might happen should a Communist government return.

As far as it is possible to measure the effect of propaganda, I believe the counterrevolutionary arguments that counted most in the twenties were the ones directed against the class policies of the Soviet Republic, and those which proclaimed that the Socialist system of production "when in the leading role, cannot possibly have a favorable impact on the economy of countries that have reached a higher degree of development and enjoy international relations" (Sándor Matlekovits).[20] In those years it would also have been difficult to convince contemporaries that the revolutions were responsible for the dissolution of the monarchy, or for the division of Hungary; for, the contemporaries were well aware that recruitment of soldiers was one of the insoluble problems encountered by those revolutions. It was not primarily the fault of the ministers of defense, nor even of the officers, or of the troops, sick and tired of the incessant slaughter which had lasted four years and a half, that Hungary could not confront the advancing opponents with sufficient effectives. Public opinion in the twenties saw Trianon in a realistic light. On the other hand, the illusions of the late thirties, the seeming results obtained by the "increasing the country" process, provided a more favorable atmosphere for spreading certain legends – such as the reason Hungary had no army after World War I was simply that Minister of Defense Béla Linder "did not want to see another soldier again," or that the signing of the November 13, 1918 armistice agreement at Belgrade was what led to the occupation of most of Hungary, etc.

The romantic recollections of Gyula Illyés pertaining to the revolutions, *Koratavasz* [Early Spring],[21] were published in 1941. Illyés, who as late as 1929 had written "we will yet march under our red, victorious flag...," definitely discarded in this work the revolutionary fervor of his youth. Not, for sure, as a renegade denying his faith, because such tastelessness would not have been characteristic of Illyés or of any of the populist writers. To him, the revolutionary days shine as a mirage of youth, which he accepts as his own, but at the same time passes sentence over them:

> The tragedy of this era was... that this time the liberty of the people and the liberty of the nation were not a single liberty... If only another Dózsa had risen from the masses! But all that rose were Toms, Dicks, Harrys and Smiths with various forenames.

He takes up the tenets of the revolutionary ideology one by one, exactly as the peasant might have formulated them at the time, and disposes of them one by one; and, along with the last remaining village Socialists, namely Péter Veres and István Dobi, he comes to the conclusion that it is no longer possible to make headway in the Hungarian villages with the help of references to 1918—19. With the March Front and similar movements, Communists and populists turned back together from one March to another: from the utopia of March 1919 to the historical anachronism of March 1848.

Between 1945 and 1956 the image of 1918—19 was relegated into the distant past. No one wanted a part of the compromising legacy, least of all the Communist party. The veterans of 1919 who, in many places, had been the first to set up the party, the "national committees" or their executive branch, were rejected or relegated to the background on the grounds of having contributed to the formation of the quaint, so-called "directoires." By so doing, however, the Communist party denied its continuity. What could the party leaders say when, upon their return from Moscow they were confronted with the question, what became of Béla Kun?... It was out of the question to publish the recollections, novels, etc., born in emigration, except for Béla Illés *Kárpáti rapszódia* [Rhapsody from the Carpathians],[22] the only memoir which carefully observed the new prescriptions. Of the two parties, it was the Social Democratic party which took better care of its revolutionary tradition, but without greater effect. Although a number of former ministers, commissars, military commanders, members of directoires took part in the cabinets between 1945 and 1953, they kept chastely silent about their revolutionary past. The public remembered the events of 1918—19 even less: it was forbidden to talk evil of it, it was not proper to praise it. In any case, the youth of the new era hardly worried about the past, inebriated as it was with the idea of "turning the whole world over," and later, bitterly disappointed, claiming that there was "nothing left to believe in."

As Marxist historiography and education evolved, it was no longer possible to leave 1918—19 out from the transcribed chronology of Hungarian history; but the reluctantly constructed appraisal of the revolutions made but a minimal impression on the public, either because of the background sketched above, or simply because an iron wheel cannot be made from wood — that is, it was not possible to give the revolutions a positive evaluation while insisting that most of their measures had been misguided, and most of their leaders were traitors. If we peruse the pertinent writings published between 1945 and 1956, we should indeed feel relieved that they did not appeal to a wider public. Thus we read:

The revolution pursued basically a Trotskyist policy in Hungary. This policy found expression: 1. In the accord between Béla Kun and the Social Democratic Party, which he concluded in the absence of the leaders of the Communist Party, and by which he surrendered the independence of the Communist Party, and ensured the Social Democrats a leading role in every aspect of the leadership of the dictatorship of the proletariat. 2. In the pseudo-radical peasant policies of the Social Democratic Party which rejected land reform, and which Kun adopted without any reservations. 3. In its underestimation of the danger of counterrevolution and the denial of the vanguard role of the Party. Béla Kun, who reached an agreement with the Social Democrats, without the leadership of the Party, by placing those leaders in front of a fait accompli and by misleading them, and gave up the independence of action of the Communist Party, even misled Lenin.

After all this author's conclusion cannot appear particularly convincing: to wit that the counterrevolution did not win as overwhelming a victory in 1919 as it had in 1848 because, among other things:

After 1848 not only the revolutionary party, but even the social class called upon to struggle consistently for revolutionary change was lacking. As regards the inner forces and conditions of the revolution in 1918–19, it was not only the class called upon to carry out the revolution that stood at the vanguard of the revolution, but the struggle of this revolutionary class brought about the next most important condition for the triumph of the revolution – namely a revolutionary part of the revolutionary workers. As regards the inner conditions for a revolution only one condition was lacking for victory: the experience of a revolutionary party, its theoretical and practical preparedness.[23]

I brought up this long quotation by way of example to show that such twisted arguments so completely unrelated to the facts could not be followed by the ordinary reader, whereas the reader with a better background simply saw through them.

The slanders with which they tried to obliterate the differences between various tendencies within the Social Democratic movement – let us say between Garami and Kunfi – after the campaign-like arrests of the leaders and officials of the United Social Democratic leaders of the MDP (Hungarian Democratic Party) may have been more effective.

The Károlyi cabinet in which two Social Democrats, Minister of Commerce Ernő Garami and Minister of Public Affairs Welfare Zsigmond Kunfi had taken part as ministers, had taken a completely reasonable attitude in the matter of the proclamation of the republic, in the matter of the creation of a Hungary independent of Austria. The Social Democratic Party endeavored to delay the immediate proclamation of the republic by bringing up the plan for the summoning of a constituent assembly...

In the days of the Soviet Republic:

The Social Democratic leaders as functionaries of the Soviet Republic worked for the Entente imperialists. Some of them, like Károly Peyer, Lajos Vanczák, Samu Jászai, infiltrating the leadership of the labor unions, committed everything possible to elicit a defeatist mood; by exaggerating the difficulties, they were internally disrupting the fabric of the defensive forces of the dictatorship of the proletariat. Many among the traitor rightwing and centrist Social Democratic leaders continued their subversive work as leaders of the Soviet Republic. Thus Vilmos Böhm, the commander-in-chief of the army, made several attempts at surrender. Zsgmond Kunfi, commissar for public education, advocated a milder treatment of the bourgeoisie, and strove for the restoration of capitalism. The leading Social Democrats, József Haubrich and Péter Ágoston, stood in the service of the British, and acted upon instructions received from the United Kingdom.

After all this, the conclusion of the chapter dealing with the revolutions does not sound particularly convincing: "The Soviet Republic is the most outstanding chapter in the history of the struggle of the Hungarian nation, of the Hungarian working class, until the liberation of April 4, 1945."[24]

Similar publications in the fifties, including the lectures at the Party High School organized by Rákosi, and the publications of the records of the 1935 Rákosi trial (from which his own speeches in front of the tribunal and, of course, the sections condemning Trianon and praising Béla Kun had to be deleted of course) spread this same schizophrenic view, which could not possibly leave a lasting impression on reasonable persons. One characteristic of this historiography was that the role of specific personalities was completely a function of the prevailing political point of view. The Communist leaders of the Soviet Republic were identified as Rákosi, who was barely known at the time, and the one who indeed played a prominent left-radical role and pushed for the faithful imitation of Soviet-Russian methods in every respect, Tibor Szamuely. It was also permissible to mention Jenő Landler, Jenő Varga, Jenő Hamburger, but only in such a way as not to interfere with the "leading role" ascribed to Rákosi; as for the real leaders — Béla Kun, József Pogány, Béla Vágó, Vilmos Böhm, Zsimgond Kunfi, Sándor Garbai — nothing or only bad things could be written about them. There was a special vaccum around Mihály Károlyi who could not be mentioned at all, whether in a favorable or an unfavorable context.

After the Soviet Union's Twentieth Party Congress in 1956 and the departure of Rákosi from the scene, these distorted points of view not longer had a reason for existing. A more reasonable approach began to prevail in historiography and in publishing, and this indeed bore its fruits; over the past 25 years we have been able to obtain more realistic pictures of the history of the revolutions than was customary earlier.

One question might come up: if this be so, why bother to ponder over the previous historical periods — after all, a quarter-century should be sufficient to educate a generation honestly. Indeed, it would be enough, but the situation is not that simple. The preceding 25 years undoubtedly had a salutary result on the image of the two revolutions. Salutary in what way? First of all, in the fact that the slanders, the distortions, the negative image were dispelled. This applies even to the Liberal Democratic Revolution about which we may now write, and which need not be contrasted with 1919, but can be described in dialectical (or contradictory) unity with it. The return of the remains of Károlyi was a positive sign, as was the return of his widow. Although the correct evaluation of Social Democracy made but slow progress, nevertheless even in this respect the compulsory curses are going out of fashion.

It would be a mistake to believe, however, that everything was suddenly made good after 1956. In the years 1957–59, we were witnesses to a certain type of "Kunist" renaissance. There were subjective reasons for this — the veterans sidelined until then came to the fore, delayed memoirs were published — and political reasons as well: the stringent mood of the restoration of order following 1956. In literature, in the official theses, in the textbooks, etc., the reckless falsifications of the preceding years were discarded, yet they were not replaced with bold concepts; their revolutionary tone was more like greyish-red. The tone was more natural, easier to assimilate, and even the passions directed against individual opponents were more normal than the mood of "everybody is under suspicion" which preceded it. Yet these writings were hardly ones to elicit enthusiasm. Some good books that deserved to be read, some good films that deserved to be viewed supported the process of the revolutions, but at the same time, plenty of dogmatic writings were published as well, until the mid-sixties (occasionally even later, but those were hardly read).

The spirit of the times found appropriate expression in József Lengyel's *Visegrádi utca* [Visegrád Street][25] and in his novel *Ferenc Prenn*[26] from which it appeared that György Lukács' wide reading was what had "paralyzed the struggle against the counterrevolution." The same line was represented by György Fukász' monograph on Oszkár Jászi and many others.[27] To be precise, the scholarly publications striving for historical accurary surpassed these even toward the end of the fifties in numbers and quality. Yet popular writings, reportages, and films dealing with the Hungarian Soviet Republic, those which reached the masses, continued to find their inspiration in romantic, simplifying presentations. The same thing may be said about textbooks, and even about the some of the party manuals.

Such publications had but minimal effect in the areas of science and politics, and even their mass effect was not as detrimental that it might influence politically, let us say, the youth; yet, with its primitiveness, its lack of credibility, it must exercise a repelling effect on the thoughtful reader or viewer. In the long run, exaggeration always achieves the opposite of the effect desired, whether dealing with the sudden leaps in the numbers of those participating in the resistance in World War II, or of those hundred thousands of Hungarians who supposedly fought in the ranks of the Red Army. The gist of the matter is, that in this case 100,000 means less than 30,000 to 40,000, for the lower figure might even appear credible.

I will not undertake the analysis of the complex influence mechanism of literature and other arts, I only wish to refer to one important aspect of it. In general in modern Hungarian literature, but more especially in the kind of literature that reaches a wider readership, the populist "village-researching" literature occupies a special place. This kind of literature flourished toward the middle and late thirties, precisely when those who practiced it (most of them trained by the revolutions) had reached the conviction, at the same time as the advocates of the Popular Front, that it is better to avoid the topic of 1918–19, for it might lead to a division in the camp of the populist writers; moreover, even without it they were subjected to more than enough official harrassment. When Péter Veres rewrote his *Számadás* [Presenting the Accounts] in 1955,[28] he returned to it "those details which he had had to leave out earlier on account of censorship, or which could not have been written at all." Yet, this otherwise excellent second edition did not have, and could not have had, the stinging effect that thrills the reading public, as did the first.

From the sixties on, the generation of eyewitnesses and participants died out, and the numbers of those who had been under the influence of the Horthy regime's propaganda was also decimated. In other words, public opinion has been dominated by the educational system of the People's Democracy for almost two decades. What changes did the evaluation of 1918–19 undergo in public opinion?

The main tenets of the former negative appraisal – "terror," "rule of the Jews," "unpatriotic," and even "treasonable" – lost their effect, or were effective in only very restricted circles. Public opinion accepts 1918–19 as a progressive tradition, but without much interest or enthusiasm. How much is too little or how much is enough is a matter of opinion (I personally consider the present evaluation realistic under the prevailing conditions). Current domestic and international issues associated with the building of Socialism are bound to reflect on the interpretation of the Soviet Republic, but not on that of the Liberal Democratic Revolution. There is even greater interest, among certain intellectual circles, in 1918 and its more outstanding leaders – Károlyi and Jászi, but not the Social Democrats! – yet the distinction does not have much significance.

If we finally ask the question, what is the reason that though 1918–19 has been assessed rather positively by the public, its acceptance is not devoid of contradictions, I would adduce the following main points: a. Since public opinion is "realist," that is, not primarily concerned with objectives and circumstance, but with results, the memory of 1918–19 is unavoidably connected with the memory of Trianon. The propaganda of the Horthy regime attempted to shift all of the responsibility for Trianon onto the revolutions; and though it was possible to eliminate by and large the effect of that propaganda, this merely meant that in the eyes of the public responsibility is *shared* between the old regime of Franz-Joseph, the revolutions, and Miklós Horthy who actually signed the Treaty of Trianon. And, this is still a relatively unfavorable assessment considering that up to today the public bears Trianon and its consequences as a deep wound.

Since Zsuzsa L. Nagy's essay has already stated what needs to be stated about the effects of Trianon, I will only complement it with a few points. Although to the observant contemporary it should be evident that within their own limits the two revolutions did everything possible to prevent the tearing away of areas inhabited by Hungarians, it was precisely this sort of activity that could give fuel to ill-intentioned criticism. If the revolutionary had taken the stand taken by the German or Austrian governments, that there was nothing to be done for the time being, this attitude could be condemned as a whole, but then it would not be possible to cogitate at length over how it might have been possible to set up a larger army, or prevent more effectively the evacuation of certain areas, etc. ... (Even today the foolish idea has its currency that, had the Soviet Republic engaged in land reform, the peasants would have rallied to its defense.) What is more, had the Soviet Republic not occupied Slovakia, it could not have been criticized by strategists for accepting the note handed down by Clemenceau, to the effect that if we are able to occupy half of Slovakia, we should also be able to occupy the other half. The best defense against naïve, speculative kind of ciriticism is for the government to take no action at all.

It is not my intention to deny that the revolutions committed mistakes, but these did not influence the tracing of the boundary lines in any way. Which does not mean that those mistakes did not cause damage. For instance, the refugee intellectuals, railwaymen, etc., had cause enough to be retroactively angry against the Károlyi cabinet, the organs of which had summoned them to refuse the oath of loyalty to the successor states for the time being: with this act of patriotism they became homeless.

A fairly large segment of the officers of the army, the civil servants, the teachers appreciated the patriotic policies of the Soviet Republic to the extent of continuing in service. This had very unpleasant repercussions later on, when they were called to account, and it became in their interest to dissociate themselves in every way from the Soviet Republic, to belittle its military achievements, etc. In contrast with 1848, of all leaders of the Soviet Republic only József Kerekess, the liberator of Miskolc, wrote his memoirs, and even these did not appear in print, for reasons that are not relevant. This could not have happened after 1849, because the victorious counterrevolution pursued a completely different policy. General György Klapka was not readmitted into the army even as late as 1868, on the grounds that he had "betrayed" it, but he did write his memoirs — on the side of the revolution.[29]

Even if the two revolutions cannot be blamed for Trianon — and this may be understood by some of the more cultured readers — their attitude to Trianon was rather different from that of the counterrevolution. Jászi's Danubian confederation, Béla Kun's Alliance of the Soviet Republics were supranational ideas, and those who believed in these could not have regarded Trianon in as unfortunate a light as those who were convinced of the impossibility of reconciling the nations confronting each other. But the fifties were the fifties not only in Hungary, but in all the neighboring countries as well; after the Hungarian minority had gained autonomy and a university in Transylvania, and some improvement in their lot took place in the other successor states as well, indeed, it was permissible to believe that, however imperfectly, Jászi's or Kun's confederation may yet come to something.

For many the present condition of the Hungarian minorities, the tensions surrounding the issue, throw a bad light, in hindsight, on Jászi and Kun, who preached that social progress automatically brings about the triumph of internationalism. If we think it over we are bound to understand one of the basic ingredients of public opinion. The critique of the "utopianism" of Károlyi or Kun is often aimed at the present.

b. A problem contributing to the above is that among all the revolutions in Hungarian history, only those of 1918–19 were explicitly directed against the churches, at least until liberation in 1945: not only as a matter of ideology, for the Soviet Republic wanted not only to nationalize the religious schools, but also spent a great deal of energy in "inventorying" and confiscating the treasures of the churches. This policy, in addition to the exaggerations of the regime's propaganda, was a tactical error almost equal in rank with its erroneous peasant policy. We do not like to talk about it, and the literature on the subject is but minimal, but it is clear that religious instruction and publications of a religious nature, etc., have certain reservations towards both revolutions, to say the least.

c. The appraisal of the Soviet Republic is also affected by the development of our Socialist ideology. We consider the Soviet Republic as our predecessor in the building of Socialism, but this was truer in the 1950s than it is today. The present method of building it departs radically from the ideology of instant and total Socialism pursued by the Hungarian Soviet Republic. Those disillusioned of our present practice would have to regard the Soviet Republic as a naïve utopia. Those, however, who accept that it is the realistic way of building Socialism in Hungary, would also have to regard as utopian that system which provided free housing to all those without shelter – without expecting any construction activity in return – and divided the existing apartments on an egalitarian basis; but it was egalitarian in other respects as well, and insisted that the workers' councils at the plants debate all relevant issues, even at he expense of productivity, etc.

d. I already referred to the matter of the remnants of the ideology of the fifties that have survived. If we consider that the majority of the stratum of today's ideological leaders – the teachers of Marxism and other subjects – learnt what he or she knows about 1918–19 in the fifties, then we should not be surprised if we keep running into the ideology of that period, in however veiled or modified form, even in the instructional materials used today. This leads not only to common pedagogical problems, but also to chaos, uncertainty, etc., which in turn diminish considerably the impact of instruction. Furthermore, at a higher level, the interpretation of 1918–19 can only become fully satisfactory if placed within the context of the international revolutionary process. To be sure, the examination of that process goes beyond the possibilities afforded Hungarian historiography.

# 502 REVOLUTIONS AND INTERVENTIONS

## NOTES

1. Zsuzsa L. Nagy, "Trianon a magyar társadalom tudatában" (Manuscript).
2. Gyula Juhász, "II. világháborús történetünk a köztudatban" (Manuscript).
3. Zsigmond Kemény, *Forradalom után* (Pest, 1850).
4. János Arany, *A nagyidai cigányok* (Pest, 1854).
5. Artúr Görgey, commander of the Hungarian Army in 1849, capitulated to the Russians at Világos, in August 13, 1848. The historical controversy concerns the act of capitulation. Was it treason or an unavoidable necessity?
6. For a general history of the revolutions and of the interwar years, see, György Ránki, Tibor Hajdu, and Lóránt Tilkovszky, eds., *Magyarország története, 1918–1919, 1919–1945* (Budapest, 1976).
7. Gyula Szekfű, *Három nemzedék* (Budapest, 1920).
8. István Tisza and his political party the Munkapárt dominated Hungarian politics during during the decade before 1918. See Gabor Vermes' article in this collection.
9. See the essay of Ivan Sanders in this collection.
10. Zsigmond Móricz, *Légy jó mindhalálig* (Budapest, 1920).
11. József Révay, *Gömbös Gyula élete és politikája* (Budapest, 1934).
12. Géza Lackó, *Szent Iván tüze* (Budapest, 1932), p. 323.
13. Cecil Tormay, *Bujdosó Könyv* Vols. I–II (Budapest, 1921–1922).
14. Ferenc Herczeg, *Északi fény* (Budapest, 1925).
15. Vilmos Böhm, *Két forradalom tüzében. Októberi forradalom. Proletárdiktatúra. Ellenforradalom* (Vienna, 1923).
16. Aladár Komját, *Válogatott versek* (Budapest, 1949).
17. Gusztáv Gratz, *A forradalmak kora. Magyarország története 1918–1920* (Budapest, 1935).
18. Lajos Kassák, *Egy ember élete* (Budapest, 1927–1935).
19. Buchinger Manó, *Tanúvallomás. Az októberi forradalom tragédiája* (Budapest, 1936).
20. Gusztáv Gratz, Sándor Matlekovits, et al., *A bolsevizmus Magyarországon* (Budapest, 1921).
21. Gyula Illyés, *Koratavasz* (Budapest, 1941).
22. Béla Illés, *Kárpáti rapszódia* (Moscow, 1939).
23. Aladár Mód, *400 év küzdelme az önálló Magyarországért* (Budapest, 1951), pp. 417, 427–28.
24. Gusztáv Heckenast, et al., *A Magyar nép története* (Budapest, 1953).
25. József Lengyel, *Visegrádi utca* (Moscow, 1932). This work was first published in Hungary in 1957.
26. József Lengyel, *Prenn Ferenc hányatott élete* (Budapest, 1958).
27. György Fukász, *A magyarországi polgári radikalizmus történetéhez 1900–1918. Jászi Oszkár ideológiájának bírálata* (Budapest, 1960).
28. Péter Veres, *Számadás* (Budapest, 1955), rev. ed.; the original edition was first published in 1937 in Budapest.
29. György Klapka, *Memoirs of the War of Independence in Hungary* (London, 1850).

Ábrahám, Dezső (1875–1973)
Hungarian right-wing politician, prime minister of the second Szeged government, July 12–August 12, 1919.

Adler, Friedrich (1875–1960)
Secretary of the Austrian Social Democratic Party.

Ágoston, Péter (1874–1925)
Hungarian Socialist publicist, state secretary for internal affairs during the Károlyi regime, assistant commissar of foreign affairs during the Kun regime.

Alexandrov, Todor
Leader of the Bulgarian State Militia.

Allizé, Henri
French minister in Vienna, 1919.

Andorka (Fleischhacker) Rudolf Dezső (1891–1961)
Hungarian officer on Aurél Stromfeld's staff in the Red Army, officer in the interwar Hungarian army, brigadier general, 1939–1941, and diplomat.

Andrássy, Gyula (1860–1929)
Hungarian monarchist politican, leader of the Constitution Party, last foreign minister of the Dual Monarchy, October 24–October 30, 1918. During the Kun regime he was one of the leaders of the Anti-Bolshevik Committee in Vienna.

Anselme, Philippe Henri (1864–1936)
French general, commander of the French troops in the Ukraine.

Antonescu, Ion (1882–1946)
Romanian colonel, operations officer for the General Staff, 1917–20; in 1933, chief-of-the-general staff and marshal; head of state, 1940–44.

Antonescu, Victor
Romanian envoy to the Peace Conference.

Antonov-Ovseenko, Vladimir Aleksandrovich (1883–1939)
Russian Bolshevik Civil War leader and diplomat, commander of the Ukrainian Front, January–June, 1919.

Apáthy, István (1863–1922)
Internationally known biology professor and Hungarian political leader in Transylvania. The Károlyi government's comissioner for Transylvania, in December 1918.

Apponyi, Albert (1846–1933)
Hungarian politician and statesman, minister of education, 1906–10, and 1917–1918; president of the Hungarian peace delegation, 1920.

Arz, Arthur von Straussenburg (1857–1935)
Austro–Hungarian general, chief-of-the-general-staff.

Babits, Mihály (1883–1941)
Hungarian poet, an editor of the progressive journal, *Nyugat* (West).

Baden, Max von (1867–1929)
Prince of Baden, last chancellor of the Wilhelminian empire.

Badoglio, Pietro (1867–1956)
Italian lieutenant general on the Italian Front, 1918; prime minister, 1943–1944.

Bakay, Szilárd (1892–1946)
Hungarian army officer, lieutenant general, 1942.

Bajcsy-Zsilinszky, Endre (1866–1944)
Founder of the counterrevolutionary Hungarian National Defense Alliance (MOVE), eventual anti-fascist, was executed by Hungarian fascists.

Balabanoff, Angelica (1877–1965)
Marxist revolutionary in Russia and in Italy.

Balfour, Arthur, J. (1848–1930)
British secretary of state for Foreign Affairs, 1916–1919.

Bandholtz, Harry Hill (1864–1925)
American general, member of the Inter-Allied Military Mission to Hungary, August, 1919.

Bangha, Béla (1880–1940)
Hungarian Jesuit publicist, editor of *Magyar Kultúra* (Hungarian Culture), 1913–1923. Counterrevolutionary propagandist in 1919, and champion of the chauvinist, irredentist, and anti-Semitic "Christian national thought."

Bartha, Albert (1877–1960)
Hungarian politician, minister of war in the Károlyi cabinet, November 9, 1918–December 12, 1919, and in October 1945–March 1946.

Barrow
British major.

Batthyány, Tivadar (1859–1931)
Hungarian politician, minister of interior in the Károlyi cabinet.

Bauer, Otto (1882–1938)
Austrian Socialist theoretician and politician, leader of the Second International and of the Austrian Social Democratic Party. Minister of foreign affairs, November 1918–July 1919.

Béldy (Bruckner) Alajos (1889–1946)
Officer in the Hungarian army, colonel general, January, 1944.

Benedek, Marcell (1885–1969)
Professor of comparative literature, translator, and literary historian.

Beneš, Edvard (1884–1948)
Czechoslovak politician, foreign minister from 1918, and president of Czechoslovakia, 1935–38 and 1940–48.

Beniczky, Ödön (1878–1931)
   Monarchist politician, minister of foreign affairs, September 1919–
   March 1920.

Beregfy, (Berger) Károly (1889–1946)
   Hungarian officer, major general, minister of defense in the fascist
   Arrow Cross government, October 1944–March 1945.

Berinkey, Dénes (1871–1948)
   Hungarian politician, minister of justice in the Károlyi cabinet, 1918,
   prime minister, January 11, 1919–March 20, 1919.

Berius, Albert
   French general, commander of the French troops in Odessa.

Berthelot, Henri Mathias (1861–1936)
   French general, head of the French Military Mission to Romania, 1916–
   18 and commander of the *Army of the Danube,* 1918–19.

Berthélmy
   French general.

Bethlen, István (1874–1947)
   Member of the Hungarian peace delegation, 1920, prime minister of
   Hungary, 1921–31.

Bétrix, Jean Joseph
   Commander of the French troops in Szeged.

Bíró, Lajos (1880–1948)
   Hungarian writer, along with Oszkár Jászi, a founder of the Radical
   Bourgeois Party in 1914. State secretary for foreign affairs during the
   Károlyi regime, president of the Writers Union during the Kun regime.

Bissolati, Leonida (1857–1920)
   Italian socialist, supporter of Italy's participation in World War I.

Blagoev, Dimitur
   Bulgarian socialist.

Boblet
   French colonel, commander of troops in Szeged.

Bobrzyński, Michal (1849–1935)
   Polish historian and conservative politician, viceroy of Galicia, 1908–
   14.

Bogár, Ignác (1876–1933)
   Secretary of the Hungarian printers union, proponent of the fusion of
   the Hungarian Social Democratic Party and of the Hungarian Communist
   Party on March 21. 1919.

Böhm, Vilmos (1880–1948)
   Hungarian Socialist leader, minister of war in the Berinkey Government,
   January–March 1919, commissar of war of the Kun regime, commander
   in chief of the Red Army, ambassador in Vienna, July, 1919.

Clausewitz, Karl von (1780–1831)
Prussian general, wrote treatise *On War*.

Clemenceau, Georges (1857–1932)
French prime minister and minister of war 1917–20. President of the Paris Peace Conference, 1919.

Clerk, George Russel (1874–1951)
British foreign office official. The first minister to Prague, 1919. Representative of the Peace Conference on a mission to Hungary, October–December, 1919.

Coanda, Constantin (1857–1932)
General, cabinet minister and premier, October 24–November 29, 1918.

Codreanu, Corneliu Zelea (1899–1938)
Romanian politician, founder and leader of the fascist Iron Guard.

Concha, Győző (1846–1933)
Hungarian lawyer and influential professor of Legal and Constitutional Thought.

Coolidge, Archibald Cary (1866–1928)
American scholar, member of the American delegation to the Peace Conference, 1919, leader of American Mission to study the conditions in the successor states for the American peace conferees.

Cornwall
British colonel.

Cramon, August von
German general.

Csernoch, János Cardinal (1815–1927)
Hungarian churchman, bishop of Csanád, 1908–1911; archbishop of Kalocsa, 1911–13; archbishop of Esztergom and Prince-Primate of Hungary, 1913–27.

Csilléry, András (1883–1964)
Hungarian dentist, extreme right politician, participant in the coup against the Peidl government. Minister of public health, August 15 to November 24, 1919.

Cunninghame, Thomas Montgomery (1877– ?)
Head of the British military mission in Vienna.

Czóbel, Ernő (1886–1953)
Hungarian Communist official of the Kun regime, headed the Soviet Republic's embassy in Vienna, July, 1919.

Daskalov, Raiko
Bulgarian left-wing agrarian leader.

Denikin, Anton Ivanovich (1872–1947)
Russian officer commander of the anti-Bolshevik *Volunteer Army* in the Ukraine, 1919.

Deutsch, Julius (1884– ?)
Austrian Socialist leader.

Diaz, Armando (1861–1928)
Italian general, chief-of-the general-staff and commander-in-chief, November 1917, signer of the armistice with the Austro–Hungarians, at Padova, November 13, 1918.

Dibenko, Pavel Iefimovich (1889–1938)
Red Army commander in the Kharkov area, February to May 1919, then commander in the Crimea, May–July, 1919.

Dimitrescu,
Romanian general, chief-of-the general-staff, 1919.

Dimitriu
Romanian liaison officer.

Diner-Dénes, József (1857–1937)
Hungarian Socialist publicist, politician, and art historian. State secretary for foreign affairs during the Károlyi regime.

Dmowski, Roman (1864–1939)
Leader of the Polish National Democratic Party, delegate to the Paris Peace Conference, 1919.

Dobi, István (1898–1968)
Hungarian Socialist, later in 1936, he joined the Hungarian Smallholder Party and became its president in 1947. Minister and prime minister in several post World War II cabinets. From 1952 to 1967 president of Hungary.

Dodge, Henry Percival (1870–1936)
American special representative to Serbia in charge of the American Legation, 1917–19; American ambassador to Yugoslavia, 1919–36.

Dovcsák, Antal (1879–1962)
Hungarian Socialist and union leader, commissar of social production, vice-president of the Soviet Republic, minister of trade in the Peidl government.

Dózsa György (1470–1514)
Leader and martyr of the Hungarian Peasant Rebellion of 1514.

Erdélyi, Mór (1877–1929)
Hungarian Socialist politician, commissioner of food supplies in the Károlyi government, commissar of food supplies in the Soviet government, secretary of state for food supplies in the Peidl government.

Exelmans, Louis Antoine
French admiral, commander of the French forces in the Kherson area.

Fenyő, Miksa (1877–1972)
Hungarian essayist, criticist, political and economic writer, founder and editor of the progressive journal, *Nyugat* (West).

Ferdinand I (1861–1948)
King of Bulgaria, 1887–1918.

Ferdinand I (1865–1927)
King of Romania, 1914–27.

Festetics, Sándor (1882–1956)
Hungarian diplomat, minister of war in the Károlyi cabinet, December 30, 1918–January 13, 1919.

Fiedler, Rezső (1884–1939)
A founder of the Hungarian Communist Party, commissar of war, and member of the Governing Council of the Hungarian Soviet Republic.

Fischer-Colbrie, Ágost (1865–1925)
Hungarian churchman, bishop of Kassa (Košice), 1907–25.

Foch, Ferdinand (1851–1929)
French general, chief-of-the general-staff, commander-in-chief of the Allied forces, 1918.

Fontenay
French envoy to Belgrade.

Franchet d'Esperey, Louis Félix (1856–1942)
French general, later marshal of France, commander of the Allied *Army of the East (Orient)*, 1918–1920.

Freydenberg, Henri
French officer in Russia on General d'Anselme's staff.

Franz Joseph I (1830–1916)
Emperor of Austria from 1848, King of Hungary from 1867.

Friedrich, István (1883–1959)
Hungarian politician, prime minister following a coup in which he overthrew the Peidl government, August 6, 1919, minister of war, 1919–20.

Frunze, Mihail Vasilievich (1885–1925)
Red Army commander on various fronts.

Gajda, Rudolf (Radola) (1892–1945)
Czechoslovak general, involved in an alleged coup in 1926.

Garami, Ernő (1876–1935)
Hungarian editor and moderate Socialist leader.

Garbai, Sándor (1879–1947)
Hungarian Socialist leader, president of the Revolutionary Governing Council of the Soviet Republic, minister of education in the Peidl government.

Gavrilović, Mihailo
Yugoslav foreign ministry official.

Gertoux
French colonel, commander of the military police in Szeged.

Giesswein, Sándor (1863–1926)

Hungarian Catholic priest, scholar, politician, founder of the Christian Socialist Party and Christian Trade Unions in Hungary.

Gömbös, Gyula (1886–1936)

Hungarian officer, counterrevolutionary leader, prime minister of Hungary, 1932–1936.

Gondrecourt, Henri Leopold de

French general.

Goodwin, Philip Lippincott (1885–1958)

Member of the International Section of the American Commission to Negotiate Peace, and a member of the American Coolidge mission to Hungary, January 1919.

Gramsci, Antonio (1891–1937)

Italian Communist activist and thinker.

Graziani, Jean Cesar (1859–1932)

French general, World War I, commander of the French troops on the Italian Front.

Grigoriadis, Neokosmos,

Greek regimental commander in the Ukraine.

Grigoriev, Nikolai Aleksandrovich (1878–1919)

Hatman, commander of Ukrainian Cossack forces.

Grishin-Almazov, A. A.

Russian anti-Bolshevik military governor of Odessa during its French occupation.

Grosfeld, Leon (1911)

Polish historian.

Győrffy-Bengyel (Bengyel) Sándor (1886–1942)

Hungarian officer, chief-of-staff of various Red Army divisions, staff officer during the interwar years, was promoted to colonel general in 1941, minister of public supplies, September 1941–June, 1942.

Haller, József (1873–1960)

Polish general, commanded the Polish Army in France, 1918.

Hamburger, Jenő (1883–1936)

Hungarian Socialist, one of the secretaries of the fused Socialist and Communist parties during the Soviet Republic, Commissar of Agriculture.

Hankey, Sir Maurice (1877–1963)

British politician, secretary of the war cabinet of David Lloyd George, 1917–18, secretary of the Imperial cabinet, British secretary of the Peace Conference, 1919.

Hardinge of Penshurts, Lord of (1858–1944)

British permanent undersecretary of state of foreign affairs, 1916–20.

Hudiakov, Nikolai Akimovich (1890–1939)
    Red Army commander of the Third Ukrainian Army in 1919.

Hus, Jan (1371–1415)
    Czech religious reformer thinker and martyr.

Huszár, Károly (1882–1941)
    Hungarian politician, minister of education and religion in the Friedrich cabinets, August 1919–November 1919, prime minister, November 1919–March 1920.

Ignotus (Veigelsberg), Hugó (1869–1949)
    Hungarian literary critic, poet, one of the founders of the journal *Nyugat* (West).

Illyés, Gyula (1902–1983)
    Hungarian poet, dramatist, essayist.

Iorga, Nicolae (1871–1940)
    Romanian historian and national leader. Prolific scholar and publicist.

Jabłonski, Henryk (1909)
    Polish historian, chairman of the State Council of the Polish People's Republic, 1972 to present.

Janoušek, Antonin (1877–1941)
    Czech communist, head of the short-lived Slovak Soviet Republic of 1919.

Jászi, Oszkár (1875–1957)
    Hungarian sociologist, publicist, politician. Leader of the Bourgeois Radical Party, minister of nationalities in the Károlyi government, 1918.

Jászai, Samu (1859–1927)
    Hungarian Socialist leader.

Joseph August, Archduke (1872–1962)
    (Jozsef Habsburg) *Homo Regius* of King Charles in Hungary, October 1918, reclaimed this title in August 1919 and appointed the Friedrich government. Resigned from his position under Entente pressure on August 25, 1919. Was an active supporter of the Horthy regime.

Jovanovic, Aleksandar
    Official in the Hungarian Soviet government.

Julier, Ferenc (1878–1946)
    Hungarian colonel, military scientist, during the Soviet Republic, chief-of-the General-Staff of the Hungarian Red Army, following the resignation of Aurél Stromfeld, commander-in-chief of the Red Army.

Karikás, Frigyes (1891–1938)
    Hungarian writer, translator; political commissar in the Hungarian Red Army.

Kalina, Antonín
    Czechoslovak politician, writer, diplomat in the interwar years.

Károlyi, Gyula (1871–1947)
Hungarian monarchist politician; prime minister of the counterrevolutionary government in Arad May 5–May 29, 1919, then in Szeged, May 29–July 12, 1919; prime minister, 1931–32.

Károlyi, Mihály (1875–1955)
Hungarian statesman; pro-Entente politician; prime minister, then president of the People's Republic of Hungary, January 11–March 20, 1919.

Kassák, Lajos (1887–1967)
Hungarian avant garde writer, poet, and painter.

Kazantzakis, Nikos (1883–1957)
Greek writer, minister of public welfare, 1919.

Kelen, József (1892–1939)
Hungarian engineer, Socialist organizer and founder of the Communist Party of Hungary in Budapest, November 1918. Commissar of socialist production during the Hungarian Soviet Republic.

Kerekess, József (1880–1961)
Hungarian officer, division commander in the Hungarian Red Army. Following the collapse of the Kun regime, he was demoted, later amnestied. In 1945, he was promoted to retired colonel general.

Kerenskii, Aleksandr Fiodorovich (1881–1970)
Russian politician, leader of the Provisional Government in Russia, 1917.

Klapka, György (1820–1892)
Hungarian officer, legendary general of the Hungarian revolutionary army of 1848–49.

Kolchak, Aleksandr Vasilievich (1873–1920)
Russian officer, anti-Bolshevik dictator of the Siberian Directorate, 1918–1920.

Komarnicki, Tytus (1896–1967)
Polish diplomat and historian.

Komenský, Jan Amos (1592–1670)
Czech philosopher, pedagogue, bishop of Unitas Fratrorum.

Komját, Aladár (1891–1937)
Hungarian poet and journalist, a founder of the Hungarian Communist Party.

Korač, Vitomir
Yugoslav minister of social welfare.

Kosztolányi, Dezső (1885–1936)
Hungarian poet, writer, and publicist.

Kozietulski, Jan (1781–1821)
Polish cavalry colonel.

Král, Václav
Czechoslovak historian, especially prominent after 1968.

Kramář, Karel (1860–1937)
 Leader of the Czech National Democrats, first prime minister of Czechoslovakia, 1918–19.

Kratochwill, Károly (1869–1946)
 Austro–Hungarian World War I military commander, passed to Hungarian service, commander of the Transylvania military district during the Károlyi regime, organizer and commander of the Transylvania Division. In April 1919 he surrendered his divison to the Romanians.

Křížek, Jurij
 Czechoslovak historian in the post-World War II era.

Krúdy, Gyula (1878–1933)
 Hungarian writer and publicist, active supporter of the Károlyi regime and sympathizer of the Hungarian Soviet Republic.

Kun, Béla (1886–1939)
 Founder of the Hungarian Communist Party, commissar of foreign affairs and leader of the Hungarian Soviet Republic, 1919.

Kunfi, Zsigmond (1879–1929)
 Hungarian Socialist leader and political writer, member of the governments of the Károlyi and Kun regimes, 1918–19.

Laczkó, Géza (1884–1953)
 Hungarian writer, publicist, and critic.

Lamaze, de
 French captain in Szeged.

Landrer, Jenő (1875–1928)
 Hungarian Socialist, later Communist, commander-in-chief of the Hungarian Red Army, opponent of Béla Kun in the 1920s.

Lavisse, Ernest (1842–1922)
 French historian.

Lazzari, Costantino (1857–1927)
 Secretary of the Socialist Party of Italy.

Lehár, Antal (1876–1962)
 Hungarian monarchist colonel, organizer of counterrevolutionary military units in Austria during the Kun regime.

Lejay, Gustave
 French colonel, commander of troops in the Kherson region.

Lengyel, József (1896–1975)
 Hungarian writer, poet.

Lenin, Vladimir Ilich (1870–1924)
 Russian Communist revolutionary.

Lenz, Albin (1878–1958)
 Officer in the Hungarian Army, lieutenant general, 1928.

Milotay, István (1883–1963)
Hungarian publicist, conservative politician.

Michta, Norbert
General in the Polish People's Army and historian.

Miklós, Béla or Dálnoki Miklós, Béla (1890–1948)
Hungarian staff officer, and military attaché during the interwar years. Chief of the military bureau of Regent Miklós Horthy, 1942–44, colonel general, commander of the I Army Corps, 1944; prime minister of the Provisional Government, December 1944–November 1945.

Mišic, Živojin (1855–1921)
Serbian field marshal and chief of staff.

Mitchel-Thompson, William
British official in the Foreign Office.

Modigliani, Giuseppe Emanuele (1872–1947)
Italian centrist Social Democrat.

Modly, Zoltán (1882–  ? )
Hungarian army officer, lieutenant general, 1930.

Mombelli
Italian general, member of the Interallied Military Mission to Hungary, August, 1919.

Móricz, Zsigmond (1879–1942)
Hungarian writer and publicist.

Münnich, Ferenc (1886–1967)
Hungarian Communist, participant of the Russian Civil War, Commander of a Hungarian Red Army division, political commissar of the Hungarian Red Army, diplomat, minister, prime minister, 1958–61.

Mussolini, Benito (1883–1945)
Italian politician, ex-Socialist organizer of the Fascist Party in March, 1919.

Nádai, István (188?–1954)
Hungarian army officer, colonel general, 1942.

Nagy, Ferenc (1880–1934)
Hungarian politican, minister of food supplies in the Károlyi government, October 31, 1918–January 19, 1919.

Nagy, Lajos (1883–1954)
Hungarian writer, publicist.

Nagybaczonyi Nagy, Vilmos (1884–1976)
Austro–Hungarian staff officer during World War I; passed to Hungarian service, colonel general, minister of war, 1942–43.

Németh, József (1883–1961)
Hungarian army officer, lieutenant general, 1935.

Nemes, Dezső (1908–1985)
 Dean of Hungarian Party historians, member of the Hungarian Politburo.

Nenni, Pietro (1891–1980)
 Italian Socialist leader, joined the Social Democratic Party in 1921, editor of the party journal, *L'Avanti*.

Nider, Constantine
 Greek officer, commander of the I Army Corps in southern Russian, 1919.

Nitti, Francesco Saverio (1868–1953)
 Italian Liberal Party politician, economist. From 1911 minister in various cabinets, Prime Minister, 1919–20, anti-Fascist emigré and political leader from 1924.

Omarchevski, Stoian
 Bulgarian minister of education.

Orlando, Vittorio Emanuele (1860–1925)
 Italian statesman, prime minister of Italy, October 1917–June 1919.

Othonaios, Alexander
 Chief of staff of Colonel Nieder.

Paderewski, Ignacy Jan (1860–1941)
 Polish pianist, premier, and foreign minister.

Palacký, František (1798–1876)
 Czech historian and political leader.

Pallavicini, György (1881–1946)
 Hungarian monarchist politician, commissioner for Transdanubia, 1919.

Pašič, Nikola (1845–1926)
 Serbian statesman, largely responsible for the establishment of the Karadjordjevic dynasty on the throne of Serbia. Prime minister of Serbia, 1891, 1904–1908, 1910–18, 1921–26.

Pastukhov, Khristiu
 Bulgarian politician, Stamboliiski's minister of interior.

Patey
 French general attached to General Berthelot.

Peidl, Gyula (1873–1943)
 Hungarian Socialist leader, leader of the Hungarian Printers Union. He opposed the Hungarian Soviet Republic and became prime minister of the shortlived Socialist government following the collapse of the Kun regime, August 1–August 6, 1919.

Pekár, Gyula (1867–1937)
 Hungarian politician and minister in several counterrevolutionary cabinets in 1919.

Pellé, Maurice (1863–1924)
French general, commander of the French military mission in Czechoslovakia, 1919–20.

Petin, Victor
French colonel, deputy chief of the French Military Mission to Romania, 1916–18. French military attaché to Bucharest, 1919.

Petliura, Semion Vasilievich (1879–1926)
Ukrainian nationalist leader of the Ukrainian Directorate, 1919.

Peyer, Károly (1881–1956)
Socialist leader, minister of interior in the Peidl government, minister of welfare in the Friedrich and Huszár governments.

Pfeifer, Ignác (1867–1941)
Chemical engineer, professor.

Picard, Emile (1856–1941)
French mathematician.

Pichlík, Karel
Czechoszlovak historian of the post-World War II era.

Pichon, Stephen (1857–1933)
French politician, minister of foreign affairs in the Clemenceau cabinet.

Piłsudski, Józef (1867–1918)
Polish soldier and statesman; marshal, chief-of-state, 1918–22, virtual dictator after 1926.

Plastiras, N.
Divisional commander of the Greek forces in the Ukraine.

Podvolskii, Nikolai Ilich (1880–1948)
Bolshevik revolutionary and military leader during the Civil War.

Pogány, József (1866–1939)
Hungarian Socialist journalist, president of the Soldiers' Council during the Károlyi regime, commissar of Various commissariats during the Soviet Republic, commanded a Red army corps.

Poincaré, Raymond (1860–1934)
President of the French Republic, 1913–20, prime minister in the 1920s.

Politis, Nikolaos Sokrates (1872–1942)
Greek jurist, diplomat, and foreign minister, 1916–20, 1922, 1936, delegate to the Paris Peace Conference. Greek foreign minister.

Polk, Frank Lyon (1871–1943)
American undersecretary of state, 1919–20; head of the American delegation to the Paris Peace Conference, 1919.

Popović, Gligorije
Yugoslav representative to Budapest following the fall of the Kun regime.

Prešan, Constatin (1861–1943)
Romanian general, later marshal. Chief of the Romanian general staff 1917–20.

Pribičević, Svetozar
  Yugoslav minister of interior.
Prohászka, Ottokár (1858—1927)
  Hungarian churchman, writer, orator, politician, bishop of Székesfehér-
  vár, 1905—27.
Prónay, Pál (1875—1944)
  Hungarian officer, major in the National Army of Szeged. Leading par-
  ticipant in the "White Terror."
Protić, Stojan
  Serb politician.
Rákosi, Mátyás (1892—1971)
  Hungarian Communist, commissar of the Kun regime; a prisoner of the
  Horthy regime during the interwar years; Stalinist dictator after World
  War II.
Rakovskii, Christian (1861—1943)
  Romanian Socialist leader of Bulgarian birth. Served the Soviet state in
  its early years.
Rattigan, Frank
  British diplomat, chargé in Bucharest.
Renner, Karl (1870—1950)
  Austrian Socialist politician, first chancellor of the Republic of Austria.
Révay, József (1905—1945)
  Hungarian philosopher and Socialist sympathizer.
Révy, Kálmán (1877—1949)
  Hungarian army officer, general, 1940.
Řiha, O.
  Czechoslovak historian, especially prominent after 1968.
Romanelli, Guido (1876— ? )
  Italian lieutenant-colonel, deputy head of the Military Mission in Hun-
  gary, 1919.
Róna, Lajos (1882—1934)
  Hungarian journalist, newspaper publisher.
Rónai, Zoltán (1880—1940)
  Hungarian centrist Social Democrat, state secretary in the ministry of
  labor and welfare during the Károlyi regime, commissar of justice in the
  Soviet government.
Rondenay
  French colonel, commander of the Szeged bridgehead.
Roosevelt, Nicholas (1893—1982)
  American captain, member of the Coolidge Mission to Hungary.
Rothziegel, Leo (1892—1919)
  Austrian internationalist in Hungary during the Hungarian Soviet
  Republic.

Rudnyánszky, Endre (1884–1943)
Hungarian Communist. As a former prisoner of war, he was one of the founders of the Hungarian Communist Party in Moscow, 1918.

Sackville-West, C. J.
British general.

Sadoul, Jacques (1881–1956)
French internationalist in Russia, ex-attaché of the French Military Mission to Petrograd, 1917.

Saint Aulaire, Charles (1866–1954)
French minister in Romania 1916–20.

Saint-Laumer,
French intelligence officer in Szeged.

Saroi Szabó, Tibor
Hungarian Red Army officer.

Shcherbachev, Dmitrii Grigorievich (1857–1932)
Russian general from 1914, one of the important anti-Bolshevik leaders, representative of Denikin in Paris from March, 1918.

Seignobos, Charles (1854–1942)
French historian.

Serrati, Giacinto Menotti (1872–1926)
Italian journalist, editor of the Socialist *L'Avanti*.

Seton Watson, Robert W. (1879–1951)
British historian and publicist, specializing on the Habsburg monarchy.

Shvoy, Kálmán (1881–1971)
Hungarian officer, counterrevolutionary, general during the Horthy regime.

Siegler, Géza (1885–1939)
Hungarian military officer, lieutenant general, 1937.

Sigray, Antal (1879–1947)
Hungarian monarchist politician, commissioner for northern Hungary in the Friedrich government.

Smuts, Jan Christiaan (1870–1950)
South African general, politician, and minister in the Lloyd George cabinet. In April 1919, he was sent to Hungary by the Peace Conference to negotiate with Béla Kun.

Sonyi (Solarz), Hugó (1883–1958)
Hungarian officer, colonel general, commander of the army, 1936–40.

Stamboliiski, Alexandur (1879–1923)
Bulgarian agrarian leader, prime minister, war and finance minister, October 1919–June 1923. He was overthrown by a coup and murdered.

Štefánik, Milan Rastislav (1880–1918)
Slovak scientist, Czechoslovak minister of war, 1918.

Steed, Henry Wickham
    British publicist.
Stojanović, Kosta
    Yugoslav peace delegation member.
Stromfeld, Aurél (1878–1927)
    Hungarian professional soldier, commander-in-chief of the Red Army.
Švejk
    Bumbling hero of Jaroslav Hasek's novel, *The Good Soldier Švejk.*
Szabó, Dezső (1882–1962)
    Hungarian novelist, essayist, important ideologist of the Hungarian
    Populist Movement.
Szamuely, Tibor (1890–1919)
    Hungarian official, deputy commissar of war then commissar of educa-
    tion of the Hungarian Soviet Republic.
Szántó, Béla (1881–1953)
    Founder of the Hungarian Communist Party, commissar of war and
    organizer of the Hungarian Red Army.
Szekfű, Gyula (1883–1955)
    Interwar Hungary's most influential historian.
Szende, Pál (1879–1934)
    Hungarian Radical sociologist, historian, minister of finance in the Be-
    rinkey government, 1919.
Szilassy, Gyula (1870– ? )
    Austro–Hungarian professional diplomat; Hungarian envoy to Switzer-
    land, February to April, 1919.
Szterényi, József (1861–1941)
    Hungarian monarchist politician, minister of trade in the Wekerle govern-
    ment.
Sztójay (Sztojakovics), Döme (1883–1946)
    Hungarian soldier; officer in the National Army, 1919; general in the
    Hungarian army; lieutenant general, 1935; ambassador to Berlin, 1935–
    44; prime minister and foreign minister, March 1944–August 1944.
Szurmay, Sándor (1860–1945)
    Hungarian professional soldier, minister of defense in Hungary in several
    cabinets, February 1917–October 1918.
Syrový, Jan (1888– ? )
    Czechoslovak general, premier, 1938.
Tardieu, André (1876–1945)
    French politican; president of the Territorial Commission for Romania
    of the Paris Peace Conference, prime minister, 1929, 1930, 1932.
Taylor, Alonzo Englebert
    Leader of an American fact-findig inter-allied commission to Hungary,
    January 1919.

Teleki, Pál (1879–1941)
Noted Hungarian geographer, conservative politician. Foreign minister, 1920–21; prime minister, 1920–21 and 1938–41.

Temperley, Harold William (1879–1939)
Historian, member of the British delegation to the Paris Peace Conference.

Thomas, Albert (1878–1932)
French politician, Socialist minister of armaments, 1915–17.

Tisza, István (1861–1918)
Leading Hungarian politician and statesman; prime minister of Hungary, 1903–1905 and 1913–17.

Todorovich, V.
Soviet aviator.

Tombor, Jenő (1880–1946)
Hungarian officer, lieutenant-colonel staff officer 1918, chief of staff of the Hungarian Commissariat of War. Forced to retire after the collapse of the Kun regime, rehabilitated in 1945; colonel general, 1945; minister of defense, November 1945–March 1946.

Tormay, Cecil (1876–1937)
Hungarian writer, founder of the irredentist National Alliance of Hungarian Women, 1920.

Tournadre, Charles Louis de
French general, last commander of troops occupying Szeged.

Treves, Claudio
Italian socialist.

Trotskii, Lev Davidovich (1879–1940)
Commissar of War of Soviet Russia, founder of the Red Army.

Troubridge, Ernest Charles (1862–1926)
British admiral, commanding on the Danube, 1919.

Trousson, Eugene
French colonel, staff officer in the Allied *Army of the East (Orient)*.

Trumbić, Ante (1864–1938)
Yugoslav foreign minister, 1918–20, represented Yugoslavia at the Paris Peace Conference.

Tsolakopoulos-Rebelos
Greek colonel, commander of the Greek contingent in the Ukraine, 1919.

Turati, Filippo (1857–1932)
Italian socialist.

Vágó, Béla (1881–1939)
Hungarian Communist, founder of the Communist Party of Hungary; commander of the Red Army's I Army Corps.

Vanczák, János (1879–1932)
Socialist leader, publicist.

List of Maps

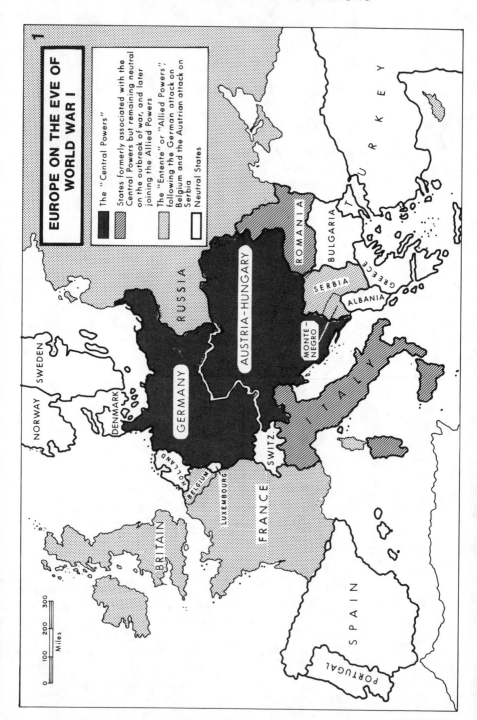

EUROPE ON THE EVE OF WORLD WAR I

The "Central Powers"

States formerly associated with the Central Powers but remaining neutral on the outbreak of war, and later joining the Allied Powers

The "Entente" or "Allied Powers", following the German attack on Belgium and the Austrian attack on Serbia

Neutral States

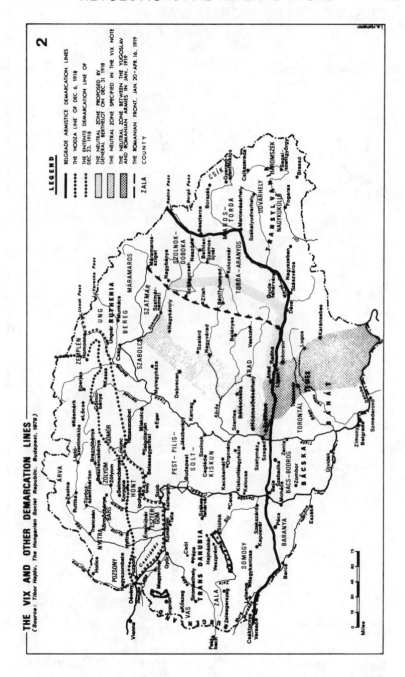

THE VIX AND OTHER DEMARCATION LINES
(Source: Tibor Hajdu, The Hungarian Soviet Republic. Budapest, 1979)

LEGEND

━━━  BELGRADE ARMISTICE DEMARCATION LINES

••••••  THE 'HODZA LINE OF DEC. 6, 1918

•••••••  THE ENTENTE DEMARCATION LINE OF
        DEC. 23, 1918

▨  THE NEUTRAL ZONE PROPOSED BY
   GENERAL BERTHELOT ON DEC. 31, 1918

▨  THE NEUTRAL ZONE SPECIFIED IN THE VIX NOTE

▨  THE NEUTRAL ZONE BETWEEN THE YUGOSLAV
   AND ROMANIAN ARMIES IN JAN., 1919

━╳━  THE ROMANIAN FRONT, JAN. 20–APR. 16, 1919

ZALA   COUNTY

# TERRITORIAL CHANGES IN CENTRAL EUROPE AFTER WORLD WAR I

**3**

FINLAND

Helsinki ● ● Leningrad

ESTONIA

SWEDEN

Riga ●

LATVIA

*Baltic Sea*

Memel ● LITHUANIA

Danzig ● Vilna ●

EAST PRUSSIA ● Minsk

Berlin ● U S S R

Poznan ●

GERMANY ● Warsaw

POLAND

Weimar ● SAXONY ● Breslau

Prague ● ● Cracow

CZECHOSLOVAKIA ● Lvov

Vienna ● BUKOVINA BESSARABIA

AUSTRIA ● Budapest

Graz ● HUNGARY TRANSYLVANIA

Trieste ● SLOVENIA ● Cluj

ROMANIA

YUGOSLAVIA

CROATIA Belgrade ●

BOSNIA SERBIA Bucharest ● DOBRUDJA

Sarajevo ● Varna ● *Black Sea*

BULGARIA

MONTENEGRO Sofia ●

ALBANIA

*Adriatic Sea* MACEDONIA Istambul ●

ITALY

GREECE *Aegean Sea* TURKEY

Athens ●

Scale: 0 100 200 300 Miles

## LEGEND

Post-war Losses of Territory By

RUSSIA

GERMANY

AUSTRIA & HUNGARY

BULGARIA

# LIST OF CONTRIBUTORS 529

György Borsányi – Researcher, Institute of Party History, Budapest, Hungary
Frank J. Coppa – Professor of History, St. John's University, New York, New
York, USA
Márton Farkas – Archivist, Hungarian Military History Archives, Budapest,
Hungary
Stephen Fischer-Galati – Editor, *East European Monographs,* Distinguished
University Professor, University of Colorado, Boulder, Colorado, USA
László Fogarassy – Librarian (retired), Bratislava, Czechoslovakia
Helén Gábor – Senior Researcher, Institute of Party History, Budapest, Hun-
gary
Dinu C. Giurescu, Professor of History, Nicolae Grigorescu Institute of Fine
Arts, Bucharest, Romania
Susan Glanz – Assistant Professor of Economics, St. Vincent's College, St.
John's University, New York, New York, USA
Peter Gosztony – Director, East European Library, Bern, Switzerland
Tibor Hajdu – Research Adviser, Institute of History, Academy of Sciences,
Budapest, Hungary
Tibor Hetés – Commander of the Hungarian Military History Museum, Buda-
pest, Hungary
Khristo Khristov – Professor of History, Institute of Balkan Studies, Bulgarian
Academy of Sciences, Sofia, Bulgaria
Béla K. Király – Director, Program on Society in Change; Professor Emeritus
of History, Brooklyn College of the City University of New York, New
York, USA
Vujica Kovačev – Researcher, Institute for Contemporary History, Belgrade,
Yugoslavia
Zsuzsa L. Nagy – Senior Researcher, Institute of History, Hungarian Academy
of Sciences, Budapest, Hungary
Lampe. John R. – Associate Professor of History, University of Maryland,
College Park, Maryland, USA
Leslie László – Professor of Political Science, Concordia University. Montreal,
Quebec, Canada
György Litván – Researcher, Institute of History, Hungarian Academy of
Sciences, Budapest, Hungary
Ervin Liptai – Commander of the Institute for Military History and of the
Military History Museum, Budapest, Hungary
Munholland, Kim – Professor of History, University of Minnesota, Minne-
apolis, Minnesota, USA
Jean Nouzille – Docteur es Lettres, Colonel, French Army, and University of
Strasbourg II, Strasbourg, France
Mária Ormos – Rector, Janus Pannonius University, Pécs, Hungary

Peter Pastor — Professor of History, Montclair State College, Upper Montclair, New Jersey, USA

György Péteri — Researcher, Institute of Economic History, Uppsala University, Uppsala, Sweden

Ignác Romsics — Group Leader, Hungarology Research Group, Széchenyi National Library, Budapest, Hungary

Ivan Sanders — Professor of Comparative Literature, Suffolk Country Community College, Selden, New York, USA

Theophanis G. Stavrou — Professor of History, University of Minnesota, Minneapolis, Minnesota, USA

Sándor Szakály — Researcher, Institute for Military History and Military History Museum, Budapest, Hungary

Leslie C. Tihany — Distinguished Service Professor Emeritus, Northern Kentucky University; Adjunct Professor of History, University of Cincinnati, Ohio, USA

Glenn E. Torrey — Professor of History, Emporia State University, Emporia, Kansas, USA

Gabor Vermes — Associate Professor of History, Rutgers University, Newark, New Jersey, USA

Martin Vietor — Professor, Chairman of the Department of Legal and State History, the Law School of Komensky University, Bratislava, Czechoslovakia (Deceased)

Piotr S. Wandycz — Professor of History, Yale University, New Haven, Connecticut, USA

Ferenc Tibor Zsuppan — University Lecturer, University of St. Andrews, St. Andrews, Fife, Scotland

# Atlantic Studies on Society in Change

# WAR AND SOCIETY IN EAST CENTRAL EUROPE

VIII. *The First Serbian Uprising 1804-1813.* Edited by Wayne S. Vucinich. 1982.

IX. *The Effects of World War II: Czechoslovak Policy and the Hungarian Minority 1945-1948.* Kálmán Janics. 1982.

X. *At the Brink of War and Peace: The Tito-Stalin Split in a Historic Perspective.* Edited by Wayne S. Vucinich. 1982.

XI. *The First War Between Socialist States: The Hungarian Revolution of 1956 and Its Impact.* Edited by Béla K. Király, Barbara Lotze, Nandor Dreisziger.

XII. *The Effects of World War I, The Uprooted: Hungarian Refugees and Their Impact on Hungary's Domestic Politics.* István I. Mócsy. 1983.

XIII. *The Effects of World War I: The Class War After The Great War: The Rise of Communist Parties in East Central Europe, 1918-1921.* Edited by Ivo Banac. 1983.

XIV. *The Crucial Decade: East Central European Society and National Defense, 1859-1870.* Edited by Béla K. Király. 1984.

XVI. *Effects on World War I: War Communism in Hungary, 1919.* György Péteri. 1984.

XVII. *Insurrections, Wars, and the Eastern Crisis in the 1870s.* Edited by B.K. Király and Gale Stokes. 1985.

XVIII. *East Central European Society and the Balkan Wars, 1912-31913.* Edited by B.K. Király and Dimitrije Djordjevic. 1987.

XIX. *East Central European Society in World War I.* Edited by B.K. Király and Nandor F. Dreisziger, Assistant Editor Albert A. Nofi. 1985.